CANADIAN WOMEN: A HISTORY

CANADIAN WOMEN

A HISTORY

Alison Prentice
Paula Bourne
Gail Cuthbert Brandt
Beth Light
Wendy Mitchinson
Naomi Black

Harcourt Brace
Jovanovich

Toronto
Orlando
San Diego
London
Sydney

Edited by Tilly Crawley
Cover and interior design by Ivan Holmes
Typeset by Compeer Typographic Services Limited
Printed and bound by Webcom Limited

Canadian Cataloguing in Publication Data
Main entry under title:

Canadian women : a history

Bibliography: p.
Includes index.
ISBN 0-7747-3112-5

1. Women – Canada – History.   2. Women – Canada –
Social conditions.   I. Prentice, Alison, 1934–

HQ1453.C36 1988   305.4'0971   C88-093357-7

5 4 3 2   89 90 91 92

Front cover: Irene Parlby (courtesy of Glenbow Archives);
Emma and Jenny (Archives of Ontario Acc. 2210,
S1949); Women in munitions factory (Public Archives
of Canada C18734). Back cover: Mattie Gunterman
(Vancouver Public Library 2276); Woman soldering
(Public Archives of Canada C75212).

To Elizabeth Smith, Lucy O'Neill, Sadie Cuthbert, Margaret Light, Frances Mitchinson, and Michal Black.

The six authors bring to this book a wide range of experience in research, writing, and teaching about Canadian women. Alison Prentice teaches history at the Ontario Institute for Studies in Education; Beth Light and Paula Bourne are research associates at the OISE Centre for Women's Studies; Wendy Mitchinson teaches history at the University of Waterloo; and Gail Cuthbert Brandt and Naomi Black teach at York University in the departments of history and political science respectively.

Contents

Preface

The idea for this book dates back to 1981, when seven historians began to plan what they already knew would not be an easy task: writing a history of women in Canada. Several of those involved were part of a women's history group that had already assembled a substantial bibliography and a vast array of documents relating to the lives of Canadian women. They and the other early participants felt the need for a cohesive account of Canadian women's past, one that would alert a wider audience to the important scholarship emerging in this exciting new field. As feminists committed to the idea of collective endeavour, the seven planned a joint project and began some of the preliminary work.

Approximately five years later, a somewhat different group of six women finally settled down to draft, re-draft, and then revise what became a more ambitious volume than first envisioned. Chapters were initially written by one or two of us; then, gathered around seminar tables and dining-room tables, or by phone and by mail, we all discussed—and often vigorously debated—every idea, word, and punctuation mark along the way. Sustained by our enjoyment of working together, our fascination with the collective process, and our empathy for the women whose lives we were exploring, we kept on with what proved to be a demanding project. In the end we hardly knew who had written what, or where a particular idea for a change of direction might have originated. The final result is a truly collective effort.

It is collective in more ways than one, for this project has provoked the most extraordinary, unstinting helpfulness from many individuals. Those among the proposed authors who were drawn aside by other commitments have continued to be extremely supportive of our work: we thank Ruth Roach Pierson, Veronica Strong-Boag, and Sylvia Van Kirk. Two intended participants were lost to death: we mourn Marta Danylewycz and Pat Schulz. Through their scholarship and organizational ideas, these five women made an important contribution to this study. We also want to thank Pat Staton for spending many hours at collective meetings, and for her valuable help with the research and illustrations.

As our text took shape, Susan Hall, Margaret Brennan, Gail Heideman, and Lucy Tantalo transformed our multiple writings, typescripts, and diskettes into consistent manuscript form. At Harcourt Brace Jovanovich, Canada, Heather McWhinney provided encouragement and support from the initial stages, and, along with Darlene Zeleney and Ivan Holmes, our designer, guided us expertly through the production process. Jean MacDonald and Sandra Peltier also provided valuable assistance. To our skilful and ever-patient editor, Tilly Crawley, who struggled with us through the process of turning sixteen essays into a single narrative, we owe a special thank you.

We are also grateful to the many others who generously shared with us their time and expertise. They include Moira Armour, Kathy Arnup, Jean Augustine, Constance Backhouse, Christine Ball, Peggy Bristow, Somer Brodribb, Valerie J. Bunn, Sherill Cheda, Marjorie Cohen, Carol Cole, Margaret Conrad, Julia Creet, Barbara Crow, Christine Donald, Muriel Duckworth, Marlene Epp, Judith Fingard, Ernest Forbes, Nancy Forestell, Frieda Forman, Ruth Frager, Isabel Gibb, Ann Hicks, Margaret Hobbs, Carol Howe, Eileen Jensen, Laura Jones, Maryon Kantaroff, Jon Kaplan, Linda Kealey, Helen Kilgour, Jeanne Lapointe, Susan Laskin, Marie Lavigne, Jeanne L'Esperance, Patricia Lilley, Kay Macpherson, Lynne Marks, Lorna Marsden, Tom Matthews, Ken McLaughlin, Angela Miles, Mary Jane Mossman, Joy Parr, Lorna Pitcher, Marian Press, Sandra Pyke, Frances Rooney, Joan Sangster, Elizabeth Smyth, Deborah Stienstra, Johanna Stuckey, Byron Wall, Shirley Wigmore, and Judith Zelmanovits. To all of them, and to the Ontario Institute for Studies in Education which funded much of the research through a transfer grant from the Ontario Ministry of Education, our sincere thanks.

Last but not least, we wish to thank our friends and, especially, our families for their encouragement and understanding. Committed supporters of the project from its inception until its completion, they tolerated a level of absence and distraction rare even in our harried lives.

Alison Prentice
Paula Bourne
Gail Cuthbert Brandt
Beth Light
Wendy Mitchinson
Naomi Black

Introduction

When feminists began to raise questions about the place of women in Canada, the absence of women from analysis became a challenge to historians. There was a growing awareness that the fact of gender made women's lives profoundly different from the lives of men. Women had an identity and a history, both barely represented in the standard studies. In the context of the women's movement and of a general widening of historical inquiry, Canadian women's history flowered. Today, in the ninth decade of the twentieth century, enough work has accumulated for us to write this general history of women in Canada.

Much that we learn from the history of men is problematic for the history of women. The very language often fails to describe women's experience. A particularly complex set of problems surrounds the word "work." To begin with, the generally accepted census definition of "occupation" omits much work that women do in the home — housework, childcare, and care of the elderly or the sick. Even less recognized is the unpaid "reproductive" work that women do in the family, both in bearing children and in providing emotional stability and support. These omissions stem directly from the failure to treat unpaid work with the same respect as work for pay. In addition, much of women's paid work goes unrecorded, from taking in sewing or boarders to doing housework or childcare for others. We have tried to uncover and discuss all of these different kinds of work, and to describe at the same time the intricate connections between them and women's involvement in paid employment outside of the home.

A second set of problems emerges with the generally accepted definitions of culture and politics. By using culture anthropologically, we move beyond "high culture" to a concept that encompasses ways of thinking and acting, ways of being in the world and seeing the world. One of our aims has been to explore the question of whether or not a separate women's culture has existed for Canadian women at different times, or among various groupings, and how such a culture or cultures might have changed over the years. We have had similar questions about women's politics. Officially excluded from the politics of men during much of Canada's history, often eschewing partisanship for broadly based coalitions focussed on goals of their own, Canadian women have had their own politics.

If accepted definitions of work, culture, and politics have been problematic, so too have been the periods into which Canadian history has traditionally been organized. Is it appropriate, for the purposes of dividing Canadian women's history into meaningful periods, to select constitutional events such as Confederation? Or would changes more directly affecting women's lives, such as the advent of the Pill, make better markers? Neither alternative seems genuinely satisfactory and yet this is an issue that we have had to resolve. Books, after all, have to be divided into chapters, however seamless the fabric of life may be in the real world. Since events of all kinds have influenced the lives of human beings, we have tried to construct a chronology that takes into account the interaction of the technological, economic, and social, as well as the political dimensions of women's experience.

After much discussion, we have identified three major turning points in the history of women in Canada. The first is the transition from a pre-industrial to an industrial society in the mid-nineteenth century. This transition brought to an end the family economies of earlier times, and ultimately had a profound effect on British North American women's lives. It is symbolized for us by the establishment in the 1840s of a cotton mill in the eastern townships of Quebec. The first corporate industrial venture in Canada, it was the beginning of an industry that was to employ large numbers of women. The second turning point occurs during World War I, which saw the achievement of two major goals of the first wave of the women's movement in Canada: prohibition and suffrage. These successes marked the end of an era: the world of the pioneer and the gentlewoman now receded from sight and gave way to that of the "flapper" and the "working girl." The third turning point was the beginning, during World War II, of the massive entry of married women into the paid labour force. Marriage, which had previously transformed the lives of women, now became a less definite transition as they worked outside of the home for a growing portion of their adult lives.

Inevitably, markers are artificial. They are the more so when it comes to the life of an individual woman, or the lives of whole groups whose participation has been on the edges of the mainstream. What did the advent of factories, the achievement of prohibition and suffrage, or the movement of married women into the paid labour force mean to women living on Canada's more isolated resource frontiers? We have tried to be attentive to those women who were far from the centres of political or economic activity. For women who did not leave written records, this has been hard to do. And even the women who did leave records of their lives wrote from inside worlds that were very different from ours. Their voices are difficult to hear and more difficult to interpret.

Like all historians, we need to face the fact of our own cultural, political, and personal biases. There is no such thing as a completely "objective" truth independent of the observers' points of view. It is therefore important to describe our shared perspective. First of all, we all consider ourselves feminists. Our feminism is a point of view that necessarily affects what we select as important and how we interpret or reinterpret the past; it is the reason for this book. There are many definitions and, more important, many versions of feminism. But underlying all is the commitment to increasing women's autonomy in a world where it has generally been less than men's. A feminist perspective recognizes that women's situation and experience are distinctive. Further, it insists that women should not be judged inferior by male standards or in comparison with men.

This is not to deny the value of all comparisons. How women have fared, compared to men, must obviously be a central question in women's history. Here we enter a difficult terrain — the question of women's status. A fundamental and related issue is the character and interpretation of the existence of "separate spheres" for women and men in any given time or place. Whether we are considering Canada's hunting and gathering communities or its Victorian households and non-domestic workplaces, we need to make judgements about how separate the so-called "domestic" or "private" and "public" spheres really were. How did their separation or non-separation affect the degree of authority men and women exercised over their own lives, as well as in their respective communities? Certainly the nature and meaning of "public" and "private" life have shifted in Canada over the years. It seems clear that much of the work of education, as well as a good deal of economic production, at first took place in what we would now call the domestic or private sphere. These activities were only gradually removed from private life as men created a new public world from which women were largely excluded. How and why this occurred, and with what results — and how the trend began to be modified — are questions that we try to address in this book.

Also intriguing are the other possible influences on women's authority and ability to control their work and their lives. Have women been more in command of their situation when their numbers relative to men were great, or when they were relatively scarce and therefore presumably especially valuable? When large numbers of women married at an early age, or when fewer married, and did so later in their lives? In addition, questions of relative power have to be examined in the context of the age structures of given populations, and of prevailing attitudes towards women's roles. Have married women — or unmarried women — been devalued at particular times and places?

We agree that the material structures of people's lives are the most important among the many factors influencing them. Yet we would not limit such influences to the economic, for we are convinced that women's bodies are an important part of the material bases of their lives. In all cultures, the lives of the childbearing portion of the community will be greatly influenced by the fact of that childbearing, and by the ideologies and practices surrounding it. But biology itself is less simple and more variable than we have been led to believe; for instance, biological clocks respond to factors such as climate and food supply, so that the age of puberty can vary widely from one place or time to another. And, as feminists focussing on the experience of women, we also recognize the power of ideas and feelings, of social and political movements, and of cultural and racial as well as gender identities, in fixing or altering how people react to the conditions they encounter.

When we consider such issues, we return to economic configurations and material culture. An important component of both is technological change. The technology of birth control has had the most dramatic potential to alter women's lives. But a host of other technologies have been important as well. From the washing machine to the microchip, how have women initiated or responded to technological transformations, and how have new technologies changed women's daily work? Who was better off, the women of earlier centuries who did little or no laundry, or the modern housewife, who washes at home, often daily, or lugs the family wash to the laundromat? Such questions are perhaps, in the end, impossible to answer.

In Canada, any such questions must also be considered in the context of the country's immense diversity. Whether we are talking about the impact of technology or the women's movement itself, there nearly always seems to be the need for multiple perspectives if we are to get the picture right. Yet, despite much diversity, or perhaps because of it, an increasingly frequent theme of Canadian women's history has been the quest for a unified women's voice. Has such a voice existed? Is there a distinctively Canadian women's experience that can be identified?

These themes and questions frame our position as feminist historians. We hope to illuminate the history of women in Canada, in all its diversity. Often faced with enormous difficulties, sometimes treated with the most cruel injustice in communities that were for the most part decidedly patriarchal, Canadian women struggled to survive, to contribute, and to make their lives meaningful. We study their lives because women have been integral to Canada's history. What they were and did made all the difference.

1 THE FOUNDING MOTHERS

Beginnings to the mid-nineteenth century

Aataentsic, according to the Hurons, was the great mother. It was for her that the earth was created, to provide a safe haven when she fell from the sky and gave birth to humanity. Similar creation stories may be found in most indigenous cultures. A recent rendering of Nootka* legend tells us of Copper Woman, the awe-inspiring figure who created the first male out of the not very promising materials at hand. With her humour as well as her strength, Copper Woman inspired her daughters to heroic feats of survival in an environment that was often hostile and was always challenging.[1]

Our knowledge of powerful mythic figures like Aataentsic and Copper Woman is fragmentary. What about our knowledge of Canada's founding women, the women of our early native and colonial cultures? Fortunately, even in the remote worlds of Canada's traditional peoples, tracings of women's lives can be discovered; indeed, archeologists, anthropologists, and historians have begun to piece these scraps of evidence together into larger studies that are of absorbing interest. Yet complete agreement on the character or meaning of women's lives in traditional societies remains elusive. First of all, from the earliest records of Canada's past to the transitional years of the mid-nineteenth century is an immensely long time. Secondly, we are considering a great many different peoples under the heading of "founding cultures."

Consider the native cultures that Europeans encountered when they first came to the northern parts of North America. In the fifteenth and sixteenth centuries, the rich fisheries of the east and west coasts supported a great number of tribal groups, some of them very populous, while in the region that was to become Ontario, agriculture sustained some 30 000 people. This figure is striking when we realize that the people of New France probably numbered no more than 70 000 by the middle of the eighteenth century. Moreover, by the time of contact with Europeans, the indigenous peoples of what was to become Canada belonged to twelve separate language families and spoke an even larger number of languages.[2]

Students of the early native peoples have also identified several different major regional economies. The hunting and gathering cultures in the north and east differed not only from each other and from the partly agricultural economies of the St. Lawrence River valley, but also from the buffalo-centred cultures on the Plains. And

A native woman, by Paul Kane.

17

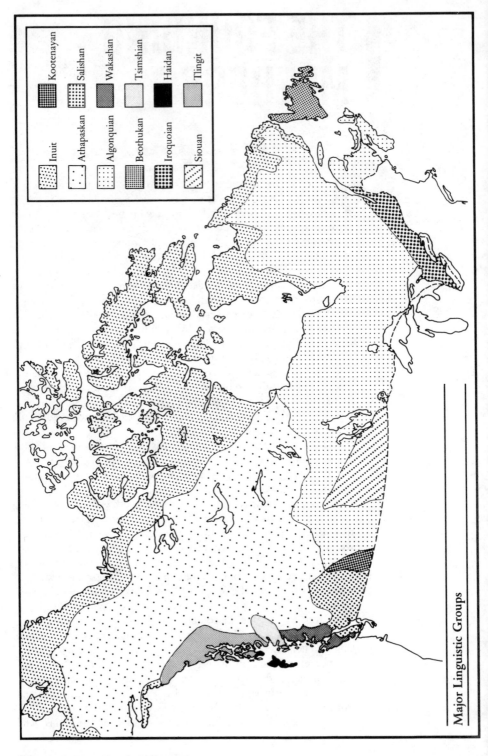

Major Linguistic Groups

Kootenayan
Salishan
Wakashan
Tsimshian
Haidan
Tlingit

Inuit
Athapaskan
Algonquian
Beothukan
Iroquoian
Siouan

An Inuit woman prepares fish for drying in the sun.

these stood in considerable contrast again to the salmon- and whale-based economies of the Pacific West Coast. Perhaps the one major factor that native economies had in common was their very delicate relationships with their various natural environments.[3]

We know that Europeans reached the shores of North America as early as the eleventh century, and Norse legends, as well as the presence of tools for spinning and sewing in a Viking archeological site in Newfoundland, inform us that women were among these early visitors. Gudrid and Freydis, according to the eleventh century "Vinland" sagas, actually gave birth to children in the New World.[4]

It was not until the sixteenth century, however, that European incursions on native territory began in earnest. The first arrivals were chiefly fishermen and traders who did not linger. Nevertheless, there is considerable evidence that by the late 1500s the development of trade on the east coast was altering native economies and, as well, the lives of women. Gradually, as European goods were introduced, women had to adapt to change. Clothing and utensils that they had once manufactured, for example, could now be purchased with furs. Settled communities were forced to move as the trade animals became depleted in any given region. In addition, European diseases were introduced, with drastic effects on the size of populations.[5]

French-speaking European women first began to arrive in North America in the seventeenth century and, like the native women they encountered, were also amazingly diverse. The France from which they sailed was ruled by a monarchy intent on extending its administrative control over a fragmented and fractious realm. From his palace at Versailles, the "Sun King" Louis XIV and his advisers sought to enhance the glory of France by laying claim to much of the North American continent. But mercantilist dreams of prosperous colonies shipping valuable resources to the mother country and importing its manufactured goods could only be realized if this vast territory were populated by French colonists. Steeped in the religious zeal of the Catholic Counter-Reformation, the court at Versailles also viewed colonization as a means of spreading the Catholic faith.[6]

Populating the French colonies was a slow and difficult process. Very soon, New France was embattled on nearly all sides, first by hostile native peoples and then by the British, locked as they were in a deadly struggle with the French for empire. Of the French colonies that developed in the northern half of the continent, Acadia had the longest history of French presence, enjoyed the best relations between the French and local native peoples, but suffered most of the consequences of French–British conflict. Despite ferocious and prolonged war with the Iroquois throughout much of the seventeenth century, it was the colony of Canada, situated on the banks of the St. Lawrence River, that became the economic and administrative centre of New France. A third major population centre developed in the eighteenth century around the fortress of Louisbourg, located on present-day Cape Breton Island.[7]

In all three colonies, the arrival of French women signalled official intention to create permanent European settlements. The women and men who came to New France brought with them the varying ideals, ambitions, and anxieties of their metropolitan patrons. French merchants sought to transform fish and fur into handsome profits; colonial administrators struggled to reproduce the political and social structures of Bourbon France in the wilderness; while nuns and priests devoted their lives to imposing a particularly austere and mystical brand of French Catholicism on natives and colonists alike. The resulting cultures reflected all of this, as well as the diverse origins and circumstances of the settlers. The Acadians, for example, were so various in their backgrounds that they found themselves living with women and men who not only spoke different dialects but had lived in communities ruled by differing laws, customs, and religious traditions in the Old World.[8] The more numerous Canadians hailed from Paris and the surrounding Île de France, as well as from coastal ports; in both colonies, there was initially considerable intermarriage between the French and the native populations. In addition, Canada's first blacks were brought as slaves to Acadia and the St. Lawrence River valley during this period. Finally, the settlers' experience varied, depending on their social rank and where they lived. Life among the upper classes in Quebec was marked by relative comfort and sophistication, features largely absent from the lives of *habitants* struggling to carve farms from the forest.[9]

Similar variety and a continuing intermingling of peoples characterized the great migrations of the eighteenth and early nineteenth centuries as well. Women who came with British soldiers, Scottish crofters, and Irish and English farmers were part of this movement, both before and after the British Conquest of New France; women were also among the Loyalist and post-Loyalist Americans of European, African, and Amerindian origin who migrated to British North America before, during, and after the American Revolution. Like their men, the women were uniform neither in their languages, which included Gaelic and German as well as the dominant English, nor in their customs or possessions.

Fixing boundaries for the founding peoples of Canada is as complex a process as attempting to delineate their cultures. Boundaries between native groups were often fluid to begin with, and major shifts occurred in their territories. To further complicate the picture, the boundaries established by both the French and their British successors were shortlived. Acadia endured as part of New France only until 1713; the Acadians themselves were finally uprooted in the Great Deportation or Expulsion of 1755–1762, when their British rulers scattered men, women, and children along the coasts of North America and Europe. Despite continuous warfare, New France survived in the St. Lawrence River valley until the British Conquest was completed in 1760; Canada was finally ceded to the British Crown by the Treaty of Paris in 1763. Yet British rule did not bring peace. The American Revolution (1776–1783), the cataclysm that set so many Loyalists on the road north, broke the peace, as did, to a much smaller extent, the eighteenth century fur trade wars. It was not until the War of 1812 was over and the nineteenth century was well into its second decade that the six colonies of British North America — Newfoundland, Nova Scotia, New Brunswick, Prince Edward Island, and Lower and Upper Canada — began to assume relatively stable boundaries. Even then, Upper and Lower Canada had still to endure the traumatic events of the Rebellions of 1837–1838. Indeed, throughout most of its history British North America, like New France before it, was essentially an armed camp.[10]

Canada's early women lived, therefore, in the midst of extraordinary conflict and change. War and the effects of war were important factors in their lives. Of equal significance was the mercantile nature of their societies. The native peoples drew the Europeans into their world; at the same time they were gradually drawn into the staple economies that the European intruders generated. The quest for furs would eventually become the driving force of many women's lives. Women were also crucial to the inshore fishery and the economies that subsequently developed around the production of lumber and wheat. In addition, they continued to be active in subsistence hunting and gathering, in farming, in craft production, and in local commerce. Most of the economies in which they participated were family-based. Women and men alike laboured for the subsistence of the family or for its improvement; generally labour was quite sharply divided along the lines of gender.

The problems historians face in analyzing women's roles in such pre-industrial economies are multiple. An outstanding one is to determine what implications the sexual division of labour had for the status of women in any given culture. Were pre-industrial women segregated in their work by choice? Did their separate work give them power or did it tend to exclude them from authority? How, indeed, do we define "power" and "choice" in these societies? Did separate work help to support a separate, gender-based culture that was different from that of men? If so, how did this cultural identity manifest itself? Equally problematic is the documentation of change and of difference. What was the impact of contact on the roles and status of native women? How did the New World affect the lives of European women immigrants to New France and British North America? And what of the many mixed-blood women who became the women "in between" two cultures?[11] Even within these larger groupings, there are often variations of ethnicity and class, and of urban and rural settings, to be considered in any assessment of how our foremothers lived.

If the contemporary sources for making these assessments are often mere scraps, it is true that the scraps are sometimes marvellous. Jesuit missionaries writing back to France, fur traders keeping track of what was going on in their trading territories for company officials or friends at home, male travellers of various nationalities writing for a variety of publics, often had fascinating things to say about women in the New World. But for the lives of native women particularly, historians have to rely almost entirely on the evidence of these men, and the evidence has to be treated with great caution, filtered as it was through the eyes of individuals who shared neither the race nor the sex of the people they were describing. For European women, the sources are more various, but are still scattered and problematic. Convent women writing the *annales* of their convents are wonderful sources for New France, but their focus is largely, although certainly not exclusively, on the lives of their communities. Notarial records and censuses have proven rich sources for historians of women, as have some groups of family business records. By the eighteenth century the diaries and letters of laywomen begin to supplement these sources, along with accounts by travellers. But if such records prove exceptionally rich for British North America by the nineteenth century, there is a distinct falling off in the quantitative sources. The superb parish, census, and notarial records of New France were to some extent carried on in Quebec and Lower Canada under British rule, but are not to be found in great profusion elsewhere for the post-Conquest years. The New Brunswick, Nova Scotia, and Upper and Lower Canada censuses of 1851 provide a wealth of information for the end of our period, however. And scattered other local surveys, coupled with what may be gleaned from individual, family, and parish records, help us to reconstruct the lives of women, especially in the first half of the nineteenth century.

Altogether, we do well to approach the history of Canadian women in this early period with caution. The temptation to use twentieth century anthropological findings and extrapolate to firm conclusions about the women of our more remote past is to be avoided. On the other hand, the studies of contemporary anthropologists are valuable guides to the historian trying to understand the beliefs or social configurations that might have influenced women in earlier times. Often it is only with the most imaginative use of fragmentary sources that we are able to construct a picture of those worlds that we, perhaps, have not quite lost.

1 The first women

Thanadelthur, an eighteenth century Chipewyan woman, was referred to by James Knight, the Hudson's Bay Company trader who wrote about her, as "the Slave Woman." Thanadelthur was both a survivor and a peacemaker, and as a result she is one of the few native women of her period whose individual lives we can document. She and a female companion were captured by Crees, long-standing enemies of the Chipewyan, in 1713. Both managed to escape from their captors but could not complete the long journey back to their own band. Narrowly avoiding the death by starvation that was the fate of her friend, Thanadelthur succeeded in making contact with Hudson's Bay Company traders at York Factory; these, in turn, quickly recognized the young Chipewyan's value as a potential link between themselves and her fur-wealthy people. The eventual result was a peace mission between Cree and Chipewyan, ostensibly led by a Hudson's Bay Company man, but actually the work of Thanadelthur herself, who proved a highly competent go-between. When the mission seemed doomed to failure owing to mounting hostility and fear on both sides, it was Thanadelthur whose courage and determination carried the day. By turns, she persuaded both sides to continue the talks, and harangued them until they were finally "forced . . . to ye peace." The trader who accompaniedThanadelthur admired her spirit. It was "Divellish," he reported. If but fifty of her people had the same "Carriage and Resolution," no other Amerindian tribe would stand a chance in Chipewyan country.

Thanadelthur's life was short. In the few years that remained to her after her arrival at York Factory, she became so valuable to James Knight as an interpreter and envoy that he despaired when, in the bad winter of 1717, she became ill and he was unable to nurse her back to health. "She was one of a Very high Spirit and of the Firmest Resolution that ever I see any Body in my Days," Knight wrote in his log; a person "of very great Courage & forecast." Clearly he was recording the loss of someone who had become more than a casual business associate.

We learn of Thanadelthur's history not from herself or chiefly from her own people but, as far as the written record is concerned, from the pen of an outsider, and his words are not easy to interpret.[1] Was there a sense in which her position was servile? Or did James Knight see her only as the powerful figure his final description implied: a woman of courage and resolution whose role was so important to his mission that he hardly knew how he would replace her? And what relationship is there between Knight's words and the reality of Thanadelthur's life? How did *she* understand her situation as an envoy between three peoples jockeying for position in a world that had once been the exclusive territory of her own people? What did the events of Thanadelthur's life mean to her?

The Slave Woman's story is instructive. It suggests, first of all, something of the power that many native women appear to have had at the time when the host peoples of North America first encountered European intruders on their territory. At the same time, it suggests the fragility of that power, especially in periods of conflict and upheaval. Native women who may have had considerable authority in their own communities were nevertheless vulnerable when men were on the warpath. Secondly, Thanadelthur was on the move. Seasonal migration was normal for hunting and gathering groups, but European contact and the fur trade brought new dimensions and additional travelling. Women acting as traders and negotiators, women travelling with husband traders, women escaping and seeking refuge — countless women might have had tales to tell like Thanadelthur's.

Other native women would see similar extraordinary changes occurring in their brief lifetimes. During the pre-contact and early contact years in the Maritime region, for example, whole populations replaced each other. By the time of contact in the fifteenth century, the Micmacs, who had only recently settled in Nova Scotia, had already given up the making of pottery and were no longer living in permanent coastal settlements, as their predecessors evidently had done. The large palisaded villages that Cartier saw in his sixteenth century explorations of the St. Lawrence River valley had already been abandoned by the time Champlain came to this region less than a century later. And it was not many years after the beginnings of French settlement in Canada that the Hurons, who had once been so numerous north of Lake Ontario, were almost entirely destroyed by disease and war. From an early seventeenth century population that might have reached 30 000, they were reduced by the 1650s to a scattered few.[2]

In spite of the disruption of their societies, there were survivors — and adapters — and they appear in the records. The questions that we are bound to ask about the native women are hard to answer but important. What were women's lives like before the coming of the Europeans? And how did women react to the changes European trade and settlement brought? The native groups whose cultures have been studied with such questions in mind are not numerous. They include the Micmac of Nova Scotia; the Montagnais-Nascapi of Labrador and Quebec among the eastern Algonquians; and the Hurons and the Six Nations of the Great Lakes region among the Iroquoians. Much of our information for these groups dates from the sixteenth and seventeenth centuries, although some is more recent. For the eighteenth and early nineteenth centuries, we can also draw on studies of the Chipewyan, Cree, and Carrier Amerindians of the northwest, who were also Algonquian, and of peoples belonging to the Salish and Haida language groups of the west coast. From the work that has been done to date, it is possible to examine native women's roles in the economic lives of their communities and, in some cases, to catch glimpses of their status.

Native women's work

Most historians and anthropologists agree that all North American native communities organized their work along gender lines. Women did work that was compatible with the task of looking after small children. This work did not require "rapt attention," as hunting did; it could be easily interrupted and resumed. It did not place children in danger and it did not require mothers and children to go very far from home. This applied even when "home" was a movable encampment. Women generally remained close to the camp; men moved farther afield on land or sea to hunt animal food that could not be obtained in any other way.[3]

Within such limits, native women's work in northern North America varied according to the resources of the region and the group. To early traders, some native women led what seemed incredibly hard lives in marginal subsistence economies. This was especially true of those groups who depended on hunting and gathering in the northern forests and tundra. On the other hand, some observers found native women in agricultural or fishing economies living in the midst of relative plenty. By the time of European contact, women did most of the work in agricultural communities; but it was the opinion of at least one eighteenth century American that this work was relaxed and convivial. A white woman who had been taken captive by the Seneca and adopted into the tribe, Mary Jemison seems to have found much to approve of in the lives of Iroquois women.[4]

Agricultural work was not only the responsibility of these women but was also under their control. Among the agricultural Iroquois/ Huron, men helped in the clearing of the land, but the corn, beans, and squash were grown entirely by teams of women organized by leaders chosen by themselves. Among the People of the Longhouse, as the Six Nations were known, the meat brought home from the hunt went to the wife's household to be distributed by her according to Iroquois rules of hospitality, which dictated that all members of the community as well as all visitors should be fed. The wealth of the community consisted chiefly, however, in its land and in the food stored and controlled by the women.[5]

The relative ease with which women's agricultural work was performed depended, no doubt, on a variety of factors, including the climate and the quality of the land, but according to Mary Jemison the labour of Iroquois women was rarely "severe." Even though they had "all the fuel and bread to procure, and the cooking to perform," she noted, their work was "probably not harder" than that of white women who had those articles provided for them. More importantly, "their cares" were not so numerous nor so great as those of white women. "In the summer season, we planted, tended and harvested the corn, and generally had all our children with us; but had no master to oversee or drive us, so that we could work as leisurely as we pleased."[6]

Jemison's observations cover only the time in which she lived among the Seneca and the region where they lived. But the evidence suggests that similar working patterns obtained among the agricultural peoples of the lower Great Lakes region generally and in previous centuries. Earlier Six Nations and Huron women were also in charge of their communities' farming; the growing of corn, squash, sunflowers, and beans had been known among the Great Lakes and St. Lawrence valley Iroquoian peoples for at least one thousand years before the arrival of Europeans. Indeed, it is the cultivation of the protein-rich bean that is believed to account for the large Iroquoian populations that the first Europeans encountered.

The Montagnais-Nascapi were among the non-agricultural hunting and gathering peoples encountered by the French of the St. Lawrence River valley.[7] It is apparent that the Montagnais-Nascapi lived in communities of varying sizes, depending on the season, but probably in social groupings that were smaller than those of the Iroquois or Hurons. In wintertime the Montagnais-Nascapi broke up into hunting bands of one or two families, who went into the bush in search of game. Women's work was different from men's; indeed, the Jesuit observers of New France noted that each sex knew the role of the other and they did not "meddle" with each other's work. Women did participate in the fishing and even, to some extent,

Women of the eastern woodlands keeping the birds away from their corn.

in the trapping of small animals, however. They were certainly involved in transporting game, preparing hides, and manufacturing clothing from them. But their main economic role was as gatherers of shellfish and other foods, supplying more than fifty percent of their people's diet by this work. Montagnais-Nascapi women, like the women of the Six Nations, were also in charge of the distribution of the food they gathered as well as of the products of the hunt and fishery.

Among the hardest lives described by European observers were those of the Chipewyan and Cree women of the northwest. Andrew Graham, who wrote about the Swampy Cree in the late eighteenth century, found that in this community, "all drugery [sic] and domestic duty is performed by the women. They pitch and unpitch the tent, cut fire-wood, dress the victuals. . . . The women also catch fish, hares, fetch all the water used in the tent, knit the snow-shoes, and make the clothes." Graham observed that the women waited on the men when the latter returned from the hunt, and that they worked as hard as ever when pregnant.[8] Alexander Mackenzie, writing in 1802, had similar things to say about Woodland Cree women. He found that they were "in the same subordinate state with those of all other savage tribes," and worked extremely hard. "They are . . . subject to every kind of domestic drudgery . . . so that when the duties of maternal care are added, it will appear that the life of these women is an uninterrupted succession of toil and pain. This, indeed, is the sense they entertain of their own situation."[9]

Such statements should be weighed against the observers' background. For whom were Graham and Mackenzie writing? Were they comparing Chipewyan, Swampy, and Woodland Cree women to European women servants or agricultural labourers, or to women of their own more privileged class? Or were they comparing the lives of these migratory Amerindians, both male and female, with the more settled lives of most Europeans? Perhaps native men viewed women's labour in a different light. Samuel Hearne quoted a Chipewyan chief, Matonabbee: "Women were made for labour," the chief had apparently told him; "one of them can carry, or haul, as much as two men can do." Their work was so important, in fact, that there was "no such thing as travelling any considerable distance, or for any length of time, in this country, without their assistance."[10]

Certainly there is no doubt that these women worked very hard. Plains women dried, pounded, and mixed berries with fat and buffalo or other meat to make pemmican. They stitched hides into bags to carry it. Nearly everywhere native women made the moccasins and leather clothes their people wore, netted the snowshoes that were indispensable to winter travel, and gathered gum and prepared birch-bark, spruce, or cedar fibres to make canoes. In many communities women were the carriers; in nearly all, they pitched the tents and broke camp when travelling. Their work, in other words, was essential.

The tasks women performed were closely related to the characteristics of their environments. The annual Micmac cycle took the people from the seal fishery on the coast in January to hunting beaver, otter, moose, bear, and caribou inland in February and March; spring sent them to the river mouths to fish and hunt waterfowl and eggs, while in summer they gathered berries and nuts. In the fall, the people withdrew from the shoreline again to take spawning eels in the rivers and, once again, to hunt the larger animals.[11] The sexual division of labour among the Micmac, described by an observer in 1612, seems to have meant that the women did nearly everything within this seasonal cycle but fight, while the men focussed exclusively on hunting and warfare.

The [women] besides the onerous role of bearing and rearing the children, also transport the game from the place where it has fallen; they are the hewers of wood and drawers of water; they make and repair the household utensils; they prepare the food; they skin the game and prepare the hides . . . sew garments . . . catch fish and gather shellfish for food; often they even hunt; they make the canoes . . . set up tents.[12]

Preparing hides and sewing garments among the Micmac amounted to more than simple tanning and stitchery. Five different techniques of working with dyed porcupine quills were known to them; early observers described their decorated clothing and other objects as "lively" in colour and, in general, "beautiful."[13]

Micmac camp.

Women trading, *circa* 1820.

Among native women everywhere in North America, the care of young children was women's work. Travellers and especially traders with the inland tribes commented on the ease with which mothers gave birth to their children. Andrew Graham noted how few of the symptoms that "afflict the delicate European" were experienced either in pregnancy or parturition by native women, "their pains being very light and soon over." Graham went on to give further details about motherhood among the Cree. Women giving birth while travelling, he claimed, simply dropped behind, brought forth "the little stranger . . . and carrying it on their backs, proceed[ed] to overtake their companions as if nothing had happened." He noted that children were "solely under the direction of the mother . . . being always esteemed the maternal property."[14]

Europeans greatly admired the wooden cradles in which infants in some tribes were tied and strapped to their mother's back. Packed in moss and soft deer hides, native babies seemed conveniently cared for in these cradles, which were sometimes decorated with beautiful designs. Native mothers nursed infants for at least two or three years, and this practice contributed to a relatively low birth rate. Native women living in their own communities rarely seem to have had on the average more than three or four children, which must have increased both their mobility and productivity.[15]

The question of women's power

European observers' interest in and admiration for native women's control of their children and the ease with which they evidently bore and cared for them is a clue, perhaps, to a certain unease. What native women controlled, native men did not; this gave white male observers pause. In addition, white women of their own acquaintance were cast in a somewhat unfavourable light, as comparatively delicate. Looking at the cultural, social, and political roles of North American native women through the eyes of such European recorders is a complex exercise, one that tells us almost as much about the observers as the observed.

There is evidence, both from contemporary anthropology and the historical record, that hunting and gathering economies like those of the Montagnais-Nascapi, and agricultural economies like those of the Six Nations and Huron, were in fact relatively egalitarian communities in which women enjoyed considerable power in three crucial areas: relative autonomy in sexual life and marriage; influence in politics or group decision making; and participation in the religious or ceremonial lives of their people. There was essentially no distinction in these societies between the "private" or domestic sphere and "public" life although, to the extent that political decisions and religious ceremonies were part of the larger communal world, these were in some sense distinct from the immediate purview of the family. Yet women were involved in both, despite their separate and distinct economic roles.

All native societies appear to have ritually secluded young women at the time of their first menstruation, and to have regarded menstruating women as powerful. Women among both the Montagnais-Nascapi and the Iroquois were evidently as free as men in their choice of spouses, although among the Iroquois, mothers formally arranged the marriages. There seems to have been considerable sexual freedom among adolescents, and both young women and young men initiated sexual encounters. Nor did the Iroquois or the Montagnais-Nascapi believe that marriage entailed sexual exclusiveness. Persons of either sex had a right to be satisfied with their unions, and so divorce was easy. This was particularly so because women had control over their children and, in the case of the Iroquois/Huron, exercised control over both agricultural property and domestic space. Polygamy, practised among the Montagnais-Nascapi, provided husbands for women who might otherwise not have had them. Iroquois and Montagnais-Nascapi welcomed children with great delight, and female children were considered a great boon.

Prior to and in the early days of contact, a young Montagnais-Nascapi man generally joined the household and hunting band of his wife, at least temporarily, thus supporting the wife's family in a subsistence economy in which skilled hunters were valuable and added to a family's strength. The Six Nations and the Huron were matrilineal as well as matrilocal: that is, to the extent that there were either property or chieftainships to inherit, inheritance was through the female line. In these groups too, husbands generally resided with the parents of their wives. The unpredictability and difficulty of Montagnais-Nascapi existence appears to have favoured a subtle and inclusive approach to decision making, taking the needs and wishes of all group members into consideration before a consensus was reached. Women's role in such decision making equalled men's, according to seventeenth century observers. Indeed Jesuits who came into contact with this group reported that the women of the Montagnais-Nascapi enjoyed "great power" in their communities. "A man may promise you something," one recounted, "and if he does not keep his promise, he thinks he is sufficiently excused when he tells you his wife did not wish to do it." The Jesuit recorders of Montagnais-Nascapi life did not approve and said as much.[16]

Reports about the detailed role of women in Six Nations government are not consistent: it is true that at tribal councils only male speakers were heard. But it is clear that leading Iroquois women not only exercised considerable power in selecting and deposing chiefs, but also had a voice in making treaties and in the councils of their tribes including, on some occasions, the power of life or death over prisoners, and in influencing decisions reached by consensus. If the structure of the household had any bearing on the structure of government, and seventeenth and eighteenth century Europeans believed that the two were closely linked, the control that women exercised in the running of the longhouses is also particularly significant. The People of the Longhouse respected the "matrons" or clan mothers who ran the houses they lived in, and this power was reflected in their higher councils. The increase in white settlement, which forced Iroquois men to travel farther and farther afield in the interest of the hunt and diplomacy, placed even greater power in the hands of Six Nations women. There is even evidence of Iroquois women, in isolated instances, engaging in warfare along with their men.

Women's authority was also reflected in the ceremonial and spiritual lives of these peoples. Among the Iroquois, women had an equal voice with men in the management of religious ceremonies and festivals or, at the very least, control over their own female ceremonial life. Among the Montagnais-Nascapi in the seventeenth century, women along with men could be shamans or people with special religious powers.

The Roman Catholic missionaries who first conducted missions among Canada's native peoples were steeped in a patriarchal tradition. They carried on intense campaigns to change the relations between the sexes, which they clearly felt were disruptive of all "natural" authority. The Jesuits complained about the lack of male control over women and connected it, in the case of the Montagnais-Nascapi, with their casual attitudes towards authority. The priests preached that wives should obey their husbands; that sexually exclusive monogamy should prevail; and that there should be no divorce. For one thing, they argued, women's sexual permissiveness confused the laws of lineage and inheritance. How could a man know which of his wife's children were his own? At least one Jesuit critic was rebuked for expressing this doubt about Montagnais-Nascapi mores. "Thou hast no sense," was the native man's response. "You French people love only your own children; but we love all the children of our tribe."[17]

The Jesuits made similar efforts to change male/female relations among the Hurons. In both cases the aim was the same: male control of women's sexuality. The alteration of gender relations in these communities was considered essential if the native people were to be brought under the control of both the Roman Catholic church and the French state. Hierarchical government could only work when hierarchy permeated the entire culture.

It may be that the mores of the Cree and Chipewyan peoples were very similar to those of the Montagnais-Nascapi at one time. Certainly these natives from the interior were hunter/gatherers, and what we know of Thanadelthur suggests that some Chipewyan women enjoyed considerable autonomy and power, at least on the edges of their communities. But there is also evidence of greater parental control over marriage among the northwestern tribes, and an attitude that young women were important elements in the vital bargaining games of the fur trade, rather than individuals choosing marriage partners on their own behalf. Among the Chipewyan, women often had no choice at all when it came to husbands; fur traders told stories of Chipewyan men wrestling with each other for wives, who became the possession of the winner. Among the Carrier Amerindians, widows became the virtual slaves of their in-laws for a period following the death of their spouses.[18]

The Hudson's Bay Company, unlike the French companies who sent their agents into the woods from the seventeenth century on, was at first reluctant to countenance any intimacy between native women and its employees. This was not an attitude that could last. It quickly became apparent that a native female companion not only fostered trade relations, but was essential to any man intending to travel great distances or to live for any time in fur trade country. Thus the employees of both the Hudson's Bay and the Northwest companies, like the *coureurs du bois*, not only travelled into Amerindian country in the course of their work, they also married there. Indeed, marriages between native women and traders "according to the custom of the country" became the rule rather than the exception. Fur traders developed long-term relationships with Amerindian women, whom they married according to native customary rites, and whom they referred to as their "country" wives. Our information, then, is about northwestern native women who were already drawn into the white man's orbit. By the nineteenth century, Chief Factor James Douglas spoke not only of the practical nature of traders' alliances with such women, but of their psychological value as well.

If these alliances were important to the traders, they were no less so to the native women and their relatives. Indeed fur trade marriages were sometimes initiated by native women, possibly in league with their families. The story of Alexander Henry's encounter with an Ojibway woman illustrates the point. Returning from New Year's festivities, Henry found the young woman in question in his rooms. When he asked her to leave, she refused, so Henry went buffalo hunting. We do not know whether or not her family initially instructed this young woman to pursue Alexander Henry. But the fact that her father, an Ojibway chief, later tried to persuade the trader to marry both of his daughters suggests a strong parental interest in the affair.

For native peoples the marriage alliance created a reciprocal social bond, which in turn was intended to consolidate economic relations. As a result of their marriages to native women, traders were supposed to be drawn into native kinship circles; in return for access to their women, native families expected unhindered access to the trading posts and their provisions. Nor did native families permit their daughters to marry indiscriminately. The Flathead tribe would only allow marriages with traders whom they particularly esteemed, and the evidence generally suggests that, by the end of the eighteenth century, parental consent to trader/native unions was considered essential. A *voyageur*, recalling his experience, was adamant on the importance of such consent. One ran the risk of getting "one's head broken" if one took an Amerindian girl without her parents' permission.

Some bride price was customary; occasionally large gifts were involved. Horses were sometimes given; blankets, guns, or utensils were also typical gifts. It is clear that traders were following Amerindian custom in the matter. There was no exchange of vows, but there was ritual: a pipe was smoked perhaps. Among some tribes the bride was lectured by her relatives on her new duties. In some cases the trader visited the home of his bride, and her relatives ceremonially accompanied her to her new home.

The special circumstances of women on the west coast add considerable complexity to any discussion of the relative power and autonomy of native women in pre-contact and early contact societies, for west coast cultures tended to be rank-differentiated. The Haida of the Queen Charlotte Islands are a case in point. Matrilineal like the Iroquois and Hurons of the Great Lakes, the Haida evidently passed all property through the female line. Yet marriages among the Haida appear to have been arranged by men. The mother might be consulted, but the mother's uncle and the father made the final decisions. Moreover, brides were expected to accept the authority of their husbands, and widows were required to take a new husband selected by their husband's relatives. Women's subordinate status in marriage was reflected in their limited access to political power. Women could be chiefs, and the number of female chiefs increased after the introduction of European diseases decimated the Haida in the late nineteenth century, but in general chiefs were male, and female participation in political activity was restricted.

Because of menstrual and reproductive taboos, the presence of Haida women was thought dangerous to men who were hunting or fishing, and women were evidently completely excluded from male work of this kind. In the crafts and arts, weaving was the work of women; carving was strictly reserved for men. Yet, despite the fact that the dominant trade role was played by men, trade deals often seem to have required a wife's consent, and women also participated in Haida ceremonial activities. They were involved in the famous feasts known as potlatches that were so important to the wealthy

Weaving, Vancouver Island, by John Webber, 1778.

Haida; mothers held potlatches for their daughters at puberty. Women were barred from the more important dances at Haida ceremonies, but they could become shamans.[19]

The behaviour of a west coast Clayoquot woman in connection with the landing of a whale illustrates her importance as a partner, although not necessarily an equal partner, in her husband's work. The Clayoquot wife was observed coming to her husband's boat and performing certain ritual actions, following which she gave a speech. In her speech she told everyone "that she and her husband had observed strict preparatory rituals for eight moons, had slept in separate beds, and prayed for strength and power." Clearly this woman's actions were vital to the hunt, even as she was excluded from it.[20]

Women seem to have had less authority in the non-matrilineal coastal tribes such as the Salish. At the time of contact, all important property in this group appears to have been held by men and was passed on from father to son. Women married men chosen by their parents and, upon marriage, went to live in the villages of their husbands. If there was a divorce, the children generally remained with the father. Although, like native women from a number of other tribes, women did go on quests for guardian spirits, possibly because they were not hunters, their journeys were not long ones, for their need for spirit helpers was less than that of men. Community decision making, in general, belonged to men, and the women appear to have been rigidly excluded from the governing councils of the Salish.

Because west coast tribes were ranked societies, some lower status native women in the West probably had very little control over their lives. This was of course the case for slaves, who existed among some of the tribes by the time the Europeans arrived. European imperialism brought increased trade and wealth, but it also brought more reason for slavery and polygamy, at least on the west coast. Wives and slaves were pressed into dressing the sea otter pelts that were required in increasing numbers for the coastal fur trade, and this may well have altered the social structure and lowered the status of native women in the Pacific Coast region.[21]

The native woman's perspective

How did native women regard the Europeans whose patriarchal culture encroached on and eventually destroyed so much of their own? As far as we can tell, the reactions of native women varied enormously, according to the time and place.

As the Jesuits themselves reported, missionaries did not always succeed in altering the marriage and social patterns of the peoples they had hoped to convert. Montagnais-Nascapi women regularly ran away from husbands who attempted to impose their Christian will on their wives.[22] And clearly more than one Montagnais-Nascapi husband came to the conclusion that the Jesuits had no sense. Yet gradually the missionaries did manage to disrupt the social patterns of those natives who were attracted more or less permanently to French settlements. In the seventeenth century, at the Amerindian settlement of Sillery, near Quebec, where native families who had been converted to Christianity were induced to engage in farming, the land was given to men who were made "captains" by their benefactors. Charity to families in want was handed out through newly created chieftains. Unmarried women were strictly controlled, and wives who disobeyed their husbands were beaten. Some native women met the Jesuits on their own ground by adopting celibacy, thus protecting themselves from the trials of European-style marriage, as did the first Canadian native woman to be called "venerable" by the Roman Catholic church. Kateri Tekakwitha, an Algonkin/Mohawk orphan who lived in the Montreal region in the 1670s, was idealized by the French authorities for her chastity and saintliness, before her early death at the age of twenty-four.[23]

The Jesuits did less well among those Montagnais-Nascapi who stayed away from French settlements, and among the Hurons, whom they attempted to convert in Huronia itself. When the natives were on their own turf, the system of economic and social dependency that the French created at Sillery could not be duplicated. The Hurons, already agricultural, and with their own complex systems of land use and inheritance, resisted the encroachment of the missionaries. Indeed, it may well have been Huron women who were at the core of the resistance. Huron men who adopted Christianity found themselves ostracized and ejected from the longhouses by their mothers-in-law. Until the 1640s, when the Hurons were dispersed by Iroquois incursions, the traditional family-oriented systems of production continued to guarantee to women, along with men, access to the necessities of life.[24] Over a century later, Seneca women living in what had once been the old province of Quebec and was now part of the United States, resisted Quaker efforts to divide up the land and assign it to their men. Clearly these later Iroquois women understood the importance of keeping control, if they could, over a major source of their livelihood.[25]

Provided one was not starving or defeated in battle (the case with Tekakwitha's people), there was little temptation for native women to adopt the missionaries' culture, which offered so little and in fact threatened so clear a loss of power. But resisting the white men who were involved in the major economic activity of the era was another matter. If marriage to a trader were a possibility, the temptation for native women must have been considerable.

The fur traders themselves were no doubt biased in the matter, but they certainly believed that native women regarded marriage to white men as preferable to marriage within their own tribes. Cree women were reported to consider it an honour to be chosen as a trader's wife. Such perceptions were reinforced by the traders' belief that the position of native women in their own societies was extremely low. To European men, the burden of Amerindian women's work appeared enormous; such women, they felt, could only welcome the relative comfort of life within the trading forts.

It is when the women married whites and moved into the trading posts that their material circumstances and their leverage with native and white men alike improved, at least initially. As Nor'Wester George Nelson pointed out, native women had a particular interest in keeping the peace, and there is no doubt that, for a time, intermarriage between fur traders and Amerindians did promote better relations between the two groups. Through their marriages, native women could gain significant power: the power to create or destroy friendly relations by their influence and good offices with both sides.[26]

In general, fur traders' wives enjoyed a life that was also physically easier than life in a migratory band. They had the benefit, perhaps illusory, of clothing made from imported textiles, and company servants did some of the heavy work that tribal women customarily did — carrying goods and hauling firewood and water. Although domestic tasks were never given over entirely to others by traders' native wives, they were able to become more sedentary and spend more time on the making of moccasins, snowshoes, and other family goods. Altogether, the material improvement must have seemed very great indeed. The "country" wife's access to European goods, moreover, generally extended to members of her family and band, who had already benefitted from the good trade relations that her marriage helped cement. Finally, there is ample evidence that many fur trade marriages were loving and life-long arrangements, and traders wrote about their Amerindian families with great affection and warmth.[27]

But there was a negative side. During the eighteenth century, some traders saw the capture and abuse of rivals' wives as weapons in the ongoing struggle between different interests for mastery of the trade. Traders' native wives were also subject to new diseases. They had longer years of childbearing, for fur traders' families, in the early to mid-nineteenth century at least, were large—from eight to twelve children compared to the four typically born to the average Cree woman. This surely took a physical toll. Childbirth itself appears to have been more difficult for traders' native wives. Unlike their counterparts in native society, country wives also had to share the raising of their children with patriarchal husbands, who had European views on discipline and education that were very different from their own. Wives of officers had to face sending children, especially sons, away to boarding schools or to paternal relatives for their education, and often these absent children died.[28]

Finally, changes in the fur trade, coupled with the arrival in the west of missionaries and European wives in the early nineteenth century, brought about a decline in the incidence of traders taking Amerindian spouses. Even before this, traders who wished to return to Europe or to the east had readily engaged in a practice that came to be known as "turning off" their native wives. At one time such women had been able to return to their tribal communities with pride, and they and their children had been welcomed; but this was to be less and less the case, and was probably not an option at all for mixed-blood women. Some wives were turned over to new trader husbands, but others found themselves abandoned and belonging to neither white nor native worlds.[29]

Such women were probably still better off than those native and mixed-blood women who, as European men moved into their territories in greater and greater numbers, found themselves involved in prostitution. The sexual freedom of women in many, if not all, native tribes was misinterpreted by Europeans, who were accustomed to purchasing sexual favours that native peoples regarded as customary. One trader noted that Cree girls were rarely virgins by the age of thirteen or fourteen; another pointed out that "fornication" could hardly be considered a vice among the Amerindians, as for them the practice was accepted as normal.[30] Coupled with the sale of alcohol to Amerindian men and women, prostitution and venereal diseases took their unfortunate toll. Accounts of the condition of Nova Scotia Micmacs point to considerable prostitution, drunkenness, and wife-beating by the seventeenth century. A French traveller saw women who had fallen into "a melancholy so black and profound that they became immersed wholly in a cruel despair. . . ." The results, he said, sometimes included suicide.[31]

Yet not all native women were victims. Many, like Thanadelthur, wove a careful and resourceful path among the options that were open to them, adapting where possible and surviving as best they could. On the east coast, Micmac women are examples of those who managed to rescue something of their former lives. Four out of five of their quill-working techniques were lost during the seventeenth century. But by the late eighteenth and early nineteenth centuries, Micmac craftswomen had developed new techniques for working quills on birchbark, and there was a new flowering of their art, which developed considerable economic importance.[32] It is also probably the case that most native women who came into intimate contact with white men did so as their tribally sanctioned "country" wives, following the customs of their own peoples, and gaining at least short-term benefits by their actions.

Finally, the vast majority of native women, like the Montagnais-Nascapi and Hurons, probably followed a more resistant path, holding on to their cultures and customs and adapting slowly to change. Most Hurons perished in the Iroquois wars. But by the nineteenth century, native groups who recognized the damage wrought in their societies by European intrusion retreated where they could, and some at least managed to avoid the tragedies that befell the Micmacs, Hurons, and other decimated groups. In 1838 in a remote part of what was to become the Yukon Territory, a Hudson's Bay Company trader met a thirty-five year old "Nahany Chieftainess" whose commanding presence and energy created a lasting impression on him. For perhaps several more generations, women of her region would remain isolated enough to continue their lives relatively untouched by European ways. Certainly by then some native women clearly understood the threat. In 1850 in the Similkameen and Okanagan areas of the territory that was to become British Columbia, a prophet was travelling through the country urging the native people to fight white encroachment and to keep their own traditions. They were told to "retain their old customs and not to adopt any of the ways of the white man," because to do this would poison their spirit. The prophet was a woman.[33]

If male observers often referred to the dreariness of native women's lives, the British feminist, Anna Jameson, put forward a different opinion when she encountered Amerindian communities in Upper Canada and adjacent regions in the 1830s. Jameson was aware of and called attention to European men's castigations of Amerindian societies for their enslavement and oppression of women. Yet, whatever the lot of the native woman, Jameson pointed out, at least she was not in a *"false* position."

When we speak of the drudgery of the women, we must note the equal division of labour; there is no class of women privileged to sit still while others work. Every squaw makes the clothing, mats, moccasins, and boils the kettle for her own family. . . . Compare her life with that of a servant-maid of all work, or a factory girl, — I say that the condition of the squaw is gracious in comparison, dignified by domestic feelings, and by equality with all around her. . . . The personal property, as the clothing, mats, cooking and hunting apparatus, all the interior of the wigwam . . . seems to be under the control of the woman. . . . The corn she raises, and the maple sugar she makes, she can always dispose of as she thinks fit — they are hers.[34]

By all accounts, Amerindian women worked hard and were strong. Among hunters and gatherers, women supplied a major share of the diet. In all native societies, women's work was essential to the survival of family and band. Should we conclude that native societies were egalitarian on the whole, at least as far as male/female relations were concerned? Perhaps it is unwise to put our query in these terms. The Amerindian world did not have the concept of individual economic rights. In small hunting and gathering bands, where decision making was often communal, women do seem to have shared some of the power with men. In the Iroquoian agricultural communities, matrons or the leading women in charge of the longhouses appear to have enjoyed great power, not only in their own realms of production, distribution, and child care, but in the larger decision-making processes of the group. In their separate female world of agricultural work and childrearing they played leadership roles, and this leadership was transferred to the larger society. Yet among the northwestern and western native peoples, the situation was more complicated. High-status women could be chieftains, evidently, but many women were relatively powerless.

The histories of these women have yet to be uncovered; perhaps much of their history is permanently lost to us. But where history is lost, legend and story come to our aid. Stories told by contemporary native and mixed-blood women about the heroines of their mythic past emphasize their ingenuity and practical skills.[35] What we know of Thanadelthur suggests much ingenuity and practical ability. What we know of Aataentsic and Copper Woman suggests a legacy also of power.

2 French women in the New World

On 25 June 1669, just one year after her marriage, a young woman in the advanced stages of pregnancy appeared before the Sovereign Council, the highest judicial body in the colony of Canada. Marie Bourgois had come to charge her husband and father-in-law with denying her the necessities of life. In her moving appeal for support, she reminded the Councillors that she was "a poor woman who had left her father and her mother and her relatives to come to this country."[1] Like Marie Bourgois, many of the women who made the arduous voyage to New France left behind the comforts of family, friends, and familiar surroundings, only to encounter disappointment and deprivation in a strange and often inhospitable land. Most, however, persevered and took satisfaction in the re-rooting of family and society in the New World. Some came from peasant groups, with their superstitions and rowdy rituals, others from bourgeois families of French coastal towns, and others still from the more sophisticated commercial and administrative centres of Paris and Versailles. We have only to think of the nuns, with their mixture of wealthy aristocrats and women with few or no economic resources, to realize the complexities of character and circumstance that marked the lives of French women who came to the New World.

Les pionnières

While many of the women who migrated to New France in the seventeenth century were married women or daughters who came with their families, there were also hundreds of single women and widows who tackled the voyage, either alone or in the company of more distant relations. Some came and went back. Marie Joly, for example, was a Parisian widow who came to Canada with her cousin. In Quebec she contracted a marriage with Antoine Damiens of Rouen, only to return to France and settle in La Rochelle.[2] Many of the single women came with the intention to marry immediately; others came as *engagées* or indentured servants, and had to delay marriage; still others, for whom the religious mission was paramount, came intending to devote their lives to God.

The first married European woman to remain in New France permanently was Marie Rollet, the spouse of the apothecary and farmer, Louis Hébert. She established a household in Quebec with her husband in 1617 and lived there with her family until his death, when she joined the farming household of her daughter and son-in-law. This first housewife of New France was on a lower social plane than Hélène Boullé, the twenty-two-year-old gentlewoman who accompanied her husband, the explorer Samuel de Champlain, to Canada in 1620. Hélène Boullé was a wealthy woman: she had been officially married to Champlain at the age of twelve, and by the time she embarked for Quebec her dowry had already paid for the out-fitting of one of her husband's earlier expeditions. There must have been a considerable gulf between Madame de Champlain's aristo-cratic Parisian upbringing and what she found in the New World, but we know little about her except that she had a brother who was in her husband's service and may have given her some companionship during her stay in Canada. She spent four years in the colony, at least some of her time performing charitable works among the natives, and then returned to France, eventually to retire to an Ursuline convent that she had founded and endowed.[3]

Hélène Boullé's retirement to a religious community is not sur-prising, for religious orders for women flourished in Counter-Ref-ormation France, and their religious zeal was transmitted to New France. Inspired by what they read in the *Relations* of the Jesuit missionaries, pious French women soon saw in the New World another and especially fertile field for their spiritual endeavours. These French women were not unique, for similar feelings inspired the Puritans of New England. They were unusual, however, in two important respects. The first was that a remarkable number of them came to New France independently as single women or as members of female religious societies. Secondly, the all-female institutions they founded played a vital role in the material, social, and spiritual development of their colony. Similar charitable and social institutions were not created in the British North American colonies until at least the eighteenth century, and even then few if any welfare estab-lishments in the British colonies were run by women.[4]

In 1639 an order of nuns called the *Hospitalières* arrived in the vicinity of Quebec. The two sisters who directed Quebec's first medical mission, Marie Grunet and Marie Forrestier, were respond-ing to a need outlined in the 1635 *Relation* of Father Lejeune, and their first thought was for the native community then living at Sillery, outside of the fortress of Quebec. In 1644 the Sillery mission was abandoned as a result of the Iroquois wars, and the hospital nuns moved into the citadel and made the French population the focus of their care. Operating at first in a small wooden structure, the sisters had acquired a larger building by 1658. Boasting eight doors and eight windows, this hospital normally held ten beds, but in times of epidemic could accommodate up to twenty. By 1672 the *Hôtel-Dieu*, as the hospital was called, had expanded to two halls — one for women and one for men — and included as well a small chamber for wealthier patients.[5]

The Ursulines also came to Quebec in 1639 expecting to devote themselves to the Amerindians, only to have these expectations crushed when many of their native charges proved resistant to their

A modern interpretation of the Ursulines' arrival at Quebec.

"civilizing" mission. The strict discipline of the convent school was alien to homesick native girls who, with the aid of their parents, slipped away to the forest. Soon the principal function of the Ursuline convent was to educate the daughters of the French colonists.

Marie (Guyart) de l'Incarnation, the founder of the Quebec Ursuline convent, had nurtured a religious vocation through adolescence, marriage, motherhood, widowhood, and a ten-year business involvement in the mercantile household of her brother-in-law. Her vocation eventually led Marie Guyart to enter a convent in Tours, but not before she had learned much in the management of her brother-in-law's business affairs that would be of practical value in her future work in New France. Indeed the creation of a convent school in Quebec involved far more than an understanding of the management of children. She had to assure the community's finances, which were only partly organized by her patron and chief fundraiser, Mme de la Peltrie; she had to oversee the construction of the first convent and then of a second one when the first was destroyed by fire; and she had to deal with the complicated matter of provisioning her community in the midst of the Amerindian wars. Somehow, while she governed the Quebec Ursulines and ran a boarding school for Amerindian and French girls, this astounding woman also found time not only to write several religious works in native languages and in French, but also some 12 000 letters to her son and to others in France who were interested in her New World mission.[6]

The lives of the women who founded religious communities in the mission called Ville Marie (Montreal) were no less demanding. In one way these women were even more unusual than the nuns of Quebec, for neither of the two key figures in the women's religious foundations of Montreal were at first members of established orders. Jeanne Mance was a single woman in her mid-thirties when she came to Canada in 1641. She first settled in Quebec in order to study the organization of the *Hôtel-Dieu* there and to learn the Huron language; only then did she move on to Ville Marie to found its first medical dispensary. As an entrepreneur and organizer she must have had few equals. Her efforts included three trips back to France to raise money and to search out an order of nuns to staff the new mission, and a major battle with the Bishop of Quebec for the right to bring a second nursing order to New France. The hospital nuns of *Saint-Joseph de la Flèche* were installed by permission of the French king against the will of Bishop Laval, who would have preferred to send a detachment of the sisters already established in the hospital at Quebec.[7]

Laval also fought with the *Congrégation de Notre Dame*, the creation of another laywoman. Marguerite Bourgeoys, who joined de Maisonneuve's Montreal mission as an educator, saw an opportunity and hit upon novel means to embrace it. Bourgeoys eventually felt the need for assistants in her educational work and returned to France to find like-minded women. The result was the secular community, founded in 1671, that was to become the *Congrégation*. The teachers of Bourgeoys' new order came into conflict not only with the local Bishop of Quebec, but with the larger church and its rules, because they preferred not to wear distinctive habits, take solemn public vows, or even cloister themselves; they argued that their guide and teacher was none other than the Virgin Mary, who had remained in the world without benefit of formal vows or, presumably, distinctive dress. She had nevertheless fulfilled her religious destiny, and so would they.[8]

At first religious communities shared with the fur trading monopoly—the Company of One Hundred Associates—the task of recruiting brides for French soldiers and traders wishing to settle in the New World. It was generally the nuns who took charge of the single women who came to the colony with the intention of marrying, until these *filles à marier* found husbands. When royal officials assumed direct control of the colony in 1663, they became actively involved in promoting the immigration of single women. Between 1643 and 1663, only 230 unmarried female immigrants had made their way to New France; in the next decade, nearly 800 single women, known as the *filles du roi* or "daughters of the king," arrived. Interested parties such as Jean Talon, the Intendant of New France during the early years of royal government, wanted to be sure that the young women selected to enjoy the king's bounty were indeed going to be useful immigrants. Talon specified that the women destined for Canada should be in no way "disgraced by nature" or have anything "repulsive about their exterior persons." He also demanded that "they should be healthy and strong for country work, or at least that they have some inclination to work with their hands." Fears were expressed by others that women brought up in cities like Paris might not adapt well to conditions in New France.[9] In fact, on the whole, they adapted well. It has been estimated that only one-half of all immigrants to New France remained for the rest of their lives, but of the single women who came to be married there, nine out of ten became permanent settlers.[10]

The social origins of the *filles du roi* were diverse. Many of them came from the Paris *Hôpital-Général*, an institution that harboured women pregnant out of wedlock, as well as orphans and abandoned children. Others were clearly young women whose parents could not, for some reason, arrange good marriages for their daughters. Certainly a great number had parents still alive. Three sisters, Françoise, Marie-Madeleine, and Marie Raclot, not only had good dowries for the time, but were accompanied to New France by their father in 1671. The latter stayed in the colony only long enough to sign the marriage contracts of two of his daughters. Aged eighteen, seventeen, and fifteen when they came to New France, the Raclot sisters settled in the vicinity of Three Rivers with the husbands they had acquired within a few months of their arrival.[11]

Most of the *filles* appear in fact to have come, like these sisters, from Paris or from other relatively large centres, and many must have been ill-prepared for the new lives that awaited them. Of those whose ages were recorded, the majority were between twelve and twenty-five, but a significant one in four was older. Their main interest, once in Canada, was reportedly a practical one: to find husbands who had already built houses or cabins on their land. That some 11 percent entered into more than one marriage contract before going through with the final religious ceremony may further suggest not only a healthy respect for their own self-interest, but a willingness to take advantage of their major trump card: the scarcity of unmarried women in New France. The women were given substantial dowries by the king, according to their station, to assist them and their husbands in setting up their households; no doubt these dowries added to their considerable bargaining power. One source values the "king's gift" at between 100 and 500 *livres*, with further disbursements for practical items that would be needed immediately in the way of clothing or equipment (including one hundred sewing needles) and later, in the way of household goods. The Raclot sisters received gifts from the king in addition to the dowry of one thousand *livres* each given by their father.[12]

At least 774 "daughters of the king" came to New France between 1663 and 1673 to join the approximately 1200 men and women colonists who had arrived earlier. In Montreal by 1681, of the 161 women immigrants, more than two-thirds were *filles seules* — women who were neither nuns nor servants and yet had come to the colony alone.[13] After the special push of the 1660s and 1670s and until the 1750s, the French colonies welcomed an average of less than fifty new arrivals a year; fewer than one in five of these were women. Altogether immigrants numbered under 10 000 for the entire French regime. In the eighteenth century trading and military fortress of Louisbourg, where the immigrants came mostly from the bourgeois and artisan classes, women were never more than one-tenth of the immigrants or one-third of the total population. In New France as a whole women were also very much a minority at first. But by 1760, of the nearly 70 000 people who made up the total population of New France, the number of men and women were finally almost equal.[14]

Family and work

Most of the women who came to New France married. As in comparable English colonies of the period, the rates of marriage and remarriage were very high — in one sample that has been studied, one-third of all widows married again. The story of Anne Le Sont of Three Rivers is perhaps atypical, but is nevertheless instructive. The employer of this middle-aged *engagée* had prevailed upon her to sign a life contract in November of 1655, and took her to court when she married one Jean Desmarais soon after her arrival. The affair was settled in Anne's favour, but only after a suitable apology for her "insulting words" and on payment of the plaintiff's costs. Perhaps more typical was the case of the young *engagée* Judithe Rigeault who, when she married a soldier and master tailor by the name of François le Maître, still owed a portion of the five years she had contracted to serve Mme Le Neuf de la Poterie. Once again a court case ensued and once again the financial obligations of both parties had to be worked out before a settlement could be reached.[15]

Anne Le Sont was much older than the average bride when she married, but this may not have been her first marriage. In general, servants who came out to New France on their own appear to have married in their early twenties.[16] But even this was older than average for girls who were born in the colony in the seventeenth century, for at first the average age at which women married in New France was very young compared to typical marriages in western Europe at this time. Young people were not supposed to marry until puberty, but there is evidence that occasionally girls as young as twelve and thirteen embarked on matrimony during the initial period of colonization when men vastly outnumbered women. Estimates of average ages at marriage have varied depending on the period or region studied. A recent one fixes them for rural families prior to 1700 at 19.6 for women and 27.3 for men. A different pattern has been uncovered for mid-eighteenth-century Sorel, however. By this time the numbers of men and women had almost evened out; the average

age at marriage for women was 22.4, and for men, 26.6. For New France as a whole, the average age at marriage has been placed at 22 for women (three years younger than was typical in France itself) and 27 for men. Relatively large groups of people delayed marriage: some 18 percent of men and women did not marry until they were 30 or older; 6 percent were 40 or older.[17]

Much has been made of the explicit legal encouragement that the royal administration gave to early marriages in New France. A seventeenth century statute provided that men marrying at 25 or younger and women marrying by 20 were entitled to a bonus of 20 *livres* from the Crown; a further law imposed fines on the parents of young people who failed to marry by the required age. Colonial authorities publicly regretted young men becoming *coureurs du bois* or fur traders, and persons of either sex remaining celibate. The married state was officially encouraged for both sexes, as was the production of children.[18]

Certainly the fundamental goal of the state in sponsoring female immigration and rewarding early marriage was to promote population growth: to seventeenth century and eighteenth century European minds, people meant workers and soldiers and these, in turn, spelled wealth and safety. If New France was to survive and prosper, the production of people was considered a vital necessity. Individual couples also equated children with wealth. Children were workers, first and foremost for their own families.

Still, for much of the seventeenth century, economic factors and the unequal numbers of men and women probably had most effect on age at marriage and the high rates of marriage and remarriage. They even affected the season of marriage, which, before 1680, was typically early autumn, immediately following the arrival of the ships from France. Later on, when the sexes were more equal in number, winter became the most popular season for weddings. Finally, the relatively low age at which women in New France married and the high rates of remarriage almost certainly helped to boost the average number of children per marriage, as did the fact that spouses lived slightly longer than they did in Europe. In eighteenth century Acadia, for example, four out of five marriages were "complete" in the sense that both spouses survived to the end of the wife's childbearing years. Infant mortality was high, but surviving children were probably healthier than they were in the Old World. So were adults. For all these reasons, it is not surprising that women in Canada gave birth to eight or nine children on the average in the early years (seven from 1700 on), and that the average "completed" family was 5.65 children per couple (compared to 4.5 in France at this time). Studies indicate that relatively large families were characteristic of other seventeenth and eighteenth century colonies in North America, where good food was generally available and European diseases not so rampant, among white populations at least. Still, the numbers of children born and surviving seem to have been particularly high in New France.[19]

Table 2.1   Marriage and birth rates, New France, 1681–1760
per 1000 inhabitants

	Marriages	Births
1681–1690	9.2	43.3
1691–1700	10.5	53.4
1701–1710	9.1	57.8
1711–1720	10.2	57.5
1721–1730	10.2	55.2
1731–1740	9.4	56.6
1741–1750	10.4	55.9
1751–1760	11.3	59.6

Nature influenced the rhythms of childbirth in New France. Historians have discovered that conception tended to occur in the winter and spring, and that there were slight differences between Montreal and Quebec in this seasonal timing. The church had an influence as well, as there were fewer conceptions during the seasons of Advent and Lent.[20] Childbirth was a major social event. Women gave birth at home, assisted by midwives, and often in the presence of a large group of people—certainly with relatives and perhaps the priest very close at hand. The event frequently took place at the home of the new mother's parents and was accompanied by important rituals: the baptism, which took place as soon as possible after the birth, and a *"repas de baptême"* or festive meal to repay and thank the assistants. A new mother might have women friends stay for a week to help after her child was born; she would usually have her mother's assistance for at least a month.[21]

From: Jacques Henripin, *Tendances et facteurs de la fécondité au Canada* (Ottawa: Bureau fédérale de la statistique, 1968).

Children meant work for women, since the labour of childbirth and early childrearing was hard in the difficult pioneer conditions that obtained in both town and country in the New World. Yet, as they grew up, many children could eventually lighten a woman's workload. Older children minded younger ones, and girls helped when they were old enough with all the tasks of the household, garden, farm, or workshop, that fell to women. These tasks were many and their value high. Few households, farms, or businesses could run without the work of women.

Women spent most of their time on the production of food. Soups, stews, roasts, and bread were standard fare and were cooked

A present-day depiction of a birth scene in New France, by Jean-Claude Dupont.

mostly in open fireplaces. Rural women probably laboured as much at the tasks of butchering, curing, and drying of meat, the various tasks of the dairy and the poultry yard, and the growing of vegetables and fruit, as they did at the work of preparing the food for the table. In the Lower Richelieu Valley by the eighteenth century, women typically grew squash, onions, cabbages, and tobacco in their gardens. Travellers in Acadia commented on the large variety of vegetables that were grown, including "cabbages, beets, onions, carrots, chives, shallots, turnips, and all sorts of salads." Even urban women kept cows and poultry and had vegetable gardens when they could, although most produce and grains were generally purchased from the surrounding countryside.[22]

Women in New France also shared in the work of their husbands. At certain busy times of the year farm women worked in the fields, and artisans' and merchants' wives were probably also skilled assistants to their spouses. Both rural and urban women often kept the accounts and managed the servants or apprentices, if there were any. Owing to the periodic absences of their husbands, soldiers' and traders' wives sometimes had to take complete charge of their households, farms, and businesses. They also occasionally found that the fur trade or the wars or both had arrived on their very doorsteps. Madeleine de Verchères was only one of many women who fired a gun, or took over when men were absent, in skirmishes with enemies. Indeed Madeleine's own mother had defended the fort at Verchères from Iroquois attack in 1690, two years before her daughter was called upon to do so in 1692. In the early days of Acadia, Françoise-Marie Jacquelin de la Tour spent a good part of the first four years of her marriage travelling back and forth between her husband's fort at the mouth of the St. John River, France, and New England, working to defend his precarious position in the Acadian trade. Finally settled in Fort La Tour during one of his absences, she not only took charge of its defence but was forced to witness the execution of nearly all of its men after its capture. Mme de la Tour herself did not survive this defeat by many weeks and died at Fort La Tour in 1645.[23]

Although not all came to grief in such a traumatic way, most seventeenth century women of New France probably experienced warfare at first hand. The eighteenth century brought somewhat more peaceful times as the Iroquois threat declined and New France expanded. It also brought economic development. Few if any women had the time or the facilities for spinning or weaving in seventeenth century Canada. Indeed, clerics and upper class visitors to the colony commented on women's "idleness," and urged the authorities to establish a textile industry. The women themselves maintained that more pressing work took up their time. But it is also true that both materials and skills were at first in short supply. Except for native-style clothing made of leather, most wearing apparel and fabrics for bedding and the like had to be imported, and early wills suggest how few clothes even the most prosperous colonists possessed. But as time went on, Acadian and then Canadian women began to be involved in the production of spun and woven goods.[24] Acadian women, especially, evidently learned many crafts from their Micmac neighbours; birchbark household utensils and leather moccasins were only a few of the items they adopted as their own. Yet it is important to stress how few farms or communities in the New World were entirely self-sufficient. Goods such as needles and metal pots and farm tools had to be imported from outside the colony, as did fancier items like silk fabrics and French shoes. Both the movement of goods and of people was considerable in New France.[25]

Women worked hard in New France. Some immigrants to the New World, according to seventeenth century witnesses, longed for the "sweetness" of life in the country of their birth. But others reported that most people were better off in New France than their social equals were in the Old World.[26]

Favoured women?

There is reason to believe that women's social/political position, both within marriage and outside it, as well as their economic position, was stronger in New France than elsewhere in the seventeenth and eighteenth centuries. As in France, the law was harsh in some respects, but it did provide a measure of protection to married women. Also as in France, women of the upper and middle classes were sometimes able to play influential (if not always "official") roles in trade, political life, and medicine. Finally, the missionary church provided opportunities for religious women, especially those in leadership roles, to organize their own lives.

The women of New France enjoyed relative freedom of choice in marriage. Among rural women in particular, there appears to have been little interference from either parents or clergy in the selection of partners, although the church was anxious to prevent the marriage of people who were too closely related, and the permission of parents was officially required.[27] All marriages were subject to the rules laid down in the *Coutume de Paris*. Under this law married women had a status inferior to their husbands and were "severely restricted in their rights and prerogatives." The law clearly regarded the man as the head of the household. Widows could not exercise guardianship over their own children. But the same law did afford some important economic protection both to married women and widows. The spouses were seen to have mutual obligations towards each other. The "community of property" that came into being at a marriage entailed restrictions on the husband, who was to manage this property with care and provide for the support of his wife and children. On the death of her husband, a wife could continue the "community" or renounce it, along with its debts if there were any. The husband did not have the latter right; certain kinds of property that the wife brought into the marriage, moreover, were in theory protected from ill-advised acts of the husband, since by law he was supposed to manage this property and could not alienate it without his wife's permission. Finally, under the Custom of Paris, married women enjoyed dower rights: a woman was expected to bring a dowry into the marriage, but when her husband died, she was entitled to the use of one half of the community property until her own death.[28]

Because of the complexity of the laws governing matrimony, it is not surprising that a significant proportion of marriages involved written contracts — indeed, as many as 95 percent in some regions of France. In eighteenth century Louisbourg 40 percent of the marriages that took place were governed by contracts, compared to 60 percent in Paris. We cannot give percentages for New France as a whole, but the length of the hundreds of contracts that have survived in notarial archives attests to their importance, at least to the wealthier segments of the population. Often signed by dozens of witnesses, they also provide a fascinating glimpse of the social networks surrounding brides and grooms, as well as evidence of their social standing in their communities. Studies of contracts have shown that there was considerable social mobility in New France. If unions among the wealthier classes were arranged with economic or political interests in mind, they nevertheless crossed boundaries between the landed aristocracy, the merchant class, and the military. A woman could make her way in the world through the right sort of marriage, as could a man.[29]

Considerable information also survives regarding the pensions of older women and widows. If a woman chose to give up her farm or her household to a son or daughter (or another person) in return for her subsistence, the *pension alimentaire* usually contained very specific provisions. The widow Thibeault, who lived in the Richelieu Valley in 1760, was to be provided with heat, light, clothing, and houseroom according to the arrangement she made with her family. Her annual allotment of food included sixteen *minots* (bushels) of flour, one quarter *minot* of salt, and one hundred and twenty pounds of salt pork. Another widow's pension specified that she should be provided with two pairs of French shoes every year.[30] It is hard to know how to interpret these documents. Did such arrangements mean security and comfort for aging widows? Or were they last-ditch stands to defend women against relatives whose goodwill could not be counted upon? Whatever the answer, at least the notarized pensions of New France did provide a modicum of support to women who otherwise might have had none.

There is considerable evidence that women played a significant role in the commercial life of New France. The introduction of the textile industry to early eighteenth century Canada is credited to Agathe de Saint-Père, Madame de Repentigny, of Montreal. Left the manager of a family of ten stepsisters and stepbrothers after the death of her mother, Agathe de Saint-Père married Legardeur de Repentigny in 1685 and produced eight children of her own. Children evidently did not take up all her time, however, for Agathe de Saint-Père was heavily involved in the buying and selling of contracts, fur trade licences, and land. Soon Mme de Repentigny was also experimenting with textiles because of continuing shortages in the colony. At first she worked with native fibres such as bark, cotton-weed, and buffalo hair; by 1705 she had already caught the attention of the king with her productions. It was the sinking of a supply vessel that was the catalyst for her most daring experiment, however. Mme de Repentigny ransomed nine English weavers who were being held captive by the native allies of the French, had looms manufactured, engaged apprentices to learn the craft, and turned her home into a workshop to make "linen, drugget, twilled and covert-coating serge." Soon there were over twenty looms in Montreal and an independent manufactory had been created.[31]

Agathe de Saint-Père was only one of several women who are known to have been active in the commercial world of New France. Marie-Anne Barbel is another. At first this Quebec housewife must have been much taken up with childbirth and childrearing: she had fourteen children altogether, although only five survived to adulthood. But she must also have had a lot to do with the business affairs connected with the store her husband, Jean-Louis Fornel, ran in Quebec between 1723 and 1737. In the late 1730s Fornel became increasingly involved in entrepreneurial activity and exploration. When he departed in 1743 on a major expedition to explore the Baie des Esquimaux, Fornel left his Quebec business affairs in the hands of his wife. When her husband died two years later, Marie-Anne Barbel did not dissolve the community of goods established at her marriage. Instead she took sole charge. She continued a business partnership with two other entrepreneurs in a fishing concession, fought law suits with the government in connection with that concession and another, and traded for furs in Tadoussac. She also bought and sold properties, quarrelled with the Jesuits over a piece of land, and established a brickworks. Not all of her undertakings were successful. The widow Fornel managed to establish only two of her five children in marriages (one of which failed), and she was not among the top-ranking "notables" of New France. On the other hand this enterprising businesswoman was able to pay off all her debts, and supported herself, three unmarried children, and the fourth daughter who had separated from her husband and returned to the family, in relative comfort until her death at the age of ninety.[32]

Women in New France could also play a role in politics, albeit an indirect one. As wives and mistresses, or through other relationships, some women did exert considerable influence. Marie-Madeleine Maisonnat, an Acadian woman married to a British officer in Port Royal after its transfer to the British Crown in 1713, was said to have influence in military circles there, which she used to help her fellow Acadians. And in eighteenth century Canada, as the French regime was drawing to a close, at least two important government officials were thought to have been under the sway of women. Mme Péan was reputedly the mistress of the powerful Intendant François Bigot, and attracted him to her salon every evening, to the envy of all the capital. The wife of Governor Vaudreuil became so influential at a certain point that petitioners began to go directly to her rather than to the governor.[33]

Women also played significant business and political roles on a much humbler level. They operated taverns, illegal as well as legal trading operations, and in one case a sawmill. Women also protested publicly when things went wrong. One group hurled insults at the governor to express their anger in the 1670s; and in the difficult period just before the fall of Quebec in 1759, women were involved in public demonstrations protesting the food shortages caused by the war with England.[34] The first of these protests occurred in December 1757. Governor Vaudreuil, away from Quebec on business in Montreal, had just ended the distribution of bread, substituting a ration of horsemeat and beef that was to be available at a reduced price. A group of women made their way to the governor's Montreal residence, demanding bread and protesting their repugnance at the idea of eating horsemeat. Vaudreuil responded by arranging for the women to be taken on a tour of the butchery in order to assure themselves that all was in order, but also by threatening to throw the women in jail and hang half of them if they rioted again. Although the ringleaders were to have been arrested, none were, probably because the authorities were more concerned about restive soldiers. In Quebec the following April, continuing food shortages again brought women out into the streets, this time to call on the lieutenant-general of the police. The arrival of ships evidently alleviated the misery for a time, but by the winter of 1758–59 rumours of further rationing of bread produced a final protest. On this occasion, some four hundred women marched to the palace of the intendant, demanding redress. Their protest was successful. Wheat was brought to Quebec from Lachine, and the intendant promised an increase in the bread ration.

We do not know whether women participated in the more formally constituted popular assemblies that were occasionally held at the local community level in New France. But their participation in the food riots of the 1750s is significant. When their own interests were at stake, and feeding their households was clearly an important concern, they did not hesitate to move into the streets in an effort to force the government's hand. By doing so, they were following a long tradition of women's street demonstrations in France.

Women also played a vital role in medicine in the colony. Experienced older laywomen were often the leading healers of their communities, and acted as midwives at births. The midwife especially was an important community figure, whose office — sometimes an elective one — was strongly supported and, as time went on, to some extent controlled by the church. By the early 1700s each territory had its official midwife, and by the middle of the century there were also four midwives in New France paid salaries by the French state. Midwives' knowledge was passed on from generation to generation, often though not always from mothers to daughters or daughters-in-law. The women who performed this role were by no means impoverished or unskilled. On the contrary, most were educated and respected members of their communities, with above average wealth.[35]

And, of course, women in religious orders were the managers as well as the founders of hospitals in Quebec and Montreal. Their work affected a great many people. The *Hôtel-Dieu* of Quebec, for example, admitted some 3297 men and 1765 women in the decade between 1689 and 1698 alone. Men probably predominated because they were more susceptible to accidents and military injury, while both sexes suffered from seasonal sickness and from epidemics. Patients of both sexes were usually young, and the hospital's death rate was low. Indeed, from all accounts the Quebec *Hôtel-Dieu* was a far pleasanter place than European hospitals of the same era, or than North American hospitals were later to become. One assumes the same was true of the hospital run by religious women in Montreal.[36]

A study of the financial dealings of the sisters who ran the *Hôpital-Général*, a Quebec almshouse founded in 1701, in particular in connection with some property left to the nuns by a generous bishop, shows a group of women deeply aware of their economic interests and prepared to defend them. The battle over the bishop's property lasted fifteen years and did not, in the end, result in a settlement very favourable to the convent. On the other hand, the nuns followed the complexities of the case (a good part of which were unravelled in France) assiduously; they refused to act hastily, and defended themselves from accepting financial burdens that might have been insurmountable. They saw their battle, moreover, as a fight for justice and the rights that were due them. Their efforts show that although they were cloistered, these women were in close contact with their world and much involved in the property struggles that were so characteristic of their times.[37] A less happy story is that of the small *Congrégation de Notre-Dame* convent school that the church founded in Louisbourg in 1727. This community was in difficulties from the start because the Quebec bishop, Monseigneur de Saint-Vallier, sent its first teaching sister to Louisbourg against the wishes of both the Crown and the mother superior of her order in Montreal. Marguerite Roy, *Soeur de la Conception*, who managed the school for its first seven years, ran the *Congrégation* into serious debt by tying up two-thirds of her income in payments for the building she bought for her new community.[38]

Most convent managers did better, although financial problems were endemic to all religious orders throughout the history of New France. Convent women made extraordinary efforts to raise money for themselves, however, and some had notable success.[39] Fundraising journeys to France were frequent; often it was the women themselves who secured the loans or gifts; often it was also women who gave. At a more modest level, there were the efforts of the nuns to support themselves in New France through extra work. In Louisbourg the teaching sisters made bedding and straw mattresses for the barracks, in order to earn much needed cash;[40] elsewhere the nuns embroidered or raised funds through other crafts.

Convent women were not only involved in the management of their communities, they also engaged in the intellectual and spiritual currents of their times. *Mère* Sainte-Hélène of the *Hôtel-Dieu* in Quebec corresponded with physicians in France who were willing to send her medical supplies, and who were also interested in the medicinal herbs and remedies discovered in New France. Marie Morin is considered to be the first writer born in Canada. Her *annales* of the Montreal *Hôtel-Dieu* are an absorbing account of the nuns' struggles for daily survival in the face of poverty and natural disasters like fires, and of the early years not only of the convent but of Montreal.[41] We have already noted the astonishing production of letters and spiritual writings by Marie de l'Incarnation. Published by her son in the eighteenth century, her writings circulated widely in French religious circles thereafter. Laywomen too were involved in the intellectual currents of their times. The daughter of the explorer Noël Jérémie sent notes about native herbs and medicines to scientists in France, and the Canadian samples she had gathered to the *Jardin des Plantes* in Paris.[42]

Although we catch only glimpses of them, there were poor and abused women in New France, particularly in the urban centres of Quebec, Montreal, and Louisbourg; and there were slaves, both native and black. We read, for example, of a woman slave in Louisbourg who was purchased by a free black so that they could marry. In the *annales* of the *Congrégation de Notre-Dame* of Louisbourg we read of a woman and her children who were taken in by the sisters because she had been repeatedly beaten by her husband. In addition, there is the fragmentary record of the slave, Marie-Joseph-Angélique who, when threatened with sale, set fire to her owner's house and ran away. Angélique was apprehended and condemned to death; her story survives in history as the first recorded resistance to the cruelty of slavery by a black woman in Canada.[43] Chiefly through the convents, the problems of poverty and abuse were somewhat mitigated in New France. But the concern for the welfare of the population evidently did not extend to those who were slaves.

It is impossible to speak about the women of New France as a single, undifferentiated entity, or to generalize about their position in society. There is no doubt that the founders of convents and the businesswomen of Montreal and Quebec had more opportunities as members of the upper classes than others to develop their skills, communicate in the world, and accomplish their goals. Yet these women must have reflected something of their larger communities. They could not have sprung unaided out of a soil that was altogether alien. Rather than making a special case for the women of New France as unusually well-off or powerful, we are better advised to take note of the circumstances of their time and place that could favour them. Their relative wealth compared to the majority of women in France, and the leverage created by their small numbers in the early years of the colony's existence, were among the circumstances that helped them survive and sometimes flourish. But theirs was nevertheless a world that officially regarded women as secondary to men in the formal hierarchies of state, church, and family, even as these evolved and changed to meet the challenges of the New World.

Education and culture

Originally the educational mission of the French religious women who came to North America was to teach the native children. Marie de l'Incarnation of the Ursulines learned two native languages and translated religious tracts for the use of her pupils and their people, but the results were disappointing. Her subjects resisted acculturation to a way of life that seemed unnatural and alien to them. Some

Marie de l'Incarnation,
interpreted by a later artist.

native girls were assimilated to the extent of marrying Frenchmen, but few were willing to stay in the Quebec convent for more than a very short time. Gradually the Ursulines modified their ambitions and turned their attention to the French girls growing up in the colony.

As in France, the order developed boarding schools chiefly for the daughters of the well-to-do, combining them with day schools for poorer children. By the time of the British Conquest, there were two Ursuline schools, one in Quebec and a second in Three Rivers. The convent in Quebec usually had about twelve boarders at any given time. Since most children attended school for only a year or so, one can argue that the brief but all-enveloping education provided by the sisters affected more girls than would at first seem likely from such a small number. Indeed, there is reason to believe that, if we include the day school, nearly all the girls who lived in Quebec came at least for a time to the Ursulines to be taught.[44]

The other great teaching order of New France was the *Congrégation de Notre Dame*, founded by Marguerite Bourgeoys in Montreal. The *Congrégation* focused all its attention at first on the creation

Marguerite Bourgeoys with her pupils, by *Soeur* Marie Elmina LaChance.

of schools for the female children of the poor. The order expanded more rapidly than the Ursulines, founding schools in at least twelve different missions, although not all of them survived. By 1760 the *Congrégation de Notre Dame* could count a total of seventy sisters in its various convents in New France, twice the number of any other order.[45]

Other religious orders also founded schools for girls, but none achieved the reputation in education of either the *Congrégation* or the Ursulines during the French period. That reputation was based on several characteristics: the ability to prepare girls for their first communion, a preparation that involved learning to read and write and to recite an appropriate catechism; and the ability to teach girls domestic arts or, as Marie de l'Incarnation put it, "all sorts of work proper to their sex."[46]

The convent schools of New France in the seventeenth and eighteenth centuries shared with all schools of their time a growing emphasis on regularity and discipline. As the schools were small and familial and pupils stayed for relatively short periods, there was perhaps little of the regimentation and rigidity we associate with educational institutions today. Yet the nuns themselves espoused the "regular" life, and days in school were certainly ordered by the ringing of bells. French nuns, Marie de l'Incarnation included, sometimes found their Canadian pupils almost as undisciplined as Amerindian children, and the taming of this wild spirit became a major goal of their schooling. Proper manners, the ability to hold a conversation, delicacy — all were intended results of convent instruction, particularly for Ursuline boarders. The gracious and lively manners of urban *Canadiennes* noted by eighteenth century travellers may have owed something to this program of social development.

Girls in rural areas, unless their parents could afford to send them to board at a convent school, were less likely to have such an intense training in the social graces, and even Montreal girls were said to be less sophisticated than their counterparts in Quebec. Yet rural women were not without formal schooling. In the villages, institutions known as *petites écoles* were at first run by the missionaries and later by parish priests or lay teachers under their direction. We know that girls were going to such schools by the 1727 ordinance issued by the Bishop of Quebec, to the effect that unmarried lay teachers should not teach members of the opposite sex. Indeed, since gender is not specified in the ordinance, there is perhaps reason to believe that young, unmarried women may also have been teachers in some parish schools. As in the convents, girls were taught to read, to recite their catechism, and possibly to write. If women were teaching, girls might also have received some instruction in sewing or knitting; the fancier sewing, the embroidery of altar cloths and the like, was probably the monopoly of the convents or seamstresses teaching in the larger centres.[47] That the *petites écoles* were not always conducted according to the ideal is suggested by the promulgation of regulations concerning them. In addition to the rule regarding unmarried lay teachers, priests were instructed to make sure that teachers were moral individuals, to supervise what went on in the schools, and to make sure that parents sent their children. There were at least twenty-nine schools of this type by the end of the French regime, a number that may seem very small for a total population of nearly 70 000, but when we recall that most children attended only briefly in order to prepare for first communion, it is possible that this schooling reached a substantial number of girls—at least those living in a region having such a school.

The people who came to New France were more likely to be able to read and write, on the average, than those who remained in France—probably because so many came from urban centres. There was initially some falling off in literacy in the New World; a study of seventeenth century Canadian parish registers suggests that there were many people, both male and female, who did not learn to read or write in the early years. But eighteenth century parish registers from Louisbourg and Three Rivers indicate that over half of the brides married in these communities could sign their names (58 percent in Louisbourg, 1722–45; 54.5 percent in Three Rivers, 1745–54).[48] Although the formal schooling of most women was brief and oriented to religion and domestic learning, some women enjoyed a measure of literary culture in New France; a few may even have been considered "learned." Religious women like Sister Morin and Sister Cuillerier, her successor in writing the *annales* of the *Hôtel-Dieu* at Montreal, perhaps had special opportunities — and a special need — for literary culture. But upper class laywomen were not all that far behind. Élisabeth Bégon, the wife of an eighteenth century Three Rivers governor, had enough leisure to write at considerable length of the salons that fashionable women attended and of the dances they held; she also wrote about the condition of the St. Lawrence River as the seasons changed, and about her grandchildren. A single letter by Marie-Angélique Hamel regarding the marriage of her son has been preserved, and indicates that even less elevated women took pen to paper when the occasion required it.[49]

For girls who did not attend school or acquire a literary training, service was probably the dominant form of education. Girls who were put into service were sometimes bound out as young as four years of age; their contracts specified that they would stay with their master or mistress until they were married or otherwise provided for. The contracts also provided, somewhat vaguely, that the arrangement was for their well-being and *"bon avancement."* A study of the contracts of domestics suggests, in fact, that binding girls into service was a way of providing for them when a natural parent was unable to do so. Formal instruction was a major part of a contract only when it was a question of apprenticeship to a trade, such as that of *couturière* or seamstress. In such cases the person bound was usually a young woman in her late teens or early twenties, the instruction was paid for, and the period of apprenticeship was only for one or two years.[50]

All girls, whether they were servants in the households of others or living at home with their own families, learned the multiple and time-consuming tasks of house and farm work from the older women with whom they lived. They began to learn from the earliest possible age — gathering eggs, holding yarn, stirring the pot, milking, spinning, and looking after animals and babies — while older women supervised or did other work. Most of their learning was directed towards their becoming competent assistants in the households of their elders, and eventually managers of their own.

Was there a separate "women's culture" in seventeenth or eighteenth century New France? Perhaps. The culture of the convent, the separate character of much of women's work, the management of childbirth and of most female education by women — all of these suggest the possibility. On the other hand, there is evidence that the worlds of women and men were in some ways less separate than they were later to become, and that even cloistered convent women bustled about "in the world" when they needed to. Then too, the society of the mid-eighteenth century, of Mme Vaudreuil and Mme Bégon, was a very different one from the seventeenth century society of Marie de l'Incarnation and Marguerite Bourgeoys. The New

World community that had been dominated by the fisheries, the fur trade, the religious mission, and the Amerindian wars had been replaced by an increasingly secular society based on agriculture and small industries. The existence of official, salaried midwives suggests that even at the intimate level of childbirth, church and state could intrude on the world of women.

Settlements along the St. Lawrence and its tributaries, in Louisbourg, and Acadia began also to have a sense of permanence as succeeding generations of French inhabitants took root. The impression of stability, however, was in part deceptive, for the final years of New France were hardly peaceful or static. The relatively quiet existence of the Acadians was rudely shattered when in 1755 the British began to force on them the long exodus known as "*le Grand Dérangement*" or the "Expulsion." Many Acadian women were separated from their families and had their lives permanently disrupted. Some were sent to England; some ended up in France; many were scattered along the shores of the eastern seaboard of North America. A few, remarkably, managed to go into hiding and stay near their homes or to return to Nova Scotia later on.[51] War with the English affected the people of Canada as well, although not so drastically. Still, war meant blockades and food shortages, and ultimately bombardments, raids, and the loss of men. The presence of troops encouraged prostitution, and the shortage of goods, smuggling. In its last years Canada as well as Acadia suffered much privation and dislocation.

Throughout the eighteenth century French Canadian clerics protested what they perceived as a moral decline. Like the Protestant clergy of New England, they found the world less pure than it had seemed in the early period of religious faith and missionary fervour. Priests no doubt complained about women's low necklines, frivolous dresses, and attendance at dances precisely because the material circumstances of women of eighteenth century New France were better than they had been for their seventeenth century mothers and grandmothers, and such extravagances were now possible. But moral attitudes had possibly shifted. Penalties for serious offenses, such as adultery, were less severe in eighteenth century Montreal than they had been in the seventeenth.[52]

Increasing numbers of illegitimate or abandoned children also suggest a society in which social controls were not as powerful as they once had been. Indeed, concern for orphans had a great deal to do with the development of a new women's religious community, founded just before the Conquest. The order of the Sisters of Charity or Grey Nuns, as they came to be called, came into being in the 1740s and received official sanction from the king in 1753.[53] Founded by Marguerite d'Youville, the *Soeurs de la Charité de l'Hôpital-Général* of Montreal had as their original focus the general care of the sick and the poor. But the problem of abandoned infants led to the admission of the hospital's first foundling in 1754, and soon more than twenty babies a year were finding their way to the Grey

Nuns' door. The infant death rate at the hostel was extremely high, 80 percent in the first decade, and would eventually match the even higher rates that were typical of similar foundling hospitals in Europe. Evidently the institution was able to do little more than stem the tide of infanticide during difficult times by giving some measure of care and baptism to infants who otherwise would have died even sooner after birth. In New France, as elsewhere in the western world, the presence of foundling hospitals with their high death rates indicated the continuing—or perhaps growing—presence of misery and the inability of institutional efforts to alleviate it.

The founding of the Grey Nuns occurred at a time of growing awareness that the existing religious orders of New France were not attracting recruits. The authorities, some critics believed in 1732, had effectively limited the numbers of women entering convents by insisting more than they had in the past on the payment of large dowries. It was pointed out in support of lower dowries that girls in New France loved liberty too much to be attracted to religious life in large numbers, and that the government need not fear the wholesale abandonment of marriage and childrearing if convent entry were made easier. A genuine social problem existed, moreover, among women who did not find husbands and whose families could not afford the high cost of their entry into the convent. The dowries finally were lowered, although women did not flock into the convents as a result. A more equally balanced population as far as gender was concerned may have meant later marriage for most women than was typical in the seventeenth century. But most women still married.[54]

The fact that marriage or convent life were the only real choices open to most women tells us much about the culture of women in New France. Totally separate or different from men's culture it may not have been. But most women's lives, especially by the eighteenth century, revolved around the demands of family reproduction and production. The majority of women also lived in a world in which both church and state had a good deal to say about how they should live. What we cannot know very well is the extent to which women paid attention. There is evidence that some did not.

The marriages of a woman whose life spanned the years before and after the Conquest tell us something of how ordinary women may have arranged their affairs in mid-eighteenth century French Canada. Félicité Audet first appears in the records in 1761. A domestic servant who was a widow with one child, Félicité married Théophile Allaire in 1761, himself a widower with one surviving child. In the six years they lived together, Félicité and Théophile had three additional children; in 1767 Théophile died and Félicité and her family were left with a farm of sixty *arpents* (acres), thirty-three of which were still bush, a bed, three chairs, a bureau, and a sideboard. Félicité married once again and had three more children, but this marriage ended in a separation. According to the settlement that was arranged with her

Canadienne   Canadien

A couple in their Sunday clothes.

third spouse, she kept from this marriage sixty *arpents* of land, a bed, a cow, and a pig. She was also allotted one half a *minot* of grain and one of the children of this final union. When we last hear of her, Félicité was selling her land in order to buy another farm and a loom, so that she could earn her living.[55]

It is hard to know how typical the three marriages of Félicité Audet were, but her life was typical in that it focused on cows and pigs, husbands and children, three chairs and a sideboard, rather than on the church or the state, the governor or the intendant, or even on events in Quebec, Montreal, or Louisbourg. On the other hand, state affairs affected the material conditions of her life, especially if there were shortages because of war. And the church probably impinged on her life as well. Her children would have been baptized shortly after they were born; she herself may have come to the priest to undergo the traditional purification ritual of "churching" at some point following each birth. Félicité no doubt shares the superstitions and beliefs regarding women of her period. Yet there was virtually no persecution for witchcraft in New France as there had been for several centuries in Europe; French people were, perhaps, afraid of the Iroquois, of soldiers, and evil spirits and ghosts; they were also afraid of poverty. But they do not appear to have been afraid of old women.

If the Conquest had any effect on Félicité Audet, we cannot know what it was. We know that, among the elite and governing families of Louisbourg, Montreal, and Quebec, many women were forced to return to France. Others stayed on and wondered how they would cope under the new regime. The lingering of many Scottish and English names in French Canadian families to this day indicates that some followed the path of Marie-Madeleine Maisonnat. Instead of marrying French soldiers they married English ones. The strength of their culture is suggested in the fact that most of their descendants count themselves French, not English Canadians. The vast majority of Acadian and Canadian women probably bided their time and continued as they had always done, coping with the authorities one day and sorting the laundry the next, as they gathered their resources for whatever was to come.

3 Carders of wool, drawers of water: women's work in British North America

The fall of New France ushered in a century of extraordinary change in North America. While the last decades of the French regime were hardly static, the advent of British government in the French-occupied territories combined with subsequent economic and political events in Europe and in the Thirteen Colonies to the south to produce a century of almost continuous political and military upheaval. One profound effect was a vast movement of peoples. A second was a rapid increase in the number of people of European origin living in the territory that was formerly New France. Single men predominated among the first arrivals to the British North American colonies. However if Britain wanted them to remain and her colonies to be settled, it was apparent that women were required. An early comment on the Newfoundland experience by a British naval officer suggests how important women were to permanent settlement. "Soe long as there comes noe women," this gentleman remarked in 1694, the people are not "fixed."[1]

The new migrants

Men and women from New England gradually began moving to the northeastern regions of British North America after Acadia was transferred to the British Crown in 1713. Not until later in the eighteenth century, however, did families begin making their way from colonies like New York and Pennsylvania to the shores of the St. Lawrence, Lake Ontario, and Lake Erie. This migration, which included Quaker and Mennonite pacifists, preceded the American Revolution (1776–1783) that would eventually result in the birth of the United States of America. The New Englanders came first to Nova Scotia, a province then encompassing much of what is now New Brunswick and Prince Edward Island. Later they and others came to the new British province of Quebec, whose boundaries for most of the late eighteenth century continued to include much of present day Ontario and vast tracts of the Ohio and Mississippi river valleys to the south and west. Despite the pacifist leanings and religious concerns of some of these American migrants, the chief motivation of most was the quest for new land and new opportunities. Nor were economic motives absent in the vast Loyalist influx into the eastern and northern British colonies that was precipitated by the American Revolution itself. Like the movements that preceded it, this too was largely a migration of families, and included Abenaki and Six Nations Indians, black slaves and former slaves, and migrants of German origin, as well as women and men of Anglo-Celtic backgrounds. These peoples were followed in turn by another generation of American migrants known to historians as "post-Loyalists," whose motives seem to have been overwhelmingly economic.

The Napoleonic Wars, economic and political upheaval in the British Isles, and famine in Ireland brought a second great movement of people to British North America, chiefly of English, Irish, and Scottish families. This influx for the most part occurred after the American migration, reaching its peak in the 1830s and 1840s.

Included in all of these movements were female immigrants travelling without families, chiefly schoolmistresses and domestics from the American states or the British Isles. Then, in the 1830s, a new group of French *religieuses* seeking to reinvigorate the Roman Catholic mission in the New World began to trickle into French Canada. They, in turn, were followed by Irish and American nuns destined for other parts of British North America.[2]

The first half of the nineteenth century also saw continuing internal migrations, some of which stirred up controversy and concern. During the War of 1812 several thousand slaves, who escaped from Maryland and Virginia when the British occupied Chesapeake Bay, made their way to British "freedom" — only to encounter much hardship and considerable prejudice in their new Nova Scotian and New Brunswick homes.[3] Later on, many more black refugees made their way to Upper Canada via the "underground railroad," and created communities in what was to become southwestern Ontario. Some came with their families, but the circumstances of their migration dictated that others, including women, would come alone.

Anna Maria Jackson and her seven children. They escaped slavery in Maryland and travelled to Upper Canada via the Underground Railroad in 1859.

Immigrants and native-born alike often lived in many different places before they settled permanently. Thus we have the countless Loyalists and others who used the Maritime provinces or the old province of Quebec or, later, Lower Canada as staging grounds for migrations farther west, as well as Maritimers who decided that the prospects were better in New England than at home. Later still, migrant French Canadians began to colonize new parts of British North America or strike out for the towns and factories of New England.

New parts of British North America began to be opened up to settlement. In the early 1800s, Scottish settlers under the leadership of Lord Selkirk planted the Red River colony in a small corner of Rupert's Land. Since French-Catholic mixed-blood families settled in the region as well, religious women were not far behind and, in 1846, a contingent of Grey Nuns established the first women's religious community in the Canadian West. Another small group of white women helped initiate the pioneer era in what was eventually to become the province of British Columbia. Their voyages by sea from the British Isles were often of six or seven months duration, rounding Cape Horn and eventually bringing them to the new settlements that were being created in Hudson's Bay Company territory on the west coast.[4]

Who were the women who were willing to sacrifice the relative comforts of home, and the frequently permanent parting from family and friends, for what were often gruelling and extraordinarily long journeys into unknown and inhospitable environments? Are there any common themes that marked their passage or characterized their lives? One thing that these women had in common certainly was the migration experience itself. Not all of them spent months at sea, for many were overland migrants. Nor did all of them walk for over one thousand three hundred kilometres, as did the the women who trekked from York Factory to Red River between 1812 and 1820.[5] But many did have extraordinary experiences as immigrants; and most of them must have found their lives enormously changed. They brought with them the work that women had customarily done in both the Old World and the New; but they also adapted to new ways of doing things in the communities they encountered or founded in British North America.

The story of Sarah McGinnis illustrates both the mobility and the need to adapt. Born in the upper Mohawk River valley to a first-generation family of German immigrants in 1713, Sarah, who had "prevailed upon her parents" to let her live for long periods among the Six Nations Indians, married an Irish fur trader and had produced four children by the time she was widowed at forty-two. Continuing to operate the family fur trading post, the widow McGinnis was in her sixties when the American Revolution swept away all she possessed and forced her to head north. She watched helplessly as her property and goods were sold to rebels, made the difficult decision to abandon an imprisoned son, and then began the long odyssey that would eventually take her to Canada. She herself spent some time in a rebel prison, lived for two protracted periods with the Six Nations, in order to perform important liaison services between the British and their Amerindian allies, and spent brief periods in Niagara and Montreal. Her ultimate "settlement" took her first to Carleton Island, then to Ernestown, and finally to Fredericksburgh (all at the eastern end of Lake Ontario), where she died in 1791 at the age of seventy-eight.[6]

Most migrants were probably younger than Sarah McGinnis. Deborah Cottnam was a Nova Scotian who was displaced twice: once to Salem, Massachusetts, when she was only sixteen, as a result of French/British conflict; and, in her middle age, back again to Nova Scotia as a result of the American revolutionary war. She too did not settle for good in one place. After running an academy in Halifax from 1777 to 1786, this enterprising Loyalist removed herself and her school to St. John, where she taught for six more years before retiring to Windsor, Nova Scotia, where she died in 1806.[7]

Many were not so successful or so lucky. Rebels not only plundered the house of Filer Dribblee of Long Island, but turned his wife Polly and their five children "naked into the Streets." "Plundered and stripped" two more times before they made their way to New Brunswick, a safe arrival in British territory did not mean the end of trouble for the Dribblee family. Filer, who had spent six months in prison during the war, succumbed to despair during the first year in St. John and committed suicide; not long afterwards the widow and her children were burnt out of their log cabin home twice in one year. In a letter to a brother in England, Polly expressed her gratitude for gifts of clothing that he had sent and recounted some of her trials as a prelude to a request for further aid.

I assure you, my dear Billy, that many have been the Days since my arrival in this inhospitable Country, that I should have thought myself and Family truly happy could we have "had Potatoes alone — " but this mighty Boon was denied us — ! I could have borne these burdens of Loyalty with Fortitude had not my poor Children in doleful accents cried, Mama, why don't you help me and give me Bread?[8]

Polly Dribblee wondered about the value of loyalty to a British Crown whose material assistance, at that stage, had been wholly insufficient; she also worried about the effect the news of her condition would have on her mother, who remained in the United States. At the time of writing (November, 1787) she had not had the courage to inform her American relatives of her recent difficulties.

Frequent moves, insufficient food, the loss of possessions, or, worse, the loss of family members—these were the lot of many migrants. Others dealt with the vicissitudes of illness and accident. Sarah Sherwood was seven months pregnant when she decided to follow a Loyalist husband into exile. Trekking with two small children and a black slave from her farm in Vermont to the British post of Fort St. Jean on the Richelieu River, Sarah and her family lived

A Loyalist encampment near Cornwall, by James Peachey, 1784.

first in a barracks, then in a house in the fort, and finally in a blockhouse on North Hero Island for the duration of the American revolutionary war, while her husband performed various services for the British government. Somehow she managed to have her baby, look after her children and the other relatives who followed her north, weave "yards of linsey-woollsey," and keep her family clothed, despite the uncertain conditions of life in wartime. Peace, however, brought a long siege when, one after another, everyone in the family had smallpox. The Sherwood family survived and eventually settled in Upper Canada, where Sarah had three more daughters, but lost her husband in a drowning accident when the youngest of this second brood was only seven. The farm was already well established by this time, however, and Sarah Sherwood carrried on, ultimately ending her days in Montreal.[9]

Accidents and illness seem to be part of many migration stories, not just those of Loyalist women. Certainly the experiences of Catharine Parr Traill and Susanna Moodie, the sisters who were two of Canada's most famous gentlewomen immigrants from the British Isles in the 1830s, were not without their traumas and tragedies. Catharine nearly succumbed to cholera in Montreal before she was able to set out for her homestead near Peterborough, and in the ensuing years lost several homes to fire. Susanna also lost a farmhouse to fire, endured attacks of intermittent fever and the loss of a son who drowned, among what seems to have been a multitude of lesser difficulties. In her famous account of pioneer life, *Roughing It in the Bush*, Susanna portrayed the rigours of backwoods life with particular flair. Commenting somewhat misleadingly on her own lack of the necessary practical skills for backwoods farming, her tale was one of continuous struggle, albeit a struggle laced with humour as well as dogged determination. As a gentlewoman, Moodie felt unprepared for much of the manual work she had to do on her bush farm. She nevertheless persevered, and in the end even admitted to contemplating her own "well-hoed ridge of potatoes" with considerable satisfaction. Moodie was also fortunate in having the knowledge and skill to take up her pen as well as her hoe. She won a government post for her husband by her petitions to the governor and was able to supplement the family income through her published writings. Finally, as a result of both initiatives, the Moodies were able to leave the hardships of backwoods life behind them. They moved to Belleville, where Susanna and Captain Moodie could more easily pursue work to which they felt better suited.[10]

Not all pioneer stories are as complete as the Moodie story, nor are they all tales of worry and woe. In 1789 an upper class Loyalist, Anne Powell, travelling through British territory to her new home in Upper Canada, recorded in her diary an encounter with a former servant who had married a disbanded soldier after the American revolutionary war and settled with him on a farm in the St. Lawrence Valley. Anne Powell was impressed with what she saw. Already Nancy and her husband had exchanged a small farm for one that was double its size, and now they were in the process of developing their new acreage and raising a fine family of three children. Asked if she was happy, Nancy replied "yes, perfectly so." She worked hard, "but it was for herself and the children."

Her husband took care of the Farm and she of the family, and at their leisure hours she wove Cloth, and he made and mended shoes for their neighbours for which they were well paid, and every year they expected to do better and better. . . .[11]

Also hopeful of bettering their lot were the many young women who were beginning to migrate on their own. Many followed relatives who had gone before them, but sometimes they moved independently of family connections. Young women immigrating from the British Isles might find their way into the countryside, but more often they would find work in urban centres like Fredericton, Halifax, Montreal, or Toronto, swelling the numbers of young single women who were already moving into these communities from rural British North America. By 1851 such centres were reporting disproportionate numbers of young women living in their midst.[12] Most of these women would take work as servants in urban households; others might follow the path of Deborah Cottnam and establish themselves as teachers. Whatever their means of support, these single women too were participating in the extraordinary mobility and change that characterized the lives of British North American women.

Not all adapted easily to the changes in their world, as the stories of Susanna Moodie and Polly Dribblee suggest. Change was particularly difficult if it brought in its wake a clash of cultures. The native and mixed-blood women of the Northwest and West suffered increasing hardship, first as these groups were forced to retreat from the pressure of colonial development, and secondly as individuals and groups found that, with the coming of white women, the old fur trade world of which they had been so important a part was coming to an end.[13]

The native and mixed-blood women who had married traders did not necessarily fare better than those who had remained with their tribal communities in the rapidly changing conditions of the nineteenth century. When white women and missionaries came to fur trade country in the early and mid-nineteenth century, some traders began to be feel encumbered by their "country" wives. These men often turned their native spouses over to others when they retired to eastern British North America or to Britain, or abandoned them. Some, like Sir George Simpson, not only "turned off" their native wives but insisted on bringing their new British spouses west. Frances Simpson's experience indicates, however, that life in the Northwest was not necessarily any happier for these white women. Only eighteen when she came as the new bride of the Hudson's Bay Company governor, Frances valiantly tried to adjust to the new and alien environment of Red River society, but in the end her health failed and she was compelled to return home to England after only a few years.[14]

Despite their own problems and insecurities, women like Frances Simpson constituted a threat to native and mixed-blood country wives. They represented a world that fur traders increasingly wanted. And when country wives were abandoned, whole families suffered. The children of country marriages might be left with their native mothers, sent off to boarding school, or put into trades; few were fully integrated into their fathers' new families.[15] Of course by no means all native wives or mixed-blood children were abandoned. Many fathers continued to care for their native offspring; others attempted to move their native and mixed-blood wives and families into the little European worlds that they were establishing in centres like Red River and Victoria. This was the experience of Amelia Douglas, the mixed-blood wife of Vancouver Island's first governor. A practical woman, who had once saved her husband's life, Amelia Douglas was the mother of thirteen children. Nevertheless, first in Fort Vancouver, then in Victoria, she had to endure the insults of the new white settlers who felt she was beneath them. Amelia Douglas probably found her new world ridiculously artificial, as well as unpleasantly prejudiced, but learned to deal with her new official role with good humour, turning some of the duties connected with it over to her daughters. She also drew on her native heritage to the end, inviting fellow native and mixed-blood men and women into her home, and telling Amerindian legends to her grandchildren. The paths of most mixed-blood women were no doubt far more difficult. They could rarely go back to their mothers' native bands, but they were not entirely welcome in white society. Truly women "in between," they were not fully accepted in either world.[16]

The most tragic stories of all were those of the native women who faced the obliteration of their cultures and, in one case, the virtual wiping out of their people. In the North and West, native peoples such as the Athapaskans still had sufficient space to maintain their distinctive migratory cultures, but this was not the case in the

Atlantic colonies. The Micmac of Nova Scotia and the Beothuck of Newfoundland had been suffering from economic and social dislocation and enduring the ravages of European-introduced diseases since at least the 1500s. During the late eighteenth and early nineteenth centuries these groups experienced death by slow starvation. Some of the Micmac migrated to Newfoundland; others survived by moving onto reserved lands or developing a tourist trade in crafts that the women managed to preserve or revive. The Beothuck, despite last-ditch efforts on the part of colonial philanthropists to save them, finally dwindled to one woman, Shawandithit. This young Beothuck was taken captive, and when she learned to communicate with her captors was able to tell them about the final days of her people: how they hid from white Newfoundlanders who seemed to be hunting them even into their last retreat in the interior; how they had watched from the woods as white men returned the body of one of their number to their camp; and how, finally, all but Shawandithit herself had died. When the last Beothuck woman succumbed to tuberculosis in St. John's in 1829, she was still in her twenties; with her death the tribal memory was extinguished.[17]

Marriage and childbearing

The majority of women in British North America probably embarked on marriage in their early twenties. The census for Canada East and West of 1851, for example, gave the average age at first marriage for females as 23. This certainly marks a considerable shift from the unusual pattern found for parts of seventeenth century New France, when the average age at first marriage was under 20, but not so great a change from the eighteenth century, when the numbers of men and women were more equal and the average age of marriage had risen to 22 in Canada. It is still about one year older on average, however, and this suggests that the cautious western European "late marriage" pattern was being reinforced by British North American circumstances. In Hamilton in 1851, marriage was considerably delayed. Only 40 percent of the city's women married by the age of 22; of the 25-year-olds, only 60 percent did so; among those older than 25 the percentage gradually continued to rise. Nevertheless, 17 percent of Hamilton's 30-year-old women remained unmarried in 1851.[18]

Late marriage is often correlated with few children, and it may well be that British North American women — especially urban women—were somewhat less fertile than the women of New France. But it is also true that these "pre-industrial" women still produced large families in comparison to average family sizes of a later period. Estimates of the numbers of children born to typical British North American families vary according to the date, locality, a id the data available, but all indicate substantial average birth rates. A study of eighteenth century French Canada reveals an average figure of over 8 births and an average family size of over 5 per "completed family" — that is, children born to women during their years of fertility —

while similar figures are given for Peel County, Canada West, in 1851. Mid-nineteenth century French Canadian women living in two Prescott County townships also had given birth to an average of more than 7 children by the time they reached the end of their childbearing years; English Canadian mothers in this sample were only slightly lower with an average of about 6. Here, age at marriage might have made the difference, for English Canadian women in these townships tended to marry a few years later than their French Canadian counterparts. Rural living also clearly made a difference. The average number of children in all of the households of the city of Hamilton when the census was taken was under 3; where heads of household were in their forties, it was under 4. Yet, for all of British North America, the average number of children born to families—slightly over 7—was still remarkably high.[19]

Numbers can only tell us so much. The story of Harriet Dobbs, who came to Upper Canada as a bride in the 1830s, illustrates how such statistics could become flesh and blood in the life of one well-to-do, urban migrant to British North America. Although we do not know her age at marriage, we do know that Harriet spent some time at the end of whatever formal education she may have had living at home with her parents in Ireland. In addition to working at the household tasks that absorbed the time even of upper class young women, Harriet painted every day, an occupation for which she said she had less time after marriage, although she did not abandon it altogether. On marrying her sister-in-law's brother, a young Upper Canadian cleric, Harriet did not immediately acquire her own separate household. She and her husband, Robert Cartwright, eventually occupied a house that had been built for them in Kingston, but claimed only one room of the house as their own. Robert's widowed sister Mary, an uncle Frank, and a doctor who does not appear to have been a relation, also lived there. Moreover, the entire household took their meals in another Cartwright family home in Kingston, while Robert and Harriet awaited the arrival of their household effects, evidently sent over from Ireland. Even when these arrived, however, Harriet cheerfully reported that the older sister-in-law Mary remained the "mistress" of the household.[20]

Harriet Dobbs Cartwright gave birth to four children, only two of whom survived to adulthood. By the time of the second child's death at the age of eighteen, Harriet was a widow. She lived for a while with a brother-in-law and his wife, and when he died one presumes that the two sisters-in-law carried on together, if not in the same household at least in close companionship. Certainly the widow Cartwright did not fade away. She was able to afford one trip home to visit her family in Dublin; she raised and educated her remaining two children, and continued to be active in church and charitable circles in Kingston until her death in 1887.

Like Sarah McGinnis, Polly Driblee, and Sarah Sherwood, Harriet Cartwright was widowed relatively young. All the evidence suggests that she was typical for this period in that she did not remarry. The census for Hamilton, Canada West, indicates that nearly one-quarter of the women over forty, and one-third of the women over fifty, were widows in 1851.[21] Early widowhood would interrupt the childbearing potential of women and refusal to remarry would curtail it. Both probably accounted for Harriet Cartwright having only four children, and would help to explain the relatively small family sizes in an urban community like Hamilton, with its large number of widows.

Harriet Dobbs Cartwright was also not atypical in her household arrangements. All studies of British North American communities indicate that, in most places and times, the majority of households consisted of nuclear families; that is, they were composed of the conjugal couple and their children. In the city of Hamilton and the predominantly rural community of Peel County, for example, the proportions of all households that were simple — that is, composed solely of nuclear families — at mid-century were 79.4 and 56.4 per-cent, respectively. But it is also clear that, over time and as a result of a variety of circumstances, households expanded and contracted. In two places that have been studied, over one in ten households were "extended" by the presence of relatives in 1851; in Moncton, New Brunswick, nearly one-quarter of all households were "multi-ple" or contained more than one conjugal couple in 1851. This astonishingly high proportion, compared to other British North American localities, is attributed to the press of population resulting from a shipbuilding boom in mid-century Moncton.[22]

The examination of the Hamilton census has shown that the extended families were often headed by young couples, suggesting that many young parents had extra adults on hand at the time when help with firstborn children would have been most welcome. This was certainly the case for Harriet Cartwright, whose widowed sister-in-law Mary clearly played a major role in the care of her first child, taking charge of him when Harriet and her husband went on a lengthy trip to the United States. The evidence indicates as well that in some communities it was the more prosperous families that were able to accommodate relatives in their households, if only because they had larger houses and therefore more space.[23] But it is also true that over any given period, the majority of families may well have been in this "extended" category at one time or another. Studies of less prosperous communities have yielded evidence that it was not always or only the very well-off who shared their households. Among the families living on Campobello Island, New Brunswick, where fishing was the main occupation, 26 percent of all households were extended by the presence of at least one relative in 1851.[24]

Wealthier families were most easily able to expand when the occasion demanded it. The Jarvis family of Prince Edward Island is a case in point. Large enough, first of all, to accommodate at least three servants, the Jarvis home also became the residence of visiting friends and relatives for various periods during the life of its patriarch, the colony's Chief Justice Edward Jarvis. When his first wife Maria died in 1841, Edward's twenty-year-old daughter Mary took over the running of the household for a while, but at her own marriage relinquished this task. In 1843 an unmarried aunt was briefly in residence; in the same year Edward married a second wife, Elizabeth Gray. Elizabeth died in childbirth in 1847, leaving several young children of her own in addition to Maria's offspring, who still remained at home. At this point Edward welcomed into his household a second unmarried relation, who evidently continued the domestic management of his household until his death in 1852.[25]

It seems safe to suggest that women raising children and managing households in this period of Canadian history were less likely than is the case today to be working at these tasks single-handedly. If they did not have female relatives on hand to help out, a substantial number had servants. A study of early nineteenth century household service in Montreal and Quebec, for example, shows that 20 percent of Quebec households had at least one servant in 1818. In mid-century Hamilton, about one-quarter of the families had a resident domestic.[26] The continuing prevalence of large families, especially in the countryside, also meant that older daughters were often on hand to help with the housework and the younger children. Frances Stewart, who settled on the Otonabee River near Peterborough with her husband and children in 1833, relied entirely on her daughters when "asthma and weakness" affected her health in 1843. Finally, a woman might have the help of visiting relatives or neighbours. Childbirth in particular brought to a woman's home not only the midwife, or the doctor if she were a wealthy or upper class woman, but also friends, neighbours, mothers, sisters, or cousins. Mary O'Brien, a pioneer wife and mother who was wealthy enough to have permanent assistance in her own home most of the time, was able to help a neighbour give birth in her isolated Upper Canadian community in the 1830s. She also helped the new mother to cope with the postpartum depression that followed. Mary herself wrote to relatives in England of her own feat of "cheating the doctor" and giving birth assisted only by her husband and children on the occasion of at least one of her children's births.[27]

Women's work

Mary O'Brien's support of her neighbour also gives us one of the few recorded examples of the charitable activities that we know pioneer women saw as part of their work as women. By helping one another and the needy, and attempting to improve the environment for their families, these women were involved from the beginning in the crucial task of community building. Susanna Moodie wrote of walking miles on a winter day to take food to a woman who had been abandoned by her husband; Moodie had learned that the woman and her children were starving. Her mission of charity was an obligation and a necessity.[28] The charitable tradition was handed down from mother to daughter. Ann Racey, a Loyalist brought to Canada as a small child, settled near what was to become Hamilton,

Canada West, and worked among the neighbouring Iroquois; her daughter, Jane O'Reilly, helped nurse the sick in the "plague" or cholera epidemic that struck the province in 1832.[29]

Childbearing and helping other families constituted a large part of women's work; another major part was what women called their "domestic employments." Older women usually managed the work and, of course, did a great deal of it. In general, however, it was the province of younger women of almost all classes and conditions to perform service tasks in the household and farmyard. Thus, girls and young women did a great deal of the spinning and preparatory work of various kinds, both inside and outside the house, whether they were daughters or servants. They also did a lot of "watching" — minding flocks or, even more routinely, younger children.

Frances Stewart's description of her daughters' work is a particularly apt illustration. All three girls were under sixteen years of age when Frances outlined their tasks in a letter to a friend. It is worth noting that work like fetching and carrying, or knitting, could begin when a child was as young as five or six.

Anna Marie is the general overseer of the household concerns, who makes all the preserves and pickles, cakes, etc. She also has the care of Johnny, the third boy, who is now five years old. . . . Ellen mends all the stockings for the little boys and repairs their clothes. She has the care of George in particular who is three; besides this she is manager and caretaker of the poultry. In spring she attends to the sowing and raising of plants and nurseries of young apple trees. Bessie is in charge of Charlie, the infant, she is always busy and can make most of her own underclothes and knits.[30]

Domestic servants were mostly young and, increasingly during the 1800s, more often young women than young men. In early nineteenth century Montreal and Quebec some 5 to 8 percent of the population were servants, and two-thirds of them were women. In Hamilton, in 1851, three out of ten girls aged 13 to 16 were servants in the homes of people who were not their relatives; 40 percent of all 17- to 20-year-olds were in domestic service.[31]

Whether they were managers or servants, mothers, unmarried aunts, or daughters, the work women did depended to a considerable extent on the occupations of the men of their households. The work of women like Frances Stewart and her children was determined in large part by the fact that they lived on a farm; but not all women lived in the countryside or occupied themselves solely with farm or housework. Eliza Ruggles, a Nova Scotian orphan who was disinherited by her Upper Canadian stepmother when she insisted on marrying a Methodist clergyman in the 1830s, helped her husband with his school for black children. Eventually their mission to the black community took the couple to the United States and then to Africa. Eliza lost first her three children and finally her husband in the course of this work, and later embarked on a second life as the wife of a Nova Scotian farmer. She gave birth to three more children and lived to tell her seven grandchildren about her missionary days.[32]

Eliza Ruggles' life was unusual, but she was not the only wife who travelled with a missionary husband. Methodist wives accompanied itinerant preacher husbands on their travels, and among the Bible Christian and Primitive Methodists, some of these missionary wives were also preachers in their own right. Frances Calloway and her husband William were Bible Christian itinerants in Prince Edward Island between 1846 and 1851, and like many English immigrants to British North America they had trouble getting used to some of the local conditions. In the summertime, heat was one problem and another was the ubiquitous mosquito. Dealing with the latter difficulty in the home was, evidently, the work of a missionary's wife, one that Frances Calloway performed indifferently. Returning from a prayer meeting with her husband one evening in June 1848, Frances found, according to William's diary, that "a number of insufferable Moschettos had taken possession" of their home. She attempted to put a "Moschetto blind" around the bed, but was not entirely successful. According to her husband's judgment of the matter, she was "not so well skilled in putting them up as the Americans. . . ."[33]

The wives and daughters of fur traders also travelled in association with their husbands' and fathers' work. Thérèse Schindler and Madeleine La Framboise, Métis sisters, accompanied their spouses in the trade; both also became independent traders when widowed. Madeleine enjoyed such success as an independent trader after her husband's death that she was able to keep servants in her home in Mackinac and pay for the education of several children in eastern Canadian boarding schools. The final triumph of her later years was teaching herself to read and write in both French and English.[34]

Other wives went to sea with husbands who were mariners. The Englishwoman Frances Hornby Barkley was with her new husband on the voyage of discovery that took them in 1787 to the Pacific Northwest and the coast of what was to become British Columbia. She journeyed there again with him in the 1790s. Similar voyages were also part of the tradition and practice of Maritime women. Indeed, Maritime women "regularly accompanied" sea captain husbands and fathers on their voyages well into the late nineteenth and early twentieth centuries.[35]

The wives and daughters of fishermen were another group of women whose work was determined by their husbands' trade. In the cod fishery on Newfoundland's northeast coast, family workers began to replace the male servants hired by the companies sometime in the eighteenth century. Women's work in the household and farmyard included preserving food, caring for animals and the garden, making butter, picking berries, preparing meals—often four or more a day—making bread, manufacturing clothing—all of this essential work and presumably very similar to that done on any farm. But it was also this work that liberated their husbands, brothers, and fathers for fishing, hunting, building boats, and other related labour. Women were "skippers of the shore crew."[36] And, in addition to this work,

they had their own tasks specific to the fishery. Ephraim Tucker, an American travelling up the coast of Labrador for his health in the summer of 1838, was astonished at how hard the women worked, noting that they engaged

A French Canadian farmwife, after a painting by Cornelius Krieghoff, 1852.

in the hard and laborious toils of fishing with as much zeal and activity as the males. When the salmon and trout fishing commences, the women and children employ themselves assiduously in the sport, and are often out night and day while the season of this fishery lasts. At the fish stands, while the cod fishery is in the full tide of operation, the women are seen among the most constant and dextrous in dressing the fish, thrown up by the fishermen. Some of these females will dress two or three thousand fish in a single day.[37]

Other British North American women were no less involved in family-related employment, even if on a less spectacular level. Farm wives and daughters continued much as their New France predecessors had done before them: taking charge of the poultry and barnyards, and of vegetable and fruit growing, in addition to their household tasks. They continued to be involved in food production at two levels: tending, growing, and gathering food; and salting, drying, or otherwise preserving it, as well as preparing dairy products such as butter and cheese. All this in addition to cooking meals for large families and regular farm servants or temporary hired labour.

In the late eighteenth and the first half of the nineteenth century,

British North American men were preoccupied with the production and transportation of lumber and wheat, as these two staple products began to make inroads on the older staples of fish and furs. While the men were off in the lumber shanty or rafting the potash down the river, or busying themselves in the fields, or taking the wheat to market, women maintained families on the products of their subsistence farming. Every pioneer diary seems to tell the same story: a frequently absent husband; wife and children as well as servants, if there were any, growing vegetables and fruits, looking after animals, and occupying themselves with the production of the family's basic food. Like Anne Powell's former servant Nancy, or Sarah Sherwood, they may also have been occupied in spinning or weaving if they had time left over. Although men seem to have been the professional weavers in most communities, women produced the "homespun," and some spun and wove for their neighbours as well as their own families. All of this work was vital. It was women's subsistence farm work as well as the production of goods for sale—spun wool, woven goods, butter, cheese, and the like — that made possible the accumulation of capital in many farm families.[38]

Mary Morris Bradley of New Brunswick left the following description of her subsistence labour after nine months of marriage to her first husband in 1790. "I had the privilege of two cows' milk," she reported.

One my husband brought home, and the other my father gave me; so that by an exchange of milk with my mother, I made plenty of cheese and butter for our use. We raised potatoes sufficient for the family, and for fatting our pork; so that with these necessaries of life, milk and butter, potatoes and pork, with but little bread, we lived; excepting particular occasions, I made little use of tea and sugar.[39]

The reminiscences of this New Brunswick housewife also demonstrate the way in which British North American women's work could make the difference to a family's survival. In the first year of their marriage, Bradley's husband got into debt over a lumber transaction, with the result that he had "no way to earn anything in the winter." Undaunted, Mary turned to her loom.

Just at this critical time, it occurred to me, I will commence the business of weaving. Accordingly, I set up my loom, and notified the neighbours, and I soon had plenty of work. I took my pay in such trade as was suitable for our family's use, which made payment easy for my customers. I soon got into the way of helping ourselves greatly. My labor was hard; but I was favoured with a good constitution, and I felt much encouraged and truly thankful for such a providential opening.[40]

Providential or not, Mary Bradley's weaving evidently saved the day. By 1805 the Bradleys were able to move into Saint John. Here Mary and her husband kept a grocery store and rented out part of their house, eventually paying off the mortgage and enjoying the "great blessing" of owning "a comfortable home."

Plain and fancy sewing provided another avenue of remunerative work that could be done in one's own household or in the homes of other women on a rotating basis. By the middle of the nineteenth century, sewing had replaced weaving as a major source of income for the single women and widows who were living without the support of a spouse. "Seamstress" is in fact one of the few employments that emerges clearly on mid-nineteenth century census returns as a woman's occupation. In 1851, 553 women in Canada East and West listed this as their source of income.[41]

Women could also take in laundry to earn money. In the eighteenth and nineteenth centuries this was probably some of the hardest physical work that women did. Hauling water, lifting water-soaked fabrics, heating irons, stirring, rinsing, and wringing were only some of the steps that could have been involved. A study of the process at its most elaborate, as it would have been done in a wealthy household in the first half of the nineteenth century, outlines some ten steps altogether, including scrubbing especially dirty clothes on a washboard, the addition of blueing to prevent linens from turning yellow, starching, and putting large items through long wooden rollers known as "mangles" to wring out the water and flatten them.[42]

Another remunerative occupation, but one that women shared with men, was schoolteaching. In the eighteenth century and the first half of the nineteenth it was relatively easy for women to teach because girls' schools were chiefly domestic affairs. Indeed the word "school" referred more to the teacher and her pupils than it did to whatever housing a school might have. The schoolmistress advertised her skills in the instruction of reading and writing, or of sewing, French, or fine arts, and waited at home for her pupils — as indeed did the vast majority of schoolmasters. When the teacher moved, so did her school; her pupils came on an irregular basis, only when they could be spared from their tasks at home. As the numbers of towns and newspapers expanded in British North America, so did the ads and the schools, which like farming or fur trading were often family enterprises. A widow and her daughters, a husband and wife, or two sisters might set up a school together; the combinations varied, as did the subjects offered and the clientele. What is certain is that these small domestic or private schools were important educational resources in their communities, as well as vital sources of income for the schoolmistresses and their families.[43]

Angélique and Marguerite Nolin are just one of many examples of sisters who taught. After their father died sometime in the 1820s, these young mixed-blood women were persuaded to set up a school in Red River in 1829 by the Roman Catholic bishop of the region, Joseph-Norbert Provencher. The record does not supply details about the content of their lessons, but their pupils were undoubtedly the Métis children of French Canadian fur traders and their native wives, whose families had started to settle in the Red River area.[44]

It was also in the 1820s that Kate Andrews opened a "private school" in the "ample basement flat of her . . . commodious residence" in Liverpool, Nova Scotia, shortly after her second marriage. Her chronicler notes that the schoolmistress was self-educated.

By conversation with broadly educated persons with whom she came in contact, by perusal of books and periodicals, as well as by practical definite study, she had informed herself on many subjects. Her reading manner was delightful, her calligraphy elegant in style. With this acquired knowledge, and her art in needlework, she at length felt well equipped for imparting instruction to the children of the town.

The school, which was mainly for day pupils but always had a few boarders as well, moved with its teacher when she moved house, but continued for some fifty years, touching nearly every family in the community for three or four generations. Kate taught with the assistance of a servant and later a niece. "Gentility" as well as the three Rs and needlework constituted the curriculum.[45]

There were many such schools in British North America by the early decades of the nineteenth century. Some catered to the well-to-do; others had a fairly representative clientele of pupils. Anne Langton, an Upper Canadian spinster who taught school two days a week in the rural household that she managed for her brother and elderly parents, saw her work as charity towards the local poor.[46] These domestic schools provided countless women with their livelihoods or a way to supplement the family income. A schoolteacher from a later era, reminiscing about her own education in Quebec and Montreal in the 1830s, was able to recall at least seven private teachers with whom she had studied during that decade, both before and after a six-year period in the Ursuline convent school in Quebec City.[47]

Perhaps the most difficult to document of women's domestic vocations in the pre-industrial era was also one of the most important, the vocation of healer or midwife. Part of the problem of documentation is no doubt the fact that healing and midwifery were arts practised to some degree by all women in caring for their families and helping their neighbours. But as there had been in New France, so in British North America there were also women who were renowned and sought after for their knowledge of herbs and their midwifery skills. The importance of the woman healer to her community is illustrated by the story of Elizabeth Doane, an eighteenth century immigrant to Nova Scotia. A thrice-married mother of eleven, Doane migrated from New England to Nova Scotia before the American Revolution, settling in the town of Barrington. Her knowledge of herbs, surgery, and midwifery was so highly prized by her neighbours that when her husband thought of returning to New England in 1770 because his business was not prospering, thirty-five petitioners supported Elizabeth Doane's request for a land grant from the town proprietors so that she could build a house and stay. There must have been hundreds of such women in British North America, although so far the detailed stories of only a few have been discovered.[48]

Almost all women who were literate kept records of medicinal recipes for use when their families became ill; the non-literate learned the recipes from watching and helping older relatives, and passed them on orally to the younger generation. Catharine Parr Traill combined her interest in the medicinal uses of plants with a passion for Canadian flora in general. As prolific a writer as her sister Susanna Moodie about life in the backwoods, Traill also made a name for herself as a botanist by sending specimens of Canadian plants to scientists in England.[49]

Women like Catharine Parr Traill and Elizabeth Doane, or the Misses Nolin and Kate Andrews, made little distinction between their housework and other activities. While much of their domestic employments were generally unpaid, activities such as weaving, teaching, and laundry could bring in income—income that was often essential. All of this work nevertheless took place in "domestic space." Countless were the women who ran small inns or taverns in their homes, or accepted boarders. The latter was an especially vital occupation for townswomen. The census for Hamilton, Canada West, records, for example, that 29 percent of all households in that community contained boarders in 1851. [50]

Since a woman who took in boarders often provided a laundry service as well as meals for her boarders, the work involved was far from minimal. Like domestic service—and even teaching and healing—keeping boarders was an expansion of women's traditional role, a way in which women could respectably earn their livings or assist in the maintenance of their families without straying very far from either their homes or their communities' expectations.

Prostitution was another, if less respectable, way of earning money. British North America was a military garrison and there is no doubt that prostitution was a temporary or supplementary employment for many women, especially in the ports and garrison towns. But "Prostitute" and "Keeper of house of ill-fame" were also among the occupations that appeared on the 1851 census returns for Hamilton, Canada West, suggesting that one census taker at least was thinking in terms of more permanent labels or identities.[51]

Interestingly enough, "Widow" and "Spinster" were also designated occupations on the census. In both cases this presumably reflected the understanding that a woman's marital status had an effect on what she did. Certainly a woman who had lost her husband would be anxious to have remunerative employment of some kind, unless she were very well off. Unmarried women too increasingly needed paid work. Even "Wife" was occasionally to be found in the column for occupations on the census, although generally this column was left blank opposite the names of married women. Did most census takers believe, therefore, that the married mistresses of households did not work? Or was their work so taken for granted that it did not need to be itemized on the census? Perhaps the answer lies somewhere in between. It may lie also in the fact that wives' roles were too diverse and variable to be easily pinned down. An additional answer is to be found in the perception, on the part at least of some by the mid-nineteenth century, of a growing gulf between two newly defined worlds: the personal, domestic world of women and the family, where it was assumed that traditional female work continued to go on; and a newly developing public world from which wives and perhaps even children were most appropriately excluded. "Work" or employment that could be dignified by the title of an "occupation" was increasingly to be seen as belonging to the latter sphere, the sphere governed and occupied chiefly by men. In the mid-nineteenth century we are still in a period when extraordinary numbers of people in British North America—perhaps the majority—had more than one occupation. To identify men or women by a *single* profession or kind of work, as the census did, was itself a move towards altering people's perceptions of what they did with their lives and who they were.

Men's occupations expanded in number and began to move out of the household; in some cases, they became specialized, full-time vocations. Women's domestic employments began to seem, in contrast, rather limited, unspecialized, and poorly remunerated.[52] Yet, in British North America this was largely an urban phenomenon and one that was only noticeable by the middle decades of the nineteenth century. Probably relatively few British North American women were greatly affected by the new attitudes towards women's work that were developing in England and New England, where things were patently changing far more rapidly.

Nevertheless, middle class emigrants from New England and England could not and did not leave their belief in the ideology of "domestic" womanhood behind them when they came to British North America. They adhered to it as best they could and aligned themselves with those in the colonies who were seemingly sympathetic. Such would be the men and women who understood women's work to be in part "ornamental," like Harriet Cartwright's painting perhaps, and wanted to believe that every woman was supported by a father, a brother, or a husband. The daughters of Upper Canada's Chief Justice William Dummer Powell and his wife Anne illustrate the power of these beliefs for some classes of British North American men and women, even in the early nineteenth century. The mother of these young women was the same Anne Powell who had admired the industry of her former servant, Nancy, and noted her ability to make money for her family with her weaving. "Working" for one's living was not appropriate for her own daughters, however. Of the two Powell girls who did not marry, Anne and Elizabeth, only Elizabeth successfully adapted to the pursuit of good works and ornamental dependency that was considered appropriate in the Powell circle. Daughter Anne clearly craved something different, but was not permitted to found the school that she coveted and thus seek a life of her own. The tragic result was serious mental illness. In an ill-fated attempt to escape from what eventually became an unbearable situation at home, Anne finally lost her life in a shipwreck off the coast of Ireland in 1822.[53]

In the upper middle class and affluent circles of families like the Powells, traditional class prejudice began to co-exist with a new ideology of domesticity that in theory, at least, emphasized the differences between women and men more than those between the classes. But in the world of British North America, this ideology denied what the vast majority of women, even of the urban middle classes, actually experienced: the absolute necessity of work and sometimes of "hard labour" in the household, on the farm, or wherever they lived, to keep body and soul together and their families going. It also denied the vital contribution that British North American women made to family and community economies by their reproductive and productive labour. In the former category, they had babies and raised children; they fed, clothed, cared for, and otherwise "reproduced" the labour force. In the second, they did work that was not only essential to the survival of their families, but often made all the difference to the family's ability to accumulate capital.

With a few exceptions, it is probable that the vast majority of British North American women were beyond the reach of the disabling beliefs that so negatively affected the life of Anne Powell. If women were not supposed to engage in productive or remunerative work, they did not know it. Or, if they thought that this was the case, they were soon disabused of the notion. Even Susanna Moodie disciplined herself "to learn and practice all the menial employments which are necessary to a good settler's wife." She admired Canadian women, who possessed the "excellent practical abilities" that were so essential on the frontier, and prided herself not only on her neat rows of potatoes, but on her ability to bring in some much-needed cash by her literary and artistic productions. Finally, Susanna Moodie learned that chaos and difficulty did not last forever and could even be productive of good. Indeed, it was when their situation appeared most desperate that "we were on the threshold of a new state of things, which was born out of that very distress."[54]

4 Women and the public order

British North Americans lived in a society regulated by popular custom and social hierarchy, by the clergy, and, of course, by government and law. In French Canada the Roman Catholic priest, the notary, and the *seigneur* exercised authority; there and in the rest of what was to become Canada clergymen, magistrates, military or company officers, and the large landowners constituted a structure of control. These authority figures were all men, and their range of activity was wide.

Sometimes they enforced unwritten codes. Such was the case at Fort Detroit in the 1780s when Pierre Frechette, the local priest, simply expelled two "disreputable" women from his parish. He reported to his bishop that he had forced the badly behaved Madame Moisseau to leave Simon's Mill; Madame Tourangu he had likewise "chased away."[1] These were not isolated or atypical events. In the absence of prisons, asylums, or police forces, vagrants and criminals were frequently driven from communities that did not want them.

Two other women who got into trouble with British North American authorities had disguised themselves as men. One, known to history as the "Orkney lad," had come by sea to the Northwest in 1806 disguised as a Hudson's Bay Company servant (possibly in order to be with the father of her expected child), and her identity was only discovered when she gave birth. Isabel Gunn was no longer allowed to do the work of a company servant—she was given employment as a washerwoman; she managed to stay in Rupert's Land for three years, but was finally shipped back to Scotland by company authorities. They were enforcing a code that still discouraged white women from entering or living in fur trade country.[2] Some fifteen years later, Mary Palmer seems to have aggravated her disobedience of the law by cross-dressing: she was arrested in Halifax for causing a disturbance on the streets one night while wearing an officer's uniform. But although Mary had to spend the night in the watch-house and appear before the magistrate in the morning, she got away with a reprimand, a small fine, and a warning.[3]

In the British colonies and in Hudson's Bay territory, women found their lives increasingly affected by British law or new legislation passed by colonial legislatures. Some of these laws perpetuated traditional sexual inequalities or divisions of labour, or extended them to the new public world that men were in the process of creating. Women were not without recourse in this world, however. Canada's first comic novel, Frances Brookes' account of manners and morals as she experienced them in Quebec in the early days of British rule,[4] reveals a community in which upper class English women exercised considerable social power, if no official authority. So did some French women, especially if they were married to British politicians or senior officers.

Regulating sexuality, marriage, and motherhood

Jane Beaver and her husband Herbert, the Hudson's Bay Company chaplain, complained bitterly of many things they found wrong with Fort Vancouver on the Columbia River in the 1840s. But their greatest grief was the country marriages of native women and traders. Because of their protests, several long-married couples, including James and Amelia Douglas, were married for a second time in the Church of England by Herbert Beaver; the church thus successfully "regulated" the custom of two centuries.[5]

Church authorities no doubt found reason to complain in other parts of British North America about casual attitudes to marriage. Owing to the shortage of persons to marry them, many couples cheerfully lived together without benefit of religious rites. As the clergy became more numerous, efforts were made to alter this state of affairs, and accounts abound of couples, from Newfoundland to the west coast, whose several children were present at their weddings. One traveller to Canada West in 1842 claimed that Canadian girls preferred this approach to marriage; he had met one informant who was proud of the fact that, when she had married, her daughter had already been two years old. He found that Canadians considered ridiculous the "correcter feelings on this subject, of females from the old country." What he either did not know or remember is that the high value placed on fertility and child labour in rural Europe had long been the source of similar attitudes. In Canada too, as he himself was quick to point out, children were "so valuable a possession" that bringing "two or three into the world in this irregular fashion, instead of being a bar to marriage, proves . . . an additional attraction, making the young lady a species of heiress." It followed, according to this account, that the producer of Canadian children was herself a valuable possession. "After marriage," he went on, the Canadian

Snowshoeing with a chaperone on the mountain at Montreal, by Charles Caleb Ward, 1841.

Walking out with a soldier, by James Pattison Cockburn, *circa* 1830.

"makes an active industrious wife, but expects from her husband much deference, and even that he should wink at occasional frailties. . . ."[6]

Courtship and parental arrangement of upper and middle class marriages also followed age-old patterns. Although the evidence is scattered and incomplete, we know that upper class parents were especially concerned to control their children's choice of marriage partners. As in Europe, in urban centres young women met men in formalized situations, at balls and parties in wintertime, and at various meetings connected with their churches. Young men requested permission to call, or were invited to young women's homes. Taking a young woman for a drive, if one was sufficiently wealthy to command a sleigh or a carriage, was a customary way to pay her court; if not, taking her for a walk, or walking her home, was another. Tradition has it that, in the County of Beauce on the south shore of the St. Lawrence, when a girl was ready for courting, her brother took her to church and escorted her to a similarly minded group of young women who stood apart from their families.[7]

In the countryside the process of daily life brought the sexes together, despite the divisions of labour that generally prevailed. Although work was hard and time for courting and lovemaking may have seemed limited, people appear to have had a relatively open approach to sexuality, albeit one in which men had greater power and freedom than women. Respectable courting went on more or less under the watchful eyes of the young woman's elders. In the Ottawa Valley as late as the 1860s, a young man named Thomas Dick and his girl friends still seemed to be operating along the old lines. Thomas Dick went to "tea meetings," to church, and to what he invariably referred to as "sinning school," although we can presume he meant "singing." He called on neighbourhood girls in their homes, sitting and chatting with them, sometimes after the parents had gone to bed. He walked them home and he discussed them with his male friends. Sometimes family sanctions operated to deter courtship and marriage rather than support them, and in Dick's case marriage may have been delayed because his mother was a widow. Despite his evident interest in courting in 1867, he waited until after his sisters had married and his mother had died before embarking on matrimony, some twenty years after the beginning of his diary.[8]

There was a clear sense of family involvement when a decision to marry was made. Mary Gapper O'Brien hesitated for some time over her engagement to be married, consulting parents and siblings to make sure that her services, as the one remaining unmarried daughter in the family, could be spared.[9] In many parts of British North America, community surveillance of marriage was to be expected. This sometimes erupted into the traditional wedding night rioting known as the "charivari." Young male revellers, often in disguise, besieged the newlyweds in their home, demanding gifts. This might happen when one spouse was much older than the other, or there was some other large social gulf between them.[10]

It is also clear that few British North American weddings were undertaken without considerable attention to the material needs of the couple. For people whose assets were few, material considerations were important. Marriage contracts carefully outlining the assets and obligations of both parties continued to govern the unions of some British North American spouses well into the nineteenth century, particularly among French Canadians.

These marriage contracts operated within a complicated system of legal regulation of marriage. In Quebec, which became Lower Canada in 1791, the French Civil Code prevailed after the British takeover, and thus French marriage law continued to apply. As revised on a number of occasions between the Conquest and 1795, the law of Quebec and then Lower Canada required the agreement of both parties, the publication of banns, and a ceremony performed by an Anglican or Catholic priest, for the marriage to be legal. The wedding also had to be witnessed and registered with the civil authorities. Eventually it became a little easier to get legally married when, between 1827 and 1845, other religious denominations were given the power to officiate. Nevertheless, the French provision for the "community of goods" prevailed, protecting to a degree the wife's interest in the marital property, regardless of the religious denomination of the couple. Contracts sorted out the details to the mutual satisfaction of the marrying parties and their friends, before the weddings of propertied individuals could take place.[11]

Elsewhere in British North America, British common law governed marriage. To paraphrase Blackstone's famously terse dictum, in common law the husband and wife were considered one person and that person was the husband. Clara Brett Martin, Canada's first woman lawyer, later summed up this doctrine of marital unity as meaning a "suspension of the independent existence of the wife, and an absorption by the husband of the woman's person and all her belongings. . . ."[12] The wife's property and person came entirely under the control of her husband. In the eyes of the law, husbands could not "rape" their wives; wives could not sue their husbands or testify against them in court. The families of well-to-do women sometimes attempted to protect them by marriage contracts similar to those used in Lower Canada, in order to keep brides' rights and inheritances from unscrupulous or incompetent husbands, and widows with property might insist on a contract to keep control of assets acquired during a previous marriage or in the interim. But contracts do not seem to have been drawn up in great numbers by English-speaking British North Americans, suggesting that most women had no such protection. Under British common law a married woman had the right to dower—a lifetime interest in one-third of her husband's property. Dower became effective only upon her husband's death, so although she was guaranteed some support during widowhood, no law protected her economic interest in the case of marriage breakdown. Most women who separated from their husbands lost not only their right to the use of whatever property the family had accumulated, but also to the custody of their children. At a time and in a place where children's labour was extremely valuable, the loss of their children constituted more than an emotional loss to women who endured such separations.[13]

Divorce was possible, but difficult, and the law varied from colony to colony. English common law applied in areas other than Quebec and the Maritimes. There were several attempts to establish divorce courts in Upper and Lower Canada between 1833 and 1859, but these failed and divorce had to be obtained through a special act of the legislature, applying the criteria of common law. Only in the Maritimes were there provisions for court treatment of divorce, and these were rarely used. As early as 1758 the Nova Scotia legislature granted the governor and Council the authority to hear divorce cases; it took a subsequent law to settle the grounds, but these were fairly extensive and included impotence, adultery, and cruelty, as well as kinship within the prohibited degree, and bigamy. This relatively liberal legislation may have had some relation to initial shortages of women; the earliest law in Nova Scotia had included desertion (for three years) as a ground for divorce, possibly evidence of legislators' desire to facilitate women's remarriage.[14] Later, the English Matrimonial Causes Act (1857), which became the basis of divorce law in most provinces, provided that a wife could be divorced on grounds of adultery. For a wife to obtain a divorce, however, her husband had to be proved guilty either of incestuous adultery, rape, sodomy, bestiality, or bigamy, or of adultery compounded with cruelty or with desertion for at least two years.[15]

Women's lack of economic protection in marriage was difficult enough. But even more damaging to some women was the common law's assumption of the husband's right to control his wife's person, which included control of the location of the household, a veto over the possibility of paid labour outside the home, the right to "confine" her to it under certain conditions, and even the right to what was considered a reasonable amount of physical punishment. Of course not everyone accepted the subordination that the law and legal marriage rites prescribed. An Upper Canadian traveller told the story of an American bride who simply walked out of the church when she discovered that the wedding ceremony required that she promise to obey, choosing to join the many couples who at that time lived as man and wife without benefit of clerical or legal intervention in their affairs.[16]

Public protests against the injustice of British laws regarding marriage and child custody were just beginning at the start of the nineteeth century; we have so far found no evidence of them in British North America before 1850. Attempts at rebellion were individual, and met with varying success. Ann Melvin, an Upper Canadian wife of the mid-nineteenth century, had a husband who would not permit her to go out of the house without his leave. She wrote to her sister in 1851 that she would rather live "in some Desert on bread and water" than remain married, but her offer to take the children away and "work out" to support them was scorned by the man who had become her jailor.[17]

Some wives in such untenable situations, especially women with economic resources, managed to arrange for legal separations, and to survive by moving back to parents or finding homes with friends. Others acted more precipitously. Ads by husbands announcing their refusal to pay debts incurred by runaway wives were by no means unusual in British North American newspapers. They testify to the fact that some women dealt with their unhappy marriages by simply walking out the door and down the road.[18]

The ad that Charles Wright placed in the *Nova Scotia Gazette and Weekly Chronicle* on September 13, 1775 described his wife's behaviour and illustrated his concern for his patriarchal rights. Hannah Wright, the ad claimed, had "been very remiss in her duty" towards her husband and children, "living in idleness and such like vicious acts and practices, as tend wholly to subvert all kind of family order and Government." Hannah had evidently not only kept bad company, but had carried off and sold a large part of the household furniture before she finally "eloped" from his "bed and board." Wright intended to prosecute anyone who harboured his wife, and declared that he would pay no debts that she contracted. On the other hand, he was willing to repay to "all good people" any money advanced on the furniture, should they return it in the same condition that it was in when taken away.[19]

Most common of all was acceptance, even transformation of personal unhappiness into yet another hardship to be conquered. Mary Bradley, whose weaving made such an important contribution to the economic success of her first marriage, sought solace in religion when she found her husband overbearing and unkind. Fortunately, after her first husband died, her second choice made her happier.

And indeed happy, even egalitarian marriages were possible under the harsh rule of common law, while some marriages were dominated by wives uncowed by conventional expectations.

Generally speaking, though, the power of married women before the law was small. They might well have envied their unmarried sisters who, if legally of age, controlled their own property and persons. But the law did gradually change, adapting to some degree to the changing circumstances of women's lives. Nineteenth century laws relating to infanticide, abortion, seduction, and rape reveal much about the changing politics of male/female relations.[20]

Early British North American law on infanticide exactly duplicated an English statute of the seventeenth century. Christian law forbade infanticide, and under English common law child murder was a felony punishable by death. But if a newborn was dead, it was difficult to establish why it had died or even whether it had been born alive. The law on infanticide therefore made it a crime, also punishable by death, to conceal the birth of a "bastard," illegitimate children being the most likely to be simply done away with. The intriguing thing about these brutal laws on infanticide is their ineffectiveness. At first the laws only applied to illegitimate births, and the cases that were heard applied only to unmarried women; very few were convicted. When Angélique Pilotte, a twenty-year-old native servant, was given the death sentence for "concealment," there was a public outcry, and later a royal pardon. Pilotte's defenders pointed out that the defendent knew nothing of Christianity and was guilty only of the "invariable custom of Indian women to retire and bring forth their children alone and in secret."[21]

In 1803, with a view to obtaining convictions where they had failed in the past, the English lawmakers decided that the ordinary rules of murder trials were to apply to infanticide; if there was an acquittal, a verdict of concealment could be substituted, punishable now by imprisonment for a maximum of two years. The British North American colonies followed suit, all passing similar laws between 1810 and 1840. Further legislation increased the scope of the law to include married women in the 1830s and 1840s; in New Brunswick and Nova Scotia, persons other than mothers were included in the workings of the law in 1849 and 1851. There were very few convictions, suggesting that legal authorities had some compassion for the women who, it must have been clear, were victims themselves. Communities were only beginning to provide for illegitimate or otherwise unwanted children. On the other hand, the very existence of such laws raises questions about male lawmakers' underlying attitudes to women's sexuality and childbearing capacity.

Before 1803, under British law, abortion had been legal before "quickening" — that is, at any stage before the child's movements were felt. British legislation in 1803 criminalized all abortion, but still maintained the distinction between abortion before and after quickening. The latter was punishable by death, the former by lesser sentences such as imprisonment or transportation; the criminal in both cases was the abortionist. Most British North American colonies gradually enacted similar legislation in the first decades of the nineteenth century, with New Brunswick the first. By 1837 British legislators had abolished the distinction between the periods before and after quickening but reduced the maximum sentence to three years. This time British North American legislators, with the exception of Newfoundland, did not follow the British model in its entirety, tending to be more severe. New laws were passed in both Upper Canada and New Brunswick in the 1840s that also eliminated the distinction, but maximum sentences remained harsh: life imprisonment in Upper Canada, and fourteen years in New Brunswick. In 1849 and 1851 respectively, New Brunswick and Nova Scotia shifted ground substantially: in a move that was unprecedented, except in the State of New York, they made it a criminal offense for the woman herself to obtain an abortion at any stage of her pregnancy.[22]

One reason for the increasing criminalization of abortion was the growth of doctors' opposition to the procedure. In 1832 the human ovum was discovered. Until then, the association between menstruation and reproduction was only speculative.[23] Since doctors no longer thought of quickening as the start of life, they were increasingly reluctant to interfere with what they now thought of as a continuing process beginning with conception. At the same time, abortions continued to be performed, for it remained difficult to diagnose pregnancy before quickening made it unmistakable. Earlier in a pregnancy, remedies to regulate or re-establish menstruation were not easily distinguishable from remedies to produce abortion, either by medical assistants or by the women concerned.

Rape, like abortion and infanticide, came under the criminal code, and was punishable by death; the related crime of seduction was a civil offense. In the case of both seduction and rape, it was not the woman who was held to be the victim, but her father. We know little about the enforcement of the law with regard to rape in British North America, although some Upper Canadian cases reported during the period between 1824 and 1850 suggest that violent resistance had to be proved and even then the all-male juries were reluctant to convict.[24] At least two convicted rapists were sentenced to death during this period, and a number of others given prison sentences of varying lengths. Infinitely more numerous than rape trials were the lawsuits generated by the unique Upper Canadian law of 1837 dealing with seduction. Under common law this had been a crime against masters as well as parents, the offense being that it deprived a young woman's master or father of her services during the pregnancy and childbirth that resulted from an illicit relationship. The 1837 law may have recognized a new situation; young unmarried women who had emigrated before their parents often worked as servants, and were particularly vulnerable to the attentions of their social superiors, men who were in fact their masters. It was thus fathers, not masters who needed to be defended against the "ruin" of their "chaste" daughters, and they needed this protection even if their daughters were no longer living at home. The law recognized also that it was not loss of services *per se* that was at issue but, as the attorney-general of Upper Canada put it, "the wound given to parental feelings, the disgrace and injury inflicted upon the family of the person seduced." The injury to the women themselves was ignored. In contrast to the punitive rape law, the law on seduction was frequently called upon in the colonies and seems to have been a fruitful source of income for lawyers and injured fathers alike.

The existence of the tort of seduction entrenched in civil law a father's right to his daughters' services. In addition, the new statute stated his property interests over her sexuality and reputation. Certainly it denied the autonomy of the woman concerned in a fundamental way. Indeed, all of the laws affecting sexuality, marriage, and motherhood might be regarded as evidence of new kinds of intrusion into women's lives, as male lawgivers attempted to reinforce or reinterpret traditional male controls over women in a changing world.[25]

As far as we know, only Anna Jameson, the British writer who visited Upper Canada in the 1830s, expressed what might be described as a "modern" reaction to the 1837 seduction law. It was only a passing comment, but she seemed to imply that women needed less to be protected by their fathers and the law than they needed to be equal and held responsible for their own persons and acts.[26] To achieve such responsibility women needed the right to earn a living. This would gradually come to mean the right to enter the public sphere and seek employment outside the home.

Learning and working outside the household

The early stirrings of industrial and urban development were just beginning to affect British North America. Although there were few factories or large cities in the colonies themselves, immigrants brought this new world with them. By mid-century a traveller would notice the decline of household spinning, as even farm women began to purchase textiles that originated in the manufactories of Britain or New England.[27] Family patterns were being changed by these trends, and daughters as well as sons would increasingly seek remunerative work outside their families. For most of British North America's history, however, the family economy continued to prevail, and a daughter's wages were a vital part of the family subsistence. Hence the view that workingmen were indeed injured if they were deprived of their daughters' earnings. The single woman's right to an independent living was an idea whose time had not yet come. But the single woman's obligation to work for the family now enabled her to move towards public employment.

The transition from domestic to public employment was a subtle one and varied according to the type of work performed. One version of the process can be seen in the development of women's involvement in public education. A first step came when a few British North

American married women, who were teaching in their own homes, applied for and received certification as teachers eligible to receive the provincial school grant; their household schools thus became public schools.[28] The more typical process in the nineteenth century, however, was in the reverse direction, as the school moved out of domestic space and into public space and the teacher moved with it. Initially the distance was not great. Most publicly employed schoolmistresses were young unmarried women or widows who taught in a schoolhouse not far from home. Often they taught only in the summer, when male teachers were less available and the pupils tended to be younger. But by mid-century women were teaching winter schools too.

Ann Stewart had been in charge of her parish school in Newcastle, New Brunswick for nearly three years when it was examined by a government inspector in 1844. A thirty-two-year-old widow, Mrs. Stewart lived in the schoolhouse and had an average attendance of about twenty girls, to whom she taught reading (but not writing) along with plain and ornamental needlework and knitting. Her discipline consisted of "admonition" and "slight corporal punishment"; she did not employ rewards. The inspector believed that the schoolbooks currently supplied by the friends of the scholars were insufficient, although under the heading of "Books and Apparatus used in the School" he commented only that "Being a female School there are few apparates [sic] needed." But this did not mean that the visitor found Mrs. Stewart's school up to standard; his final assessment was that Ann Stewart was not really competent to teach either reading or writing, and was only employed by the local community "with a view to the wants of the female children of the neighbourhood." It was because of these "peculiar circumstances" alone that the Board of Education had "passed" Mrs. Stewart and permitted her to collect the government allowance for elementary schoolteachers.[29]

By 1851 almost one-fifth of Nova Scotian parish or common school-teachers were female; in Upper Canada the proportion was about the same. But in New Brunswick almost half of the teachers were women by mid-century, and in Lower Canada the proportion was higher still.[30] Both the Lower Canadian and the New Brunswick examples alert us to the fact that the trend towards women teaching in the public schools did not necessarily originate in cities. Urban schools were beginning to be interested in employing female teachers as assistants, but even at mid-century their numbers were still tiny. Indeed, a study of teachers in central Canada during the middle of the nineteenth century suggests that rural poverty and the lure of resource industries for young men explain in part the preferential hiring of young women in the common schools. In addition, as rural school trustees and commissioners candidly admitted, female teachers could be got for "half the price"; when local funds to match the government grant for salaries were pitifully small, male teachers were simply beyond the community's reach.[31]

Some Upper Canadian schoolmasters, bent on improving the

status of the profession for men, railed against the advent of the woman teacher, claiming correctly that the entry of women into public-school teaching prevented the payment of good wages to men. But these critics did not stop the hiring of women in the schools. Increasingly, public-school teaching vied with domestic service as an occupation for girls seeking employment after their own schooling was over.

Less significant numerically than the female teachers of publicly supported elementary schools, but highly influential all the same, were the women teachers who were employed in the larger Protestant academies and colleges or in their Roman Catholic convent equivalents. Many elite Protestant families sent their daughters to the Lower Canadian convent schools that the sisters of the *Congrégation de Notre Dame* and the Ursulines continued to operate in the late eighteenth and early nineteenth centuries. Some of the new Protestant institutions may well have been created in response to the obvious attraction of these Catholic schools. But the new non-Catholic institutions that began to appear in British North America in the 1820s also had their roots in the American and British academy movements. And despite their apparent competition, Protestant and Catholic schools for young ladies differed very little in their educational offerings. Both emphasized the genteel arts, strict timetables, and social supervision. In both Catholic and Protestant girls' schools, and even in the co-educational academies, girls were offered a basic instruction in English or French; arithmetic, geography, and perhaps history; and a wide variety of the practical as well as the "ornamental" arts. Generally unavailable to girls were such subjects as higher mathematics or classical languages, subjects that educators tended to define as "masculine." In the same way, in the public schools that girls attended and that were often co-educational, girls could be denied access to advanced arithmetic. In elementary schools, wherever female teachers were employed, girls were nearly always taught sewing in addition to the three Rs.[32]

Whether they were in public schools or domestic schools, Protestant academies or Catholic convent schools, women participated in varying degrees in a female culture that increasingly valued "learning." Women were taught what was considered suitable to their sphere, and by the middle of the nineteenth century it was much expanded from what had been made available to most women of previous generations. Those women who were aware of the growing international agitation for female "improvement" believed that a more advanced education was essential to fit women for their vital and enhanced educational role as mothers and teachers.

Mary Electa Adams was affected by this movement. The daughter of Loyalists who had settled first in Lower, then in Upper Canada, Mary Electa was educated by her parents until, at the age of seventeen, she was sent to the Montpelier Academy in Vermont, the school that had been attended by her mother. There Mary Electa was admitted to the study of the classics and advanced mathematics.

After a year at Montpelier, the young scholar returned to Upper Canada to study at the Cobourg Ladies' Seminary, founded when girls were excluded from the newly created Victoria College. The Seminary offered a diploma thought suitable for young ladies: the MLA or "Mistress of Liberal Arts." Mary Electa Adams obtained the diploma and remained at the seminary to teach until its director and her husband moved their school to Toronto, where it reopened as the Adelaide Academy in 1847. It is not clear if Adams made this move as well, but by 1849 she had embarked on a career of her own in the administration of girls' academies. She went from the Picton Lady's Academy in Prince Edward County, Upper Canada, to Michigan, and then to New Brunswick, where she was "Lady Preceptress" of the women's department of Mount Allison University, before returning to Canada West to head first the Wesleyan Female College in Hamilton, then an academy of her own known as Brookhurst, and finally the Ontario Ladies College in Whitby.[33]

The educational impulse took women in two somewhat contradictory directions. On the one hand it led to an expansion of all-female institutions, like those with which Ann Stewart and Mary Electa Adams were associated. This was particularly true in Roman Catholic Lower Canada, where seven new female religious communities were established between 1842 and 1851, four of them devoted to the provision of schooling for girls or for poor children. English-speaking convents devoted to education were also established in centres like Halifax and Toronto at mid-century.[34] Like the larger female academies and the small girls' parish schools, these institutions took women out of the private household, but remained all-female enclaves. They provided forums where women could exercise power, but only by isolating women and girls from the public world of men.

The alternative route, which affected more British North American women in the long run, was the move into co-educational public schooling, where women appeared to be working in closer proximity with men. This avenue was made possible by the admission of young women to most of the "normal schools"; these were opened by the governments of nearly every province in the 1840s and 1850s for training teachers. In French Canada, the normal schools remained strictly male institutions and the training of women teachers was undertaken by female religious orders, most notably the *Congrégation de Notre Dame* and the Ursulines. Indeed, convent women had been engaged in the formal training of teachers in Lower Canada since the 1830s.[35] But elsewhere in British North America women moved into the same institutions and buildings as the men. Their position was by no means the same as that of their male counterparts, however. In Toronto, when women were admitted to the newly founded normal school in 1848, they were much younger on the average than the male teachers training there; they were also less advanced in their preparation, for many of the men had already taught school. Finally they were treated differently, streamed into lower levels of teacher certification. Outside of school, they were strictly supervised.

Martha Hamm Lewis, the first woman to attend New Brunswick's normal school in Fredericton in 1849, was required to wear a veil when attending the school. She also had to arrive in class before the arrival of her fellow students, and leave well after they had left.[36]

Interpreting what educational innovation meant for British North American women in the first half of the nineteenth century is a subtle exercise. There is no doubt that the more rapid advancement of education for boys and young men put girls and young women at a disadvantage. The first colleges and universities were exclusively male institutions. When Upper Canada Academy was transformed into Victoria College, women were no longer admitted. Yet, as mid-nineteenth century observers recognized and the early normal schools demonstrated, simply admitting girls to boys' schools or colleges could also be problematic. Should young men and women study the same things together? Or should they be in separate departments studying different things? The latter was the solution chosen by most of the early co-educational academies. Government-funded grammar schools, on the other hand, often admitted girls. Some did not differentiate between their male and female students. More often, girls were simply admitted on sufferance.

In the end, no solution really worked in the context of a society in which the worlds of men and women seemed to be drifting apart. Advanced education for men was obviously intended as a grounding for professional roles. If this was so, what was the purpose of advanced education for women, who were essentially excluded from the professions? The new medical schools that began to be founded for men in the 1830s and 1840s did not admit women; nor did the law schools. Nor could women train for the ministry. The established denominations placed great emphasis on learning and a proper training in theology at a college or university, an ideal in which women had no place.

Prophesying and preaching women did appear among the more radical Christian sects. In the great religious revival, known as the Second Awakening, that swept across North America in the late eighteenth and early nineteenth centuries, women and children were active participants. "Protracted" revival meetings engulfed communities for weeks and prayer meetings went on day and night; both appeared to provide release and even leading roles for the young and female members of communities whose lives were normally more constrained.[37] As well, religious revivalism encouraged more permanent ministries among women. Bible Christian and Primitive Methodists, and some Wesleyan Episcopals, briefly supported women missionaries, and some of these made their way to the British colonies in North America. Elizabeth Dart Eynon came to the Cobourg area in the 1830s with her recently converted husband, John Hicks Eynon; both were itinerants in that region for several decades, often travelling and preaching separately. Eliza Barnes was a Wesleyan Episcopal who preached in the Canadas in the 1820s, but settled down to running a school for native children when she married her fellow Methodist missionary William Case in 1833. Perhaps the most vibrant-sounding of the Methodist women preachers was the American Ellen Bangs, also an Episcopal, who "exhorted like a streak of red-hot lightning" on the Niagara circuit at the turn of the century. And it is an American woman, Barbara Heck, who is credited with founding the first Methodist congregation in Upper Canada.[38]

But even among Methodists the woman preacher was an anomaly. By the middle of the century the evangelical sects began to adopt more conservative notions about the need for a professionally trained ministry. Women called to preach rarely had access to the kind of education church leaders had in mind. Preaching women, moreover, were probably associated with "religious enthusiasm," itself identified by many British North Americans as a Yankee import and a danger to the dignity and safety of the imperial state. In the end women remained largely excluded from the evangelical ministry, as they did from the other learned professions.

Women and government

The other great exclusion of the period was the barring of women from participation in government. Men were active in politics in larger and larger numbers as the imperial authorities established elected assemblies in the British North American colonies and introduced franchises based on increasingly generous property qualifications. The franchise was exercised, in this period before the secret ballot, in public election meetings — rowdy and highly contentious events that could last several days. At first it was not entirely clear what women's position might be under the rapidly changing political conditions of British North America. New Brunswick specifically excluded women from voting in 1791; in the other colonies it seems to have been simply assumed that women would not exercise the franchise. According to one constitutional historian, women had not voted in British elections "for centuries," although there was no formal legal restraint.[39]

Yet, intriguingly, in Lower Canada — and perhaps elsewhere — it appears that propertied women were not fully aware of their exclusion. A nineteenth century history of the Papineau family described Montreal women voting in the election of 1809, noting particularly one "elderly lady, long a widow, but notwithstanding her age, still fresh and vigorous." When she was asked for whom she wished to vote, "she answered with a voice strong and filled with emotion 'For my son, M. Joseph Papineau, for I believe that he is a good and faithful subject.' "[40] Evidently there was no protest, and the voter's son, Louis-Joseph Papineau, was elected for the East Ward of Montreal. Women in Bedford County and the borough of Three Rivers exercised the franchise in the election of 1820. The Bedford County case was disputed, however, because the votes of twenty-two married women had duplicated the votes of their husbands on the same properties. The Assembly declared that the election was void, and that voting by wives was illegal whether or not the husbands voted. Clearly the notion of an individual franchise was meaningless to these early nineteenth century legislators. It was property that voted, as represented by male heads of families.[41] By the late 1820s the question of women at elections began to arouse more extensive controversy. In 1828 the election of the previous year in Quebec Upper Town was called into question because a widow had been refused permission to vote. Petitioners called this a lapse of justice, declaring that "it would be impolitic and tyrannical to circumscribe [woman's] efforts in society, — to say that she shall not have the strongest interest in the fate of her country, and the security of her common rights. . . ." Pointing out that women were responsible for rearing and educating men, they added that "Widows exercise, generally, all the rights of men, are liable to most of the same duties towards the State, and can execute them as well. . . ."[42]

Public opinion and the views of British North American legislators and their imperial governors were moving inexorably in the other direction, however. In that same election in the "Borough of William Henry," a counter-petition claimed that there had been a miscarriage of justice because "many women" had in fact been permitted to exercise the franchise. In the debate, one of the two members for Quebec Upper Town based his objection to women's participation in politics on historical tradition: "it was incontrovertibly the practice of all representative governments, both ancient and modern, to exclude women from any share therein," he explained; therefore he could not "decide in favour of the ladies." In 1832, as part of an act concerning controverted elections, the Assembly included a measure prohibiting the exercise of the franchise by women; the Reform Act in Britain made the same provision in the same year. The Canadian law was disallowed by the British authorities for reasons unrelated to its content, and there seems to be no further record of women going to the polls in Lower Canada. In 1844, shortly after the union of Upper and Lower Canada, seven women evidently managed to vote in Canada West, and the election was upheld. But in 1849 a Reform government finally passed a law specifically excluding women from the franchise in both of the Canadas. Prince Edward Island had passed a similar law in 1836 and Nova Scotia was to do so in 1851.[43]

Something of the flavour of male attitudes to the idea of women voting comes through in an account of an election that took place in Nova Scotia well before women's official exclusion. The incident was a hot contest in Annapolis County, reported in the *Novascotian* of December 3, 1840 by a supporter of the Reform party. He had gone into Annapolis in the middle of the election to see what the Tories there were doing and found that they were up to mischief:

Getting all the old women and old maids, and everything in the shape of petticoats to be carried up to the hustings the next and last day to vote for [the Tory candidate] Whitman. As it was 9 o'clock in the evening no time was to be lost. I . . . rode all Tuesday night, and roused up every farmer;

Queen Victoria, a painting
with embroidery, by Ann
McLean and Agnes Wallace,
1841.

*and what was the result, they harnessed up their horses, went off, and each
one by 10 o'clock, was back with a widow or a fair young fatherless maid,
to vote against the Tory women from Annapolis Royal.*[44]

It is not clear, in the end, if any of the women actually managed to
exercise the franchise. What is clear is that the attempt of women
to vote was finally to be dismissed as no more than a "manoeuvre"
or perhaps, at the most, an occasion for a clever story. Reformers in
the colonies did not take up votes for women for any length of time
as a serious political cause. Louis-Joseph Papineau and other Lower
Canadian Reformers evidently espoused the idea in the 1820s, but
a violent by-election in Montreal West in 1832 changed Papineau's
mind. Men and women alike were intimidated, he claimed; three
people were killed, and women were being "drawn to the hustings
by their husbands or their guardians, often against their wills." Papineau finally concluded that such scenes were against the "public

interest, decency, and the natural modesty of the sex."[45] It has been suggested that he was also responding to the fact that, unlike his mother, the majority of qualified female property-holders in Lower Canada were anglophones who could not be expected to support his party.[46]

Women in British North America were now disenfranchised, but it would be wrong to imply that they played no political role whatever. On the contrary, the women of the colonial political elites and even women who were not in the official governing classes sometimes had considerable influence, particularly in times of stress. Probably Molly Brant was the most effective female political actor during the American revolutionary war. The third wife of the British Indian Agent, Sir William Johnston, and the sister of the Mohawk chief Joseph Brant, Molly Brant was a leading matron of her extensive and important tribe. She exerted a steady influence on her people and helped to persuade them to continue their support for the Six Nations' alliance with the British. When the war forced the Mohawk to abandon their ancestral territories in New York State for a new home in Upper Canada, she continued to work for the best possible conditions for their settlement.[47] Laura Secord also won fame for warning British officers of an impending American attack during the War of 1812. The record is unclear, but it appears that Secord walked the entire day of June 22, 1813, and a distance of some thirty kilometres, to carry this message. The entire American detachment of about four hundred men was captured. The British officer in charge later described the event and his indebtedness to Secord: "The weather on the 22d was very hot and Mrs. Secord whose person was slight and delicate . . . no doubt was much exhausted by the exertion she made coming to me." He added that, as Secord and her family were "entire Strangers" to him before the twenty-second of June, her "exertions . . . could have been made for public motive only." He therefore recommended her to the "favourable consideration" of the provincial government. But no reward was forthcoming and Secord was left to live in poverty with the husband she had earlier saved from death in battle. In 1828, finally, he — not she — was rewarded with a series of local offices. Left with nothing at her husband's death in 1841, Laura Secord taught school in her home in Chippewa until, at the age of eighty-five, she received a small reward of her own from the Prince of Wales.[48]

For French Canadian women, the 1837–38 uprising against the British brought the need to supplement individual initiatives by organization and collective effort as well. It was women who formed the *Association des dames patriotiques du comté des Deux-Montagnes* in the summer of 1837, and began a campaign to boycott the goods of British merchants. Soon women in Montreal were copying the determination of these *patriotes* to wear only French Canadian homespun clothing and to avoid all but the most necessary purchases. Individuals and groups of women made flags, manufactured armaments, lent their homes for meetings, and even carried arms. Cordelia Lovell, a

Lower Canadian who wrote to her sister about her alarm at the deteriorating political situation in November of 1837, wondered if her sister would think she had become a *"politicienne."* She assured her that she had not, but that on the other hand it was not possible to avoid politics altogether. The political question preoccupied everyone and was "the subject of all conversation."[49]

After the fighting was over, women did what they could to assist imprisoned rebels and win better treatment or reprieves for them, or to influence the climate of opinion in favour of the defeated *canadien* leaders. Eugénie Saint-Germain petitioned the wife of the governor in 1838, begging that her husband be spared from death for his part in the rebellions.[50] Her pleas had no effect; under the law, neither Madame Saint-Germain nor Lady Colborne was in a position to exercise genuine political power, despite their membership in the elite circles of their respective societies. For such women power was, at the most, influence on those in a position to make decisions. During his exile in the United States in 1839, Louis-Joseph Papineau wrote to his friend Louis Perrault about the passionate defense of the rebel cause by Perrault's mother. She had exerted such an influence that an important American official had written to England, attempting to explain the extent of nationalist feeling in Lower Canada and urging a more moderate policy towards the *patriotes.*[51] But the rebel cause was already lost and the flags of the *patriotes* had to be put away.

In other settings, however, women's political action could sometimes be crowned with success. Women were active in the underground railroad that brought runaway slaves to Canada because, by the imperial statute of 1834, slavery was abolished in British territory. Usually they worked in clandestine ways, but when necessity demanded it their actions could be overt. Anna Jameson reported the excitement that developed among both white and black inhabitants of the Districts of Gore and Niagara when Upper Canadian authorities were preparing to deliver an escaped slave to his former owner. Because the man had stolen a horse to effect his escape he was a felon, and by agreement of the British and American governments all felons had to be extradited. A black mob assembled and began to riot when the man was led out of jail; in the ensuing melee, he escaped. What fascinated Jameson was "the conduct of the women":

They prevailed upon their husbands, brothers, and lovers, to use no arms, to do no illegal violence, but to lose their lives rather than see their comrade taken by force across the lines. They had been most active in the fray, throwing themselves fearlessly between the black men and the whites. . . . One woman had seized the sheriff, and held him pinioned in her arms; another . . . held [one of the artillery-men] in such a manner as to prevent his firing.[52]

A woman had been the mob's leader, a former slave from Virginia who had been treated well by her owners, but had nevertheless run away when her master died and it appeared that she would be sold. To Jameson she expressed a fiery determination to live only where she could be safe. If blacks could not be safe on British ground, she would go "to the end of the world" to find a country where they could be.

Formalizing collective action

Women were largely cut off from official political action, but they were not necessarily cut off from each other. Pioneer women were lonely in British North America because farms were often isolated from one another and travel was difficult. But as quickly as they could, women attempted to re-establish their traditional patterns of female sociability and co-operation. Thus quilting and sewing bees, co-operative cooking for festivals, all-female gatherings to attend a birth, and long-term visiting by aunts and sisters, mothers and daughters and friends, powerfully reinforced women's sense of community and common interest in a world in which, as a sex, they may have perceived themselves as increasingly isolated.

New outlets in religious work offered opportunities for individual expression as well as for collective action. Very few Protestant women could become itinerant preachers, but many more were able to immerse themselves in the Sunday school movement that began in the Maritime colonies and had spread to the Canadas by the early nineteenth century. Young middle class women wanting useful religious work found it in teaching poor children the three Rs and giving Bible lessons at Sunday schools, which often lasted for the whole day.[53] Occasionally religious conversion provided the possibility of escaping from a patriarchal religious atmosphere at home or made possible a marriage in the face of parental disapproval. Such was the case for Nancy Lawrence, the daughter of a Nova Scotian Congregationalist minister; she became a "New Light" in the 1780s and, to her parents' distress, married a widower with three children because he shared her new-found religious enthusiasm.[54] For Roman Catholic women, the revival of religious, and particularly of convent life in the 1830s and 1840s, provided similar opportunities for individual choice and socially useful work.[55]

Women turned to social activism when they saw around them what seemed to be increasing levels of social distress and crime, as migration and economic dislocation wrought major changes in town and country. It is unclear whether the growing numbers of people arrested and jailed in the nineteenth century represent real increases in criminal activity or a growing unwillingness in urban centres to tolerate public drunkenness, prostitution, and vagrancy.[56] But there is no doubt that more women were being jailed.[57] Protestant and Roman Catholic women alike responded to urban problems by banding together to create new charitable and religious associations to address the problems of unwed mothers, starving families, or orphaned children. In this way they continued and extended the well-established tradition of mutual assistance and care for the needy.

In small communities, home visiting continued to seem adequate to meet the needs of the poor and destitute; in other, larger centres women began to move towards the institutional solutions that were beginning to be popular in Great Britain and the United States.

Institutions such as orphanages were easier to found in Roman Catholic communities, where the structural support of religious congregations probably strengthened women's efforts. In French Canada, Roman Catholic religious organizations already existed to serve the needs of the poor, but even as these expanded it was apparent that new structures were called for. By the middle decades of the nineteenth century, Protestant women's benevolent or missionary societies had sprung up in nearly every major town or city. The Prince Town Female Society for Propagating the Gospel and Other Religious Purposes was founded by Presbyterian women in Prince Town, or Malpeque, Prince Edward Island, in 1825, and included among its missions the distribution of Bibles to the families of isolated fishermen in the colony.[58] Other Protestant women's associations known to exist by the 1840s include The Ladies' Total Abstinence Society of Saint John, and an interdenominational Ladies' Society of Montreal, the latter dedicated to co-operating with a similar Roman Catholic missionary society operating in the city. In Canada West, the major towns also had their Protestant women's associations. Hamilton's Ladies' Benevolent Society was, like its Montreal counterpart, interdenominational and devoted to visiting and distributing assistance to the poor. Toronto's Queen Victoria Benevolent Society was probably largely a Methodist organization. Serving the needs of indigent black women in the city, this association was founded by Ellen Abbott, herself a former domestic servant who had married a free black in the United States and immigrated to Upper Canada in 1835.[59]

Many of the new associations involved women ministering to women, but some had children as their special care. Both groups were sources of concern to philanthropically minded women in Montreal. The Montreal Protestant Orphan Asylum came into existence in 1822; in 1824, the Montreal Benevolent Ladies' Society was founded to help both women and children. Both were associations of laywomen. Another group of laywomen under the direction of Emélie Gamelin had sick and destitute women as its special concern in a charity that dated from 1828; it was transformed into the Sisters of Providence in 1843.[60]

The need for such charities demonstrates that British North American society, for all its increasing idealization of motherhood and of women's educational role, was a less than ideal world for many women. Unmarried mothers and poor widows did not fit the idealized view of the family that was emerging in the third and fourth decades of the nineteenth century, nor did the few women who chose not to marry and attempted to live independently. Even the Protestant and Catholic women's associations that tried to alleviate the poverty and distress they saw around them sometimes ran into male opposition. In French Canada, the church discouraged lay-women's organizations and channelled women's efforts into the development of religious orders.[61] The French Canadian women who gathered around the Montreal widow, Rosalie Cadron-Jetté, in the early 1840s, ministered to unwed mothers. Persuaded by the city's Bishop Ignace Bourget that their work could best be accomplished if she and her assistants were bound by religious vows, this fifty-year-old midwife became the founder and first mother superior of the *Soeurs de la Miséricorde*, a community devoted not only to the assistance of unmarried mothers, but eventually to the care of their "orphaned" children as well.[62]

Eventually, some women began to recognize that their charitable and educational efforts, for all their worthwhile character, were to some extent "bandaids" in a social system that required more radical attention to the causes of social distress. This certainly was the view of the Saint John Ladies' Total Abstinence Society. In 1847 the society petitioned the legislature of New Brunswick, asking for a ban on strong drink, the evil that this group identified as the source of social dislocation. Their petition met with no response.[63]

2 THE NEW PIONEERS

The mid-nineteenth century to the end of the Great War

H istorians have been fascinated by the period that stretches from the middle of the nineteenth century to the end of the Great War. The tremendous changes that occurred in those years laid the groundwork for Canadian society as we know it. In 1867 the colonies of Canada East and Canada West, New Brunswick, and Nova Scotia, joined in Confederation; in the decades that followed the goal of a Dominion from sea to sea was completed. During the same era, the burgeoning women's groups that existed across the country began to unite in more formalized associations, and formed in the National Council of Women of Canada a single umbrella organization that joined in the unifying and expansionist impulses of the nascent national community.

The background to these political events was the continuing economic development of the nation. The staples economy expanded into the new pioneer areas of the North and West. In the settled regions, household production gave way to the beginnings of a factory system that co-existed with sweatshops, the "putting out" of industrial work into workers' homes, and artisan workshops. The vast forest, mineral, and hydro-electric resources of central British Columbia, Ontario, and Quebec helped fuel this development, as did foreign capital from Great Britain and increasingly from the United States. By the end of World War I a full-blown industrial society had emerged, albeit with strong remnants of the earlier economic systems still in place in various regions and locales.[1] The resulting regional disparities are still with us.

The two decades following Confederation saw a boom in the Maritime economy, and it appeared that the provinces of New Brunswick and Nova Scotia in particular would benefit from industrialization. But the boom was not to continue, and by the early decades of the twentieth century the eastern regions had lost ground to the more industrially developed southern regions of Quebec and Ontario. Westerners too had their complaints about the distribution of economic benefits, specifically the effects of the 1879 Conservative National Policy. High protective tariffs had the result of filling the coffers of eastern banks and enriching central Canadian industrialists at the expense of agricultural producers.

Class differences and ethnicity also created inequities. Industrial development was predicated on cheap labour; thousands of immigrants, especially those from non-English countries, paid a high price

Alberta Woman, 1917.

107

for their "free" entry into Canada. They and other working class Canadians endured harsh and unsafe working conditions and low pay with little public acknowledgement of their plight or appreciation of their efforts. Yet they continued to come, underlining the even harsher realities of the societies they were leaving behind.

Gender cut across regional, class, and ethnic divisions, for women participated fully in the economic transformation of Canada in all regions and in all groups. Indeed, without them it is unlikely that the transformation would have occurred. As well as bearing children who were the workforce of the future, women provided a cheap and efficient workforce in themselves. Most of their work was unpaid, absorbed into the family economy; but even when irregular or unpaid, it was vital.

A massive growth in Canada's population accompanied and contributed to these economic changes. From approximately 2.5 million people in 1851, the population grew to nearly 9 million by 1921.[2] But growth was not even. During the economic recession of the 1880s and early 1890s hundreds of thousands of Canadians left the country to seek their fortunes elsewhere. Nevertheless, as a result of a high birth rate, the population did increase, and by 1900 the exodus had been stemmed. At the turn of the century, new immigrants flooded into Canada, not only from Great Britain and the United States, the two nations from which Canada had always attracted settlers, but now also from all parts of the European continent and some parts of Asia and the West Indies. As a result, Canadians of British origin decreased from 60 percent of the population in 1871 to 55 percent in 1921, and those of French origin from 31 percent to 28 percent.[3] The host community sometimes displayed overt hostility to these latter immigrants, but most Canadians could see the benefits of a growing population, and immigrants, including young women whom the federal government viewed as potential childbearers, continued to be encouraged to settle here.

Many of the immigrants who came in the early years of the twentieth century were attracted by the offer of free homestead land in the region west of Ontario. Not only did they help open up and develop this area, but their presence was strongly felt, since the host community was so small. In 1901 the foreign-born share of the population of British Columbia, the Northwest Territories, and Manitoba was 26, 30, and 15 percent respectively. For the country as a whole it was only 3 percent.[4]

Added to the ethnic shift was one of gender. Between 1851 and 1891 young men flocked to the Prairies, the Northwest Territories and the United States in search of greater economic opportunities; as a result women of marriageable age outnumbered men in the same age range in the original British North American provinces. In Manitoba and British Columbia on the other hand, the 1881 and 1891 censuses revealed that men significantly outnumbered women.

At the same time as new regions were being settled, many Canadians and immigrants moved into urban areas. In 1851 more than four-fifths of the British North American population lived in rural regions; by 1901 the proportion of rural dwellers had declined to two-thirds. By 1921 the number of rural and urban Canadians was about equal.[5] Women continued to lead this shift in the population, because they moved to the cities for employment opportunities that the rural areas could not offer them. Consequently women outnumbered men in most cities, just as men tended to form the majority in rural and frontier areas.[6]

The tremendous changes in the demographic and economic make-up of Canada — from an economy that stressed the ownership of land to one that emphasized wage labour, and from a society in which prestige devolved from who one's parents were to a society that placed value on what one did — gave many Canadians a sense that they were part of a modern and developing nation, and that this called for some adjustments in their institutions. One example was the franchise, which was changed to almost universal manhood suffrage. The general enfranchisement of women, however, continued to be denied until after the outbreak of World War I; indeed the Dominion Franchise Act that governed the federal franchise between 1885 and 1898 specified that an eligible voter was "a male person, including an Indian and excluding a person of Mongolian or Chinese race."[7] It took nearly half a century of determined struggle on the part of women activists and their allies to secure votes for women.

Problems arose from Canada's expansion and industrialization. Rapid urbanization resulted in densely populated areas that accentuated the problems of poor sanitation and contagious disease. The concentration of factories in certain sections of the larger industrial centres created pollution and filth in the areas surrounding them. Social problems — intemperance, crime, delinquency, and prostitution — appeared to be worsening. Nor was life in the rural areas idyllic. Many farmers' sons and daughters were lured to cities by the prospect of paid employment, a trend that resulted in rural depopulation in some regions, and to a sense of an agrarian lifestyle under siege.

Canadians responded to these problems in various ways, and by the turn of the century a vigorous reform movement was in place in which thousands of Canadian women were active. The existing women's organizations expanded the range of their activities. Improved transportation and communication networks began to counteract the geography of Canada, and some women began to develop an enlarged sense of common identity. The growth of a female paid workforce in education, health, business, and industry also strengthened this spirit of sisterhood and increased the potential for organization. The isolation of rural women often made getting together difficult; nonetheless, their efforts to counter this isolation led to an enhanced awareness of shared experiences and problems, and ultimately to the creation of their own organizations.

At the same time, the women's movement responded to the nationalism and imperialism of the era, sharing in a patriotic concern both to protect the country's stability and future vitality, and to maintain and reinforce strong links with the British empire. Most English Canadians hoped that the territorial expansion of Canada would lead to a glorious future for the nation at the centre of the British empire, and the more imperialistic among them pressured the Canadian government into supporting the British in the 1899 Boer War. Women who shared these aims formed the Imperial Order Daughters of the Empire to look after the graves of those Canadian soldiers who had fallen on the foreign battlefield. Women were also enthusiastic supporters of Empire Day celebrations in the various schools throughout English-speaking Canada. Such patriotic activities reached their zenith during World War I.[8] The more extreme imperialist and nationalist attitudes could shade into nativism, which at times rested on theories based on eugenics. Canadian-born, English-speaking Canadians worried about the growing numbers of non-English-speaking immigrants, and the high birth rate of French Canadians. Women activists frequently shared these anxieties.

At the opposite end of the political spectrum, some women supported socialist solutions to Canada's problems. Pacifism was attractive to some women, who saw it as a natural expression of women's nurturing role. French Canadian women in particular had reason to be opposed to war for, unlike their anglophone sisters, they did not identify with imperialist dreams of grandeur. French Canadians proudly asserted that their loyalty was undivided, and that their identity was rooted solidly in Canadian soil. Any affinity they had once had with Great Britain was largely destroyed as English Canadian imperialists invoked their belief in the superiority of the Anglo-Saxon race, and of all things British, to justify their attacks on French Canadian rights outside Quebec. School crises in New Brunswick, Manitoba, the Northwest Territories, and Ontario, the violent reactions of English Canadians to the two Riel uprisings (1869–70 and 1885), and the ongoing debate over the status of the French language underscored anglophone intentions to limit the French presence to Quebec. The result was a turning inward, a concentration on *la survivance*. A key element in the French Canadian strategy for survival has been dubbed "the revenge of the cradle" — an emphasis on large families to offset the tide of immigration that was swelling the ranks of non-French Canadians. This strategy was, of course, dependent on the labour of women, and reinforced an ideology that exalted women's role in the home. The reforms of an Anglo-Protestant society that accorded women increasing economic and eventually political rights were generally unacceptable in Quebec. Nonetheless, as elsewhere in Canada, French Canadian women did organize, and challenged the existing constraints on women's activities. French-speaking Catholic women too concentrated on initiating social reforms in response to the problems generated by industrialization and urbanization.

The grand themes for the nation as a whole during this period have been identified as "urbanization" and "industrialization." But only local studies can reveal how people integrated change into their lives; not everyone experienced urban or industrial development in the same way: the pace varied depending on region, class, ethnicity, and gender. Canadians were active participants in the process, not the passive victims of inevitable economic, political, or demographic forces utterly beyond their control. Many nevertheless experienced change through the eyes of a bygone age. Attitudes had a tendency to shift more slowly than social reality, especially when the social reality was altering at a pace hitherto unknown.

Contemporary historians, including historians of women, have studied this period of our history more than any other. As a result we have been able to draw on a wealth of secondary literature that reflects rich primary sources. The number of newspapers and magazines expanded dramatically during these years. So did interest in women: the proper sphere of women was an obsession of Victorian and Edwardian Canadians, and they delighted in writing about it. Women were told what it meant to be a woman and the proper way to behave. At mid-century, religious authorities were the most significant voice in this discussion. However, with the increased commercialization of society, with the challenge to accepted faiths presented by Darwin's evolutionary theory, and with the questions that the biblical higher criticism posed to the literal truth of the scriptures, new experts appeared. Science in particular gained an aura of authority in the late nineteenth century, and those who invoked it, such as physicians, could bask in its reflected glory.

More reliable than the stereotypes in the written materials produced by male pundits are the records generated by women themselves: their actions, their words, and their artifacts. Diaries and letters were generally written by educated women, however, and by no means reflected the lives of all. This is true as well of the abundant records belonging to women's groups of this period. The evidence of material culture that has come down to us—the kitchen utensils, the new household appliances, the dresses—is also from relatively affluent homes. Not all women could afford to save things or not wear them out before new purchases were made. Yet these items are important, for they allow us to get closer to individual women and to flesh out impressions based on less personal data.

The evidence from such sources can be supplemented by that contained in census returns and other quantifiable data. The first comprehensive censuses of the British North American colonies were taken in 1851, and at ten-year intervals thereafter. In Catholic parishes manuscript census returns augment the continuing parish records; in non-Catholic communities these returns are often the only source of demographic data. Such information enables us to estimate with greater accuracy than for the period before 1851 the number of children women had, the age at which they married, and their life expectancies. From birth intervals we can even infer whether or not they used birth control.

It is from many kinds of evidence, then, that we are now beginning to piece together a picture of women's experience in the second half of the nineteenth century, and in the early decades of the twentieth. It is not always easy, however, to interpret that experience, for it is difficult to know how much women internalized the ideal concept of themselves. This is particularly true when it is remembered that the ideology of domesticity applied to a private or intimate culture, one that historians are only now probing. We know more about women's public activities, their involvement in the paid labour force, and their participation in a myriad of women's organizations. But what did such experiences mean for women? Did they perceive any contradictions between the popular perceptions of women and the reality of their own lives?

5 Continuity and change in women's work

When two young sisters of Irish descent, Hannah and Alice Bailey, were wed in a double ceremony in Ingersoll, Ontario on February 26, 1908, neither could possibly have imagined how utterly different their lives as married women would be. Hannah's marriage was an unhappy one, but fortunately Hannah was a plucky and hard-working woman who not only outlived her first husband, but two others as well. She raised seven children, and lived past the age of ninety. Fate, however, was not so kind to her younger sister Alice. Buoyed by the dream of owning their own farm, she and her husband Thomas set out for Saskatchewan shortly after their marriage. In the little loghouse they constructed on their homestead, Alice subsequently bore two daughters but, worn out by the hard work of pioneer life, she died of consumption when she was only twenty-nine years old.[1]

In the period between 1851 and 1921, women's lives were marked by an intriguing interplay of continuity and change. Increasingly, young women in rural areas sought work off the farm. For most of the period, the major employment for women was the traditional one of domestic service. The primary or resource sector of the economy had not in the past afforded women significant opportunities for earning wages, but women were moving into new areas of wage labour after 1850. With industrialization and the growth of secondary industry, thousands of women found paid work within labour-intensive manufacturing enterprises. Moreover, by the end of the nineteenth century, the tertiary or service sector of the economy was expanding rapidly, and it afforded women additional employment opportunities in fields such as teaching, nursing, and clerical work. Indeed, by World War I, there were more women holding down white collar jobs than there were engaged in manufacturing.

For all women, there was the tension between the ideal of the woman at home and the reality of women's work. Canadian women from the mid-nineteenth century on protested some of the conditions that working women faced, married or single, young or old. They did not always speak with a united voice; women in one class were not always sympathetic to the protests of women in another class. But isolated as their voices sometimes were, the emerging picture is one of a growing, if tentative, strength. Women workers began to recognize common problems and a common cause. Their collective efforts and the increased visibility of women's employment outside of the home prompted public awareness of the new shape of women's lives.

Migration

Pioneer experience did not disappear with the beginning of industrialization; thousands of Canadians and immigrants continued to move into the unsettled reaches of the new nation. For many women the opportunities migration afforded outweighed the disadvantages, but for others, giving up a home in a settled part of the country was not easy. Some refused to move, like Rebecca Ells of Port Williams, Nova Scotia, who with her son ran a mixed commercial farm while her husband went off to the Klondike for twelve years. Some did not want to move but had no choice. This was the situation of Mrs. Carmichael of Sunnyside, New Brunswick. Her husband insisted on selling the family farm and moving farther north. Her daughter recalled her mother's tears and her initial refusal to sign away her share of the farm. But in the end, seeing no alternative, she signed and the family made their move.[2]

By the late nineteenth and early twentieth centuries more and more single women were also moving west. Some came on their own or with migration agencies; some were motivated by the high wages offered to domestic servants in a labour-scarce region; others were attracted by matrimonial offers. One such woman, the bride-to-be of a Mountie, made the trip out west; but when she arrived in town, her prospective groom, unbeknown to her, was looking her over from a distance. Deciding she did not suit his needs he sent a message to her and paid her way home.[3]

Immigrants also continued to move to Canadian farms from other countries. Between 1901 and 1921 alone, 644 089 men and women came from the British Isles and 246 125 from the United States.[4] Although Canadian customs and environments must have seemed very different, at least there was a shared language. Women speaking languages other than English or French had more to contend with. Between 1901 and 1921 some 500 000 immigrants entered Canada from southern, central, and northern Europe or from Asia.[5] In addition to the language barrier itself, they often faced cultural, racial, or religious hostility.

One of the largest groups of non-Anglo-Saxon immigrants to arrive during this period were the Ukrainians. From less than 6000 in 1901 their numbers swelled to over 75 000 just ten years later. The influx of Ukrainian women to the prairie provinces, particularly to Alberta, was a source of great concern to local women's organizations there, appalled as they were by the "low status of immigrant women" and the "abomination of child marriages among the Galicians [Ukrainians]."[6] A similar concern was expressed about the Japanese "picture brides"—young women who arrived in Canada to marry, sight unseen, Japanese men who had decided to settle permanently in this country. Community reaction to Asian settlement was extremely hostile, for Canadians considered "Orientals" to be unassimilable. From 1886 until 1923, when they were barred as permanent settlers, nearly all Chinese wishing to come to Canada had to pay a head tax. Beginning in 1904 the fee was set at the very high level of $500. This measure effectively kept female immigration to a minimum, since most Chinese men could not afford to bring their wives, and most single women did not have the resources to pay for themselves. Only Chinese women who had non-Chinese husbands, or were the wives of Chinese clergymen or merchants, were exempt from the tax. As a result, many of the women who did immigrate were "slave girls" brought in by Chinese businessmen, who claimed them as either wives or daughters. These young women were bought from their impoverished parents in China to work as domestic servants, waitresses, or prostitutes in British Columbia.[7]

Women from all cultures often experienced dire poverty in the course of their immigration. In the spring of 1905 Ottilia Tetzlaff Doering, pregnant with her eighth child, left Russia for Canada with her husband and seven children. En route the wagon in which all their possessions were packed caught fire and only a samovar survived. During the voyage over on what was essentially a cattle boat, Ottilia became ill and would have died but for the captain taking the entire family into his quarters. With only fifty cents to their name on arrival, the family accepted the help of an immigrant aid committee, which provided the fare to Manitoba. There Ottilia's husband taught and ran church services, her sons worked as farm labourers and her daughters as kitchen helpers, until the family saved enough to build a loghouse on a homestead in Chevlin. Ottilia died of tuberculosis a few years later and did not see the fruits of these efforts.[8]

At least Ottilia had a family with whom to share her trials. Single women of all groups lacked even that comfort, although their willingness to move suggests an independence and strength that would serve them well. Not all single women, however, moved freely. The Chinese "slave girls" and the Japanese "picture brides" of the early twentieth century clearly did not. Nor did the thousands of young "home girls" sent to Canada from various agencies in Great Britain, who were apprenticed out to local families as domestic servants.[9]

Migration to agricultural or northern frontiers was not the only migration of the era. Women also left the rural areas to seek their fortunes in the cities, pushed by the difficulties or loneliness of country life and pulled by new economic opportunities. By the turn of the century and increasingly afterwards, columnists writing in farm newspapers acknowledged this rural exodus and blamed it on the harshness of farm life for young people, and especially for young women, who felt they had no prospects on the farms, particularly in the less prosperous regions. Few wanted to end up as one forty-year-old farm woman did — left on her father's death with only a cow and one hundred dollars to show for her life-long work on the farm, when each of her three brothers had inherited a 320–acre farm.[10] At least the cities offered women a chance to work for pay. Soon women were moving to urban centres in massive numbers. By 1871 women in Montreal outnumbered men in every age category.[11] Nor was Montreal an anomaly. By 1921 women between the ages of 15 and 29 outnumbered men of the same age in most urban centres in Canada.[12]

Migration to and between cities was equally the experience of immigrant women and Canadian women. Despite the fact that government policy encouraged immigrants to settle in agricultural regions, many chose cities or towns instead. The average rate of increase in the urban population after mid-century was 34 percent per decade.[13] As well, many urban Canadians were transients in the decades after the middle of the century: in the centres that have been studied, 50 to 75 percent of city residents cannot be traced ten years later.[14] The cities of Canada did offer opportunities to women. Between 1891 and 1901 women in the paid labour force increased by 41 959 or 21.4 percent, and most of these were in the urban centres.[15]

Women's work on the farm

Women in rural regions and on the frontier continued to perform labour-intensive work for little or no pay. They scrubbed clothes on scrub boards (if they were lucky enough to have one), hauled water from the creek or the well, cooked on wood stoves, and made most of the family's clothes. In addition, they grew vegetables, gathered fruit, preserved and baked, and looked after their children. Susan Dunlap's diary of 1866–1868, written when she was a young girl in Stewiacke, New Brunswick, details the household chores performed by her sister, her mother, and herself. These included churning butter, washing fleeces, picking and carding them, spinning, weaving, and also "pulling, setting, breaking, hackling, and scutching of the flax." Even Christmas day was not free from labour. In 1866 she wrote, "Christmas day and a rainy one. Mother and Mary scoured fifty skanes [skeins] of filling. Mother spun 2 skanes. Mary made Howard's cap. Aunt Ellen was over. Mother stitched a sack [dress] for Mary." These chores not only saved money but in some families generated income. The butter Susan churned every day was sold and the money used to help support the family.[16]

Micmac women in the 1890s in Nova Scotia continued to bring in money with their basket work, and this money tended to be the most dependable source of family income. In addition, many of these women were doing most of the work on their farms. As the Indian Agent in 1893 noted, "Those Indians living on the reserve have done much more planting this spring than at any time previous, the women doing a large part of the work while the men are employed on the streets [in Yarmouth] at good pay."[17] Half-way across the continent Dominko Roshko and her mother, pioneering in early twentieth century southern Manitoba, dug seneca roots and sold them at 35 cents a pound for medicinal purposes, or traded them for supplies.[18]

The money these women earned helped their families to survive and their farms to prosper. Their success usually came from hard physical work, but ingenuity also played a role. In 1884, when her hens and a rooster were killed by a mink and her one remaining hen froze its foot, Harriet Neville fashioned an artificial leg and foot for it out of whalebone, wire, and a kid glove. The hen went on to raise several clutches of chicks.[19]

Although farm women, particularly pioneer women, continued many of the work patterns of their mothers and grandmothers, change did occur during the second half of the nineteenth century. When farms became prosperous, the money women generated was no longer as necessary for survival, although it still often represented a regular source of income for the family. Those women who continued to bring in money welcomed it for the independence it gave them, and the chance to buy things for their families and homes without feeling they were "robbing" the farm.

At the same time that the financial needs of the farm were shifting, large-scale and centralized production often took over some of the

Carrying on the tradition of Abenaki basket-making.

work that traditionally had been women's, such as spinning and weaving, and the making of cheese and butter. In 1851 32.4 million pounds of butter and 4.8 million pounds of cheese were home-produced in Canada. By 1891 it was 111.6 million and 6.3 million respectively. The increase, however, occurred simultaneously with and tended to camouflage the transfer of cheese and butter production from home to factory, especially in Ontario. In 1864 the first cheese factory in Canada opened in that province. By 1900 there were 200 cheese factories in Oxford County alone, and during the single decade of 1871–1881, the share of cheese produced on Ontario farms declined by 50 percent. As dairy farming increased in importance, so too did the size of dairy herds, and caring for them passed from the hands of the farm women into the hands of their husbands and farm labourers.[20] In general, there was a decline in skilled work for farm women and a resulting decline in the money a farm woman was able to earn, leaving her with very little visible or recognized economic input.

Many farmers acknowledged the work women did, and in rural areas it was well known that bachelors were not as successful farmers as married men because the work done by wives and children remained so essential. In the early 1860s the Agricultural Association of Upper Canada stated explicitly that "a good wife" was "indispensible" to a farmer.[21] Seeing firsthand the work that women performed in early twentieth century Saskatchewan, settler Georgina Binnie-Clark could only concur with this judgement. She believed she owed one important debt to her life on the prairie: "a fair appreciation" of her own sex.[22] Yet few farm wives received *tangible* recognition. Farmers were notorious for purchasing new equipment for the barn or fields but refusing to buy anything for the house. Nor did the government of Canada recognize the work farm women did: in the census, farm wives—like other wives who worked in their homes—had "no occupation."[23]

According to both law and custom, a farm wife had little or no legal claim on family property that had been acquired partly as a result of her labours. The land was owned by her husband, and he had the right to sell it at any time unless she was protected by dower right. Increasingly, Canadian men viewed the buying and selling of land, including the family farm, as a way to get ahead, and saw dower right as an anachronistic holdover from an earlier time when agricultural property seldom changed hands. The hostility to dower was particularly strong in the Territories, where the right was abolished in 1886.[24]

Even if the land was not sold, women who outlived their husbands often found their position tenuous. Frequently, widows found that the farm had been left to a son, and they had little beyond their dower portion and some form of limited maintenance. Sometimes this was conditional on the wife's "good behaviour"—in particular her willingness to remain a widow. In Richibucto, New Brunswick, in 1856, a widow discovered that her husband's will specified she would lose her right to the use of the family property if she remarried.[25] Control "from the grave" continued in many farming regions well into the twentieth century, as Lucy Maud Montgomery observed in connection with her grandmother in 1905.

Uncle John and Prescott have been using grandmother shamefully all summer. In short, they have been trying to turn her out. . . . Grandfather's absurd will put her completely in their power — the power of selfish, domineering men eaten up with greed. Grandmother told them she would not leave the home where she had lived and worked for sixty years and since then Uncle John has never spoken to her or visited her. . . .[26]

In the West the situation was worse, for widows had no legal rights of inheritance.

The relative lack of financial control over their future added to the decline in status that widows frequently experienced. Often the widow was no longer the mistress of her own house but, like Lucy Maud Montgomery's grandmother, a guest of her son and daughter-in-law, or other younger family members. Nor were her daughters any better off. They too rarely inherited family farms, and their portions of estates were usually smaller than those given to their brothers. The idea of women farming on their own did not appeal to Victorian public opinion — or legislators for that matter, as the 1872 Dominion statute governing public lands made clear. Only women with dependent children were permitted to homestead on their own. At least one woman is known to have disguised herself as a man when, after her husband died, she decided to carry on with the couple's scheme to raise horses on the Canadian Prairies, possibly in order to get access to public land. For the most part, women who

Farm work in early twentieth century Manitoba.

wanted to be farmers had to accumulate enough capital to purchase land that had already been developed.[27]

Few farm women actually sought public recognition for their work. Their reward was not the plaudits of government officials but the well-being of their families, even if they personally did not always have an equal share of the material benefits. Many delighted in living close to nature and building something for the future. One woman captured this faith in these terms:

I no longer utter a mental protest against the prairie as a final resting place. Our western life is too real, too vital to waste time in gloomy speculation. It is enough that you are alive and can take your chances in the great future that lies just at hand.[28]

Knowing that they were working for the good of their families helped offset the loneliness felt by many women in farming and rural communities. In the older, more prosperous, farming areas, roads and railways gradually made access to and from rural areas easier, and speeded the delivery of mail. Yet even in these communities, women could be isolated because they had too little leisure to enjoy contact with neighbouring friends and kin. In the outport villages of Newfoundland and in other remote regions, women were cut off from their sisters in other places; in the case of frontier towns dependent on single resources such as mining and lumbering, the problem for women was the sense that they were living in a largely male environment. Of all women, perhaps those on prairie homesteads were the most isolated. Neighbours were not close, and often women were hundreds, if not thousands, of kilometres from extended family members and childhood friends. Johanne Fredericken, who came from Denmark in 1911 to join her husband homesteading in Saskatchewan, described the implications of this isolation: "Everything depends on the mother, one cannot share the responsibility with the shoemaker, tailor and baker, school or priest, and therefore, one stands by oneself poor and powerless."[29] As a sympathetic male commentator noted in 1913, the isolation of the frontier was difficult for all but "especially for the women to whom the little amenities of social intercourse mean so much."[30]

It was an isolation not all could tolerate. While many women coped with the support of husbands and children, newly made friends, and a belief in their contribution to the future, heartbreaking stories abound of women whose physical and mental health broke down. Letitia Youmans noted in her 1893 autobiography that farm women seemed to be particularly numerous in one Ontario asylum because, according to the superintendent's laconic observation, of "hard toil and monotonous mode of living."[31]

Many women worked vigorously to lessen their isolation and to improve their situations, by maintaining ties with friends and family from whom they were separated, and by creating new ones with other women in their adopted communities, especially with those of the same ethnic origin. Together they ensured that there were schools for their children, libraries for their neighbourhoods, and social occasions for people to meet, talk with, and court one another. Women were often the chief supporters of institutional religion and were among the first to encourage the establishment of churches in isolated areas. Their interests encompassed the quality of life and thus the support and preservation of ethnic cultures. Unfortunately, their efforts in this direction were not without victims, for they often closed out those who could not or would not conform. Amerindian and mixed-blood women were among those who suffered particular discrimination at the hands of English-speaking settlers in the West, convinced as the latter were of the superiority of their culture over all others.[32]

Women's work in the city home

Farm women's lives, while changing, maintained a strong continuity with the past. The work performed in the home by urban women changed more. Industrialization had the effect of accentuating the division between paid and unpaid work, with most paid work now being performed outside the home. There was an increasing acceptance of the idea that it was the husband's responsibility to bring home a "family wage" — one that would support both the worker and his family — and a wife's to see to it that the wage covered the needs of the family. Even traditional cultures were affected by these developments. At the turn of the century, Micmac women in Nova Scotia were excluded from industrial employment and considered suited only for domestic work.[33]

In other regions, women became involved in the network of home manufacture created by the "putting out" system. Employers avoided the necessity of renting or buying factories and passed on overhead costs to workers, employing subcontractors or middlemen who distributed work to women in their homes. In the garment trade, for instance, the employer or his agent might sell or rent sewing machines to home workers; he often deducted the cost of the needles, thread, or material from the women's wages. Domestic manufacture was paid by the piece, so that it was the worker, not the employer, who absorbed the cost of low production because of faulty equipment, crowded or difficult working conditions, or irregular demand. Many women who had families to care for at home, however, were willing to put up with this situation, for they could make some money without leaving home, and even their small children could be conscripted to accomplish simple parts of the work.

In towns and cities, there were other ways women at home continued to receive an income, such as taking in laundry or boarders. The income earned by such work came in irregularly in some cases, but it was often crucial for the continued well-being of the family.[34] Yet, because the income generated by women in the home was not as visible as wages earned outside it, few Canadians recognized the important role women's earnings played in a family's survival. Certainly the government did not. Its statistics on women's employment never acknowledged this kind of income, with the result that the percentage of women in paid employment was greatly under-estimated.

Even more significantly, official statistics did not acknowledge the unpaid work that women did and its contribution to the wealth and prosperity of the country. And women continued, of course, to work extremely long hours at the traditional tasks associated with house-keeping, childrearing, and general family management. As the life of the family increasingly ran on a cash basis, the stretching or reorgan-ization of funds became an important part of women's work. Many working class women stretched the family budget by keeping gardens, raising animals, making their own soap, and once glass bottles became reasonably priced, by canning their own fruits and vegetables. Some even stinted on their own food intake to ensure that the principal breadwinner was sufficiently fed. This self-denial could become extreme in some cultures. In 1888 an elderly Inuit woman, whose health had been declining for several years, decided to follow the custom of her people, and asked her son to abandon her on an island to die. What prompted her to this decision was not only her failing health, but the knowledge that if she died in her son's home he, by custom, would have to throw away his clothes. His wife had already died that year; the mother decided her son could not afford to lose a second set of clothes. Elsewhere in Canada women assisted their husbands by their savings. They saved on medical costs by "doctor-ing" those around them, using Balm of Gilead for blisters, mustard plasters for colds, milk and bread poultices for boils, soda for bites, cold tea leaves for burns, salt water for sore throats, and senna tea for constipation.[35]

For urban women, however, the character of housekeeping and childcare was gradually changing. As children spent more time at school and families became smaller, fewer children were at home to help with household chores or mind younger siblings; as well, fewer young girls were looking for jobs as domestic helpers. Partly in response to the fact that there were fewer hands to do the housework, and partly because of a whole new range of technological develop-ments, housework was becoming more mechanized. The develop-ment of technology applied to domestic work had the potential to change household routines radically. The ideal woman portrayed in advertisements had at her disposal a factory: her servants were the workers, and used machines such as carpet sweepers and washing machines. The only problem was that few of these ideal women — those having both the servants and the money necessary to purchase the new appliances — existed.

All women had to contend with apparently ever-rising expecta-tions as new standards of cleanliness and efficiency developed. The recently discovered germ theory of disease propagation made dirty clothes or a dirty house seem tantamount to family neglect, as public health nurses and doctors tied childhood illness and high infant mortality rates to mothers' ignorance of the need to keep their households and children clean. The introduction of the hand-powered washing machine in the 1890s made washing easier, and so laundry could be done more often. There seemed little or no excuse for soiled clothing or linens: "labour saving" technology combined with new standards could actually mean an increase in the housekeeper's work load. For the poor, it was becoming more difficult to keep their households clean. Even if they could have afforded the new technology, in the working class sections and slums of Canada's growing industrial and commercial cities and towns, dirt was endemic. If women opened the windows to let in fresh air, as recommended by the health authorities, dirt would come in as well. Even in rural areas, opening windows to fresh air could, depending on the season, let in all sorts of infestations.

Technology was a double-edged sword, and not always the progressive change that manufacturers claimed.[36] Women's traditional lore and experience declined in value with developments in household technology, and also as new consumer goods replaced the products that women had once made themselves. In the cities, for public health reasons, municipal by-laws ended the keeping of the pigs, cows, and hens that had been so important to the traditional household economy. As stores distributing mass-produced goods proliferated, and as "store-bought" became the standard by which to measure "home-made" products such as bread and dresses, the items women used to make for their families in the home were increasingly replaced by factory-produced goods. As a result, women's work in the home declined in variety although not in intensity. The noted feminist Nellie McClung recalled seeing her first ready-made dress, which a "daring" Manitoban woman had ordered from Montreal. She and other women waited with bated breath to see this "new" phenomenon, and were pleasantly surprised when it turned out to be attractive.[37] More and more, women entered a new world where it was possible to consume without directly producing goods, and where "it was wonderful to imagine everything coming from a store."[38] But shopping carefully and effectively was itself work, as was accumulating the cash necessary to buy the new goods that seemed increasingly necessary.

Old and new kinds of work

Domestic service continued to be the single most important paid employment for women in Canada; in 1891 41 percent of all working women were employed in this type of work. But it was work that increasing numbers of Canadian-born women spurned. As early as 1868 the *Globe* reported that "our working women dread household service, and hundreds would perhaps rather famish than apply at a servants' agency."[39] By 1921 only 11 percent of working women were in domestic service.[40] Domestics tended to be young girls, more often than not immigrants, with little or no training. However, for immigrant women, particularly the Irish of the nineteenth and the eastern Europeans of the early twentieth centuries, domestic service was at least a paid job and could represent upward mobility. The demand for servants was so great that the federal government and many women's organizations in fact encouraged British and European domestic servants to come to Canada. Domestic service provided an entry into the Canadian workforce not only for European women, but for many farm girls. It was a job for which they were considered ideally suited since they were familiar with household work and with conditions in Canada. From their parents' point of view, the occupation sometimes seemed preferable to others since it took place in a family environment. Above all, domestic service was considered suitable for women since it prepared them for their eventual role as housewives.

Yet domestic work was only as good as the mistress for whom one worked. Since there were no employment standards to govern either work or living conditions, both could be very bad. Living in meant that one did not have to pay room and board, but employers of live-in servants were known to hold back wages to ensure that servants would remain.[41] Some domestics had to spend entire days bent over the washtub; others were given next to no time off, and few servants had any privacy. Life could also be lonely, since few families could afford more than one servant, and class and ethnic differences frequently prevented warm servant/mistress relationships. A former servant, recalling the 1880s, stated that when a girl was hired for a term, she was for that period "as much the property of her mistress as was ever a slave in the cotton fields of the south."[42] Not all were willing to play a subservient role, however. Nellie McClung recounted the story of a servant girl who was told that she must take a bath on her day off at the YWCA—not in the family tub. Her response was, "No bath, no work."[43]

Perhaps the most serious problem of the domestic servant, if far from the protection of friends or family, was her vulnerability to sexual exploitation. Olive Savariat, a seventeen-year-old domestic in the Clarenceville, Quebec home of James Collins in the early 1860s, was one of countless servants who were made pregnant by their employers. Olive's story ended tragically in her employer's barn, where she died as a result of an abortion he had arranged.[44] Yet not all young women were as easily victimized as Olive. In 1915, Carrie Davies, an eighteen-year-old servant of Charles Albert Massey, a scion of the wealthy Toronto family, shot and killed her employer because of his sexual advances. Davies did not escape trial, but about one thousand sympathetic supporters contributed to her defence fund, and the jury acquitted her.[45]

The more typical response of the exploited servant, whatever the form of exploitation, was simply to leave. The turnover rate in domestic service was very high, as domestics searched for better positions or left to get married. It was better to leave than to be fired, since all servants depended to some extent on personal references. Most domestics lived in the homes of their employers; if they lost their jobs, they also lost their homes. For this reason, servants who were dismissed by their employers were extremely insecure. Those who had lost their virginity and might have difficulty making a "respectable" marriage, and lonely immigrant women who were far from family and friends, were particularly vulnerable to the entreaties of madames and pimps who offered them lodgings and companionship. The low status accorded domestics probably facilitated the entry of former servants into prostitution. For many, prostitution was one of the few options available for earning a living, especially in areas where there were few employment opportunities for women. A national scandal broke out in 1886 when some employees of the federal Indian Affairs Department were charged with trafficking in Indian women.[46] One of the positive features of domestic service that governments and women's organizations liked to stress was the level of remuneration. In 1900 a "general" servant could earn $8 to $14 per month in eastern Canada, and from $10 to $20 monthly in western Canada. These wages were comparable to, and in some cases higher than, those earned by women in other occupations, because domestics did not have to pay for room and board. Nonetheless women were looking for new kinds of work and finding it.

With the development of Canadian industry after mid-century, young women were increasingly employed in factories or at piece-work in the home. By 1871 women and children comprised 42 percent of the industrial workforce in Montreal and 34 percent in Toronto.[47] Women played a particularly important role in the Canadian textile industry. Girls entered the mills as young as eleven and twelve in the 1880s and at thirteen and fourteen at the turn of the century. In the Quebec cotton industry in 1908, almost half the operatives were women. Indeed, so tied to the industry were Quebec women that when jobs were scarce a veritable exodus occurred to the mill towns of New England. Single women and men were often the first to go, and as they became established other family members followed. In 1909 alone, over 10 000 of Quebec's population left for the United States in search of jobs.[48] This exodus was of particular concern to the church and government in Quebec, sensitive as they were to the issue of *la survivance* of the French culture within the larger English milieu of Canada. Priests and politicians alike did not want to see future childbearers leaving the province. However, Quebec was not the only province to see many of its energetic young people leave. Between 1881 and 1921, over 165 000 Maritime women also left Canada to try their luck in the more industrialized and lucrative job markets on the eastern seaboard of the United States. And jobs did seem easy to get. When Ada Williams left her fishing village in Nova Scotia for Boston in 1907, she quickly gained employment in a box factory, and when laid off had no difficulty finding another job, this time in an ice-cream parlour.[49]

By 1901 women represented 25 percent of the Canadian workforce engaged in manufacturing and mechanical work, and in 1921 they still comprised 24 percent of a much expanded industrial labour

Spinning and weaving, New Brunswick.

force.[50] Factory work was hard and involved long hours, despite the introduction of legislation to protect women and adolescents employed in industrial establishments. In 1884 Ontario was the first province to pass such a law; for young women it set the age at which they could begin factory work at fourteen, and for young men, at twelve. The hours that women, girls, and youths could work were limited to 10 per day or 60 per week, with one hour provided for a noon meal. Employers could apply for, and often received, special permits that enabled them to work their employees up to 72 hours per week for a maximum of 6 weeks each year. Concern for women's safety and especially for their reproductive potential was reflected in the portion of the law that prohibited them being employed in situations in which their health might be permanently damaged; however, the principal onus was placed on the worker to protect herself. Rather than require employers to install guards on dangerous machines, the law stipulated that women workers should wear hairnets to prevent themselves from being scalped.

Similar protective legislation applicable to factory work was passed by the Quebec Assembly in 1885. It took the government of Ontario two years to set up a system of factory inspectors to enforce its 1884 legislation, and the government of Quebec three years before it appointed its first factory inspector. By the 1890s both governments had appointed female factory inspectors to visit those manufacturing establishments that employed large numbers of women and children, but as late as 1913 there were only two badly overworked female factory inspectors in each province. In 1913 women in Ontario and Quebec factories still routinely worked 55–60 hours a week and up to 70 hours in rush seasons.[51] But at least the hours were defined and at the end of the working day the time remaining was a worker's own. Factory work also seemed more "modern" and therefore more exciting than domestic employment. It usually provided the opportunity to talk and make friends with other women. In the factory, and during free time after work, a young woman was able to meet young men, and perhaps develop a relationship that would lead to marriage and the establishment of her own home.

The hierarchical work relations of factories proved as potentially abusive as those in domestic service. When the Royal Commission on the Relations of Capital and Labor reported in 1889, it described the case of Georgina Loiselle, a worker in a Montreal cigar factory. When this young woman refused to make another hundred cigars, her employer attempted to spank her; she fell to the ground, where he pinned her and struck her with a cigar mold. However, it was not the beating that concerned the Commission, but the propriety of "a man placing a girl of eighteen in that position."[52]

Whatever the concerns women might have about the relations of men and women in the work place, they continued to seek industrial jobs. Many working class families depended on the wages of their children. In 1891 over 7000 women under the age of sixteen were in industrial establishments.[53] Unfortunately, women's ability to contribute to the family income was limited by the comparatively poor wages they received. According to early twentieth century census returns, average earnings for women in central and eastern Canada, where most female industrial workers were situated, remained at 55 to 60 percent of male earnings.[54] In 1901 a Toronto woman was working for the equivalent of 2 cents per hour, and as late as 1921, factory women in Montreal received only half the wages men did.[55] One of the reasons for this large discrepancy was that women were employed on piecework more often than men. Since employers based piecework rates on the output of the fastest workers, the less fast — that is, the majority — earned less than a living wage.

In fact, most female workers barely made a living wage. In 1889 the Ontario Bureau of Industries provided a cost of living analysis for women workers without dependents. Average annual earnings were calculated to be $216.71, and average annual costs to be $214.28, leaving a grand surplus of $2.43! Female workers with dependents faced a yearly deficit of $14.23.[56] This situation did not improve greatly with time or with the introduction of new technology. Although machines did away with brute strength as a prerequisite for many jobs, sexual stereotypes remained. Women working machines were not identified as skilled operatives as their brothers were, but only as "alert" and "nimble" workers who were paid accordingly.[57]

Other new areas of work for women emerged in the clerical and retail sectors. For all of the nineteenth and even in the early decades of the twentieth century, clerical work was still considered men's work. When the Bank of Nova Scotia in St. John's, Newfoundland hired a woman stenographer in 1898, it was described as an "'experiment' . . . courageously and gallantly undertaken."[58] But gradually women found openings. In 1901 only one in twenty female workers were clerical workers, and they accounted for only one-fifth of all clerical workers; ten years later, approximately one in every ten gainfully employed women was a clerical worker, and one-third of all such workers were female.[59]

Clerical work at first seemed to offer considerable opportunity for upward mobility, and was valued as clean, "white collar" work. And indeed, some women were able to launch innovative careers by taking advantage of the need for clerical workers. For instance, Mary Frances Forbes, a student at Dalhousie University in 1896–97, eventually made a career for herself as principal of the Forbes Shorthand School in Halifax.[60] When the typewriter was introduced, women quickly made it their own, opening up a new area of employment for themselves. When Cora Hind first moved to Winnipeg, she created a job for herself as a "lady typewriter" by renting a typewriter and teaching herself how to work it. She eventually moved on to journalism and a career as a wheat crop forecaster.[61] However, for most women, access to office work was less fulfilling. Clerical work, once an avenue to learning the business, gradually became routine and mechanical, characterized as women's work, and without prospects for advancement. Women did not replace male clerical workers so much as they filled a need for a new type of office worker. Secretarial work, while requiring special skills, was not always recognized as skilled labour, although in the years 1901 to 1921 those women in higher status clerical jobs such as stenographers and bookkeepers were paid on a par with women teachers and nurses.[62]

Retail work quickly grew in the late 1890s with the re-emergence of economic prosperity. Women were preferred to men as sales personnel because they were considered to be more polite to the customers, particularly now that women were increasingly the purchasers of household goods. Even more to the point, perhaps, women sales clerks accepted low wages compared to men. By 1921 one in every four clerical and sales workers was a woman.[63] These jobs were seen as a step up for many young working class women, for as sales clerks they could at least work in a clean environment compared to women in factories. Their work was less isolating than domestic service, less menial, and more respectable. In reality, however, the pay was low, hours were long, often longer than in a factory, and the physical strain was high, as they were required to stand for hours on end. Such jobs, too, required a certain outlay of money for clothing. Owing in large measure to pressure from women's organizations concerned about the long hours "shop girls" had to stand— and the possible negative effects on their capacity to bear children— some provincial governments introduced legislation setting minimum standards for women working in the retail trade. By 1897 Ontario had amended its original Shops' Regulation Act (1888) to limit women's employment to the hours between 7:00 A.M. and 6:00 P.M., and to require employers to provide seats for sales clerks to use when they were not working.[64]

Women in the "professions" and business

By the last few decades of the nineteenth century, the occupation that engaged most women, after domestic service, was teaching. Indeed, the number of women teachers became so great that they were largely responsible for the high percentage of individuals designated "professionals" in turn-of-the-century census returns. In 1901, for example, almost half of all professionals were women and well over 80 percent of these were teachers.[65] Yet the status of the teacher was ambiguous; it might represent upward mobility for a farm girl, but not for a middle class girl.

As public schooling expanded and became more complex after mid-century, educational systems provided increasing opportunities both for work and training. There were more normal schools, and some provinces also provided model schools authorized to give temporary teaching certificates. The development of secondary schooling and the continuation of private schooling provided additional opportunities. Overall, the need for teachers vastly increased, and employing women continued to be the solution for schoolboards hard-pressed for funds. In addition, educators and trustees alike were convinced that women made ideal assistants in schools where the senior grades and the schools as a whole were governed by men. Not all schoolboards agreed with this approach. Catholic boards in Quebec obtained higher provincial grants if they hired male teachers, and in 1903 the board in Victoria, British Columbia, determined "that in the interests of tactful discipline and the cultivation of strength and character in the boys," they should hire more male teachers.[66] Nevertheless, at the turn of the century, women dominated the profession numerically: in 1901 three-quarters of all those engaged in the educational profession were women.

But was teaching really a profession? Teachers, whether women or men, did not control entry into their field, nor did they make the regulations that controlled their work place; they had little choice respecting the curriculum or the books used in their classrooms, and they were increasingly subject to extraordinary regulation by their local schoolboards, as well as by provincial school authorities.[67] The conditions of work may gradually have improved in some urban centres over time, but many teachers in rural areas continued to teach all ages in one classroom. Given the deeply rooted belief that women teachers were best supervised by men, it is somewhat ironic that they were entrusted with complete responsibility in rural schools, although the trustees were never very far away. Rural teachers boarded with students' families and so, like domestics, had little or no privacy. Indeed, the parallel with domestic service can be taken further: many teachers had to do the cleaning in their schools, and in the early years, even perform light duties for the families with whom they boarded.

Still, teaching was a respectable job and one that provided some upward mobility and a modicum of financial security for women who needed to work in order to support themselves or their dependents. A noted Canadian historian remembered that when he started school, the women teachers of his community exuded authority. They had been to normal school in Brandon, Manitoba, and the fact that they had done so and were teaching meant "that they had been out in the great world, had met its demands and had proved themselves. They were, even after only a year, professionals and knew their job. It was an unusual thing for students, encountered only, and that rarely, in the local doctor and the local lawyer."[68] But there were limits to women teachers' prestige. Women continued to be paid less than men even when equally qualified. In Toronto in 1870, the average salary for a woman teacher was $220–$400 per year while a man earned $600–$700. In rural areas of Ontario the average pay for women and men teachers respectively was $187 and $260.[69] Astonishingly, many women were able to save enough money from teaching to further their education and their careers. Dr. Elizabeth Margaret MacKenzie from Prince Edward Island taught for three years before attending the Dalhousie Medical School, from which she graduated in 1900.[70] Certainly there was little room for advancement within the teaching profession itself. A few women became principals and even inspectors; in the Catholic school systems, where the sexes were segregated and many of the teachers were nuns, there were far more opportunities for such administrative positions. But overall, promotions were rare. They were certainly the preserve of the unmarried career teacher. Indeed, as the occupational structure of teaching changed in the second half of the nineteenth century, so did the employment opportunities for married women in schools. Gradually, schools taught by married couples or married women working with sisters or daughters disappeared; more and more often, women teachers lost their jobs if they married.

The higher up the educational ladder one went, the scarcer women teachers became. In 1901, of the 857 professors listed in the census, only 47 were women. One of the most successful was scientist Carrie Derick, who received her B.A. from McGill in 1890 and her M.A. in 1896. She also studied at leading institutions in the United States, Great Britain, and Germany. In 1891 she became the first woman appointed to the academic staff of McGill when she became a demonstrator in botany, and in 1912 she became the first woman in Canada to be named a full professor. Her own struggle for recognition within academe led Derick to an active involvement in the women's movement, and to her assertion that "the professions should be open to men and women alike. It is just a question of the survival of the fittest."[71]

Like teaching, nursing had an ambiguous and changing status. For generations religious nursing orders had enjoyed a high reputation, along with individual nursing sisters, who became legends in their communities. When soeur saint-Thérèse, who acted as a pharmacist in the Red River settlement, was recalled by her order to Bytown (Ottawa) in 1859, the father of Louis Riel voiced the objections of the people who had depended on her, and had her kidnapped and returned to the settlement.[72] Unlike nursing sisters, lay nurses at mid-century were not held in such esteem. Hospitals were designed for the poor and destitute; the nurses who worked in them were essentially servants who were unable to find employment elsewhere. Florence Nightingale's campaign to make nursing respectable began to have an impact in Canada by the latter part of the century, and with the opening of their first training school in St. Catharines in 1874, nursing began a new era. But change was slow. The young nurses in training were used as a source of cheap labour in the hospitals, taking their classes in between their regular duties, which could last from 7:00 A.M. to 7:00 P.M. And, as long as hospitals continued to depend on nursing students for their labour force, the only work for graduates was private duty nursing, which also shared many features with domestic service.

Nurses made various attempts to change their situation. Some tried to expand their area of expertise: the Victorian Order of Nurses (VON) was formed in 1897 with the intention of allowing some of its members to act as midwives. The medical profession opposed this proposal so vigorously, however, that it never became a reality. Nonetheless the VON created a model national public health nursing service, dedicated to sending trained nurses to people's homes, particularly in sparsely populated communities. Trained nurses in Alberta were legally permitted to attend births in 1919, but only in remote areas where a physician was not available.[73] Doctors were also hostile when nursing education seemed to take a professional turn. As one physician put it in 1906, nurses ought to forego scientific study and return to the "gentle touch."[74] Municipal public health nurses, who emerged as a separate group in the early twentieth century, were more successful in exerting their power, perhaps because they tended to work in teams and were able to control their work with little interference from doctors. As a result, they were also able to develop an *esprit de corps* that gave them a sense of worth and identification with their calling.[75]

While teaching and nursing remained the largest professions to attract women, others gradually opened up, although not without a struggle. Jennie Trout and Emily Howard Stowe, the two women most responsible for advancing medical training for women in Canada, were both trained as physicians in the United States, since no medical school in Canada in the 1860s and mid-1870s would accept women. Women had traditionally been healers, and caring for the sick was not a departure from woman's traditional sphere; but being highly educated to do so and being paid for it were. When they had finished their training and returned to Canada, Trout and Stowe pushed for the admission of women to medicine. The major obstacle to medical training for women was the problem of co-education, particularly when the subject was the human body. So antagonistic were Canadians to the idea of allowing women into existing medical schools that two separate women's training facilities were established in 1883. The Kingston Women's Medical College was affiliated with Queen's University, and Woman's Medical College, Toronto, was affiliated with the University of Toronto and with the University of Trinity College. Beginning in 1890, women in Montreal were also able to study at the Faculty of Medicine established by Bishop's University. But the required education was only the first barrier women had to face in their quest to practise medicine. Few hospitals would provide them with the opportunity to gain clinical experience. To be admitted to the Quebec College of Physicians and Surgeons in 1903, Dr. Irma Levasseur, who had trained in the United States, had to win authorization through a private member's bill in the legislature. Once licensed, women doctors were unlikely to attract enough patients to make private practice economically viable. In the early years many women doctors chose to leave Canada and become medical missionaries.[76]

Despite the obstacles, many of these early women physicians went on to distinguished careers. Maud Menten, who graduated with a medical degree in 1911 from the University of Toronto, travelled to Germany where, with Dr. Lenore Michaelis, she studied the properties of enzymes; together they devised the Michaelis-Menten Equation, which provided a theoretical framework for further studies and research on enzymes.

Law degrees came later than medical degrees, perhaps because there was no equivalent in the legal profession to the image of woman as healer. In *The Canada Monthly* in 1872, the distinguished journalist and former academic, Goldwin Smith, argued that the physical attraction between the two sexes made it highly improper for women to be admitted to the bar for "it would be present when a female advocate rose to address male jury men and judges; and perhaps the class of women who would become advocates would not be those least likely to make an unscrupulous use of their power of appealing to emotions subversive of the supremacy of justice."[77] As a result of this kind of opposition, Clara Brett Martin, the first woman trained in law in Canada and in the British Empire, had to face much opposition.

An exceptionally bright student, Martin graduated at sixteen in 1890 from Trinity College with an honours degree in mathematics. The following year she applied for admission as a student to the Law Society of Upper Canada, but was rejected on the grounds that the Society's regulations restricted admission to "persons," and as women were not legally "persons," they were ineligible to study law. This decision failed to dampen Martin's determination. Championed by Dr. Emily Stowe and the Dominion Women's Enfranchisement Association, she used all the means in her power to pursue her goal. She succeeded in having a bill passed by the Ontario legislature making it possible for women to study law. Martin's victory was partly owing to the personal support she received from Sir Oliver Mowat, the premier and attorney-general, who had been under pressure from the suffragists for some time to enfranchise women. His support appears to have been a compromise measure designed to appease the suffrage forces without succumbing to their more controversial demand. The new legislation allowed women to be considered by the Law Society for admission, and to be permitted to practise as solicitors but not as barristers. This meant they could not appear in court to present and argue cases. Even so, the Law Society responded by declaring that it was "inexpedient" to frame rules for the admission of women.

Persistent as ever, Martin persuaded Mowat to intervene with the Society on her behalf. This he did, and by 1892 Martin was able to pursue her studies. But her troubles were not yet over. Throughout her student years she endured the taunts and ridicule of male classmates, teachers, and the press. Before graduating in 1895 she decided to petition the Law Society for admission as a barrister. She received extensive public support, including that of Lady Aberdeen, the wife of the governor-general, and the recently formed National Council of Women of Canada. Premier Mowat again brought pressure to bear on the Law Society. Finally the Society grudgingly amended its regulations, thereby allowing Clara Brett Martin to become, in 1897, a fully fledged member of the legal profession, and the first woman to practise law in the British Empire.[78]

Women aspiring to careers in the law were not as successful in Quebec. Although the first woman to graduate with a law degree did so in 1914, women were not allowed to practise law in that province until 1941.[79] Other professions that opened up to women did not need the intensive training that law and medicine required. Isabel Grant, an honours mathematics graduate from Dalhousie University, became, in 1911, the federal government's first woman actuary and insurance expert. Family lore has it that she applied for the job using her initials, and when her application was accepted and she reported for work, her employers were shocked when a woman appeared.[80] Many women made their living or supplemented the family income with their novels and poetry; one, Margaret Marshall Saunders, was the first person in Canada to sell one million copies of a book (*Beautiful Joe*, 1894).[81] Women also entered journalism. When Cora Hind applied for a job on the *Free Press* in Winnipeg in 1881, she met with shocked disbelief on the part of the editor. "It would never do to have a woman in the newspaper business," he argued; it was a business "marked by hard, rough work, late hours, and sometimes involved meeting not quite nice people."[82] Nevertheless, women before and after Cora Hind flocked to work that was respectable, clean, a bit daring, and different, and that offered them a public vehicle for their thoughts. Many exploited the fact that women were major consumers of reading material by writing columns for and about their sex. Some of these were shortlived, but others, like Francis Beynon's column in the *Grain Growers' Guide*, became an essential part of their papers' popularity. One of the most famous journalists was "Kit" Coleman, whose "Women's Kingdom" page in the Toronto *Mail* helped boost the circulation of that paper. Her work, however, went beyond the women's page. In 1898 she made her way to Cuba to cover the Spanish–American War, and in 1906 she described the aftermath of the San Francisco earthquake.[83] Women journalists became so successful and numerous that they set up the Women's Press Club in 1904. Some women even helped establish and edit newspapers. Mary Ann Shadd Cary edited the *Provincial Freeman* in Toronto in 1854–55 to publicize the plight of the black people of Canada and to give them a voice.[84] Two other women editors were Mme Josephine Marchand of *Le Coin du Feu*, 1893–99, and Robertine Barry of *Le Journal de Françoise*, 1902–1909.[85] Sara McLagan published the Vancouver *World* after her husband's death and became the first woman newspaper publisher in Canada.

Other creative fields attracted women, particularly the visual and performing arts, both at the amateur and professional level. At least twenty women worked in professional photography in Ontario alone by the 1860s. In 1894 women were admitted to the newly formed Toronto Camera Club, although until 1943 they were prohibited from using the darkroom, and then only during the day.[86] Emma Lajeunesse from Chambly, Quebec, took the late nineteenth century opera world by storm as Mme Albani. When she retired in 1896, she had performed forty-three starring roles.[87] Canadian-born actresses such as Marie Dressler, Mary Pickford, and Margaret Anglin found success in the United States and became household names. For the few who won acclaim, however, most went unsung. Canadians tended to view the stage as not quite respectable, and associated actresses with dancehall girls.[88]

Kate St. John accompanies the Wolsey expedition during the first Riel uprising, 1817.

Women visual artists also had difficulty achieving public recognition and supporting themselves with their art. Emily Carr ran a boardinghouse for a number of years because she felt she received little encouragement, financial or otherwise, to continue her painting. And Mary Riter Hamilton, whose realistic scenes of World War I won her acclaim from the French government, was ignored by her own.[89]

Even less known than women artists are women who were in business. Yet we know that women were hotel and tavern keepers, ran their own millinery and dressmaking businesses, operated their own private schools, or ran their own ranches. However, census returns often did not distinguish between those working for someone else and those working for themselves, and thus the extent of entrepreneurial endeavour is difficult to trace. Needless to say, it was difficult for women to gain access to capital or credit. Nevertheless there were startling success stories. For example, Belinda Mulrooney came to the Klondike during the Gold Rush from Pennsylvania on a steamship, working as a stewardess. In the exceptional circumstances of boom-town Dawson, she ran a lunch counter, started a contracting business, and later a roadhouse. She then built the elegant Fairview Hotel in Dawson and subsequently became part owner of a mining company and a telephone syndicate.[90]

Women workers organize for change

Women workers had little power to improve their working conditions. Yet some did become involved with unions or form their own associations; they were also involved in protests and strikes. In the textile and garment trades, unions had to come to terms with the presence of large numbers of women workers. The Knights of Labor, a unique trade union organization in the late nineteenth century, believed that all workers, whether skilled or unskilled, male or female, should be organized. As a way of attracting women workers to the union, the Knights held "socials" that brought together female and male workers. They also asked Leonora Barry, who was the General Investigator of Women's Work and Wages for the Knights in the United States, to come to Toronto to help organize female workers. These efforts met with some success. In 1884 Local Assembly 3040 of the Knights was formed among the woollen mill operatives in Hamilton, and included women within its ranks. The women later broke away and formed the exclusively female Excelsior Local Assembly 3179, led by Katie McVicar. McVicar was a young, single worker, totally devoted to improving the lot of women workers. She stressed the need for organized labour to change its usual techniques of recruiting to meet the needs of women, who were unlikely to participate in mass rallies, or to be swayed by vague promises of improved conditions. Unfortunately her untimely death at the age of thirty robbed the women's union movement of one of its most forceful leaders. In 1885 another women's local, the Hope Local

Assembly, was established in Toronto, primarily by garment workers.[91] Unfortunately, the Knights were a shortlived phenomenon, whose impact in provinces other than Quebec greatly diminished after 1890. By 1902 they had been reduced to a mere remnant in Quebec also.

The majority of women workers were not members of male trade unions; nonetheless, on many occasions they demonstrated a high degree of militancy, devotion to working class solidarity, and a commitment to advancing their own economic interests. In 1880 in Hochelaga, Quebec, female weavers initiated a strike to protest an increase in the work week. Although the strike included some men, the Montreal *Gazette* reported that the men "were not nearly so demonstrative as the women."[92] White collar workers were in a different situation. The public perceived their "respectable" work as less onerous, and so it was with surprise that Toronto citizens faced a strike by 400 Bell telephone operators in 1907. In fact, the job of a telephone operator was fatiguing, stressful, and could even be dangerous, for severe electric shocks on the long distance lines gave some workers convulsions. The strike began when the company decided to increase the hours of work and eliminate overtime. The workers protested and eventually went out on strike on January 31. The women's solidarity during the strike was impressive, and so was public support for them, for the telephone monopoly had earned little sympathy. William Lyon Mackenzie King, the deputy minister of labour, intervened in the strike and persuaded the women to go back to work in return for a public inquiry. Most of the testimony at that inquiry supported the workers, and Bell agreed to a settlement that lessened their hours of work. Take-home pay, however, remained inferior to what it had been under the overtime system.[93]

In 1912 almost 1000 workers from the T. Eaton Co. factory in Toronto, many of them women, went out on strike to protest the firing of some co-workers. The strike spread to Montreal, and in Kingston sympathetic garment workers threatened to strike firms doing business with Eaton's. In addition, Toronto's immigrant Jewish community ran an effective boycott of Eaton's goods, thanks to the support of its women.[94] Even among the most isolated of female workers, there were attempts at organization. In British Columbia, a group of domestic workers established the Home and Domestic Employees Union in 1913 to work for the nine-hour day and minimum wages. Given the enormous obstacles that the union had to confront in its attempt to organize domestics, most of whom worked alone in individual households, it is not surprising that the union dissolved within two years.[95]

Despite their militancy, women did not play a significant role within the union movement. This was partly because of tʜe practical problems involved in organizing them. Even women in manufacturing were frequently employed in such small shops that they were difficult to bring together. For example, in 1891 over 2000 Toronto women worked in either dressmaking or tailoring, but they were divided among 614 different work places.[96] Unions were generally restricted to workers who were "skilled," of whom few were women. The work performed by women, whatever its characteristics, was usually labelled "unskilled." Unions during this period were very fragile and vulnerable, and had more than enough to do trying to organize male workers. Women workers presented union organizers with additional problems: compared to men, women had high turnover rates, as many left their jobs when they married. In addition, female wage earners often had family or domestic obligations that prevented them from attending union meetings in the evenings.

Of equal significance, however, was the ambivalence or outright hostility many union members and leaders felt towards the idea of women working in the public labour force. In 1898 the Trades and Labour Congress, the largest grouping of organized labour, declared its support for the "abolition . . . of female labor in all branches of industrial life such as mines, factories, workshops, etc."[97] By the turn of the century, male workers claimed that women were competitors for their jobs, even though statistics indicated women and men workers seldom performed the same kind of work. Even when both sexes worked in the same industry, a closer examination indicates that the separation of the sexes into specific job categories was maintained. In the cotton industry, while female and male operatives worked alongside each other in the weave rooms, other departments were overwhelmingly composed of either female or male workers. Ring spinners looked after a stationary frame on which the cotton yarn was drawn onto spindles by means of a ring travelling around a small circular track; such spinners were almost exclusively female since manual dexterity was the principal requirement for the successful ring spinner. Mule spinners, by contrast, were always male since the mule spinning frame was a large, complex machine with a moving carriage, which was considered too difficult for women to operate. Not surprisingly, this job and that of loom fixer, another exclusively male occupation, constituted the highest paying manual work in the mills.

Male workers also believed that women workers caused wages to be low. If the only way to stop this was to bring women into a union it would sometimes be done, but often more for the benefit of the male members than the female ones. As the *Palladium of Labor* pointed out in 1894, "place the sexes upon equal pay for the same kind of service and man has the advantage."[98] Indeed, insistence on economic equality with men in the workforce often cost women their jobs. This seemed to be the case in the cigar industry of late nineteenth century Toronto. As one commentator explained, "In Toronto there are very few women employed in cigar-making. The reason being that all the employés [sic] belong to a union which insists on all workers being paid alike, and the employers prefer to employ men, because they are likely to remain longer in the business."[99]

Underlying much of the uneasiness towards women workers was the growing belief in the latter half of the nineteenth century in the idea of the "family wage." Workers believed that if a family wage was paid to men, women would not need to seek paid employment. They could remain in their proper sphere — the home. The belief, of course, assumed that most women had a male protector, and overlooked the fact that many women did not, that many wanted to work, and indeed had dependents of their own for whom they were responsible. Women continued to flow into the paid work force, especially into the service sector and into the new or growing women's "professions."

In these fields also, conditions of work and low pay brought women together in an effort to improve their situations. The first associations of women teachers were formed in towns and cities, where it was easier both to organize and to see the extent to which women were discriminated against compared to the men who taught in the public schools. Eight women created the original Women Teachers' Association of Toronto in 1885; teachers in Montreal and in several smaller Ontario cities soon followed suit.[100] Teachers were ambivalent about their organizing efforts, caught as they were between an image of "professionalism" and the realities of their working conditions and pay. In Toronto, for example, the more radical members of the Women Teachers' Association toyed with the idea of affiliating with the Trades and Labour Council in the early 1900s, but caution won out and the affiliation never happened. Energies went, rather, into campaigns for better wages and working conditions, and into making connections with other groups. In 1918 the various Ontario groups formed the Federation of Women Teachers' Associations of Ontario and began the long process of building a province-wide organization.[101] In the same year, the Saskatoon Women Teachers' Association was formed by fifteen teachers. Campaigning for better contracts, equal pay for equal work, and the retention of married women teachers, they too demonstrated an awareness of women's disabilities in the labour force and of the need to organize in order to seek improvement.[102]

Catholic teachers were also struggling to improve their lot. In Montreal there was a Catholic association for laywomen teachers, as well as a separate association for women teaching for the Protestant schoolboard, but they represented only a minority of teachers. In Quebec urban centres the majority of women teachers were members of religious orders, and they perhaps had a greater sense of control over their conditions of work. On the other hand, teaching sisters were not immune from the interference of school officials and bishops. In Halifax the Sisters of Charity came into conflict with their new archbishop in 1876 when he attempted to prevent the attendance of the laity at the graduation exercises of Mount Saint Vincent Academy, and to institute other reforms not to the liking of the teaching sisters. A deputation to Rome eventually succeeded in having the order placed under the authority of their friend, the Bishop of Antigonish.[103] In Montreal, the Sisters of the *Congrégation de Notre Dame* fought a battle with a Catholic school commission that was perennially short of money and seemed to believe that nuns did not need to be paid a living wage for their work.[104]

Nurses also organized to improve their working conditions. In 1905 the Alumnae Association of the Toronto General Hospital School of Nursing inaugurated a journal called *The Canadian Nurse*, which concerned itself with issues such as the need for registration. Nurses believed that registration would attest to their training and skill, thus raising their status in the eyes of other professionals and the public.[105] From 1912 the Canadian National Association of Trained Nurses, formed originally to affiliate with the International Council of Nurses in 1897, struggled to obtain registration laws in the various provinces.

Work and war

The involvement of Canada in World War I had important repercussions for women's work, especially after 1915 when the recruitment of thousands of young men into the armed forces resulted in serious labour shortages. As Canada increased its agricultural exports to hard-pressed Britain, women were called upon to assume an even larger part of farm work. During the summer months, farm wives and daughters were aided in their efforts by hundreds of female students housed in camps and hostels run by the Young Women's Christian Association. In 1917 and 1918 there were over 2000 young women in these camps in Ontario alone. They worked at every job: "besides picking and packing fruit, [they] handled horses, pitched hay, drove motor trucks to market and sold the fruit . . . took charge of chicken houses, worked in canning factories, put handles on baskets, [and] hoed for ten hours a day."[106]

Urban working women saw their employment opportunities change. Although many continued to enter domestic service, still the largest employer of women, new jobs opened up as the wartime economy moved into full gear after 1916. The most widely publicized were in the munitions industry, since before the entry of the United States into the war in 1917, Canada was a major supplier of munitions to Great Britain. To meet its commitment to supply arms, the Canadian government actively recruited female workers for the munitions factories, and by 1917 over 35 000 women in Ontario and Quebec were producing shells for the Allies. Although the munitions manufacturers paid wages well above those earned by women in traditional occupations, female munitions workers in 1917 earned only 50–83 percent of what their male co-workers earned.[107] In addition, the wartime emergency was used to justify extremely long hours (13–14 hours a day) and deplorable working conditions.

The brief but impressive economic boom and the manpower shortage engendered by the war enabled women to move into areas of employment normally reserved for men. In Montreal alone, over 2300 women were employed by the railways and by the steel and cement industries in jobs formerly held by men only.[108] In October 1917 Maude Chart made history in Kingston by becoming the first

street railway "conductorette" in Canada; soon all male conductors in Kingston had been replaced by women. The insatiable demand for men to serve overseas, which resulted in conscription late in 1917, also facilitated the entry of women into white collar work previously performed by men. Between 1911 and 1921 the number of female clerical workers nearly tripled (33 723 to 90 577); by 1921 they accounted for nearly 42 percent of all clerical workers and for over 18 percent of all paid women workers in Canada. Even the most renowned bastions of male clerical work, the banks, were compelled by a combination of male labour shortages and increased task specialization to hire women as tellers and clerks. In 1916 over 40 percent of the clerks employed by the Bank of Nova Scotia in Ontario were women, compared to less than 10 percent five years earlier. In western Canada also, the marked movement of women into clerical work during the war resulted in a doubling, between 1911 and 1921, of the female workforce employed in clerical occupations.[109]

The proportion of married women working in industry also increased in these years. In 1921, for example, 22 percent of the female munitions workers in the Montreal area were married, although married women comprised only 2 percent of all gainfully employed women.[110] Of course, young single women continued to constitute the vast majority of female workers. But, once and for all, the war established the propriety of women working for wages before marriage, even when the young woman belonged to the middle class.

Women boat builders, Baddeck, Nova Scotia, 1918.

In "respectable" work like teaching, women continued to replace men teachers at the elementary and secondary school levels. In Alberta, for example, there were 630 more women teachers in 1916 than there had been in 1914.[111]

The armed services also recognized the potential of women's work, but only as nurses. In 1885 during the Riel Rebellion, at the invitation of the minister of militia and defence, seven nursing sisters had travelled to the Northwest Territories to tend the wounded. The Boer War presented Canadian nurses with another opportunity to serve in battlefield hospitals, and in 1901 the Canadian Nursing Service was created as a part of the Army Medical Corps. During World War I, 2504 members were actively involved in overseas duties; all told, forty-six nurses died while in the service of their country.[112] The dedication and heroism of the wartime nurses contributed much to enhancing the status of the nursing profession.

Many of the trends in women's employment were reversed at war's end. Women were treated essentially as a "reserve army of labour." When there were labour shortages, women were pulled into the workforce, including into jobs from which they had been traditionally excluded. But when the special need was over, the traditional gender division of work roles was re-established.[113] Nonetheless, owing to the terrible casualties among the young men of Canada, many women could not expect to marry. With these women in mind, the Women's War Conference of February 1918, which had been convened by the federal government to ensure women's continued support for the war effort, passed resolutions in favour of equal pay for equal work, technical training, and a minimum wage for women.[114]

Although the war focused increased attention on women in paid employment, it was difficult for many Canadians to accept with equanimity the idea of the working woman. Nevertheless, as more and more women entered the workforce from the mid-century to the end of the Great War, the reality of their doing so could not be ignored. It seemed increasingly acceptable for young women to work before marriage, and a small but important group of women were already making life-long careers for themselves. They represented the "new woman" of the late Victorian and Edwardian periods.

More representative of women of this era were those who married, bore children, and devoted themselves to ensuring a better life for the next generation. In untold cases this seemingly simple task involved enormous courage and sacrifice, as it did for Lillie Davis. It was during World War I that she and her husband, DeCourcy, decided to emigrate with their two young children from England to Canada. Just before they set sail, however, DeCourcy died. Undaunted by her loss, Lillie decided to emigrate anyway. After surviving a German attack on her ship during the crossing, she began a new life for herself and her children in Canada.

6 Women's sphere

Distressed by the Canadian government's failure to recognize the contribution of Laura Secord to her nation's sovereignty in the debate over pensions for veterans of the War of 1812, Sarah A. Curzon took up her pen in 1876 and wrote a play focussing on Secord's heroic deeds. In her preface to "Laura Secord, the Heroine of 1812," Curzon pointed to the injustice of showering so much attention on the male heroes of the war. "To save *from* the sword is surely as great a deed as to save *with* the sword; and this Laura Secord did, at an expense of nerve and muscle fully equal to any that are recorded of the warrior." In the play itself, Curzon had Colonel Fitzgibbon, the officer who made his military reputation as a result of Secord's warning, deliver the moral that Canadians ought to draw.

Men, never forget this woman's noble deed.
Armed, and in company, inspirited
By crash of martial music, soldiers march
To duty; but she alone, defenseless,
With no support but kind humanity
And burning patriotism, ran all our risks,
Of hurt, and bloody death, to serve us men,
Strangers to her save by quick war-time ties.
Therefore, in grateful memory and kind return,
Ever treat women well. [1]

With these words and by her play, Curzon acknowledged the link between her generation and Secord's, a link that many Canadian women of her time felt profoundly. For all their sense that they were living in a new era, they recognized how close they still were to the women before them.

It was true that women were increasingly entering the labour market. But they tended to do so when they were single and young, working between the ages of fifteen and twenty-four. In 1891, in fact, only 11 percent of women over fifteen were "employed," according to the official record of the census; in 1911 the figure had risen to a mere 14 percent. [2] What such statistics ignored, of course, were the thousands of women who toiled in their own homes as their mothers and grandmothers had done before them.

That women were crucial to the household had long been recognized, even—perhaps especially—in the days when the household and the workforce were less clearly separated. Women's identity had always been centred on the family. But in the nineteenth century, as some women moved into an identifiable, non-domestic world of work, the family and women's role in it seemed threatened. In response, nineteenth century ideologues promoted the concept of separate spheres for women and men and, most significantly, prescribed a domestic and maternal role for women that was highly idealized. Clergymen, doctors, and other male "experts" in fact had much to say about the nature of womanhood and what the ideal woman should or should not do.

Nor were women silent on the subject. In the second half of the nineteenth century, Canadian women too began to propose solutions to what was increasingly identified as the "woman question" or the "woman problem." Many argued that education was the way to improve women's condition, but two different directions were proposed: one sought for a more practical training geared to the reality of woman's work in the home, and led to the domestic science movement; the other demanded access to higher education and to the professions, and led to the movement of small numbers of women into the universities. Another burning issue was women's reproductive behaviour. Since motherhood was so inextricably linked to the image of the ideal woman, it was with great consternation that many realized that women were apparently abandoning this role and having fewer children.

The idealization of domesticity

Victorian Canadians were assaulted by an ideology that saw women as the embodiment of purity, and as both physically and financially dependent. Home was a woman's "proper sphere." Woman, the ideal proclaimed, was man's equal, but equal did not mean identical. Women were different, and from this difference complementary roles and responsibilities naturally evolved. The Reverend Robert Sedgwick was an early proponent of such views. As he explained to a group of young men in 1856,

Woman is the equal of man, alike in the matter of intellect, emotion, and activity, and . . . she has shown her capabilities in these respects, ... It would never do, however, from these premises, to draw the conclusion that woman . . . is bound to exert her powers in the same direction and for the same ends as man. This were to usurp the place of man — this were to forget her position as the complement of man, and assume a place she is incompetent to fill, or rather was not designed to fill.[3]

Two decades later another commentator could only concur. "Woman's first and only place is in her home," this writer explained. "She is destined by Providence to make her home . . . a cloister wherein one may seek calm and joyful repose from the busy, heartless world. . . . The land she governs is a bright oasis in the desert of the world's selfishness."[4] Since most women married and indeed expected to make home and children their main concerns, the ideal was not completely divorced from reality. If it had been, it would not have

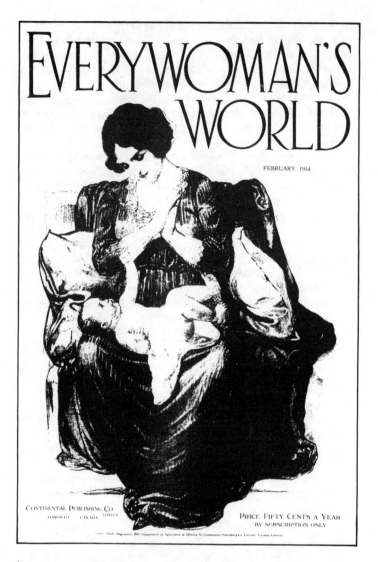

EVERYWOMAN'S WORLD

FEBRUARY, 1914

CONTINENTAL PUBLISHING CO
TORONTO   CANADA   LIMITED

PRICE FIFTY CENTS A YEAR
BY SUBSCRIPTION ONLY

Trade Mark Registered, 1913, Department of Agriculture at Ottawa, by Continental Publishing Co. Limited, Toronto, Canada.

been so powerful. What was new and confining about the ideal of domesticity was the increasingly sharp distinction it made between the domestic world of women and the public world of men, the growing emphasis on the mothering role, and the negative reactions that greeted most deviations from the norm.

Several groups of men were heavily involved in public discussion of the question of woman's proper sphere. Among the first to take up the issue were clergymen like Robert Sedgwick. Clerics continued to preach and write on women's place and possibilities throughout the latter part of the nineteenth and on into the twentieth century. Within the Roman Catholic church, there were two possible roles for women: wife and mother, or member of a religious order. For

Motherhood is idealized on the cover of a popular women's magazine.

members of religious communities, a variety of paths was possible, for the church fostered and supported comtemplative orders like the Carmelites as well as more active ones involved in teaching or social work. What the church frowned on, evidently, were sisterhoods of laywomen. Women who tried to organize communal life for charitable purposes were urged to take permanent vows and bring their associations under church control. Catholic religious orders expanded phenomenally between the middle of the nineteenth century and the first two decades of the twentieth century —at least thirty new orders were formed.[5] These orders were responding to the needs not just of the church but of the women who entered them. But male clerics continued to see themselves as the proper interpreters of women's roles, both inside and outside the convent. Women were "naturally" separate and different from men, as a French Canadian priest explained in 1918.

Equality, whatever it is before God, in no way implies the parity of roles in society. One forgets that woman, by her very sex, by her physical structure and her moral qualities, by her tastes, talents, and tendencies, absolutely differs from man, and that this radical difference between the sexes results in no less a difference in their duties.[6]

Protestant clergymen of all denominations also felt called upon to pronounce on women's proper roles and duties. Whereas earlier in the century some sects had encouraged women to speak out at meetings or even to preach, by the third quarter of the nineteenth century the practice was condemned. Woman's Christian vocation was to be silent; the woman's place was in the home. "Bad" mothers, moreover, were increasingly held responsible for children who turned out delinquent, whether drunken sons or fallen daughters. By the early twentieth century, the leading Methodist reformer and social gospeller, J.S. Woodsworth, had no doubt that mothers who went out to work were to blame for a good deal of "truancy and juvenile crime."[7]

Physicians were a second group of men who had much to say on the subject of women and their roles. And in an era when religious faith was being challenged and when physicians were working very hard to upgrade their profession and gain control of health care, the voice of doctors was an increasingly powerful one. Like clergymen, they wrote in the popular press. But they also wrote a great deal for each other in the professional medical press.

Physicians tended to emphasize women's physical frailty, reflected in every aspect of the biological life cycle. The weakness began with puberty. This difficult and mysterious stage appeared to heighten the physical, mental, and emotional differences between the two sexes. A pubescent woman's energies evidently became so concentrated on the development of her reproductive system that there was little energy left for anything else, certainly not for higher education or for sports. Some doctors warned that the woman who did continue her studies during this crucial stage might well damage her reproductive system forever, as her vital energies would go to her brain instead of her uterus. Medical experts encouraged girls to engage in appropriate physical activity, but the sports recommended were very different from those recommended for their brothers. Walking was good for girls; running was not.

Even when a woman passed the precarious age of puberty, her reproductive system continued to control every aspect of her being. "Woman exists for the sake of the womb," declared a popular health manual of the 1890s.[8] Doctors also believed that the complexity of a woman's reproductive system made her especially subject to disease. This placed women at risk throughout their lives, and the risk permitted the medical profession to speak out on a number of topics. Women were urged, for example, to cast off their corsets and wear clothing that was both more comfortable and healthy, and less likely to damage their childbearing capacity.

Physicians acknowledged woman's sexuality but interpreted it in their own way. They comforted themselves by arguing that it existed to encourage conception, and they developed fascinating theories about the relationship between sexual excitement and its results. The *Canadian Practitioner* of 1886, for example, republished a review from an American journal, which solemnly informed its readers that "at the generation of male offspring the mother must be in a higher state of excitement than the father. And, conversely, at the generation of female offspring the father must be in a higher state of such excitement than the mother."[9] In general, doctors believed that a woman's sex drive was not nearly as strong as a man's, and that it was a woman's responsibility to keep both under control. Nor should women attempt to avoid the repercussions of their sexuality. If they remained virgins or practised birth control, they risked physical breakdown.

Even after the childbearing years were over, medical experts thought that woman's reproductive system continued to exert its unremitting control—menopausal women were irrational and liable to "every form of neurasthenia, neuralgia, hysteria, convulsive disease, melancholia," and even insanity.[10] Doctors believed women to be highly susceptible to emotional disorders, particularly hysteria. Their belief in "reflex action"—that is, the tendency of healthy parts of the body to be weakened by diseased parts — persuaded some doctors that certain cases of insanity in women could be reversed by curing them of their gynecological disorders. As a result, hundreds of insane women were given gynecological operations, from simple curettage or cleansing of the diseased surface to complete hysterectomies. A middle-aged woman who was subjected to "curettage and amputation of the cervix" in the London insane asylum in 1898 had been diagnosed as suffering from a "subinvoluted uterus and cystic and hypertrophied cervix" as well as a perineum that was "slightly torn." She reported that her husband neglected and abused her and consorted with other women. According to her file, her insanity was a form of pyromania: she "gathers anything she can and burns it." Whatever the relationships between the various aspects of her case, the operation was declared to have been a success and the patient discharged.[11]

Performing operations on women judged insane was an extreme approach. More typically, physicians avoided discussing the causes of women's emotional disabilities. It was simply accepted that women were weaker and less emotionally stable than men. This led easily to the view that they needed to be both protected and controlled. Yet at the same time, it was believed, because women were more moral and less sexually excitable, they should be able to control themselves. Such contradictory views permeated the thinking of lawmakers and judges, another group of men who routinely differentiated between the sexes and made pronouncements, both overt and implicit, about women's capabilities and roles. Their views had practical as well as ideological force.

Adolescent girls who were convicted of offences, for example, received longer sentences than boys did in the new reformatories that were being set up for young offenders. Magistrates and legislators were also more willing to incarcerate adult women for "moral" offences than men. An 1871 statute stipulated five years imprisonment for Quebec women convicted of vagrancy for a second time; no such law applied to men.[12]

Canadian divorce law also continued to embody the double standard. In 1857 the British Matrimonial Causes Act was adopted in the province of Canada; similar laws were in effect in most of the other provinces at the time of Confederation. Typically, a husband might win a divorce if his wife was proven to have committed adultery. It was still the case that a wife could only obtain a divorce if her husband was proven guilty of adultery coupled with desertion without reason, extreme cruelty, incest or bigamy, or if he was convicted of raping another woman or of sodomy.[13] In general, the law and its enforcement seemed to be saying that men needed some freedom; women should be content with their lot in the home, no matter what their circumstances. For them, no transgressions were permitted. However, in Quebec it was declared in 1866 that marriage for Roman Catholics was only dissoluble by death.

Laws governing native women also reflected the view that a woman's place was with her husband. Thus in 1869 the federal government altered the Indian Act to exclude native women from Indian status if they married non-status men. White husbands of native women were seen as a threat to the resources of various bands; white wives of native men did not constitute such a threat.[14] The government did acknowledge the validity of Amerindian marriages according to their own customs, but it refused to sanction their traditional practices with respect to divorce.[15]

The double standard in many provinces regarding divorce extended to the status of married women. After the 1870s, a woman could sue her husband, but only for damages to her property, not to her body. Wives who attempted to sue for divorce after repeated beatings were chastised for failing to leave after the first beating — they were held to have condoned their husbands' actions. On the other hand, wives who did leave after only one or two beatings were chastised for being insufficiently patient with their husbands. In both murder and assault cases where wives were the victims, judgements often suggested that the women involved were somehow themselves to blame for inciting their husbands to these acts. An 1844 court decision stated that it was a wife's duty "to conform to the tastes and habits of her husband, to sacrifice much of her own comfort and convenience to his whims and caprices, to submit to his commands. . . ." If the husband was violent, it was the wife's role "to endeavour . . . to induce a change and alteration" in his behaviour.[16] Ontario judges continued to cite this extraordinary decision for decades afterwards. And, for all the increasing emphasis on motherhood and the importance of this role for women, women did not have equal guardianship rights over their children. Only unwed mothers had rights over their children, and even then an 1859 Upper Canadian statute prevented the prosecution of any man who abducted a child, and who "claim[ed] to be the father."[17] Finally, the wife's disability and the double standard extended beyond her husband's death. In any province that provided relief for widows, the woman was deprived of her right to it if she had committed adultery.[18]

The courts had little sympathy for women who deviated from the domestic ideal. In the case of prostitutes, the women who solicited, not their clients, were viewed as the criminals. They, after all, were the ones who made the money. Nor were the courts particularly sympathetic to women who were the subjects of men's violence outside of marriage. It was still rare for rapists to be prosecuted, and even more rare for them to be convicted.[19] As in an earlier period, the courts were reluctant to find women guilty of infanticide, but the reason for this leniency was the demeaning view that women were uninformed and therefore morally incapable.

In looking at this kind of evidence, we have come a long way from woman as the embodiment of purity and gentleness, a creature in need of man's protection. In fact, a good deal of what late Victorian Canadians said about women suggested that they were to be feared rather than protected. At the very least, a woman outside her "place" was a woman in danger or a woman who did not deserve protection.

Women's lives

Women themselves had a much richer, more complex and positive concept of their own roles and lives. They recognized the importance of their ties to other women, particularly the relationships between sisters and between mothers and daughters. As a young girl in boarding school in the late 1870s, Marshall Saunders wrote to her mother in Halifax quite explicitly about her feelings. "I do not believe a child ever loved her mother as much as I love you. I would be willing to die to ensure your happiness, my darling. I hope the dear Lord Jesus will keep you safely till I come back."[20] There was also a sense that

A Klondike dancer.

family obligation fell more on women than on men, and that this was appropriate; it seemed right that they should help to care for younger siblings or for their parents as they aged. When Elizabeth Smith wanted to enter medical school in 1877, her best friend Maud Rankin tried to dissuade her because of the duty she owed her parents. "Lay aside those silly thoughts and you will be a better woman," Rankin urged. "I know that you are wishing to do something grand something that will carry your name on to further ages . . . but are you neglecting no home duties . . . ? Lizzie your first duty lies there, you never can repay your father and mother for all they have done for you. . . ."[21] At times, caring for parents delayed or prevented any chance a woman had to lead a full life of her own. In her personal recollections, Alice Chown had much to say about the constraints on women. Only after the death of her widowed mother, when she was 40, did she finally have some control over her own fate.

During the next few months I shall have all the struggle for life and breath that an infant has, for I shall be breaking away from all the old walls that have surrounded me, from all the old environments that have enfolded me, that have kept me hidden from life and have forced me to live only through others. . . .[22]

Chown celebrated her liberation by throwing herself into labour politics. Other women, forced almost against their will into domesticity, reacted more dramatically. Flora McPhee was a single woman who had made her life in Montreal, but was called home to Campbellville, Ontario, to nurse her mother, who treated her like a servant. When her mother died in 1920, free at last, McPhee expressed her rebellion by going out to the barn and chopping "into little pieces the old spinning wheel and loom. . . . She said she needed kindling." What she really needed, the niece who tells her story believes, "was to destroy the symbols of her bondage."[23]

The role of the helping daughter, sister, or aunt was one that not all enjoyed. Many single women admitted that they coveted domesticity, and they usually meant married domesticity. Marriage represented a sense of place, of creating a family of one's own, and of shaping and controlling the next generation. In the words of a woman banker quoted in the 1915–16 *Journal of the Canadian Bankers' Association*, "When the opportunity offers the most successful banking women amongst us will cheerfully retire to her own hearthstone, preferring the love of a husband and little children to thousands a year and a seat in the council of the mighty!"[24] Indeed professional single women were sometimes the most vociferous promoters of the domestic ideal. They were sure that the employment of the married woman outside the home meant that her family would suffer. In her "Report on Infant Mortality in Toronto" (1910), Dr. Helen MacMurchy took these sentiments to their ultimate conclusion: "Where the mother works," she stated, "the baby dies."[25] Certainly most women agreed about the importance of the family and of their own role in keeping it together. They argued that, as the family went, so went the nation. So focussed were women on their role as mothers that Nellie McClung felt she could safely declare that "every normal woman desires children."[26]

Unfortunately, to the extent that they accepted their role as the exclusive moral guardians of children and the family, women left themselves open not only to the barbs of male moralists and clergymen when their children transgressed, but to feelings of guilt and self-blame. Even "good" mothers puzzled over how best to train their children. One Victorian mother, who kept a running diary of her child's development, recorded a constant state of worry over her daughter's moral health. How was she to train her daughter and ensure that she would "grow up a good woman?"[27] Women were also not above blaming each other. In 1911 the Presbyterian Woman's Home Missionary Society criticized Ruthenian immigrant women for lacking the ideals and morals needed to raise their children as proper Christian Canadians.[28]

Despite the primacy of family for most, women did not define themselves solely by their familial roles and obligations. Victorian and Edwardian women also saw themselves increasingly as individuals in their own right, with obligations and friendships outside the family. The opportunity to make female friends was one reason unmarried working class women gave for preferring factory work to domestic service. Friendships were also formed through the numerous organizations and clubs that were developed by women and for women during this era. Some women's friendships became passionate attachments, but such relationships between women were becoming suspect and the object of repression. In a small village in Quebec in the 1880s, a teacher named Elizabeth Hébert was persecuted because of her intimate friendship with an older woman in the community; she lost her position as a result, but was "exonerated" in the hearing that the Quebec Department of Public Instruction held at her request.[29]

Family and close friendships do not constitute the total picture. For many women — perhaps most of the women who put their thoughts on paper during this period — religion was a major focus. For some it was the foundation for their work in the larger world. In 1878 medical student Elizabeth Smith thanked God in her diary for her religion. "It is my rock of strength — it has never failed me yet — it never will."[30] Others — particularly those newly emigrated to the country — found special comfort in their religion in a strange and often uninviting land. Still others found in religion the route to collective action, for women frequently outnumbered men in their congregations, and saw themselves as the special carriers of the Christian message. Laura Haviland was a Quaker for whom religion led to a mission to former American slaves. In addition to aiding fugitive slaves to escape the United States, she set up a Christian Union church for blacks in the Puce River area of Canada West in the early 1850s.[31] Women were particularly active in the Social Gospel movement at the turn of the century, a movement devoted to the establishment of God's Kingdom on earth and thus to the reform of the temporal world. To work for social reform seemed to the women in the movement a logical extension of their maternal role. The Social Gospel also opened up new areas of endeavour for women. Beatrice Brigden in 1913 was hired by the Methodist church to work with girls, and became a travelling lecturer on sex, hygiene, and young women's social problems.[32]

Catholic women similarly found their roles expanding through their work in the church. Between 1851 and 1911 the number of nuns in the province of Quebec increased from 650, representing just over 1 percent of single women over the age of 20, to 13 579 or 9 percent. Through the church, nuns could find and maintain a status in society outside of marriage. After the 1890s laywomen as well found in the church more than a spiritual source of strength, as they joined with nuns to further Christian education or supported the social activism of the sisters.[33]

Although women were very active participants in organized religion, they were not necessarily unquestioning believers. Through the diaries and letters of some Canadian women we can glimpse a refusal to be told what to believe. Henriette Dessaulles, who grew up in the village of St. Hyacinthe in the 1870s, went to confession, but she learned to tell the priest only what she wanted him to know. And when he criticized her friendship with a young man, Henriette rejected his opinion out of hand. Henriette was also critical of the conformity to rules and formalized ritual that she found among the nuns at her convent school and in the church generally. Similarly, in 1910, Lucy Maud Montgomery made it clear that church attendance for her was part of a social ritual and a way of focusing on her own spiritual development. It did not signify acceptance of the formalized doctrine that her church espoused, even though she was engaged to be the wife of a minister.[34]

Women saw themselves as more than spiritual beings; they were physical beings as well. Victorian Canadians seldom discussed their bodies openly, but there are suggestions of what they thought. Privileged young women who had leisure to do so engaged in a variety of physical activities, and revelled in the opportunities they had for play. In their diaries they wrote about the pleasure they derived from walking, riding, playing hockey, curling, skating, dancing, and, at the end of the century, from the new craze of bicycling. In 1893 the Brampton *Conservator* felt the idea of a woman riding a bicycle was novel and important enough to report. Miss Lillie Roberts had "the proud distinction of being Brampton's first lady bicyclist," the paper noted. "The graceful appearance she presents while passing through the town on her wheel will no doubt lead others to take up the healthy pastime." For many women the bicycle represented increased mobility and independence. Predictably, some men disapproved, among them the trustees of the Toronto Public School Board when one of the city's teachers was seen riding in public.[35] Opportunities for team sports were also increasing. By the 1890s there were lawn

Field hockey, Manitoba, 1912.

tennis and curling championships for women, and in 1903 a women's rink from Quebec City defeated a men's curling team from the Royal Caledonian in Scotland.[36]

Nor were women averse to showing off their bodies. At mid-century the bustle accentuated the hips; then and later corsets not only emphasized the hips but the breasts as well. Yet the dictates of fashion could interfere with healthy activity. Increasingly, when dress interfered with what women wanted to do, it was altered. As women started to bicycle, play tennis, and swim, new and more comfortable fashions made their appearance. Bloomers or a divided skirt were worn for bicycling. The shirtwaist, a slightly more comfortable and plainer garment than the fitted bodice, reflected the impact of the working girl on the fashion industry. The shirtwaist had the additional advantage of being inexpensive because it required less measuring and sewing and could be mass-produced.

Victorian and Edwardian women rarely discussed their sexuality; when they did, it was usually to emphasize their own self-control. Control seemed necessary to most women who wrote on the subject, since it was women who paid the price of sexual pleasure in the fact of childbirth. Women gained moral stature and a certain amount of domestic power through affirming their sexual purity, and some were willing to carry that image into public life. They were particularly concerned about the fate of innocent young girls attracted to urban centres and susceptible to the sexual entreaties of immoral men. In 1894 the Ontario Woman's Christian Temperance Union threatened to publish the names of prostitutes' clients so that mothers could protect their daughters from such men. In 1911 the National Council of Women of Canada supported the case of Angelina Napolitano, who killed her husband because he had tried to force her to become a prostitute and give him her earnings. When she refused, he beat her so severely that she was admitted to hospital. The courts convicted him of assault, but when freed he once again tried to force her into prostitution, at which point Angelina murdered him.[37]

Many women felt they had the right to protect themselves and their daughters against sexual exploitation by unscrupulous men of this sort. Venereal disease was recognized as threatening prostitutes and, indirectly, all women. Indeed, the danger from venereal disease was very real and gradually became another topic that women were willing to discuss. Some physicians in the late nineteenth century estimated that 15 percent of gynecological disorders, including sterility, were the result of women contracting venereal disease from their husbands, who had acquired it before or outside of marriage.[38] Perhaps for this reason, the National Council of Women in 1917 urged "a Dominion campaign for the study and control of venereal diseases."[39]

Concern about the dangers of sexuality and the belief in the need for control over sexual feelings should not be equated with the non-existence of sexual feelings among Victorian women, however. Lucy Maud Montgomery poured out her feelings about an early love in her diary on April 8, 1898. Looking back on her passion for Herman Leard, a man with little education and few prospects, she recalled that she had loved him "with a wild, passionate, unreasoning love that dominated my entire being and possessed me like a flame — a love I could neither quell nor control — a love that in its intensity seemed little short of absolute madness. Madness! Yes!" But she controlled the madness for, as she concluded, Herman had been "impossible, viewed as a husband."[40] Montgomery eventually chose to marry someone she deemed more suitable and who, she believed, could provide her with the kind of home and family life she wanted.

With Montgomery, we come full circle to the centrality of marriage and family to Victorian Canadians. Montgomery tempered her own emotions and chose a marriage partner on the basis of practical realities. The vast majority of women, pioneer and working class women especially, must have had similar practical notions and probably took the idealization of their situation with a grain of salt. Certainly Alberta farm women seldom romanticized their positions as wives. When reflecting on their marriages later in life, they tended to focus on the economic nature of these partnerships. Bella Harris, a Cree whose parents arranged her marriage in 1913 when she was fifteen, recalled the event with a certain wry humour.

Your parents choose the guy you going to marry. You don't even know the man. Here comes your husband. I was fifteen. After the dance some people came to visit and they were having dinner. I was in the kitchen washing dishes and all at once I heard my mother say, "Oh yes, she'll marry him." And that's it. And I'm wondering who was going to marry who. And it was me they were talking about.[41]

As well, the idealization of home and family made a mockery of some women's lives. Women, looking at the realities that many of their sex faced, began to criticize society's unwillingness to support women's domestic role with something more concrete than rhetoric. The women's column of the *Grain Growers' Guide* in the early twentieth century chastised farmers who took advantage of their wives' good will and self-sacrifice. Labour papers and women's testimony before various government commissions spelled out the harsh conditions under which many married and single women in paid employment worked and lived. The domestic ideal depicted a woman with a man to protect her. But in Winnipeg in 1916, over 20 percent of women between the ages of 35 and 64 were single, widowed, or divorced.[42]

The ideal also had little to offer a woman like Mary Gorman, who never really had a chance to aspire to it. Born in 1858 in Ontario to a mother who was a prostitute, Mary had few advantages and certainly little if any chance to learn the codes of Victorian respectability. Arrested at the age of nine for being drunk and disorderly, she served thirty days at hard labour. By the age of ten she had been convicted at least three times and served more time at hard labour. From age ten to fourteen, she worked as a servant but was also convicted four more times. At the age of fourteen the gaol records listed her as a prostitute and noted that she was also illiterate.[43] For this young girl, the cult of domesticity was irrelevant; life in Victorian Canada was ugly and hard.

The quest for education

That Mary Gorman's illiteracy was noted was symptomatic of nineteenth century concern for education. Everywhere the socially concerned were promoting more regular and improved schooling for both sexes as a solution to many of the social ills of their time. Educators were another group that spoke at length about the differences between men and women, focussing on the kind of training appropriate to each.

Educational reformers believed that more systematic school attendance, in state-supported institutions designed to uplift as well as inform, had the potential to prevent the social, economic, and moral ruin of girls like Mary. The hope was that they would grow up to follow the ideals that men were putting forward for the women of their time. Governments worked to achieve the aims of educational reform by legislating free schooling and compulsory school attendance, along with programs designed to improve what went on in schools. By 1905 all provinces except Quebec had laws requiring young children (initially those between the ages of seven and twelve) to attend school for certain minimum periods. Although some families resisted, many parents saw the economic and social value of schooling, and were motivated to send their children to school more regularly and for longer periods. Attendance continued to be sporadic and geared to the requirements of the family rather than the school, but gradually more young people did attend classes for more months of the year and stayed in school for more years altogether. Canadian girls and boys typically spent almost 8 years in a classroom by 1911. Nevertheless, in the same year, only slightly over 44 percent of all fifteen-year-old girls were attending any school.[44]

Old patterns persisted, especially in rural areas. Many working class and immigrant families who needed their girls at home resorted to traditional practices, such as rotating school attendance among their daughters. Where young women had access to jobs, as they did in towns with textile mills or food-processing plants, working class girls tended to leave school early. Attendance also varied according to race, ethnicity, and class.[45] Immigrant children who came to Canada through organizations such as the Barnardo Homes were less likely to attend school than Canadian-born children. In 1896 a woman who migrated to southern Ontario through another child immigration agency, Annie Macpherson's House of Industry, was made an apprentice and evidently obtained no schooling whatever. She wrote back to the house, saying that she was ashamed of her poor writing.

The people you let take me and raise as their child they would not sent me to school and mistreat me . . . . I run away when I was 15 year old I wish I could see you.[46]

Beyond the common or elementary school level, access to education was uneven and varied. After mid-century there were still many small private schools for girls, and a number of grammar schools, academies, and colleges that either admitted girls or were designed for them alone. But in the co-educational institutions girls were often treated as second-class citizens. In the 1860s a debate developed in Ontario over the admission of girls to state-subsidized grammar schools, in the course of which the government declared that female students who were not studying the classics were only worth half the subsidy paid for male students.[47] By 1871 Ontario had a new system of secondary education that was more accessible to girls; but few secondary schools in any province were free and few parents could afford to subsidize the costs of their daughters' attendance even when they were. In all provinces the number of teacher training institutions increased, and so did the number of young women who attended them. These schools opened up to women the prospect of teaching jobs and, through teaching, the chance to save money to further their education in other fields. Still, the normal schools contributed to the doctrine of separate spheres in their unequal treatment of the sexes. In Toronto, a separate training institute was founded in the 1880s, chiefly for men who would go on to teach in the secondary schools.[48] In Quebec, all Roman Catholic teacher education continued to be segregated by gender.

Girls' academies, while often providing an excellent grounding in academic and cultural areas, varied in quality. Many saw their primary task to be the training of young ladies. Such goals did not necessarily negate good scholarly training, and the calendars of some of these colleges reveal a rigorous academic program. In 1883–84 the Dunham Ladies' College in Quebec required its honour students to take Latin, Latin Prose Composition, Greek Grammar, Geometry, History of Rome, Great Events of History, Logic, Rhetoric, First Principles of Natural Philosophy, Moral Philosophy, English Literature, Analysis of English Authors, French Literature, French Composition and Christian Evidences.[49] Many such schools seemed designed, however, to keep particular groups of girls apart from the less "respectable" parts of society. And the All Hallows School for Girls in Yale, British Columbia, which had once mixed its native and white students, was by 1891 advertising its strict separation of the two groups.[50]

In English Canada, public elementary schools initially appeared to make no distinction between the sexes as far as curriculum was concerned, but separate playgrounds, school entrances, and seating in classrooms proclaimed the message that boys and girls needed to be separate. In urban schools largely taught by female teachers labelled "assistants," the male principals and superintendents provided a message of masculine authority that was not lost on the children who attended. At the high school level, a further message was embedded in differing curricula for young men and young women. Only the former were encouraged to take the classics or the more advanced mathematics required for university entrance and the professions. When physical education was introduced, it was segregated, with the girls engaged in calisthenics and excluded from the rougher games of boys, while the latter were also given military drill. Finally, the latter years of the nineteenth century witnessed the beginning of a new educational campaign: the campaign to provide practical training in the schools for young men and women, in the form of domestic science for girls and manual training for boys.

There were at least two fundamental motives behind the domestic science movement. On the one hand, there was the problem of girls like Mary Gorman, who so clearly and tragically lacked any kind of schooling and who required some practical training. On the other hand, there was the housewife and mother, who increasingly laboured alone and could use trained help. Young girls were reluctant to choose domestic service if they could find paid work elsewhere; too often those who did go into service seemed poorly educated or socially unsuited to the work. Commentators offered two solutions to the servant shortage. One was to encourage the government of Canada to bring over immigrant women to replace the dwindling pool of Canadian-born domestics. The second and more innovative project was to improve the status of domestic work through domestic science education. Young women would be attracted to domestic service because the work would be considered educated, professional work. At the same time, those trained in domestic science would be properly prepared for their future roles and more capable of running their own households and families.

Needlework had always been taught in girls' schools. In Quebec the convent schools had been renowned since the seventeenth century for their teaching of fine embroidery and other kinds of needlework.[51] But the way in which sewing was taught began to change towards the end of the nineteenth century as the domestic science movement took hold. Teachers were now given detailed and often rigid instructions about the needlework lessons they were to teach. By the early twentieth century classes in the new subject of "domestic science" were formally established in most school systems, and cooking and nutrition were added to the subjects girls studied. By 1903 advanced training in domestic science was being provided at the Macdonald Institute in Guelph, Ontario, and Macdonald College in Ste. Anne de Bellevue near Montreal; later it was made available at the University of Toronto, and at McGill, Acadia, and Mount Allison universities. Although the expansion of domestic science classes was impressive, it was largely an urban phenomenon. In 1905–1906 fewer than 6 percent of the girls in elementary school took formal domestic science classes in Ontario cities; by 1920–1921 the figure had risen to 70 percent. In rural schools, however, it remained less than 7 percent.[52]

Obviously the courses were not popular with everyone. The supporters of domestic science education argued that with more young women entering the workforce, daughters would no longer learn household skills from their mothers, and had to be trained in scientific and hygienic ways. But these courses emphasized woman's domestic role to the exclusion of all others, and critics complained about their lack of intellectual content, as well as their remoteness from some girls' realities. Domestic science courses promoted the latest technology, technology that girls rarely found in their homes, and also subtly undermined the work women had traditionally done and the way students or their mothers still did it. The emphasis was on what women were doing wrong, not on what they were doing right. And as governments sponsored lectures and organized leaflet campaigns designed for adult learners, mature farm women and housewives joined schoolgirls as recipients of the messages of the domestic science movement. Many women were grateful that someone was taking enough interest in what they were doing to proffer advice, and they certainly enjoyed the excuse to meet and chat with other women. But their own wisdom and experience was often ignored. As one woman complained to the *Grain Growers' Guide* in 1916, such educational programs seemed designed "for very young schoolgirls." She had more than one question to ask. "Does this program speak to your head and intellect? Does this program give us a larger field than the usual 'women's yard'? Always suggestions about housework, knitting, and the main woman's destination 'preparing of dainty side-dishes and salads'. Kitchen, kitchen, and again kitchen!"[53]

The most vociferous and lengthy debate in education was over the question of women at university. When in 1875 Mount Allison University in New Brunswick granted a B.Sc. degree to Grace Annie Lockhart, it was the first university in the British empire to graduate a woman.[54] Acadia University in Nova Scotia soon followed. Other universities in the country were not as open to change, but eventually yielded to pressure as more women acquired the necessary entrance qualifications. Young women desperately wanted the chance to learn. Quebec's Maude Abbott, who eventually became a renowned doctor and medical researcher, wrote in her diary in 1884 about her "selfish" desire to go to school.

I do so long *to go. And here I go again, once begun dreaming of the possibilities and I become half daft over what I know will never come to pass. Oh, to think of studying with other girls! Think of learning German, Latin, and other languages in general. Think of the loveliness of thinking that it entirely depended on myself, whether I got on and that I had the advantages I have always longed for. . . .[55]*

Such women would not be denied, and their campaigns for advanced schooling initiated a wide-ranging discussion on woman's role in society and the kind of education she needed.

Some ridiculed the idea of the educated woman. In 1872 the *Christian Guardian* snidely remarked that "very intellectual women are seldom beautiful; their features, and particularly their foreheads, are more or less masculine."[56] Others were concerned about the more serious effects of educating women. Dominion statistician George Johnson announced that the decline in the birth rate was "due to the spread of education which enables females to become better wage earners and therefore less interested in marriage."[57] Johnson's perception was not inaccurate—about half of the 392 women who studied at Dalhousie University between 1885 and 1900 remained single, a high figure compared to the 10 percent of the whole population that did not marry.[58]

Most Canadians who wrote on the subject supported higher education for women, as long as women were educated separately and differently from men. But the question of separate facilities remained an issue of critical importance. Many feared that it was dangerous to educate young women and men in the same classrooms during the years when they were reaching sexual maturity. Although there were some attempts to found ladies' colleges, few succeeded in establishing themselves as university level institutions. One of the institutions that came closest to success in English Canada was Mount Saint Vincent Academy in Halifax. Established by the Sisters of Charity in 1873, it was recognized by the government in 1895 as a teacher-training school for the members of its order. By 1915 many of the teaching sisters had obtained advanced degrees, and the Academy, in association with Dalhousie University, was permitted to offer university level courses for a degree that the latter would confer.[59] In Quebec, the Sisters of the *Congrégation de Notre-Dame* also moved into higher education for women when they founded the *École de l'Enseignement Supérieure* (later the *Collège Marguerite Bourgeoys*) in 1908.[60]

Heavy costs prevented the development of other colleges for women; but heavy operating costs at the universities, along with a shortage of qualified male students, were also partly responsible for the fact that women were finally admitted to those once exclusively male halls of learning. The process of women's acceptance was slow, however. In the case of McGill, women's education began in 1857 when the new McGill Normal School admitted both men and women. In 1870 a meeting of Montreal citizens convened by the McGill Board of Governors unanimously adopted a resolution to extend university benefits to women as soon as possible, and the following year, the Ladies' Educational Association was formed to provide lectures for women and to look into the establishment of a women's college connected with the university. The founding of a high school for girls by the Protestant Board of School Commissioners in Montreal was a necessary first step. Girls at that school took exams that McGill considered matriculation or successful completion of high school, but they were still not permitted to enter the university. Only in 1884, when Donald Smith gave McGill a substantial sum earmarked for the higher education of women, did the university finally open its doors to them. Even then, the step was taken reluctantly, and for many years the university did all it could to educate

its women students, nicknamed "Donaldas," separately and differently from the men.[61]

St. Mary's Academy, 1890.

The three Rs, domestic science, art, music, and literature were generally accepted as appropriate subjects for women. Few objected to their training to be teachers or to be better wives and mothers. But opposition was acute to the idea of women entering the medical or law schools, for this suggested that women intended to be doctors and lawyers rather than wives and mothers.

Emily Howard Stowe, along with Jennie Trout, did most to break down the barriers to the entry of women into medicine in Canada. Born in 1831 in Norwich, Upper Canada, the eldest daughter of a Quaker family, Emily Howard was raised to believe in religious freedom and the equality of women. Like so many young women of her era, she began teaching school when she was fifteen. But like no others in her period that we know of, she also had the audacity to apply for admission to the University of Toronto. Her application rejected, Howard continued to teach and save money so she could attend the provincial Normal School in Toronto, from which she graduated in 1854 with a first class certificate. Armed with her certificate and no doubt, by this time, a reputation for her ability, Emily Howard captured a job as the principal of a Brantford elementary school, and thus became the first Canadian woman to hold such a position in the public school system. Two years later she married, and by 1863 she was the mother of a daughter and two

Ladies are reminded that the wearing of hats at lectures, &c., very much interferes with the comfort of those sitting behind. They are therefore politely re

McGill University, *circa* 1912.

sons. It was the illness of her husband, who contracted tuberculosis, that led to Emily Howard Stowe's decision to become a doctor. She returned to teaching to support her family and to earn the money she would require for further study. Again denied admission to the University of Toronto, this tenacious woman finally earned her degree from the New York Medical College for Women in 1867.[62]

This was not the end of Emily Stowe's battle. When she tried to establish a practice, she found herself at odds with the provincial requirement that all doctors obtain a licence from the College of Physicians and Surgeons of Ontario, which refused certification to doctors who had trained outside the province until they had first attended a series of lectures given by a provincial school of medicine, and then been examined by the College. The problem was that no medical school in Ontario yet admitted women. Finally, in the 1870s, Stowe was allowed to attend the necessary courses, but she refused to submit to the required examination and practised without a license until 1880, when she finally received provincial accreditation. Jennie Trout, who attended the courses with Stowe, did take the exams and so became the first licenced woman physician in Canada.

The first women admitted to Canadian medical schools did not necessarily have better experiences. When Elizabeth Smith and a handful of women colleagues attended medical lectures at Queen's in the 1882–83 session, some of the male medical students staged a revolt and threatened to transfer to another school. This and other hostile behaviour on the part of the professors as well as of the male students, took their toll. The women felt excluded. As Smith put it, her early medical school experience was like going through a "furnace fiery & severe."[63]

Similar resistance was encountered across the country, some universities refusing to admit women altogether, others denying their entry to particular faculties. Nevertheless, by 1900, 11 percent of college and university students in Canada were women, and by 1919–20 the percentage had risen to 13.9. The majority of women students were concentrated in the undergraduate faculties of arts and education, but some found their way into other faculties and a few even braved graduate study. In 1903 Emma Baker became the first woman to gain a Ph.D. in philosophy from a Canadian university when she graduated from the University of Toronto.[64]

Women (and men) who attended university were a tiny fraction of the total population. But despite their limited numbers and the fact that, for many, higher education for women was only accepted reluctantly and with a view to reinforcing women's traditional roles, the new graduates began to alter women's public image. Certainly there was now evidence that women could be the intellectual equals of men. Bigotted views could still be openly expressed, however. In Quebec a vice-rector at Laval University warned of the dangers of failing to measure out knowledge according to "the nature and scope" of young girls' minds, and of what would happen if women students were not immunized against "stupid pride or ambition." This cleric believed that higher education might easily be the means of launching such young women "on a disastrous course . . . no longer preparing them to be generous and devoted companions of man, but rather his inhibiting and, in all instances, misunderstood rivals." The news that the first graduate of the new *Congrégation de Notre-Dame* college for women had come first in the Quebec provincial examinations was deliberately kept quiet, as were similar "compromising incidents."[65]

Women proved in their university work that they were the intellectual equals of men. They also proved that educated women could marry and have children, even if they did so less frequently than other women. After all, half of Dalhousie's women graduates had in fact married. A university education also opened up new employment possibilities and careers to women. While a woman lawyer or doctor was still atypical in 1920, she was no longer an anomaly. The first generation of women graduates also had a sense that they were special. They formed long-lasting friendships with each other, and codified them through the formation of the Canadian Federation of University Women in 1919.

Childbearing and childrearing

Women graduates provided a new dimension to the concept of womanhood but did not change its underlying premises. Women continued to be seen in terms of their destinies as wives and mothers. Indeed, on one level, the world of women was remarkably stable: the majority of women married and had children. But on another level, women's family lives were dramatically altered. The timing of family events changed. The age when women experienced puberty was dropping in the western world — according to British studies, from about 16 to around 15.[66] Yet, despite the lengthening of the potential childbearing years, the fertility rate for legitimate births underwent a marked decline. In addition, fewer women in fact married; in Canada the percentage of single women between the ages of 45 and 49, which was 8.2 in 1851, rose to 11.1 by 1921.[67]

The number of children women bore varied according to region and ethnicity. The newly settled prairie provinces had a higher birth rate than the older provinces, and Quebec also maintained a high rate, although in the 1850s and 1860s Nova Scotia's was higher still. A study of the 1871 census has shown that throughout those parts of Canada where the census was taken, women of Scottish and French Canadian origin had higher marital fertility rates than women of Irish and German backgrounds who, in turn, had higher rates than women of English origin.[68] Between 1900 and 1910, the birth rate of native people increased, but then began a slow decline.[69] The general decline in fertility rates was also a result of older women limiting the number of children they had, for women under 25 continued to have high rates.[70] The net result of declining fertility may be seen in the changing average size of completed families. Whereas in 1851 a woman who had come to the end of her childbearing years on average would have borne 7.02 children, by 1921 the average had dropped to 3.54.[71]

Wedding party, Nova Scotia.

Another important factor contributing to the declining birth rate

was the rising average age at marriage; later marriage shortened the total number of years that a woman might bear children, and also resulted in the by-passing of several years of potentially high fertility. In 1851 the average age at first marriage for women had been 23; by 1871 it was 25.4, and by 1891 it had risen to 26. The economic depression of the 1880s was a possible related cause.[72] Although the average age of first marriage for women declined again to 24.9 in 1911 and to 24.3 in 1921, it still remained higher than it had been at mid-century, reflecting both a cautious approach to the future and the increasing material aspirations that accompanied the expanding economy.[73]

Among some groups, delayed marriage was a deliberate strategy to limit family size. Some Canadians were also intentionally limiting the sizes of their families by using birth control. *Coitus interruptus* or withdrawal was probably the most widespread birth control method used during this period. But many others were also known. Advertisements in late nineteenth century newspapers attest to the use of condoms, which, when rubber was vulcanized at mid-century, became less expensive than they had been previously. Condoms were not deemed respectable, however, as they were associated with prostitution and the prevention of venereal disease. Abstinence from sexual intercourse was another method of birth control that couples practised. Women also shared information about how to prevent pregnancy through the use of herbs or the insertion of vaginal sponges or pessaries, often home-made. One recipe that a young woman actually passed on to her mother called for cocoa butter, tannic acid, and boric acid.[74] It has been suggested that the declining birth rate in other countries in this period could be construed as evidence of a kind of "domestic feminism," as married women achieved a greater measure of control over their bodies and over an important area of their lives through insistence on the use of birth control.[75] This may well have been true for some Canadian women.

Not all birth control methods were reliable, however, nor were all men co-operative. Women frequently faced unwanted pregnancies, and many continued to seek abortions. As with birth control, women's traditional knowledge included ways of inducing miscarriage using herbs. Among the Nuu-Chah-Nulth Amerindians of the west coast in the 1870s, women mashed the roots of "a three-leaved plant" in water and drank the infusion once or twice a day to induce abortion.[76] Elsewhere a variety of home remedies were known, although they were not necessarily effective or safe. These ranged from jumping off a hay wagon, taking excruciatingly hot baths, or drinking carbolic acid or a mixture of turpentine and sugar, to even more dangerous methods involving the insertion of instruments like scissors or knitting needles to bring on miscarriage. Scores of patent medicines were thinly disguised abortifacients, among them Dr. Holloway's Pills, which were advertised as designed to cure "female irregularities."[77] Throughout the period, women who could afford to also sought the services of abortionists.

Table 6.1 Average age at first marriage and sex ratios, 1851–1891

	Average age at marriage Men	Women	Number of men aged 20–49 per 100 women aged 17½–47½
1851			
Quebec	25.4	23.7	89.1
Ontario	26.7	22.4	103.7
1861			
Nova Scotia	28.8	26.8	85.2
Quebec	26.5	24.7	91.9
Ontario	27.2	23.9	97.5
1871			
Nova Scotia	29.4	26.6	87.0
New Brunswick	28.8	26.0	90.8
Quebec	26.9	25.3	86.0
Ontario	28.4	25.0	92.5
1881			
Prince Edward Island	30.1	26.9	88.1
Nova Scotia	29.8	25.9	89.0
New Brunswick	29.4	25.4	91.4
Quebec	26.7	24.9	87.5
Ontario	28.0	25.3	91.4
Manitoba	28.3	20.1	147.7
British Columbia	29.3	20.0	173.7
1891			
Prince Edward Island	31.1	27.9	89.6
Nova Scotia	30.1	26.4	92.0
New Brunswick	29.4	26.3	90.8
Quebec	27.5	25.3	89.1
Ontario	29.3	26.6	91.9
Manitoba	29.8	23.8	134.7
British Columbia	32.7	22.3	231.2

From: Ellen M. Thomas Gee, "Marriage in Nineteenth-Century Canada," *The Canadian Review of Sociology and Anthropology* 19, 3 (August 1982) 321.

While abortion before quickening had once been legal and had not been regarded by the society at large as a moral problem, the practice was increasingly condemned in the course of the nineteenth century. Gradually everywhere in the western world, moral and legal barriers were raised against it. Nativists of British origin worried about what they and other middle class moralists referred to as the "race suicide" of the Anglo-Saxon population. The logical outcome of such thinking was to condemn not just abortion but all methods of birth control. In 1892, Section 179 of the Criminal Code of Canada read:

Everyone is guilty of an indictable offense and liable to two years' imprisonment who knowingly, without lawful excuse or justification, offers to sell, advertises, publishes an advertisement of or has for sale or disposal any medicine, drug or article intended or represented as a means of preventing conception or causing abortion.[78]

This law remained unchanged until 1969.

But the birth rate continued to decline, particularly among the middle classes and in urban centres.[79] By 1921 the fertility of urban couples was approximately 20 percent lower than that of rural couples. Children were not as useful in the urban economy, where family costs were higher, as they were in the countryside. Child labour laws, compulsory education laws, and parents' changing attitudes to children all conspired to make large families seem impractical, if not irresponsible. And even farm families experienced pressures to limit their fertility as the future on the land, especially in older settled regions, seemed less promising than it had in the past.[80] The decline of the family as a unit of economic production accounts for the variation in fertility patterns by region. It was in Ontario that the rate plummeted most sharply; in Nova Scotia, the rate dropped between 1871 and 1891 when industrialization was first a major factor there. Elsewhere the decline came later; for cultural reasons, the decline was especially delayed in Quebec.

A further reason for declining family size was the more positive factor of declining mortality rates. Many couples still experienced the tragedy of children dying young. But by 1920 infant mortality had decreased significantly to approximately 102 deaths per thousand population, compared to 184 per thousand in 1851.[81] The decline in the birth rate predates, by at least a generation, the decline in infant mortality, however. Thus we know that the expectation that more children would live can only be part of the cause of family limitation. However, declining infant mortality did mean that fewer women would undergo the heartbreak of losing a child and living with the loss, as did one woman who, eight years after the death of her son, wrote in her diary: "Oh how I miss him yet — that dear sweet face — but God knows best and I am sure he is better off — But O I miss him all the time."[82]

A positive result for women of the decline in fertility was the reduced physical toll of childbearing, which in turn increased women's average life expectancy. However, childbirth still remained the single greatest cause of death among women of childbearing age, and puerperal infection continued to be common, despite the medical knowledge that it was preventable with the use of antiseptic techniques. In 1921 the Canadian maternal mortality rate was 4.7 per 1000 live births, a rate higher than that experienced in most other western countries.[83]

Physicians argued that their scientific expertise and access to medical technology justified their increasing control of childbirth, and made it safer. In 1874 the medical journal, *The Canadian Lancet*, explicitly called for women's gratitude to the male medical profession.

But if woman could only be made intimately acquainted with the truth, that the cultivation of obstetrics by men has been to their advantage by immense odds over what could have been expected of its continued practice by women, what a debt of gratitude would the sex be sensible of owing to man. . . .[84]

Many women accepted such arguments, believing that the scientific knowledge of doctors was more valuable than the experiential wisdom of midwives and grandmothers. Childbirth came to be regarded more as a medical than a natural phenomenon and as a matter for a woman and her physician, rather than for midwives, women friends, and families. Midwives continued to practise in remote regions and among some immigrant groups, but doctors were taking over childbirth in urban centres. Almost all births, however, still took place in the home. Only the unmarried or the very poor gave birth in hospitals, or lying-in homes, where infant mortality rates were shockingly high, although by the second decade of the twentieth century, medical authorities were beginning to persuade other women that hospitals were the safest places to give birth.

Childrearing began to change as well. For much of the nineteenth century there was typically a forty-year span between the birth of a woman's first child and the departure of the last one from home.[85] Smaller families did not alter this situation; the tendency for children to stay in the home longer and marry later initially meant little change in the number of years that women devoted to children at home. Now mothers coped with the newly defined period of "adolescence" in their children, as earlier puberty and later marriage resulted in young people who were sexually mature but still dependent. Native people had always recognized the significance of puberty with celebratory ritual.[86] But among other Canadians, the onset of puberty began to be seen as a "problem," as there was less work for the young to do, on the farm, in the home, and in the public labour force, and schooling extended longer into the teenage years.

At the end of their lives, many women faced widowhood. There was a great difference in life expectancy among people over sixty. At mid-century, men outlived women at this age level, but by the end of the century this trend was reversed. Some old age homes were built to cater to predominantly female paying customers. Poorer women most likely depended on their families to take care of them, perhaps in return for assistance with childcare. Otherwise they were dependent on charity or the poorhouse to look after them in their old age.[87]

Unfortunately we know very little about the situation of elderly women at the turn of the century. Perhaps this is because so much emphasis was placed on woman as mother, and when she stopped being mother, she was regarded as no longer significant.

What women experienced during this period, then, was an intensification of the role of motherhood. Books devoted to advising women on childcare as well as books for children proliferated. The number of children might be fewer, but the task of raising them became more complex. Where women had once seen raising children as part of the many things they did, it now seemed their most important responsibility, and one that, according to the prescriptive literature, belonged chiefly to them. The tensions produced by this new vision were multiple, but two were particularly important. Women were told that they bore the responsibility for their children's lives, but the reality was that more and more of their children's time was in fact controlled by schools. Women were to take responsibility for the young; but at the same time, their sphere was the separate one of the home. The public world, the world that affected all their children and in which their grown sons would have to spend their working lives, was controlled by men.

It was these realities that late nineteenth and early twentieth century women faced and turned to account as they began to demand a voice in the public realm. Many of them were already "voting with their wombs" as they recognized the complexities of childrearing in the new industrial age. Drawing on the powerful ideology of separate spheres and on a culture of womanhood that celebrated not only the home but the bonds between women, they now proclaimed that as mothers and the managers of families they had both the need and the right to play a role in influencing what went on in the world outside the home.

7 The "woman movement"

For Canada's women reformers, the impulse for social change often began with a personal experience. Letitia Youmans recalled how, as a child, she saw the rotting body of a local drunkard, "swarming with worms" after he had lain dead and unmissed for several days. "This was my first impressive temperance lesson," she wrote, "and I still look back to it with horror."[1] While not all women activists could recall such an early and telling awakening, like Youmans they could document a growing awareness of needs and problems in the society surrounding them. They coupled these concerns with a growing dissatisfaction with the constraints of their prescribed roles. And co-operation with and for other women became also an identification with shared problems.

As Canadian women organized to change society, they found it necessary to defend explicitly the goals they had always taken for granted; as their charitable and benevolent efforts expanded in scope and scale, becoming visible and effective, activists became the objects of public criticism and even abuse. The arguments they used in response were the basis of the "woman movement," incorporating the two perspectives that continue to be influential today. The first of these, and the most characteristic of Canadian feminism, was "maternal" or "social" feminism, based on woman's role as guardian of the home. Arguing that women had special experience and values that would be crucial to society, if society would only allow them free rein, women activists insisted on their responsibility to establish order and well-being, not just for their families, but for the country. Indeed, how could they care for their families unless conditions were improved in the country? And they came to believe that, unless women had the same political rights as men, and particularly the vote, society would never be reformed as they wanted.

At the same time, a version of feminist beliefs often called "equal rights" or "equity" feminism focussed more directly on arguments of simple justice. It was a viewpoint that stressed how much women resembled men, and how unjust it was that they should have fewer rights. As human beings, women were endowed with souls and abilities, but they were barred by custom and law from participating in public life. In such a context the vote became the symbol of citizenship. A number of women had the property qualifications that would have let them vote if they had been men. Yet assemblies of men, elected by other men, continued to decide what women might or might not do. It was infuriating, quite apart from noble ideals for reforming society. Amazingly, the vote was at that time a "radical" issue that respectable women hesitated to endorse, mainly because respectable, otherwise reasonable men, found the idea outrageous.[2]

While the arguments used by the women can be labelled, the women themselves cannot. Most accepted both feminist arguments, emphasizing one or the other as seemed most useful or appropriate, apparently without feeling any contradiction. Most of them would have been reluctant to adopt the term "feminist," which at that time meant a quite extreme degree of commitment to women's issues. They preferred instead to speak of what was then called the "woman movement"; in this all kinds and groups of women could co-operate.

The "woman movement" was not unique to Canada. Similar ideas and reform movements were present in other western societies. Leading feminists toured each other's countries and read each other's publications, and there is evidence of considerable cross-fertilization.[3] However, the development of the women's movement in Canada was distinctive in a number of ways. Tactics involving deliberate flouting of the law were never used in Canada, and only a few of the Canadian leaders approved of the attacks on property and politicians organized by the British militants. The traditional methods of the disenfranchised — petitions, lobbying, publicity, and private efforts at influence — remained their preferred weapons. Secondly, although a national umbrella organization, the National Council of Women of Canada, played a signficant role, the Canadian women's movement derived its success from the diversity and strength of many organizations rather than from a single unified or national force. Finally, in Canada, winning the franchise did not become the obsessive goal it did in some other countries.

The politics of womanhood

Given the power of religion in their lives, it is not surprising that Protestant women reformers were active first in associations affiliated with the churches. These organizations were originally directed by the male governing bodies of the various denominations, but eventually some of them became truly independent. In the Maritimes, for example, evangelical Protestantism stimulated the growth of church societies with local women's auxiliaries. As the local Protestant churches joined together into larger national organizations, their proselytizing efforts expanded to include overseas missions in areas such as the West Indies, India, China, and Japan. The male-controlled missionary societies refused, however, to sponsor women missionaries. In Canso, Nova Scotia, Baptist women inspired by Hannah Norris formed the first separate female missionary society in 1870; similar local groups then grew rapidly. Norris was a teacher active among the poor; she learned the Micmacs' language in order to work with them. Converted as an adult and baptised in the cold waters of Canso harbour in March, 1869, she applied to go to "Burmah" as a missionary. When the Baptist Foreign Mission Board rejected her application, she turned to the women of the church, who established the first female fundraising society. Soon there were thirty-two Baptist Woman's Missionary Aid societies, and with their guarantee of financial support, Hannah Norris sailed for Burma, where she served for forty-two years, as well as marrying and raising three children.[4]

The women's missionary societies grew rapidly and were successful in all the Protestant denominations. Although Baptists comprised a smaller percentage of the population in Quebec and Ontario than they did in the Maritimes, a Baptist board was formed for these provinces in 1876. And by 1885 there were 123 Baptist Woman's Missionary Aid societies in small towns and villages across the Maritimes, operating under a central regional board after 1884. Presbyterian women in Quebec established a Ladies' Auxiliary (1864), which became the Ladies' French Evangelization Society (1875), and then in 1882 became part of the Montreal Woman's Missionary Society for Home, French and Foreign Work. The Presbyterian Woman's Foreign Missionary Society, with a Western Division for Ontario, Quebec, and the western provinces and an Eastern Division for the Maritimes, was established in 1876. As for Methodist women, they created a similar association in 1881. The Anglican women's efforts were the last to get underway, starting in 1885, when seven women approached the Domestic and Foreign Missionary Society to offer the services of women as an auxiliary. The Anglican women were unable to get independence from their general missionary society until 1911.[5]

Women's roles in the new societies differed significantly from their earlier ones in church auxiliaries. They now raised funds for their own organizations, which they controlled. The amount of money raised was truly remarkable, considering that most of it came from women themselves through weekly pledges, special collections, donations, and the sale of literature and reports. In 1899 Presbyterian women from the Western Division collected no less than $45 513 from 21 000 members; in 1900 Baptist women collected $10 000 in the Maritimes alone; in 1901 Methodist women raised over $50 000.[6] With this money the societies supported female missionaries throughout the world, and by 1899 the Western Division of the Presbyterian Woman's Foreign Missionary Society was supporting seventeen women in India and four in China. Many of the early women missionaries trained as teachers or doctors specifically for this work; one of the first three women who graduated from the Kingston Women's Medical College, Dr. Elizabeth Beatty, went to India under the sponsorship of the Presbyterian Woman's Foreign Missionary Society.[7]

Female missionaries were valuable because they had access to other women in cultures where the missions were established. In addition, not only did the women increase the overseas effort, they did so at no cost to the churches.[8] The missionary society women in practice challenged the men's control of important work both at home and abroad, but most women did not see themselves as part of a larger movement. Nevertheless, co-ordinating female missionary societies' activities provided many women with their first chance to develop leadership and administrative skills. Their societies were the first large-scale women's organizations in which women were able to act independently and to develop confidence in their own abilities.

Unlike the female missionary societies, the Woman's Christian Temperance Union (WCTU) was from the very start strongly identified with Canadian women's causes and concerns at home. It began as a women's group and closely guarded its independence from male intrusion, allowing men to be honorary members but not to vote. Yet there were similarities between the women's missionary and temperance movements. Both were deeply Christian and drew heavily on rural communities for their members; both provided a valuable training in public speaking and in parliamentary procedure. And both were crucial to the development of the women's movement in Canada.

Letitia Youmans founded the first Canadian local of the WCTU in Picton, Ontario, in 1874. Although a women's temperance society called the Ladies' Prohibition League was established early the same year in Owen Sound, Ontario, by Mrs. R. J. Doyle, Youmans is rightly regarded as the pioneer organizer of Canadian women's temperance activities. A former ladies' academy teacher who, at the age of twenty-three, married a widower with eight children, Youmans was inspired to form the Picton local after attending the founding meeting of the American WCTU. As a Methodist Sunday School teacher, she had been horrified by the harm caused by alcohol among her students' families, and in response started a non-denominational temperance group for children. Youmans then progressed from local community involvement to leadership at the provincial and national level, eventually becoming first president of both the Ontario and the Dominion Unions (in 1877 and 1883 respectively).[9]

Letitia Youmans was one of a number of Canadian women activists to have a considerable international reputation. She was prominent in the world WCTU, whose founder, Frances Willard, wrote of how the Canadian woman had been "loved and honored" in the United States as well as Canada, and how her powerful voice "electrified . . . her American sisters."[10] It obviously electrified Canadians also, for by 1891 there were over nine thousand members of WCTU locals in Canada. While Ontario claimed the largest number of paid members — over 4000 — British Columbian women participated to the greatest extent in proportion to the female population in that province.[11]

At its beginning stages, the WCTU focussed on the evils associated with alcohol consumption. Members were convinced that government intervention was necessary: only complete prohibition could save society from crime, family breakdown, political corruption, and immorality. For WCTU women, the beliefs and the cause they espoused grew out of their roles as wives and mothers, and their acknowledged responsibility as women to protect the family from the results of male intemperance. Most members had seen the tragic results of drunkenness, even if less horrific than Letitia Youmans' tale of a maggot-infested corpse; Youmans herself recounted many, more commonplace episodes of family disruption and domestic violence. Practical concern for the victimized wives and children led the organization to a truly radical departure from women's traditional charity to the needy. WCTU members believed they had identified the cause of want and disorder, and they hoped to eradicate misery at its source. Gradually, the organization enlarged its analysis to advocate a wide variety of reforms.

Until the 1890s the WCTU directed its energies towards membership recruitment, individual temperance pledges, and petitions to various levels of government to adopt prohibition. These were formidable tasks. Thousands of signatures are witness to the endless hours of trudging from door to door. Attending and addressing public meetings was also a triumph for many women, who faced audiences

A typical family temperance pledge.

unaccustomed and frequently hostile to the idea of women speaking in public. The members of the Picton WCTU were typical as they presented their first prohibition petition to the all-male town council. Fearing that their appearance would be regarded as "bold . . . and unwomanly," they met and prayed before entering the council chamber "with palpitating hearts." When the mayor insisted that the ladies should defend their own petition instead of having a Council member do so, they "looked at each other in blank despair." But Letitia Youmans rose to the challenge and aroused the room with an account of "the suffering families, the freezing in the snow-drift under the influence of drink, and the amputations resulting therefrom."[12]

WCTU members also sought to have temperance teaching and materials used in both Sunday and public schools, and tried to influence doctors to cease prescribing liquor as medicine. Gradually, as all these activities proved unfruitful, the Union became convinced that the major obstacle to the achievement of its goal was the political powerlessness of women.[13] This conviction was increasingly shared by other women activists, some of whom focussed more directly on women's rights.

The quest for political power

In the years 1852 to 1857, three groups of women petitioned the legislature of Canada West, requesting the passage of a married women's property act giving them some degree of freedom from control by their husbands. These are the first records we know of women going to the legislature on behalf of their own rights. Anne Macdonald "and other ladies" made the appeal in 1852, Elizabeth L. Hawley "and others" petitioned in 1856, and Elizabeth Dunlop "and others" did the same the next year. We know little about the petitioners, though Elizabeth Dunlop, at least, was apparently active in women's issues; her name appears on the list of prominent women attempting to incorporate the Toronto Magdalen Asylum and Industrial House of Refuge in 1858, to provide assistance to prostitutes and unmarried mothers.[14] These sources show that by the 1850s some Canadian women were concerned about their economic dependence and had organized to seek remedies. And they seem to have produced results. The 1856 petition had asked for legislation like that in New York State. In 1859 an Upper Canadian law without any British precedent permitted married women to own property. Although a wife could not sell it, her consent was now required if the husband wished to make the sale. There seems to have been concern for cases where drunken or improvident husbands would dispose of women's earnings, savings, or other assets, and the Women's Rights petition supporting the measure noted specifically "the injury sustained by women of the lower classes" whom common law deprived "of all pecuniary resources."[15] The drafts of the law even included permission for married women to retain their earnings. But a more moderate version was passed, and judicial interpretations tended, in practice, to restrict women's right to manage or get benefits from their property.[16] In 1872 an Ontario statute—this time following a previous British one—gave married women control over their own earnings.

At approximately the same time as the earliest known groups of women were presenting petitions relating to married women's property, there is the first evidence of public interest in women's rights. The Toronto *Provincial Freeman* reported in 1855 that Lucy Stone, the well-known feminist, "held forth to crowded audiences on the subject of 'WOMAN'S RIGHTS'." Editor Mary Ann Shadd was encouraged that "in Toronto, with the strong attachment to antiquated notions respecting woman and her sphere, so prevalent, she was listened to patiently, applauded abundantly, and patronized extensively."[17] In 1871 Susan B. Anthony, the American suffragist, gave a series of lectures to enthusiastic Victoria audiences. She "thundered out, night after night" that the local women were "meek, milk and water and had no rights of their own."[18] Although there is no record of a British Columbia woman's suffrage organization during the 1870s, a bill supporting the provincial vote for women was introduced into the provincial legislature in 1872. It received the support of only two members. British Columbia women property holders did receive the municipal franchise in 1873, however, the first women in Canada to be granted the right to vote. Moreover, the right was given to both married and unmarried women. In January, 1875, three eligible women, organized by the doughty widow Silvestria Theodora Smith, actually voted in the municipal election in spite of "jibes and catcalls."[19]

Only in 1876, it seems, was an organization formed explicitly to address women's lack of access to the political process. A small group of women founded the Toronto Women's Literary Club, whose name and subsequent history suggest that the founders felt the need to disguise its major political objectives. Discussions of educational, social, political, and economic issues, however, supported the conviction that little could be done to advance women's status—literary or otherwise—until they acquired the vote. The dynamic leader of the Toronto Women's Literary Club, Dr. Emily Howard Stowe, had confronted women's exclusion from the public realm in her own struggles to enter the medical profession. Along with her fellow Literary Club members, she was concerned about women's educational and professional rights, the inadequate protection of women in the work place, married women's property rights, and the need to acquire the vote. The Club facilitated the discussion of these topics; although small, it became an important catalyst for reform. Its educational program was enhanced in 1881 when one of its members, the witty and urbane Sarah Curzon, became associate editor of *Canada Citizen*, a weekly temperance newspaper, and started a regular column outlining the Club's activities and urging the adoption of woman suffrage.[20]

The Club's members must have been pleased when, in 1882, an

Ontario law gave the right to vote on municipal by-laws to spinsters and widows with the requisite property qualifications, even though the full municipal franchise and the eligibility to hold office were still denied to women. In spite of, or perhaps because of, the partial character of this victory, the Literary Club discarded its disguise and publicly proclaimed the suffrage cause, adopting the following motion on the 1st of February 1883:

That in view of the end for which the Toronto Women's Literary Club was formed, having been attained, viz., to foster a general and living public sentiment in favor of women suffrage, this Club hereby disband, to form a Canadian Woman Suffrage Association.[21]

To implement this motion, a quite remarkable turnout of 130 men and women attended a meeting in the Toronto City Council Chamber and agreed to organize the Canadian Women's Suffrage Association, as well as a Toronto local named the Toronto Women's Suffrage Association; both endorsed equal suffrage as their major aim.

The next two years, which saw no progress in respect to the vote, nevertheless saw additional gains in Ontario in the quest for legal equality with men. Women were admitted to the University of Toronto (1884), and medical colleges for women were established in both Toronto (1883) and Kingston (1883). In 1884 the full municipal franchise was extended to unmarried women with the appropriate property qualifications, although without the right to hold public office. Married women were once again excluded, although in that same year Ontario passed a Married Women's Property Act giving married women the right not only to own separate property but also to deal with it — rent or sell it — without their husbands' consent. In addition, married women were for the first time allowed to enter into contracts with respect to their separate property.[22] Although this Act was limited in its effect because few married women actually owned property, its provisions did substantially improve on existing rights. It was not until 1897 that the Ontario law was changed to permit a married woman to sign a contract whether or not she owned property, a provision that was a crucial condition of carrying on business independently.

On the Prairies, isolation, the sparseness of population, and the strenuous work of frontier homesteading and community building delayed the establishment of reform or feminist networks until the twentieth century. Nor did Quebec's French-speaking women succeed in establishing non-religious women's organizations before 1893. The major growth of women's activism took place, rather, within the Catholic church and the women's religious orders, which were growing vigorously by the second half of the nineteenth century. Old orders expanded and new ones were founded as French Canadian women confronted the social problems that Protestant women were tackling in their benevolent and missionary societies or through the WCTU. There is intriguing evidence that some nuns and laywomen fashioned feminist alliances to address the problems and inequities confronting women in Quebec society. But the primary responsibility for the care of the needy resided with the nuns, and their efforts in social and political reform always remained under the control of male-dominated church hierarchies.[23] Not suprisingly, convent women for the most part immersed themselves in the necessary social work rather than pressuring government to pass social reform legislation. The *religieuses* nevertheless did important innovative work; in Montreal, for example, the Grey Nuns organized and operated urban *salles d'asile* or daycare centres for the children of working women.[24]

Public service often led women to a deeper involvement in the political questions of the day. In 1885 the national WCTU formalized an effective nationwide structure. The reform impulse had generated other socially concerned groups; by the 1890s they too had been transformed into national organizations. An especially important example is the Young Women's Christian Association (YWCA), while the Girls' Friendly Society, an Anglican organization very like the YWCA, was also prominent at this time. Both provided reception centres, shelters, and educational programs for single working class women.[25] The varied objectives of these organizations capture the dynamism of the women's movement; together, they provided a range of opportunities for women wishing to expand their concerns beyond the home. Membership in such groups appealed to women at different stages of their life cycles. Those with young families and little free time tended to join local organizations focussed on issues affecting children. As their family responsibilities diminished, women involved themselves with broader issues at the provincial and national levels. Letitia Youmans, for instance, waited until all of her step-family was grown before becoming heavily involved in the public domain. But she was unusual in having not just the approval but the active support of her husband, who eventually accompanied her on temperance lecture tours.

The YWCA, the Girls' Friendly Society, the missionary societies, and the WCTU all adopted a maternal or social feminist stance, imbued with a strong sense of Christian morality. The WCTU was initially the only group espousing this philosophy that also articulated the demand for equal political rights to achieve its objective, and then only within certain locals. In Victoria, British Columbia, the local WCTU unsuccessfully petitioned for the provincial vote in 1883 and repeated the process with the same result in 1885. On the east coast the Nova Scotian WCTU locals succeeded in pressuring their legislators to introduce a municipal suffrage bill in 1884. The bill failed, but three years later unmarried women were at last granted the municipal franchise; New Brunswick women had obtained this right the previous year. These suffragist initiatives of WCTU locals were always tied to reform goals; the vote was not viewed as an end in itself but as a means for the improvement of society by legislating prohibition.

Indeed, pragmatism more than unquestioning adherence to any particular feminist philosophy guided most women activists.

Between 1884 and 1893, the Woman's Christian Temperance Union continued its educational program and intensified political activities through its national, provincial, and local organizations. In 1891 it formally endorsed woman suffrage at all levels of government. Repeated petitions, delegations to provincial and federal governments, and demands for plebiscites kept the question of votes for women before the public. This tireless work played a crucial role in bringing Canadians to accept the notion of political rights for women.

The Toronto-based Canadian Women's Suffrage Association, in the meantime, seems to have been relatively inactive in the second half of the 1880s, after a very energetic and effective first year. There are a number of possible explanations for this hiatus. Activists may have been temporarily satisfied with the real, though limited, gains that women had made. The leaders may well have felt the need to rest, to recharge their energies, and to plan future directions for the movement; Emily Stowe and her daughter Augusta Stowe-Gullen were both heavily involved in their professional lives at this time. In addition, according to Stowe, the presence of men sapped the organization of its vitality:

We admitted the opposite sex as members and the effect was demoralizing. The old idea of female dependence crept in and the ladies began to rely on the gentlemen rather than upon their own efforts.[26]

Whatever the reason for the lull, the Canadian Women's Suffrage Association entered into a renewed phase of activity in 1889. Meeting in Emily Stowe's home, members agreed to engage Dr. Anna Howard Shaw, the eloquent American suffragist and preacher, to address a Toronto public meeting. The enthusiasm generated by this event led to the creation of a renewed and more effective suffrage organization, the Dominion Women's Enfranchisement Association. Stowe was elected the group's first president.

Immediately after its founding, the Association took action, along with the Toronto WCTU, to support passage of a suffrage bill for Ontario sponsored by John Waters, a Liberal member of the provincial legislature. Waters had introduced suffrage proposals every year from 1885, some aimed at extending the municipal franchise to married women, others at giving the provincial vote to unmarried women; it was clear that his efforts needed organized support. But although Emily Stowe was described as addressing legislators "in a style that would have done justice to an Oxford lecturer," the bill was defeated; Stowe commented tartly that she wished Attorney-General Mowat, who had voted against woman suffrage, had been "less the politician and more the Christian."[27] During its first year, the Dominion Women's Enfranchisement Association also mounted a lecture series to educate and arouse public sympathy for its causes, bringing Dr. Shaw back and ending with a stirring presentation by

Susan B. Anthony. The success of this series convinced the Association that it could command broader support; it hired an American organizer to establish branch associations, and in 1890 it held its first national convention. A number of Canadian delegates from outside Ontario attended as well as several representatives of the American movement, but only a few branches were organized. The Dominion Women's Enfranchisement Assocation's national aspirations remained elusive. Like the earlier Canadian Women's Suffrage Association, it was Toronto-based, was directed and dominated by Toronto members, and never fully succeeded in the difficult task of organizing a nationwide suffrage group.[28]

The 1890s: consolidation

In the 1890s the women's movement continued to pursue other political goals. Toronto feminists celebrated a notable success in 1892 when three women won election to the Toronto School Board as trustees. Arguing that education was of particular interest to women because of their maternal role, movement activists had evidently persuaded a larger public that women should participate in school management. The right was of particular interest to women teachers, who felt that female trustees would understand their problems and work harder to improve their conditions of work. One of the first women trustees was Augusta Stowe-Gullen. As a young woman she had participated in the discussions of the Toronto Women's Literary Club; she later became the first woman doctor to graduate from a Canadian medical college and the first woman staff member of the recently established Toronto Woman's Medical College. A founding member of the Dominion Women's Enfranchisement Association, she followed her mother as its president in 1903.[29]

The 1890s witnessed a general broadening of women's reform aspirations and activities. The Dominion Women's Enfranchisement Association was one of the women's groups that supported Clara Brett Martin's arduous, successful struggle to become a lawyer. The 1892 Ontario statute permitting women to study and practice law in the province was the fruit of sisterly solidarity, now more than ever characteristic of the women's movement.

It was increasingly apparent that women's roles and status in society were undergoing a transformation, a transformation that, although uneven across the Dominion, was in evidence everywhere as Canada changed from a rural to an urban society. For city women, the problems associated with urban industrial development gave rise to a variety of new causes. Women reformers responded to the problems of immigrant women and founded hostels for them; housekeeping and health standards became an issue; conditions in jails and prisons developed into another. Nor did temperance and suffrage cease to be important issues. Rather, they became the central foci for a variety of concerns emphasizing woman's role as protector of the home. As Canadian women approached the end of the century, they asserted their right and responsibility to be "housekeepers" of the public realm.

The flowering of reform interest led, in 1893, to the establishment of the National Council of Women of Canada (NCWC), an umbrella group of representatives from national women's organizations. Affiliated Local Councils of Women served as umbrella groups for organizations operating within their communities, usually including branches of national women's groups like the YWCA, and local societies such as women teachers' associations. The Council's major objective was to encourage and support the extension of women's domestic roles into the larger society, as its constitution made clear:

We, Women of Canada, sincerely believing that the best good of our homes and nation will be advanced by our own greater unity of thought, sympathy, and purpose, and that an organized movement of women will best conserve the greatest good of the Family and State, do hereby band ourselves together to further the application of the Golden Rule to society, custom and law.[30]

The founder of Canada's National Council was the indefatigable Lady Ishbel Marjoribanks Gordon, Countess of Aberdeen. Lady Aberdeen was elected president of the International Council of Women during its Congress at the Chicago World's Fair in 1893. She was an enthusiastic and energetic supporter of reform causes, and her work on behalf of British women and children was well known to many Canadian women reformers. She first visited Canada with her husband in 1890 and helped found the Aberdeen Association to provide reading materials for isolated settlers. She came to

Inside the Ottawa Home for Friendless Women, 1895.

Canada for a longer stay when her husband was appointed governor-general in 1893. Another of Lady Aberdeen's initiatives, the Victorian Order of Nurses, was established in 1897 to provide visiting nurses for areas not served by trained medical help. Lady Aberdeen held the dual presidency of the Canadian and International Councils of Women until her husband's tour of duty in Canada ended in 1898. Devoting both time and money to the National Council's development, she remained a staunch supporter of its activities until the 1920s.[31]

Local Councils of Women spread rapidly across the country, aided no doubt by the prestige of its formidable founder, but also by the Council's intention to be non-partisan and non-sectarian. Aware of the potential divisiveness of political and religious differences, Lady Aberdeen got agreement at the outset that Canada's National Council would avoid activities or positions that allied it with any particular creed or political organization. Although personally sympathetic to woman suffrage, she refrained from publicly endorsing it so as not to alienate more conservative women. Largely through her influence, the National Council also adopted silent instead of spoken prayer in the hope of attracting Catholic, Jewish, and other non-Protestant women's groups while still remaining acceptable in an overwhelmingly Protestant society.

The non-denominational stance of the National Council, however, lost it the support of the WCTU, the largest and the only effective nationally organized women's reform association at the time. Although the Woman's Christian Temperance Union was non-denominational, its members believed that their Union and its causes

Lady Aberdeen and a farm woman, Manitoba, 1890.

were essentially Christian, as their name stated. For them, silent prayer was an unacceptable denial of the need for an explicit religious commitment. The Dominion WCTU consequently refused to affiliate with the newly formed National Council, as did other Christian women's associations including the National YWCA.[32] As it turned out, the National YWCA eventually affiliated in 1914 and the Dominion WCTU in 1921; some local branches of the YWCA joined Local Councils of Women even earlier. The early hostility between the Dominion WCTU and the National Council reflected in part the different origins of the two groups' leaders: the WCTU tended to draw on small communities and the middle or lower middle class; the urban National Council was led by upper middle class women. Lady Aberdeen herself disapproved of some aspects of the WCTU, noting acidly in her journal, "They train their younger women to be so painfully aggressive and self-asserting on all matters & on all occasions. They are essentially *American*."[33]

Although the National Council had difficulty encompassing all women's groups, its organizational structure did create a nation-wide network for organized women's activities. Within six years of its founding, seven Dominion-wide societies affiliated: the Victorian Order of Nurses, the Girls' Friendly Society, the Dominion Women's Enfranchisement Association, the Dominion Order of King's Daughters, the Lady Aberdeen Association for Distribution of Literature to Settlers in the West, the Women's Art Association of Canada, and the National Home Reading Union. Also, within six years, twenty-three Local Councils were set up in cities from Charlottetown to Victoria. Once the basic structure was in place, local and national resolutions determined Council programs. Members discussed, studied, and recommended reforms relating to such diverse areas as dental and medical health, "pernicious" literature, truancy, prostitution, and the "white slave trade," the provision of recreational facilities, and immigration policy. In some instances they set up standing committees to examine a cluster of related concerns, as with the important committees on laws for the protection of women and children, and issues related to public health. The Council's approach reflected its basically Christian, upper middle class, and urban membership, but its programs, while cautious, nevertheless contained the seeds of significant reform.

For rural women, physical isolation created different sets of problems and responses to those of city women. At the same time, they too were affected by the changing commercial and industrial scene. Concern for their children, for themselves, and for other rural women, and a sense that rural problems also demanded political solutions, drew rural women into new organizations focussing on their own particular needs. As with many urban activists, it was often a personal experience or observation that prompted a reform response. Such was reportedly the case for Adelaide Hoodless, whose youngest child died as a result of drinking impure milk. Galvanized to action, she determined to eradicate this common cause of infant mortality. Working initially through the Hamilton, Ontario, Young Women's Christian Association, Hoodless concentrated on the need for educational programs dealing with nutrition and sanitation. She soon became an influential advocate of public school domestic science courses, pure milk legislation, and the public health movement. Already familiar with the activities of the Farmers' Institutes, a men's organization designed to improve agricultural practices, she told an audience of Wentworth County women that they too needed an organization to promote their interests; she proposed an affiliated institute to foster homecraft and educated motherhood. Spurred by this suggestion, the women established in February 1897 a separate, rather than an affiliated organization, the Women's Institute of Saltfleet (Stoney Creek). Its stated objectives were ambitious and optimistic, emphasizing the role of science in the home: "to promote that knowledge of household science which shall lead to the improvement in household architecture with special attention to home sanitation, to a better understanding of economics and hygienic value of foods and fuels, and to a more scientific care of children. . . ." Their goal was "raising the general standards of health of our people."[34]

Although Hoodless was made honorary president of this first Women's Institute, she did not become involved in its work, concentrating instead on promoting school-based domestic science. The Women's Institutes spread slowly at first, hampered by the problems of organization within isolated rural communities, and by the lack of money to hire qualified resource people. By 1900 there were only three branches. Convinced of the advantages to rural society, the Ontario provincial government offered assistance in organizing Women's Institutes, including cash subsidies for hiring lecturers and demonstrators to teach courses in hygiene, nutrition, cooking, home nursing, and sewing. The response was overwhelming, and by 1903 there were fifty-two branches throughout the province, with a paid membership of 4151. As their popularity suggests, the Women's Institutes met important needs for rural women. They also played a significant role in the early development of continuing education for adults, as branches extended their initial concerns beyond the farm home itself, seeking to improve rural schools, introduce preventive health measures for children, and set up cultural programs for both men and women in their communities.[35]

Other women reformers shared the Women's Institutes' interest in improving household management and childrearing practices. The National Council of Women had already resolved in 1894 to lobby for domestic science courses in the schools, an initiative designed not only to further women's education as wives and mothers, but also to provide better trained domestics for those who could afford them.[36] Similarly, during the 1890s the Woman's Christian Temperance Union expanded its plan for a "moral society" to include domestic science education and manual training.

All women's organizations of this period had an expanding and diverse range of reform interests. The WCTU, for instance, initiated "social purity" campaigns in the hope of ridding society of perceived evils such as prostitution and gambling, both of which all too often accompanied excessive drinking. Some carried such programs further, worrying about the effects of nude art or even of allowing young women and men to dance together in modern dances such as the waltz. Members urged mothers to protect their daughters from temptation for their own sake and in society's interest. By 1900 the WCTU boasted twenty-six different departments organized around separate issues but united in the belief that social reform could be achieved through female activism. Yet prohibition remained the primary goal. The federal government's refusal to enact temperance legislation prompted the WCTU to pursue its suffrage campaign with increased vigour.

The tactics of reform

Endorsement of suffrage as the means of achieving prohibition quickly became part of the platform of the Manitoba WCTU, organized in the early 1890s by a committed group of Winnipeg women. This innovative group, which included Dr. Amelia Yeomans, journalist E. Cora Hind, and Mrs. J.A. McClung, a temperance advocate who was the future mother-in-law of Nellie McClung, staged a "Mock Parliament" in 1893 with the women taking roles for and against suffrage. The event forcefully demonstrated the absurdity of much of the opposition to female suffrage and received favourable publicity in the local press, as did a similar 1896 Mock Parliament staged by the Dominion Women's Enfranchisement Association in co-operation with the Ontario WCTU. While these tactics did not result in legislation, they did serve to draw attention to the suffrage cause. In Manitoba the renewal of publicity, fired by WCTU disillusionment with the negative legislative response to a prohibition petition, led to the founding of the Manitoba Equal Franchise Club in 1894. The crucial factor in the founding of this, the first English-speaking suffrage organization west of Ontario, was the appointment of Yeomans as the provincial president of the Dominion Women's Enfranchisement Association. The Winnipeg-based club provided information and public education about women's political rights, although it cannot be described as exerting a lasting influence.[37]

The Icelandic community in Manitoba generated a more radical expression of pro-suffrage opinion. An Icelandic population was firmly established in the province by the 1890s, but it remained isolated from the Anglo-Saxon majority by its different language and culture. A major distinction between the two communities was the role and status of women. The cultural, economic, and political participation of Icelandic women drew not only on a solid community base, but also on a long tradition of equal rights for women. Determined to regain in Canada the status that they had enjoyed before emigrating, Icelandic women formed suffrage associations and

petitioned the legislature. Between 1898 and 1910 Margret Benedictsson and her husband Sigfus published a magazine called *Freyja*,
or *Woman*; its articles advocated political, social, legal, and economic
equality for women. Despite a concern for temperance shared with
anglophone women, and contacts with the Manitoba Equal Franchise Club, Icelandic feminists remained relatively separate from the
wider woman's movement. Certainly Benedictsson's outspoken
views on women's rights tended to set her apart from many suffrage
supporters. For their part, Anglo-Saxon women seem generally to
have been unwilling to accept immigrant women's initiatives, thereby
ensuring that the Canadian reform movement remained a middle
class phenomenon. They tended to exclude non-Anglo-Saxon and
working class women, although they were not necessarily unresponsive to their concerns.[38]

The difficulties of building a strong common front among women
of different economic and cultural backgrounds are further illustrated
in Quebec. However, while the mainstream Manitoba suffrage activists appear to have made little effort to communicate or co-operate
with Icelandic women, the very active Montreal Local Council of
Women initially consisted of both French and English women's
groups. It strongly supported suffrage from the outset. Local Council
women struggled valiantly, if largely unsuccessfully, to open the
professions and higher education to women, to effect urban reforms,
and to abolish legal discrimination against women. Eventually, however, the French women involved in the Montreal Local Council
came to realize that the Council's ideas and activities reflected British
Protestant values unacceptable to the vast majority of French Canadian Catholic women. Influenced also by the Catholic feminism then
developing in France, in 1907 Marie Gérin-Lajoie, Caroline Béique,
and Joséphine Marchand-Dandurand, all prominent leaders in French
Canadian society, founded an explicitly francophone, Catholic, and
separate organization. Organized along lines similar to the Montreal
Local Council of Women and often collaborating with it, the *Fédération Nationale Saint-Jean-Baptiste* linked the few existing French-
speaking laywomen's groups and established three areas of concern
— charity, education, and economics. Under the latter heading, the
association sought to improve the plight of working women, and
fostered the establishment of associations for store employees, factory
workers, office employees, servants, teachers, and business women.
These associations acted as mutual aid societies and provided members with religious support as well as technical and homemaking
courses. While the need for political rights was recognized by *fédération* members, and they encouraged women to exercise those municipal rights that they had obtained, escalating opposition by the
Catholic church inhibited full support for suffrage.[39]

The role of religion in relation to women's public activities was
also evident in the Maritime provinces. There Protestantism provided the major outlet for female energies; women perhaps felt less

need for involvement in reform causes, such as a major campaign for the vote, that would take them beyond the church.[40] Nevertheless, WCTU locals in Nova Scotia actively supported suffrage from their formation in the early 1880s through the mid-1890s. Leaders of the Halifax WCTU organized a Local Council of Women in 1893, which continued support for the cause. Their zeal and work for the franchise is shown by the annual doubling of pro-suffrage petition signatures from 3000 in 1893 to between 6000 and 7000 the next year, and over 12 000 names in 1895.[41] After 1895, interest in suffrage apparently waned in the midst of a wave of anti-feminist propaganda, much of it emanating from the Roman Catholic archbishop of Halifax. The evidence suggests that Halifax feminists did not abandon the suffrage question but avoided confrontation by making a pragmatic shift of emphasis to achievable social reform goals, such as the organization of a branch of the Victorian Order of Nurses. These tactics enabled the Halifax Local Council to attract support, and eventually, in 1910, when progress appeared more likely, once again to endorse suffrage.[42]

Suffrage was also a topic on the mind of a New Brunswick-born Acadian woman teaching in Nova Scotia. Between 1895 and 1898 Emilie Carrier LeBlanc, under the pseudonym of "Marichette," wrote a series of thirteen letters about the lives and aspirations of Acadian women to *L'Evangéline*, the major French Maritime newspaper. An avowed supporter of temperance and of women's education, in a February 1895 letter Marichette addressed the question of the female franchise, punning on the word "suffrage," to describe the "suffering" of Acadian women impatiently awaiting the suffrage. And in March she supported women's claim to vote by a witty and impertinent version of God's creation of Eve:

When He was making woman, He found Adam, "le boss" of all men, dozing with the sun shining on his belly, too lazy to work in his garden. He ripped out Adam's brain and took the best stuff out of it and made woman, who has saved man from disaster.

For Marichette, women were superior to men, and should have "worn the pants and governed the country."[43] Evidently her stance provoked *L'Evangéline's* readers, editors, or owners, for within two months the paper editorially opposed woman's suffrage and announced its intention not to publish favourable views from other writers on the question. However, owing to Marichette's popularity, the newspaper did continue to publish her letters, in spite of their controversial content.[44]

The only recorded separate women's suffrage association to exist in the Maritimes before the First World War, the Women's Enfranchisement Association of New Brunswick, was organized in 1894 and articulated equal rights arguments to advance its cause. The provincial WCTU remained the major pro-suffrage supporter, doing so from a social-feminist perspective focussing on women's special nurturing and domestic roles. These ideological differences prevented a close relationship between the two groups, while the Saint John Local Council of Women refused to support suffrage for any reason. The Women's Enfranchisement Association attempted to co-operate with both the Local Council, of which it was an affiliate, and the WCTU. Increasingly frustrated by the Council's unwillingness to endorse woman suffrage, the Association developed its own political agenda. Between 1899 and 1902, it expressed support for equal pay for equal work and argued the need for more collectivist approaches to social life, as well as for equality between men and women. The alienated Local Council responded by being outspokenly critical of such ideas at its 1902 annual meeting, precipitating the withdrawal of the Enfranchisement Association. The withdrawal, though only temporary, was nevertheless evidence of the way in which feminist forces could polarize. In Prince Edward Island, even women active in the WCTU showed little interest in the question of suffrage. By 1900 the province had already adopted prohibition; evidently less radical tactics had succeeded in achieving WCTU members' most cherished goal.[45] The situation in British Columbia was very different. There suffrage and temperance reform remained closely linked. Until the formation of the Political Equality League in 1910, the only formal voice petitioning and supporting bills in the cause of suffrage was that of the anti-liquor lobby. In this respect British Columbia resembled Manitoba and Ontario, where temperance women continued to be the primary suffrage agitators between 1896 and 1905.

As time went on, Canadian women demonstrated their distinct and separate ability to perceive and respond to social problems. Although disagreements existed between individual women and women's groups, a measure of unity was fashioned at the community, provincial, national, and even international levels. The WCTU, missionary societies of various denominations, and suffrage organizations affiliated formally or linked themselves informally with other organizations such as the YWCA, Women's Institutes, and NCWC, to take advantage of the power that comes with organization and to break down the isolation of women in their homes. Together they moulded a lobby committed to reform.

The work of enrolling members and developing organizations that dominated these years taught women the techniques of public speaking and pressure politics. Although the provincial and federal franchises had yet to be won, a number of other political efforts bore fruit. Women became eligible to be elected to school boards, and could vote in municipal elections in many jurisdictions. Between 1872 and 1907, Married Women's Property Acts were passed in all the common-law provinces except Alberta.[46] A married woman's personal property, including her earnings, were at last her own.

Laws were also passed to help deserted wives. In Newfoundland, legislation dated from 1872, and in 1888 Ontario followed suit, pegging assistance at $5 per week. Wives who left husbands because they were cruel or refused to support them were not eligible for the assistance, because they rather than the husbands had technically deserted. Still such laws were a beginning, and between 1900 and 1911, Manitoba, British Columbia, and Saskatchewan also passed laws designed to help women who had been abandoned by their husbands.

The legislation that women reformers lobbied for and won was designed to uphold the family and to protect women. In the context of the times and given the conditions that many working, married, or deserted women had to contend with, the laws constituted progress. They also showed that organized women could have an influence. Although the activist groups never represented all Canadian women, they nevertheless provided a resource for representation and sisterhood. There was a clear continuity of women's traditional interests in the new, wider view that they brought to problems concerning other women, children, the family, the church, and the community. And in that continuity reform-minded women found a respectable, acceptable rationale for their activities and for the expansion of their field of endeavour.

8 Marching into the twentieth century

The dawning of the new century stimulated many Canadians to assess formally and informally the country's past, present, and future. After half a century of collective endeavours, the time was propitious for Canadian women to reflect on their progress. Judging by sheer numbers and diversity of activities, women's organizations were a great success. Female reform groups representing a wide range of causes were thriving in urban and rural communities throughout the country. Alongside them existed a rich mosaic of women's cultural and artistic organizations dedicated to personal and communal improvement.

The progressive optimism voiced by many Canadians at the start of the new century was not shared by everyone. While some suffragists believed that the tide of public support and legislative debate on the vote had turned in their favour, and that female enfranchisement was imminent, others expressed concern about the rising anti-suffrage voice and the conservatism of provincial and federal legislators. Nevertheless, members of social and reform organizations could and did take great pride in the scope of their activities and achievements, and in the expansion of organizational activity among concerned women. Nowhere was this self-confidence more evident than in the National Council of Women of Canada and its written assessment of the roles and status of Canadian women produced for the Paris International Exposition in 1900.

This report, *Women of Canada: Their Life and Work*, was funded by the federal government, and was the first published national portrait of Canadian women.[1] As well as documenting women's status, roles, and condition, it also set an agenda for mainstream women's reform activities in the years to come. *Women of Canada*'s program for change was not stated in so many words; it was, rather, implied by the careful chronicling of achievements and remaining challenges. Introducing this survey of the organizations in which the Canadian woman "realizes the power of a corporate life," the compilers signalled their confidence in organized, activist women.[2] The book reviewed women's group activities and problems in the legal and political realms, the professions, in trades and industries, education, literature, the arts, the churches, charitable and reform work, and social life. As a comprehensive reflection of women's associational life in Canada, *Women of Canada* was less than perfect. Short sections were devoted to non-Anglo-Saxon immigrants and native women, but apart from a note by native poet Pauline Johnson, the volume did not provide them the opportunity to present their own personal or group perspectives. Nor was there any reference to labour unions, although the volume did refer to protective legislation for working women. What *Women of Canada* did provide were insights into the leadership and the themes that would dominate the mainstream Canadian women's movement in the next two decades.

The flowering of the woman's movement

The vast majority of organized women belonged to local groups, frequently developed by local women themselves and devoted to the improvement of the quality of community life. This was particularly so in the frontier areas of the nation. Mrs. McNeil of Leslieville, Alberta, is a case in point. When the McNeils arrived in Leslieville in 1907, most of the residents were preoccupied with homesteading. The determined Mrs. McNeil, convinced that her community needed an interdenominational church, set about organizing local women. The women held a series of community "bees" at which the menfolk constructed the building while the women did finishing work such as plastering and painting; the women also supplied the meals. When interest lagged at various stages of the construction, Mrs. McNeil rose to the occasion, one time mailing cards around and another posting a placard that read "WANTED — 1,000 men for a worthy cause! Payment — Virtue is its own reward." Mrs. McNeil got her church built and the women's group continued as a spiritual, educational, and money-raising force in the community.[3]

Women's auxiliaries, like the one in Leslieville, proliferated across the country and became the mainstays of many churches, schools, and other community activities. Depending on their denominational affiliation, the women called themselves sewing circles, ladies' aids, mothers' meetings or guilds. While designed to tend to the social and spiritual needs of their members, these groups also engaged in charitable work, and did much to advance the material circumstances of their communities. Native women in Split Lake, Manitoba, for example, formed an Anglican auxiliary in 1913 to supply equipment necessary for their church and to co-operate with other women's auxiliaries in local and international mission work.[4] In Nova Scotia, black women in a Halifax Baptist church constituted themselves informally in 1914 as the "Women at the Well," with the purpose of supporting education for their community through the development of an industrial and normal school. That work completed in 1917, they formally organized themselves into a Workers' Missionary Society to undertake other forms of social development.[5]

Already by 1900, clubs promoting social interests—the arts, handicrafts, drama, music, history—had been established in such great numbers as to occupy one-tenth of the 442 pages in *Women of Canada*. The founders in most cases had a particular interest or expertise in the arts and sought to extend their enjoyment and knowledge to other women in the community. A variety of cultural interests occupied Anna Leonowens during the decade she spent in Halifax. A former teacher in the court of Siam, whose story became the basis for Margaret Landon's book, *Anna and the King of Siam*, and later the musical *The King and I*, Leonowens organized a women's book club and a Shakespearean Society as well as playing a leadership role in the Local Council of Women.[6] By 1920 all the major centres and many of the smaller communities as well could boast a host of women's clubs devoted to the various arts and crafts.

In the first two decades of the new century, Canadian women became more active in their professional organizations. As they advanced in fields such as teaching, journalism, social work, and public health, and began to make advances in medicine and law, their involvement in the political reform movement also increased. Toronto female teachers, for example, formed a separate teachers' franchise club in 1909. Activity to gain the franchise also grew within the National and Local Councils of Women, and culminated with the National's endorsement of suffrage at its 1910 annual meeting. New and expanded suffrage undertakings, including visits by American and British suffrage leaders, also brought energy to the movement. The Dominion Women's Enfranchisement Association changed its name in 1907 to the Canadian Suffrage Association. One of the earliest groups to affiliate with it was the Icelandic Suffrage Association. In 1909, the Canadian Suffrage Association collaborated with the WCTU in a monster demonstration at the Ontario legislature. A vigorous group of new progressive and professional members were attracted to the cause, along with members of the Toronto Local Council of Women, most of whom were wives of the city's leading businessmen.[7]

A new unorthodox participant in the Toronto movement, Flora MacDonald Denison, quickly made her voice heard. Born in 1867, she spent her childhood and youth in impoverished circumstances brought on by her father's business losses, drunkenness, and unemployment. Although she taught for a short time, she eventually trained in a private commercial school and worked for a Toronto insurance company, later moving on to journalism in Detroit. There she met and married Howard Denison in 1892. After the birth of a son, the family returned to Toronto, where Flora Denison worked as a dressmaker, then as a "modiste" for Simpson's, and eventually opened her own dressmaking business. By 1898 Denison was also writing for *Saturday Night*, frequently drawing on her experiences and observations of the sweated needle-trades for her articles. In 1903 Denison met Emily Stowe, who introduced her to the Toronto women's movement and encouraged her to become actively involved in it. Within three years, Flora Denison held the post of secretary of the Dominion Women's Enfranchisement Association and was appointed the official Canadian delegate to attend the third World Conference of the International Woman Suffrage Alliance in Copenhagen. Denison increasingly expounded a widely democratic, egalitarian feminism, adopting a position that was intensely critical of capitalist society and orthodox Christianity, a position that most Canadian women found unacceptable.[8]

The majority within the small Canadian suffrage movement wanted to continue the cautious route of petitioning, issuing pamphlets, public speaking, and letter writing campaigns. They argued for restraint and the pursuit of other reforms in times of anti-suffrage hostility, moving towards more active pressure when the public sentiment seemed less hostile to female enfranchisement. Some of the new members, particularly Denison, increased tension by advocating more militant strategies for getting the vote. They were impressed by and sympathetic to the arguments, slogans, and strategies adopted by the Women's Social and Political Union founded in Manchester, England in 1903. Led by Emmeline Pankhurst and her daughters, Christabel and Sylvia, the "suffragettes," as they were eventually labelled, conducted a militant campaign for votes for women, heckling politicians, chaining themselves to fences, breaking shop windows, and resorting to arson. Like the majority of Canadian suffrage supporters, Flora MacDonald Denison initially rejected the tactics of the British suffragettes, labelling them "unwomanly" in a 1906 interview. However the International Woman Suffrage Alliance conference that same year, which she attended, changed her mind. Speaking on her return she explained:

I am inclined to think that the press has woefully exaggerated the behaviour of the women who are not lunatics or fanatics, but earnest women anxious and willing to sacrifice themselves that the race may be benefitted and moved nearer to an ideal civilization of cooperative brotherhood and sisterhood.[9]

Denison helped to arrange for Emmeline Pankhurst to speak in Toronto in 1909, and Denison's column in the *World* regularly and sympathetically reported the activities of the British suffragettes. In 1913, at the height of the Women's Social and Political Union campaign of violence, Denison changed the name of her column to "Stray Leaves from a Suffragette's Notebook," becoming one of the few Canadian women to identify herself publicly as a suffragette. The hostility engendered by Denison's open espousal of British militant suffragette tactics led to a split in the Toronto movement. In 1912 members of the Toronto Local Council of Women founded a separate franchise organization, the Equal Franchise League. Unlike Denison, this group of women did not argue for the vote as a natural right but rather as a means of achieving other necessary reforms. A letter in Denison's papers suggests that some may also have been uneasy with her working class background and connections.[10]

Hostilities and tensions among reformers were not new. A rift over ideological differences occurred in 1902 in New Brunswick between the Women's Enfranchisement Association and the Saint John Local Council of Women. Class, rural/urban, philosophic, and ethnic differences also worked against female unity. The influx of large numbers of non-Anglo-Saxon immigrants, especially after 1896, heightened nativist concerns. The larger families and higher birth rates of the newcomers encouraged xenophobia, as did immigrants' supposedly lenient attitudes towards alcohol and prostitution. Some women activists were strongly attracted to eugenics, which, at its most extreme, advocated selective breeding of the fittest and compulsory sterilization for those considered inferior.[11] Their aim was the "regeneration" of the "Anglo-Saxon" race, a cause that could only alienate those belonging to other groups.[12] Only a minority of reformers thoroughly supported eugenics; its premise that heredity determined all was contrary to the belief in social change. Most hoped that, through education and improvement of their social environment, immigrants' problems—or the "problem" of the immigrant—could be overcome.

Yet the overtly Anglo-Saxon and Christian identification of the majority of Canadian women's reform organizations clearly excluded women of other races, religions, and ethnic groups. These women most frequently identified with, and organized within their own cultural or racial settings, either separately or as auxiliaries to male associations. In Montreal, for example, black women began to meet informally in 1900 for mutual support and friendship, the first known example of organized black women's solidarity in that community. Although the census recorded only 191 Montreal blacks in 1901, by 1902 the women had formalized their organization as the Coloured Women's Club of Montreal.[13] The members recognized that social agencies in the city were not paying attention to the hardships and problems suffered by black families, especially by new arrivals from the West Indies. The Coloured Women's Club initiated a number of relief and benevolent services, providing warm clothing for newly arrived families, introducing them to the existing black community, and suggesting strategies to deal with discrimination.[14]

Rural/urban differences further divided female social reformers. The Winnipeg Political Equality League was founded in 1912 and subsequently renamed the Manitoba Political Equality League in 1913. Like its defunct predecessor, the Manitoba Equal Franchise Club, it did not attract many members among ethnic or rural women. Rather it appealed to urban Social Gospellers, who believed that the church should play a major role in eradicating the problems of cities, and saw women as an essential force for social and political reform. Progressive women's campaigns for temperance, social purity, improved public welfare, the franchise, and urban renewal meshed with the evangelical impetus to rid society of its imperfections.[15] Reformers were also joined by businessmen who supported a moral reform movement that would increase the respectability of their cities and so promote expansion and investment in them.[16]

The Manitoba Political Equality League's success in attracting male support and involvement is aptly illustrated in the Mock Parliament staged at the Regina Walker Theatre in Winnipeg in 1914. Men were not only well represented in the audience but participated in the entertainment itself. Presented the day after Manitoba Premier Roblin had rejected the suffrage petition of a women's delegation to the Legislative Assembly, the play was entitled "How the Vote Was Not Won." To the tremendous amusement of all, this Mock Parliament, like its two predecessors, forcefully exposed the sanctimonious and contradictory arguments used by male politicians to deny female suffrage. The curtain parted to reveal the women sitting at desks, posing as legislators receiving a deputation of vote-seeking men who were pushing a wheelbarrow full of petitions. The "Premier," the witty and well-known Nellie McClung, congratulated the men on their "splendid appearance," but told them that "man is made for something higher and better than voting":

Men were made to support families. What is a home without a bank account? . . . In this agricultural province, the man's place is the farm. Shall I call man away from the useful plow and harrow to talk loud on street corners about things which do not concern him! Politics unsettle men, and unsettled men mean unsettled bills — broken furniture, and broken vows — and divorce . . . . When you ask for the vote you are asking me to break up peaceful, happy homes — to wreck innocent lives. . . .

"It may be that I am old-fashioned," she concluded. "I may be wrong. After all, men may be human. Perhaps the time will come when men may vote with women." And she assured them solemnly that "The man who pays the grocer rules the world."[17] She was faithfully echoing the words and tone of Premier Roblin speaking to the suffragists the day before, and the crowd roared in recognition.

The public debate

The Mock Parliament was but one vehicle for the supporters of the suffrage cause to get across their message to the public. They, and their opponents, also expounded their views in lectures, sermons, books, magazines, and newspapers. One of the earliest and least known contributors to the debate was Ontario schoolmaster Donald McCaig, who published in the United States a yawn-inducing 241-page attempt to rebut John Stuart Mill's *On the Subjection of Women*.[18] Better known was the Toronto journalist and former academic Goldwin Smith. In an essay entitled "Woman Suffrage," Smith acknowledged that some women's reform work was a logical extension of their mothering role, but argued that the exercise of political rights was men's business and quite inappropriate for women. Woman's enfranchisement would, he suggested, lead to "national emasculation" and the disruption of home lives, as spouses supported different candidates and fought over politics. Smith, who prior to coming to Canada had resigned his Cornell University post in protest against that institution's decision to admit women, claimed that women did not need the vote. They already had equal access to education and equal opportunities in the professions.[19]

Some twenty years later, Canadian economist and humourist Stephen Leacock expressed his opposition to women's suffrage. He argued that woman's true and only role was motherhood, and society

VALENTINE GREETINGS

BACK TO THE "BACKGROUND"

Be careful, men, of the advocate
Of woman's rights in the single state.
If you marry one,
Your trouble's begun—
You'll count for less than half your weight!

THE CLUB WOMAN
'Mid a clatter of tea-cups and spoons
And an atmosphere suited for swoons.
The President hen
Rails at the men,
And talks of prisms and prunes.

Anti-feminist postcards
circulating in Canada, 1913.

should recognize and uphold women in this role. The problem was that society did not truly value or support women's work in the home or deal adequately with the visible fact of women's necessary dependency in a harsh and frequently uncaring world.

Women need not more freedom but less. Social policy should proceed from the fundamental truth that women are and must be dependent. If they cannot be looked after by an individual (a thing on which they took their chance in earlier days) they must be looked after by the State. To expect a woman, for example, if left by the death of her husband with young children without support, to maintain herself by her own efforts, is the most absurd mockery of freedom ever devised.[20]

Quebec anti-suffragists voiced their opposition to suffrage even more strongly. Alarmed by the threats to family life posed by industrialization and urbanization, Henri Bourassa, an outspoken French Canadian nationalist and founder of the influential Quebec newspaper, *Le Devoir*, condemned anything that drew women's attention from the home, including the vote.[21]

Male anti-suffrage writers were not alone in their views. Their theories and arguments were echoed across the country and struck a chord not only in the minds of anxious men, but in those of concerned women as well. Adelaide Hoodless was one of the women who were never persuaded that the vote was the answer to women's problems. She believed that women exerted their most effective influence on government through the education of their sons. Although she admitted a possible role for unmarried women in municipal affairs, the role of the married woman was essentially domestic. Proper training would reveal this to be true; "any girl or woman who has been brought face to face with the great truths presented through a properly graded course in domestic science or Home Economics in its wider interpretation," Hoodless felt sure, would never be found "in the ranks of the suffragettes."[22] French Canadian women who were against the franchise may have been influenced by nationalist writings to see women's suffrage as an Anglo-Saxon, foreign idea, inimical to the interests of their people.

On the other hand, supporters of the vote for women could be found in all provinces. In general, the progressive press was supportive, and in some cases ran separate women's columns addressing the need for improving women's status. The *Manitoba Free Press*, for example, devoted articles to these concerns from at least 1890 on. The existence of separate women's columns facilitated both the debate on women's issues and the emergence of women journalists, such as Francis Beynon and Isabel Graham and others, who were usually strong advocates of reform. Labour, farm, and socialist newspapers also provided a forum for discussing the unequal treatment of women. The *Grain Growers' Guide* actively promoted suffrage along with a host of other feminist reforms, including reformed dower law and improved homesteading, property, and guardianship rights for women.

Men in western Canada appear to have been especially sympathetic to the suffrage cause. Dissatisfaction with government policies towards farmers was strong, and female suffrage would have strengthened the farm vote: this motivation probably affected both men and women in the prairie provinces. It is possible also that western men were aware of the pioneering efforts of their spouses, regarding them

Finnish women in Northern Ontario march for voting rights.

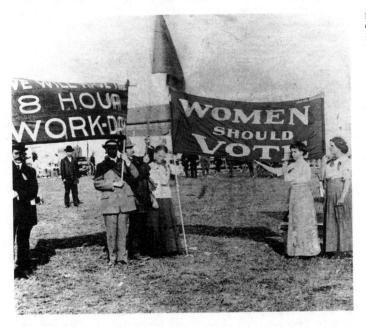

as equal partners entitled to the vote. However, some of these men adamantly opposed the granting of equal property rights to women, and it was in these areas that women lost their already meagre dower rights. It seems more likely that some men, at least, were responding to women's role as moral and spiritual guardians of the home, who would use the vote for reforms essential for the maintenance of a stable social order. Certainly this was the motivation of the supporters of temperance and, more widely, of the Social Gospellers.

The possible influence of the massive and relatively recent immigration into the prairie provinces should also be noted. The experience of resettlement may itself have played some liberating role, and so may the fact that a significant number of western settlers came from those American states where women had already won the vote. Finally, there is the less positive influence of nativism. There was growing prejudice against the non-Anglo-Saxon immigrants, accompanied by concern about purchase and manipulation of votes. Some were offended that illiterate "foreign" men could vote while rela- · tively well-educated women could not. They were convinced that foreign women, educated or not, would counterbalance their more easily corrupted spouses. But whatever their motivation, western rural men, individually and collectively through such organizations as the United Farmers of Alberta, the Saskatchewan Grain Growers' Association, and through newspapers like the *Grain Growers' Guide*, vigorously supported the suffragist efforts.[23]

For its part, organized labour was ambivalent in its support for suffrage. When it was supportive, it generally equated the franchise with workers' rights. Labour newspapers emphasized the need to increase the power of labour generally, and also hoped that working class women might help elect a labour government and bring about reforms that organized labour endorsed. Socialist writers discussed a variety of women's issues in the press. *Cotton's Weekly*, a socialist newspaper published in the eastern townships of Quebec, included columns in its first year (1908–1909) on the problems of working women, as well as on women's "emancipation" and the problems of women in the home. Its columns addressed prostitution, sexuality, and even "free love." The paper strongly supported suffrage, and advocated both socialist and feminist activism to bring it about. On the other hand, the Socialist Party of Canada and its newspaper, the *Western Clarion*, displayed considerable uncertainty regarding both suffrage and the "woman question," arguing that the task of replacing capitalism should take precedence over addressing women's issues.[24]

The publicity for the suffrage cause was heightened by the development of a separate women's press. Periodicals like Quebec's *Le Coin de Feu* and *Le Journal de Françoise*, the Icelandic women's paper *Freyja*, and British Columbia's *The Champion*, produced by and for women, devoted all of their pages to an examination of the major issues facing women. In addition, most of the women's organizations had papers, bulletins, or reports, which were widely distributed.

Suffragists Nellie McClung, Alice Jamieson and Emily Murphy.

Female supporters of suffrage continued to move easily between causes, all of them connected to their concern for reforming society. Nellie Letitia Mooney McClung worked for prohibition, factory laws for women, compulsory education, prison reform, and changes to the existing laws affecting women and children; it was to effect reforms in these areas that she and other feminists fought so hard to get the vote. A particularly vibrant personality, McClung has come to epitomize the first wave Canadian feminist movement.[25] Certainly she has become its best known advocate from the west. Born in Grey County, Ontario in 1873, McClung participated in the Ontario migration to the west, moving with her family to Manitoba in 1880, and later as an adult to Alberta and British Columbia. By the time she reached her forties McClung, the mother of five children, had become a best-selling novelist, and rip-roaring public speaker. Basing her approach on social feminism, McClung explained women's public role in terms of their special capacity as women. Addressing the argument that politics were too corrupt for women, she retorted:

What would you think of a man who would say to his wife: 'This house to which I am bringing you to live is very dirty and unsanitary, but I will not allow you — the dear wife whom I have sworn to protect — to touch it. It is too dirty for your precious little white hands! You must stay upstairs, dear. Of course the odor from below may come up to you, but use your smelling salts and think no evil. I do not hope to ever be able to clean it up, but certainly you must never think of trying.' . . . Women have cleaned up things since time began; and if women ever get into politics there will be a cleaning-out of pigeon-holes and forgotten corners, on which the dust of years has fallen, and the sound of the political carpet-beater will be heard in the land.[26]

McClung was similarly comfortable advocating women's right to participate equally with men in the political realm and frequently voiced the equal-rights appeal to plain justice:

We went there to the Manitoba Legislature asking for plain, common justice, an old fashioned square deal, and in reply to that we got hat-lifting. I feel that when a man offers hat-lifting when we ask for justice we should tell him to keep his hat right on. I will go further and say that we should tell him not only to keep his hat on but to pull it right down over his face.[27]

Nellie McClung saw no contradiction between arguments from women's special gifts and arguments from justice. Women and men were different but equal.

Working for legal change

The campaign for legal reform gained momentum in the second decade of the twentieth century. The laws relating to property continued to be a concern everywhere, but were particularly in need of reform in the prairie provinces, where women were still largely excluded from homesteading rights and, unprotected by dower laws, had no control over the disposal or use of family property. In addition, widows had no legal guarantee of inheritance. The first success came in 1910, partially through the efforts of writer and reformer Emily Murphy: Alberta legislators passed the Married Women's Relief Act, entitling a widow to receive through the courts something of her husband's estate if he had not adequately provided for her. Between 1910 and 1919, all three prairie provinces passed legislation guaranteeing wives' inheritance rights and restricting a husband's ability to sell or mortgage property without his wife's consent.[28]

The law governing homesteading was a harder nut to crack. The homestead act provided that all men, but only widows and women with dependents under the age of twenty-one, had the right to homestead, entitling them, when they met specified conditions, to free legal title to lands. The movement for reform to allow wives and unmarried women homestead rights began as sporadic, uncoordinated protests in a number of communities. The issue was eventually taken up by two influential activists, Georgina Binnie-Clark and Isabel Beaton Graham. Isabel Graham, who emigrated west from Ontario with her husband in 1885, was a founding member of the Winnipeg Women's Press Club, honorary secretary of that city's Women's Canadian Club, and women's editor of the *Grain Growers' Guide* from 1909 to 1911. Her November 1909 column featured a theoretical and practical discussion with Georgina Binnie-Clark on women's right to homestead. Binnie-Clark, a British journalist turned prairie wheat farmer, was the most prominent advocate of equality in homestead laws, and through her two books, *A Summer on the Canadian Prairie* and *Wheat and Woman*, the major publicist of this cause.[29] Although some western men supported the extension of homesteading rights to unmarried women and wives, the campaign for this reform encountered strong, highly organized and politically influential opposition. In 1912, for example, delegates to the annual meeting of the Saskatchewan Grain Growers' Association rejected a motion to extend homesteading privileges to women. The battle continued unresolved until the 1930s, when control of public lands passed from the federal to the provincial governments. Manitoba and Saskatchewan eliminated homestead rights for everyone; Alberta drew up its own legislation allowing "every person" who met specific conditions the right to obtain a homestead.

Important legal battles were also fought in the early twentieth century in British Columbia. Leaders such as Helen Gregory MacGill studied, discussed, and lobbied for improvements in family law affecting the lives of women. Born to an elite family in 1864 in Hamilton, Ontario, Helen Gregory graduated from Toronto's Trinity College with the degrees Bachelor of Music, Bachelor of Arts, and Master of Arts. She became a journalist, and while travelling across the Prairies met and married her first husband. Pregnant and with a broken leg, she continued to Japan on her own to complete a newspaper assignment. After her return she lived with her husband in San Francisco and subsequently Minnesota. When her husband died she was left to support two young sons and her mother. Two years later, Helen married lawyer James MacGill, and by 1901 they had settled in Vancouver. There, as she had in San Francisco and Minnesota, she involved herself in women's organizations, including the Women's Musical Club, the Vancouver Women's Press Club, and the Women's University Club. In working with and for other women, Helen Gregory MacGill followed a family tradition established by her mother and grandmother. Her daughter and biographer, Elsie MacGill, recalled:

In each new society [i.e. community] a compulsion forced her to work toward a particular goal of her own, the radix of the force being that disturbing thrust of intellect that had pushed her into Trinity, over to Japan, into writing, publishing, crusading.[30]

In British Columbia, that goal came to be the protection and improved status of women and children. In 1912, with the backing of the Vancouver University Women's Club, MacGill produced a booklet outlining the inequities women faced before the law. British Columbia became the first province to enact an equal guardianship and custody law in 1917, giving mothers the same rights as fathers with respect to their children. Later the same year the province established a juvenile court and appointed MacGill as one of its first two judges.

The plight of women workers was another focus of attention in British Columbia. Low wages, long hours, and miserable working conditions motivated suffrage and labour activist Helena Rose Gutteridge to work to unionize women and to demand improved conditions. This militant British suffragette, socialist, and Labour Party member arrived in Vancouver in 1911 and quickly immersed herself in reform activities. Gutteridge helped organize city laundry and garment workers, took a prominent role in the Vancouver Trades and Labour Council, and campaigned for the minimum wage for women as well as pensions for mothers left without other means of support. The passing of a 1918 law restricting hours of work for women was, in part, the result of her efforts. Similar campaigns to ameliorate women's working conditions were continuing in other provinces, and by 1920 a variety of further protective measures for female employees had been legislated in the Maritimes, Ontario, Quebec, and the Prairies.[31]

Hand in hand with British Columbian women's interest in legal and labour law reform went a renewed commitment to suffrage. From its founding in 1911, the provincial Political Equality League organized delegations, circulated petitions, and ran public meetings. It garnered support from various men's and women's organizations, including the British Columbia Federation of Labour, the Local Option League, the WCTU, and the provincial opposition Liberal Party, but could not unite all political rights reformers. After 1911 a variety of more radical but shortlived suffrage associations appeared in the province. One in particular, Gutteridge's British Columbia Woman's Suffrage League, objected to the Political Equality League's conservatism, its failure to involve working class women, and its use of exclusively maternalist arguments. The aims of Gutteridge's group extended beyond obtaining the vote to dealing "with all matters connected with the interests of women, particularly those things that affect women out in the labour market."[32]

While support for women's suffrage in British Columbia appeared to grow, women activists in the Maritime provinces continued to struggle against a current of strong anti-feminist sentiment. Although sporadic attempts to raise the franchise question continued to come from WCTU or Local Council women in all three provinces, the separate suffrage associations floundered. Internal division apparently crippled the cause in New Brunswick, where there is no evidence of activity by the Saint John Women's Enfranchisement Association between 1903 and 1907.[33] Revitalized in 1907, the Association began to work for the passage of a suffrage bill drawn up by one of its own members, Mabel French, New Brunswick's first female lawyer. In this effort and subsequent ones, the women met with increasingly overt mockery, insult, and even sexual harassment from some provincial legislators. The presence in 1909 of seven suffrage supporters at a hearing by the legislative Committee of the Whole on a bill to enfranchise unmarried women brought catcalls of "Help," and "Police," the ringing of the division bells, and open laughter at a coarse "verse" directed at the women. Despite this public abuse, the Local Council of Women and the Sons of Temperance endorsed suffrage in 1910, and a well-publicized visit to Saint John was made in 1912 by British suffragette Sylvia Pankhurst.

The same year saw the establishment of an Equal Franchise League in Moncton, and the publication by the Saint John *Globe* of a cogent letter to the editor, simultaneously rebuffing the abusive legislators and aggressively supporting equal political rights for women. The writer of the letter, Ella Hatheway, secretary-treasurer of the Women's Enfranchisement Association and wife of a sympathetic member of the legislature, recalled the appalling treatment of the 1909 delegation, of which she had been part, and outlined the similarly uncouth reaction she had encountered when an attempt was made to introduce a bill in 1912. Maintaining that women refused to be intimidated and would never abandon their just cause, she went on to outline her reasoning:

The woman suffrage movement, the world over, has broadened and intensified during the past year. In no way is this shown more than in the growing demand from women that they shall no longer be regarded by men as sex beings, but as human beings; that they shall be recognized, politically and economically, as persons, not as females merely.[34]

In Nova Scotia, the local newspapers' prominent coverage and condemnation of the growing violence of the suffragettes in England inhibited overt suffrage support. Following the defeat of the suffrage bills in the 1890s, the movement's leaders had made a pragmatic decision to pursue other reform work through the Local Council of Women until some later date when, as leader Eliza Ritchie put it, "the time was ripe" for a return to explicit suffrage activities.[35] Certainly there was plenty to be done, and the council members had used their time and energy to advocate and advance a number of reform programs. From 1908 they lobbied local and provincial authorities, and later the federal Royal Commission on Technical Education, for the establishment of a vocational school to train women for a variety of industrial occupations. Halifax Local Council women also engaged in a major public health campaign. They raised funds for the Victorian Order of Nurses through tag days, formed an anti-tuberculosis league, and educated the public about the causes and prevention of infant mortality. Through such activities they hoped to dispel public criticism of the women's movement, and particularly that coming from the city's Catholic clergy.[36]

The lack of separate suffrage organization and activity in Prince Edward Island during the first two decades of the twentieth century may have similarly stemmed from women's concentration on alternative reform work; or the winning of prohibition may have taken the wind out of the reformers' sails. The only documented motion in favour of the franchise was passed in 1913 at the regional WCTU convention in Summerside. Otherwise, women activists in Prince Edward Island appear to have maintained a discreet silence on the subject.[37]

Like their Maritimes sisters, Quebec's women activists experienced a severe anti-feminist backlash prior to the First World War. At the turn of the century French Canadian lay and clerical elites increasingly responded to urban industrial growth, social dislocation, growing Anglo-American influences, and new public initiatives by women with an aggressive, conservative nationalism. In their blue-print for a better society there was no place for the "new woman." Yet, in fact, concerned nationalists, the leaders of the Catholic church, and the emerging lay feminist organizations were all addressing, albeit in different ways, perceived threats to the social order and its basic unit, the French Canadian Catholic family. In some cases, they co-operated in social, charitable, and educational action, but with increasing frequency both lay nationalists and church leaders allied themselves against feminism in any form. French Canadian women's organizations nevertheless persevered.[38]

The founding of the *Fédération Nationale Saint-Jean-Baptiste* in 1907 provided francophone women's associations with a united voice and a public alliance with their sisters in the convents. Although the *fédération*'s feminism was not overt, it successfully co-ordinated Catholic women in their work to benefit society. Members' and affiliated groups' activities before the First World War were diverse. Some, for example, set up commercial, technical, and household science classes; others addressed the problems of factory women, establishing sickness and mutual aid funds, employment bureaus, and boardinghouses for working women. Partly as a direct result of *fédération* work, by 1914 Quebec women teachers' pensions had doubled, factory lighting had improved, pure milk depots or "*gouttes de lait*" had been established to reduce rampant infant mortality, and legislation passed making it mandatory to provide female store clerks with chairs. Perhaps the *fédération*'s greatest contribution, however, was in uniting with the Sisters of the *Congrégation de Notre-Dame* to achieve in 1908 the establishment of the *École d'enseignement supérieur pour les filles*, the first institution to offer higher education to Fran-cophone women.[39]

There was little explicit franchise activity in Quebec's Franco-phone community. It was the members of the Anglophone Montreal Local Council of Women who founded the Montreal Suffrage Asso-ciation in 1913. Their major efforts were educational, involving the distribution and sale of literature about suffrage and about the legal inequities affecting women.

War

By the outbreak of the First World War, Canadian women had organized around a remarkable number of social, political, cultural, and economic issues. Overlapping memberships in women's associ-ations were common, and female voluntary organizations frequently adopted and supported each others' causes. Involvement in specific social reform often seemed to lead individual women into a broad reform program.

Emily Murphy was an excellent example of this progression. The daughter of a well-to-do Ontario family, Murphy married a popular preacher. By 1910 she had settled with her husband in Edmonton and was beginning to find her niche as a journalist and popular novelist, known to her large public as "Janey Canuck." In addition to an active participation in the Canadian Women's Press Club, the effervescent Murphy lent her name, acumen, and energy to the cause of reform. She worked to establish a local Victorian Order of Nurses, police courts for female offenders, public playgrounds, and municipal hospitals, as well as the right for women to be elected as school trustees in Edmonton. Campaigns for a provincial dower law and tuberculosis prevention also occupied her attention, as did provincial and national drives for suffrage. During the war years she added to her list of activities the registration of female wartime volunteers, and participation in the War Council of Women.[40]

National commitment to the war effort provided many opportunities for individual and group endeavours. Spurred on by personal economic need as well as patriotic fervour, thousands of women entered the paid workforce, filling jobs vacated by enlisted men.[41] Others undertook a host of volunteer labours designed to aid the overseas campaign. They knitted socks, preserved foods, and salvaged clothing. Prominent Canadian women such as Lady Drummond, the first president of the Montreal Local Council of Women and widow of the president of the Bank of Montreal, offered their English homes as hospitals and created an Information Department of the Canadian Red Cross Society, which became the main channel of communication between the soldier and his family. They also established Maple Leaf clubs for soldiers on leave. Two Toronto women, Mary Plummer and Joan Arnoldi, formed the Canadian Field Comforts Commission to oversee the distribution of clothing and other supplies assembled by women throughout Canada to soldiers in England and on the Continent. Although many women worked separately, most joined existing, pro-British women's groups or reform organizations that adapted or enhanced their programs by emphasizing war service. Some suffragists persisted in their campaign, but established Suffragists' War Auxiliaries, which became involved in local recruitment drives and organized women to fill available jobs vacated by male service volunteers.[42] In some communities suffrage activists planned future suffrage campaigns during sessions for making soldier comforts and bandages for the Red Cross.

The visible, publicly acknowledged wartime work of women encouraged many reformers to press their more comprehensive demands. Despite the opposition of local employers, the Halifax Local Council of Women created a women's employment bureau in order to promote better industrial career training, occupational access and advancement.[43] A Canadian Patriotic Fund was set up through which women's groups could work together to provide financial help and advice for families of enlisted men, and, as the war went on, it became what can only be described as a national welfare service for them.[44] Reformers pointed to the example of the improved living conditions of soldiers' dependent wives and children achieved by the Fund, and lobbied for mothers' pensions, day nurseries, improved urban housing, and health inspection. Wartime inflation and deprivation revived interest in the economy and domestic consumption, and Household Leagues, formed just prior to the turn of the century and affiliated with the National Council of Women of Canada, became particularly visible in Victoria, Halifax, and northern Ontario. Members demanded government regulation of prices and quantity, the standardization of sizes in manufactured and canned goods, and the control of local food production and distribution. The Ottawa League investigated co-operative buying, while a similar association, the Calgary Consumers' League, put that idea into practice. Particularly concerned by high prices for the necessities of life in the fall and winter of 1914–15, the Calgary women brought carloads of flour and frozen fish into the city market, which they sold to members at substantial reductions. They also counteracted soaring fuel costs by arranging for discounted coal purchases.[45] Strategies such as these expanded in the later war years as the government launched thrift, food conservation, and "self-denial" campaigns. By 1917 the Quebec Housewives' League had 10 000 members, and other leagues had expanded on a similar scale.[46]

Wartime patriotism directly benefitted many of the established women's organizations by attracting new members. The National Council of Women, the YWCA, the Women's Institutes, and the Imperial Order Daughters of the Empire all experienced spectacular increases in membership. By 1915 the Women's Institutes had attracted 29 045 women to a total of 892 branches. During the First World War, the Institutes spread beyond the Canadian borders to England and eventually to other European countries.[47] The IODE's first chapters had been founded in 1900 in Fredericton and Montreal in response to the Boer War, and by the end of World War I it had become one of the nation's largest women's voluntary associations. In just three years, 1915–1917, IODE membership increased by 10 000, and nearly one hundred new chapters were formed. The IODE's primary purpose was to mobilize women and children to support the British empire, and to appreciate its history. During World War I the IODE founded Red Cross branches, organized the Canadian Women's Hospital Ship Fund, sent gifts to soldiers overseas, assisted in recruitment, badgered those who did not enlist, and organized material and emotional support for soldiers' families. By 1917 the Daughters had collected over $1.5 million to finance their efforts.[48] Although its members were concerned about women's problems, the IODE's pronounced patriotism and enthusiasm for things British occasionally put its members at odds with other women's organizations. They protested, for example, the National Council of Women of Canada's affiliation with the International Council of Women, which, they argued, also included "enemy" affiliates.[49]

Through their organized reform activities in the late nineteenth and early twentieth centuries, women had developed and refined the skills of organizing and fundraising. In the war years the government needed civilian assistance in drives to recruit men and to raise war funds, and found ready-made support in existing women's organizations. Prime Minister Borden estimated in 1916 that Canadian women had raised the immense sum of between $40 million and $50 million since the war began.[50] Women also responded when wartime disaster struck. The Halifax explosion of December 6, 1917, which destroyed over 2000 homes, killed 1600, and injured an additional 9000, activated the city's women and their organizations. Women from all walks of life participated in the rescue work under the leadership and initiative of prominent feminists and Local Council leaders. Leading women's movement activists such as May Sexton, Eliza Ritchie, and Agnes Dennis organized nursing care and co-ordinated the distribution of food and clothing.[51]

In a symbolic recognition of the huge range and intensity of women's voluntary and emergency efforts, a Women's War Conference, also known as the War Council of Women, was convened in 1918 at the request of the Cabinet War Committee. Conference resolutions ranged widely, covering the major unachieved reform platforms, including suffrage, that the National Council of Women of Canada, its affiliates and supporters had been espousing for over two decades.[52]

While the First World War had a positive effect on the image and prestige of organized Canadian women, it also accentuated old divisions and raised some new ones. In Winnipeg in 1918, the Local Council of Women, concerned about maintaining communications necessary to the war effort, acted as scab workers, replacing and undermining the cause of women telephone operators who were on strike.[53] Organized women also divided sharply on the issues of conscription and the Union government, which federal Liberals and Conservatives formed in 1917 to pursue the national war effort. In Saint John the refusal of Women's Enfranchisement Association members to endorse Prime Minister Borden's Union government sparked the resignations of its president and vice-president.[54]

It was perhaps involvement in the war in the first place that presented the greatest challenge to female reformers. Central to the ideology of feminism lay a strong condemnation of violence, associated with men and male power. The Maritimes WCTU had been involved in the 1890s, for example, in a campaign for peace through international arbitration.[55] Flora MacDonald Denison was among the prominent women reformers who had written on the subject in the years before the war. Her *War and Women*, published by the Canadian Suffrage Association in 1914, blamed militarism on the domination of public life by men.[56] Nellie McClung's *In Times Like These* (1915) included one of the most eloquent condemnations of all forms of war.

But although men like to fight, war is not inevitable. War is not of God's making. War is a crime committed by men and, therefore, when enough people say it shall not be, it cannot be. This will not happen until women are allowed to say what they think of war. Up to the present time women have had nothing to say about war, except pay the price of war — this privilege has been theirs always.[57]

McClung and Denison were two feminists for whom the reality, as opposed to the abstraction, of war presented painful problems of personal conscience. Both had been against war; both had dearly loved sons who enlisted; both eventually came to support the Allied cause. Only a few Canadian women sustained their pacifist opposition to violence. These included Winnipeg writer Francis Marion Beynon, British Columbia's Helena Gutteridge, and Toronto peace activist Laura Hughes, all of whom consistently and publicly condemned Canada's participation in the war. Beynon's refusal to alter her pacifist stance resulted in the loss of her job as a respected journalist on the *Grain Growers' Guide*, and led to her self-imposed exile in the United States. Early in the war pacifism also inspired the president of the Toronto Business Women's Club, Mrs. C. R. Barker, to resign her presidency rather than share in the club's war work. But these women and others who spoke or wrote publicly against the war found themselves increasingly isolated. Looking back, Nellie McClung recalled in 1945:

The fall of 1914 blurs in my memory like a troubled dream. The war dominated everything. Some of my friends were pacifists and resented Canada's participation in a war of which we knew so little. . . . Chief among the Empire's defenders among the women was Miss Cora Hind. Her views were clear cut and definite. We were British and must follow the tradition of our fathers. She would have gone herself if women were accepted. Miss Hind saw only one side of the question and there were times when I envied her, though I resented her denunciations of those who thought otherwise.

The old crowd began to break up, and our good times were over.[58]

Victory

In spite of obstacles and disagreements, women continued to campaign for the suffrage. The turning point in the long battle finally came in 1916, when the vigorous suffrage campaign waged by western women culminated in their enfranchisement in Manitoba, Alberta, and Saskatchewan. A year later British Columbia and Ontario followed suit, and women in Nova Scotia, New Brunswick, and Prince Edward Island won the vote in 1918, 1919, and 1922 respectively. In all cases, except New Brunswick and Ontario, the right to vote was accompanied by the right to hold office; New Brunswick women became eligible to hold office in 1934 and Ontario women in 1919. Only Quebec and the British colony of Newfoundland held back and refused to grant the vote to women.

At the federal level, women's franchise was achieved in three phases. The Military Voters Act in 1917 gave the vote to women nurses serving in the war. Later that year the Wartime Elections Act extended the franchise to wives, widows, mothers, sisters, and daughters of those, alive or deceased, who had served or were serving in the Canadian or British military or naval forces. This act, designed to help re-elect Borden's Union government and endorse its mandate for conscription, drew both praise and outrage from suffrage advocates.[59] Support came primarily from people who, in the wartime context, believed in the superiority of the Anglo-Saxon race and saw the vote as a way of reshaping society according to their values. Opponents, like the Victoria and Regina Local Councils of Women, both of which passed resolutions protesting the law, also saw the vote as an instrument for achieving social change, but objected to the act's discriminatory provisions, maintaining that valid change could only be achieved when all women acquired equal political rights with men.[60] Their political objective was finally met in 1918 with the passage of the federal Women's Franchise Act, which gave the vote to every woman who was over the age of twenty-one and a British subject, and who possessed the same qualifications as men required for the provincial franchise. Canadian women had achieved the franchise before women in Great Britain and, as far as the federal government was concerned, in the United States as well. The following year the federal government enacted legislation enabling women to be elected to the House of Commons.[61]

The timing of these victories has been the source of considerable discussion by historians. Why did most of Canada's governments acquiesce to the campaign for the suffrage between 1916 and 1922? Why, in contrast, did Quebec and Newfoundland not participate in the general trend? The first question is perhaps the easiest to answer. Certainly "political motives" are obvious major factors in the 1917 federal decision. Borden's Union government clearly had much to gain from the prospect of a loyal voting block of newly enfranchised women, at the height of bitterness over the conscription issue. In British Columbia and Manitoba, suffrage had become a partisan issue and newly elected Liberal governments were simply fulfilling their campaign promises. In Ontario the incumbent Conservative government under Premier William Hearst gradually recognized the expediency of accepting female suffrage; in addition he was evidently pressured by Prime Minister Borden to adopt the cause. Concern to capture women's votes undoubtedly motivated Alberta and New Brunswick Liberal governments as well.

International influences may also have played a part. After 1910 a revitalized feminist movement was sweeping Europe and North America, making it more difficult for Canadian legislators to justify women's continued exclusion. A negative stance became even harder to defend in the light of women's acknowledged and valued contributions to the war effort. Speeches introducing franchise measures certainly often cited these contributions as a major rationale. It has also been suggested that the growth of a female labour market increased women's visibility as an independent force and gradually paved the way for the acceptance of equal political rights. Ultimately, the extraordinarily persistent efforts of the suffragist campaigners paid off. The campaign, after all, had taken some sixty years to win. From the time it began, thousands of women and hundreds of organizations had been involved in the fight for political rights. Even during periods of apparent inactivity and division, the movement never completely lost its focus or momentum.

The reform movement that had claimed over half a century of women's attention could boast other important victories by 1920. Through their work to counteract the problems associated with urbanization, to improve the status and well-being of women in the work place, and to eradicate the inequities faced by women in family law, Canadian feminists never lost sight of the importance of family and children. They idealized the family and believed that a stable family life could both prevent and counteract "social degeneration." This led to a call for state support for the family. Rather than providing for children in state institutions, feminist reformers and their allies sought and won channels for legal adoptions, and in some provinces the establishment of Children's Aid Societies. By 1920 allowances for mothers to tide them over economically difficult times were available in Manitoba (1916), Saskatchewan (1917), Alberta (1919), and British Columbia and Ontario (1920). Reform-minded women had also been involved over the years in the kindergarten movement and the founding of home and school associations. They had advocated and achieved separate courts, trials, and institutions for the group of children and adolescents increasingly identified as "juvenile delinquents." Gradually various provinces accepted the need for separate facilities for female offenders.[62]

Reformers could take pride in all these accomplishments, but by far the greatest victory they achieved was the implementation of prohibition throughout Canada during the war years. The spirit of sacrifice, the strong commitment to the reformation of society, and the growing acceptance of government intervention into the lives of its citizens, all evoked by the war, created a climate of opinion extremely favourable to the prohibitionists' cause. Supporters equated the corrupting liquor trade with the evil enemy, Kaiser Wilhelm, arguing that both were scourges of western civilization. Why sacrifice innocent young men to the Allied cause, only to have them frequent "wet" canteens and fall victims first to drink, and then in their vulnerable state, to prostitution and venereal disease? Moreover, prohibition advocates argued that it was inefficient to use valuable grain for the manufacture of alcohol when it might better be sent to the starving allied nations.

On the basis of these and similar arguments, the prohibitionists' long-standing cry for the banishment of bottle and bar caught the attention and support of unprecedented numbers of Canadians, many of whom had previously been indifferent or overtly opposed to the temperance movement. Prohibitionist sentiment was strongest in the prairie provinces, and there politicians were unable to ignore it. New-found allies for the prohibitionists included the Imperial

Order Daughters of the Empire, the Orange Lodge, and the Anglican church. Even among non-Anglo-Saxon immigrants, long immune to temperance overtures, significant numbers converted to the cause. Following the holding of provincial referenda, by the end of 1916 all three prairie governments had enacted prohibitory legislation. Within a year, all other provinces, with the exception of Quebec, also endorsed prohibition. In 1918 the Dominion government used its powers under the War Measures Act to apply prohibition to that province also, and to stop interprovincial trade in liquor.

Victory was now complete, but was prohibition the panacea that the WCTU and other supporters claimed it would be? Initially at least they could take great satisfaction in the results: in Manitoba during the seven months following the introduction of prohibition, "drunkenness" fell by 87 percent, and all other crimes by nearly one-third; in Alberta, arrests for drunkenness declined by 90 percent in 1917 and 1918. People also praised the effectiveness of the new legislation in creating a safer and more wholesome environment. One enthusiastic Saskatchewan farm wife proudly informed the provincial premier that her small community, "formerly a drunkard's paradise, since the banishment of the bars and dispensaries has assumed an air of thrift and sobriety."[63]

The women's associations of the late nineteenth and early twentieth centuries met important needs. Accessible both to women who were able to make a full commitment and to those who could only be involved part-time, the women's movement reached out to nearly all women in Canadian society in one way or another. By 1916 journalist Marjorie MacMurchy could proclaim that one out of every eight women in the Dominion belonged to the network of women's societies.[64] Organized activity not only provided a sense of purpose for women, but prevented their personal isolation, and through exposure to and participation in the community of like-minded women, intensified their common identity. Within all the clubs, whether social or issue-oriented, members learned the organizational and public skills essential to their greater participation in the urbanized and industrialized world of the twentieth century.

Although Canadian women reformers personally claimed victory for many of the social, economic, and political reforms of this period, the extent to which these can be described as uniquely women's victories is debatable. In certain areas, such as the temperance and suffrage movements, a direct relationship between women's efforts and the reform in question can be traced — although the efforts of male supporters of these causes clearly cannot be dismissed. In others, perhaps, men's and women's efforts were about equal. Male collaboration in feminist reform reflected the acceptance of women's movement goals by increasing numbers of Canadians. The thrust of the movement, with its emphasis on protecting the home and family life, perhaps posed no threat to male supremacy. But it did challenge the exclusive nature of men's public power. In the end, feminist thought radically challenged the division of the world into men's and women's spheres by eroding the boundaries between public and private activities. In the context of turn-of-the-century Canadian middle class Christianity, the work of female reformers was genuinely radical. If their efforts fell short of social revolution, they nevertheless paved the way for more revolutionary activity to come.

In the final analysis, although most historians identify "maternal" feminism as the dominant philosophy of this first wave Canadian women's reform movement, the radical character of some aspects of the movement cannot be overlooked. From an early expression by the Toronto Women's Literary Club, the argument for equal rights evolved with, and often merged with, the idea of women's special maternal and nurturing role. Canadian women believed that, as mothers and as homemakers, they had knowledge and skills that were as valuable as and equal to men's knowledge and skills. In a just society their value ought to be acknowledged and rewarded. The issues of the times appeared to call forth women's talents; between 1850 and 1920 a growing body of educated women were sensitized to the need for public action. Ultimately, realistic appraisals of what was practical and generally acceptable guided women reformers.

3 THE PROMISED LAND?

The end of the Great War to the beginning of World War II

O n a moonlit evening in May, 1918, Allied encampments near Etable in France suffered a prolonged bombardment. By the time the seemingly endless attack was over, two Canadian field hospitals had been seriously damaged and four Canadian nursing sisters were dead or lay dying. Other nurses made heroic efforts to save the wounded: among them were the first nurses to receive the Military Medal for bravery.[1] The activities of the Canadian nursing sisters overseas dramatically illustrated the new responsibilities Canadian women had assumed, and the sacrifice they had made for the war effort. Women's wartime contribution was one of the principal arguments used to justify the granting of the federal franchise to the majority of women in Canada, which occurred in May 1918.

The contribution of both women and men to the Allied cause was used by the Canadian government to claim a more prominent position for the Dominion within the British Empire. Prime Minister Robert Borden was one of the signatories to the Versailles Treaty at the end of World War I, the first Canadian representative to sign an international treaty in his own right. The subsequent gradual recognition of Canada as an entity with its own identity and interests laid the foundation for the evolution of the British Empire into the Commonwealth. In 1931, the Statute of Westminster officially confirmed Canada's transformation from a dependent colony into a sovereign state.

World War I, then, was a turning point for Canada as a nation. The Canada of 1919 was profoundly different from the Canada of 1914 in several fundamental aspects—demographic, economic, political, and social. Wracked internally by divisions between French and English, East and West, labour and capital, and plunged into a serious recession, the emerging nation stood poised on the brink of an uncertain future. Most Canadians could scarcely imagine that only twenty years later they would be at war again, or that many would welcome war's arrival as a way to escape the grinding poverty and unemployment produced by the Depression of the 1930s.

The Canadian inter-war experience can best be described as turbulent. The transition from a wartime to a peacetime economy was a painful one, particularly for women workers; jobs generated by wartime production ceased, and both unemployment and inflation rose during the post-war depression. In this difficult economic climate, labour militancy intensified as working men and women

A military nursing sister, 1917.

sought to protect or improve their standard of living. New, radical organizations, such as the One Big Union, brought together industrial workers regardless of their trade or skill, and led many Canadians to fear that Bolshevism, recently triumphant in Russia, was about to wreak havoc in their own backyard. Thus, when workers initiated massive walkouts across the nation in the spring of 1919, the full weight of the Canadian state was ranged against them. The ensuing defeat of labour precipitated a rapid decline in union membership throughout the 1920s, and left the labour movement dispirited.

The expanding economy of the mid- and late-twenties, particularly buoyant in central and western Canada, did result in new job opportunities and unprecedented prosperity for some segments of the Canadian population. The most significant economic growth occurred in the resource-related industries, especially in pulp and paper, and mining, but these industries provided few employment opportunities for women. Women had been encouraged by public officials to give up their employment at war's end; with the return of prosperity young single women were once again actively recruited into the workforce, mainly in the growing clerical and service sectors. In the manufacturing sector, owners and managers used new technologies and "scientific management" techniques to rationalize their operations and to reduce labour costs. Many skilled jobs were eliminated and replaced by repetitive assembly work; skilled worker was often pitted against unskilled worker, female worker against male worker.

The improved economic conditions of the mid-1920s did make it possible for some male workers to support their families on their own wages—the "family wage" was becoming a reality. Conversely, the traditional family economy, to which all able-bodied members of the family were expected to contribute, was under attack. Smaller families, and legislation in most provinces extending compulsory school attendance, reduced the number of children in the paid labour force, and reinforced married women's roles as mothers and consumers; their participation in the economy as paid workers was increasingly criticized as unnecessary and ill-advised.

Yet with the onset of the Great Depression in 1929, few families could rely on one male wage earner. Canada was one of the most adversely affected of the western industrialized countries by the economic downturn, since its economy was so dependent upon the export of commodities. Between 1926 and 1933 the price of wheat fell from $1.09 to 35 cents per bushel, and that of newsprint from $70 to $41 per ton. [2] Entire single-industry towns were abandoned as families moved, usually to the larger urban centres, in a frenzied attempt to find jobs. In many families, only wives and daughters were able to find employment; but as the Depression deepened, women found it extremely difficult to keep their paid work, and as unemployment soared, married and single women were blamed for contributing to the nation's problems by taking jobs away from men. Thousands of men, and some women, jumped on freight trains and travelled across the nation searching for jobs. Although there were several indicators that the worst of the Depression was over by 1937, for hundreds of thousands of Canadians conditions improved only after Canada entered World War II in September 1939.

The wildly alternating cycles of bust–boom–bust from 1919 to 1939 created enormous fluctuations in population growth. Although the population increased from nearly 9 million in 1921 to 11.5 million by 1941, the pace of growth slowed and was at its lowest during the Depression years. For the first time since official records were begun in 1851, the number of births dropped during an intercensal period: between 1931 and 1941 there were only 2.29 million compared to 2.42 million during the previous decade. The most startling demographic change was the sharp decline in immigration after 1931, as economic conditions worsened and the Canadian government restricted immigration: a mere 149 000 immigrants arrived between 1931 and 1941, the lowest number recorded for any decade since 1851. Just as immigration plummeted during the Depression, so too did emigration, most notably to the United States. During the 1920s, 970 000 residents left Canada; but in the following decade, the United States tightened its immigration policies, and less than a quarter of a million Canadians left their native or adopted land to re-establish themselves elsewhere.

The impact of the Depression was most noticeable on the population of Saskatchewan. The collapse of wheat prices, prolonged drought, and the plagues of grasshoppers that devoured the few existing crops proved too much for many of the province's residents. Over 150 000 more people left the province than entered it, and in spite of natural increase, there were 25 000 fewer inhabitants in 1941 than there had been ten years earlier. The pace of urbanization also slowed during the Depression: the proportion of all Canadians who resided in urban settings grew only 3 percent to reach a level of 55.7 percent in 1941. As in the past, there were more women than men in the urban centres, especially in the 15 to 29 age group. For the first time since the census began in 1851, there were also more women than men urban residents in the 30 to 34 age group, reflecting both the increased employment opportunities for women in this age group in the cities, and the departure of some of the men to perform military service.

Fluctuations in the nation's economy and population in the interwar period created an atmosphere conducive to political change. Discontent with the Borden administration's wartime policies combined with the economic and social turmoil that enveloped the nation immediately after the war to produce new political movements and parties. Across the nation farmers deserted the traditional parties to support emerging organizations such as the Progressive movement in western Canada and the United Farmers of Ontario. Workers, returned veterans, and other disaffected groups variously sought to register their protest during federal and provincial elections by supporting socialist and labour parties, or independent candidates. The formation of the Communist Party of Canada, at a secret meeting held in a barn near Guelph, Ontario in 1921, provided those on the left with yet another vehicle for political protest. These alternate political parties gave newly enfranchised women new avenues of political involvement. It soon became apparent, however, that women and men voters preferred the two traditional parties, particularly the Liberal party. For most of the 1920s, federal politics were dominated by the back-and-forth struggle for power between the bland but adroit Liberal leader, William Lyon Mackenzie King, and the brilliant but hapless Arthur Meighen, who had replaced Borden at the helm of the Conservative party in 1920. With the exception of a few brief days, King managed to hold onto power for the Liberals by his skilfull courting of the West and Quebec.

Even King's political finesse, however, was no match for the cataclysmic impact of the Great Depression, and in 1930 he was defeated by the Conservatives, now led by millionaire R.B. Bennett. Before King left office, however, Canadian women had the small satisfaction of seeing him name the first woman senator. The Liberal defeat was only a preliminary indication of a substantial political upheaval engendered by the Depression. At the federal level, the Co-operative Commonwealth Federation (CCF), formed in Calgary in 1932, and the Reconstruction party led by maverick Tory H.H. Stevens, offered new alternatives for voters in the election of 1935. Like most other leftist political organizations, the CCF officially endorsed the full participation of women and provided many women with a forum for involvement in the political process. Canadians, however, were in a cautious mood and preferred reinstating King and the Liberals to engaging in political experimentation. The advent of new parties and colourful leaders was more momentous at the provincial level. Duff Patullo and the Liberals in British Columbia, "Bible Bill" Aberhart and the Social Credit in Alberta, Mitchell Hepburn and the Liberals in Ontario, and Maurice Duplessis and the Union Nationale in Quebec all rode to power on a wave of protest against incumbents long ensconced in their respective legislatures.

One of the new tools that this generation of politicians had at their disposal was the radio. Radio broke down much of the isolation that had been a hallmark of living in Canada, and put Canadians in contact not only with one another but also with the rest of the world. It often provided women at home with their only form of entertainment, and served as a powerful instrument for the dissemination of information and mass culture. The other major technological innovation of the inter-war period that brought Canadians into closer contact was the automobile; by 1930 there were over 1.2 million motor vehicles registered in Canada. The car made it possible for workers to commute longer distances and so stimulated the growth of suburban areas. This one development alone had important ramifications for thousands of married women, whose own work place, the home, was consequently changed. Households tended to become smaller and more private; increased emphasis was put on the nuclear family as a unit of consumption rather than production, and on married women's role in making the home a haven in an increasingly complex society. As scientific management principles were applied to the household, women were expected to save time and energy through more efficient home management, and spend more time with their children and husbands.

Capturing the essence of women's experience during this exciting phase of Canadian history is both easier and more difficult than for earlier periods. Oral sources now become available, and several feminist scholars have begun to use them to supplement traditional written sources. New magazines directed chiefly to middle class women made their appearance during the 1920s, and provide a fascinating window on women's domestic and public life. This period also saw the first tentative steps towards the welfare state, with the implementation of programs such as mothers' allowances and old age pensions. Government bureaucracies generated masses of documents on many aspects of women's lives. On the other hand, it is more difficult to locate personal letters and diaries for the inter-war years. Women probably wrote fewer letters because the telephone was becoming more available, and new forms of entertainment took up their limited spare time. Moreover, personal documents such as diaries and letters may not yet be deposited in archives. This period has also received somewhat less attention from historians than that between 1850 and 1918. The study of women's organizations after World War I, for example, is much less extensive than it is for the earlier period.

This may explain the belief—only recently challenged—that the women's movement in Canada disappeared after the achievement of suffrage. Careful reconstruction of the activities and issues that women's organizations pursued during the inter-war years is beginning to reveal that, on the contrary, many groups continued to work actively for the transformation of Canadian society in accordance with feminist principles. This finding raises the important question of why women's issues failed to generate the public attention they had attracted during the suffrage campaign.

Other questions focus on technology. What was the impact of the changes that were introduced into the home and factory in the name of improved efficiency, as far as women were concerned? New and improved appliances and products became available in the majority of middle class urban households as the distribution of electricity widened. Did their use significantly lighten women's load, or did these changes create new demands on their time and energy? Finally, recent studies of women during the Depression have raised questions about how major economic change affects the role and status of women over time.

9 New opportunities, old obstacles: women in the corporate economy, 1918–1939

"It is a natural conviction that enfranchised Canadian women will apply themselves intelligently and with energy to the basic economic problems of national existence. It is only through the help of women that the future can be made secure. The co-operation of Canadian women in industrial life and reconstruction is indispensable,"[1] wrote Marjory MacMurchy, a well-known journalist, at the end of World War I. The gains women had made in the labour force during the war inspired considerable optimism; reformers such as MacMurchy and Nellie McClung believed that, since women had proved invaluable to the war effort and had won the vote, a new era of social reform and advancement for women was certain to follow. For them "reconstruction" did not mean the restoration of Canadian society as it existed prior to 1914, but rather its reorganization and renovation into a more perfect society.

At the same time, most Canadians remained convinced that women's primary place was in the home. It was taken for granted that when the hostilities ceased and the men returned, women would cheerfully surrender their newly acquired positions in the workforce. To make certain that women understood this, the federal government bombarded them with a poster campaign. "Do you feel justified in holding a job which could be filled by a man who has not only himself to support, but a wife and family as well?," one such poster demanded. "Think it over."[2] Women were urged to seek "feminine" areas of employment where they would not threaten the position of male workers.

Much attention was now focussed on new opportunities for single, educated women to engage in work that was light, clean, and non-threatening to their womanhood. Education was stressed for all young women; if women were transient, low-wage workers, it was because they had failed to equip themselves adequately for the work place.[3] Occupations such as nutritionist, social worker, journalist, sales clerk, stenographer, and librarian were highly recommended for the educated woman. One brochure extolled the advantages of secretarial work for university-trained women and, lest any old-fashioned prejudice remain against higher education for women, an American study was cited showing that the infant mortality rate for mothers with university training was less than half that for mothers of similar social standing but with less schooling.[4]

Indeed, most commentators continued to stress motherhood as

the principal and most rewarding career for Canadian women. While there was a new emphasis on vocational training and higher education for women, and a wider acceptance of single women in paid employment, women were only to work at jobs for a few years before marriage. Women were reminded that "No other work that a woman can do is as important to Canada as making a home and taking care of children."[5] Given the loss of 60 000 Canadian lives during the war, motherhood acquired an enhanced practical and symbolic importance.

The modern "working girl"

The tremendous social and economic dislocation the nation experienced at war's end reinforced the belief that women should not compete for men's jobs. Massive unemployment, labour unrest, and political ferment characterized the last years of the war and the immediate post-war era. By 1918 female unemployment had risen significantly, and was one of the issues discussed at the Women's War Conference in February of that year. Thousands of female workers suffered enormous hardships as jobs became scarce, wages were cut, and inflation soared. Although the Women's Department of the Reconstruction Association proclaimed that this was the age of the woman at work, it too counselled women to avoid direct competition with men for jobs: experienced female munitions workers were not to take employment in machine shops where there was already an excess of male workers. Only highly skilled, extraordinarily strong women with exceptional financial needs, it was argued, were justified in continuing to work in the metal trades, and even they were cautioned to avoid undercutting male wages. When women could secure employment, they often had to be content with traditional female jobs and inadequate wages. According to a sympathetic observer in Hamilton, Ontario, some were forced into prostitution to support themselves and their dependents.

And they are all working girls! Here was the dressmaker's apprentice who could not live on nothing a week, there the worker in the jam factory who was out of work for three months and had to find her bread on the street.... Clerks, barmaids, factory hands, servants, laundry workers, every trade was represented in which women are over-worked and exploited.[6]

Given women workers' low wages and acute vulnerability to the ravages of post-war inflation, it is not surprising that they played an active part in the labour unrest that swept through many communities after the war. Women were the first to walk out in the Winnipeg General Strike on May 15, 1919, when some 500 telephone operators left their jobs shortly after dawn; hundreds of confectionery workers and sales clerks subsequently joined them. One of the most visible strike organizers was Helen Armstrong, president of the city's Women's Labor League. Its members provided up to 1500 meals daily to women strikers and others in need. In addition, the League gave cash grants to women on strike to cover the cost of their rent.

Merchants or their agents who sought to carry on business as usual incurred the wrath of women supporting the strike; one company had three delivery wagons destroyed, and its drivers assaulted. A detective sent out to investigate warned men not to go to that district for "his life is in danger if these women find out that he is at work, or had been working during the strike." Not all women, however, supported the strike; some worked to undermine it by crossing picket lines to provide what they considered essential services.[7]

The telephone operators in Vancouver played a visible but costly role in the general strike called there to support the Winnipeg workers. They did not join the initial walkout since they were classified as essential workers by the strike committee, but 300 operators left their jobs at the peak of the strike in the middle of June. Although the Vancouver General Strike came to an end on July 3, the operators remained on strike until the middle of the month to protest the telephone company's policy of replacing striking supervisors and senior employees by strikebreakers. In the end the operators had to return to work on the company's terms, and within a year the telephone operators' union disappeared.[8]

In Toronto some women workers actively supported the union movement, especially the attempt of less-skilled workers to organize on an industrial rather than on a craft basis. By the end of 1919, hundreds of women telephone operators had secured substantial improvements in their working conditions through unionization, and a newly established union of bank employees claimed that over half of all bank clerks, many of whom were women, had joined its ranks. Other groups of women who had traditionally been considered unorganizable, such as domestic servants and waitresses, also joined unions. During the sympathy strike called in mid-May to support Toronto metal workers, approximately 2000 garment workers joined in a show of solidarity.[9]

By 1921 over 17 percent of all Canadian women over the age of 15 were counted as members of the paid labour force, and they

The staff of the Newfoundland Hotel dining room in the 1930s.

comprised 15 percent of all paid workers. There was considerable regional variation: female labour force participation rates were higher in Ontario and Quebec (19 percent), and considerably lower in Prince Edward Island (13.5 percent), Saskatchewan, and Alberta (13 percent). In the latter two provinces, there were so few jobs for women that they constituted fewer than one in ten paid workers. Even after the severe recession of the early 1920s gave way to the relative national prosperity of the latter part of the decade, female workers everywhere continued to experience the injustices arising from the ghettoization of women's work: domestic service, the textile, clothing, and food industries, clerical work, teaching, and nursing were all characterized by low wages, poor working conditions, and limited job opportunities.

As in previous decades, the majority of women who worked outside the home were young and single. According to one Vancouver survey, eight out of ten working women in that city were under twenty-five years of age. The 1920s has been portrayed as a period during which young people asserted their independence and challenged the moral and social dictates of their parents; but in reality the lives of working class daughters throughout Canada largely replicated those of their mothers.[10] Economic necessity still compelled thousands of girls under the age of fifteen to go out to work. Most unmarried employed women continued to live at home or under the watchful eye of relatives or other surrogate parents, and to hand over a significant portion of their meagre salaries to their families. Quebec textile workers in the 1920s, for example, reported that they kept only a small portion of their bimonthly pay for themselves; in some cases this amounted to only a few cents. Single Jewish women working in Toronto's garment industry did the same.[11] Because family was considered so important, young working women did not generally object to this custom. Even had they wanted to live away from home, their low wages would have prevented most of them from doing so.

For women living in small or remote communities, domestic service frequently continued to be the only form of employment available. "I had to go out and earn my own bread," Elizabeth Goudie of Labrador recalled.

I never was home much after the age of fourteen. The wages were very low. I went to work for two dollars a month. If the family was very poor you only got your food or maybe the makings of a new dress. This work wasn't easy. You had to do everything by hand: scrub, wash, bring wood and water, help to cook and mend clothing.[12]

As most Canadian-born women continued to reject the long hours, low wages, demeaning status, and lack of privacy of household service, the federal government increased its efforts to encourage the immigration of foreign-born domestics. The majority still came from Great Britain; in the decade after the war, some 80 000 British women entered Canada as domestic servants. Indeed, domestic service was still being advocated as a suitable occupation for British "gentlewomen," who were provided accommodation in hostels such as the Queen Mary's Coronation Hostel in Vancouver, where they were also given six to eight week training courses to enable them to secure employment as "home helps." The promoters of this type of work, usually pursued in rural areas for twenty to twenty-five dollars per month, claimed that it was appropriate for British "ladies" since they were to be placed with families of similar social standing to their own, and to be treated as one of the family.[13]

There was a substantial increase in non-British domestic servants during the 1920s, however. One quarter of all immigrant domestics in Ontario in 1931 were from continental Europe; those from Germany and the Scandinavian countries were preferred. For all its constraints, domestic service had several positive features: it offered steady employment, room and board, and, for non-British women, an opportunity to learn English and become familiar with Canadian customs. Finnish servants, 8 percent of all immigrant domestics in the 1920s, took great pride in their work; for them, to be a servant was to be far from servile. When conditions proved unsatisfactory, they reacted energetically and in a variety of ways, ranging from frequent changes of employer to collective organization. Indeed, during the 1920s Finnish maids' organizations were established in a number of urban centres.[14]

The newly created Woman's Branch of the Department of Immigration also recruited women from central and eastern Europe for household service. All unaccompanied immigrant women were put under the supervision of federally appointed train conductresses, who were to prevent their charges from being enticed away with offers of employment before they reached their intended destinations. Yet escapes occurred. From one party of twenty-five women, three ran away in Montreal, and another two were caught trying to climb through the window minutes before the train's departure.[15]

Domestic service was also the lot of many of those Chinese and Japanese women who managed to circumvent the severe restrictions placed on immigration from Asia. In 1923 even this trickle of female immigrants from China was stemmed when the federal government, in response to the deep-rooted racism of most Canadians and continuing hysteria about the "yellow peril," passed the Chinese Immigration Act, which excluded all Chinese from permanent settlement in Canada. This legislation remained in force until 1947. Although Japanese and East Indian women were not explicitly barred from entry into Canada, a number of policies adopted by the Department of Immigration effectively kept their numbers low during the interwar period.[16]

The trend away from live-in domestics to household helpers hired on a daily basis became firmly established during the decade following World War I. After the war many married immigrant women were engaged as daily household workers when their husbands were unable to find employment; the men stayed home to look after the children. Such arrangements made it possible for the family to survive, but could result in strained relationships.

In western Canada, immigrant husbands and wives were frequently employed together as agricultural labourers. When Helen Potrebenko's parents first arrived in Alberta in 1928, her mother "fed the pigs in the morning, milked five cows, separated the milk, washed the separator, then repeated the whole thing in the evening. In between, she picked roots on newly-broken land," all for $1 per day. Even when women stooked grain all day long in the fields as efficiently as their husbands, they were paid less than the men.[17] Women also comprised half the seasonal workers in the fruit-growing areas of the Erie and Niagara regions in 1930.[18]

Women workers in urban areas could usually count on better wages and shorter hours than they could obtain as domestic or agricultural workers. However, they remained clustered in certain industries and confined to low-paying jobs. Even in industries where they formed a significant proportion of the workforce, women rarely posed a direct threat to male employment, since jobs were generally assigned on the basis of gender. A complex interplay of factors determined the sexual division of labour in this period. In general, women were excluded from skilled positions or from exercising control over the work process or over other workers. "Foreladies" were rare, and exercised authority only over other female operatives. In work resembling that done in the home, women were still relegated to positions with less control and fewer rewards than men. In the clothing industry, men had more prestigious and better paying positions as cutters and pressers, while women lined, hemmed, and finished the garmets. When women and men did the same work they often worked on different shifts — the women during the day, the men at night. Most factory departments were therefore predominantly of one sex, thus enhancing solidarity among workers of the same sex but impeding a sense of common interest between the sexes. When women and men performed the same tasks and were paid on an hourly basis, the men were nearly always paid at a higher rate. In the Toronto garment industry, the average female wage was one-half to two-thirds that of the average male wage.[19]

During the 1920s, industrial workers of both sexes had to contend with the consequences of an increased emphasis on efficiency and scientific management techniques. As a result of time studies and technological innovation, operatives faced speed-ups and ever-mounting production quotas. Women workers, on the whole, were more vulnerable to the negative effects of technological change since they were virtually excluded from the decision-making process, and more often paid piece rates. When workers consistently achieved their quotas, unscrupulous employers cut their piecework rates. Prostitutes were always paid "piece rates," but at least their rates were higher. In some Montreal brothels the prostitutes were said to entertain up to forty clients a night, and they were able to keep half of the $1 each client was charged.[20]

The nervous strain created by the hectic pace of production in manufacturing took its toll on the workers' health. In one Winnipeg clothing factory, a labour newspaper reported that the "girls" were seated side by side on long benches, and all sewing machines were operated by a single motor. As a result, the individual operators could not leave their machines or else all would fall behind. The only respite from this incredibly arduous regimen was the half-hour the workers were allowed for lunch, which they were compelled to eat in the workroom.[21]

Despite the introduction in most provinces during the 1920s of legislation setting minimum standards for wages, hours, and conditions for female workers in industrial establishments, abuses were rife. There were too few factory inspectors to provide effective enforcement, and the worst injustices occurred in individual households under the system of sweated labour. Entire families, often recent immigrants, basted, hemmed, cut out appliqués, or sewed on buttons at wages well below those paid in factories. Such workers were generally at the mercy of the clothing subcontractors, and were not protected by legislation of any sort. Home work, for all its problems, was nevertheless the preferred form of employment for Italian women, since it allowed them to work with other family members, and to combine paid employment with domestic responsibilities. Nor was such work confined to the garment trade; in Toronto one food company sent out bushels of onions to Italian women for peeling and washing, and then collected them for further processing at its plant.[22]

Given the difficult conditions, limited opportunities, and low status of women workers in manufacturing, clerical work was an increasingly attractive option. Indeed, by the early 1920s there was already a glut of stenographers and typists who, ironically, shared a common fate with their supposed social inferiors, the "factory girls." Although some stenographers and secretaries continued to perform skilled work, with the increased specialization that took place after 1920, many female office workers were relegated to subordinate positions that were routine, low paying, and dead-end. Like the factory operatives, clerical workers experienced the negative effects of mechanization: work became fragmented, the pace of work increased, and supervision intensified.[23]

The influx of women into the federal civil service during the first decades of the twentieth century had been a source of great concern for male bureaucrats, who feared the large numbers of women would deter bright young men from pursuing careers in government. After 1910 the most important positions were reserved for men. In 1918 additional restrictions had been placed on female employment, and by 1921 women were virtually excluded from all permanent positions in the federal bureaucracy. Female employees who married were required to hand in their resignations. These stringent measures achieved their goal: between 1921 and 1931 there was a 13 percent decline in the number of female civil servants working in Ottawa, while the numbers of male civil servants increased by over 6 percent.[24] Other white collar occupations generally regarded as appropriate for women were those of sales clerk and telephone operator. In these positions too, women were subject to a rigid sexual division of labour, intense competition from other women workers, low wages, and long hours.

Women's opportunities for advancement in the business world were extremely limited. Deeply rooted misogynist views surfaced in articles such as "Woman in business is still at heart a woman," in which the author pontificated, "A man can do business very successfully with someone he dislikes but I have never met a woman who could."[25] Since it was assumed that women were destined for marriage, it seemed a waste of time and money to train them for more responsible positions. Nevertheless, wives, especially those in ethnic communities, were often indispensable to the successful operation of small family businesses such as restaurants, laundries, grocery stores, and shoe-shine parlours. As one Canadian-born Chinese woman recalled, "My mother helped out for many long hours in the laundry. She did not even go out to shop. She worked the longest. My mother worked six days and also Sunday. . . . Sometimes she had to cook for thirteen."[26] In the outports of Newfoundland, wives earned much-needed cash through their berry-picking, and continued their management of the complex, all-important processing of the cod catch on shore.[27]

The majority of "professional" women during this period were teachers and nurses still struggling to obtain self-regulation, status, and appropriate monetary rewards. The extraordinary heroism of the Canadian nursing sisters who served overseas during the war, and the important role nurses played in combatting the horrendous Spanish influenza epidemic of 1918-19 that resulted in 50 000 Canadian deaths, greatly enhanced the public image of nursing, especially in English Canada. Attempting to capitalize on their new respectability, nurses engaged in an intensified campaign to control their profession. In 1919 the first university degree program in nursing in the British Empire was established at the University of British Columbia. Similar study programs designed to meet the urgent need for nursing teachers, administrators, and public health nurses were initiated at the University of Toronto and McGill during the 1920s. These initiatives did not win unanimous approval either inside or outside the profession. Most nurses could not afford to take the five-year degree course and opted instead for the three-year courses offered by the hospitals. They often resented what they perceived as the preferential treatment of the select number of students who were enrolled in the university programs. Of greater concern to the proponents of higher education for nurses was the opposition they encountered from doctors. In 1920, for example, the College of Physicians and Surgeons in British Columbia stated that two years of training was quite sufficient for nurses and proclaimed that "the overtraining of nurses is not desirable and results largely in the losing of their usefulness."[28]

Nurses throughout the country did achieve some success in gaining control over who could be members of the profession. By 1922 all provinces had enacted legislation setting out the education and training required for registered nurses, and investing the power of registration in the hands of the provincial nursing associations. In Quebec, however, the 1920 legislation, which had given the anglophone registered nurses' association exclusive control over registration, was amended two years later at the insistence of francophone nurses and doctors, diluting the criteria for registration and breaking the association's control over registration.[29] A national survey of nursing education reported in 1929 that the *raison d'être* of the nursing schools continued to be the provision of cheap labour for the hospitals. Most student nurses put in a twelve-hour work day, consisting of nine hours on the wards, and three hours of lectures and study. During their first year of training, in particular, they were required to perform many heavy housekeeping duties. Once trained, most were replaced in hospitals by a new group of unpaid student nurses; in 1929, 60 percent of graduate nurses continued to be employed as private duty nurses in patients' homes, where domestic work often was expected of them. During times of economic crisis, private duty nurses found it difficult to secure full-time employment and had to compete with untrained women who were willing to provide similar services for lower wages. Among the private duty nurses who participated in the 1929 survey, 60 percent stated that they were not able to save for their retirement. Since nine out of every ten nurses were unmarried, their futures were bleak.[30]

During the 1920s, a general shortage of nurses was keenly felt in the area of public health nursing, as provincial and some municipal health services grew. Still, by 1922 there were over 1000 public health nurses in Canada.[31] In addition to receiving higher wages than nurses working in hospitals or private homes, these specialized nurses also enjoyed a greater degree of autonomy from physicians, especially when they were posted to remote areas. Nonetheless, public health nurses frequently met hostility or indifference from doctors and other male community leaders when they sought to establish much-needed services that were primarily aimed at women and children. After three years of a provincially supported program undertaken in 1920 to place nurse educators in Ontario communities, only eight communities had engaged public health nurses. When two provincially sponsored nurses arrived in Kenora in northern Ontario, they were advised not to ask the prosperous town for money, and so used their bedrooms at the local hotel as their offices.[32]

Attempts at improvement: minimum wages and unions

During the 1920s, there was little improvement in female workers' hours and wages. Responding to pressure from women's groups to protect and improve the position of female workers, and from organized labour to limit female competition, provincial governments extended "protective" legislation. Alberta was the first province to adopt a minimum wage law for women in 1917. Most provinces followed suit: British Columbia and Manitoba in 1918, Saskatchewan and Quebec in 1919, and Nova Scotia and Ontario in 1920. By the end of the decade, only New Brunswick and Prince Edward Island had still not passed such laws. But it took Alberta until 1924 to set up a permanent wage board, and minimum wage legislation was not actually put into force in Quebec until 1927, and 1930 in Nova Scotia.

The stated purpose of minimum wage laws was not only to ensure "the right of the worker to live from her work," but also "to preserve the health, morals and efficiency of that large class of women dependent on their daily wage for a living."[33] As the number of young, Canadian-born women entering the labour force continued to mount, so did concern over the future of the Anglo-Saxon race: those very same women who toiled in industry, it was pointed out, would one day be the mothers of the nation. As in other industrialized nations, women in Canada remained divided on the issue of protective legislation. Some prominent feminists, such as Helen Gregory MacGill of British Columbia, served on provincial wage commissions, but others were firmly opposed to minimum wage laws, and the pros and cons of protective legislation for women became the focus of vigorous debate. Maud Petitt Hill, a middle class journalist and reformer, declared that protective legislation was highly desirable because women workers were even less unionized than men. In 1912 Hill had disguised her origins and had gone to work in a Toronto biscuit factory. Using the pseudonym "Videre," she had written a series of articles about female factory workers in which she expressed an overriding concern for their moral condition and their weakness for "finery."[34] In the 1920s she continued to argue that working "girls" had to be protected from themselves, or otherwise they might "overwork with the mere ambition of owning silken hose and patent pumps," and subsequently "produce an inferior race." Further, it was undesirable to have women working night shifts and "walking the streets alone at night."[35]

Other supporters of minimum wage laws for women, such as the British Columbia union activist Helena Gutteridge, were more clearly motivated by concern for the female worker's economic status.[36] They firmly believed that such laws would result in improved wages and a better standard of living for women. Other concerned women criticized protection as unwarranted privilege and a poor substitute for equality. Because protective laws would render women less competitive, the principal beneficiaries of the maximum hours and minimum wages that applied only to women would be male workers. Moreover the argument that such legislation would help preserve their morality was insulting to the women workers.

Minimum wage commissions began their work by establishing

the basic weekly amount a single female worker required to keep herself in a respectable, if somewhat impoverished state. There was no acknowledgement that many female wage earners had dependents to support. The budget the commissioners invented was based on a full year's employment, an unattainable goal for many women. A third highly questionable assumption was that only a few unscrupulous employers were paying unconscionably low wages. There was no provision for retirement savings or vacations. Minimum wage rates varied from province to province and from industry to industry, and a separate order had to be issued to cover women in each trade. Within a province, the rate for women in the same type of employment might differ according to the size of community in which the worker resided, her age, and her experience. By the end of the decade, the majority of provinces had set minimum wages for most large groups of female employees. The exceptions, however, were notable: all those engaged in agriculture, domestic service, banking, teaching, and nursing. Initially, the wage commissions had no authority to regulate hours, a situation that many employers exploited by simply offsetting mandatory higher wages with longer hours. Eventually, however, this power was conceded to all provincial commissions except the one in Quebec.

In Ontario and Quebec, the highest minimum wage (for experienced female workers in certain industries in the largest urban centres) was set at $12.50 per week; the lowest (for the youngest and least experienced) was $8.00. In Alberta, the minimum was set at $12.50. Unfortunately the minimum rate rapidly became the maximum most women could earn, and even these low wages were not guaranteed to all workers. In Ontario, for example, inexperienced workers or minors under the age of eighteen, who did not have to be paid the minimum, could legally constitute up to half of an employer's workforce, depending upon the type of industry. In the case of piece workers, only 80 percent had to attain the minimum rate. Exemptions were also granted for "handicapped" workers, the elderly, and some juvenile workers under 18 years of age.[37]

The problems created by the legal loopholes were exacerbated by those related to enforcement. There were few inspectors, and the fines for contravening the law were paltry: $50.00 in Quebec, for example, and $100.00 in Saskatchewan. Employers frequently claimed ignorance of the law, and many employees were unaware of its existence or were too intimidated to invoke it. In the needle trades, those piece workers who were furthest from earning the minimum wage at week's end, and therefore would be the most costly for employers to "bonus up" to the required level, were subject to layoffs or dismissal. Several other methods employers used to contravene the legislation included having more than one employee punch in on the same time card, switching workers from job to job or firing and rehiring them so that they could continue to be classified as inexperienced, or using so many different piecework rates that it was virtually impossible for workers and inspectors to comprehend how the wages had been calculated. Although wage commissions continued to claim that employers who resorted to such practices were rare exceptions (and primarily of "foreign" origin), many respectable and well-known establishments such as the T.E. Eaton Company and Robert Simpson Company were also among the offenders. The Minimum Wage Boards had initially reassured nervous employers that female wages would not rise drastically, and they were right; women workers continued to earn on average 54 to 60 percent of what men earned.

Was there a better alternative to government intervention to improve the lot of women workers? Many believed that there was: unionization. Outspoken female champions of working women, such as Communist activists Annie Buller, Becky Buhay, Bella Hall Gauld, and Florence Custance, argued that only by recognizing the class origins of their exploitation and by organizing themselves could working women effect significant changes in their lives. Buller, who had been sent at the age of thirteen to work in a Montreal tobacco factory, worked her way from a sales clerk to department store buyer; in the end, however, she turned her back on what appears to have been a highly desirable position and devoted herself to Marxist politics and labour activism. She and her friends, Buhay and Gauld, were instrumental in setting up the Montreal Labour College in 1920 to promote the study of Marxism and to provide a meeting place for workers. Florence Custance was similarly involved in the Toronto Labour College. Through their writings, speaking tours, participation in various important strikes — and in some cases their arrests — these women worked on behalf of both female and male workers in industries as diverse as the needle trades and mining, and became well-known figures in the labour movement in several regions of Canada. Jeanne Corbin, a young francophone woman from northern Alberta, was another important activist. Recruited by Buhay and Buller in 1929 to contribute to Communist labour publications in both Ontario and Quebec, Corbin became an organizer among miners and bush workers in northern Ontario and Quebec, and was later imprisoned for her involvement in the 1934 miners' strike in Noranda, Quebec.[38]

During the 1920s, however, few Canadians of either sex embraced communism or unions; after 1923, only one out of every eight nonagricultural paid workers was a union member. According to one estimate, less than 1 percent of female wage earners was unionized.[39] Employers had a variety of tactics at their disposal to discourage unionization, including threatening workers with dismissal, moving their factories, and establishing "shop" unions that were pro-management. The craft unions of skilled workers continued to dominate the Canadian labour scene, confining their activities to industrial settings in which there were few women. In any event they had a tradition of excluding women. Many male unionists still considered female workers unlikely and undesirable union members; one concluded that because women did not have a long-term commitment to paid employment, and because they did not "possess that spirit of solidarity, characteristic of men in industry," female workers were "the most difficult workers to organize."[40]

Such negative assessments failed to recognize that it was often male unionists' indifference or overt hostility to female workers, and their failure to deal with issues of importance to women such as sexual harassment or unhygienic working conditions, that caused many women to spurn unions. In the 1920s unions made little effort to eliminate the pay differential between male and female workers, and by insisting on across–the–board raises they effectively increased the wage gap. Union halls were primarily male clubs. Although women were hired occasionally by the international unions to act as organizers in industries with large numbers of female workers, they suffered the familiar inequities in pay. In the early 1920s, for example, Mary McNab was hired as an organizer by the Amalgamated Clothing Workers in Hamilton, and paid half the salary typically given to male organizers.[41]

Despite the obstacles to organization, women in manufacturing did score some notable successes during the 1920s, especially in the garment and textile industries, although inter-union rivalries as well as ethnic divisions complicated organizational efforts among the garment workers. Three major unions with American or international connections — the Amalgamated Clothing Workers of America, the International Lady Garment Workers of America, and the Communist-supported Industrial Union of Needle Trades — sought to establish their pre-eminence. In Quebec these unions also faced a strong challenge from the newly organized *Confédération des travailleurs catholiques du Canada* (Canadian Catholic Confederation of Labour). Formed in 1921 under the aegis of the Catholic church, this organization sought to protect Catholic workers not only from the exploitation inherent in unfettered capitalism, but also from what many French Canadians perceived as essentially atheistic, foreign-controlled international unions. By 1921 there were eight women's locals of the Catholic Confederation in Hull, and one in Montreal; in addition other female workers were organized along with their male co-workers into "mixed" locals. All told, approximately 2200 women belonged to exclusively female Catholic unions, and another 600 to the mixed Catholic unions; but together they accounted for only 3 percent of all the women workers in Quebec industry and commerce.[42]

Despite women's membership in the union movement, male leaders continued to regard the presence of women in the labour force as symbolic of an unhealthy industrial order in which a man could not earn enough to support his family. Once the "family wage" was secured, they argued, there would be no reason for daughters and wives to desert hearth and home. Such arguments ignored the continuing economic contribution made by working women, their right to work for wages outside the home, and the fact that many women workers had no male "breadwinner" to rely on.

Women workers, whether unionized or not, were far from passive. As individuals, they reacted to unsatisfactory work situations by changing jobs or getting married; collectively, they helped each other meet production quotas or engaged in militant activities such as slow-downs, walkouts, and strikes. In August 1921 hosiery workers in Stratford, Ontario set up picket lines to try to win union recognition and improvements in wages. As in most labour-management disputes, the full force of the law was used against the strikers: fifteen were arrested, two of whom had to be tried in Juvenile Court. Despite widespread local support, after two months the strike failed. Another example of female workers' activism occurred in Hull, Quebec in 1924. In this instance, without notifying their union, the women at the E.B. Eddy factory walked off the job to protest the firing of their female supervisors and management's attempts to force them to sign "yellow dog" contracts renouncing union membership. They were more successful in pummelling the plant manager into temporary submission, however, than in achieving their long-term goals. Although a settlement was reached and the workers were rehired, the Company refused to reinstate the female supervisors or to permit on-going union activities.[43]

For those women engaged in the clerical and retail trades, both unionization and strike activity were rarer, partly because of the safer working conditions, and because of their perception of themselves as a better educated, higher status occupational group for whom trade union activities were inappropriate. Moreover, managers often pre-empted attempts at organization by providing employee welfare schemes such as company cafeterias, recreational facilities, pensions for loyal long-term workers, and piecemeal benefits for the "deserving." In Montreal the associations for women in white collar occupations that had been created by the *Fédération Nationale Saint-Jean-Baptiste* before World War I continued to operate. But total memberships never exceeded a few hundred women, and the major objective of these associations remained the educational and moral betterment of their members rather than fighting for better working conditions or pay.[44]

In some regions, on the other hand, female white collar workers recorded considerable progress in organizing during this decade. In 1918 local women teachers' organizations had formed the Federation of Women Teachers' Associations of Ontario. Given the chronic post-war inflation and inadequate salaries for its members, the federation assigned top priority to equal pay for equal work and contract protection. Within a year, over one-third of the province's women teachers had joined the federation. The militancy of some women teachers was demonstrated in 1922, when several in Owen Sound threatened strike action to support their demands for a decent wage. The local board of education conceded by raising the minimum salary for female teachers to $1200. In western Canada female teachers also sought to improve their position by joining forces. The Saskatoon Women Teachers' Association continued to campaign for

better contracts, equal pay for equal work, and the retention of married women as teachers. This activism notwithstanding, women in the teaching profession were still treated as second class citizens. Their salaries lagged significantly behind those of men teachers; those who married generally lost their permanent contracts or were dismissed, while their male counterparts received bonuses. Enrollment in the women teachers' associations remained strictly voluntary, and only a minority of rural teachers belonged, which restricted both financial stability and bargaining power.[45]

Similarly, nurses continued to press for better working conditions and a greater degree of professional recognition and self-regulation. In 1928 student nurses at Guelph General Hospital reacted to the heavy workload and the regimentation by launching a strike that lasted for two days. Although it appears to have resulted only in the departure of some of the nurses involved, the strike demonstrated that even the most powerless of women were prepared on occasion to strike back at the "system."[46]

Women's militancy in the 1920s was not confined to those who worked for wages. In several instances workers' wives, mothers, and daughters lent both immediate and longer term support to their male family members' labour struggles. In coalminers' strikes in Nova Scotia (1922) and Alberta (1923), the militancy of the miners' wives was a significant factor in the collective demonstration of solidarity the men were able to mount. One Ukrainian woman in Edmonton recalled her first involvement in a labour dispute: "In 1921 there was a strike. We walked the picket line. We left at four in the morning. The police prevented us from going and pushed us with rifle butts. I was afraid. There I met other women, and we went to the Labour Temple for meetings." In Cardiff, Alberta, women armed with sticks engaged in a pitched battle with police and strikebreakers

Miners' wives barricade the entrance to the Flin Flon community hall to stop a back-to-work meeting during the 1934 strike.

Working in a lobster cannery, New Brunswick, 1920.

or "scabs," and some were subsequently arrested and convicted of disturbing the peace.[47]

A most depressing decade

If the 1920s were difficult years for women workers, the 1930s were disastrous. Wages plummeted, working conditions deteriorated, union membership declined, and women's right to work was even more seriously challenged. For women who worked at home there was enormous pressure to replace unemployed family members in the labour force, to supplement the reduced wages of those still working, and to intensify their domestic labour to make ends meet. As the Depression deepened, millions of Canadians experienced unprecedented deprivation and an immeasurable loss of dignity. Although governments clumsily attempted to attenuate the worst effects of the economic crisis, they directed most of their efforts to aiding men. Once again it was assumed that the vast majority of women would be looked after by their families, and those women who had none able or willing to support them were initially left to fend for themselves.

At first the world-wide economic crisis that began in October 1929 appeared to stimulate the entry of women into the labour force. In many families the role of breadwinner was transferred from men, who were now unemployed, to daughters and wives able to find work in traditional female areas of employment. By 1931 there was already a 2 percent increase in the labour force participation rate of women aged ten and over, compared to ten years earlier. However, much larger increases occurred among women in their twenties and thirties; there was a 7 percent increase for those aged 20–24 years, and a 4.5 percent increase for those between 25 and 34 years. Evidence presented in 1934 before the Special Committee on Price

Spreads and Mass Buying emphasized the vital role women were playing:

Of 30 women from one non-union shop, practically all of whom were earning less than $12.50 per week . . . 21 were married and were the sole providers for the family or were helping to support them; eight were single, but were helping to support their families, while only one girl had no dependents and no family obligations.[48]

As the crisis grew and the national unemployment rate mounted to almost one-third of all workers, resentment against wage-earning women increased. The deep-seated prejudice against married women working outside the home intensified, and the appropriateness even of single women working for wages, widely conceded during the 1920s, was now called into question. These convictions transcended regional, ethnic, class, and, to some extent, gender boundaries. Whether it was the westerner who counselled Prime Minister R.B. Bennett to end unemployment by firing all single young women, or the leaders of the Canadian Catholic Confederation of Labour, including those representing female textile workers, who petitioned the Quebec government to bar all women from working for wages except in cases of absolute necessity, the message was the same: get the women out of the paid labour force. Men contended that they were being replaced by unskilled female workers. Women in business and the professions were also accused of taking away men's jobs. Stories abound of women who had to be content with lengthy engagements, clandestine relationships, or secret marriages in order to retain their jobs. For ethnic women the discrimination encountered in securing employment was exacerbated by the pervasive prejudice against non-Anglo-Saxons. Anti-Semitism was especially rife during the 1930s: one woman in Winnipeg was able to obtain and keep an office position only because, as she was tall and blonde, her employers did not realize that she was Jewish.[49]

Despite the widespread perception of the threat women posed to male employment, there is incontrovertible evidence that desperate male workers were undercutting women's wages and supplanting them in several industries. In the garment, textile, and leather industries, the practice of giving preferential treatment to male workers was common. Married female operatives, some with many years' experience, were dismissed so that their work could be reallocated to male workers, often at rates of pay well below the minimum required for women workers. In the cotton industry, ring spinning, a job consisting of minding sets of spinning frames, was previously considered women's work. During the Depression years it was assigned to men as well, and female spinners at the Magog mill in Quebec reported being replaced by male textile workers from Sherbrooke. Thus the minimum wage legislation that had been intended to protect women often proved their undoing. At one textile mill in Valleyfield, Quebec, a group of female apprentice weavers signed a petition imploring the provincial government not to apply minimum wage legislation to them so that they could keep their jobs. The substituting of lower-paid male for female workers became so widespread that, in order to maintain male wage levels, the provincial governments of Ontario and Quebec extended their minimum wage legislation to include men. British Columbia had already made a similar move in 1934. Legislation originally affecting only women thus finally generated an important new category of wage support for industrial workers. In Paris, Ontario, skilled female operators constituted the majority of the knit goods workforce, and they continued to enjoy greater security of employment than their male relatives.[50]

But often, when women were successful in securing or maintaining positions, they experienced drastic wage cuts and deteriorating working conditions. In Ontario, the Factory Act was amended to allow the implementation of a double shift for women and youths between 6 A.M. and 11 P.M. The fact that so many of Canada's female wage earners were concentrated in industries characterized by low capital investment and intense competition rendered them all the more vulnerable to exploitation. This was particularly true of the garment trade, where many small, undercapitalized entrepreneurs fought to maintain their markets by slashing production costs. Even large, well-established companies such as the T.E. Eaton Company cut wages, reduced the number of employees, and increased production quotas. Mrs. Annie Wells, an examiner who began work at Eaton's in 1916, testified before the Price Spreads Commission that she was not allowed to sit down during her eight-hour shift, and after 1931 she was not able to make the minimum wage because the piece rates had been so greatly reduced. The price for sewing a dozen dresses was cut from $5 per dozen before 1929 to $1.35 by 1934. The resulting physical and nervous exhaustion of the workers led another witness, Miss A. Tucker, to declare that "the girls were just about insane. In fact it got to such a climax that they were threatening to commit suicide and even I myself was contemplating the same thing. . . ." Another employee revealed that she had gone out only once in 1934 — to celebrate her birthday — the only time she attended a movie in three years.[51] But once again it was home workers who suffered the most. In one Quebec home, a woman and her daughter produced a dozen pair of boys' short pants for 30 cents minus 5 cents for the thread they used. Their average daily production was one dozen pants.[52]

Whatever limited occupational mobility had existed for women workers now vanished. In one large Quebec cotton mill, young girls who normally would have progressed from learners to weavers within a few months, now spent several years toiling at unskilled jobs. For many women there was only downward mobility into domestic service; between 1921 and 1931, there was a 7 percent increase in female wage earners employed as domestics, and a 6 percent decline in those engaged in manufacturing. For Canadians with fixed or steady incomes, the standard of living improved as prices dropped, and many families found they could afford a domestic helper. In Vancouver, a domestic servant could be engaged for as little as $10 per month plus room and board. Local relief officers encouraged young women without jobs or families to support them to become servants, and the only major initiative to reduce female unemployment undertaken by governments was the development of domestic training programs.

Municipalities did not initially provide relief for single women; indeed their first priority was to try to provide what limited assistance they could afford to married men. This usually took the form of make-work projects such as street improvements, and highway and sewer construction, projects that required the use of many unskilled labourers. Similarly, the federal government gave subsidies to the provinces to undertake highway and railroad construction work, which provided jobs almost exclusively for men. Although municipal relief for single men was often poorly organized and inadequate, usually some attempt was made to provide food and hostel accommodation; responsibility for single women was generally relegated to their families or to private charitable organizations. Women were not perceived as posing a serious threat to the social order, as did the roaming bands of unemployed young men who "rode the rods," in spite of the fact that "girl hoboes were frequently encountered."[53] Even when women could qualify for financial assistance, relief officers could be sexist and insensitive. Some women were told that "with figures like theirs" they did not need relief. According to C.G. MacNeil, the member of parliament for Vancouver North, relief payments to women were so inadequate that "they are compelled to live in only the most disreputable parts of the city, denied any chance to dress respectably . . . ready material for prostitution in its most sordid forms."[54] For some women, prostitution was the only way they could eke out a livelihood during the Depression. Immigrants who could not get jobs faced double jeopardy. If they had been in Canada less than five years they could be deported if they went "on relief."

Wives of men who lost their jobs strained to cope with the financial, social, and psychological repercussions of living with an unemployed breadwinner. Husbands frequently left their families to search for work elsewhere, and sometimes deserted them altogether rather than face the humiliation of failing to provide. The number of female heads of households in Edmonton, for example, rose from 978 in 1921 to 2653 ten years later.[55] The social stigma associated with being "on the dole" was crushing: the relief authorities confiscated all possessions they considered luxuries, such as cars, radios, and jewellery. Persons receiving relief had to hand in their liquor permits, and if they owned a telephone it was removed. The limited financial assistance successful applicants received usually took the form of food and rent vouchers; no provision was made for the replacement of clothing or for the sundry items most Canadians considered essential. When their silk stockings wore out, women powdered their legs and drew a black line down the back. Wives, mothers, and sisters made clothing from flour bags, and mended, patched, and darned until the cloth disintegrated; sometimes women and children became virtual prisoners in their homes because they lacked suitable clothing to go out. Women also often lacked the cooking facilities and fuel they needed to prepare what little food they had. They substituted chicory or roasted grain for coffee, game for the butcher's cuts, and invented an endless variety of "mock" dishes. In order to obtain additional milk and clothing for her children, one woman consented to have sexual relations with her relief officer.[56] When their myriad and continuous efforts to sustain the family failed, a few women appealed directly to the prime minister for help. Their letters reveal not only the pathetic state to which many had been reduced, but also their habit of putting husbands and children first, and their unshakeable faith in God and country. The moving entreaty from Mrs. C.L. Warden of Lambert, Saskatchewan, written in the winter of 1934, speaks for itself:

Your Honor:
I am writing you regarding Relief. Will you please tell me if we can get Steady Relief and how much we should be allowed per week we have three children, 2 of school age. . . . There are times we are living on potatoes for days at a time. . . . I am five months pregnant and I haven't even felt life yet to my baby and its I feel quite sure for lack of food . . . the two oldest children and I are suffering from abscess teeth can we get them out and have the town pay for the Dental Bill. . . .[57]

For some women even the opportunity to appeal to public authorities was brutally denied. When Stepan Chiruk was imprisoned for three months for killing a moose and her calf in order to feed his family of six, his wife was told that she must agree to have him sterilized, or else the entire family would be deported. Zosya Chiruk refused, distributed her children among the neighbours, and went into hiding in the bush in northern Alberta. Eventually Zosya hired a lawyer, who advised her to return home with her children; this she did, only to find the police at her doorstep. Since there were many neighbours present, the police promised Zosya that the family would not be deported, and that her husband would be allowed to return. Later that same night, the neighbours now all gone, the police returned and took away Zosya and the children. The entire family was sent back to the Ukraine.[58]

Life during the Depression was also very harsh for many older women who were separated, divorced, or widowed. Their sex and age combined to reduce their chances of employment. One particularly poignant story involved a needy and resourceful seventy-seven-year-old English widow who advertised for a pensioner husband to supplement her small income. Although she did find a husband by this means, he was under seventy and therefore not yet a pensioner; consequently, when his son reneged on a promise to provide his father twenty dollars per month until he reached pensionable age, the woman's financial situation was ironically made more precarious.[59]

Women of all ages and regions fought back against the indignities and deprivations with whatever limited means they possessed. Rural women on the Prairies, who confronted drought, dust, grasshoppers, sheriffs' writs, and bank foreclosures, found support in women's organizations and new political parties such as the CCF (Co-operative Commonwealth Federation) and Social Credit. In 1932 Jewish women in Toronto, including labour militants, factory workers, and housewives, organized a boycott of kosher butchers who were charging exorbitant prices for their products. "Every butcher was picketed each morning by small groups of women, often starting at 6:00 A.M. They tried to prevent anyone from going in, and often ripped the meat out of the hands of those who did buy, and threw it into the street."[60]

As for unions, membership fell sharply during the worst years of the Depression as competition for jobs intensified. Workers were afraid to join unions for fear of losing their jobs; they often could not afford to pay the union dues. Nonetheless, there were some significant organizational initiatives. In 1936, Laure Gaudreault, who had started teaching thirty years earlier at the age of sixteen, formed an association of female rural school teachers in the Chicoutimi area of Quebec. Created to protest the provincial government's failure to implement a promised salary increase, this group developed within a year into the *Fédération catholique des institutrices rurales*. Under Gaudreault's leadership, it undertook a vigorous campaign to improve the desperately low salaries and primitive working conditions that women teachers in rural schools had so long endured.[61] In the cities of Montreal and Toronto, leftist activists such as Lea Roback and Pearl Wedro worked to attract garment and fur workers into unions. The only unions to demonstrate any increase in membership during the early 1930s were those affiliated with the Workers' Unity League, which had been organized in 1929 by the Communist International and the Communist party. In 1934 alone, the Workers' Unity League organized 109 strikes involving some 50 000 Canadian workers. Prominent among its affiliates was the Industrial Union of Needle Trades Workers, which was involved in the Toronto Dressmakers' strike in February 1931, and the Montreal garment workers' strike of August 1934. In the latter, thousands of young women, primarily of Jewish and French Canadian origin, took to the streets, and when attacked by mounted police, fought back by stabbing the horses with pins.[62] It was surely no coincidence that, during the course of this violent strike, which lasted over six weeks, the Quebec Minimum Wage Commision announced a slight upward adjustment of wages for female operatives in the garment industry, and reduced the work week from 55 hours to 48 hours. When the workers returned to work, however, the battle for union recognition was lost, and within a year the Workers' Unity League had been disbanded.

Cross-class solidarity among women was vividly illustrated in 1934 during a strike in the Eaton's dressmaking department by the workers who belonged to the International Ladies' Garment Workers' Union. Members of the Toronto Local Council of Women and other middle class women's organizations raised funds for the strikers, lobbied government officials to force a settlement, and even joined the picket line. When the strike failed, the Local Council provided funds to help some of the strikers set up their own co-operative dressmaking shop.[63]

In April 1937 it was the International Ladies' Garment Workers' Union that led yet another strike of Montreal women's garment workers, popularly called "midinettes." After four weeks on the picket line, the workers won a general wage increase of 10 percent, a forty-four hour work week, and more importantly, the "closed shop" — only workers belonging to the union could be engaged by those companies that signed the collective agreement. Subsequently, further significant improvements in salary were established through arbitration, but the workers' victory was shortlived. Many employers simply reneged on the terms of the agreement. Among the first to join the union was Yvette Charpentier. Sent to work at the age of ten, she became an active organizer among workers in the dress industry, and eventually became the union's director of educational services. Four months later, in August 1937, even more women were on strike in Quebec as a result of a province-wide walkout in the textile industry. This strike, led by the Canadian Catholic Confederation of Labour and lasting over a month, ended with an agreement arbitrated by Cardinal Villeneuve, which won only minor improvements for the workers.

After long and bitter conflicts, the immediate gains of these strikes were either negligible or minimal, but such confrontations constituted important demonstrations of female workers' solidarity. The strike of the "midinettes" or female garment workers in Montreal was especially significant, for it demonstrated the militancy of women previously considered unorganizable, and their ability to transcend the ethnic and linguistic divisions that employers had previously exploited to keep the workers from uniting. Moreover, a new generation of female organizers, such as Lea Roback, and Yvette Charpentier, emerged from the strike to carry on what would become a successful struggle for unionization over the next two decades.

10 At home

The disruption to family life brought about by World War I strengthened the desire for a return to peacetime lifestyles. For women, this meant a reaffirmation of traditional roles as wives and mothers at a time when increased educational and job opportunities appeared to offer more choice than ever before. These seemingly paradoxical attitudes and assumptions about women's place did not, however, result in any major changes. Rather they coalesced as the image of the "new woman" was incorporated into a value system that reasserted and redefined the female traits of femininity, domesticity, and dependence.

Whether women wanted or expected a return to pre-war "normalcy" or not, social, economic, and demographic changes were shifting what was normal. By 1921 nearly half the Canadian population was living in urban centres, and this trend continued throughout the inter-war years. As urbanization increased, family size continued to decline, particularly among the working class. Analysts of 1931 census data suggested that working class couples were making a conscious decision to limit the size of their families in order to escape poverty and to improve their social position.[1] The average number of children born per Canadian woman fell from 3.2 in 1930 to 2.7 during the Depression decade, in large part because of delayed marriages.[2]

Better public health practices altered the life expectancy of both men and women, primarily by reducing infant mortality. A Canadian woman born in 1931 who survived infancy could expect to live to 62.1 years, and a man to 60 years; a woman born a decade later had a life expectancy of 66.3, while that of a man was 63.[3] Since most Canadians got married, their longer life expectancy increased the average length of marriages. This, combined with smaller family size, extended the time between children leaving home and the death of the husband or wife. Couples who married in 1920 could expect this post-parental period to be almost seven years longer than it was for those who had married in 1900.[4]

While none of these changes altered women's major role within the family, the nature and performance of that role was subjected to increasing scrutiny and pressure during the inter-war years. Through educational systems, newspapers, books, and magazines, new ideals and standards for women were created, all aimed at preserving the "best" of the old attitudes and assumptions about proper female roles while accommodating the "best" of the new.

Creating the educated housewife

Training for adult roles was increasingly the concern of formal educational institutions and systems, as young people generally spent more of their formative years in school. School-leaving age varied from province to province, and even within provinces, ranging from fourteen in New Brunswick and Manitoba to sixteen in Ontario, Alberta, British Columbia, Saskatchewan, and cities in Nova Scotia. There was still no compulsory attendance law in Quebec. Attendance requirements reflected rural or urban realities and economic conditions—legislation allowed exemptions if children were required during the fishing and fruit-picking seasons, or for other seasonal labour on farms, for necessary household duties such as the care of siblings, or for "personal maintenance" to support themselves or their families.

A young person's ability to take advantage of education continued to vary according to class, gender, race, ethnicity, religion, and rural or urban residence. Nevertheless, by their early teens, virtually all children had received some formal schooling.[5] On average, Canadian boys and girls spent almost 10 years in the classroom by 1931.[6] Even those living in remote areas could participate through correspondence courses, which were introduced across the country during the 1920s, and in the 1930s through school radio broadcasts.[7] Instruction, however, for most girls in remote areas continued to be interrupted by seasonal farm or domestic labour. The letters of twelve-year-old Edna Snyder of Ashcroft, British Columbia to her correspondence teacher provide a typical example. In the first month of 1927 she wrote to her teacher explaining, "I have only been to school for three years. I have gone since I was nine years old and only had one whole year, [as] the others were only parts. I am also teaching my brother." Two months later Edna had to abandon her lessons to help her father haul hay. The 1934–1939 correspondence between Alma Paubst and her teacher reflects the similar frustration this teenager experienced. Alma routinely had to put up with interruptions in her formal learning during the farming season or when family members were ill. Non-routine farm tasks also claimed her time, as she noted in a letter dated May 14, 1937: "I haven't much time to do lessons now. We have to build a new barn before haying time and now that we have a cow we have to put up all new fences and plant the garden."[8]

Urban girls too, and not exclusively in working class families, were expected to sacrifice lessons when other chores, paid or unpaid, demanded their time. Nevertheless, increasing numbers of girls completed elementary school, and more young women enrolled in secondary schools and in the universities than in the pre-war period. Enrollment of women undergraduates reached its peak in 1930, when 23.5 percent of all undergraduate students were women. The ratio of female to male undergraduates declined throughout the

1930s, although in absolute numbers, undergraduate female enrollment increased from 7428 in 1930 to 8107 in 1940. The proportion of women in the total graduate enrollment also dropped during this decade, going from 26 percent in 1930 to 20 percent in 1940. Unlike undergraduates, the actual number of women graduate students declined slightly, from 352 in 1930 to 326 a decade later.[9] Within the universities and colleges, moreover, women were channelled into "female" departments: home economics, nursing, and courses such as the secretarial science course first offered at the University of Western Ontario in 1925. In the prestigious faculties of medicine, law, and engineering, women remained a tiny minority.

In addition to basic literacy skills, elementary and secondary school curricula emphasized the development of vocational skills designed to prepare women for marriage and motherhood, and for careers that complemented these roles. Throughout the 1920s and 1930s, provincial departments of education, pressured by the established women's organizations and new ones like the United Farm Women of Alberta, expanded domestic science programs in the public elementary and secondary schools. These programs now reached greater numbers of girls than previously and could be followed to a higher degree of specialization. For girls in Quebec, domestic science classes frequently replaced academic subjects like science in the province's secondary and normal schools.[10] British Columbia appointed its first director of Home Economics in 1926. At that time, fifty-five home economics teachers were employed in elementary and secondary schools, teaching some 11 955 students, or close to one in four of the girls enrolled in public schools. In keeping with the application of scientific principles to household management, British Columbia's courses stressed order, cleanliness, and the use of "good" equipment. Classroom visitors and reporters remarked upon the regimentation and attention to detail. As one commentator noted after visiting a class, the teacher gave her students

a thorough training in systematic methods, the work of her classes being performed with almost military promptness and precision, each dish in each girl's cupboard being in its exact place, and even the knives, forks and spoons being ranged like a row of little soldiers.[11]

Many parents and taxpayers criticized the programs as a waste of time and money. Some complained of the lack of attention to practical activities and the overemphasis on order and theory, as in prescribed lectures on hygiene and nutrition. Others worried about students' possible frustration and dissatisfaction when they were unable to apply the prescribed theories and practices in their own homes. In class, girls cooked on modern electric stoves and ironed with electric irons, but rural and working class girls went home to the reality of wood or coal stoves and flat-irons. Teachers stressed standardization of recipes, a practice impossible in a home without measuring utensils, and at odds with family recipes handed down from generation to generation and calling for a "handful" of this and a "pinch" of that. Interviews with students exposed to domestic science training in British Columbia's schools during the 1920s suggest that most school-taught practices and recipes were rejected in favour of the training received at home. One former student recollected the dreadful indigestion she suffered after eating a Waldorf salad prepared at school. Her digestive system could not tolerate the celery and nuts, ingredients beyond the financial means of her family and new to her.[12] The tension between home and school created by the content of domestic science curriculum was exacerbated by the perception of many working class mothers that such classes undermined their authority and denigrated their personal role in educating their daughters.

Proponents continued to stress the role of domestic science in training working class girls, both to ensure "better run" working class households and to provide a supply of trained servants for middle and upper class households. This latter rationale became particularly important in the 1920s, when the women who once might have gone into service increasingly opted for factory or other jobs. Many girls, including those from middle class homes, now spent their formative years in classrooms and moved on directly from school into the working world. As a result, it was believed that girls of all classes had insufficient opportunity to learn household skills from their mothers. Increasingly, middle class "professional" women, such as teachers, nurses, and secretaries, married after living away from home in boardinghouses or other non-domestic settings. Without school-based instruction, domestic science advocates maintained, these women would lack the necessary skills in scientific homemaking when they needed them. Paradoxically, they were implicitly accepting women's increased participation in the workforce while simultaneously developing various rationales for domestic science training that reinforced traditional attitudes about women's domestic role.[13]

Outside the school, youth clubs developed their own educational programs. Organizations such as the Girl Guides of Canada, the Canadian Girls in Training, and the Girls' and Boys' Clubs of Canada (later the 4-H Club), added new objectives to their earlier goals of developing moral, upstanding citizens. They encouraged female independence while at the same time emphasizing domestic activities related to girls' future roles as wives and mothers. In 1935, some 1200 4-H Club girls in Manitoba independently organized and ran their own clothing and food projects. Although there was no prize money, the girls set up competitions and sold home-made goods, using the profits to assist themselves and their families.[14] Paralleling the pattern of groups for older women, organizations like the 4-H and the Girl Guides provided opportunities for camaraderie, leadership, and the development of decision-making skills.

The stress on the development of both domestic skills and independence was in keeping with the expectations held for adolescent girls once they left school. Canadians increasingly assumed that nearly all girls, whether working class or middle class, would seek employment. Organizations like the YWCA, business girls' clubs, and settlement houses continued their educational and support services for single working women living away from home, attempting to recreate a family atmosphere by fostering individual and group morality as well as homemaking skills.

These services were regarded as essential in the 1920s in a society alarmed by the media image of the "flapper"—the girl who indulged in "immoral" pursuits such as drinking, smoking, wild dancing, and party-going. The author of the 1922 *Maclean's Magazine* article, "Is the Flapper a Menace?," confirmed society's worst fears, even though she admitted that the majority of young Canadian women followed more "chaste" lifestyles. Three flappers, aged seventeen, eighteen, and twenty, all from middle class homes, had described to the author a motoring outing where such large quantities of bootlegged liquor were consumed that one of the flappers declared, "It was a wonder we got back without an accident." Another told of "fussing" parties "where each girl sits on a boy's knee and lets him kiss her all he wants to do. Sometimes the kissing goes on for hours." According to the flappers, unchaperoned parties were commonplace and mothers were too innocent to know what was going on at them.[15] In her book, *The Black Candle*, Judge Emily Murphy combined anecdotes from her courtroom experience with national and international statistics to link contemporary evidence of youthful women's moral laxity to drug trafficking, prostitution, and the white slave trade.[16]

Ultimately, the "independence" Canadian women gained from paid employment was considered by most to be temporary; marriage and leaving the labour force remained the goal for most women. The media bombarded women with anxious pronouncements on the virtual impossibility and, above all, the undesirability of combining marriage with a career. Short stories telling of independent young women happily trading their jobs for marital bliss appeared frequently in widely read magazines like the *Canadian Home Journal* and *Maclean's Magazine*. Sometimes the stories related the unhappy lives of married women who attempted to be both housewives and paid workers, but eventually found true happiness by staying at home. Given that the circulation figures for these magazines were relatively high, the impact of such stories was potentially significant.[17] Canadian women's interest in having their own magazine was illustrated by the fact that 70 000 entries were submitted in the contest to name a new magazine. The winner, Mrs. Hilda Paine of British Columbia, received a cheque for $1000. Her suggestion, *The Chatelaine*, was chosen because it "seemed to have about it a feminine grace . . . in one word, it expressed women and Canada."[18]

For those working women who traded their jobs and careers for marriage, a real or a potential conflict did exist. Given women's typically low pay, their social and economic status usually improved with marriage. But it now reflected their husband's position, not their own. A number of factors helped to ease the transition from a limited form of independence, where women had some money of

Table 10.1		Household amenities, 1941			
	% Electric lighting	% Inside running water	% Telephone	% Refri- geration	% Flush toilet (private)
Rural					
Farm areas	20.2	12.2	29.3	22.2	8.1
Rural non-farm	59.5	41.0	27.8	35.9	32.8
Urban					
< 1000	75.0	35.0	24.7	35.0	27.7
1000–5000	94.1	81.6	34.0	56.3	66.5
5000–15 000	97.2	94.4	45.0	66.1	82.8
15 000–30 000	98.7	96.4	53.8	67.4	85.2
> 30 000	99.4	98.5	57.3	79.2	88.9
Canada Total	69.1	60.5	40.3	50.9	52.1

Source: *1941 Census*

their own to spend, to marital dependence. First of all, most young women from the working class did not experience independence as we know it, since they continued to reside at home and contribute most of their wages to their families. In addition, women continued to be socialized and trained from their earliest years for their wifely role, and many preferred this role to the alternative of poorly paid work and spinsterhood. Relatively new forces were also at work. The burgeoning household technology industry and the mass media increasingly defined homemakers as new "professionals"; household management itself was touted as a "career." The customary, supposedly haphazard, approach to housework and childcare were to be replaced by the principles of science and business.

The promises of the new technology were especially appealing to those middle class women who could not find or afford to employ domestic servants. The growth in the number of families with disposable income coincided with the application of new technologies developed during World War I to domestic uses. Products such as instant coffee, tinned goods, and rayon were aggressively advertised in the mass media, and increasingly these ads were directed towards women, a recognition of the family's growing role as a unit of consumption, and that a woman's job was buying.[19] The key to the new domestic technology was electricity, which became available in the majority of built-up areas by the end of the 1920s. According to the 1941 census, nearly all urban homes had electricity. Some 60 percent of rural non-farm homes used electricity, but only one in five farm households had it.

Electricity meant a clean, safe, and efficient method of lighting and cooking. The electric stove not only cooked food but helped ensure a constant supply of hot water; the electric refrigerator preserved food more efficiently than iceboxes, and made less mess; the electric washing machine, in conjunction with the new easy-care fabrics, abolished many heavy and time-consuming laundry chores. Women greeted these appliances with enthusiasm. At the same time, however, standards of family nutrition and cleanliness continued to rise. Appliances like the washing machine also brought back to the urban household tasks that had been removed during the earlier industrial period. Urban women who had sent laundry out to commercial laundries or self-employed home laundresses now found themselves washing clothes. The actual benefits of appliances such as vacuum cleaners and floor polishers are questionable. There is no doubt that the new appliances greatly decreased the physical effort involved in household labour, a fact much appreciated by housewives, most of whom now worked alone. But rising standards of housekeeping meant that they won little free time as a result.

The acquisition of all these appliances required a reorganization of the kitchen, and a new art of kitchen planning evolved based on convenience and efficiency, borrowing from organizational principles used in industry. For the minority of families able to afford such renovations, built-in cupboards replaced movable cabinets and open shelves, providing increased storage space. Cupboards, countertops, and appliances were positioned to minimize unnecessary walking, bending, and climbing. Articles and intensified advertising in women's magazines and local newspapers praised the advantages of the changing technology and the streamlined kitchen. As a result of the media and advertising campaigns, and of the exposure in domestic science classes, many women became convinced of the benefits of change.

Women's actual financial control over household purchases was, of course, limited by their economic dependence and their ability to persuade husbands to spend the money. This was clearly demonstrated in the advertising campaign by the Dominion government in connection with its 1936 Home Improvement Plan. Designed as a means of promoting employment within the depressed construction industry, and clearly directed at middle class men, the plan provided low-interest loans to property owners for repairing and modernizing homes. The government also recognized women's vital importance to the plan's success, however. Promotional literature focussed on their role as financial managers and consumers; the advertising assumed that women needed little convincing of the advantages of modernization. Joined by the media, and by manufacturers of house-

A new electric washing machine and iron, Ontario, 1921.

hold equipment, the government urged women to convince their husbands to take out loans to create new kitchens, bathrooms, dens for men, "rumpus" rooms for children, or "recreation" rooms. Only after meeting the needs of husbands and children was it suggested that women plan rooms entirely for their own use, perhaps a sewing room in the attic.[20] Certainly, women who could afford to do so welcomed opportunities to modernize their homes and equip them with the latest technology. Consumer credit companies such as Household Finance Corporation also promoted the idea of borrowing money for these purposes. Many women found the advertisements' claims appealing, and believed that they would be happier, freer wives and mothers as a result of spending less time on household chores.

The educated mother

The time women supposedly saved from domestic toil was to be spent on the now magnified responsibilities of caring for husband and children. During the 1920s and 1930s, medical and other experts bombarded women with popularized versions of new theories relative to childbirth and childcare. Scientific approaches were to replace instinct, intuition, and informal advice. The new methods, like those for household management, required more time, but smaller families meant that the mother could pay more attention to each child. High maternal and infant mortality rates had worried late nineteenth and early twentieth century social reformers, but their efforts at reversing these trends at first met with limited success. The loss of life in World War I motivated a renewed and systematic campaign to ensure "the production of future generations of healthy Canadians."[21] The campaign was fuelled by the findings of a number of studies on maternal and infant mortality by Dr. Helen MacMurchy, perhaps the best-known publicist of the infant welfare movement in Canada.

Appointed by the Ontario government in 1910 to study and make recommendations on the problem of infant mortality, Dr. MacMurchy produced reports that brought her to national prominence as a doctor, writer, lecturer, and government official. When the federal government created the Child Welfare Division of the Department of Health in 1919, MacMurchy became its chief.

Her 1926 report confirmed the extent of maternal mortality, but did not address itself to solutions. A number of women's organizations, medical associations, and government agencies then studied and recommended ways to combat the problem of infant and maternal mortality. Three major needs emerged: formalized pre-natal education and care, increased medical competency, and improved socioeconomic conditions. Government and other appropriate agencies directed their efforts towards the first two areas; for the most part they ignored the low standard of living that jeopardized the health of many pregnant women and their babies.

Reformers adopted the strategy of educating women and providing them with what was perceived as the correct information. Health care authorities advised that women should improve their physical health long before they became pregnant. Pregnant women should be monitored by a doctor or through medically supervised pre-natal clinics. Government and public health agencies published and distributed brochures written by doctors. The most famous of these, *The Canadian Mother's Book*, available in English or French from the Child Welfare Division of the federal Department of Health, had over 200 000 copies in print by 1922. Childbirth itself was to be supervised by a doctor; it increasingly took place in a hospital, until half of all births took place in hospitals in the larger provinces: in British Columbia by 1928–29, in Ontario by 1938, and in Quebec by 1945.[22] For many women the hospital experience was a positive one, providing them with a chance to rest and be looked after before returning home to normal household activities, care of the new baby, and in most cases, other children. Leila Middleton's March 29, 1930 diary entry expressed this fact. After one miscarriage, one stillbirth, and two home deliveries, she gave birth to her third and fourth children in the hospital in Clinton, Ontario. Since she also had three stepchildren at home, it is not surprising that she wrote, "I enjoyed my hospital stay."[23] The drawback was that doctors increasingly treated the process of giving birth not as a natural event but as a medical one, undermining traditional support networks and practices.

Once the child had been born, experts from the fields of psychology, education, and social welfare prescribed correct methods for mothering. Women who failed to heed this advice were viewed as irresponsibly endangering the survival, health, and character of their children. Popular articles, well-baby clinics, radio talks to mothers, pamphlets produced by governments and businesses, visits by public health nurses, and lectures to women's organizations, all ensured that more and more Canadian women received instruction in "approved" childrearing practices.

No aspect of infancy, childhood, or adolescence remained untouched by the new scientific authorities. Beginning at birth, prescribed feeding times, especially for bottle-fed babies, allowed for no deviation. Breast feeding was preferred, but for those who could not or would not, the correct methods of formula preparation were widely publicized. Unless there was a good reason to the contrary, weaning was to take place at nine months of age. Age rather than the baby's state of readiness also determined toilet training. Regimented sleeping and exercise patterns rounded out the infant's schedule. Strict adherence to all these methods, mothers were told, would promote not only physical but also emotional health. Behavioural and other problems in later life were attributed to the mother's failure to establish the discipline required by industrial society. Anything that detracted from the formation of appropriate regular habits was frowned upon.

While the literature urged parents to love their babies, it advised against outward signs of affection, such as hugging and kissing, on the grounds that this behaviour would likely produce spoiled, nervous, and irritable children. Furthermore, medical experts suggested that excessive handling of infants could lead to a variety of physical problems, including bone deformities and spinal curvatures.[24] Of course, not all women followed the advice of the experts. Discussing the rearing of her first-born infant, Phyllis Knight, a working class woman who had immigrated to Canada in the late 1920s, rejected "silly psychological books," preferring instead instinct, tradition, and observation.[25] But not all mothers may have been so strong-minded.

The mother of school-aged and older children also received instruction about how to oversee their physical, emotional, and intellectual development. Children's prompt and regular school attendance, their cleanliness and health, and their attitudes to school and learning all demanded the mother's co-operation with, and support of, the educational and public health professionals' efforts. The authorities insisted on their right to intervene in the parent-child relationship by virtue of their scientific approach.

Mothers were also active in disseminating these values. In Baddeck, Nova Scotia, they formed the first Canadian Home and School (or Parent-Teachers') Association in the 1890s; during the first two decades of the twentieth century, the movement slowly spread. The major expansion of these associations occurred during the 1920s and 1930s, when both local groups and provincial federations flourished. A national federation, devoted to the training and guidance of children and youth both during and after their school years, was established in 1929.[26] The federation's growth during the inter-war period indicates an acceptance of the partnership of parents—usually mothers—and experts, while the fact that recommendations for changes in the school curriculum frequently originated with parents shows that their involvement was not purely passive. Music and home economics, for instance, were two subjects vigorously promoted and actively organized by parent members of Home and School groups. Rural mothers also became involved in the education of their children through women's organizations. The United Farm Women of Alberta's Education Committee, for example, sought to improve rural education both inside and outside the classroom by emphasizing educational experiences that were both social and practical.[27]

The duty of monitoring the time children spent outside school was no longer the parents' alone. Social reformers and professionals railed against the effects of child employment, against unchaperoned, co-educational activities, and against idleness. They advocated instead protected, supervised home or group cultural pastimes.[28] A particularly strong media campaign in the 1920s linked the social immorality of modern life and the problems of youth to parental failure in rearing and supervising their sons and, particularly, their daughters.[29]

One proposal to combat problems caused by idle time was to convince school and municipal authorities to allow the use of school equipment and playground facilities after hours and during vacations for activities organized by trained instructors.[30] Another, perhaps more successful one, was for the organization of athletic clubs and youth sport groups.[31] Interest and participation in sporting activities promoted healthy alternatives to evil temptations, it was argued, not only during the school years but also into adulthood. Although the question of women's biological fitness for physical activity continued to be debated, physical education teachers and medical authorities generally agreed that suitable types of exercise programs were beneficial. Sports for girls were encouraged so long as they were neither too aggressive nor too competitive. Organizers were cautioned about the possible adverse effects of strenuous activities during puberty. Care was to be taken to ensure normal menstruation patterns were established and maintained, and that no damage occurred to the female reproductive system. Menstruation continued to be viewed as a disabling time, during which girls were excused from gym classes and other sporting events. At the same time, gentle calisthenic exercises were promoted as a relief from menstrual pain and as a contribution to the development of good posture in young women.[32]

Parental acceptance of the experts' views concerning the limitations that should be placed on girls' physical activities cost at least one young Maritimer the opportunity to compete in the 1928 Amsterdam Olympic Games. Gertrude Phinney, Canadian champion in the 220-yard dash, qualified for the games but did not participate because her father believed "that strenuous exercise such as that demanded of a track athlete would most certainly have adverse effects on child bearing and cause perhaps 'irreparable harm' to the mysterious workings" of her female body.[33]

It was generally the mother's responsibility to administer the experts' prescriptions for the proper physical, mental, and social adjustment of children, and the ultimate responsibility for a child's success or failure remained with her. Motherhood was promoted as a woman's patriotic and moral duty, as well as her life-long profession. As Dr. Helen MacMurchy put it in 1922,

Being a mother is the highest of all professions and the most extensive of all undertakings. Nothing that she can know is useless to a mother. She can use it all. The mother reports for special duty about 250 days before the baby is born and she is never demobilised until she meets the Bearer of the Great Invitation. Mother, at ninety years, is still Mother.[34]

Fearing the harmful effects of feminist politics on Quebec families, Monseigneur Georges Gauthier, archbishop and coadjutor of the Montreal Diocese, used his 1930 New Year's Eve sermon to stress the moral aspect of women's proper role "as queen of the home, creator of the race." Monseigneur Gauthier concluded that, "through their noble maternal functions," women held in their hands "the education and moral formation of the future generation."[35]

The experts who extolled the virtues of the scientific, informed approach to motherhood promised that, if their advice were followed, it would not only produce well-adjusted and healthy offspring, but would also reduce the time involved in raising children. Little cognizance was taken of the contradiction in these arguments. In reality, acquiring, updating, and applying this information took more time than mothering had in the past. Mothers were now expected to read books, pamphlets, and relevant articles in the popular press, to attend baby and child health clinics, and to participate in mothers' clubs, parent–teacher associations, and the running of youth activities. Mothering, if one followed the experts, was becoming a full-time job. At the same time, experts ignored the economic reality of many women's lives. The literature advocated lengthy rest periods before, and recuperations after pregnancy that were impossible for most working class and farm women, or for those with other offspring and no domestic help. Similarly, doctor care and hospitalization cost money, as did the long list of baby articles considered necessary for a baby's layette. But what choice did a mother have? If she believed in the literature, she might see her failure to provide the idealized home for her baby and growing child as seriously endangering its physical and emotional survival.

While the role of fathers was neither as circumscribed nor as scrutinized as that of mothers, it too was subjected to considerable attention. Preparation for "perfect" fatherhood, as with motherhood, was to begin long before birth. The ideal father was physically and morally fit, and a good provider. While mothers were assigned primary responsibility for childcare, and for character and personality development, the father's role was to be supportive in every way possible. The literature accepted that men lacked their wives' patience, understanding, and time to study the new training methods, but suggested they use their own business skills of efficiency and understanding to develop friendly relations with their children. The age of the tyrant father was over; instead he should provide an inspiring influence for his children. This meant taking time from his busy schedule to initiate and participate in such activities as ball games, fishing expeditions, and visits to the zoo or the circus. However, although experts did not assign father's role the importance of mother's with regard to the daily childcare responsibilities, they clearly recognized the father as the final authority and head of the family. "Bringing up children is a two parent job," commented one writer, "and almost always father sets the pace."[36]

The ideal marriage

The experts intended that mothers' time, allegedly freed up through scientific childcare and household management, should be used primarily for the pursuit of an ideal home life. Family planning and birth control advocates suggested that reduced family size would lead to improved marital happiness; removing the fear of unwanted pregnancy, moreover, could lead to more satisfying sexual relations. Indeed, books and birth control advice frequently included counselling aimed at enhancing the sexual aspect of marriage. *Sex, Marriage and Birth Control*, a 1936 Canadian guidebook written by an Anglican clergyman, stated as a fact that, "In the life of love that marriage implies, satisfactory sexual intercourse is the prime factor."[37] Intuition and instinct were no longer sufficient for couples to achieve the desired sexual relationship. They now were expected to study marriage manuals in order to learn about the workings of their bodies and the correct sexual responses. For most women, however, cultural taboos continued to shroud the subject of menopause, and the attitudes of medical authorities towards menopausal problems remained the same as they had been in previous decades.

The expanding cosmetics industry emphasized the role of physical attractiveness in promoting a satisfactory marital state. It advocated the use of face creams, cosmetics, mouthwashes, and deodorants as a means of promoting and maintaining an acceptable body image. Beauty parlours proliferated as new, shorter hairstyles required the attention of trained hairdressers. In fact, employment opportunities for women in this industry increased even during the severe unemployment of the Depression. Advertising downplayed the relationship between beauty and sexuality in favour of more acceptable campaigns stressing the retention of a youthful appearance and enhanced femininity. This theme was echoed in women's magazines, in articles in the popular press, and in books. In *Margaret Currie — Her Book*, the author, a columnist for the *Montreal Star*, devoted a chapter to "Beauty," outlining methods for skin care, weight loss, and hair styling. Other chapters dealt with household financial management, laundry, cooking, and the "Middle Aged Wife."[38]

The focus on weight loss reflected another aspect of the contemporary, preferred body image — slimness. World War I had a liberating effect on women's clothes; short, loose dresses that de-emphasized breasts and hips became fashionable, giving rise to the

A typical advertisement for patent medicines for women.

pursuit of a slim, boyish look. Corsets had earlier been discarded by young women; girdles had replaced them. Now women were advised to maintain a "trim" figure through careful diet and exercise programs as well. For the plump or big-breasted woman, this translated into painfully binding her breasts and starving herself into the fashionable silhouette. Aging or even mature women were out of style in the heyday of the cinema vamp.

Physical and sexual attractiveness was not all that was required of a wife. While it was acceptable for middle class, married women to engage in hobbies such as bridge, golf, and tennis, and cultural pursuits like piano playing, amateur acting, and painting, most "free" time was to be devoted to being a loving, supportive companion for their husbands. Women's magazines frequently exhorted their female readers to take up their husbands' interests and educate themselves in order to augment their wifely roles.[39] The idea of the wife as a husband's "best friend" became increasingly popular. Young people were counselled to seek marriage partners whose interests, education, and values reflected their own. Even in Quebec, where the Catholic church adamantly opposed any form of birth control, the clergy stressed the importance of friendship and companionship within marriage. Newly implemented marriage preparation courses used these ideas to reinforce the old prohibition of marriage outside the faith.[40] Other churches were perhaps less explicit, but also encouraged marriage within the fold, by sponsoring chaperoned activities for young adults.

The idea of companionate marriage may in part have been a response to demographic factors. As family size fell and longevity for both sexes increased, it became more and more likely that couples would spend a longer time together after their children had grown up. The idealistic view of marriage as a more equal partnership was also supported somewhat by changes improving the legal status of wives within marriage. These included provincial equal guardianship laws, and the federal 1925 Divorce Law, which for the first time

A bridal party, Montreal, 1920.

allowed a woman to obtain a divorce on the same grounds as a man — namely, simple adultery. Yet equality and companionship often translated into support of, and submission to, husbands who continued to be the heads of families both in theory and in fact. Husbands were rarely encouraged to take up their wives' interests; women continued to be responsible for the home. According to editorials in *Chatelaine*, it remained a wife's duty to create a smoothly run haven for her hard-working husband. When problems arose it was her responsibility to solve them.[41] Fearing possible rising divorce rates after the enactment of the divorce laws in 1925, the popular press constantly reminded women that it was their duty, honour, and privilege to preserve family stability for the benefit not only of the family but also of the nation. Throughout the Depression, this same press exhorted women to budget wisely, and to provide emotional support for unemployed husbands. Self-sacrifice and restraint of selfish desire were the hallmarks of the "good" wife in the ideal family setting.

Difficult as it was for middle class women to attain the high standards expected of them in all areas, for most working class, rural, or immigrant women, the ideal was impossible. Almost all rural families still used outhouses and depended on outside water supplies.[42] Gwen Lefort, a sixteen-year-old, World War I war bride, discovered as much upon her arrival in Canada in 1918. Her French Canadian husband had told her "glowing stories" about Canada, none of which prepared her for life in Cheticamp, Cape Breton, where she spent fifteen years before moving to the nearby town of New Waterford. In Cheticamp she raised nine children and, as she later recalled:

I cooked meals and scrubbed floors and washed my kids clothes on the scrubbing board you know. And drew water from the well—there was no indoor plumbing or anything.[43]

Many of the basic amenities lacking in her Canadian home were ones she had taken for granted while growing up in an English city. Her experience was not unique. Many Canadian women coped with similar conditions. Even those who enjoyed comfortable material conditions had little time for reading, let alone practising the experts' advice on being an ideal wife or perfect mother. In addition, of course, the advice literature could not be understood by women who were unable to read either English or French.

For most Canadians, moreover, the husband's wages, supplemented by a wife's or children's pay or other household economic strategies, were barely enough to provide housing, food, and basic necessities. By 1928 it was for the first time theoretically possible for the average male manufacturing worker to earn sufficient wages to provide for a family on his own. But in 1929, 60 percent of Canadian working men and 82 percent of working women earned less than the minimum necessary for the support of a family of four.[44] The concept of the family wage was unrealistic at the best of times, and when strikes or unemployment hit, many women faced debilitating hardships. Following her 1925 visit to inspect conditions during the Glace Bay coalminers' strike, Canada's first woman MP, Agnes Macphail, criticized the federal government for its "neglect of humanity," particularly its failure to address the problems of the emotional and physical effects of this strike on women.

I could not help but be struck by the tragedy of womankind in that place. Their youth is brief. Some young women are hotly resentful . . . but for the most part, especially if they have many children, their attitude is subdued and apathetic.[45]

For the working wife or the wife raising livestock or taking in boarders to make family ends meet, the time required to achieve the ideal household, children, or marriage was simply not available.

The Great Depression placed additional strains on women when the ideal became bread on the table, not a sparkling General Electric kitchen. One Winnipeg immigrant woman's inability to cope had a particularly tragic ending in December 1934. Despondent over her husband's continual lack of work and the prospect of a poverty-stricken Christmas, according to the newspaper account,

She had just completed the hanging of Christmas decorations in her little home. Then with the home bravely adorned and spotlessly clean, she strangled one child, drowned the other in the bath, and killed herself by drinking a powerful germicide. There had not even been enough money in the house to buy the poison that killed her. She left a farewell note on the kitchen table bearing this out. 'I owe the drug store 44 cents; farewell,' it said.[46]

Help for wives and mothers

Meeting the new standards was difficult for women who were poor, and impossible for poor women with large families. Yet the distribution of information and the sale of birth control devices were both illegal, and for the women themselves the subject was often embarrassingly taboo. Throughout the 1920s, desperate Canadian women wrote seeking contraceptive advice from *The Birth Control Review*, a journal published in New York by Margaret Sanger, founder of North America's first birth control clinic. The following letter from a Saskatchewan woman was typical:

I am a young married woman nineteen years old and I have a dear little baby boy five and a half months old, and I am expecting another baby in four months. Now, we are not in a position to support more than two children as my husband and I both work hard for a living. I love my baby and I want to give him a fair chance in life. I have a good husband and he don't want to see a big family in want any more than I do. I have good health at present, but oh! Mrs. Sanger, how long would it be good if babies came to me that fast, and once health and happiness are gone, what is the use of asking help then? Now is the time, and if you could only tell me how to prevent conception you would make me the happiest woman in Canada.[47]

The pleas came from across Canada, from working and middle class women and also from men. A college-educated woman related how, after three pregnancies, she had followed a neighbour's totally inadequate advice about birth control and given birth to two more children. Her health gone, she had decided, "not to go back to my husband unless I can know of an absolutely certain contraceptive." Physical separation was the best advice that some doctors were willing to give, and many still warned that mechanical methods of birth control were dangerous as well as disreputable.[48]

Women used a variety of contraceptive measures. But as the two letters to *The Birth Control Review* illustrate, their knowledge was limited and often incorrect, and such information was only made available by being passed privately from one woman to another. During the inter-war years, the question of limiting family size moved from the private to the public arena, but there too it was surrounded by controversy. Believers in the superiority of British stock continued to argue that the practice of family limitation among the Anglo-Saxon middle class would gradually but ultimately lead to "race suicide," because they would be outnumbered by the larger immigrant and working class families. A similar argument was put forward by French Canadian nationalists, who feared for the survival of their culture should the francophone population decline. The United Church of Canada emphasized the use of contraception by married couples as essential for the promotion of companionate, Christian marriages, but members of fundamentalist religions condemned the use of birth control as immoral and likely to contribute to sexual promiscuity, while the Catholic church proclaimed that marriage existed for procreation and that any attempt to thwart this purpose was a sin.

Despite these arguments, birth control advocates worked to educate couples. Initially, public debate and support came from the Canadian left. Particularly influential were American birth control leaders like Margaret Sanger, or the anarchist Emma Goldman who, during her exile in Canada, expounded her view that birth control was an individual woman's right, part of the right to control her own body, and a necessary weapon in the workers' struggle against capitalism. This latter argument found favour among some socialist groups, who were convinced that the capitalist system encouraged large families in order to have a cheap source of labour for its factories and cannon fodder for its armies.[49] In 1924 the Canadian Birth Control League was founded by British Columbia socialists, who recognized the need for education among the working class.[50] Equally concerned about the physical and mental toll of unwanted pregnancies on farm and working class wives, the women's branch of the United Farmers of Canada's Saskatchewan section passed the first public resolution on the matter at a 1929 convention. Calling upon the government to rescind the ban on the distribution of birth control information, delegates requested the establishment of birth control clinics staffed by trained doctors.[51]

A birth control clinic founded in British Columbia in 1932 also counted among its objectives the need for "good breeding," and recommended the sterilization of the "unfit."[52] The use of such eugenic arguments became increasingly popular in the 1930s, when the ranks of the unemployed caused rising relief costs, and deteriorating economic conditions raised fears of social unrest. Birth control clinics were established in at least three provinces: Ontario, Manitoba, and British Columbia. Rising relief costs also concerned Dr. Elizabeth Bagshaw, the pioneering medical director of a clinic in Hamilton, Ontario from 1932 to 1966. But her main motivation — like Margaret Sanger's in the United States — was her genuine concern for the plight of working class women facing repeated unwanted pregnancies. Founded and largely financed by Mary Hawkins, a wealthy Hamilton widow, the clinic was a godsend to many women, some of whom were given the contraceptive devices they were unable to pay for.[53]

The debate about family limitation received national attention in 1936 when Dorothea Palmer was charged under the Criminal Code for distributing birth control information and devices to women in Eastview, a working class, French Canadian suburb of Ottawa. Palmer was employed by Alvin R. Kaufman, the wealthy owner of the Kaufman Rubber Company. Inspired by a growing personal conviction that limiting family size was essential for maintaining social order in a depressed economy, Kaufman had established the Parents' Information Bureau in Kitchener, Ontario in 1929. The bureau hired married women as field workers in many parts of Canada; at the time of Palmer's arrest it employed fifty-three field workers to visit the homes of poor women and counsel them about birth control. During the Palmer trial, experts testified that it was "in the public good" to provide contraceptive information in areas such as Eastview, with its large French Canadian families and population of unemployed who were receiving public relief. More telling still were the twenty French Catholic women who testified that Palmer's work was appreciated and that they saw nothing wrong with the contraception methods the Parents' Information Bureau promoted.[54] The defence was successful, Palmer was acquitted on March 17, 1937, and an appeal of the verdict was dismissed. Yet, although the trial provided a platform for opponents and proponents of birth control, and had an undoubted effect, the law regarding the distribution of birth control information and devices was not rewritten.[55]

The economic hardships suffered by some families had been recognized in a limited way by governments through the introduction of mothers' allowances in Manitoba, Saskatchewan, Alberta, Ontario, and British Columbia between 1916 and 1920. Nova Scotia introduced them in 1930 and Quebec in 1937, leaving only Prince Edward Island and New Brunswick without this assistance during the inter-war years. Mothers with families who, through no fault of their own, were left alone with the responsibility of raising children, were eligible for the allowances, which were to be short-term sup-

Table 10.2   Mother's allowance and pensions as compared to adequate standard of living, 1939

	Adequate standard/ mother and two children $	Mother's allowance $	Adequate standard/ aged person $	Average monthly pension $
P.E.I.	—	—	25.70	10.94
N.S.	53.80	30.00[1]	25.90	14.71
N.B.	—	—	27.10	14.16
Que.	54.60	40.00	26.30	17.85
Ont.	59.00	40.00[2]	28.40	18.51
Man.	58.90	50.00[3]	28.30	18.66
Sask.	54.20	12.00	26.10	16.59
Alta.	53.20	31.25[4]	25.60	18.44
B.C.	58.20	47.50[5]	28.00	19.27

[1] this was in fact the average monthly payment per family; the amount for a mother and two children was probably somewhat lower, since the average number of children was 3.3.
[2] this was the sum given to mothers in cities; the amount was $5 less in towns and $10 less in rural areas.
[3] not including $10 a year for winter fuel allowance.
[4] approximate.
[5] more was in fact allowed by the act, but $5 less was given to home owners.

Source: Historical Atlas of Canada. Funded by the Social Sciences and Humanities Research Council Toronto: University of Toronto Press, forthcoming).

plements, not regular income. Both the eligibility requirements and the amounts provided varied from province to province. Widows were eligible recipients in all provinces; some provinces also paid allowances to deserted wives, wives whose husbands were physically and mentally handicapped, or wives of prisoners. Mothers with one dependent child qualified in certain provinces but not in others, and the maximum age of dependency varied from fifteen to sixteen. In all provinces, except Alberta and Saskatchewan, to qualify for assistance the mother had to be a British subject, or the widow or wife of a British subject. This resulted in the disqualification of many immigrant women, as well as those women who lost their status as British subjects upon marriage. All recipient mothers were encouraged to earn additional income when they could do so without neglecting their family responsibilities. Applicants were scrupulously scrutinized and recipients supervised to ensure that they were truly deserving.[56]

The replacement of voluntary philanthropy by state assistance reflected the growing concern of the English-speaking middle class to enlist the state in the campaign to support Canadian family life. Institutions such as orphanages, refuges, and training and reform schools, and even foster families were increasingly under attack for their failure to produce good results. It was best, it was now argued, to use means that encouraged mothers to remain at home and keep their families together. There was, however, no recognition or financial support for women who were responsible for elderly or handi-capped adults and dependents. Mothers' allowances, like compulsory school attendance laws and child labour legislation, represented exam-ples of direct state involvement in family life.

An astonishing case of state intervention in an individual family occurred in Corbeil, Ontario in 1934 with the birth of the famous Dionne quintuplets. The poor, rural, French Canadian parents of these children were completely "relieved" of the responsibility for raising their five girls, implying quite clearly that provincial author-ities disapproved of the parents' values and lifestyle. Within two months of the birth, the provincial government placed Yvonne, Annette, Cécile, Emilie, and Marie Dionne under the control of a board of guardians, which did not include their parents.[57] In Septem-ber of that year, the five-month-old babies were moved from the family farmhouse to a separate, specially equipped "hospital" build-ing, and placed under the care of Dr. Allan Roy Dafoe, the doctor who had delivered them. Dafoe instituted what he called, in the foreword to his mothers' guidebook, "medical control," typified by rigorous monitoring of every aspect of the quints' lives and environ-ment.[58] Although their parents might visit the girls, Elzire and Oliva Dionne could not interfere in their care, despite Elzire's protests in favour of her own cultural practices and her desire for an active role. In 1936 Dr. William Blatz, Canada's leading child psychologist, took control, introducing his own system of disciplined, scientific routine and child study. Only in 1938 did the Dionne parents' arguments, combined with those of Catholics and Franco-Ontarian nationalists, succeed in restoring the parents' authority. But the damage had been done. It was too late to heal the rift that had developed between the quints and their family. The saga of the Dionnes represented more than intervention on the part of the government. The experts involved made their reputations and fortunes, and all Canadian women were treated to yet another campaign designed to convert them to perfect, germ-free childrearing.

Unconventional women

Some women did not or could not conform to the idealized maternal role, with its emphasis on self-effacing femininity or on scientific child-management, and righteous moral indignation continued to haunt the lives of many of these women. Unwed mothers were seen as "weak and ignorant, strong-minded and wicked, or simple-minded."[59] The only exceptions tended to be those who were the victims of sexual abuse. The nuns who ran Montreal's *Hôpital de la Miséricorde* shielded their inmates from the outside world, but expected them to perform domestic duties both for their keep and as atonement for their transgressions. Wherever possible the unwed mother was encouraged to marry, even if the prospective husband was unsuitable, because marriage was seen as the only means of achieving a respectable living other than entering the convent. A more direct response to illegitimacy, in this case among women deemed mentally ill or feeble-minded, was sterilization. Between 1935 and 1945 fifty-seven of the sixty-four patients sterilized at a British Columbia hospital were women. Of these, forty-six were single women and the mothers of thirty-three illegitimate children.[60]

Little or no attention was paid to the situation of those women, who for reasons of choice or circumstance, did not marry. Yet some women challenged society's right to control their sexuality and restrict it to marriage. As knowledge of birth control spread, some women separated their sexuality from procreation. As early as 1928, a Canadian female university student questioned the assumption that she would marry, arguing that women should have the option to remain independent but not necessarily celibate. Introducing her discussion as a "protest and an explanation," this anonymous critic noted that she was not against marriage as a social institution, but against having it thrown in her teeth as an "inevitable goal" or as "the simple panacea for all one's difficulties and ambitions."[61] A few women chose to fulfill a desire for motherhood and children despite their single status. Most single, immigrant women came to Canada with cultural beliefs emphasizing the overriding importance of marriage, family, and motherhood. Some of the Finnish women who had come to Montreal as domestic servants seem to have consciously chosen to have children despite their unmarried state. From 1936 to 1938, the average unmarried Finnish mother's age at her child's birth, as registered at Montreal's St. Michael's Finnish Evangelical Lutheran Church, was over thirty-seven.[62]

Most people, however, believed that the only respectable lifestyle for an unmarried woman was celibacy. Many such women chose life in a Roman Catholic (or Anglican) religious order, and the number of sisters and the number of female orders, inside and outside Quebec, continued to expand. Over 15 000 women entered full-time religious life between 1921 and 1941. The convent still represented an important form of economic security, especially during the Depression years, as well as offering a spiritual role, the possibility of self-development, and a career. For some, it even provided a certain degree of independence.[63] But not all Catholic women wanted to join a religious order, and for most Protestant women, this option did not exist. In both French and English Canada, independent unmarried laywomen constituted an important group. This lifestyle was economically viable only for those few women whose occupations would support separate households or joint establishments with other women. Charlotte Whitton, a social worker and later executive secretary of the Canadian Council on Child Welfare (who gained further renown and some notoriety as mayor of Ottawa during the 1950s) lived with Margaret Grier, another federal civil servant, for almost thirty years until Grier's death in 1947. Their relationship involved not only an economic partnership, but also provided emotional support, in a period when such relationships between women were increasingly suspect.[64]

Even married women could deviate from the conventional ideal of the housewife and mother depicted by the glossy magazines. The New Glasgow, Nova Scotia, temperance inspector, Clifford Rose, ran into a number of women who made ends meet for themselves and their families in ways that hardly accorded with the ideal. He recalled the notorious women, known as "mothers," who ran the "worst dives" in town. One, whose name was Delores, "was a mite of a woman [but] . . . her obscene and profane tongue was feared by friend and foe." Delores escaped prosecution for running an illegal tavern by smashing her rum bottles in the sink when the inspector was hammering on the door. The most famous of the women rum-runners, known as the Queen, was the object of veiled admiration. A former nurse, horsewoman, and part-time movie actress in the United States, the Queen had returned to her native Nova Scotia with her husband in order to care for her aging parents. Attracted by the money to be made in smuggling rum, she used her commercial acumen—and her ability to bribe highly placed government officials — to create a business that even the inspectors had to admit was successful.[65]

Clearly, women like Delores and the Queen had not been able to depend on their husbands to make ends meet. Many other women did not have husbands and nonetheless had children or other dependents to support. A family in which the mother stayed at home to look after the house and her children, while her husband, as the sole breadwinner, supported the entire household, was an ideal to which many—perhaps most—families could not conform.

The inadequacy of the family wage was finally recognized with the introduction by the federal government in 1944 of the family allowance, a monthly sum to be paid for each child. This controversial measure, as the debate surrounding its passage showed, focussed on the need to supplement the wages of the male breadwinner. Underlying the initiative was the assumption that, except in emergency situations, married women were responsible for children and ought not to be wage earners. Family allowance cheques were to be made out directly to mothers, a rule that initially was to be applied in all provinces but Quebec. There the cheques were to be made out to the fathers. It was Quebec feminist and politician Thérèse Casgrain who discovered this extraordinary plan and managed to stop it in its tracks before the first cheques were issued. After a delay of three weeks, Quebec women also received the family allowance cheque.[66] Family allowance legislation did benefit families in all provinces; and it was important that the money was controlled by women. At the same time, it reinforced the traditional view that the man was the wage earner, and that woman's proper role was a domestic one.[67]

11 Proving themselves in public life

Buoyed by their achievements and the recognition they had received during World War I, women's organizations entered the post-war period determined to solidify their gains and extend their social, economic, cultural, and political influence. Even in the depths of the Depression this optimism was never completely abandoned. Speaking to the Canadian Federation of Business and Professional Women's Clubs in 1933, Josephine Dauphinee of Vancouver challenged the members to "study, read, discuss, . . . and learn to draw conclusions from your thinking. The men will welcome you to their councils and with equal rights, men and women will confer together over the problems of the day."[1]

Women's suffrage, of course, was no longer a shared goal once the federal and all provincial governments except Quebec had granted women the vote. Temperance had also ceased to be a major issue with the introduction in many provinces of government regulations controlling liquor distribution and sales. The child welfare and public health programs long advocated by women's groups gradually moved forward with the establishment of the Federal Department of Health and its Child Welfare Division (1919), and the development of similar provincial and municipal agencies. Staffed in some cases by former activists of the women's reform movement, these agencies also opened up career opportunities for women as professional social work gradually replaced voluntary efforts.[2]

Professional organizations

Career aspirations prompted many women to join organizations focussing on an occupation and seeking to establish women's equality with men.[3] One example was the Federation of Medical Women of Canada, established in 1924 to provide women doctors with a forum in which to meet, exchange ideas, and discuss problems. A founding member was Dr. Elizabeth Bagshaw, who subsequently became the driving force of a birth control clinic in Hamilton. Within a year of its founding, the federation had sixty-five members on its rolls, drawn from all provinces. Another example of separate organizations for professional women was the Canadian Women's Press Club, which by the 1920s had branches in Winnipeg, Edmonton, Toronto, Vancouver, Ottawa, Halifax, and Saint John. These and other groups, such as the Federation of Women Teachers' Associations of Ontario and the Canadian Nurses' Association, were now able to launch

Sculptors Frances Loring
and Florence Wyle.

vigorous campaigns to enhance the status of their members as professionals. Women doctors, teachers, nurses and journalists worked to improve their salaries and to develop special training and career opportunities. Their primary identification was with their chosen occupations; most members of these groups were single women, brought to activism through their professional connections.[4]

Local business and professional women's clubs had started before the war, beginning in Alberta in 1912; in 1930 they joined together in the Canadian Federation of Business and Professional Women's Clubs, chaired by Dorothy Heneker of Montreal, then the only Canadian woman to hold both Bachelor of Civil Law and Bachelor of Common Law degrees. Active in business, and working as a subordinate in her father's law firm because Quebec regulations would not allow women to practise law, Heneker was keenly aware of the disadvantages endured by working women. Others shared her concern, for by 1937 there were over 2000 members in Business and Professional Women's Clubs in centres across Canada.[5] These clubs sought to improve the social and economic conditions of working women by promoting training and advancement for women in their careers. From their inception, the clubs were committed to equality between men and women. Armed with their own survey on unemployment, in 1933 the National Board endorsed the principle of unemployment insurance, but added the proviso that "any legislation which might be introduced in respect thereof shall apply equally to men and women."

The local clubs provided opportunities for women with similar jobs to meet socially and discuss issues of common interest. In the

Montreal club, biweekly talks ranged from parliamentary procedure to industrial working conditions for women in China and Australia. The club worked to establish a national health insurance scheme, lobbied the Quebec government for provincial and municipal political rights for women, provided funding and volunteers for other groups such as the Big Sisters' Association and the Montreal Girls' Association, and during the Depression, co-operated with the YWCA in registering unemployed women and locating jobs for them. During the Depression the federation also protested the dismissal of female bank clerks.[6]

Professional organizations separate from men's did not, however, suit the aims and objectives of all career women. Rather than organize their own groups, women in the arts tended to join men in founding mixed societies dedicated to the promotion of their work. Possibly their limited numbers, along with the struggle for recognition and acceptance experienced by all artists, male and female alike, encouraged collective strength. A number of female writers participated in the founding convention of the Canadian Authors' Association held in 1921, and women artists were among the founders and active members of the Canadian Group of Painters. In 1933 nearly one-third of the members belonging to the latter group were women, and six years later, landscape artist Isabel McLaughlin was elected the first female president.[7] Women painters participated as founders in nearly all the major artistic organizing efforts of the inter-war years. In Montreal, the Beaver Hall Hill group (1920–21) brought together ten female and eight male artists, who not only shared studio space, but also contributed to the development of a co-operative modernist movement. Several women artists were invited by the all-male Group of Seven to include their works in its exhibitions and, in 1924, fifty-four works by thirty women artists were selected to represent modern Canadian art at the prestigious British Empire Exhibition held in England.[8] Among Canada's internationally acclaimed visual artists were sculptors Frances Loring and Florence Wyle. Together with colleague Elizabeth Wyn Wood and two men, they established the Sculptors Society of Canada in 1928, chartered in 1932.[9] Female sculptors had benefitted from the post-war enthusiasm for municipal and other patriotic memorials, and for the first time they competed equally with men to produce major public pieces.

The apparent breakdown of society during the Depression, and the emergence of new forms of political and social activism challenged some women artists to address the question of the relationship of their work to social change. Arguing for political involvement, painter Paraskeva Clark wrote, "those who give their lives, their knowledge and their time to social struggle have the right to expect help from the artist. I cannot imagine a more inspiring role than that which the artist is asked to play for the defense and advancement of civilization."[10] A similar consciousness stirred poet Dorothy Livesay, who with thirty-four others began the Progressive Arts Club in 1932, linking writers and the Left. Committed to social action in both her poetry and her life, Livesay described the summer of 1932, after her return from Paris, as "a crucial one for friendship and love . . . . My political convictions became the dominating obsession of my life. This lost me friends, split me away from parents, disrupted my relationship with my lover."[11]

Community groups

Other women who were not artists worked within the community to advance Canadian culture and art through existing and new organizations. The Women's Art Association of Canada carried on the tradition of promoting public interest in art, and among its varied activities, encouraged the work of women artists. By the 1920s it had active branches in large and small urban centres throughout the nation, and in 1927 it arranged the first meeting between Emily Carr and the Group of Seven.[12] Local groups like the Heliconian Club in Toronto sponsored a variety of cultural activities, and others like the the Hawthorn Women's Club, established in Winnipeg in 1923, worked to foster the study of the arts. Women's auxiliaries provided funding and promotion for many theatrical companies, musical organizations, art galleries, and schools of art. In 1936, Madame Athanase David organized the first Montreal Music Festival.[13] The local literary clubs, and Shakespearean and musical societies that had been common in the later nineteenth century continued, or new ones were formed.

During the 1920s, the older, reform-oriented organizations declined in membership, if not in activity. In the immediate postwar years, the National Council of Women of Canada continued to focus on motherhood and the protection of home life as necessary stabilizing factors after the upheavals of war. It largely ignored female career aspirations, or criticized them as a threat to the home, and promoted occupations such as domestic service, nursing, and teaching as suitable work for unmarried women. The National Council of Women of Canada's orientation discouraged many young professional women from joining, and even antagonized former supporters. The Canadian Women's Press Club, for instance, disaffiliated from the National Council of Women in 1925, and twenty-three Local Councils made the same choice within the next five years.[14] During the Depression years, when jobs were scarce, the National Council joined other Canadians in arguing that working women should not be competing with men for jobs. Both the National and Local councils did debate the plight of unemployed women, and undertook relief work in many localities; the concern, however, that jobless women would turn to prostitution or the suspicion that they preferred relief to domestic service jobs, pervaded council discussions. To counteract these perceived problems, the council endorsed the upgrading of domestic work, and the creation of self-help groups where unemployed women could come together to knit, sew, or quilt. Member associations were encouraged to establish domestic training courses, and the National Council adopted a Code for Household Workers, designed to improve working conditions and combat women's reluctance to accept domestic jobs.[15]

Within its family-oriented frame of reference, the National Council continued its reform work. The council backed and monitored mothers' allowance legislation, and continued to address the issue of child welfare in the home, in institutions, and in schools. It urged equal treatment for male and female divorce petitioners, the establishment of divorce courts in all provinces, an increase in the age of consent for marriage, the treatment of adultery as a criminal offense, and enhanced legal remedies for deserted wives. To safeguard the financial position of wives and mothers, it proposed amendments to the provincial dower acts.[16] Local councils also became involved occasionally in consumer issues, such as boycotts to eliminate large commercial and industrial profits on some products. The National Council's consumer policy, however, generally resembled that of the Canadian Manufacturers' Association, endorsing its "Made–in–Canada" campaign and accepting, uncritically, the growing role of advertising and the cult of household efficiency. The pro-manufacturing and central Canadian outlook of the national organization alienated many rural and western members.[17] Still, by the outbreak of World War II, National Council members had reason to feel that their work had helped to achieve considerable improvement in the quality of life for Canadian women. The care of the old and the sick had improved, women had benefitted from mothers' allowances, infant mortality and tuberculosis rates had declined, new urban parks served children's recreational needs, and in some regions innovative education programs had been put into place.[18]

The Woman's Christian Temperance Union continued to make prohibition its primary focus, and to work on a variety of fronts. Prison reform occupied some members, and during the 1930s, a number of western locals were involved in the Canadian women's peace movement. After the defeat of absolute prohibition in various provinces in the 1920s and the introduction of government liquor control, the union directed even more attention than previously to educating the public about the dangers of alcohol. Members continued their campaigns for temperance textbooks and courses in schools, held essay contests, and encouraged teachers to inculcate the virtues of temperance in their classrooms. Their gains are hard to assess. Public drunkenness may have become less visible in Canada as a result of the organization's efforts, but a ban on alcohol consumption was impossible to achieve. Prohibition was increasingly out of step with a society that no longer regarded the use of alcohol as a major social evil. [19]

The difficulties faced by the WCTU and the National Council of Women of Canada were not shared by all volunteer women's organizations during this period. Some, notably the United Farm Women of Alberta and the Women's Institutes, expanded their membership, influence, and programs. Rural women were disillusioned with the essentially urban orientation of the National Council of Women and turned to associations whose aims and objectives reflected their own needs. Established in 1915 both to educate members for self-realization and to improve rural health services and education, the United Farm Women of Alberta was directed by a central board. It nevertheless encouraged its member groups to undertake local projects such as the construction of libraries, to which the central body donated books. Locals organized lectures and study groups on literature, music, immigration, rural health care, and schooling. Irene Parlby, elected as a United Farmers of Alberta provincial member in 1921, recognized the constraints of rural life and saw the farm women's organization as a vehicle for a lifetime learning process, a practical outlet for her idealism and that of her peers. One of those very active and visionary peers was Susan Gunn, a former teacher, president of the United Farm Women of Alberta from 1924 to 1929, and a dynamic member throughout the twenties of the education committee of both the women's organization and the men's association, the United Farmers of Alberta. Parlby and Gunn were dedicated to progressive educational reform, and through their countless speeches and writings, did much to promote improvements in the province's rural schools. Speaking of her involvement in the agrarian movement during the inter-war period, Susan Gunn recalled:

I was caught up in the work of the UFA *and the* UFWA. *It was like a crusade, through co-operative effort we envisaged a new Heaven and a new earth, co-operative stores were started, municipal hospitals, the great wheat pools. . . . Then along came the devastating thirties and we were flat on our backs. It took us a long and weary time to get on our feet.*[20]

As Alberta's minister without portfolio from 1921 to 1935, Parlby supported and encouraged farm women to think beyond domestic questions and to broaden their horizons. One of the many ways that the United Farm Women promoted this objective was to organize, in conjunction with the provincial Department of Agriculture, annual conferences known as "Farm Women's Week" at the University of Alberta. Efforts to make this event as accessible as possible included the provision for pre-school children to attend at no extra cost.[21]

The goal of providing continuing education for rural women, and close co-operation with provincial departments of agriculture, were also central characteristics of the Women's Institute movement that flourished after the war. The institutes or homemakers' clubs engaged paid lecturers to speak about household science and agriculture, and these proved extremely popular. Although the development of domestic skills was a primary concern, many local institutes broadened their interests. The British Columbia Women's Institutes, for example, included business methods for young women as well as health care among the many other topics studied. When the province's Department of Health decided in the late 1920s to establish provincial health centres, it called upon the institutes for support to carry out its plan.[22]

In Quebec, the convergence of government, clerical, and rural women's interests in strengthening rural life had fostered the development and growth of French Canadian Women's Institutes, known as *Cercles de Fermières*. In 1919 there were already thirty-four locals amalgamated under a provincial council, and the *cercles* were among the founding members of the Federated Women's Institutes of Canada established in that year. The Quebec council initiated the publication of a review, *La Bonne Fermière*. Through this journal, and through lectures, study groups, and exhibitions, the *cercles* promoted the upgrading of homes and the development of farm skills.[23] Like the Women's Institutes, the *cercles* were encouraged by the state; also like the institutes, they reinforced the philosophy of separate spheres. They nevertheless provided opportunities for female organization and self-development. Perhaps more important, the institutes and the *cercles* opened new economic ventures for their members, and by publicizing rural women's traditional activities through exhibitions and sales, they validated farm women's work and attempted to professionalize it. Théodora Dupont, the vice-president of the Saint-Denis *cercle*, established in 1921, recalled the economic advantages of her membership:

The Minister of Agriculture gave us two hives of bees per circle. Selected by lot, I was the happy winner of one of the hives with all the necessary operating equipment . . . . The first beneficiaries of these gift hives had to give their first swarm to another farm woman who did not have one, in my opinion an excellent idea. After that, an inspector came several times in the season, without charge, to give us the required instructions. The following spring, each farm woman received fourteen Plymouth Rock chicken eggs . . . for us to incubate, which gave us the chance to improve our flock.[24]

During the 1920s, Canadian rural women's organizations served as a model that women from other countries copied, and in 1933 women from around the world met to create the Associated Country Women of the World.

The established women's organizations did not, for the most part, seriously court or attract minority women, who continued to organize their own associations. Most of these had three related objectives: to preserve and enhance their group culture, to help members of their ethnic community adjust to Canadian life and overcome prejudice, and to maintain contacts with and assist members of their group outside Canada. Ukrainian women, under the auspices of the Association of United Ukrainian Canadians, formed a Women's Section in 1922, and branches were organized in many localities.[25] Lillian Rutherford, a black woman in Montreal, organized the Phyllis Wheatley Art Club in 1922 for young black women and, in the mid-1930s, this club was reconstituted as the Negro Theatre Guild of Montreal.[26] Another black women's group, the Hour–A–Day Study Club, was established in Windsor, Ontario in 1934 to bring women together for self-improvement, to organize cultural programs and the study of black history, and to foster mutual understanding through involvement in the Windsor community.[27]

Jewish women, mainly of western European origins, worked together in the twenties and during the Depression in the National Council of Jewish Women. Through fundraising and volunteer work they supported schools, scholarships, orphanages, care for the aged, and summer camps. Another group, the Zionist Hadassah, formed during World War I and dedicated to providing social services to Jews in Palestine, attracted more recently arrived eastern European Jewish women. For their part, women in the Ladies' Section of the Macedonian Political Organization, founded in Toronto in 1927, dominated church and community social life. They raised funds and animated the community to support the achievement of a free and independent Macedonia while at the same time promoting and maintaining awareness of the Macedonian culture.[28] Armenian women, although also few in numbers, joined the Armenian Relief Society, which had Canadian branches even before World War I. As survivors of the Turkish massacres arrived during the 1920s, membership and activities expanded to include assisting Armenians internationally and locally, supporting Armenian choirs, theatre, poetry and lectures, and expanding knowledge of the language.[29]

Although group policy decisions were most often made by males, ethnic women made a vital contribution to the maintenance of group identity and adaptation. Moreover, not all women were content to play merely supportive roles. The Pioneer Women's Organization, a Jewish socialist group composed mainly of working class women born in eastern Europe, disaffiliated from the male-dominated Labour Zionist movement in 1925 because the women were disenchanted with their exclusion from the political process. This independent group pursued overtly feminist goals, supporting programs in Palestine and North America aimed at increasing women's and children's political and social awareness.[30]

Women's clubs were the training ground for many of the women who were to become active in public life. Florence Bird, later head of the Royal Commission on the Status of Women in Canada, gained organizational experience in Montreal and Winnipeg during the 1930s and early 1940s. An occasional columnist and magazine writer, Bird was "lonely and disoriented" when, in her twenties, she arrived with her husband from the United States.[31] They quickly developed friendships with the circle of Montreal progressive intellectuals who formed the League for Social Reconstruction. Bird also worked at a women's food depot several days a week, and joined with friends to form a women's Peace Study Group. At their semi-monthly meetings, members heard papers and discussed the causes of and cures for war. She later remembered preparing several talks for the group:

Evidently some of the members thought well of them, because I was invited to give four lectures on current events by the Montreal Junior League. I worked hard preparing those lectures. I was excruciatingly nervous beforehand and was seized with violent diarrhoea before each.[32]

Her talks were the beginning of a "most interesting and rewarding career." Bird was paid to lecture to other organizations, although she continued to speak before groups of working women without charge. In 1937 Bird's husband accepted the job of assistant editor at the *Winnipeg Tribune*. The uprooted Florence once again found herself isolated, and again found solace within women's organizations. She became active in the Social Science Study Club, an organization similar to the Peace Study Group she had left behind, and in the Winnipeg Junior League. Her early assessment of its members as "fat-cat women who amused themselves by playing the role of Lady Bountiful" changed as she underwent the requisite social work training course, and saw at first hand their community contributions. In her autobiography, she gives credit to these associations not only for their obvious contributions but also for their role in developing individual women's awareness of their potential.[33]

The pursuit of equality

Women's organizations, whether volunteer, cultural, or professional, shared a common theme: a desire for continuing self-education. Through formal and informal learning, women strove to improve their lives and those of other women. Many also recognized that self-realization for women required that young girls be trained to make decisions. With this goal in mind, the Canadian Girls in Training was founded in 1917 by the Young Women's Christian Association and the Protestant churches. Initially, the YWCA had sponsored Girl Guide companies, but its dissatisfaction with the Girl Guide's perceived secularism, imperialist and competitive spirit, and the lack of opportunity for girls to participate in decision making, convinced the YWCA that a different organization was necessary. Canadian Girls in Training was the result. These groups met with their leaders at Sunday School and at mid-week sessions. Their activities reflected progressive educational theories, emphasizing research and discussion, co-operation, and independent thought. Adolescent girls from twelve to seventeen were encouraged to participate in physical, religious, intellectual, and service activities, not for reward but for their intrinsic value. The enthusiastic response to the movement can be measured by its numbers; in 1925 there were 30 000 members in 3000 groups from Vancouver Island to Newfoundland. During the Depression (1933–34), numbers peaked at 40 000 in 1100 communities. Although the organizers assumed that marriage and motherhood were the ultimate goal for women, Canadian Girls in Training groups urged girls to pursue their educational studies as far as possible.[14]

Most youth-oriented groups, particularly the YWCA, stressed participation in physical education. Indeed, the 1920s and 1930s have been labelled the "Golden Age of Sports" for young women, in contrast to the previous generation. Organized physical activity and games for girls and women had the additional advantage that participants were supervised and kept out of mischief. School athletic programs expanded, and team activities such as basketball and baseball were popular, although after 1930 in eastern Canada, these games were usually played using "girls' rules" that restricted physical contact and limited physical exertion. The greatest development in women's sports was the expansion of women's amateur sports and athletic clubs. These separate organizations provided for women's participation as coaches, fundraisers, and administrators, as well as players. Women's sports caught the imagination of spectators and the press; business sponsored them to an extent that has only recently been matched. Phyllis Dewar of Moose Jaw, Saskatchewan became the first Canadian woman competitor to win four gold medals for swimming at the 1934 British Empire Games, a record until 1966. Perhaps the most famous team accomplishment was that of the Edmonton Grads. Formed from students and graduates of an Edmonton high school, this basketball team amassed 502 wins and only twenty losses from 1915 to 1940. Recognized four times as world champions at international tournaments, the Grads were forced to disband at the beginning of World War II because the military took over their practice facilities.[35]

At universities, women's sports thrived as well, but there was a significant difference in levels of support for men's and women's activities. Although the number of women students had increased, campus facilities for women generally remained non-existent or pitifully inadequate. As early as 1911, female students at the University of Toronto had petitioned for a gymnasium. When Hart House was finally built in 1919 for sports and extra-curricular activities, women were excluded. Although women at McGill had their own athletic facilities at Royal Victoria College, these were crowded and inadequate for the compulsory physical education program. The new Currie Gym, built on the McGill campus in 1939, assigned last priority to women's space requirements and accepted women only "on sufferance."[36]

Student activities were not all organized for each sex separately. The Student Christian Movement, which was formed in 1920 from the student departments of the YWCA and YMCA, provided university and normal school students of both sexes with an opportunity to examine and reflect upon the real and potential problems they faced. At some universities, the Student Christian Movement was co-educational; at others, men and women met separately. An offspring of the Social Gospel movement, this Christian reform association organized study groups on most Canadian campuses throughout the 1920s and 1930s to address social problems, and became an outlet and training ground for students interested in social change.[37]

Through their Student Christian Movement activities, many women sharpened inter-personal relations and developed organizational skills that were useful for their future successful participation in public life.[38] One such woman, Marion Royce, was a driving force in the YWCA both at the national and international level during the 1930s and 1940s, and later (1954) the first director of the federal

Learning to ski, Ontario.

Department of Labour's Women's Bureau. The applied Christianity learned in the SCM also led some women into political activism. Both Marjorie Mann and Avis McCurdy, later active members of the Co-operative Commonwealth Federation, credited the student organi-zation, at least in part, for their later political perspective. McCurdy, who came from a middle class Maritimes family, recalled in a 1982 interview, "I came straight to the CCF because I was convinced I had to be my brother's keeper. It was right out of my religious background — CGIT and SCM. I had also worked in business in my summers, and was overcome with the injustice and inequality."[39] Women's desire for equal participation extended into the major Protestant churches. Both the Methodist and Presbyterian churches had admitted female deaconesses from the 1890s, giving women an opportunity to participate in church life in a manner that mirrored their separate sphere: deaconesses visited the poor and the inmates of prisons, workhouses, and hospitals, and nursed the sick. Their limited training and lack of financial compensation reflected the churches' continuing perception of women's volunteer role. Though there were some improvements in training and salary by the 1920s, the failure of the female diaconate can be partially attributed to its inferior status within the church hierarchies. When a shortage of ordained ministers developed during and immediately after World War I, deaconesses had been called upon to take over many minis-terial duties and responsibilities, but at the same time were prohibited from administering the sacraments or performing marriages. Dissat-isfaction with these limitations in role and status caused many dea-conesses to leave and take jobs in the expanding fields of nursing and social work, areas where their skills were clearly welcomed. By 1925, the year of the Methodist, Presbyterian, and Congregational union as the United Church of Canada, there remained only sixty-seven Presbyterian and forty-seven Methodist deaconesses in Canada.[40]

Separate auxiliaries and charitable associations within their churches remained the avenue for most Protestant women's achievements. Mennonite women's organizations, like the Women's Missionary Society of the United Church, provided an example of how women's strength could be perceived as a threat to the male establishment. Informal Mennonite sewing circles had long provided social contact while producing clothes for the needy. In 1908, however, Ontario Swiss women formalized their circle as a mission society, possibly the first Ontario Mennonite group to do so. By 1917 the various female Mennonite and Amish societies had expanded sufficiently to unite as a district, preceding the formal male conference unions by several years. Unification increased the strength of the women's missionary group and was perceived as a challenge to the power of the male Mennonite Board of Missions and Charities. In the late 1920s, the church reacted by placing the women's societies under the control of the board. At about the same time new and strict dress regulations, much more prescriptive and restrictive for women than men, came into effect.[41]

Frontier areas attracted women missionaries, some of whom, like Eva Hasell and Monica Storrs, were British. Hasell began her work immediately after World War I. Trained in nursing, car maintenance and driving, she conceived a plan to spread the Anglican Sunday School movement to remote sections of the Canadian Prairies and British Columbia, using vans as mobile churches. Financed partly by her own money and partly by the Western Canada Sunday School Caravan Fund, Hasell's commitment and personal work continued until 1972 when she was eighty-four. In England in 1928, Eva Hasell met Monica Storrs, the then middle-aged daughter of an Anglican dean. Hasell convinced Storrs to undertake the mission of religious training in the Peace River area. Monica Storrs left for Canada in September 1929 to begin organizing Sunday schools, Boy Scouts and Girl Guides for the children of Peace River.[42] These women saw their work as sufficient reward and did not aspire to equality with the men of the church.

Other church women, however, were involved more directly in the fight for equality in their denominations. The slowly growing campaign for equal status within the Protestant churches realized one goal when the Methodist Assembly admitted women delegates for the first time in 1922. Nellie McClung, the seasoned women's rights activist, was instrumental in pushing forward this reform. She also urged that women be admitted as regular clergy. After the founding of the United Church in 1925, she devoted a major part of her energy to lecturing and writing on expanding the role of women in the church.

The standard response of the church leaders — that they were willing to consider female ordination only if and when there was a candidate seeking it — was first put to the test when a request for ordination was received from Lydia Gruchy in 1926. Gruchy, a theology graduate and preacher, served three large Saskatchewan congregations. Her acceptance by the congregations, and her endurance of the physical exertions involved in tending to their spiritual needs, ought to have defused arguments that women ministers were unacceptable to church members and could not withstand the hardships of extensive travel necessary in many rural areas. Still, Gruchy's application was refused by the 1926 meeting of the United Church's General Council, which instead recommended a new diaconate to which women could be ordained. This compromise was rejected both by Gruchy and her employer, the Saskatchewan Conference, which required a fully ordained minister capable of performing all the functions of that role. Continued requests for her ordination, made by the Saskatchewan Conference, were backed by Nellie McClung and a small but forceful group of supporters.[43]

The campaigners were disappointed by the lack of support received from the United Church's Women's Missionary Society, however. This society, created, supported, and administered by women, raised and controlled a million-dollar budget in the 1920s and maintained nearly 300 female missionaries in Canada and overseas. Perhaps the society perceived that competition between itself and the ministry for female recruits would have an adverse effect upon Women's Missionary Society membership and work. The society may also have opposed female ordination because it believed that its own expanding organization provided sufficient career opportunities for capable, well-educated church women.[44] The fact that this strong organization was outside the control of the male church leaders certainly engendered feelings of anxiety if not outright hostility in the men. Indeed, the eventual reluctant acceptance of female ordination by the 1934 General Council has been attributed to the church leaders' determination to assimilate women's growing strength into the male-dominated church structure rather than tolerate it outside. Even after the ordination of Lydia Gruchy in 1936, the fight for equal rights in Protestantism was only beginning. Although in 1946 married women were also accepted as United Church ministers, most Protestant churches still remained closed to the idea of women assuming genuine leadership roles, whether married or single.

Perhaps the lack of leadership and equal roles for women in the established Protestant churches partially explains women's numerical dominance in the variety of religious sects that mushroomed, particularly in western Canada, before World War II.[45] One well-known example was the International Church of the Foursquare Gospel and its charismatic leader. Born on a dairy farm near Ingersoll, Ontario in 1890, Aimee Semple McPherson was exposed to popular religion as a child through her mother's involvement in the Salvation Army, and in evangelical camp meetings. By the age of nineteen she had completed elocution lessons, won numerous medals in WCTU public-speaking contests, and married a Pentecostal preacher, Robert Semple. She travelled with him to China, where he died; she then returned penniless with an infant daughter to North America. Several years later, after an unsuccessful marriage to New York grocer Harold McPherson, Aimee left this second husband and returned with her children to Ingersoll to preach. Now known as Sister Aimee, she launched a continent-wide religious campaign, combining evangelism and drama. By the mid-1920s she had established a church, the Angelus Temple, in California. Her ability to attract followers was enhanced by her use of the media and by its infatuation with all aspects of her life, particularly her mysterious "disappearance" in 1926, and the numerous court cases related to her various marriages and her church's finances. In western Canada, McPherson founded and ran several churches and a bible school. During the Depression she discovered a new vehicle in the radio, and became as well-known a radio preacher as the Social Credit Premier of Alberta, William Aberhart.[46]

Within the Roman Catholic church, women appeared to accept their separate, subordinate role. The church assigned service roles in health and education to the female religious orders, as it assigned similar roles to women within the family. Especially in Quebec, this view of the appropriate activities of lay and religious women solidified in the 1920s and 1930s, as the perceived threat to French Canadian nationalism posed by urbanization and industrialization intensified. Equal political, social, and economic rights for women continued to be viewed with horror by the male church hierarchy. To counter these ideas, the church assiduously promoted initiatives to enhance women's family role. In 1937 Cardinal Villeneuve directed Abbé Albert Tessier to spare no effort in mounting a campaign to persuade the public of the need to educate girls "to the vocation of wife and mother." For women to fail in their "great mission" would irreparably damage the Christian order. Under Tessier's leadership, the écoles ménagères (domestic science schools) were reorganized into instituts familiaux (family institutes), popularly called "schools for happiness"; the primary objective, however, remained unchanged — the education of women in a manner completely different from that of men.[47]

Clerical insistence on the maternal role left few respectable career alternatives for Catholic laywomen. Such attitudes may have contributed to the remarkable increase in the number of nuns and the expansion of the church's female orders, especially in Quebec, where ten new women's orders were added to the existing ones in the interwar period.[48] The immense growth in the numbers of women entering convents provoked little comment — unlike the entry of women into politics.

Women and politics

For the women who had fought for the vote, a key question of the 1920s was how women's suffrage would influence the political process. Initially, politicians were eager to court the new female electorate, for they believed suffragists' arguments that women would vote as a bloc to reform society. It became apparent within the decade, however, that regional, class, cultural, and other differences divided women's political allegiances as they did men's. In 1918 a group of Ontario women from the National Equal Franchise Union attempted to form, through the National Council of Women of Canada, a non-partisan Woman's Party.[49] Their efforts were strongly opposed, especially by western council members; the result was a shortlived and ineffective organization. More pragmatic was the practice that the National Council began of adopting a Canadian Women's Platform to identify women's issues to be pursued through the established political parties. The 1920 platform incorporated reform positions on the political equality of the sexes, equal pay for equal work, equal child guardianship, and a female minimum wage.[50] The council also continued to mount campaigns to educate women about their political responsibilities, and to encourage their participation in partisan politics.

Such activities were more important than might be thought at first, for many women still found it very difficult to cast their ballots. According to Elsie Inman, a founder of the Women's Liberal Club in Prince Edward Island, and later a senator, when Island women finally did get the provincial vote in 1922, many had to overcome their husbands' opposition in order to use it. In one case that she recalled, the woman "was scared to vote because her husband threatened her if he saw her at a poll." Working on the assumption that the man would not recognize his wife if she were attired differently, Inman took the woman home, dressed her in Inman's own clothes, coat and veil, and successfully conducted her to the polling station. When Inman went to accompany another woman to vote, she was met by the irate husband, who accused her of trying to lead his wife astray. He sternly admonished her, "You're from a nice family, and have a good husband, you should be ashamed of yourself."[51]

Although a number of local women's auxiliaries to the two major political parties existed as early as 1906, they were not formally integrated into party structures. This changed in 1928 when the Liberal party formed a national women's auxiliary, the Federation of Liberal Women of Canada, to attract women to the party. The Conservative party followed suit shortly after. Both women's organizations were established to bring women to the parties as voters, with no intention of integrating them into strategic or leadership roles. Within the party organization, they were expected to carry out the essential day-to-day tasks of party maintenance, serving as the staffers who raised small-scale party funds, stuffed envelopes, distributed literature, answered telephones, and "minded" campaign offices. During elections, they became indispensable as canvassers, poll clerks, and scrutineers. In riding associations, they became secretaries and occasionally treasurers.[52] Valuable as these activities were, they were unlikely to provide opportunities for women to gain the skills, reputation, or political contacts necessary for party or public office.

Many of the third parties that emerged or grew into prominence in Canada after World War I were relatively receptive to having women participate; these included the United Farmers' parties in Alberta, New Brunswick, Nova Scotia, and Ontario. The National Progressive Party and the Co-operative Commonwealth Federation (CCF), as well as the even smaller Socialist Party of Canada and Communist Party of Canada, were also less steeped in traditions of male dominance of politics. In addition, the philosophical orientation of many of the third parties embraced social and economic issues such as equal pay, protective labour legislation, and birth control — issues that had long been dear to reform-minded women.[53]

In their quest for members and for citizens willing to stand for office when there was little hope of winning, the newer parties actively recruited women. Agnes Macphail, Canada's first woman MP, was among the founders of the CCF, and the party relied heavily on the organizing work of women like Louise Lucas and Gladys Strum. Unlike their male colleagues, however, women organizers were not always paid.[54]

The parties' support of women's issues was limited in other ways also. The example of the Communist Party of Canada illustrates the point. In the 1920s this party took up the "woman question"; by the middle of the decade the party had inaugurated a women's department with the object of advancing communism among women, established a women's column in its newspaper, and formed a national organization of working class women. The Women's Labor Leagues, led by Florence Custance, numbered thirty-seven by 1937. Finnish, Jewish, and Ukrainian leagues predominated, reflecting the party's important ethnic connections. The leagues emphasized the economic exploitation of women and attributed their subordination to the capitalist system. Despite this activity, women's issues never became a major priority for Canadian communists; like other organizations, the party could not avoid reflecting structures of inequality in the larger society.[55]

Members of the Winnipeg Women's Labor League prepare relief bundles to support Nova Scotia coalminers, 1925.

The more influential Co-operative Commonwealth Federation was also committed to the emancipation of women but had similar difficulty living up to its promise. Concerned primarily with overcoming class inequality and getting candidates elected, the party relegated the cause of equal rights for women to the background. Nonetheless many women worked at the local level for the CCF, as did Nellie Fraser. Fraser was widowed at the age of thirty-two in 1919. Her husband, who had been an agent with the Great West Life Company in Saskatchewan during the wheat boom, left her enough money to live on and to support their three children. In 1938, with her family grown up, she sold her home in Winnipeg, moved to Toronto, and became involved with the party, speaking on its behalf on local radio. A commitment to peace activism led her to work with the Women's International League for Peace and Freedom, eventually becoming president of its Toronto branch.[56]

During the Depression years, when unemployment and economic problems dominated political life, socialist and communist women co-operated with each other and with women of other political persuasions on social and economic issues. In 1935, when relief camp internees in British Columbia went on strike and occupied the Vancouver post office, women from various local groups, including the Vancouver Communist party, the CCF, the Local Council of Women, and the WCTU joined together to form a Mothers' Council. It passed a resolution urging the federal government to provide genuine work and a living wage for the strikers. Led by women from the CCF and the Communist party, the Mothers' Council participated in rallies and demonstrations supporting the unemployed, and organized the distribution of food, clothing, and shelter to the destitute. Similar groups in Saskatchewan and Alberta established women's committees to aid the "On–To–Ottawa" trek of unemployed workers. After the 1935 crisis passed, interest in the Mothers' Council waned, although Communist Party of Canada involvement remained strong. In 1936 the Mothers' Council affiliated with the Local Council of Women and became the socialist voice on the latter's Unemployment Relief Committee.[57]

After 1921 women had another more direct avenue to making their views known; they could be elected to legislative office federally and in most provinces. There were many hurdles to be overcome, however. The first woman seated in the federal House of Commons, Agnes Macphail, faced discrimination during all stages of the political process. Although Macphail won the United Farmers of Ontario federal nomination over ten men at the South-East Grey convention in September 1920, protests against her candidacy flooded the riding executive. Called before the executive and under pressure from some quarters to resign, she refused, arguing that she had been duly selected by the accredited delegates. During her election campaign, opponents attacked her religion — the Church of Jesus Christ of the Latter Day Saints — her sex, and her "mannish" behaviour, but on December 6, 1921, Macphail was duly elected. As a member of a third party

and as the only woman member of the Commons, Macphail was an alien novelty, commented upon and scrutinized by other MPs, the public, and the press. Her first session, she herself admitted, was "miserable . . . . I was intensely unhappy. Some members resented my intrusion, others jeered at me, while a very few were genuinely glad to see a woman in the House. Most of the members made me painfully conscious of my sex. . ."[58]

She did not shrink from the responsibility she had accepted, taking it so seriously that she rejected several marriage proposals in order to continue her work. Sensitive over being a "spinster" in an era when marriage was highly valued, Macphail took pains to announce the marriage offers publicly. She sat as the South-East Grey member, initially for the United Farmers of Ontario from 1921 until 1940. While she never lost sight of the interests of her agrarian constituency during her years in Parliament, Macphail also came to see herself as representing and acting for the women of Canada. In her day she was regarded, and criticized, as a feminist. She supported the struggle for women's suffrage in Quebec; fought successfully for the Archambault Royal Commission on prison reform and then for the implementation of its findings; and worked for peace and social welfare provisions, including unemployment insurance, family allowances and pensions for the old, blind, and disabled. Defeated in 1940, partly because of her pacifism, Macphail later served as one of the first two women to sit in the Ontario legislature.

Only five women were elected to the federal parliament before 1950. Like Macphail, Dorise Nielsen and Gladys Strum, both from Saskatchewan, represented third parties; the other two, who sat for the major parties, were both cases of "widow's succession" — replacements for previously elected husbands. However, both Cora Taylor Casselman, elected in an Alberta by-election following her Liberal husband's death, and Martha Black, who represented her

Vancouver women demand the abolition of relief camps for the unemployed, 1935.

Conservative husband's Yukon riding for five years when he was incapacitated by poor health, turned out to be excellent parliamentarians in their own right.[59] An American immigrant, estranged from her first husband, Black had walked across the Chilkoot Pass in 1898 while pregnant with her third child. She settled near Dawson City and became a successful sawmill owner and operator. In 1904 she married George Black, who later became the territory's commissioner, and in 1921 its Member of Parliament. When sixty-nine-year-old Martha ran in his place in 1935, she faced a hard battle. Despite her husband's popularity, her victory was far from assured, and she won by only 134 votes. In her autobiography she recalled how she had to confront her hecklers:

There were the younger women who said, 'What can this damned old woman do for us at Ottawa?' That was hard to take, yet I hurled back, 'You'll be lucky when you reach my age if you have my sturdy legs, my good stomach, my strong heart, and what I like to call my headpiece.'[60]

Once in the Commons, she concerned herself with pensions and unemployment, and supported both cadet training and the imperial tie with Britain. When her husband was well enough to replace her in 1940, she retired.

At the provincial level, twenty-three women managed to win legislative seats between 1916 and 1949; nearly all were from Ontario and the West, for with the exception of one woman in the legislature of the newly created province of Newfoundland, no women had been elected in the Maritimes or in Quebec. Most of these MLAs represented third parties. The CCF sponsored a number of female candidates, two of whom, Dorothy Steeves and Laura Jamieson, were elected during the 1930s to the British Columbia legislature.[61] Steeves' primary commitment was to socialism rather than women's issues, but Laura Jamieson, like many of the early women's activists, associated herself with a broad range of feminist causes and groups, including suffrage, the women's peace movement, the British Columbia Parent-Teacher Association, the Business and Professional Women's Club, and the Women's School for Citizenship. Before her election in 1939, Jamieson had been employed for eleven years as a Burnaby juvenile court judge.[62]

The United Farmers of Alberta was one of the few third parties to form a provincial government in this period, and therefore to gain the opportunity to legislate on women's issues. After its election in 1921, it appointed Irene Parlby as minister without portfolio. She became a spokesperson for women's issues, such as the provision of a minimum wage for women, married women's property rights, mothers' allowances, and children's welfare. The United Farmers of Alberta government passed eighteen acts positively affecting the welfare of women and children during its term. Parlby's activities were both aided and endorsed by her close association with the organization she in turn so keenly supported, the United Farm Women of Alberta.

A campaign of great symbolic significance that was visibly initiated and led to a successful conclusion by women was the action taken to gain Senate appointments for women. At issue was the exclusion of women from the upper house; some reform women also believed that the Senate could be used as a platform from which to exert influence on public policy. In 1919 the first conference of the Federated Women's Institutes of Canada, presided over by Judge Emily Murphy, passed a resolution requesting that the prime minister appoint a woman senator. Surely women, now voters and eligible for election to the lower house of Parliament, ought to be among those "persons" who, if qualified, could be summoned to serve in the Senate. The National Council of Women and the Montreal Women's Club renewed the request, settling on Judge Murphy as their candidate. But the governments of both Arthur Meighen and Mackenzie King stalled, apologetically pointing out that women were precluded from eligibility under the terms of the British North America Act of 1867. After eight years of requests, refusals, and lack of progress, Murphy got together with four other prominent women, including Nellie McClung, Louise McKinney, and Irene Parlby, all of whom had served in the Alberta legislature, to mount a legal challenge. The fifth petitioner, Henrietta Muir Edwards, was very well known in women's organizations for her many years of service as convenor of laws for the National Council of Women. These women used an obscure section of the Supreme Court Act to petition the government for an Order–in–Council directing the Supreme Court to rule on the constitutional question of whether the term "qualified persons" in section 24 of the BNA Act included women, and therefore whether women were eligible to be summoned to the Senate. The Supreme Court ruling in April 1928 held that the term "qualified persons" did not include women. The five petitioners then asked the government to allow an appeal of the judgement to the Judicial Committee of the Privy Council in England, at that time the highest court of appeal on questions related to Canadian law. The government agreed and the appeal was heard. On October 18, 1929, the Judicial Committee unanimously reversed the judgement of the Supreme Court of Canada and held that the word "persons" in section 24 of the BNA Act did (in 1929) include women as well as men. Unfortunately, Emily Murphy was never invited to sit in the Senate; being a well known Conservative, she was passed over by Mackenzie King in favour of Liberal Cairine Wilson, who was appointed the first woman senator in 1930. Even when the Conservatives returned to office later that year, and a Senate vacancy was created in 1931 by the death of a Catholic senator from Edmonton, Murphy was once again denied a seat, this time because she was a Protestant. Two years later, Emily Murphy died without achieving the appointment for which she had fought so long and hard. In 1935 a second woman, Iva Fallis, was named to the Senate.[63]

Montreal-born Cairine Wilson had not achieved the same recognition from the general public and the women's movement as

Murphy, but she had devoted her married life to social and charitable reform causes, and more importantly from the point of view of the Senate appointment, to Liberal party politics after 1921. An active volunteer with the Red Cross, Victorian Order of Nurses, Presbyterian Women's Missionary Society, Salvation Army, YWCA, and the Ottawa Welfare Bureau, Wilson was a founder of the National Federation of Liberal Women. As a senator, she involved herself in divorce legislation, immigration, and the League of Nations. She was president of the Canadian League of Nations Society, and also one of the few Canadians to protest the government's restrictive immigration policies, which prevented the entry of Jews fleeing Nazi persecution in the 1930s.[64]

Women were still unable to vote and ineligible to hold public office in Quebec until 1940. Under pressure from the Roman Catholic church, the *Fédération Nationale Saint-Jean-Baptiste* had abandoned its support for women's suffrage by 1920. For a short period there was no separate suffrage organization in Quebec, a situation remedied in 1922 by the formation of the Provincial Franchise Committee at the initiative of Marie Gérin-Lajoie, president of the *Fédération Nationale Saint-Jean-Baptiste*. This organization consisted of two sections, one English and one French, the heads of each sharing the new organization's leadership. Gérin-Lajoie became president of the French section and Anna Lyman headed the English section. The Provincial Franchise Committee sent delegations to the provincial government, mounted education campaigns, and supported attempts to introduce the suffrage question in the province's Assembly.

Hopes for a continuing women's suffrage movement, uniting Local Council of Women and *Fédération Nationale Saint-Jean-Baptiste* members, were dashed in short order. When Archbishop Paul-Eugène Roy denounced suffrage in a 1922 pastoral letter, Gérin-Lajoie took her case and that of the women of Quebec to the International Union of Leagues of Catholic Women, hoping to win papal support. Although she was successful in getting the council to pass two favourable resolutions, one encouraging enfranchised women to exercise their rights, and another approving the civic, moral, and religious education of women, a third resolution tied any new suffrage activities to prior approval of the church in each country. When Gérin-Lajoie and the *Fédération Nationale Saint-Jean-Baptiste* attempted to interpret the clause as relating to a local authority — the relatively progressive bishop of Montreal — the international body responded that approval was required from all the province's bishops.[65] The position of the Quebec church hierarchy was made clear by Cardinal Bégin in a letter supporting Archbishop Roy and sent to the newspaper *Le Canada* on March 19, 1922. "The entry of women into politics, even by merely voting," he emphasized, "would be a misfortune for our province. Nothing justifies it, neither the natural law nor the good of society."[66] This pressure forced the *Fédération Nationale Saint-Jean-Baptiste* to withdraw its support for the Provincial Franchise Committee and Gérin-Lajoie to resign her presidency of the committee.[67]

After this serious setback, the Provincial Franchise Committee marked time. In 1928 it was revitalized under the dynamic leadership of Thérèse Casgrain, and renamed the League for Women's Rights the following year. The daughter of an upper class political family from Montreal, whose husband served as speaker of the House of Commons and secretary of state in the Mackenzie King government, Casgrain used her influence and public prestige to campaign for political and professional rights for Quebec women throughout the 1930s. She was a tireless worker, championing the cause of Quebec women through her writings, lectures, and radio broadcasts.[68]

In 1927 a separate organization, *l'Alliance Canadienne pour le Vote des Femmes du Québec,* had been formed under the leadership of Idola Saint-Jean, a McGill language professor. An original member of the Provincial Franchise Committee, Saint-Jean had resigned in January of that year to initiate her own campaign for the vote. The *Alliance* attracted working class francophone women, and operated alone and sometimes in unison with other suffrage forces, to build what its founder called "a militant campaign."[69] Idola Saint-Jean was at the heart of the struggle, writing for newspapers, magazines, and the group's own publication, lobbying the legislature, and presenting briefs to government commissions. By courageously running as an independent candidate in the 1930 federal election, Saint-Jean generated a great deal of publicity for the suffrage cause; although she lost, she did manage to win the support of nearly 3000 electors. The work of the various Quebec suffrage organizations and the support of other provincial women's associations, like the Montreal Local Council of Women, culminated in the endorsement of women's franchise by the Quebec Liberal party at its 1938 convention, and the subsequent passage of the enabling legislation when that party assumed power in 1940.

Quebec women were battling on a number of fronts during these years. Their inferior legal and economic status was also a major focus for organizational effort. Spurred on by improvements in the status of women in other provinces, both anglophone and francophone women sought similar reforms for themselves. In response to these demands and to divert attention from the suffrage issue, the Liberal government of Louis-Alexandre Taschereau set up the Commission on the Civil Rights of Women in 1929, headed by Judge Charles-Edouard Dorion. The women who appeared before the commission did not demand radical changes in their civil rights. Rather they sought to lessen restrictions on married women, and to equalize authority within the marital relationship, changes similar to those under discussion in France at the same time. A particular change they sought was the elimination of the double standard for legal separation. Under Quebec law a husband could seek a separation if his wife committed adultery, whereas she had to prove that her husband kept his concubine in the family home to be granted the same right. The primary demand, however, was that married women be legally entitled to control their own earnings. Even though no more than 10 percent of Quebec wives earned wages, witnesses testified regarding the hardships caused to women and children by husbands who refused to provide the necessities of life for their families, and squandered their wives' earnings.

Most briefs presented by delegations were extremely moderate, stressing the need to limit a husband's right to dispose of "community assets," without consulting his wife, for frivolous purposes. No individual or group appearing before the Commission seriously challenged the patriarchal structure of Quebec families. No one threatened the sacrosanct role of the husband as *chef de famille* by suggesting that he no longer be accorded his wife's obedience, or that mothers and fathers share responsibility for family affairs. Nevertheless, faced with the hostility of the church, the legal profession, and the government, the Dorion Commission produced arguments for retaining the status quo, stating that, "Women themselves have not really evolved. Created to be the companions of men, women are always, and above all else, wives and mothers."[70] In the light of such sentiment, it is not surprising that the minor changes recommended by the commission affected few women. They did include giving women the right to control their salaries and any goods or property brought with them to marriage. But no other changes in the law respecting legal separations were recommended. The commission, like the clerical and nationalist forces that opposed Quebec feminists in the first four decades of the twentieth century, echoed the powerful view that women had to remain in subordinate and familial roles if the French Canadian nation was to survive. Assessing the commission in her autobiography, Thérèse Casgrain wrote that "while the Dorion report brought a few amendments to our Civil Code, it did not go very far." She also believed that in the report's arguments against change, it was easy to observe the "scornful and haughty attitude of our masculine elite towards women."[71] The feminists were deeply disappointed, even though the commission's deliberations and reports did provide a forum for the discussion of women's rights.

Peace work

World War I provoked for many an altered awareness of the nation's position in the world, and in the 1920s and 1930s some Canadian women developed and acted on a new international perspective. In 1929 Agnes Macphail was a member of the Canadian delegation to the League of Nations. Rejecting pressure that she sit on the committee dealing with welfare, women, and children, Macphail successfully insisted on becoming the first woman delegate to sit on the Disarmament Committee. Charlotte Whitton, while the executive secretary for the Canadian Council on Child Welfare, represented Canada on the League of Nations' Commission on the Protection of Women and Children, and later on the League's Advisory Committee on Social Questions. She also served as a member of the Advisory Committee of Experts on the Protection of Women created by the International Labour Organization. Another prominent activist, Nellie McClung, was one of Canada's delegates to the 1938 session of the League of Nations.

These individual efforts were part of a larger movement of international co-operation among women and their organizations, which was by no means new. Connections between women's groups in Canada, the United States, and Great Britain were long-standing, as was the international outlook of the various Protestant missionary societies. The promotion of a world view and the eradication of racial prejudice and intolerance became a goal for many groups. Within the various missionary societies, for instance, new theories of individual self-worth and cultural relativism replaced old ideas about Christian superiority.

Canadian involvement in the war had not only highlighted the interdependence of nations but also produced a profound reaction to war itself. In the aftermath of war, Canadian women and men had established in 1921 a national organization to support the efforts of the League of Nations in Geneva. Membership in the Canadian League of Nations Society reached a peak in 1929 as a result of the work of women's organizations such as the WCTU and the National Council of Women of Canada, especially in the West. Although initially dominated by a male elite, the society owed its survival to the efforts of its many women members. By the 1930s it had become in effect a women's peace organization, led by Cairine Wilson. In addition to taking up the League of Nations Society's cause, Local Councils of Women sponsored lectures, study groups, essay and speaking contests to promote the spirit of international understanding. Despite its tradition of avoiding controversial issues that could create tensions for some members, the National Council of Women of Canada lobbied Ottawa on peace issues, urging government support for the 1932 Disarmament Conference.

Even before the end of World War I, a group of women who were dissatisfied with the efforts of existing organizations had formed a separate peace party, the Canadian Women's Peace party. It was one of the founding groups for the Women's International League for Peace and Freedom. By the late 1920s Canadian branches of the Women's International League were active in Ontario and the West. More left-leaning than other peace organizations, the Women's International League for Peace and Freedom did not involve a large number of Canadian members, but it did attract women of high calibre. Violet McNaughton, editor of the women's page of the *Western Producer*, became a propagandist for the league, and she is credited with creating strong support for its activities among rural women in the West. Laura Jamieson, aided by various women's organizations, organized peace conferences in Vancouver, Winnipeg, and Saskatoon, and together with McNaughton and Agnes Macphail, represented Canada at the International Congress of the Women's International League for Peace and Freedom in Prague, Czechoslovakia in 1929. Upon their return they determined to build a stronger movement in Canada, and in 1930 seventeen locals of the United Farm Women of Alberta and the Alberta WCTU joined the league.

A major goal for women's peace groups was the reorientation of Canadian education. They campaigned to replace cadet training in schools with physical education; to change textbooks and curricula that glorified the military and war; and they tried with some success to elect their own members as school trustees in Winnipeg and Toronto in the 1930s. Although members co-operated with the League of Nations Society, the WCTU, and Local Council of Women branches, for the most part they found these groups unwilling to adopt many of the pacifist positions they promoted.

The increasing sympathy among the members of the Women's International League for Peace and Freedom for radical social change accelerated during the Depression. McNaughton became active in the League for Social Reconstruction; Jamieson joined the Co-operative of Unemployed Workers and later the CCF. Pacifists faced a dilemma at the outbreak of the Spanish Civil War, when commitment to non-violence conflicted with commitment to social justice. Their dilemma intensified as dictators assumed power in Germany and Italy. Sharp divisions occurred within the membership of the Women's International League, with some persisting in their opposition to all war, while others concluded that war against the Nazis and Hitler was a regrettable necessity. Perhaps for this reason, by the late 1930s the organization had lost its base across the country and ceased to attract younger women.[72]

For Canadian women, as for all Canadians, peace and international understanding were elusive goals. The optimism that characterized the women's peace movement faltered in the face of deteriorating world conditions. Looking back over nearly two decades of women's active participation in domestic politics, some observers also felt discouraged. Even the normally irrepressible Nellie McClung was disillusioned.

When women were given the vote in 1916–17 ... we were obsessed with the belief that we could cleanse and purify the world by law. ... But when all was over, and the smoke of battle cleared away, something happened to us. Our forces, so well organized for the campaign, began to dwindle.[73]

Not all suffragists concurred; Helen Gregory MacGill wrote an article in 1936 entitled "Canadian Women Have Not Failed in Politics." To prove her point, she cited a long list of important social and legal reforms enacted at both the provincial and federal levels, which were directly attributable to women's public involvement.[74] Women's organizations had indeed continued to play a crucial role in extending the horizons of Canadian women, and when Canada found itself at war in 1939, the women's organizations once again responded enthusiastically to the patriotic call for their selfless, unpaid efforts.

4 THE UNFINISHED REVOLUTION:

World War II to the
Charter of Rights

*The New Feminist 2, 2
(May 1971) 6.

"Our revolution is the most important revolution in the history of human beings."* With this ringing proclamation, a small group of women calling themselves the "New Feminists" declared their intention to achieve a fundamental transformation of society — the destruction of gender roles for both Canadian women and men. The New Feminists came together in 1969, at the end of a turbulent decade of dramatic change. Yet for them, as for many groups in Canadian society, the changes had not been as fast or as sweeping as they desired. Francophones, native peoples, students, and women struggled, sometimes together but most often on parallel or even conflicting courses, to achieve a larger share in the "Just Society" promised by the newly elected prime minister, Pierre Elliot Trudeau. The social and political ferment represented by separatism, native rights, the student movement, and women's liberation led many puzzled Canadians to look back longingly to the "good old days" when people seemed to know their place. Then, everyone had been content to bask in unprecedented national prosperity, and to pursue single-mindedly the good life: a home of one's own, a car in the driveway, a fridge in the kitchen, and 2.5 kids in the "rec room" watching "*Les Plouffes*" or "Father Knows Best."

The prosperity they were still enjoying in the late 1960s began when World War II brought the Great Depression to a close. Canadian participation in the war depended heavily on women's voluntary activities, their work in the paid labour force and, for the first time, in the armed services. After the prosperity of the 1950s and 1960s, the economy experienced a slowdown, characterized by inflation, rising unemployment, and sky-rocketing interest rates. By the late 1970s and early 1980s, the country was fighting a full-fledged recession.

From a small, staid, overwhelmingly white Anglo-Saxon Protestant country of just over 11 million inhabitants in 1939, Canada was transformed into a dynamic, officially bilingual, and multi-cultural society of over 25 million inhabitants by 1987. The components of this population growth were three: high fertility rates, the entry of Newfoundland into Confederation in 1949, and a massive influx of immigrants — some 5 million in forty years. Population growth varied from region to region; Ontario and Quebec attracted the bulk of the immigrants, but the highest percentage increases in population

A karate black belt, 1983.

after the war were recorded in northern and western Canada, a result of the growth of resource-based industries there. In contrast, the proportion of the Canadian population located in the Maritime region declined, despite the addition of Newfoundland. At the time of Confederation in 1867, more than one in five Canadians had lived in the Maritime provinces; by 1981, less than one in ten was located in the Atlantic region.

Although the wave of immigration that began immediately after World War II was still overwhelmingly British and American in origin, by 1950 this was no longer the case. Immigrants made their way from the displaced-persons camps of war-torn Europe, and subsequently fled internal upheavals such as the Hungarian revolution; in 1951, seven out of every ten immigrants came from countries other than the United States and Great Britain. More importantly, the ethnic composition of these "other" immigrants was increasingly diverse, as European immigrants were joined by large contingents from the West Indies, Asia, and Latin America. Not only was Canada a multi-cultural society, but a multi-racial society with significant visible minorities. Initially, after the war, the majority of those arriving at Canadian points of entry were men, but after 1958 female immigrants outnumbered male immigrants until 1981.

The female immigrant experience was remarkably unchanged in the jet age. Successive groups of young, single women — Italian, West Indian, then Filipina — were recruited for domestic service, and suffered the same hardships of isolation and generally poor working conditions that British and other European-born domestics had experienced in previous generations. The principal way for most women to enter Canada was as wives or fiancées. Until the late 1980s, this meant that the majority of women immigrants were ineligible for the benefits and programs, such as government-sponsored English-language courses, that were available to adult male immigrants.

Immigrants of both sexes continued to prefer the cities to the country, and during this period the inexorable transformation of Canada from a rural and agricultural nation to an overwhelmingly urban and industrial society was completed. According to the 1981 census, seven out of every ten Canadians lived in an urban setting. It is important to note, however, that the rate of urbanization varied considerably; Ontario remained the most highly urbanized province — 82 percent of its population were urban — while Prince Edward Island was the least urbanized at 36 percent. Increasingly, Canadians lived in very large cities. In 1981, 16 percent of the total Canadian population were to be found in centres with populations of over 500 000, almost double the proportion of those living in such large municipalities only ten years earlier. Toronto replaced Montreal as the nation's largest metropolitan centre, and movement west, especially to Alberta during the years of great prosperity that followed the oil strike at Leduc in 1948, resulted in extremely rapid growth for Calgary and Edmonton.

Within these internal migration patterns there were some interesting cycles. During the 1950s, the greatest growth rates occurred in the suburban areas of the metropolitan centres; by 1961, 45 percent of all city residents lived in the suburbs. The ecological movement of the late 1960s and the early 1970s, however, sparked a small but not insignificant movement to rural areas beyond the cities and their suburbs, especially among the urban middle class. Then, within a decade, middle class Canadians, sometimes even the same individuals, were turning to the inner city for housing. These affluent "Yuppies" — young, urban professionals — played a role in the transformation of the inner cores of many metropolitan centres during the 1970s and 1980s.

The changes in the composition and distribution of the population were in large part responses to the ebb and flow of economic life. In general terms, Canadian economic development followed that of other western industrial nations, from the age of Sputnik to that of Star Wars. The rapid pace of technological change was dramatically demonstrated by the development of computers; from bulky constructions taking up the space of a large room, they evolved into ever-smaller microcomputers that transformed the ways in which Canadians lived, thought, and communicated. The movement from an industrial to a post-industrial society was signalled in the 1950s by the declining importance to the national economy of primary, resource-based industries and secondary industry, such as manufacturing, and the continuous growth of the service and clerical sectors. This shift created employment opportunities for women, so that in spite of widespread opposition to their working for wages, increasing numbers of married women entered the labour force. Although public attitudes towards married women in gainful employment changed slowly, by the 1960s it had become widely accepted that childless married women, or those whose children were in school, could be in the labour force. However, it took another decade before it became common for women with pre-school children to work outside the home.

Married women's labour force participation was greatly stimulated by the renewed emphasis on the production and purchase of consumer goods at war's end. Increased consumer spending and the creation of a national social welfare system were integral parts of the plan developed by C.D. Howe, the federal Minister of Reconstruction, for Canada's post-war recovery. Industries were encouraged to convert their tremendous capacity for wartime production to the manufacture of automobiles, appliances, and other household goods. The advent of television provided yet another and more powerful medium through which advertisers could convince Canadians that such products were essential to an improved standard of living. For most families, the purchase of expensive consumer items was possible only if there were more than one wage earner in the family. This role was increasingly filled by wives, since prolonged education for children, and legal restrictions on child labour, greatly reduced the

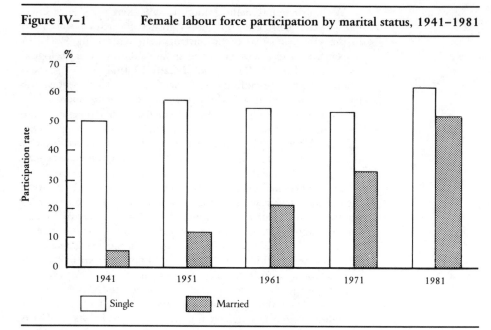

Figure IV-2   Composition of female workforce by marital status

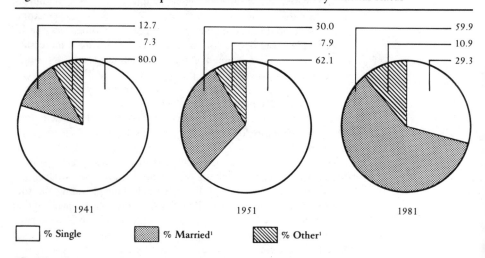

¹ *For 1941 and 1951, separated women are included with married women, while for 1961, 1971, and 1981 they are included in the "Other" category, that is, along with widowed and divorced women.*

number of young adolescents active in the full-time workforce.

The master plan of Mackenzie King's Liberal government for ensuring Canada's prosperity after the war also involved a massive development of the nation's natural resources, particularly in the West and North. To expedite this process, it encouraged Americans

From: Pat Armstrong and Hugh Armstrong, *The Double Ghetto: Canadian Women and their Segregated Work*, rev. ed. (Toronto: McClelland and Stewart, 1984) 169.

to invest in projects such as the construction of a pipeline to carry gas and oil from Alberta to eastern Canada. As American investment in Canada grew by leaps and bounds, so too did concerns about the nation's sovereignty. Prominent Canadians, such as economist Harold Innis, warned that the country was now in the process of becoming a colony once again, this time of an increasingly powerful American empire. In 1950 the royal commission appointed to report on the state of the arts and sciences in Canada, the Massey Commission, documented just how fragile Canadian culture was as a result of the pervasiveness of the American influence. The negative impact of Canadian reliance on the United States was a favourite theme of the Conservative opposition leader, populist John G. Diefenbaker, who made it a major issue of the 1957 general election campaign. After forming a minority government in 1957, and calling an election the following year, the Conservatives swept into power in 1958 with the largest parliamentary majority up to that time in Canadian history. Thus ended the federal Liberal rule that had been uninterrupted since 1935, and only briefly broken since 1896.

Diefenbaker's love affair with the Canadian electorate soon turned sour, however. Just four years after his apparently decisive victory, Diefenbaker was defeated at the polls by the Liberals, now led by the internationally renowned diplomat, Lester B. Pearson, who formed a minority government in 1962, and then obtained a majority a year later. Scarcely in office, Pearson found himself embroiled in controversy over the issue of Canadian sovereignty. Should the Canadian government permit the installation of nuclear warheads on missiles stationed in Canada? After much soul-searching, the prime minister permitted their installation, a decision that alienated Canadian women involved in the peace movement. Canadian women, in growing numbers, participated in the protest against the war in Vietnam. More generally, a new dimension of women's lives was their greater participation in conventional and protest politics. Soon a resurgent women's movement would be launching public actions on behalf of women themselves.

The many changes in women's lives affect our study of them, as we move into the present. Because of the importance our culture assigns to public and political activities, the historical sources dealing with such activities are relatively abundant. In addition, autobiographical and biographical accounts of prominent women continue to be a valuable source, although the regional, ethnic, and class biases of such sources are obvious. The political activities of women on the margins of society — the poor and the powerless — are only now starting to gain attention. When we turn to other aspects of women's experience, the material is even more difficult to find. When the study of women's history began in earnest in the 1970s, the recent past was not much studied; researchers were preoccupied with exploring the historical roots of the Canadian women's movement. As a result, there is as yet very little scholarly analysis of many dimensions of women's lives in the period from 1939 to 1987.

The task of locating sources for the most recent decades has been rendered more difficult by the fact that the telephone continues to replace the personal letter as a major means of communication. If diaries exist for this period, we have not been able to read them, compounding the problem of gaining access to the private worlds of ordinary women. The newer women's organizations, committed to informal procedures and non-hierarchical structures, do not seem to be generating the organizational records so valuable for interpreting the first wave of feminism. Even their newsletters and briefs are difficult to locate. Rarely collected in public libraries or archives, they are even more rarely reprinted. Although oral history is now becoming a crucial tool of research, the results are not yet widely available. We have supplemented written and oral personal sources by using the magazines and newspapers, which are an expanding and invaluable resource for exploring women's lives and times in this period, but the spread of mass culture, particularly through the medium of television, has made it more difficult to identify regional, ethnic, or class variations.

In addition to the problem of sources there are new problems of interpretation. Historians venture into the realm of the present with considerable trepidation; the subjectivity involved in choosing personalities, events, and issues on which to focus is all too apparent. Here there is no accumulated body of historical scholarship to use as a reference point, and no consensus on what should or should not be included. The treatment of the contemporary women's movement embodies these problems, as does the whole question of possible improvement in the lives of women. Can we assert that women are better off today in Canada than they were forty years ago? Or is it the case that the "superwoman syndrome" has forced women to take on an overload of roles and responsibilities, increasingly unsupported by family or by women's culture? And what part, if any, did the women's movement play in those changes, for good or for evil?

12 The "Bren gun girl" and the housewife heroine

By 1939 the Dominion was slowly recovering from the devastating impact of the Depression. On September 17, however, Canadians found themselves yet again engaged in an overseas conflict not of their own making. And once more Canadian women played a key role in the war effort through their domestic activities, voluntary organizations, and participation in war-related industries. In addition, they were recruited for the first time into that most venerated of male establishments, the quintessential expression of patriarchal power — the armed forces.

After the war, government and media focussed on the need to get women back into the home. But the structures of Canadian women's lives changed rapidly by the late 1950s. Earlier age at marriage, reduced fertility rates, and earlier completion of childbearing combined with increased longevity and economic opportunities to promote women's participation in the labour force. Most Canadian women with pre-school children continued to withdraw from the labour force to devote themselves solely to their families, but the average length of time spent doing so contracted. Though few noticed it, a new era had begun for women.

War work

Women were indispensable to the Canadian war effort, and most contributed in the familiar surroundings of the household, the family farm, or women's voluntary organizations. As individuals and in their associations, women initiated extensive and varied war work, as they had in the Great War. This time, however, their activities came to be closely co-ordinated and controlled by the federal government through the Women's Voluntary Services Division, created in the autumn of 1941. Since they had already begun their own programs, some women's organizations were irked by what they considered government intervention.[1] The Department of National War Services ran an extensive publicity campaign in both French and English to involve Canadian housewives in the war effort. One advertisement, entitled "From the frying pan to the firing line," depicted three women pouring a panful of grease, which magically turned into bombs, over an enemy ship. "Work at munitions production in your own kitchen," the accompanying copy exhorted.[2] In response, thousands of women collected fats, paper, glass, metals, rubber, rags, and bones for recycling in war production.

World War II poster emphasizing homemakers' role in the war effort.

The government's management of the war economy depended on women: some 2 285 000 homemakers were responsible for over 80 percent of the nation's retail purchases.[3] For many Canadians, the war effectively ended the Depression. As wartime production expanded, employment levels soared, and the average Canadian's purchasing power grew rapidly. At the same time, there were fewer civilian goods available, resulting in shortages, a sharp increase in the cost of living, and the spectre of an uncontrollable price-wage spiral. To control inflation, as soon as war was declared the federal government created the Wartime Prices and Trade Board to establish production quotas and maximum prices for many civilian goods. Various women's organizations, such as the National and Local Councils of

Women, made it their responsibility to see that the board's price guidelines were followed. Impressed by their price-monitoring activities, the board moved to create a Consumer Branch with the well-known editor of *Chatelaine*, Bryne Hope Saunders, as its head. Subsequently fourteen regional committees co-ordinated the efforts of over 10 000 liaison officers supplied by women's voluntary organizations; these women informed consumers of the board's regulations, policed prices, and laid the basis for the establishment of the Canadian Consumers' Association when the war ended.

The federal government also relied on women to support its rationing system and wartime savings program, and to maintain the nation's nutritional standards. In addition, hundreds of thousands of women planted victory gardens, knitted and sewed articles of clothing for the troops, made up parcels for prisoners of war, ran hospitality centres and canteens for members of the armed forces, organized blood banks, practised civil defence procedures, or acted as spotters of enemy aircraft.

In the rural areas the Women's Institutes were especially active in promoting women's war services, and in mobilizing women for agricultural production. Across the nation wives and daughters supplemented the declining male agricultural workforce, as men signed up for military service or gravitated to more attractive industrial work. In British Columbia and Ontario, dominion-provincial programs were established to mobilize farm labour, and in Ontario three separate women's groups were created. The Farm Girls' Brigade included farm women under the age of twenty-six; the Women's Land Brigade recruited working women and housewives to help whenever they could; and the Farmerette Brigade brought together students and teachers to help out during the summer months. In 1943 nearly 13 000 women were enrolled in the three groups.[4] For some farm wives, the war years brought not only an increased burden of work and responsibility, but also new opportunities for personal growth and accomplishment. "Dorothy," for example, tackled the heavy farm work during her husband's absence overseas, maintained the equipment, looked after the house and children, taught Sunday school, and still found time for curling and hunting. On her husband's return, she handed him the family bankbook and proudly declared, "There is more money in there than we ever had in our lives."[5]

The recruitment of women for agricultural production was part of a federal government campaign to manage the wartime labour force and to cope with labour shortages. Initially little government intervention was required, for there were some 900 000 unemployed Canadians when the war broke out. By 1942, however, this labour pool had been depleted as both industry and the armed forces expanded. In March of that year, Mackenzie King's government established the National Selective Service agency to oversee the recruitment and allocation of labour. Two months later, the Women's Division of the Selective Service agency was created under the direction of Fraudena Eaton of Vancouver, and in September 1942 it undertook a national registration of women aged twenty to twenty-four. The primary objective was to identify young single women who could be recruited into war industry. Although married women in this age category were also required to register, the federal government hoped that, by creating a pool of single workers, wives could be kept at home. Once the registration exercise was complete, the National Selective Service initiated programs to relocate single women from the Prairies and Maritimes to central Canada to work in war industry. In order to accomplish this, massive publicity campaigns were also launched to encourage single women to participate in war production. By June 1943, some 255 000 women were employed in war industry, and thousands more had entered military service.

The urgent demand for workers continued to grow, however, particularly in those industries that had traditionally employed large numbers of women. Workers were exchanging low-paying positions in garment and textile factories, in hotels, restaurants, hospitals, and private homes, in laundries and dry cleaning establishments, for the high wages offered by war industries. Now there was no choice but to turn to married women to take up the slack. Throughout the summer of 1943, with the help of Local Councils of Women, Selective Service mounted ambitious drives to recruit married women for part-time work in service industries. Housewives were also asked to work evening shifts created specially for them in essential war industries. Still the labour shortage remained acute, and the government in Ottawa was compelled to widen the scope of its recruitment plans to include full-time employment for married women. Yet another extensive campaign was undertaken, and the King government agreed to offer a few incentives: in July 1942, the Income Tax Act was amended so that working wives were treated as full dependents no matter how much they earned. Previously a wife could only earn up to $750 before her husband lost the married status exemption.[6]

The other major initiative was the provision of government-funded daycare services. Well before the promotion of employment for married women with children had begun, many mothers had availed themselves of the unprecedented job opportunities, despite the absence of adequate childcare services. In Ontario, where there was growing public concern over the lack of proper supervision for children, the blame for juvenile delinquency was laid squarely on the mothers of "latch-key children."[7] In July 1942, the federal government acknowledged the need for institutional childcare by introducing the dominion-provincial Wartime Day Nurseries Agreement. It provided for the two senior levels of government to share equally the costs of daycare services for children whose mothers were employed in war industries. However, only three provinces signed the accord—Ontario, Quebec, and Alberta—and after further study Alberta decided not to implement the program. Eventually, twenty-eight day nurseries were established in Ontario and six in Quebec. These nurseries accommodated children between two and six years of age, and in Ontario, homecare was arranged for children under the age of two and after-school daycare for those between the ages of six and sixteen. In keeping with the government's commitment to provide such services strictly to cope with the wartime emergency, only one-quarter of the available spaces could be given to the children of working mothers not employed in war industries. Eventually public pressure forced the government to amend the legislation to provide services for the children of all working mothers, but priority was still assigned to war industry employees.

In Quebec, the few day nurseries established under the program primarily served the anglophone population, a situation that reflected the vocal opposition of French Canadian Catholic leaders in that province to the employment of mothers. French Canadians now appeared to be among the most prejudiced against daycare centres, even though some childcare services had been available since the nineteenth century when the Grey Nuns opened their *salles d'asile*. Part of this negative reaction was the result of opposition to the war itself, particularly after conscription for home service was introduced in June 1940. In the national plebiscite that released the King government from its pledge not to institute conscription for overseas duty, the overwhelming majority of French-speaking Quebeckers had voted "No." Well before the implementation of the Day Nurseries' Agreement, which occurred three months later, French Canadian opposition to the war effort had solidified. Religious leaders and nationalists in Quebec roundly condemned those married women who "deserted" their families for lucrative work in munitions plants, and articles published in the influential Jesuit publication *Relations* branded government-sponsored daycare facilities as communistic and destructive of the family. Provocative but unfounded reports of thousands of abandoned children in Montreal, and of infant deaths occurring in unlicenced nurseries, flooded the newspapers. In an impassioned speech, one member of the Quebec Assembly condemned all women's work outside the home. Such work, he claimed, created a desire for emancipation; it was destroying the family and "sabotaging what is most precious to us." [8]

Despite these vehement denunciations, thousands of French Canadian mothers took on paid employment. Their primary reasons for doing so were economic, according to Florence Martel, Fraudena Eaton's Quebec assistant:

We were coming out of the Depression. There were no longer sheets on the beds, the children had no shoes and there were no more kitchen utensils. . . . Women lacked everything for a long time and they did not go to work to buy luxuries, as certain people accused them of doing. [9]

Indeed, Canadian women themselves indicated that an improved standard of living, not the call to loyalty and service, was their primary motivation for entering paid employment. In a 1943 survey conducted among married women over the age of thirty-five who were applying for paid work, only one in ten gave patriotism as their "prime object," while well over half said they wanted to add to the family income. The rest cited "personal needs."[10]

By July 1, 1944, some 42 000 women in Quebec and Ontario were engaged in munitions works, where their much-vaunted ability to perform repetitive, precise work was fully exploited. One male journalist explained why women were able to persist at such work long after men had grown weary from the monotony — after all, they had long been accustomed to the boring routine of daily house-keeping! Analogies between women's war work and domestic tasks were rife: running a lathe was even easier than operating a vacuum cleaner, while filling a shell was no more difficult than making a cake.[11] Although working conditions had improved substantially compared to those endured by munitions workers during World War I, hours were long and the work often dangerous. Average wages for women workers were 10 cents an hour less than for men. Although women employed in the dangerous explosives department were paid from 5 to 13 cents an hour more than other female munitions workers, the amount seemed small for the additional risk.[12]

As the labour shortage grew, women were admitted in increasing numbers into the dominion-provincial War Emergency Training Program, and into non-traditional employments. By the end of 1942, nearly half of all full-time participants in pre-employment training were women who were being taught skills normally reserved for men, such as machineshop work, welding, aircraft assembly, ship-building, electronics, drafting, and industrial chemistry.[13] The aircraft industry, which by itself provided employment to 33 000 women, contained the largest proportion of women employed in any war industry.[14] But these apparent opportunities were only of limited value. Government training programs were shorter for women than for men, and most women received only two to six weeks' instruction. Women who entered directly into industry without such training were often expected to acquire the skills they would need during their first shift. Consequently there was little opportunity for them to secure the specialized training that would ensure long-term employment or upward mobility.

A few women did assume positions of authority; they immediately became the focus of media attention and were held up as living examples of the emancipating effects of the war. Such was the case of Elsie Gregory MacGill, who was put in charge of all engineering work for Canadian production of the Hurricane and Helldiver fighter planes. The daughter of Helen Gregory MacGill, Elsie MacGill had been the first woman to graduate in electrical engineering in Canada. Far more typical of war workers were young women like Veronica Foster, the 1941 "Bren gun girl," who worked on the assembly lines.[15] If, like Foster, they worked in war industry, they too might be singled out and glamourized for publicity purposes.

"You're in the army now!"

The image of the emancipated woman was further enhanced by the entry of women into the armed forces, but here, as in war industry, equality was never gained. Even before war began, women across the nation had organized themselves into paramilitary groups. One of the earliest and largest was the Victoria Women's Service Club, created in October 1938. Subsequently other units were formed in British Columbia, and by 1940 such groups boasted a total of 1200 members. The movement spread eastwards to other Canadian cities, and by 1941 nearly 7000 women were enrolled. Modelled on the women's auxiliary of the British army, these organizations taught their members military drill, first aid, map reading, signalling, and transport driving; some even included rifle practice. Shortly after their formation, the women's corps lobbied vigorously for official recognition from the Department of National Defence, but this was withheld. Only when the manpower shortage grew serious did the government decide to form the Canadian Women's Army Corps (CWAC). Established in August 1941, it provided only partial recognition of the existing women's corps, which were used primarily as a source of recruits.

Once again women's war initiatives were taken over and directed by a male-dominated bureaucracy. Since the CWAC was initially not integrated into the army, but comprised a separate organization, its officers did not enjoy the same ranks, authority, or insignia as men in the army. The women officers' ranks were indicated on their uniforms by an array of beavers and maple leaves. Only in March 1942 was the Canadian Women's Army Corps integrated into the Canadian armed forces, and its members entitled to use the usual military titles and insignia.[16] In the same year as CWAC was formed, the federal government established the Canadian Women's Auxiliary Air Force, largely as a result of British inquiries about recruiting women to assist at Commonwealth Air Training Plan centres; in February 1942, the auxiliary was transformed into the Women's Division, Royal Canadian Air Force. In the following July, the Women's Royal Canadian Naval Service was created.

Women who entered the armed forces encountered many of the obstructive attitudes and practices confronting women in civilian life. In all ranks, the women received only two-thirds of the basic pay of men with equivalent rank. Initially, there was no provision for servicewomen to receive dependents' allowances, and women recruits married to military personnel were not eligible for a separation allowance. Confronted by vehement protests against these practices by servicewomen themselves and the National Council of Women, and by the negative impact the poor pay was having on female recruitment, the Department of National Defence raised women's basic pay to 80 percent of that received by men of similar rank. In addition, women were to receive the same trades pay as men in each category, and a servicewoman with a husband in the military was to receive a separation allowance—provided her annual income did not exceed $2100. Dependents' allowances for parents and siblings were also to be provided on the same basis as to servicemen, but women continued to be denied such allowances for spouses or children.

Job segregation also remained a fact of life in the armed forces. It was understood that only the war emergency and the necessity to release able-bodied men for active duty justified the creation of the women's services. From the beginning, military authorities intended to use female recruits to replace support personnel such as clerks, cooks, telephone operators, drivers, mess waiters, and canteen helpers. In all areas men remained firmly in charge. In the CWAC, for example, eventually close to fifty occupations were opened to women recruits, but the vast majority worked at typically female jobs: of nearly 6000 CWAC tradeswomen surveyed in March 1945, 62 percent were working as clerks. Although most women who enlisted hoped to satisfy their spirit of adventure through an overseas posting, only one in nine servicewomen served outside Canada, with the exception of the nursing sisters. We can well imagine the anger and disappointment felt by one group of WDs (Women's Division, RCAF) at Rockcliffe, who found themselves scrubbing the floors in the governor-general's residence. When they did manage to make it overseas, most CWACs found themselves assigned to work as clerks, laundresses, and cooks; in fact, the first call for Canadian servicewomen to serve overseas came when Canadian Headquarters in London was unable to find sufficient laundresses, and requested 150 CWACs to make up the shortfall.[17] The sexual division of labour remained intact.

Indeed, traditional attitudes towards women were ultimately reinforced during the war, in spite of initial challenges. The sight of women dressed in overalls and bandanas, swinging lunch pails on the way to work, or of women in trim military uniforms, caused many Canadians considerable consternation. Those responsible for recruiting women into the labour force and the armed forces felt called upon to reassure the public that the new tasks women were undertaking were short-term, necessitated by the current emergency, and did not constitute any real threat to existing gender roles. Military authorities undertook a massive educational and publicity campaign to reassure Canadians that the femininity of the women recruits was not being jeopardized, emphasizing the attractive uniforms and the homey atmosphere of the women's barracks. Female recruits were allowed to wear make-up, were encouraged to be attractive and feminine, and were reminded "at all times to act in a becoming and lady-like manner."[18]

As part of their campaign, the authorities also had to reassure the public about the respectability of the women under their command. There was a persistent belief that servicewomen were promiscuous; rumours abounded that some were former prostitutes, that many were getting pregnant, and that a large proportion were suffering from venereal disease. Despite the fact that venereal disease was far more common among Canadian servicemen, who also accounted for nearly 90 percent of the fathers named by CWACs discharged for pregnancy, the reputations of the men were unaffected. Indeed, it is only too evident that a double standard of sexual behaviour was transferred from civilian to military life. Servicewomen who contracted venereal disease were much more likely to be discharged than servicemen with the same condition, and much greater effort was expended on setting up preventive programs for men. The latter were constantly reminded that it was predatory, unprincipled women who caused venereal infection.[19]

By the war's end, more than 43 000 women had enlisted in the armed forces: 21 000 in the Women's Army Corps, 16 000 in the Women's Division of the air force, and 6600 in the Women's Naval Service. In addition, some 2500 women joined the Nursing Service and 38 women doctors signed up for medical duty. Despite the limitations and discrimination that women in the services frequently encountered, for many their wartime experience was exhilarating. "When you passed your exams and you received your flags," one member of the Women's Naval Service recalled, "it was like getting your degree. It had a big effect on our lives. We were proud of ourselves as individuals as well as women, for we succeeded under the same conditions as the men, and for many this changed our outlook toward our place within society."[20] Nonetheless, the official mottoes of the women's services — "We are the Women behind the men behind the guns"; "We serve that men might fly"; "We serve that men might fight" — cast them in a subsidiary role. Although the women's naval and military units played a crucial role in the war effort, and considerable pressure was exerted on the government to maintain them as part of Canada's reserve forces, once the hostilities ceased they were promptly disbanded. Concurrently, the government abandoned the wartime incentives to attract women into paid employment. Women were expected to return to their primary sphere of activity — the home.

What should women do after the war?

Canadian policy makers were merely reflecting prevailing public opinion — that women's labour force participation during the war was a temporary phenomenon. Even before peace was achieved, most Canadians expected women, especially those who were married, to rededicate themselves to work in the home. In 1944 Dorise Nielsen, CCF member from Saskatchewan, gave Parliament a sardonic summary of men's attitudes towards women's appropriate role: "Well, girls, you have done a nice job; you looked very cute in your overalls and we appreciate what you have done for us; but just run along; go home; we can get along without you very easily."[21]

A Gallup poll conducted in 1944 indicated that 75 percent of the Canadian men polled, as well as 68 percent of the women, believed men should be given preference in post-war employment.[22] Given the limited opportunities for women to move out of female work ghettos during the war, the physical and emotional strain endured by those who combined paid employment with domestic labour, the aggravation of wartime shortages, and the anxiety caused by the absence of loved ones, many Canadian women themselves looked forward to a return to full-time home life at war's end. "When the Johnnys and Joes come marching home," a woman journalist noted, "just shopping for ham to cook ham and eggs — if she can get eggs — is apt to be important to a woman . . . even if she drops an odd pay envelope along the way."[23] Not surprisingly, both governments and industry quickly adjusted their policies and practices to encourage women to stay at home.

Planning for the post-war economy and society began well before the Allied victory in Europe in May 1945. Many Canadians feared a resumption of the severe recession and massive unemployment of the 1930s, or of the inflation and social unrest of the years immediately following World War I. Spurred on by these concerns, in March 1941 the Liberal government named an Advisory Committee on Reconstruction, consisting of six prominent men, with Principal Cyril F. James of McGill University as chairman. Almost immediately, women began to petition for representatives of their sex in the planning exercise, on the basis of women's important contribution to the war effort. Finally, in January 1943, the government bowed to the women's lobby, and established a new subcommittee to deal with the problems women in war industry were likely to encounter once war ended. This subcommittee, whose terms of reference were soon expanded to allow it to report on post-war problems for all Canadian women, was headed by Margaret Stovel McWilliams, journalist, Winnipeg councillor, and prominent women's organization activist, and included nine other women from across the nation.[24] They were all well-educated, almost exclusively of British Protestant background, middle-aged, and mostly upper middle class. Although these women had considerable experience and expertise as a result of the organizational work in which nearly all were involved, several were clearly chosen because of their husbands' prominent positions and political connections.

At its initial meeting, the subcommittee adopted as its first principle the precept that women's war work entitled them to the same possibilities as men for post-war training and employment. Each woman, its members believed, should have the right not only to choose her work, but also to obtain equal remuneration, working conditions, and opportunity for advancement as men. Although the subcommittee's effectiveness was undermined by being ordered to avoid publicity, and by the sudden shortening of its term to eight months, it produced a comprehensive report.

The report itself was a mixture of old and new. Assuming that marriage would greatly reduce potential female unemployment, the subcommittee nevertheless recommended that the federal government assume responsibility for the training and retraining of women workers, and provide low interest loans to help needy women upgrade their skills. Training should be available to women on the same basis as it was to men, but most women would be trained in distinctive women's occupations, such as domestic service, nursing, teaching, and social work; to avoid duplicating the work of another subcommittee, proposals on training programs were given only for domestic workers. Somewhat radically the subcommittee proposed that "household workers" be included in any national labour code that might be forthcoming, including minimum wage legislation, unemployment insurance, and workmen's compensation. Such workers were to be protected further by means of written contracts with their employers. The subcommittee echoed again the hope that domestic work would be raised to the status of a vocation, a development that would benefit housewives as well as their employees. In respect to married women at home, the subcommittee members proposed measures intended to improve their status: they should be viewed as economic partners with their husbands, be included in social security schemes such as health insurance, receive family allowances, and have access to government-funded morning nursery schools. Hoping that the rural way of life would attract back to the countryside many of the 95 000 women who had left the farm during the war, they urged governments to extend electricity to rural areas, supply household appliances at cost, improve communication networks, and expand rural educational, health, and recreational facilities.

The important new elements in the subcommittee's recommendations led some journalists to describe their report as a "charter of rights" or a "bill of rights" for Canadian women.[25] Yet, despite its innovative character, the report received little public attention apart from a few press accounts that were usually consigned to the "women's pages." The federal government ignored most of its recommendations, as it did most of the recommendations of the Advisory Committee's other subcommittees.

Instead, governments now moved to cancel the incentives they had created to draw women into the workforce. The Quebec government discontinued its participation in the Day Nurseries Agreement in October 1945, and the federal government ended its agreement with Ontario in June 1946. Although the total number of children accommodated in these nurseries was small—some 1000 in the pre-school programs and 2500 in the school-age programs—their existence had been extremely significant symbolically. The federal government also amended income tax regulations so that after January 1, 1947, if a wife earned more than $250—not the pre-war $750—her husband could no longer claim the full married status exemption.[26] Although the tax amendments appear to have had little effect on married women's employment in some regions, in others they were reported as having a significant negative impact. In Prince George, British Columbia, the local employment office manager noted that no fewer than eight married women had indicated their intent to resign their nursing positions at the local hospital owing to the new tax regulations, aggravating an already "grim" shortage of trained nurses. There were also reports that labour shortages were occurring in the fruit packing and canning industry in the Okanagan Valley because married women were quitting work once they had earned $250.[27]

Another post-war policy that worked to women's disadvantage was "veterans' preference," giving priority in government employment to Canadians who had performed active duty overseas. Relatively few women met this criterion, since only 7000 Canadian women had served overseas.[28] There was a general effort to limit women's employment in the public service. The prime minister went so far as to request his cabinet ministers not to employ female secretaries. The Minister of Agriculture, W.R. Motherwell, is reported to have responded "To —— with him. I couldn't get along without her."[29] Within the public service, the married women who had been implored to help run the burgeoning wartime bureaucracy were now discharged. Married women continued to be barred from the federal civil service until 1955.

When the government disbanded the women's military services in 1946, post-war training programs for discharged members paid lipservice to the principle of equal opportunity for training for women and men, but in reality focussed on "suitable" occupations such as stenography, homemaking, dressmaking, and nursing. Of the female veterans who took vocational training, over half took commercial training courses.[30] For young women who had learned a trade in the armed forces, the return to civilian employment was often frustrating. The experience of one French Canadian telegraphist was typical. Since railway companies and airlines gave preference to men, Monique Comeau Gauthier was counselled to take a course in how to use an adding machine; eventually she found work as a telephone operator.[31]

For women who had been engaged in war industry, there were few opportunities to retain the skilled jobs or the high wages of the war years. The National Employment Service considered that low-paid, unskilled labour was suitable for female war workers: in one case brought to the attention of the House of Commons in July 1946, the service was accused of offering an elevator operator's job that paid $15.30 per week to a woman who had been earning $30.80 per week as an instrument mechanic in an aircraft factory. The new wage was below the prevailing minimum wage.[32] Moreover, women were to be redirected from manufacturing, where their continued presence might constitute a threat to male employment, into domestic service, where there was a dearth of workers. By going into domestic service, women also lost the opportunity to receive unemployment insurance benefits. The 1941 unemployment insurance legislation did not include domestic servants, teachers, or nurses, although some categories of nurses were included in 1944. The oft-repeated but unrealistic objective of attracting throngs of women into paid domestic work by improving the status and wages was tried once more under the label of the "Home Aide" program. And once again, Canadian women workers responded by virtually ignoring the program.[33]

Disillusioned by public failure to recognize women's contribution to the war effort adequately, one female reporter wondered whether married women would "go to war" again:

We made munitions, served overseas or at home, whenever we were needed. And loved doing it. Then what happened when the war was over? We were patted on the head and told, "Good show, girls, but now back to kinder, küche and kirche. . . ." If married women are people in emergencies, why can't they be people when there isn't an emergency?[34]

Once more, women's role as a "reserve army of labour" was unmistakable. When workers were urgently needed, even married women were encouraged to take on paid employment; once male labour became more plentiful, women were encouraged to shift back to traditional female occupations or to the home.

Media messages

The Canadian government's massive campaign to encourage women to enter the labour force and military service during World War II made use of newspapers, periodicals, radio, and the newly created National Film Board to modify the image of the ideal Canadian woman. At war's end, the image changed again: women's productive role disappeared, and it was domestic duties that were the central feature of the idealized woman's life. Canadian media portrayals of women in the post-war years stressed an all-pervasive stereotype of women as happy homemakers, winsome wives, and magnanimous mothers. Woman's role as consumer was re-emphasized.[35] In *Maclean's* magazine between 1939 and 1950, the proportion of all advertisments that directly appealed to women as homemakers rose from about 40 percent in the period 1939–43 to over 70 percent in 1950. And the emphasis shifted. No longer did the advertisements merely offer to free the housewife from the drudgery and boredom of her work; now they promised her a life of personal fulfillment — provided she wisely purchased the right products.[36]

The Francophone media followed a similar pattern, but adopted an even more traditional version. The representation of the ideal French Canadian woman was thoroughly unidimensional: she was portrayed as a fervent Catholic, a devoted wife and mother, and attached to the rural way of life. This characterization was consistently presented in *La Terre et le Foyer*, the official organ of the *Cercles de fermières* after 1945. Designed for women in the smaller urban centres as well as farm women, most of the articles in this magazine discussed women's handicrafts (*artisanat*), and promoted the primary objective of the *cercles*: the professionalization of country women's work. *La Terre et le Foyer* also made it clear that it adhered closely to church directives. During the 1950s, articles dealing with women and the family thoroughly reflected the ideas of the Catholic church: that nature destined women to perform domestic work, and that women's paid employment outside the home was a negative influence.

The media did not question whether or not the normal and desired fate of most women was marriage and motherhood. Although a rare editorial in *Chatelaine* did champion a woman's right to remain single, and some articles in Canadian mass-circulation magazines such as *Saturday Night* strongly advocated education for women that would enable them to pursue certain "women's careers," spinsterhood was not a highly regarded state. Advertisements aimed at the single young woman counselled her on how to catch a man, and glamour was decreed her most highly prized attribute. The 1950s were the decade of Yves St. Laurent's "New Look," the sweater girl, and Marilyn Monroe. St. Laurent designed clothes, he said, "for flowerlike women, clothes with rounded shoulders, full feminine busts, and willowy waists above enormous spreading skirts."[37] For many women, such feminine appearance required encasing themselves in padded bras and waist-cinchers. In addition, the essential requirement for a glamorous image was impeccable personal hygiene. Advertisements for soaps, deodorants, and sanitary napkins were numerous: one deodorant advertisement showed a tearful young woman under the caption, "She lost her man because of *that*." It was not enough, however, to be clean and odour-free; a woman's chances of romantic success depended on improving her appearance by using the plethora of products the cosmetic industry had to offer her.

Once she had used her beauty to effect the desired change in marital status, it was a woman's duty to continue to be sexually attractive to her husband. An advertisement for disinfectant showed a distraught wife whose husband was walking out the door, suitcase in hand; if only she had used Lysol in her douche to keep herself fresh and dainty! The married woman's role as a tension manager was also highlighted in the advertisements. Under a picture of a beaming middle-aged couple, the manufacturers of Ovaltine proclaimed that this twosome was "still in love after years of marriage." But it had taken "more than love to reach this blissful state of trust and devotion." The "thoughtful wife" had made a cup of Ovaltine their "nightly custom," thereby "melting away the nervous tensions of the day."[38]

It was still only with her transformation into mother, however, that a woman was able to reach her full potential. Weston's Bakery paid tribute to the Canadian mother as the "heart of her home," responsible for the moral and civic training of her children.[39] The message of this advertisement is remarkably similar to that delivered by Dr. Hilda Neatby, Canada's pre-eminent woman historian of the 1950s. A professor at the University of Saskatchewan and member of the Massey Commission on cultural affairs, Dr. Neatby never married. However, she confidently assured other women that the

GUARDIAN OF HER FAMILY'S HEALTH

Today, more than ever, this wise mother knows that even well-balanced meals often do not contain all the vitamins needed by growing children, and adults too! Her family starts each day by taking ONE-A-DAY (BRAND)* MULTIPLE VITAMINS. Each tiny tablet contains seven essential vitamins that help maintain normal resistance to infection, which is so important at this time of year when colds and similar ailments are so prevalent.

Keep the smart, attractive apothecary bottle of ONE-A-DAY (BRAND)* MULTIPLE VITAMINS on *your* table . . . Provide each member of *your* family with an important extra margin of vitamin protection, for less than 4¢ a day.

* Reg'd trademark

100 TABLETS

for only $**3**95*

Post-war magazine advertisement reinforcing women's maternal responsibilities.

establishment of "a moral tone and moral practices in her family is a woman's first obligation to society. . . . Women, gifted and otherwise, are the individuals who in the present state of society have a large, perhaps the largest share in determining the cultural atmosphere of the home." [40] Neatby's arguments were echoed by many others who sought to expand opportunities in higher education for Canada's future mothers.

The belief that marriage and motherhood were the normal goals for women was reinforced by medical experts. As Freudian views about women became more widespread in the 1950s, as did the psychosomatic approach to medicine, doctors stressed the importance of women's reproductive and maternal roles. The growing tendency for women to work outside the home fuelled concern about the preservation of the family. Women suffering from gynecological disorders were considered to have rejected their traditional roles. According to the *Canadian Medical Association Journal* in 1958, women who experienced pre-menstrual tension tended to resent their femininity and to envy men. Another doctor asserted that women exaggerated the extent of their menstrual pain "in order to get revenge on men for their easy lot in life and to shirk their own work responsibilities." Specialists in obstetrics and gynecology were advised to determine the extent to which their patients accepted themselves as women.[41]

For those women who did become mothers, feature articles and regular columns appearing in the women's magazines offered advice —frequently conflicting—about how to deal with the myriad problems inherent in raising a child. The expansion of the middle class in the prosperity of the post-war years created an enlarged audience of well-educated parents receptive to childrearing advice. Childcare experts emphasized the emotional bonds between mother and child, and as infant mortality rates for the general population continued to decline, middle class mothers could be increasingly confident that this emotional investment would not be destroyed by the untimely death of their children.

Many mothers were anxious about their abilities as parents, increasingly so with the popularization of the work of child psychologists such as Dr. John Bowlby. Bowlby was the British psychologist who coined the phrase "maternal deprivation," a notion central to his book *Child Care and the Growth of Love*, and discussed widely in women's magazines in North America. On the basis of a study of orphaned children who had to be cared for in institutional settings or foster homes, Bowlby argued that irreparable damage was done to young children when they were separated from their mothers for a prolonged period. He counselled mothers not to leave children under three years of age in the care of others except for the most urgent reasons. Even "the holiday whilst granny looks after the baby" was "best kept to a week or ten days." Many mothers interpreted Bowlby's dictum about the "absolute need of infants and toddlers for the continuous care of their mothers" as meaning they should always be on call for their children.[42]

The conflicting advice mothers of infants received further complicated their lives: should they feed baby according to a strict time schedule, as their own mothers had done, or when baby demanded it? Although infant care experts pointed out the advantages of breast feeding, and counselled mothers to try it, they assigned an inordinate amount of space in the literature to describing the procedures to be followed in bottle feeding. Given the overwhelming importance accorded motherhood, and the confusion about how best to meet the demands of this role, it is small wonder that Canadian women relied on books such as the free government publication, *The Canadian Mother and Child* (1940), and Dr. Benjamin Spock's *Baby and Child Care* (1945) for authoritative answers. By 1953 Canadian public health nurses had handed out to new mothers over 2 000 000 copies of the former; by 1975 it was in its third edition.

Although the image of women as homemakers and mothers was

all-pervasive and powerful, and undoubtedly exercised a considerable influence, increasing numbers of Canadian women did not conform to its fundamental specifications. Once again, it is important to underline the gap that existed between what women were told they should do and what women actually did. The very vigour with which the "happy homemaker" image was promoted by the media may well have been a reaction to women's growing involvement in activities outside the home.

What women really did

Immediately after the war, there was little apparent discrepancy between the image and the reality of women's lives. Canadians' desire to return to familiar roles combined with the reduced opportunities for women in paid employment to produce a sharp decrease in the female participation rate in the labour force. By September 1945, nearly 80 000 women in war industry had been laid off and thousands of servicewomen discharged.[43] In 1944, at the peak of wartime employment, one-third of all women over the age of 15 were in the paid labour force. Two years later, only one-quarter were working for pay. Only in 1967 did women's participation rate surpass the 1944 level. However, the decline in the period immediately after the war appears to have been caused less by the withdrawal of women already in the workforce than by the lower participation rate of younger women. Prolonged education, earlier age at marriage, and earlier age for starting a family together produced this result. One estimate placed the number of women who withdrew from the workplace at war's end at approximately 102 000, under 10 percent of all female war workers.[44] In the United States, women's labour force participation rate had reached even higher levels during the war, only to drop by 19 percent between 1945 and 1947. The decline in Canada was much less pronounced—less than 9 percent during the same period. [45]

After the war, marriage rates soared, especially among younger women. For those aged 15 to 19, the rate more than doubled, climbing from 30 per 1000 in 1937 to 62 per 1000 in 1954.[46] Canadian women were also marrying earlier. The average age of brides at first marriage fell from 25.4 years in 1941 to 22 years by 1961.[47] In addition, they were having more children, and having them earlier than women of the previous generation. There was a sharp increase in the number of births per 1000 population, which rose from 20.1 in 1937 to 28.9 in 1947. It is important to note, however, that significant increases in the birth rate were recorded only among married women under 30, and most strikingly among those under 25. As one observer pithily commented, "Young girls are more interested in raising families than jobs; not-so-young girls like jobs better than children."[48] In the younger groups of married women, birth rates continued to climb until 1956; for women over 40, the rates continued to decline compared to those established by women in the same age category during previous generations.[49]

These patterns initially produced the renowned post-war "baby boom" in the late 1940s and early 1950s, the result of a combination of earlier age at marriage, earlier births of first children, and larger completed families. In 1956, nearly one-half of all live births consisted of third or later children.[50] Nevertheless, after 1956, substantial declines in birth rates were recorded for all age groups.

Despite the general absence of young mothers from the workforce in the post-war era, the proportion of married women among paid female workers continued to rise. In part, this was owing to the lower age at marriage and the growing acceptance of young married women working, providing that they did not have children; in part, to the presence in the labour force of older women with school-age or older children. In 1941 only slightly more than 10 percent of all employed women were married; during the war the estimated proportion was from 25 to 35 percent. By 1951 the percentage had dropped slightly, but by 1961 nearly half of all female workers were married. This dramatic increase can also be measured by looking at the proportion of wives who were in the paid labour force: from only one in twenty-five in 1941, the figure changed in twenty years to a remarkable one in five. Changes such as these led the Dominion Chief Statistician to declare in 1954, "The woman's place is no longer in the home, and the Canadian home is no longer what it used to be."[51]

In spite of the initial post-war setbacks, women's involvement in the labour force increased steadily from the mid-1950s on. For the first time in Canadian history, the number of women entering the workforce was greater than the number of men.[52] During the recession from 1957 to 1961, a *Financial Post* reporter noted that married

Aspiring clerical workers, Henderson Secretarial School, Calgary.

women's wages were being used to supplement their husbands' unemployment benefits. He concluded, "This is a woman's world all right and getting more so. More and more married women are going to work and they are quickly being snapped into jobs. . . . Keep your eye on Mom."[53] Unemployment rates were lower for women than men owing to the rapid expansion of clerical and service positions, largely filled by women.[54] With the post-war baby boom and the failure of teachers' salaries to keep pace with inflation, an acute teacher shortage developed, and once more women, including married women, were actively recruited. To cope with the unprecedented numbers of students crowding into schools in Ontario, the provincial government dropped the entrance requirement for teachers' college from grade 13 to grade 12, and encouraged high school graduates to "qualify" as teachers by taking a brief, five-week summer course. Other provinces adopted similar policies: in Nova Scotia, for example, in a practice reminiscent of the nineteenth century, women as young as sixteen were recruited for rural schools.[55]

The increasing numbers of working mothers became the source of much controversy and, possibly as a result, in 1955 the Department of Labour conducted a survey of employed married women in eight Canadian cities. Over 50 percent of those interviewed had dependent children, and some 80 percent worked full-time. They had evidently taken jobs for economic reasons: only 15 percent of their husbands earned a relatively high income of $4000, but when the wives' wages were included, over half of the families reached this income level. One-third of the workers in the Department of Labour survey were born outside Canada.[56] For some immigrant groups such as the southern Italians, married women's paid employment was central to the family's strategy for improving its financial situation.[57] The higher labour force participation rate of married women in the late 1950s compared to the immediate post-war years was, it seems, owing in part to the massive post-war wave of immigration. The authors of the eight-city survey were eager to refute the public perception that most married working women had children who were being neglected — so eager that, instead of stating that 56 percent of the women interviewed had dependent children, they declared that 44 percent had none.[58]

Women workers with pre-school children had to make their own childcare arrangements, and generally preferred family or friends. Highly placed women such as Marion Royce, director of the Women's Bureau of the federal Department of Labour created in 1954, persistently argued the need for better daycare facilities and more part-time work for married women with children.[59] However, no level of government felt an obligation to provide such facilities, and most Canadians continued to believe that married women with young children should not be employed outside the home. It was still assumed that the vast majority of women could not successfully combine work and family. In 1955 one woman who tried but failed concluded vehemently,

I don't care who you are or how well organized you are, you can't be a good wife and mother, hostess and housekeeper and also do a good job for your employer all at the same time. When you try, someone is bound to get cheated — your husband, your child or your boss — and in most cases, all three.

Her solution: quit your job to save your marriage.[60]

Most married women in the paid labour force could not choose to quit their jobs. It was essential for them to work to maintain their families' standard of living in an increasingly consumer-oriented society. The strong desire of Canadians to improve their material situations, frustrated by years of depression and war, was not to be denied. In the 1950s, television revolutionized mass advertising techniques, stimulating the demand for major consumer items such as cars, appliances, and furniture. To purchase these things, which most Canadians now considered essential, and to ensure access to higher education and better health care for their children, many married women had to supplement their husbands' wages through paid employment.

The pronounced emphasis on consumption may also have increased the workload of most homemakers. As the standard of living rose, and the volume and diversity of consumer goods increased, the tasks associated with household management became more complex. The work entailed in managing the family budget, trying to balance family income against family needs, was even more difficult in the new suburbs that mushroomed on the fringes of Canadian urban communities. Frequently isolated and without transportation, suburban housewives had little opportunity to engage in comparison shopping or to buy at the lowest prices. Shopping plazas, the first of which was constructed in Toronto in 1946, were somewhat helpful, but they provided only a limited choice of shops. Women were also responsible for dealing with the countless salesmen, repairmen, public officials, and community representatives who showed up on their doorsteps.[61]

For women who continued to participate in the workforce, there were some significant attempts at organization, a consequence of the continuation of labour militancy generated during World War II. During the war, as the demand for workers expanded, so did workers' bargaining power; union membership soared, especially with the expansion of industrial unionism. Even the more conservative international unions became involved in organizing semi-skilled and unskilled workers, within whose ranks were to be found thousands of women. In the textile industry, Madeleine Parent and her future husband, Kent Rowley, made impressive inroads. Parent, the daughter of a prosperous French Canadian retail manager, graduated from McGill in 1940 and became a labour activist while still a very young woman. In 1942 Parent and Rowley started to organize Quebec cottonmill workers in Valleyfield and Montreal. They faced formidable odds, for they had to confront not only the might of the textile cartel headed by Dominion Textile, but also the overt hostility of the Roman Catholic church, which branded them Communists. Because of the wartime ban on strikes, the workers had to wait until 1945 before they could walk off the job in an attempt to win union recognition, a shorter work week, and improved benefits.

In June 1946, some 3000 workers at Dominion Textile's Montreal mills and an additional 3000 workers at the Valleyfield mill staged a walkout. Approximately one-third of the workers were women. Although the Montreal strike was grudgingly accepted as legal by the blatantly pro-business government of Maurice Duplessis, it declared the Valleyfield strike illegal since not all the bargaining procedures required by law had been followed. The authorities made a concerted effort to break the strike, using the provincial police to protect strikebreakers and intimidate the workers. The Valleyfield strike was long, bitter, punctuated by violence, and marked by the arrest of the union leaders, including both Parent and Rowley. However, it finally terminated in September and resulted in a first contract, improved wages, and other benefits for the workers.

There was another effort in 1946, equally concerted but less successful, to unionize a segment of the workforce containing a large proportion of female wage earners — the campaign undertaken by the Retail, Wholesale and Department Store Union to organize the 15 000 T.E. Eaton Co. workers in Toronto. A key figure in this drive was Eileen Tallman, a Toronto CCF activist and crack organizer for the United Steelworkers. One of the major obstacles in recruiting workers to the union was their high rate of turnover, over one in four leaving each year. It took one and a half years of painstaking efforts to contact Eaton's employees working at various outlets throughout Toronto before the first union meeting could be held. Equal pay for equal work became a principal objective: the starting salary for married women was $20 per week, while it was $24 to $26 for single men and $30 for married men.[62] Although the Canadian Congress of Labour created a special organizing committee to support the union in this monumental task, and there was a prolonged attempt to win certification, the drive was unsuccessful. It was finally called off in 1952. The company managed to undercut the strength of the campaign by improving wages and establishing pensions for some long-term employees. The failure of the Eaton's drive was a clear indicator of how difficult it was, and would continue to be, to organize white collar workers. And this was the sector where women workers were increasingly to be found.

The importance of women's support for the trade union movement grew during and after World War II, as production workers saw many of their material gains threatened by the rising cost of living, and women's consumer roles expanded. Some women's auxiliaries were also involved in the bitter internal struggles between local Communist union leaders and their international leadership that bedevilled many unions after the war; such a situation occurred in Lake Cowichan, British Columbia, where the ladies' auxiliary supported the local "red" faction of the International Woodworkers of America. The political activities of this auxiliary also led it to support the "rolling pin brigade," a protest movement largely composed of housewife consumers, which culminated in a march on Ottawa after the war to demand price and rent controls, low-cost housing, and the establishment of a peacetime agency to regulate prices. More importantly, on an individual level, women active in the auxiliary acquired a greater awareness of the interconnections between men's paid labour and women's unpaid domestic labour. One delegate to a 1947 district auxiliary convention aptly summarized the relationship:

I didn't just marry a meal ticket, and that's what it amounts to if my husband works more than forty hours a week! Wives also need a shorter work week and the only way that most of us can get it is if our husbands pitch in at home to give us a break, spend a little time with the children and (incidentally) learn a bit of housekeeping.[63]

By the end of the 1950s, it should have been clear that women were in the workplace to stay. Instead, what was mainly noticed was the continuing emphasis on women's role in the home. Certainly, wartime did not have any "liberating" effect for the Japanese Canadian women who spent the war years imprisoned in internment camps, or "resettled" thousands of kilometres away from their homes. Nor was the war a period of personal fulfillment for those

Community kitchen, Slocan City Japanese internment camp, 1943.

who lost sons, husbands, or lovers. Nevertheless, a more optimistic assessment may be in order. For some Canadian women, the opportunity to expand their activities did have a positive impact. According to one woman,

The war killed all this servant business, being a maid, and I think it did a lot to finish off the idea that a woman's place and her only place was in the home . . . . The war and working in plants so changed me I became an entirely different person. I wish I'd kept a diary.[64]

Such women gained an increased sense of self-worth, leading them to chafe at the more traditional and limited notions of women's appropriate roles that re-emerged at war's end.

13 Prelude to revolution

Dramatic demographic, social, and economic transformations reshaped women's lives beginning in the 1940s. More and more women entered the public realm previously identified as male, while the confinement of adult women to the home lessened. There was increased emphasis on the husband–wife relationship, and intense female friendships were discouraged. Yet vestiges of an earlier women's culture remained, and to some extent this culture was reformulated in a number of contexts: the post-war changes in women's everyday life, their education, their sport and recreational activities, their organizations, and their artistic goals — all these combined to define an identifiable women's world.

Demographic patterns

The everyday lives of Canadian women changed greatly between 1945 and 1970. There were shifts in the life cycle — the timing of leaving home, of marriage, and of starting a family; the duration of childrearing; and of old age. One of the most striking changes in the lives of young women was the greater degree of independence they enjoyed. In the past, if young people left their families before marriage, they usually went to live with a surrogate family so that their lives were still carefully monitored. During the late 1950s and 1960s, it became more common and more acceptable for the young to leave home to live on their own or with people their own age while working or completing their education. The increase in apartment construction, particularly rapid between 1961 and 1970, facilitated this trend.[1] During the five-year period from 1966 to 1971, the total number of households in Canada increased by 17 percent, but there was an amazing 92 percent increase in households with single, never-married heads.[2] The increased tendency for young people to live on their own was a manifestation of the unprecedented freedom — economic, social, and sexual — enjoyed by the generation of Canadians coming of age in the 1960s.

There is some evidence to suggest that by the early 1960s young Canadians were using this new-found freedom to postpone marriage. The high marriage rate immediately following the war declined gradually until 1963, when it reached a low of 6.9 per 1000 population, the same level as in 1925.[3] In the late 1960s, the marriage rate climbed again, reaching 8.9 per 1000 by 1971. The reasons for these variations between 1940 and 1971 are not entirely clear. One con-

Table 13.1	Average age at first marriage, 1941–1981	
	Women	Men
1941*	24.4	27.6
1951	23.8	26.6
1961	22.9	25.8
1971	22.6	24.9
1981	23.5	25.7

* Does not include Newfoundland, Yukon, or Northwest Territories until 1951.

tributing factor may have been changes in sexual mores. In the 1950s, pre-marital sex continued to be socially unacceptable for "respectable" young women. Sexual intimacy before marriage became more widespread by the late 1960s, although most women limited such relationships to the man they hoped eventually to marry. In addition, young women and men were increasingly likely to live together without marrying. The age structure of the Canadian population also played a role, since the increase in the marriage rate in the late 1960s occurred when the large group of children born after the war reached marriageable age. At the same time, the average age at first marriage continued to decline throughout the entire period. For women, the average age dropped from 24.4 years in 1941 to only 22.6 years in 1971; for men, the average shifted from 27.6 to 24.9.[4] The greater autonomy young people experienced in directing their lives extended to decisions about when as well as whom to marry. The decline in the age at marriage was also related to the general prosperity of the post-war years, the growing acceptability of married women without children working outside the home, the availability of social assistance programs, and easier access to credit. At the same time, the growing affluence of Canadians may also have led many parents to give financial support to young people who, a generation earlier, would have been considered too dependent to marry.[5]

The rapid formation of new and larger families in the prosperity of the immediate post-war period resulted in an increase in the percentage both of nuclear family households and of owner-occupied dwellings. In 1951, 90 percent of Canadian families maintained their own households; by 1966, 96 percent did.[6] Typically, the newly formed families were moving into detached houses located in the suburbs, with more rooms than houses built before the war, and spacious yards for the children to play in. But there were negative aspects to these changes. Canadian women in the 1950s were increasingly cut off from traditional women's support systems. Young

Sources: 1941–71: Gail C.A. Cook, ed., Opportunity for Choice (Ottawa: Information Canada, 1976) 18; 1981: Women in Canada: A Statistical Report (Ottawa: Statistics Canada, 1985) 10.

women with small children, living in the suburbs and performing their own domestic work, could no longer easily turn to more experienced adult women for help and advice. Their response was to seek female companionship and support networks through "coffee klatches," bridge clubs, women's organizations, and mixed volunteer groups.

The birth rate, which began its downward spiral after 1957, had fallen by 1971 to 16.8 per 1000 total population. Women were having fewer children, and they were compressing childbearing into a shorter space of time. By 1970, less than one-third of all live births were third or later children. The average number of children per family declined from 1.9 in 1961 to 1.7 in 1971.[7] In addition, the likelihood that children would be born in a hospital rose significantly after the war: in 1941 just under half of all babies were born in hospital, but by 1951 four out of every five births were hospital births. Ten years later, 97 percent of all Canadian babies were born in hospital.[8]

Despite nativist anxiety about the fecundity of post-war immigrants, families headed by individuals born outside Canada had fewer children (1.6) on average than those headed by the native-born (2.0). There was also considerable regional variation: in 1966, Newfoundland had the highest average of 2.6 children per family; British Columbia and Ontario had the lowest average of 1.7. The number of children per family also varied considerably according to place of residence. In urban areas, families had on the average only 1.7 children, while in rural farm communities, they averaged 2.2 children. More significantly, the proportion of rural families with 4 or more children under the age of 25 living at home was nearly double (26.2 percent) that of urban families (13.4 percent). Overall, however, the size of the Canadian family was becoming more uniform. Between 1941 and 1966, the percentages of small families (0–1 child) and of very large families (6 or more children) had decreased.[9]

Fertility rates also provide indicators of change in women's lives. In the Northwest Territories, the Yukon, and Newfoundland, fertility rates remained well above the national average from 1951 to 1970, while those of Ontario and British Columbia were slightly below.[10] The continued higher rates in the Territories can be accounted for by the higher birth rate among native women, a rate significantly higher than that recorded for the Canadian population as a whole. Moreover, Indian fertility rates continued to rise throughout the 1960s, while those for the Canadian population fell; in 1965, the birth rate for Indians was 43.5 per 1000 compared to 21.3 for all Canadians. Within the native population there were important variations: Indians living in the eastern provinces recorded birth rates similar to the provincial rates, while Indians in the prairie provinces and the Territories had very high rates.[11]

By contrast, a dramatic decrease in the birth rate occurred in the province of Quebec: between 1959 and 1969 the birth rate was cut in half, a change that in the rest of the country took place over the span of a century.[12] By 1970 Quebec had the lowest birth rate of any of the provinces (15 per 1000). This stunning change was an integral part of the "Quiet Revolution," the amalgam of demographic, economic, social, and political transformations that, although beginning in the 1940s, was only fully realized after the death of Premier Maurice Duplessis in 1959. The rapid rate of urbanization and the modernization of Quebec agriculture during the 1950s rendered the traditional natalist arguments of French Canadian nationalists increasingly irrelevant. Mechanization of farms reduced the need for abundant labour, and consequently, even in rural areas, the benefits of having very large families evaporated. Among Quebec women born between 1922 and 1926, who would have completed their families by the late 1960s, only 3.5 percent had more than 10 children and fewer than 20 percent had more than 6 children.[13] As urban couples in particular increasingly chose to limit the size of their families during the 1940s and 1950s, the Roman Catholic church was compelled to recognize the "natural" forms of birth control, such as the "rhythm method" and the "thermometer method." In fact, by organizing marriage preparation courses in which these methods were discussed, the clergy played a key role in the dissemination of at least some forms of birth control information.

In Quebec and elsewhere, the decline in fertility was the result in part of increased knowledge of and access to birth control devices. The birth control pill had been developed by the early 1960s but was only available on prescription to married women in the larger urban centres. Legal penalties for displaying and selling contraceptive devices remained in force until 1969. In fact, the conviction and jailing of a Toronto pharmacist in 1960 for selling condoms was one of the factors that motivated Barbara and George Cadbury to organize the Planned Parenthood Association of Toronto one year later. By 1963 they had succeeded in establishing both the Planned Parenthood Federation of Canada and the Canadian Federation of Societies for Population Planning. In Quebec, the decline in the social power and moral authority of the Catholic church translated into an increasing willingness on the part of Roman Catholics to ignore church doctrine. Like women throughout North America, *Québécoises* adopted the birth control pill and other methods of contraception officially condemned by the Vatican, as a means of asserting more effective control over their own lives. When Pope Paul VI condemned the use of artificial means of birth control in his 1968 encyclical, *Humanae Vitae*, Canadian Catholic bishops dissociated themselves from his stance by stating that the use of birth control was a matter of individual conscience.[14]

The social and political ramifications of such intimate and individual choices soon became apparent. The rapid decline in the birth rate in Quebec from the late 1950s became a central issue for Quebec nationalists. Demographers predicted that Quebec's influence within Confederation would diminish as its population dropped, and that the *Québécois* might eventually be reduced to a minority in their own province if immigration rates, the birth rate, and language transfers from French to English remained at the prevailing levels.[15] Not surprisingly, these fears helped fuel separatist demands for the creation of a sovereign state that would have complete freedom to determine its own immigration and language policies. The widespread use of family limitation practices in Quebec, and the stand taken by the Catholic bishops in 1968, also made it politically posssible for the federal government to amend the following year the provisions of the Criminal Code dealing with contraception and abortion. The urgent need for changes in the existing abortion laws was all too obvious: between 1954 and 1965, there were 226 therapeutic abortions performed in Canadian hospitals, and an estimated additional 50 000 to 100 000 illegal abortions. In British Columbia, abortion-related deaths accounted for one in every five maternal deaths occurring between 1946 and 1968.[16]

Like birth control and abortion, divorce was another controversial issue. Divorce rates in Canada almost tripled at the end of World War II, from 56.2 divorces per 100 000 married persons 15 years of age and over in 1941, to 131.9 in 1946. The dramatic increase was largely the result of the dissolution of unhappy wartime marriages and those weakened by long separations; it may also have reflected the economic independence acquired by some married women during the war. The divorce rate rose steadily from 1951 to 1968 (88.9 to 124.3), and then dramatically after the liberalization of the divorce laws in 1969.[17] By the end of the 1960s, marital breakdown was becoming a familiar occurrence in Canadian society, and was a factor in the increased labour force participation of women who had to support themselves—and in many cases their dependent children—after their marriages had been dissolved.

Despite the increase in the incidence of divorce, the vast majority of Canadian marriages in the 1960s were still brought to an end by the death of one of the spouses rather than by marriage breakdown. Canadians were living longer, however, owing to continued advancements in public health and medicine. The most significant advance was the reduction of infant mortality. The infant death rate almost halved between 1946 and 1960, dropping from 48 per 1000 live births to 27 per 1000. Furthermore, fewer adult women died in childbirth as maternal mortality rates fell dramatically after 1940. The likelihood of a Canadian woman dying because of pregnancy fell from one in 150 in the 1930s to one in 3000 by the 1960s.[18]

By the 1960s, it was apparent that the difference in life expectancy for women and men was increasing. In the 1930s, women could expect to live about 62 years, and men to about 60 years; by 1971 life expectancy for women had increased to 76 years and, for men, to only 69 years. The reasons for the continuing difference in female and male life expectancy are complicated and still not well understood, for they encompass genetic, social, and environmental factors.[19] For Canadian Indians of both sexes, life expectancy remained disturbingly short: in 1970 it was only 37 years for Indian women, and 34 years for Indian men. The principal reason for this was the continuing high infant mortality rate among Indian children. By the end of the 1960s, the mortality rate for Indian children two years of age and under was still eight times that of the white infant population. An Indian woman who survived the first two years of life could look forward to a life span of 53 years, while her male counterpart was likely to survive only until the age of 50.[20]

On the national level, the age composition of the population changed. An increasing proportion of the population was over the age of 65 and women predominated in that group. As the gap between female and male life expectancies widened, the years a woman was likely to spend as a widow increased. As the numbers of solitary elderly women grew, so too did the problem of female poverty.

Educating women

The ideal of equal opportunity for the sexes that had been so widely touted during the war became a dominant theme in post-war education. It appeared that the remaining obstacles to higher education for women had been removed, and that women's education was increasingly similar to men's as proportionately more women took up secondary and post-secondary studies. Full equality, however, remained an elusive goal.

Even at the elementary school level, the experiences and expectations of young girls and boys continued to differ. Sex-role stereotyping was pervasive in the materials used by the students. In the American *Fun with Dick and Jane* reading series that was used well into the 1960s in some provincial school systems, Dick engaged in active play, such as running and jumping, playing with boats, and flying his kite, while Jane played with her dolls. Their father was away at work all day, and drove home in his late-model automobile just in time to eat the dinner that had been prepared by his stay-at-home, smiling, aproned wife. In Quebec, *Guy et Yvette* gave the same message of female subordination. Even mathematical problems reinforced the dominant images; in one text, students were asked to determine whether a girl who could type 48 words per minute could type 2468 words in 45 minutes.[21] The heavy emphasis placed on science and mathematics in the post-Sputnik era seems only to have increased the marginalization of girls and women in the texts and books that children were likely to read. By the mid-1970s, seven out of ten of the people portrayed in Quebec school texts were male. Gone were the references to the outstanding women of the past found in the old manuals, especially those used by the teaching nuns in previous generations. The earlier images were not replaced: women simply disappeared.[22] Parents reinforced the messages implicit in the textbooks. An "Attitude Study," undertaken in 1966 by the Federation of Women Teachers' Associations of Ontario, reported that parents considered nursing, teaching, and social work to be the best occupations for their daughters, but favoured medicine, engineering, science, architecture, the law, and business for their sons.[23]

Divergent expectations for girls and boys continued to influence both the extent and type of education they received at the secondary and post-secondary levels. There is evidence, however, that some of the egalitarianism promoted during World War II had an effect. The teaching of home economics in Ontario schools, for example, had as one of its primary objectives the fostering of "a conception of homemaking as an undertaking in which all members of the family co-operate." Ten years later, home economics teachers were advised that their students would be pursuing "two future careers — wage-earning employment, and marriage with the establishment of families and homes of their own." Suggested class topics included "Fathers as wage-earners and homemakers," and "Mothers as homemakers and frequently wage-earners too." By 1964, however, guidelines stated unequivocally that it was the wife and mother who formed the nucleus of the family, and that she bore the principal responsibility for achieving either "an organized and artistic way of living or a chaotic and unattractive existence within the home."[24]

By the early 1960s, sex-role stereotyping was an important topic of discussion for women journalists. The new editor of *Chatelaine*, Doris Anderson, was writing thought-provoking editorials that linked stereotyping to married women's domestic work and paid employment, and the death of women in public life. June Callwood was also among those who attacked the notions of femininity that

Domestic Science class, Boulton Avenue School, Toronto.

Figure 13.1   Women at universities, 1920–1968

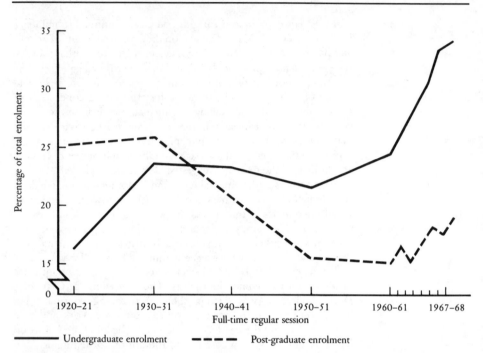

Source: Royal Commission on the Status of Women, *Report* (Ottawa: Information Canada, 1970) 168.

constrained the activities of so many Canadian women. In Quebec as well, there was a subtle yet significant shift in the orientation of the women's press after 1960. With the appearance in 1960 of the French version of *Chatelaine*, and the appointment of Francine Montpetit as the new editor of Montreal's fifty-year-old magazine, *La Revue populaire*, Quebec women were offered more realistic appraisals of their situation. An article on birth control published in *La Revue* in September 1962 resulted in an avalanche of mail. Montpetit was fired two months later and within a year the magazine had disappeared, leaving *Châtelaine* as the only commercial publication directed to Quebec women.[25] During the 1960s, while English Canadian general interest magazines contained a declining proportion of articles about women and work, *Chatelaine/Châtelaine* and the *Canadian Home Journal* continued to focus on women's changing roles.[26]

At the university level, women's educational experience in English Canada immediately following the war closely resembled that of women in the labour force: female students constituted a "reserve army." During the war, they represented a larger proportion of the student body than previously, and were seen as a means of maintaining enrolment—keeping places that would be occupied by men once the war was over.[27] A prime example of this trend occurred in the University of Toronto's Faculty of Medicine. During the war, women as young as sixteen and seventeen found it relatively easy to gain admission. The resulting increase in female students facilitated the Women's Medical Society's successful petition in 1948 to have the yearly quota for female interns at Toronto's largest hospital raised —from one to two.[28] Nonetheless, most women continued to enroll in traditionally female courses of study: arts, nursing, household science, and physical and occupational therapy.

Once the veterans returned, their needs were assigned top priority. Although ex-servicewomen such as future cabinet minister Judy LaMarsh, who had been a translator and decoder during the war, used the veterans' educational programs to acquire a university degree, only 2600 of the approximately 50 000 servicewomen joined her. The vast majority of the veterans at university were men.[29] Consequently, although the actual numbers of women attending university increased, they quickly constituted a smaller proportion of the post-war university students overall. In 1940 some 8000 women accounted for 23 percent of all full-time undergraduate enrolments at Canadian universities; in 1945, the nearly 14 000 female undergraduates represented only 21 percent.[30]

Despite this brief setback, after 1951 there was a steady increase both numerically and proportionately in university attendance by women. By 1970 they accounted for 37 percent of full-time under-graduates. However, women continued to be concentrated in certain areas considered appropriate to their sex. In 1969–70, they represented over 95 percent of the students enrolled at Canadian universities in undergraduate programs in household science, nursing, secretarial science and physical and occupational therapy, but only 1 percent in applied science and engineering.[31] By 1982–83, women students were in the majority both in community colleges (52 percent) and university undergraduate faculties (56 percent), and by 1985, 52 percent of all B.A.s or first professional degrees awarded were to women.[32] The increase in enrolment was particularly rapid in non-traditional areas such as engineering—where women reached 11 percent of total enrolment by 1983–84. Their participation was increasing most rapidly, however, in part-time studies: in 1983–84, 44 percent of all women undergraduates were part-timers. Women still remained largely clustered in traditionally female fields that did not require scientific or mathematic training at the pre-university level.[33]

Mount Saint Vincent College in Nova Scotia, which in 1925 had become the first and only English-language women's college to grant its own degrees, briefly offered a different model of higher education for women. Many of the teaching sisters at the Mount possessed doctorates, at a time when few women pursued Ph.D.s. Nevertheless, because of the shortage of teaching nuns after World War II, the college began to hire lay faculty members, and in order to take advantage of government subsidies the university opened its doors to non-Catholics. By 1969 the dream of an independent Catholic women's university came to an end: Mount St. Vincent affiliated with Dalhousie University, and admitted its first male students.[34]

In post-war Quebec, where secondary and post-secondary education were under church control until 1964, home economics remained a standard feature. There is little evidence of adjustment to the changing times, even though French Canadian women were experiencing demographic and economic transformations even more dramatic than those affecting other Canadian women. The *instituts familiaux* continued to stress the necessity to educate women differently than men. By 1947 there were forty *instituts*, and enrolment had increased eight-fold. The building, maintenance, and staffing of these schools were entrusted to the female religious orders, who were given financial assistance by the provincial government. Their primary purpose was to train young women for their domestic role "with all that this implies of personal charm and culture as well as a knowledge of technical domestic skills." In 1957, of some 4000 hours of instruction spread over a four-year program, well over half were devoted to sewing, cooking, French, child psychology, and religious education. Graduates from the family institutes were able to pursue post-secondary studies in domestic science offered in Montreal and Quebec City. The Anglophone woman journalist who produced a detailed study of the *instituts* could not contain her enthusiasm for this particular type of education for women: it promised them "real freedom and happiness," whereas women's quest for equality with men gave them, in her view, only higher wages, more career choices, and dissatisfaction.[35]

While the church was promoting domestic science education for Francophone women, the provincial government was providing other options. After the introduction of compulsory education by the Liberal government in 1943, the number of normal schools for Francophone Catholic women grew rapidly; between 1940 and 1950, the annual number of graduates from such institutions rose from 712 to 1636. The implementation of compulsory education also resulted in the extension and reform of secondary schools, including the provision of free secondary education. By 1959, most young Francophone women, regardless of class, could acquire some secondary school education. Between 1954 and 1962, the possibility of continuing studies up to the university level was also increased by the establishment of an additional 15 classical colleges for women. The opening of the professions of lawyer (1941) and notary (1956) to women reflected a growing demand on the part of the Francophone bourgeoisie that at least a few exceptional women be provided with the same educational and career opportunities as men.

Québécoises had to wait for additional reforms in the provincial educational system, undertaken in the wake of the comprehensive Parent Commission Report (1964), before it became common for women to attend university and to obtain advanced education in the same disciplines as men. The commissioners, two of whom were women, recommended substantial changes, including the recognition of women's right to obtain the same type of education as men. Among the results were the abolition of the domestic science schools and the creation of co-educational CEGEPs (*Collèges d'enseignement général et pratique*). By 1970, women accounted for one-third of all full-time undergraduates in the province, and for nearly half of all part-time university students.[36]

At the graduate level in Canadian universities, although there was also a steady increase in the number of female students after 1955, the proportion of students who were women (22 percent) was still lower in 1970 than it had been in 1921 (26 percent). Women earned about one-fifth of the masters degrees, and under one-tenth of the doctorates awarded in 1969–70. In 1982, women received 40 percent of the master's degrees awarded, a quarter of the doctorates, and 36 percent of the medical degrees earned.[37] One reason for the reluctance of women to pursue studies in non-traditional areas, especially at the graduate level, was the lack of "role models." In the mid-1960s only slightly more than one in ten university teachers in Canada was a woman, and most were in the faculties of education, nursing, household science, and arts. By 1980–81, women still represented only 15 percent of the full-time faculty; they had their highest representation (24 percent) in education, but only 1.3 percent of the faculty members in engineering and applied sciences were women.[38] In the university as a whole, proportionately more women than men were located in the lowest ranks and non-tenured positions. Faculty women's second-class status was symbolized in some universities by exclusion from full Faculty Club privileges; at McGill, a few determined women faculty fought to eliminate the rules that prevented their use of the Faculty Club's dining room, a battle they finally won over objections of one-third of the club's members. Dr. Virginia Douglas, one of the principal organizers of the campaign, recalled meeting an elderly colleague at the Faculty Club a few weeks after the vote: "Placing a fatherly hand on my shoulder, he said, 'Dr. Douglas, it is such a pleasure to see you here, although I must admit I voted against having ladies in this dining room. But Dr. Douglas, I didn't mean you'."[39]

Sports

Old myths about women's biological weakness were still used to justify the many restrictions on what kind of sports women could participate in, and with what intensity. The development of professional sport as big business, which had begun in the inter-war period, intensified after World War II. In the world of mass spectator athletics, there were few opportunities for women and significantly fewer material rewards. Even in recreational athletics and sport, girls and women encountered exclusion or discrimination; on the playground, in the schools and universities, and in community and privately owned recreational facilities, they were consistently denied equal facilities and financial resources. The media provided little coverage of women's athletics and thus helped perpetuate the view that women's sports were of secondary importance.

During World War II, athletics for both women and men had a low priority. The cancellation of all international competition until the Summer Olympics of 1948, also reduced the incentive and opportunity for participation for top athletes. With the return to peace and the resumption of international competition, women's involvement in both competitive and recreational sport remained limited. Although a few women continued to win medals at international meets, they did so in individual events that were considered appropriate female activities, such as figure skating, swimming, skiing, and gymnastics. The association of female athletes with individual pursuits was reinforced by the lack of opportunity for women to compete in team events at the Olympic level: it was not until 1964 that the first such event for women, volleyball, was added to the Olympic roster.[40]

Nevertheless, the Canadian public idolized outstanding female athletes in the 1950s such as Barbara Ann Scott, who won the Olympic, World, and European figure skating titles in 1948, and Marilyn Bell, who made history in 1954 at the age of sixteen by being the first person to swim across Lake Ontario. They were admired, however, less for what they did than for what they were. The former epitomized feminine grace and beauty; the latter, "the girl next door."[41] In track and field, the pre-eminence that Canadian women had achieved in the late 1920s was not regained; in fact, after 1948, not one Canadian woman reached a final track and field event in Olympic competition until the Tokyo games of 1964. Despite the relative lack of support, Canadian women athletes' overall performance at international events from the late 1920s to 1980 managed to remain on a par with that of Canadian men.[42]

Women's participation in sports within Canada was completely overshadowed by men's after the war, and was less extensive than in the 1920s when women's leagues and inter-school sports programs had flourished. Professional team sports, geared to men's interests and needs, syphoned off most of the financial support and public interest previously given to amateur athletics. The opportunities available to young boys to enjoy team sports such as hockey, baseball, and football were few or non-existent for girls. Only occasionally could exceptional girls, such as future Olympic runner Abby Hoffman, register for a boys' team; she was only able to do so as A. Hoffman and because she had a slight and boyish frame. The few team sports that girls were encouraged to play were carefully designed to preserve their femininity; for instance, baseball was made less dangerous by the institution of a "no sliding" rule. For most teenage girls in the 1950s and early 1960s, being a cheerleader was considered a more appropriate achievement than excelling in sport. The view that active participation in sports was somehow incompatible with femininity was unwittingly reinforced in some cases by female physical educators themselves. One university instructor, writing in 1961, suggested drawing attention to "the most charming looking students through the election of baseball queens, field hockey queens and

archery queens." The idea was to counteract the una
image of female athletes: the successful candidates v
tographed in non-sports clothes, and to have their p
nently displayed.[43]

By the late 1960s, a growing number of Canad ... girls and women were actively involved in recreational and competitive sports, challenging the stereotypes of what constituted "appropriate" female physical activity. Their increased participation can be attributed to a number of factors: the greater consciousness of most Canadians about the benefits of physical fitness, the increase in leisure time, and a renewed women's movement. Nonetheless women's participation at all levels continued to be eclipsed by that of men, for reasons both structural and attitudinal. Working women with families found it difficult to take time from their hectic schedules to take part in sports, and few evening sports programs offered childcare. Participation levels are directly related to income, and on average women had less money than men; moreover, some women continued to believe it was "unladylike" to sweat or to develop muscles. There were also proportionately fewer female coaches and physical education teachers than in the past, and women continued to be woefully under-represented among sports administrators and executives.[44]

Women's organizations

Women involved in separate women's organizations after the war were laying the basis for the resurgent women's movement of the late 1960s. Assessments of women's voluntary associations in the immediate post-war period have tended to be essentially negative, accepting patronizing interpretations of critics in the 1950s. A typical account of Canada's premier women's organization, the National Council of Women, characterized the group's members as being "like most club women everywhere . . . great hands for passing resolutions." Their "resounding outcries against strong drink, atomic warfare and the traffic in Chinese slave girls," the report went on, "had come in for some gentle kidding." In this way the important social issues with which the members of the National Council were grappling were trivialized.[45] Women's groups were also identified as outlets for the idle rich.

But women's organizations in the 1950s were involved in much more than holding social events or fighting rearguard campaigns to maintain the nation's morality. While they continued to engage in activities traditionally associated with women's volunteer organizations, they also focussed their attention on issues ranging from the status of women, economics, and taxation, to urban planning, peace, and the arts. The National Council and the Canadian Federation of Business and Professional Women's clubs (BPW) lobbied the federal cabinet annually, and played a significant role in advancing the political and economic status of women. During Margaret Hyndman's term as the national president of the BPW from 1946–48, that group successfully protested a federal government advertisement, which

.ed that the position of regional director of family allowances for New Brunswick was open only to male residents of the Maritimes. As a result of the BPW protest, the job went to its nominee, Muriel McQueen Fergusson, who subsequently became the first woman Speaker of the Senate. Similarly, the BPW inundated the Cabinet with requests to place women on the Civil Service Commission, the Unemployment Insurance Commission, the board of the CBC, the Board of Broadcast Governors, and various royal commissions, as well as calling for the appointment of a woman senator from each province. Since these requests were invariably accompanied by an up-to-date list of qualified women candidates, the BPW was sometimes successful. Nor was the private sector spared, for the federation called for the appointment of women to the boards of institutions such as chartered banks.

The campaigns of the middle class women's groups extended well beyond the appointment to prominent positions of a few token women from their own class or from their own organizations. In concert with other women's organizations, the BPW played a leading role in obtaining the right for women to sit on juries. They petitioned the federal government to open the competition for diplomatic appointments to women, and succeeded in having the federal Civil Service Commission drop the wording "for men only" from its advertisements for many of its positions. Concerted lobbying by women's associations, including the BPW, resulted in the creation of the vitally important Women's Bureau within the federal Department of Labour, a bureau devoted specifically to gathering and disseminating information on all facets of women's employment.

Undoubtedly the great achievement of the post-war organizations was the passage of equal pay for equal work legislation by the federal government and nearly all the provinces. It was Margaret Hyndman who assumed a key role in this campaign. As national president of the BPW, she submitted a brief on equal pay to the Ontario government immediately after the war. The Women's Committee of the Ontario CCF was instrumental in having legislation tabled in 1949 that would have made "sex" a forbidden basis for employment discrimination, and that would have required equal pay, but it was defeated.[46] One year later, twenty-one YWCAs set up Public Affairs committees to promote anti-discrimination employment laws. It was against this background that Hyndman led a delegation in 1951 to meet with the provincial premier, Leslie Frost; Hyndman argued for inclusion of the principle of equal pay in the forthcoming Fair Employment Practices law, designed to prohibit employer discrimination on the basis of nationality, race, or creed. In spite of the growing pressure from women's organizations, Frost expressed his reservations about the effect that the implementation of equal pay might have on the economy of the province, and invited the women to present a brief outlining what the likely impact would be. Since Hyndman was a lawyer, he also asked her to draft an equal pay bill.

Within a week, not only had these submissions been delivered, but every member of the provincial legislature had been lobbied and supplied with a copy of the Universal Declaration of Human Rights, with the appropriate sections dealing with discrimination on the basis of sex and equal pay underlined. Co-sponsored by Agnes Macphail, the Female Employees Fair Remuneration Act was introduced on the symbolically significant date of March 8 — International Women's Day—and on January 1, 1952 Ontario became the first province to put equal pay legislation into effect. Provincial equal pay committees were created in 1952 by the BPW to petition other provincial governments to enact equal pay legislation. These committees helped produce similar laws by the end of the decade in all provinces except Quebec and Newfoundland.

In 1955 the BPW asked one of their own members, Ellen Fairclough, the Conservative labour critic, to introduce in the House of Commons a private member's bill requiring equal pay for equal work. Although the bill was defeated, the Liberal government took up the cause. According to the federal minister of labour, Milton Gregg, the government's 1956 decision to implement equal pay legislation to cover over 70 000 women working under federal jurisdiction was taken largely because of the pressure exerted by representatives of the National Council of Women, including Gregg's own wife, and of the BPW. And once again Margaret Hyndman, who was appointed to represent both women's groups, was instrumental in helping frame the ensuing legislation.[47]

In Quebec, it was pressure from organized women's groups that led the provincial government to set up a commission in 1963 to re-examine the legal disabilities that the Civil Code continued to impose on married women. Before the commission could complete its work, Claire Kirkland-Casgrain, who in 1961 had become the first woman deputy and then minister in the Quebec Assembly, introduced legislation that terminated the legal incapacity of married women. Known as Bill 16, the legislation was passed by the Legislative Assembly on July 1, 1964. Many hailed the new law as a progressive measure that finally made it legal for a wife to exercise a profession in her own right, to sign contracts on her own behalf, and to exercise several other rights regarding property and taking legal action. In some ways it was simply confirming current practices, for married women had already been engaging in their own professions.[48]

Other women's groups were addressing important issues during this period. In addition to helping Jewish refugees settle in Canada, and to supporting many projects in the newly created state of Israel, the National Council of Jewish Women was deeply committed to promoting social legislation and creating social services, especially for the elderly. The council gave considerable financial support to the Canadian Mental Health Association, the Canadian Red Cross, and other volunteer groups. As with other nationally federated women's organizations, resolutions passed at the biennial national meetings were forwarded to the relevant federal and provincial politicians; the issues they treated included a Canadian bill of rights, family planning, and equal pay for equal work for both sexes.[49]

The elitist Junior League was transformed during the 1950s and 1960s; the membership, which had formerly been composed mostly of young, unmarried society women, was increasingly made up of middle class, married women. Members made a concerted effort to shed the league's snobbish image; drafting new regulations to ensure that all leagues would provide training courses in community work for new members, they set up minimum standards for volunteer work. In the post-war period, leagues worked to reduce the shortage of trained teachers, to improve health services and television programming for children, and to provide much-needed social services. The Junior League was also actively involved in penal reform for women. In Toronto, it set up the Elizabeth Fry House for recently released women prisoners, and created a Special Lectureship on Corrections at the University of Toronto's School of Social Work, a lectureship that formed the nucleus for the university's Centre of Criminology.[50] In Vancouver, the organization undertook a detailed survey of the city's cultural activities, which culminated in the creation of the first arts council in North America.

In the decade following the war, rural women belonging to the Women's Institutes continued to expand their activities in an attempt to improve the quality of life for women. Stories abound of the extraordinary lengths to which rural women went to attend WI meetings, especially in winter-time. One devoted New Brunswick member, Mrs. J.D. Ross, found herself "snow-bound at home atop a hill and unable to persuade her husband to shovel her out." Undaunted, she climbed aboard her son's "flying saucer" sled; "with a half-knitted afghan in one hand and a fresh pie in the other she sped downhill and thumbed a ride" to the institute meeting. By the time she arrived home, the path had been shovelled.[51] In conjunction with universities and provincial departments of agriculture, local institutes offered evening courses for married women who worked. The Women's Institutes also lobbied governments to introduce equal pay for equal work.[52]

After experiencing a decline in membership during the war years, churchwomen's groups also flourished during the 1950s. In the United church, the combined membership of the Women's Missionary Society and of the Women's Auxiliary almost doubled between 1942 and 1955, rising from 278 789 to 401 757. However, by the late 1950s, membership started to decline again as more and more married women took on paid employment outside the home. In 1962 the two organizations were amalgamated into the United Church Women. The purpose of this merger was ostensibly to prevent unnecessary duplication of work; more importantly, the decision taken by the General Council, composed overwhelmingly of men, was to incorporate the new organization into the existing church structures. This change meant an end to the autonomy that the influential Women's Missionary Society had always exercised in relation to its missions, for they now fell under the control of the national mission boards. On the surface, it appeared that the amalgamation of the women's organizations with the men's would guarantee women greater access to all levels of church life; in practice, however, men assumed control of what had previously been women's work and women's financial resources.[53]

The achievement of international peace, a prime concern of Canadian women's organizations in the past, assumed a new urgency in the atomic age. Characteristic of post-war women's associations was the special interest they took in international affairs, and particularly in the work of the United Nations. According to Gladys Manness, a woman from a small rural community in Manitoba, membership in the Women's Institutes that she shared with some 95 000 other Canadian women was important because it gave her an opportunity to discuss national and international issues. "It's broadened our outlook," she concluded.[54] The Women's Institutes and other women's voluntary associations also mounted vigorous campaigns to have the federal government ratify the Declaration of Human Rights passed by the United Nations General Assembly in 1950. The ties that organizations such as the National Council of Women, the Women's Institutes, and the BPW developed with the United Nations and its agencies were even closer. Women who were prominent in these associations served as Canadian representatives to the UN and its affiliated organizations, largely as a result of pressure from women's groups on the Canadian government to make such appointments. In 1958, Adelaide Sinclair was named deputy director of the UN's Children's Fund (UNICEF), and Josie Quart, later Senator Quart, acted as Canada's delegate to the UN. Six years later, Margaret Aitken, a former Conservative member of Parliament and an active member of the Toronto BPW, was appointed Canadian representative on the UN Commission on Human Rights. In addition, both the National Council of Women and the BPW either belonged to, or actively supported the United Nations associations within Canada. The familiarity of the executive members of the BPW with events at the UN led them, in 1954, to petition the federal government for ratification of Convention 100 of the International Labour Organization, requiring equal pay for work of equal value, and of the United Nations Convention on Political Rights of Women.

It was around the issue of peace that one of the most significant new women's organizations was born. In May 1960, just after the Paris Summit Conference on disarmament broke up, Toronto columnist Lotta Dempsey wrote about the failure, and asked what women could do. The response to her article in the *Toronto Star* was overwhelming, and subsequently a mass meeting was organized. It led to the formation of Voice of Women in July and, by the fall of 1961, membership had grown to 5000. This non-partisan organization won general acceptance from the Canadian public; even the Canadian government politely listened to its representatives. Both the external approval and the internal unity of the group were severely eroded, however, when the newly elected Liberal government, led by Lester Pearson, decided to place nuclear weapons on Canadian soil. Many women active in the Liberal party, including Maryon Pearson, resigned from Voice of Women when it openly criticized the government's policy, and the media increasingly insinuated that the organization was "soft on Communism." The identification of Voice of Women with the radical left was no doubt reinforced by the political connections of several of its most active members with the NDP, and by the arrest of two of its well-known leaders, Thérèse Casgrain and Kay Macpherson, by the Paris police when the two women attempted to deliver a letter to the secretary-general of NATO.

Throughout the 1960s, Voice of Women actively pursued its goal of fostering peace through a wide variety of activities, such as writing briefs, sending delegations to international conferences, sponsoring peace conferences within Canada, and organizing campaigns against war toys. During the Cuban Missile Crisis in 1962, women delegates from Voice of Women travelled to Ottawa to pressure the federal government not to support the American position. Later, Howard Green, who was external affairs minister at the time, attributed the government's decision to delay putting the RCAF on the same NORAD alert as the Americans to the vigorous lobbying that Voice of Women had initiated. Voice of Women also helped inspire the United Nations to declare 1965 International Co-operation Year, and played a key role in organizing Canadian opposition to the war in Vietnam.

As it pursued its primary goal of the prevention of war, Voice of Women became involved in a number of other issues. A good example was its early involvement in the issue of bilingualism and biculturalism. Voice of Women's 1962 Peace Train delegation to Ottawa, led by Thérèse Casgrain and including hundreds of Francophone women, was met by the unilingual Howard Green. Not only did the group gain media attention by demanding a government representative who spoke French, but two members of the delegation— Solange Chaput-Rolland and Gwethalyn Graham—were motivated by this incident to write *Dear Enemies*, an innovative contribution to the public discussion of French-English relations.

The activities undertaken by Voice of Women to gain peace led its members to question Canada's relationship with the United States, especially in the area of foreign policy. By so doing it placed itself at the forefront of the nationalist movement of the 1960s. Voice of Women activists were also prominent in many of the other issues of the 1960s involving the environment, human rights, science policy, and the status of women. The Halifax Voice of Women undertook a study of discrimination against blacks in Nova Scotia that initiated an anti-discrimination movement in that province. As Muriel Duckworth, a long-time member, recalled,

Somehow we're always having to make these choices of how to separate what is strictly the Peace Movement and what is the Women's Movement,

*what is the Ecology movement and what is the Human Rights movement.
I think these movements are alive and effective because more and more of
us see these things as interrelated.*[55]

The briefest glance at women's organizations clearly reveals both
the important services that women's organizations were performing
in post-war Canada, and their relevance to their time. Clearly rooted
in the first women's movement, these groups formed the bridge to
the resurgent feminism of the late 1960s. In some ways they were
simply carrying on a tradition of good works developed by women
over the centuries; yet in many other ways, they were breaking new
ground, identifying and addressing important new issues, and lobbying for change. They helped effect tangible improvements in the
lives of Canadians, especially among children, women, and the
elderly. In some instances, they called for a thorough restructuring
of government policies. Women's organizations were often ahead of
governments. They established and maintained innovative programs
until governments were ready to assume responsibility. As one journalist concluded, "Every town and hamlet is jam-packed with worthwhile activities, all existing on woman-power. . . . Strawberry social
thinking is dead."[56]

The arts

A great deal of women's associational life and volunteer work continued to be related to the arts and the development of Canadian
culture. In 1950 the federally appointed Royal Commission on
National Development in the Arts, Letters and Sciences (Massey
Commission) reported that the precarious state of cultural life in
Canada might easily be further undermined by the all-pervasive
American influence. American radio and television did not recognize
the existence of the 49th parallel and, for many Canadians, it was
increasingly difficult to distinguish between what was Canadian and
what was American. It was in this difficult environment—before the
establishment of the Canada Council in 1957—that women initiated
some of the most important projects in theatre, dance, and the visual
arts. As organizers, fundraisers, and administrators, they made a vital
contribution to nearly all aspects of Canadian culture.

At galleries throughout the country, women had their own committees to promote the visual arts. By their fundraising, the pioneering of picture loan programs, their encouragement of young artists,
and the pressure they exerted on gallery boards to make new acquisitions, they had a major impact. As one noted art critic, Elizabeth
Kilbourn, pointed out, "these women, perhaps more than any other
group . . . consciously pioneered the public acceptance of contemporary art."[57] Jean Sutherland Boggs was the first woman appointed
director of the National Gallery of Canada in 1966, and launched
the museum on several bold new initiatives regarding acquisitions
and exhibitions. Women's committees also played a vital role in the
development and support of the performing arts, especially opera,

music, and ballet. Without their enthusiasm and extensive fundraising efforts, the nation's cultural life would have been greatly diminished.

In English Canada, Dora Mavor Moore played the role of "theatre's fiery godmother." Beginning in the 1920s, she organized amateur theatre productions and gave drama lessons in Toronto, but her most important contribution to the dramatic arts came in 1946 when she formed the New Play Society. Planned as a permanent, professional, non-profit company, it scored a number of theatrical "firsts," including the first performance of a Canadian play at the Royal Alexandra Theatre in Toronto. Moore's role in the success of the New Play Society was central:

A classic diva, she begged, browbeat, improvised, scrimped, borrowed, wheedled and worked for years to keep theatre alive .... Moore used to put on classical productions costumed entirely in crepe paper and, when there was no money for crepe paper, presented Shakespeare in modern dress.[58]

Dora Mavor Moore was also one of the moving spirits behind the establishment of the Stratford Shakespeare Festival in 1952. A year later, her own company went into semi-retirement, largely as a result of Stratford's success.

In Montreal, Yvette Brind'amour developed a permanent professional theatre. In 1949 her newly formed company, *Le Rideau Vert*, gave its first performance; it subsequently commissioned several new plays by French Canadian playwrights, including *Encore Cinq Minutes* by Françoise Loranger, which won a Governor General's award. The company established an excellent international reputation. Joy Coghill and Jane Heyman in Vancouver, and Susan Rubes in Toronto played active roles in developing children's theatre. In Montreal, women formed small theatres to present avant-garde drama, and by 1970, according to one critic, summer theatres in Quebec were "almost entirely the preserve of women."[59] From these and other regional theatres emerged many superb women actors who performed to national and international acclaim. Another innovative project was the establishment of the Montreal Women's Symphony, founded by Ethel Stark in 1940. Stark, the first Canadian to hold a scholarship at the Curtis Institute of Music in Philadelphia, was a violinist and conductor. In 1947 this critically acclaimed group became the first Canadian orchestra to play in New York's Carnegie Hall. Despite its success, it was a shortlived venture, mainly because of the lack of financial resources — unlike many symphonies of the period, the Montreal Women's Symphony did not have a supporting women's committee to raise funds.[60]

Women also founded three major ballet companies in Canada in the post-war era. In 1949 two British ballet teachers resident in Winnipeg since 1938, Gweneth Lloyd and Betty Farrally, organized the Royal Winnipeg Ballet, the country's first professional dance company; two years later, it received its royal charter. At about the same time, ballet enthusiasts in Toronto engaged Celia Franca, a principal dancer with the Sadler's Wells Company in Britain, to found a national company. The National Ballet of Canada gave its first performance in Toronto in 1951, but struggled throughout the decade to establish itself as a truly professional and permanent company. Funds were initially so scarce that Director Celia Franca had to work part-time in a department store.[61] One of the factors that contributed to the success of the National was the establishment of the National Ballet School in 1960 under the direction of Betty Oliphant. Nor was Montreal to be denied its own ballet company for, thanks once again to the vision and energy of a determined woman, *Les Grands Ballets Canadiens* became a reality in 1957. It was founded by Latvian-born Ludmilla Chiriaeff, who had trained with the Bolshoi Ballet and who had worked with a small group of dancers after her arrival in Canada in 1952.

As creative artists and performers, women faced special obstacles. Few artists, especially in the days before Canada Council grants, could support themselves on their artistic endeavours, and few women could easily combine motherhood and a career. A notable exception was Maureen Forrester, the famous contralto and mother of five, who later became the first woman head of the Canada Council. She delighted in telling people, "I can sing the morning I'm giving birth, and even during. It doesn't bother me. It's just the conductors who get nervous."[62] Women visual artists, already disadvantaged, were rendered a further disservice by the system of funding established by the Canada Council after 1957. If their work borrowed techniques associated with women's traditional handicrafts, it was likely classified as craft rather than art. The artificial distinction between art (male) and craft (female) served to devalue women's artistic endeavours and diminished their chances of securing financial assistance. Ironically, the agency established in the 1960s to promote greater support and recognition for the crafts was named the Canadian Crafts*men*'s Association.

Despite such obstacles, women played an activist role, both individually and collectively, in the development of the visual arts after the war. In 1948 the arts world in Montreal was stunned by the publication of *Le Refus Global*, a ringing manifesto that called on all artists to reject the fetters of the past and to "break out of the walls of the common mould." Written by abstract painter Paul-Emile Borduas, it was signed by fifteen other *Québécois* painters, five of whom were women.[63] Quebec became a centre for abstract art, and with artists such as Rita Letendre, Suzanne Bergeron, Marcelle Ferron, and Lise Gervais, it had what one critic described as "more active women painters of the first rank than any other arts centre in the world."[64] These young artists were encouraged by women such as Agnes Lefort of Montreal who, in 1950, opened the first art gallery in Quebec committed to displaying contemporary work.

Although there were a number of gifted women artists in postwar English Canada, none achieved the recognition that was by that time finally being given to Emily Carr. Hamilton's Hortense Gordon was one of the first painters in Canada to experiment with abstraction and, by the 1970s, Joyce Wieland was attracting considerable public attention with her strongly nationalistic and feminist art. Her 1971 show at the National Gallery was the first solo exhibition of the work of a living Canadian woman. An extraordinarily versatile artist, at home in a variety of mediums from collage to film, she drew inspiration from women's history and daily experiences, especially in her quilt works. Wieland's 1971 show, with its interwoven themes of nationalism, ecological concerns, and women's issues, was an early, important statement of feminist aesthetics.[65] Like Wieland, Newfoundland artist Mary Pratt turned to the world of women for much of her subject matter. Her best-known paintings had as their focus items from her own kitchen, such as cod fillets and aluminum foil.

Sculptors too drew from their own female experience. As she became involved in the feminist movement, Toronto sculptor Maryon Kantaroff began to question the male aesthetics she had tried so hard to apply to her earlier sculptures. From strident, angular shapes she moved to rounder, softer, and more fluid ones. Characteristic of her attempt to reconnect her work with the female experience was the appearance of the egg in her works, a form she described as "a symbol of the beginnings of life, the essence of life, the seat of all potential, awareness . . ."[66]

It was in the area of literature that women perhaps made their best-known contribution to Canadian cultural life and, by the 1960s, issues related to women's lives and experiences were explicitly woven into their work. To speak of "Can Lit" was to speak primarily of women writers and of women's experience. Authors such as Gabrielle Roy, Germaine Guèvremont, Marie-Claire Blais, and Anne Hébert in French Canada, and Margaret Laurence, Margaret Atwood, Alice Munro, and Marian Engel in English Canada won national and international critical acclaim for their work. In poetry also, women's concerns and imagery were incorporated in the work of writers such as Dorothy Livesay, Miriam Waddington, and Margaret Atwood.

With the evolution of Canada into an ethnically diverse society in the post-war era, and the heightened awareness of the need to preserve and promote more than anglophone culture, thousands of women contributed to the cultural mosaic that was becoming a cornerstone of the Canadian identity. Within their ethnic communities they organized language classes, choirs, theatre and dance groups, and cultural festivals. The role that women assumed in the promotion of native and black culture is representative of this contribution. Alanis Obomsawin, an Abenaki woman from Quebec, a professional singer who subsequently became a successful film-maker, was among those who celebrated and worked to preserve native traditions. Thousands of kilometres away, Victoria Kildaw Calihoo recorded stories relating to Métis pioneer life in Alberta, while Maria Campbell drew a disturbing picture of contemporary Métis women's experience in her autobiographical work *Halfbreed*. In 1946, Carrie Best began the publication of a church bulletin that grew into a bimonthly newspaper for Nova Scotian blacks, and that evolved into *The Negro Citizen*, a newspaper that gained national circulation between 1949 and 1956.[67] Five years later, a newly formed Canadian Negro Women's Association made the promotion of the black heritage one of its principal objectives. Among others, Anne Packwood in Montreal and Grace Price Trotman and Ola Shanks in Toronto worked throughout the 1950s and 1960s to preserve and reinforce black culture through drama, music, dancing, and fashion design.[68]

Many of the old patterns and rituals that had formerly dominated the lives of women disappeared in the post-war era. Women's roles were no longer ordered sequentially — work–marriage–family — but were increasingly intertwined. Marriage, once the great dividing line in women's lives, became a less significant event since it no longer

Armenian Church workers' gathering.

involved the end of employment and almost immediate initiation into motherhood. The role of wife and that of mother became increasingly distinct; it was now possible to be one but not the other. Moreover, there was less physical separation of the sexes. If home was still where many Canadian women's hearts were, they no longer spent most of their time in that female-oriented space. The media still stressed heterosexual relations and close conjugal ties to the exclusion of female friendships, and ignored or trivialized women's activities in groups. By the 1960s, women's efforts to achieve equality with men appeared to require a denial of a separate female identity.

By the end of the decade, however, awareness of the need for that identity re-emerged. More and more women recognized how necessary and desirable it was for women to draw upon their own experiences, and to work in their own groups if they were to bring about the changes they sought. Increasingly as well, women's contribution to Canadian culture either had a feminist bent, or was used by feminists to demonstrate the creativity of women and their essential role in making life more humane and enjoyable.

14 A bomb already primed and ticking

The late 1960s and the 1970s witnessed in Canada, as elsewhere in the modern world, a resurgence of feminist activity. Old groups re-emerged into public visibility, supporting and assisting newer ones in what has come to be called the "second wave" of feminism. The women's movement had worked its way through something like the trough between two waves, and the tide of change was ready to move further up the shore. There was a highly visible proliferation of women's groups, more varied and more extensive than had ever occurred before. Although their aims were recognizable, the groups often had new labels and even new ideologies. Moreover, millions of women who identified with no particular group or ideology became increasingly aware of their identity as women and their need for autonomy and recognition. Looking back over her experiences in the women's movement, one young woman writing in 1980 raised a fundamental issue: "How to measure the ripple effect generated when one person in transition touches another who touches another, the ripples colliding, intersecting, overlapping and causing further ripples?"[1]

New initiatives

The beginning of the public process of change can best be dated in 1966, when existing Francophone and Anglophone women's organizations began to regroup and reorganize in a way they had not done for over a generation. In Quebec, after the celebration of the twenty-fifth anniversary of full enfranchisement, representatives of women's groups called together by Thérèse Casgrain agreed to found a new coalition of women's organizations. The result, the *Fédération des femmes du Québec*, was the first substantial, enduring new organization of Quebec women since the formation of the suffrage leagues in the 1920s. An umbrella group structured very much like the old Councils of Women, the *fédération* was limited by the need to reach consensus among its members, but was undeniably feminist. Unlike its French Canadian predecessor, however, the *fédération* had no religious ties. This important change reflected the reduced influence of the church in Quebec and especially its decreasing importance for women.

In the same year as the founding of the *fédération*, the *Association féminine d'éducation et d'action sociale* was also formally established, combining two old organizations: the *Union catholique des femmes*

Table 14.1	Chronology of the second wave, Canadian women's movement
1960	Voice of Women; Quebec branch 1961
1961 ·	Planned Parenthood of Canada
1966	La Fédération des femmes du Québec L'Association féminine d'éducation et d'action sociale Committee for the Equality of Women in Canada
1967	Royal Commission on the Status of Women Toronto Women's Liberation
1968	Feminist Action League, Simon Fraser University; Women's Caucus, Vancouver First edition of McGill Birth Control Handbook Indian Rights for Indian Women Birthright
1969	Montreal Women's Liberation starts at McGill University and Sir George Williams College
1969–70	Women's Liberation groups in Regina, Saskatoon, Winnipeg, Ottawa, Kingston, Guelph, "Hamilton district," Halifax, Sudbury, Thunder Bay
1969–71	Le Front pour la libération des femmes du Québec; Québécoises deboutte!, no. 1.
1969–73	Toronto New Feminists
1970	Abortion Caravan organized by Vancouver Women's Liberation (February 14–May 10) Report of the Royal Commission on the Status of Women
1971	National Ad Hoc Committee on the Status of Women Ontario Committee on the Status of Women
1972	"Strategy for Change" Conference (Toronto) and founding of National Action Committee on the Status of Women (NAC) Women for Political Action Le Centre des femmes (–1975); remaining issues of Québécoises deboutte!
1973	Federal and Ontario Advisory Councils on the Status of Women Le Réseau d'action et d'information pour les femmes (Montréal) First national lesbian conference, YWCA, Toronto; first Canadian lesbian journal: Long Time Coming (Montreal) First national conference of black women
1974	Canadian Association for the Repeal of the Abortion Laws (CARAL; after 1980, Canadian Abortion Rights League) Native Women's Association of Canada L'association des femmes autochtones du Québec
1975	Canadian Association of Women Executives National Association of Women and the Law
1976–79	Les têtes de pioches published by radical feminists in Quebec
1976	L'association des femmes collaboratrices Lesbian Organization of Toronto

rurales and the *Cercles d'économie domestique*. The *association*'s first president, Germaine Gaudreau, was a member of the *fédération*'s first executive, and the two organizations worked closely together, the *fédération* concentrating on urban women, the *association* on rural. The *Cercles de fermières* remained unaffiliated, celebrating their fiftieth anniversary in 1965 and continuing to represent the relatively traditional aspects of the Quebec women's movement as it existed on farms and in small towns.[2]

The new coalitions of Quebec women's groups produced a surge of reform activity. Focusing on housewives, the *association* pointed out that all women worked, even though not all of them got paid. It developed a special interest in the women who worked in family businesses; in 1976 it produced a daughter group, the *Association des femmes collaboratrices*, as well as, two years later, an important study of women's work in the home, *Pendant que les hommes travaillaient, les femmes elles. . . .* For its part, the *fédération* had wider interests; becoming steadily more radical, by 1975 it was able to take a public position in favour of removing abortion from the Criminal Code.[3]

A similar organizational process was also beginning in the rest of Canada. Here the focus was a concerted campaign to obtain a royal commission on the status of women. Early in 1966, Laura Sabia, then president of the Canadian Federation of University Women, called together representatives of some thirty national women's organizations to discuss their common concerns. Forming themselves into the Committee on Equality for Women, the women who attended decided to call for a royal commission and to incorporate their request in a brief to the prime minister. Doris Anderson, editor of *Chatelaine*, attended the meeting, and in July 1966 she launched a public call for such an enquiry. She was reluctant to suggest that "one more be added to the groaning shelfful of past Royal Commissions," but was firm in her belief that it was time for a study on the status of women in Canada. She justified the request by referring to the rising level of women's participation in education and the workforce. "What we don't need in a commission," she concluded, "is an all-woman witch-hunt. We do need a forward-looking commission composed equally of impartial men and women prepared to take a cool twentieth-century approach to our problems."[4]

Laura Sabia, who spearheaded the push for the royal commission, was far less temperate. Educated in a Montreal convent school, she had been appalled by what she considered as the nuns' stifling lives. "I think that had a lot to do with my revulsion towards a male-dominated society," she told an interviewer. Sabia's father had raised her to be self-confident and independent, taking her out of school to play hookey at the Stock Exchange. But when she graduated from McGill University, instead of following her plan to go to law school, she married and raised four children in St. Catharines, Ontario. She participated in the Catholic Women's League, the Parent Teachers' Association, City Council, and a hotline radio show; by 1966 Laura Sabia was already a redoubtable charmer and rabble-rouser, endlessly energetic as a campaigner and organizer.[5]

The thirty-two-member Committee on Equality for Women that Sabia drew together in 1966 consisted of leaders of the large continuing women's organizations, including groups who had earlier been the most vocal and consistent campaigners for woman suffrage. Most important among the long-established national women's organizations represented on the committee were the WCTU, the YWCA, the National Council of Women of Canada, the National Council of Jewish Women, the Imperial Order Daughters of the Empire, the Federated Women's Institutes, and the Canadian Federation of Business and Professional Women's Clubs.[6] Their feminism can be inferred from their ready response to Sabia's appeal; in the same year, similar organizations in the United States had explicitly refused suggestions that they become publicly involved in issues of women's equality.

In addition, Voice of Women was actively involved in the committee through Kay Macpherson, its national president in 1966. Although the *Fédération des femmes du Québec* did not take part in drawing up the presentation to the prime minister, its leaders shared the committee's concern that the women of Canada should appear united by having representation from both Francophone and Anglophone women's groups. The official delegation that went to Ottawa therefore included Thérèse Casgrain and Réjane Laberge–Colas; Laberge–Colas, the *fédération*'s first president, was to be, in 1969, the first woman appointed judge in a Canadian superior court. Women's groups from all three federal political parties also supported the brief calling for a royal commission, as did a considerable number of well-established women's professional and service groups. Some sixty observers accompanied the five official delegates.[7]

The Pearson government ignored this first decorous, mildly posed request of the committee, provoking Laura Sabia into what the Toronto *Globe and Mail* described as an "ultimatum to the Government: establish a royal commission or face the consequences." Sabia's son, Michael, recalled the incident:

Picture, if you will, a typical scene from our household in the 60s. Mother is preparing dinner. Father, a surgeon, and his 10-year-old son are waiting to be fed. The phone rings, and a brief discussion ensues, mother calmly saying: "Tell the Prime Minister that I will lead an uprising of Canadian women."[8]

She said she would march two million women on Ottawa; in later accounts, the figure escalated to *three* million. Sabia has since noted repeatedly that she would have been lucky to mobilize three women for an actual march.

This gesture has become legendary, with Sabia and others convinced that it produced the Royal Commission on the Status of Women that was formally established in February 1967. Certainly Sabia's bravado captured the headlines. And in terms of specific timing, it seems clear that the activities of the committee served as a catalyst for the commission. The Honourable Judy LaMarsh, who had followed Ellen Fairclough as the second solitary woman in the cabinet, had been arguing in vain for a commission of enquiry into the status of women; she credited the Committee on Equality with the results she had been unable to achieve.[9] In fact, the explanation for the commission is probably to be found in the inter-related patterns of education and work that characterized women's lives in the 1960s, patterns that also explain women's renewed responsiveness to feminism. Strains had developed as a result of the combination of unchanged attitudes with changing employment and educational patterns. The women's movement was to articulate the grievances that resulted.

In the 1960s, the government seemed unaware that women had any causes for dissatisfaction, whether subjective or objective. From the perspective of the state, what mattered about women's situation was the negative impact on the expanding economy of the slow movement of women into the labour force. It seemed likely that this translated into reduced possibilities of national growth. By 1966 ten industrialized nations, including the United States, had already begun to look into the problem. The head of the Women's Bureau, Sylva Gelber, was concerned that the failure "to utilize our human resources" (meaning women) to their full capability was "to deny to the nation the productivity essential for the maintenance of a high standard of living."[10] It was now desirable once again to mobilize the "reserve army of labour," and women made particularly good recruits. They had the skills and attitudes required for the ever-expanding clerical and service sectors of the economy. Within a few years, governments would find it necessary to provide a whole range of new rights and services for women, in order both to placate and mobilize them. In 1966, agreeing to their request for a commission of enquiry seemed like a sufficient first step.

In addition, there were political reasons to respond to the Committee on Equality's initiative. By 1965 Canadian women were voting at approximately the same rate as men, and participating in election campaign activities almost as frequently.[11] In Parliament, where the Liberal government lacked an absolute majority, the New Democratic Party held the balance. Urged on by their only woman MP, Grace MacInnis, the NDP used the issue of a women's commission as a weapon against the government. The committee's specific request—for a royal commission—was ideally suited to the double purposes of getting the necessary information about fully integrating women into the workforce while appeasing and, if necessary, defusing feminist complaints. It was a truism of Canadian politics that an excellent way to deal with insistent claims was to "royal-commission them to death."[12]

The general mandate of the commission, announced early in 1967, was "to inquire and report upon the status of women in Canada, and to recommend what steps might be taken by the Federal Government to ensure for women equal opportunities with men in all aspects of Canadian society. . . . "[13] The presidency of the commission was handed over to Florence Bird, now a professional broadcaster working under the name of Anne Francis; she had already spoken on the air in support of it. Bird was the first woman to head a royal commission in Canada. The prime minister had met her through the Canadian Institute for International Affairs, for which she had written a pamphlet on the rights of women in 1950. The commission she headed included two men: Jacques Henripin, a well-known Quebec demographer, and John Humphrey, a lawyer who had represented Canada for twenty years on the United Nations' Human Rights Commission.[14] Another member, Quebec academic Jeanne Lapointe, was selected because of her experience with the Parent Commission on education in Quebec and her political connections. Her experience on the women's royal commission was to transform her into an active radical feminist.

Elsie Gregory MacGill, an informed and persuasive third-generation feminist, and past president of the Canadian Federation of Business and Professional Women's Clubs, was effectively the vice president of the royal commission. Since MacGill had been born in British Columbia, her appointment had a regional significance; as well, she represented both women in business and women in science, a counterpart to the Quebec/education representation of Lapointe. Lola Lange, active in the Alberta Farm Women's Union, and juvenile court judge Doris Ogilvie from New Brunswick also obviously represented regional and professional interests. There were no minority, native, leftist, or even young women in the group. Their interests were set out in the 469 briefs, approximately 1000 letters, and, above all, the public hearings, held in fourteen cities in all ten provinces and the Territories. These hearings had a major impact on those members of the commission who had previously been relatively uninformed about women's situation; all ended with, at the least, a commitment to some measure of feminist reform. The commission's young research director, sociologist Monique Bégin, a founding member of the *Fédération des femmes du Québec* and a protegée of

Thérèse Casgrain, worked diligently to strengthen their recommendations.

The commission deliberately used its unprecedentedly wide-ranging public sessions as a device for public education. Initial media responses were sceptical if not frivolous. We provided "a field day for some cartoonists," Elsie MacGill recalled:

These were so out of touch with reality about women's shapes and styles that they depicted women in the audience as simpering, large, bosomy, and wearing hats, although simpering had gone out with Queen Victoria, the popular fashion model was the very thin, very narrow, very flat-chested Twiggy, and hats had vanished from daily wear.[15]

But the media and public alike moved to a grudging interest and respect. "The petitioners weren't just strident suffragettes in garden-party hats," wrote one woman journalist who went to the commission's first Ottawa meeting as a self-described "lapsed feminist": they included "airline hostesses, university professors, nuns, nurses, beaded hippies, whores and farm wives." They were not the women preoccupied with "female neuroses" but "the dispossessed of Canadian society . . . The Other Canada":

In Yellowknife a Métis girl asked if the Chairman of the Commission could come to her prison cell; eighteen years old, pregnant and in despair, she'd been jailed for trying to kill herself by swallowing hairspray.[16]

The commission reported in 1970, having expanded its mandate to cover the many important areas of policy under provincial jurisdiction, such as health, education, and family law. Its report spelled out four principles: (1) women should be free to choose whether or not to take employment outside their homes; (2) the care of children is a responsibility to be shared by the mother, the father, and society; (3) society has a responsibility for women because of pregnancy and childbirth, and special treatment related to maternity will always be necessary; and (4) in certain areas women will for an interim period require special treatment to overcome the adverse effects of discriminatory practices.[17]

Deliberately published as a single, inexpensive volume, the report was a bestseller. After a careful reading of the 167 recommendations it contained, a *Toronto Star* columnist told his readers that the report was nothing less than "a bomb already primed and ticking. . . . packed with more explosive potential than any device manufactured by terrorists . . . a call to revolution. . . . "[18] Such terminology hardly seemed to fit the sober, middle-aged commissioners. But it was accurate. The second wave of feminism in Canada now had its agenda, an agenda that could transform Canadian society.

Feminists had produced the royal commission and its report through a familiar process of coalitions and pressures on government. Those who had been active both in demanding and serving on the royal commission remained at the forefront during the follow-up period. Impatient when the government did not produce immediate responses to the commission's report, Laura Sabia led the Committee on Equality for Women as it evolved into the National Ad Hoc Committee on the Status of Women in Canada, which met during 1971 and early 1972. This coalition now included representatives of new status of women groups as well as of the women's liberation and radical feminist groups that had begun to appear. The ad hoc committee presented a substantial brief to the government, incorporating three priority goals: expansion of daycare, insertion of "sex" as a prohibited basis of discrimination under Canadian human rights provisions, and decriminalization of abortion. The adoption of the third priority lost the ad hoc committee the support of Catholic groups, but added several groups that supported freedom of reproductive choice.[19] Early in 1972, the ad hoc committee became the continuing umbrella organization, the National Action Committee on the Status of Women (NAC).

NAC dropped the optimistic "ad hoc" from its title because the government would not otherwise supply the money essential first for the "Strategy for Change" conference that inaugurated NAC in the spring of 1972, and then for continuing funding. This pattern of dependence on government money has continued, with constituent groups making only token contributions. "Strategy for Change" also set a pattern of co-operation among widely differing feminist groups, with Voice of Women president Helen Tucker in the chair, Elsie Gregory MacGill as keynote speaker, Toronto New Feminists running the workshops, and over 500 women from more than forty groups present. A group of militants gave the organizing committee its first taste of disruption, as they protested what they viewed as the excessively moderate approach of the conference. A "radical caucus" grabbed the microphone and called for, among other things, all-women media crews. In the end, the conference agreed to endorse all of the royal commission's recommendations except the proposal for status of women councils to be appointed at all levels of government.

Beginning in 1971, new women's organizations oriented specifically to the royal commission's report began to appear. These were the voluntary status of women groups whose major concern was implementation in each province of the commission's recommendations. The Ontario Committee on the Status of Women, established in 1971, seems to have been the first, and by the end of the decade most provinces had a similar group. They varied so greatly that is is difficult to generalize about them, although they were often described as "liberal" feminist. Alberta's Status of Women Action Committee, founded in 1976, transformed itself into a collective in 1982; it also allowed men to join as members.[20] But in general, status of women committees (or action committees) tended not to include men, to be small, sometimes completely unsubsidized, and informal in internal structure. Oriented towards lobbying provincial cabinets and civil servants, they were made up of young professional women without explicit ideological commitments. Their members were actively involved in NAC and also influential on the provincial level, where some of them participated in the provincially appointed advi-

Kay Macpherson of the National Action Committee on the Status of Women.

sory councils on the status of women. Their professional competence and expertise seem to have given them an entry to governments, especially to the bureaucracies.

In Quebec, no status of women committee developed, in part because the *Parti québécois* itself had an active women's committee and included influential, though not always feminist, women. Lise Payette, Quebec's first Minister Responsible for the Status of Women, pushed hard for change from 1976 to 1980, and helped to produce major improvements in areas like family law. In 1977 a resolution favouring decriminalization of abortion was passed by the General Assembly of the *Parti québécois*, but the PQ government disregarded it, and moved instead to a natalist and family-oriented platform relating to women. From this time on, the appeal of the *Parti québécois* for feminists declined, encouraging the diffusion of women's groups and activities.[21]

One of the central projects of the voluntary status of women groups and of the *Fédération des femmes* was to have the governments set up the official, state-funded advisory bodies on the status of women recommended by the royal commission. In 1973 the federal Advisory Council on the Status of Women was accordingly established. Later in the same year, the government of Ontario set up its own advisory council, and Quebec did so in 1974. The latter, relatively well funded for research and action, prepared in 1978 a full and useful document on the status of women, *Pour les Québécoises, Egalité et indépendance*. Eventually, such advisory councils were set up in all provinces except Alberta and British Columbia; the latter generously funded other feminist structures until the arrival of a Social Credit government in 1976.

Such councils played a necessarily limited role; governments probably saw them as a means of channelling and controlling women's demands. Laura Sabia, who used the Ontario Advisory Council to force action on family property law, finally resigned in frustration, exploding in her *Toronto Sun* column: "Today is the day of my liberation! Allelujia! I have tossed the albatross of the 'Status of Women' from around my neck and resigned as chairman of Ontario's Status of Women Council." She felt that women had been outmanoeuvred: "From 'Royal Commission' to 'Councils' we have been kept busy pushing paper. 'Do advise us,' say the astute politicians, 'we're such numbskulls; tell us what to do.' And we fell for it, God help us, hook, line and sinker."[22]

The women's liberation movement

The establishment of the Royal Commission on the Status of Women in 1967 was the first publicly recognized success of the second wave of Canadian feminism. Simultaneously, what looked like an entirely new sort of feminist activism was beginning. The women's liberation movement, initially the outgrowth of the international student movement of the mid-1960s, became public towards the end of the decade. The media were fascinated by the more or less outrageous street demonstrations, often about such seemingly novel issues as abortion and sexuality. Its members were happy to be described in the inflammatory language of "revolution," and they distrusted the co-operation with government in which the rest of the Canadian women's movement still had such confidence.

Women's liberation grew out of the informal meetings of young women sharing their dissatisfaction with the treatment of women in the leftist student movement, and also with this movement's failure to take seriously the problems of women in the larger society. Illustrative of this failure were the events that unfolded at a conference held in Montreal in 1969 to protest American involvement in Vietnam. According to participant Naomi Wall,

On the final day . . . all hell broke loose. Women refused to discuss the resolutions or the war until every woman present who had something to

say about the conference was heard. The men went wild. How could these women insist on addressing their concerns as women when men were dying in Vietnam? . . . Who gave a damn whether they were listened to? . . . [23]

Eventually the leftist women's caucuses broke away from their mixed-sex origins. But they kept their vocabulary—the "liberation" of women echoed the liberation of colonial peoples, with Quebec included by Quebec theorists. They brought with them to the women's movement the views of the 1960s counter-culture, a preference for openness and self-expression, and a rejection of customary standards of dress, behaviour, and sexuality.

Furthermore, the members of women's liberation groups kept the analytic and organizational preferences of the student movement. Unlike the majority of women's groups, which inclined to formal structures and to the conventional tactics of lobbies and pressure groups, the liberationists, whose goal was revolutionary change, relied on consciousness-raising through small, unstructured cells and through demonstrations. And where the older feminists had a perspective that combined women's maternal and family concerns with a liberal concern for equality, the beliefs of the younger feminists tended to be closely connected to Marxism or socialism. By the end of the 1960s, significant groupings of Canada's women activists were committed to leftist belief systems.

In 1967 a women's caucus at the University of Toronto rebelled against the male chauvinism in the student organization, the New Left Caucus. As a result, Toronto's was one of the first five women's liberation groups existing in North America. In 1968 Toronto Women's Liberation was joined by the Feminist Action League at Simon Fraser University, followed by the Women's Caucus in Vancouver. Toronto Women's Liberation's first public action was a protest against a "winter bikini" contest in 1968. The protesters displayed meat-cutters' charts to show that the contestants were involved in marketing their flesh. But few understood.

A beautiful sister . . . stunned the organizers and onlookers by emerging fully clad under her borrowed furs, with a sign: "I Have A Mind" . . . . The winner, a McMaster University philosophy student, was asked to comment on the incident. She was uncomprehending. Disgusted with being treated as a sex object? "That's what a girl wants most." [24]

In 1969 additional women's liberation groups started in Regina, Saskatoon, Winnipeg, Ottawa, Guelph, Hamilton, Halifax, Sudbury, Thunder Bay, and Edmonton.[25] Some apparently drew membership, not just from student groups, but also from other radical groups.

In Quebec, Anglophone women's liberation is usually seen as beginning in October 1968, when the McGill Student Society began to publish the illegal but widely distributed *Birth Control Handbook*, and then became publicly involved in the even more controversial activity of abortion counselling. Swamped by the demand for services, late in 1969 they turned for help to Montreal Women's Liberation, which had begun meeting that October at McGill and Sir George Williams universities. These referral services continued under liberationist auspices until 1975. Francophone liberationist groups had a somewhat different origin, growing out of the Quebec student groups committed to Quebec nationhood. Montreal's *Front pour la libération des femmes du Québec* dated its own start to a public protest in Montreal by women in 1969, a response to the fact that the Montreal city administration had banned all demonstrations after a wave of trade union and other leftist activity. This street action, initially an attempt to exploit possible police chivalry towards women, suggested to the leftist, nationalist women involved that women could, and should, move out of a passive role in politics. They decided to set up a women-only organization, whose first feminist action was a demonstration on Mothers' Day in 1970 in support of free access to abortion. Francophone liberationists also arranged to have the McGill *Birth Control Handbook* translated into French, and participated in the abortion referral service started at McGill.[26]

The national Canadian women's liberation movement, for its part, made its first significant public appearance with the 1970 Abortion Caravan, a protest against the inadequacy of the reforms of the previous year. According to the 1969 revisions of the Criminal Code, abortion remained illegal unless performed by a doctor in an accredited hospital under specified conditions. Among these was certification by a three-doctor committee that continuation of the pregnancy would threaten the life or health of the mother; the pregnant woman was not allowed to appear before this therapeutic abortion committee to present her own case. The royal commission, reporting in 1970, had recommended abolition of the therapeutic abortion committees and, in general, easier access to the service. The Abortion Caravan was probably the most innovative of a wide range of activities and organizations that responded to the 1969 legislation. Organized by the new women's liberation groups, demonstrations occurred across the country while the caravan was en route from Vancouver to Ottawa; it ended with women disrupting Parliament by chaining themselves to the Visitors' Gallery in the House of Commons. Abortion was an issue that moved rapidly to the top of the agenda for feminists in Canada, as women who had found the rhetoric of the women's liberation movement daunting responded enthusiastically. "Here was something I could support unequivocally," wrote Cerise Morris, a student at that time. "The right of a woman to legal abortion affects me personally — affects women of all classes and political beliefs." And she reported, as did many other women, "the shared anger, pride and love" she felt as she joined with other women for action.[27]

Women's liberation was initially a continent-wide movement and also an international one. The abortion caravaners who disrupted Parliament recognized that they were using tactics militant suffragists had previously used in the United States and Britain. But the Canadian movement was at the same time significantly different, even though some of its early leaders were American immigrants to Canada. For one thing, the Abortion Caravan was also modelled on the "On to Ottawa" trek of the Great Depression.[28] When the future members of Toronto Women's Liberation first considered secession from the New Left Caucus in 1967, they ended with a very traditional Canadian declaration: "We are going to be the typers of letters and distributors of leaflets (hewers of wood and drawers of water) *no longer*."[29]

Members of Montreal's *Front pour la libération des femmes* reacted with the same attention to local context and meanings. Their 1971 *manifeste* was written in the colloquial French of Quebec, and focussed on "colonization" rather than "oppression." Looking at the secondary, supportive role of the few women active in the *Front pour la libération du Québec*, they asked, "Why are there so few women in our revolutionary movements?" Their answer: "The majority of women in Quebec are trained to be housewives."[30] Their manifesto was an explicit response to the experience of women in the independence movement, and to the absence of any mention of women in the earlier *manifeste* of the *Front pour la libération du Québec*, on whose name they had modelled the name of their own organization.[31]

Also specific to Canada was the way that the student activist women of the early Canadian women's liberation groups generally avoided the overt anger their U.S. counterparts expressed towards male comrades who had been unresponsive. The women intended to rejoin the men, or assist them as allies in the struggle for change. Here, as in other ways, Anglophone Canadian women deliberately evoked a specifically Canadian tradition, the history of reform movements in Canada. They also looked back to the roots of Canadian feminism, embracing leaders like Nellie McClung as heroines for the movement. Later, socialist feminists were to be more selective about their history, praising pacifists like Francis Beynon, and criticizing some of the first wave feminists for racism or class bias.[32]

In Quebec, the history of women was initially unhelpful to feminists. The earlier foremothers, such as Marie de l'Incarnation, presented a problem because they had supported the church and represented tradition. Quebec suffragists like Thérèse Casgrain, still alive and active in the 1970s, supported federalism, which was anathema to separatist or nationalist women's liberationists.[33] Not even abortion, the issue that brought all sorts of feminists together, could over-ride the importance for Quebec women of the independence struggle that dominated politics in the late 1960s. The refusal of the *Front pour la libération des femmes* to join the national Caravan march on Ottawa was a denial of the legitimacy of federalism. As many commentators have noted, this decision made it possible to place the women's struggle squarely in the centre of independentist politics in Quebec: it challenged the present Quebec government and the future Quebec nation to be more responsive to women than the federal government.[34] Such views made collaboration with Anglophone liberationists virtually impossible, even when linguistic barriers could be surmounted. Furthermore, with the Marxist elements of the national liberation struggle so powerful in Quebec in the early years of the second wave, relatively few leftist French Canadian women were likely to join separate women's organizations that might divert energy away from that struggle.[35]

The early days of women's liberation in Quebec were characterized by a succession of small action groups. The *Front pour la libération des femmes* staffed abortion referral services, participated in a number of political actions including a protest against the exclusion of women from juries in Quebec (1971), and produced one issue of the feminist newspaper *Québécoises deboutte!* before dissolving late in 1971, with most members returning to the mixed-sex nationalist and socialist groups they had originally left. The next year, a very small group of successors to the *front* picked up its projects as the *Centre des femmes*, carrying on with a revived, more explicitly Marxist *Québécoises deboutte!* and the abortion referral service. The *centre*'s final dissolution in 1975 left behind the Marxist-feminist publishing house, *Editions du remue-ménage*, as well as the *Théâtre des cuisines*, a feminist resource centre, and a women's community health group in Montreal. This was the end of attempts in Quebec to work out a "non-affiliated" nationalist or Marxist feminism.

Outside Quebec, Canadian issues and Canadian nationalism were crucial to the women's movement, accounting to a large degree for the co-operation, and even convergence, between the supporters of women's liberation and other women activists. Anti-Americanism played a significant role, since the closest threat to Canadian national identity had always been American. Within the student movement, there was increasing hostility to American war resisters who had come to Canada expecting to lead the Left. Women's liberation groups shared the concerns of the student organizations. "The problem the Canadian left faces is not the draft," stated a 1969 pamphlet of the Toronto Women's Liberation Group; "It is American imperialism."[36] Those who founded Canadian women's liberation also shared with Voice of Women, as well as the surviving first wave groups, the Canadian feminist conviction that women were better able than men to protect Canadian values. For the new groups, central issues included the equal treatment of women, and active resistance to American influence.

In addition, the leftist women's groups turned increasingly towards direct services for women. Class analysis of women's oppression led the women's liberationists to set up organizations to assist poor and needy women, much as reform activists had done in previous generations. The services focussed on issues related to women's bodies and sexuality, which now meant abortion referral and counselling, rape crisis centres, and transition houses and other facilities for battered women, all deliberately organized in a consensual model designed as a contrast to male-style hierarchy. The motive was new — a political attempt to sensitize women to the abuses of the patriar-

chal state. The result, which some found dismaying, was similar —
women volunteers providing social services the state neglected.

Radical feminism and socialist feminism

In some ways all feminist groups constituted a radical challenge to
the status quo, but only one branch of feminism chose to label itself
"radical." The organizational origins of radical feminism are to be
found in the women's liberation movement. By the early 1970's
women's liberation groups were experiencing breaks and schisms,
producing a feminism that considered gender rather than class structures as central to women's oppression. Radical feminists chose "to
concentrate exclusively on the oppression of women *as women* and
not as workers, students, etc."[37] Canadian liberationists dissented
from this stance; they eventually settled on the term "socialist feminism" to describe their focus on the ways in which capitalism and
patriarchy were related so that both acted as systems of oppression
for women.

Independent socialist feminist groups became a major element of
the women's movement in English Canada, participating in NAC but
also influential on a local or provincial level. A key slogan was "A
socialist who is not a feminist lacks breadth. A feminist who is not
a socialist lacks strategy."[38] A major focus on women in the industrial
labour force produced an emphasis on workplace activism, including
attempts to found women's or feminist unions. Support of strike
actions by women, especially the immigrant women who worked in
the textile and electronics industries and as cleaning women, led to
a broader concern for immigrant and Third World women, and for
questions of women's pay. Socialist feminists also devoted major
attention to childcare, which they understood as necessary to facilitate women's paid labour; co-operative daycare centres were among
the earliest projects in both Vancouver and Toronto. Along with
reproductive rights, women's health care, including sexuality, also
became a priority.

Radical feminism did not grow out of any existing form of mainstream theory; its relationship to the other sorts of feminism became
a major theoretical problem for second wave feminists.[39] In Canada,
as elsewhere, one of the characteristics of the second wave was
eventually the insistence that activist women identify themselves at
the very least as feminists and, in many circles, as feminists of a
particular sort. Bonnie Kreps, who had been active in New York
radical feminism, appears to have started the first radical feminist
group in Canada in 1969, by walking out of a Toronto Women's
Liberation meeting that refused to accept that "women were
oppressed in the household."[40] She was followed or later joined by
women somewhat older than the liberationists, young faculty or
faculty wives, or sometimes career women, who felt uncomfortable
with both the youth and the Marxist orthodoxy of women's liberation.[41] For the radical feminists, liberation was related to asserting
the uniqueness of women's situation; their earliest goal tended to be

obliteration of gender roles as a basis of oppression. In the words of the Toronto *New Feminist*, New Feminists were "a group of women in search of their humanity." They had a variety of views about marriage but agreed that, "our society is fundamentally built on separate but unequal sex-roles for men and women. The first, fundamental step in the liberation of women is the rejection of a society so ordered."[42] This logic produced efforts to get permission for girls to wear jeans instead of skirts to school, as well as participation in a campaign by a coalition of women's groups, finally successful in 1972, to have the category of "sex" added to the Ontario Human Rights Code. Over time, radical feminists tended to shift from the goal of abolition of sex roles to a focus on the value of women's specific experience and values. If patriarchy was the oppressor and was embodied in men's values, it was reasonable to conclude that female values and practices were preferable.

Radical feminists tended to be unconventional, explicitly theoretical, insistent on consciousness-raising, and on linking the personal and the political; it was out of radical feminism that some women moved to personal or political lesbianism and separatism. Such a style made them very different from non-liberationist feminist groups, while their rejection of class analysis separated them from the original women's liberation movement. Yet in their various campaigns they were able to co-operate effectively with a wide range of other women's organizations. Kreps submitted a radical feminist brief to the royal commission and later, in the early 1970s, prepared for *Chatelaine* magazine a "Cope Kit," so that the magazine's readers could educate themselves about the women's movement in Canada. In the kit Kreps focussed on "women's subservient role in society" and the concept of "sisterhood," beginning with a description of a parents' group that had briefed the Ontario minister of education on their concerns about sex-role stereotyping in primary school readers. "Feminism," she concluded, "has become a state of mind rather than a political movement."[43]

Toronto New Feminists seem to have been the only radical feminist group outside Quebec to have left records; they voluntarily dissolved in 1973, agreeing that their raised consciousness ought now to be applied in their daily work, which tended to be in academic and artistic circles. There is no trace of the groups in Sarnia, Oshawa, and Saskatchewan mentioned by their newsletter, the *New Feminist*, in May 1970. Certainly, radical feminist groups or fragments must have existed elsewhere; at least one Anglophone group can be traced in Montreal. The Feminist Communication Collective, as it was called, issued a radical feminist newsletter aimed primarily at immigrant women.[44] Groups such as Women Against Violence Against Women (WAVAW), which started in Canada in 1977, were clearly radical feminist in orientation. The first, Toronto-based WAVAW described itself as organized around the conviction that "this world is profoundly misogynistic"; its activities were "spontaneous street action with a firm political base."[45] Such groups, including very active ones in British Columbia, protested "snuff" movies, sadistic pornography for which actual violence, including murder, was committed against the women being filmed. Their activities included "Take Back the Night" marches calling for streets safe from violence against women.

Nationwide, the influence of radical feminism could, in general terms, be traced in second wave groups organized around women's specific experience and values. For instance, in 1979 a number of women attempted to found a Feminist Party of Canada. "Traditionally, politics has not been one of the areas defined by society as the sphere of women," they noted, going on to draw a familiar conclusion: "But although the role that women play in society has historically been imposed on us and defined for us, it has in effect made us the custodians of those concerns that are most fundamental to a functioning society." In short, "The vision women will contribute to politics is that same vision we have always been depended on to bring to our more traditional spheres."[46]

Both radical and socialist feminism had a major impact on Women's Studies, as the field developed in Canada, beginning in the late 1960s and early 1970s. Academically separate programs of Women's Studies were in part the result of awareness of male domination in the universities. A hostile discussion in *Homemaker's Magazine* called this a self-inflicted "ghettoization," and made the charge that feminists often hear: "The predominant theme . . . is that to be female is burdensome. The stress is on the inadequacy of the female and the power of the male, her oppressor/enemy."[47] This attack was not accurate. It also overlooked the strong role played in Canadian Women's Studies programs by socialist feminists, and their analysis of women's paid and unpaid work. An important paper originating in the discussions of the socialist Vancouver Women's Caucus and written by Margaret Benston in 1969 identified housework as a significant category of labour; from this beginning, Canadian socialist feminist analysts developed interpretations of "reproduction" as a parallel to "production." Socialist feminists consequently came to argue for an economic reinterpretation of domestic labour very remote from the conventional Marxism it grew out of.[48]

The radical feminist emphasis on women's "difference" — not "inadequacy" — served as a major intellectual justification of study and research focussing on women, as did the need to integrate women's experiences and perceptions into existing academic disciplines. By the 1980s, Women's Studies were well established in a number of Canadian universities, supported by three journals and by five regional Women's Studies chairs endowed by the Department of the Secretary of State. Many of the instructors were previous or continuing women's movement activists.

Finally, radical feminism was influential in the development of feminist separatism in Canada, both in its cultural dimensions and in the form of radical lesbianism or lesbian separatism. These connections were most obvious in Quebec, where both radical feminists and feminist lesbians were relatively unconstrained by the loyalties to other political organizations that had such serious implications for other Quebec feminists. Radical feminist attention to male dominance encouraged feminist attention to the question of heterosexuality and to lesbians' situation in a society dominated by heterosexual values. Lesbian sociability in turn seems to have been a basis for cohesion among feminists, while lesbian perspectives deepened feminist analyses of patriarchy. Under the auspices of the YWCA, the first national lesbian conference was held in Toronto in 1973 and, shortly afterwards, *Long Time Coming*, the first lesbian newsletter in Canada, started in Montreal. The Lesbian Organization of Toronto was founded in 1976; *Coop-femmes*, a Francophone lesbian group, started in Montreal in February 1977.

By 1976 the Montreal newsletter *Les Têtes de pioche*, founded by a small group of radical feminists, was able to present itself as simply a feminist publication. For *Les Têtes de pioche*, the main criterion for feminism was "autonomous" organization, a crucial term and concept for Quebec feminism. The next important feminist journal, *Pluri-elles*, founded in 1977 and renamed *Des luttes et des rires des femmes* in October 1978, indicated by its names the tendency towards pluralism, greater diversity, and mutual tolerance. From this time on, Marxist and nationalist feminists, respectively, concentrated on action in the women's committees of the trade union organizations, and in the *Parti québécois*, as well as in extreme-left Marxist fragments.[49]

For other Quebec feminists, the influence of *Les Têtes de pioche* and *Des luttes et des rires des femmes* was major, amplified by the extraordinary role of women writers and performers in the literary explosion of Quebec in the 1970s. The *Théâtre des cuisines*, active from 1974 to 1976 and again from 1980, presented two plays, the "pro-choice" *Nous aurons les enfants que nous voulons* and *Môman travaille pas, a trop d'ouvrage*, about housework. In 1979 the scandalous *Les fées ont soif* presented the Virgin Mary flanked by a housewife and a whore, all three lamenting women's situation; Mary complained, among other things, of the boredom of being kept up on a pedestal and the irritation of not being able to have a normal female body. Plays like this were both feminist and centrally significant in the artistic world of the era. An important element in Quebec feminism, from this time, was the work of exploratory writers such as Jovette Marchessault, Louky Bersianik, and Nicole Brossard, one of the founders of *Les Têtes de pioche*.[50]

Nationwide, feminist publishing, writing, and theatre also flourished. In 1972 the Corrective Collective published an eighty-page feminist history of Canada, *She named it Canada: because that's what it was called*, and the next year saw the formation of the Saskatoon Women's Calendar Collective, which began in 1974 the annual publication of *Herstory: A Canadian women's calendar*.[51] Literary and political journals and newspapers multiplied, struggled against the hazards of distance, underfunding, and burnout; they tended to be shortlived but crucial for communication within the women's movement. Feminist publishing companies, developments of socialist or radical feminism, had somewhat more success in surviving. By the 1980s, they included The Women's Press (Toronto), Press Gang (Vancouver), and Ragweed Press (Charlottetown, P.E.I.)[52]

Convergence and coalitions

The different sorts of feminist and other women's organizations managed to co-operate on specific projects, even though they had different ideological perspectives. Women's liberation groups thought of "femininity" as an ideology used to trick women into economic dependence. As a result, they became involved with "women's issues" such as education, childcare, and the family, which had always been central to the continuing activities of the more traditional women's organizations. Similarly, Voice of Women's orientation towards maternity, as in its continuing campaigns against war toys, aligned them with radical feminists in the effort to eliminate sex-role stereotyping. Socialist feminist interest in the economic dimension of domestic labour was an additional basis of possible agreement among women's groups, for the household, always central for the maternal feminists, was also crucial to the analyses made by radical feminists.[53]

The result was often joint action on specific issues, however much socialist feminist theory condemned the concept of "sisterhood" as apolitical and inimical to class analysis.[54] In the 1970s, campaigns to include "sex," "sexual harassment," and "sexual preference" in human rights codes mobilized groups ranging from women's auxiliaries of the industrial unions, through liberal feminists, to the most

Montreal march for abortion rights.

extreme of radical feminists. A similar spectrum of groups protested sexism in advertising, in textbooks, and in the media more generally. But the most persistent coalitions responded to the violence and hostility to women expressed in the widely distributed, increasingly sadistic hard-core pornography.

Like rape and battering, pornography, in the view of radical feminists, encouraged both men and women to think of women as weak, submissive, and taking pleasure in being mastered. They accordingly argued for drastic controls on the availability of such material. A few women took direct action: in British Columbia, in December 1982, the "Wimmin's Fire Brigade" firebombed three video outlets that specialized in the distribution of pornographic films. More common, and effective in moblizing women of a wide range of beliefs, were the lobbying and pressure groups found in all parts of the nation. In 1983 a newly formed national Coalition Against Media Pornography launched a protest against a new pay TV channel owned by *Playboy* magazine, which intended to show soft-core pornography. The country-wide hearings of the Fraser Commission, a parliamentary task force that reported in February 1985, drew attention to the problems involved in limiting pornography.

But major disagreements, including some concerning the proper role of government, emerged among second wave feminists in response to the pornography question. The issue seemed to line radical feminists up on the same side as the groups that defined all explicit portrayal of sexuality as pornographic, and against other feminists who shared civil libertarians' views that no prior control should be exercised over any form of communication.[55] Views about the nature of women's sexuality were central, for some of the anti-pornography groups, often church-supported, were repressive of all forms of sexuality. The complexities of this particular issue were highlighted in 1981: *Not a Love Story*, a feminist film on pornography produced by Studio D, the women's unit of the National Film Board, gained publicity because the Ontario Film Board restricted its presentation — on account of the explicit material within it.

By the end of the 1980s, although some feminists saw any controls on pornography as dangerous, they agreed that pornography was a women's and a feminist issue. A 1984 account identified the *Front commun contre la Pornographie* as "the most important location for the advancement of the [women's] movement" in Quebec.[56] Most feminists also agreed in opposing sections of a bill proposed by the federal government in 1987 that would label all depictions of sexual activity as pornographic.

The cause of abortion law reform also mobilized a very wide range of groups, including NAC, as well as women's liberation and mixed-sex groups including unions and the organized left. From November 1974 CARAL (called the Canadian Association for the Appeal of the Abortion Laws until 1980, and then the Canadian Abortion Rights League) co-ordinated the struggle nationally. But

Table 14.2	Abortions in Canada, 1971–1982		
	Abortions	Abortion rate per 1000 females ages 15–44 years[1]	Abortion rate per 100 live births
1971	30 923	6.6	8.6
1972	38 853	8.2	11.2
1973	43 201	8.8	12.6
1974	48 136	9.5	13.7
1975	49 311	9.5	13.7
1976	54 478	10.3	15.1
1977	57 564	10.6	15.9
1978	62 290	11.3	17.4
1979	65 043	11.6	17.8
1980	65 751	11.5	17.7
1981	65 053	11.1	17.5
1982	66 319	11.1	17.8[2]

[1] *Rate based on abortions of women of all ages.*
[2] *Abortion rates for 1982 are based on estimated live births.*

From: A. Romaniuc, *Fertility in Canada: From Baby-Boom to Baby-Bust* (Ottawa: Statistics Canada, 1984) 53.

the provincial and national coalitions also had to deal with internal contradictions. Those who wished to liberalize or abolish the Criminal Code provisions ranged from supporters of "abortion on demand," to those whose major concern was the injustice of a system that denied abortions to women who were poor, or lived in isolated communities.

In addition to alliances around specific issues, there were a few on-going coalitions incorporating a variety of goals. One important example was the British Columbia Federation of Women, a regional coalition of a wide range of women's groups set up by socialist feminists in 1974 in order "to bring about the liberation of women through fundamental change in our society." This group organized a number of significant feminist demonstrations, including in 1976 the first systematic, well-publicized "lobby" of legislators. Similar tactics were adopted by NAC for its annual general meetings in Ottawa, and turned out to be effective for educating activists and the public. Representatives of a women's centre in Port Coquitlam, British Columbia reported their experience, which was typical of participants in legislative lobbies:

By nine o'clock we went to our appointments armed with briefs, dressed for the occasion and feeling rather nervous. We had no idea that there were so many doors and halls in the Parliament Buildings . . . . In general, we found that [the MLAs] were not well informed and that their attitudes ranged from indifference to a positive desire to learn.

The women came away feeling that they had "been in control and had an impact. . . . "[57]

Another socialist feminist project of collective action was Toronto's International Women's Day Committee. Beginning in 1978, it planned rallies and marches of several thousand participants, including representatives of sympathetic unions and other leftist groups, on or around International Women's Day. March 8th became something of a feminist holiday when thousands of supporters of the women's movement showed up to march every year. Early in the group's history, the decision was made to allow male supporters to participate in the celebration, a practice radical feminist groups did not usually allow.[58] This is a striking contrast with what happened in Montreal, where International Women's Day became a forum of competition between feminist groups, women's committees of unions, and the far left. In 1975 these three factions co-operated, but in 1976 "the women found themselves robbed of their only spot on the revolutionary calendar" as the far left and the union committees each organized separate celebrations without the participation of the non-aligned feminists.[59]

The closest to a national representative of all this varied activity was NAC. Over the years, it grew into an effective lobbying group, a coalition that operated on a basis of consensus among its widely differing components. What was unusual and possibly typically Canadian about NAC was the organization's inclusion from the start, not just of new voluntary status of women groups, but also of many of the surviving older women's organizations and, surprisingly, of representatives of a whole range of second wave service and cultural groups such as rape crisis centres, transition houses, and women's centres. By 1987 NAC had over 500 member groups, and through them, indirectly, could claim to represent 5 million Canadian women.

Opposition

Whatever its form, feminist political action had to contend with a growing organized opposition. The first signs began to appear in the 1970s in the form of anti-abortion groups. These seem to have begun as responses to the liberalized law of 1969, reinforced by the simultaneous campaigns in favour of freer access to abortion. The first active anti-abortion group, Birthright, had been started in 1968 to provide support for unmarried mothers. It was in 1971 that anti-abortion groups became publicly visible, with the first of annual demonstrations in Ottawa calling for an end to all abortions. Much of the activity focussed around the activities of Henry Morgentaler, who became the chief symbol of the "pro-choice" movement. Morgentaler, a concentration camp survivor who defined himself as a humanist, told the Commons Health and Welfare Committee in 1967 that abortion should be allowed freely to women through the end of the first trimester of pregnancy. After the passage of the 1969 amendments, he continued to perform abortions in defiance of the law, announcing that he was carrying on legitimate acts of civil disobedience. Although he was repeatedly arrested and brought to trial, three Quebec juries and one in Ontario refused to find him guilty.[60] Finally, on January 28, 1988, the Supreme Court of Canada invoked the Charter of Rights to strike down the federal law on abortion as unconstitutional.

The support the women's movement gave to freedom of reproductive choice made some conservative women's opposition to abortion turn into a wider anti-feminism; the earliest group seems to have been the Alberta Federation of Women United for the Family, founded in 1981, but nationally visible only a few years later.[61] In 1984 a national group headed by women formerly prominent in the "right to life" movement began to get media attention. Calling itself REAL Women, an acronym for Real, Equal, Active, for Life, and claiming that NAC represented only a small number of "radical feminists," the group announced that it spoke for the "real" women of Canada. It opposed not just abortion but also the equality clauses of the Charter of Rights, no-fault divorce, legislation on equal pay for work of equal value, publicly funded childcare, affirmative action in employment, and legal protection of the rights of homosexuals. The group's "pro-family" program included joint income tax returns for spouses, tax credits for homemakers, public funding for marriage counselling, job-sharing, benefits for part-time workers, extended maternity leaves, and more use of short-term contract work. They also proposed a million dollar annual sustaining grant for REAL Women, to replace the grants of approximately $400 000 per year NAC was then receiving from the government. Their tactics included handing out pink brochures and muffins, presumably freshly baked by "real" women, to legislators. "What are we? plastic women?" asked Judy Erola, previously Minister Responsible for the Status of Women. She noted sadly how much energy the women's movement now had to spend in answering the accusations of anti-feminists.[62] A number of feminists proclaimed themselves to be FAKE Women — Feminists for All Kinds of Equality.

Given the dependence of women's groups on government funding, REAL Women represented a genuine threat: they went to the Secretary of State's Women's Program for funds, were refused them, and then attacked that program. Some conservative members of Parliament declared that REAL Women were "a breath of fresh air."[63]

It had to be recognized that anti-feminist groups also responded in part to the surviving inequities in the treatment of women: REAL Women stated that they too "support the equality and advancement of women." There could be no disagreement among feminists with the wish to adapt the workplace to the needs of the family. Even in their defence of an idealized traditional family, anti-feminist women were attempting to obtain recognition and reward for the distinctive abilities and activities of women. But they seemed unable to appreciate any alteration in values or life styles. Florence Bird summed up the problem:

REAL *Women wants to recreate the beautiful and happy society of the '50s ads—the happy mother, the beautiful, shining kitchen and the three happy children who never get sick . . . . It's nostalgia for the good old days that were never very good.*[64]

Contrary to the claims of the anti-feminists, nostalgia for a mythical past was not generally shared by Canadians in the 1980s. In 1982 a national poll showed 72 percent of the respondents supportive of women's access to abortion. By 1986, Canadians saw women working for pay as, at worst, a "necessary evil," and the majority of them favoured both pay equity legislation and public support for daycare.[65] Increasing numbers of women were prepared to identify themselves as feminists—47 percent in a poll taken among *Chatelaine* readers in 1986.[66] Also in 1986, a poll of the wider public showed 73 percent agreeing that over all "the feminist movement" had had a positive, rather than a negative, effect on Canadian society; only 11 percent disagreed. And fully a quarter of them, when given a list of five "problems facing Canadians today," put "improving the rights of women in Canada" either first or second.[67] However it had operated, the impact of feminism had apparently been considerable.

15 Work in the electronic era

Looking back from the 1980s, most observers were struck by the enormous changes in the work patterns of Canadian women, both within the three most recent decades and in comparison to earlier periods. The typical married woman of the 1950s was still usually remembered as a homemaker, isolated from the world of work, and living out her destiny with her husband and children in suburbia. In sharp contrast was the upwardly mobile, childless career woman of the 1980s, a glamorous "gladiatrix" in designer clothes off to do battle in the executive suite. These stereotypical images were the creation of the mass media, and like most stereotypes they contained just enough truth to perpetuate themselves. The first image reflected the reduced role of women in the labour force in the immediate post-war era; the second, the greatly increased proportion of Canadian women in the labour force in the 1980s, and the somewhat greater likelihood of their attaining positions of power and prestige in traditional male preserves. However, both images masked other significant facts. The dramatic speed up of married women into the paid workforce actually began in the 1950s. Furthermore, the woman worker of the 1980s was much more likely to be a secretary with dependent children than a corporate lawyer with none. Regional, class, and ethnic variations were also obscured by these distilled images. And both these images of women ignored the individual women and groups who organized to transform the world of work.

Work patterns and problems

Changes in women's participation in the labour force began in the 1950s and increased in the 1960s; in the next decades, significantly larger numbers of married women with small children began working for pay. In 1961 Canadian women's participation rate remained at a lower level than that of most other industrialized countries; it was high enough to be contentious though not changing fast enough to satisfy either individual women or the state. The percentage of women fifteen and over who were in the labour force continued to climb, moving from 24 percent in 1952 to 37 percent in 1971; the proportion of men in the labour force declined from 84 percent to 79 percent, the result of prolonged education among younger men and earlier age of retirement for older men. Between 1951 and 1971, the proportion of women workers who were married also rose

Figure 15.1   Labour force participation of women with children, 1967–1985

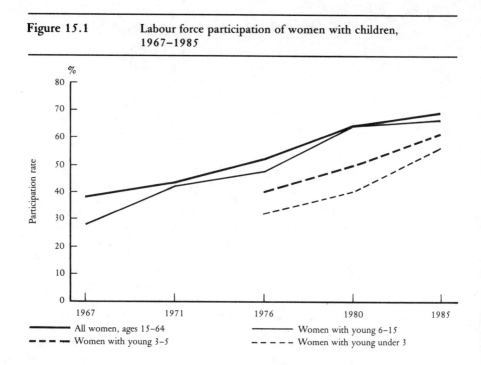

Source: Statistics Canada, Characteristics of Women in the Labour Force, 1984; The Labour Force, #71-001. From: Canadian Congress for Learning Opportunities for Women, *Decade of Promise: An Assessment of Canadian Women's Status in Education, Training and Employment 1976–1985* (Toronto, Avebury Research, 1986).

dramatically, almost doubling. By the latter date, for the first time more than one-third of all married women were members of the labour force.

These employment trends of the 1950s and 1960s reflected the fact that increasing numbers of women now completed their families by the age of thirty, and had reduced childcare responsibilities once their children were in school. They could undertake as many as three additional decades of paid employment to assist their families in the unremitting struggle to maintain their standard of living. As older children prolonged their education or left home at an earlier age than in the past, it was mothers who assumed the role of secondary wage earners. In previous decades, women's adult life typically had two distinct phases: paid work before marriage and then permanent withdrawal to the domestic realm. Now, for a relatively brief period lasting until the middle 1980s, women's life cycle had three distinct phases: employment until birth of the first child, childrearing at home, and re-entry into the workforce once the children reached school age. This significant change was illustrated by the labour force participation rate for the group of women who were aged 15–24 in 1951. In that year, 42 percent were in the labour force. By 1981, when their age ranged from 45 to 54 years, 56 percent were working.[1]

Generally, women's new work patterns were accepted as legitimate. In 1970 a Gallup poll found 77 percent agreement with the proposition that married women might "take a job outside the home" if they had no "young children." But if women did have young children, 80 percent were opposed to them working outside the home. In 1976, 81 percent still thought that "when children are young a mother's place is in the home."[2] Since public opinion expected childcare to be undertaken by mothers, few support systems such as daycare existed. Nor was it expected that any but single women would undertake a lifelong career for pay.

Not surprisingly, women's labour force activity varied considerably according to region, ethnicity, and level of education. In 1985, when the national participation rates for women reached an average of 52 percent, women in Alberta had the highest rate (60 percent) while women in Newfoundland had the lowest (41 percent). Women of Chinese and other Asiatic origins were the most active in the labour force (60 percent); native women were the least active (37 percent). The latter statistic reflected the few job opportunities available to native women in their communities, as well as the discrimination they routinely encountered. All too common were situations such as that experienced by Irene Desjarlais when she entered nursing:

My first day at Brandon General I was so scared I felt like turning around and running down the steps and home. This was the first time away from my people. I heard someone say that I'd be just like the rest of the Indians and quit, wasting the government's money.[3]

Fortunately, in Irene's case, these racist remarks only strengthened her resolve and she established a very successful career in nursing.

By 1981 for the first time more than half of all married women were wage earners, and 60 percent of all female workers were married. More surprisingly, well over half the married women with preschool children were in the paid labour force. For these women, adult life was not divided into separate phases of employment and childrearing; rather, they combined them. By 1985 most women were remaining continuously in the labour force, without leaving for extended periods.

As in past generations, the majority of working mothers with young children had to fend for themselves to arrange childcare, which was all too often either prohibitively expensive or of dubious quality. In 1975 there were daycare spaces for 13 percent of the children under six whose mothers were in the labour force, about one out of eight, and by 1982 this had increased only to 16 percent.[4] For some women, especially those with high levels of education who intended to pursue life-long careers, one strategy for combining work and family was to postpone both marriage and childbearing, and then to reduce family size. By 1984 Canadian women were making their first marriages at the average age of 24.3 years, so that they were almost two years older than comparable women had been at the beginning of the 1970s. The fertility rate continued to decline, dropping to 1.7 births per woman. Only one family in twenty contained four or more children compared to one in six twenty years earlier.

How the loaf is sliced. Who is earning the family income?

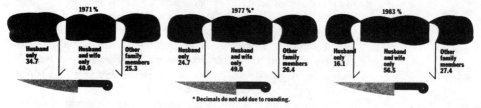

1971 %
Husband only 34.7
Husband and wife only 40.0
Other family members 25.3

1977 %*
Husband only 24.7
Husband and wife only 49.0
Other family members 26.4

1983 %
Husband only 16.1
Husband and wife only 56.5
Other family members 27.4

* Decimals do not add due to rounding.

The importance of married women's contribution to family income through paid employment increased substantially during the 1970s and 1980s; therefore, women with young children continued their paid employment. In 1971 husbands working as sole bread-winners earned 35 percent of all income generated by families — by 1983 they produced only 16 percent.[5] Wives' paid labour was especially crucial for low income families: the lower the husband's earnings, the more likely it was that the wife would be in the labour force. In 1979, in families whose income would have been under $5000 if the wife did not work, two-thirds of the married women under the age of forty-five were in the paid labour force. Less than half of the wives in the same age group worked for pay in families that would have earned $25 000 or more without their contribution.[6] A Portuguese textile worker, married to a construction worker who worked only part of the year, explained her role proudly: "That's life. I need money. I go to the factory . . . . The wife help, is good because I buy the house, need to pay . . . need the money." A farmer's wife in Saskatchewan gave a similar explanation:

[I wanted] to get little extras . . . well, like things I want for the house. And sometimes we have bills that we can't meet . . . . That's why I started working in the first place . . . grain sales were so low that we couldn't make ends meet and I had to get a job.[7]

Greater female labour force participation can also be related to the increase in "non-traditional" families. In 1981 only 52 percent of Canadian families consisted of two parents with children, 32 percent were couples with no children, and 11 percent were headed by a single parent who, in four cases out of five, was a woman. In the nineteenth century, widowhood was the primary reason that women with children went out to work; now it was marriage break-down. The divorce rate remained high, though it was about 5 percent lower in 1985 than in 1984. In 1982, 53 percent of divorces involved dependent children, whose custody was still awarded to the wife in over 85 percent of the cases.[8] Over 80 percent of divorce settlements were defaulted on; by the middle of the 1980s, provinces were discussing central registries of divorce settlements and the possible use of tax and employment data to trace or garnishee defaults.

Whatever her marital status, the female worker in Canada experienced many problems similar to those encountered by her mother

Source: The Royal Bank *Reporter* (Spring, 1986).

Figure 15.2   **Divorce rates, 1941–1981**

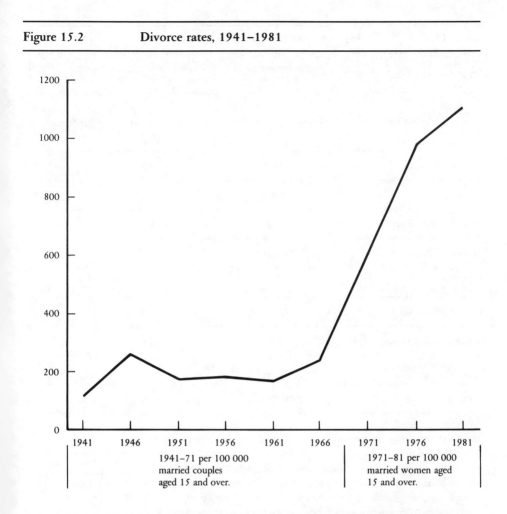

1941–71 per 100 000
married couples
aged 15 and over.

1971–81 per 100 000
married women aged
15 and over.

Sources: Based on data from
Gail C.A. Cook, ed.,
Opportunity for Choice
(Ottawa: Information
Canada, 1976) 22; *Women
in Canada: A Statistical
Report* (Ottawa: Statistics
Canada, 1985) 10.

and grandmother. The most significant were the continued assignment of work according to gender, and the lower rewards that
accompanied work classified as female. From 1951 to 1981, the
massive influx of women into the paid workforce occurred primarily
in clerical and retail jobs, the expanding areas where the demand for
their services was highest. By 1981 clerical, sales, and service occupations employed over 60 percent of all female workers. Men were
much more evenly spread across occupational categories: the three
leading men's occupations had less than one-third of all employed
males.[9] Within their white collar occupations, moreover, women
were confined to lower level positions; for example, only one woman
in twenty was classified as a manager or administrator, compared to
about one of every ten men. As one study of women in business
concluded in 1977, few "have made it to the top. . . . For the most
part they are the shadowy invisible army of workers who keep

Table 15.1		Top ten jobs for women in Canada, 1981	
Jobs	Number of females employed	% of total female employment	Female % of job
Secretaries & stenographers	368 025	7.6%	98.9%
Bookkeepers & accounting clerks	332 330	6.9	81.9
Salespersons/clerks	292 915	6.0	59.4
Tellers & cashiers	229 325	4.7	92.7
Waitresses & hostesses	200 710	4.1	85.7
Nurses	167 710	3.5	95.4
Elementary & kindergarten teachers	139 620	2.9	80.4
General office clerks	115 015	2.4	80.5
Typists and clerk typists	102 970	2.1	97.8
Janitors, charworkers, and cleaners	96 735	2.0	41.2
Total	2 045 355	42.2	79.1

business running, occasionally sergeants, rarely, very rarely, generals."[10]

Moreover, within broad occupational categories, women continued to be clustered in lower paying, less prestigious "female" areas or "pink collar ghettos"; for example, the vast majority of women "professionals" were teachers or nurses rather than lawyers or doctors. In the early 1980s, less than 10 percent of women in teaching and related activities were employed at the post-secondary level, compared to nearly 30 percent of men in teaching; nearly 80 percent of women health or medical workers were nurses or therapists compared to just over 30 percent of the men. In specific jobs in 1982, among health care professionals only one doctor in five was a woman, while nine out of every ten nurses and therapists were female.[11] Women doctors tended to be family physicians or specialists treating women and children; women lawyers were much more likely to practise family rather than corporate or criminal law; women clergy were more frequently chaplains and educators than rectors of parishes.

The concentration of women in positions that conferred the least control and monetary rewards resulted in large part from the goals they were urged to set for themselves, which persuaded them to

From: Rosalie Silberman Abella, *Equality in Employment: A Royal Commission Report* (Ottawa: Ministry of Supply and Services, 1984) 405.

view the less authoritative and less remunerative positions as their most appropriate career choices.[12] A dental hygienist from British Columbia commented, "In my undergraduate years, I was sort of channelled into thinking that as a woman I would be a hygienist or nurse or something like that."[13]

The situation of dental hygienists was broadly illustrative of the gender dynamics of work. An almost exclusively female profession, it was subject to regulation by the dental profession in every province except Quebec. In spite of their considerable training and expertise, hygienists in all provinces except British Columbia were required to have a dentist present while they performed their work; their average annual earnings ranged from $30 000 to $40 000, while dentists earned two or three times as much. A report released by the federal government in 1986 suggested that the current restrictions on the type of work hygienists might perform were excessive, limiting public access to much-needed preventive health care. Representatives of the dentists responded that the regulations were necessary because hygienists lacked the intensive training that dentists had to undergo. But the president of the Ontario Dental Association also said that there were already too many dentists. Given the general improvement in dental hygiene, dentists themselves were spending less time repairing cavities, and more time cleaning teeth and treating gum disease, the kind of tasks that hygienists were trained to perform — and that made them a threat to the dentists.[14]

While there was some movement of women into non-traditional occupations in the nation's mines, forests, steelworks, and railyards, progress was slow. The proportion of women among blue collar workers increased only marginally, from 12 percent in 1975 to 15 percent in 1985. Companies such as Stelco in Hamilton, Ontario, and Cominco in Trail, British Columbia, which had hired women as production workers during World War II, dismissed them when male workers became available after the war, and subsequently stopped offering production jobs to women. Faced with negative publicity from feminist coalitions such as "Women Back into Stelco," and court challenges under human rights legislation for their failure to hire female production workers, in the late 1970s companies began to accept female applicants for blue collar jobs. However, the few women who did secure employment were often isolated, the objects of sexual harassment by male co-workers, and among the first workers to be laid off when the economy slowed down a few years later.

Many of the newly hired women agreed in blaming management for most of their difficulties: they "put me in the blast furnaces really to get even with me," said Jeannette Easson, one of the first women Stelco hired under pressure from the Human Rights Commission. "They put me in the dirtiest places." Another woman at Stelco, Joanne Santucci, told of the sexual harassment, which commonly took the form of pornographic pin-ups, but also told how it could be combatted:

*There was a really gross picture, eh? I saw it one day, and the next night
I went in again and looked, and there was this little paper bikini taped to
the girl's crotch . . . and up on her top . . . .Later* BJ *said she did it. The
guys thought that was hilarious. Instead of ripping it down, she added to
it. Turned it into something different.*[15]

Publicly owned enterprises were equally slow to accept women into
non-traditional occupations. It was 1981 before the Halifax Transit
Commission hired its first permanent female bus driver, and only in
1987 did Air Canada hire a female cargo-handler in the Atlantic
region.[16] In the case of Canadian National Railways, it took a ten-
year legal battle, initiated by a small Montreal women's group —
Action Travail des Femmes, dedicated to finding jobs for women on
welfare — to force the company to hire more women in non-traditional jobs. The unanimous decision handed down by the Supreme
Court in June 1987 in support of the women was a precedent-setting
case, establishing that the Human Rights Commission could require
companies to hire a specified percentage of women, and so increase
their access to jobs.[17] Many of the blue collar positions that women
were fighting for were dangerous jobs involving hard physical labour;
however, the wages and benefits paid for such work were twice those
paid for "women's work."[18] The decline in job opportunities for
women and men in the primary (agriculture, forestry, fishing, and
mining) and the secondary (manufacturing and construction) sectors
of the Canadian economy after 1950 made it unlikely that a large
proportion of the female workforce would be found in "non-traditional" jobs in these sectors.[19]

What, then, are we to make of the media accounts of women
entering "male" areas of employment, and the attention given to
such women as Roberta Bondar, the first Canadian woman astro-
naut? Certainly, women increased their representation in the "male"
professions: from 11 to 19 percent between 1971 and 1981. But in
the 1980s, it was still true that, even when they entered male-
dominated professions, women tended to be clustered in areas that
conferred less prestige or lower earnings.[20]

On the other hand, a striking development was the progress
women made as entrepreneurs in the 1980s. In 1986 nearly one-
quarter of the new businesses registered in Ontario were started by
women, many of whom took advantage of the increasing trend
towards franchises. Of the 145 Molly Maid franchises in Canada,
for example, only one was owned by a man. This company, the
largest maid service in the world, with franchises in the United States
and Great Britain, was started in Canada by a woman in 1979.
Despite the lower bankruptcy rate among female owners of small
businesses, however, women generally experienced more difficulty
than men in securing the credit they needed to start up their enterprises. In one telling incident, Elizabeth Tower, who headed her own
company, was asked to get her husband to co-sign a loan when in
fact he was *her* employee.[21]

Non-traditional work.

Few of these "success" stories of women's forays into previously prohibited occupational territory involved immigrant women, particularly those belonging to visible minorities, and native women. They continued to be over-represented among low-status, low-paying employees such as domestic servants, hospital, restaurant, and laundry workers, and garment and textile workers. "It was so disappointing," said "Ziddah," a young Palestinian woman, "I went around and made all these applications and no one called. I felt so badly because they hired Canadians after me, that I was too dark. Then K-Mart called me and I was so excited and so happy."[22] Yet in the 1980s, a few women entrepreneurs emerged even among these marginalized groups. For instance, Gerry Many Fingers, head of commercial development of the Blood Tribe of southern Alberta, produced and marketed women's cloth coats with fur trimming, elkhorn buttons, and caribou hair tufting, and she hoped to develop an industry employing other native women.[23]

Given the sexual division of labour, technological change — and the microelectronic revolution in particular — had a differential impact on women's and men's work. Just as employers during the Great Depression sought to use technological innovations to reduce labour costs, during the recession of the early 1980s many managers promoted the use of microtechnology to reduce their staffs. In 1982 a study commissioned by Labour Canada predicted that secretarial, sales, and clerical work — occupations where women were concentrated — would be the most vulnerable to job loss owing to computerization.[24] For women who managed to retain their jobs, there were further threats: a dilution of skills required to perform the work, increased use of monitoring devices to record their rate of work, more shift work, alienation from other workers, and health problems such as backache, eye strain, and high levels of stress. The office worker hired to do word processing for other employees she did not even know, or the grocery store clerk pulling items over optical scanners while the electronic cash register at her counter monitored her speed and sales volume, illustrated the dehumanizing effects of microtechnology. Conditions such as these led one researcher to coin the phrase "the electronic sweatshop." In addition, as clerical work became more fragmented and standardized, it became increasingly difficult for clerical workers to acquire the skills necessary for upward job mobility.[25]

A remarkable example of the continuity of work patterns from pre-industrial times was the growing numbers of women working at home on microcomputers — a modernized version of the cottage industry. A representative of a company employing a large clerical staff declared in 1982 that his company had the capability of transforming half of its clerical jobs into home work jobs. At first glance, working out of one's home could appear an improvement; after all, many women as well as men were taking advantage of the technical advances in microelectronics to set up their own small businesses at home. However, the prospect of the wholesale transfer of clerical work to the home was a serious issue for women. The clerical home worker employed by a company would be working under an entirely different set of conditions, for she would not be self-employed. It seemed likely that she would share many of the problems that women home workers in the past had experienced, as well as some new ones. These included a lack of contact with other workers; the strain of simultaneously performing paid work and childcare, if there were pre-school children at home; payment on a piecework basis; the absence of fringe benefits; and being monitored by a machine.[26]

The trend for women to be over-represented among part-time workers increased by the early 1980s, when one of every four women in the labour force worked part-time, compared to only one in twelve men, and women accounted for over 70 percent of all part-time

Working on
microcomputers.

workers. While many women chose part-time work so that they could more readily combine domestic tasks and paid employment, for many others part-time employment was under-employment.[27] Since few part-time jobs offered fringe benefits or job security, many women would have preferred full-time work, but they were unable to obtain it. A large number of big employers in the service sector, such as the multinational fast food firms, successfully combined franchising, computerized work processes, and reliance on a predominantly part-time workforce to generate impressive profits. The high rate of turnover among most part-time workers, and the tendency for labour relations legislation to require that they should be represented by bargaining units separate from those representing full-time workers employed at the same location, made it extremely difficult for part-time workers to organize. Nor were most part-time workers covered by equal pay, unemployment, or maternity leave legislation.

Women also continued to perform much of the taxing seasonal work in Canada in agriculture, in fish and fruit processing, and in retail establishments. Working conditions under these circumstances tended to be extremely trying, because of the long hours necessary during short-season employment, and the lack of job security. "You work for the season, however long it lasts," explained Gina Vance, who worked in a seafood plant in Nova Scotia:

This year it was only ten weeks; they didn't do any crab. But my first season was six months, six days a week, nine, ten hours a day. . . . During the season you only get Sunday off, but even Sunday is geared towards the factory because of washing uniforms, aprons and gloves.

In that plant in the late 1970s, workers stood on concrete floors in rubber boots up to ten hours a day with their hands submerged in cold water for most of their shift, unable to talk with co-workers because of the noise of the machinery and the oppressive discipline imposed by management.[28] Conditions for agricultural workers, many of whom were native or immigrant women, were generally even worse. The back-breaking toil, long hours, very low wages, and deplorable living quarters provided on some farms ensured that people became agricultural labourers only as a last resort.

Wages and benefits

In the 1980s, the persistence of segregation by gender was a major cause of the continuing wage gap between women and men. After social class, gender had the most effect on differences in wages and salaries.[29] There was only a slight improvement between 1970 and 1986 for full-time female workers, as their average annual incomes rose from approximately 60 percent to 66 percent of the average annual incomes of full-time male workers. This differential was greater in Canada than in several of the industrialized European countries: in Sweden in 1986, a working woman made on average 80 cents for every dollar earned by a male worker, and her French and West German counterparts earned 75 cents. More disturbing than the slow pace at which the wage gap decreased in Canada was the fact that, within some of the most common female occupations, the wage gaps stayed large, and in some cases increased. In fact, during 1986 the overall wage gap widened for the first time on record.[30] The reasons for the continuing differential were complex. In the retail sales sector and food services industry, for example, women had lower average wages because they were often assigned work that earned them lower commissions. Selling lingerie did not carry the same financial rewards as selling refrigerators or automobiles. On the other hand, the smallest wage discrepancy occurred in teaching and nursing, occupations that were attracting growing numbers of men and that were strongly organized.[31]

In the 1970s and 1980s, analysts using the concept of "human capital" insisted that the wage gap was not caused by discrimination. Women were less qualified for the paid labour force, they were convinced. Further, this lack of qualifications was the result of choices women had made at key points in their lives: women, unlike men, did not decide to "invest" in what would make them valuable to employers.[32] Yet even after allowing for women's lower educational levels, briefer and less continuous job experience, overall lower productivity and somewhat higher rate of absenteeism, women's wages still remained significantly lower than men's.[33] Explanations based on the concept of human capital relied, moreover, on faulty assumptions: women did not freely choose their educational experiences, nor did they choose to work part-time or in undercapitalized areas like the garment industry, where worker productivity was low. Instead, there were very subtle but nevertheless real constraints on women, including the manner in which girls and women were social-ized. Women's participation in the labour force was also directly affected by the fact that they bore the children and still retained the primary responsibility for childcare; female absenteeism, although it was only slightly higher than among male workers, was in large part a result of the unequal family responsibilities they shouldered. Absen-teeism was also related to the type of work performed, in that all workers with low-status, low-paying jobs who exercised little control over their work had significantly higher rates of absenteeism than those who enjoyed high status, high pay, and authority—and women workers were concentrated in the type of work likely to produce a lower level of commitment to the job.

Education was certainly an important influence on women's employment. Seven out of ten women with university education were gainfully employed in 1985, compared to one in four of those with only primary school education. A smaller proportion of the female population held university degrees (6 percent in 1981 com-pared to 10 percent of the male population) although proportionately more women (44 percent compared to 38 percent of men) had completed high school. Nonetheless, when age and educational levels were held constant for full-time female and male workers, the wage gap persisted. Women workers between the ages of 25 and 54 years with a university degree earned an annual average of $21 000 in 1981; their male counterparts earned over $30 000. In fact, men in the same age category with only a high school education also earned an average of $21 000 per annum.[34] Even when differences in edu-cation, labour force experience, degree of unionization, and number of hours worked were taken into consideration, women still earned 15 to 20 percent less than men.[35]

The wage differential continued to exist despite the enactment between 1951 and 1973 of equal pay for equal work legislation by the federal government and all the provincial governments except Quebec. The primary weakness of these laws was that they applied only when women performed the same or very similar work to men in the same establishment, a situation that the existence of female work ghettos precluded. Equal pay laws sometimes actually rein-forced the sexual division of labour, since employers in industries highly reliant on female labour could benefit from employing only women and paying them low wages.[36] This major flaw in the equal pay laws led women activists to demand legislation on equal pay for work of equal value. Under this approach, endorsed by the Inter-national Labour Organization in 1951 and ratified by Canada in 1972, women were not required to do the same or similar jobs as men in order to receive equal monetary rewards. Jobs were to be evaluated according to a number of criteria, usually skill, effort, level of responsibility, and working conditions; similarly rated jobs were then to receive equal wages regardless of the gender of the worker. In 1977 the federal government passed such legislation for all workers under federal jurisdiction, which meant mainly those working in the federal public service and the crown corporations, including banks.[37] Although this legislation did not immediately have a major impact, its potential usefulness for female workers was demonstrated on a number of occasions: for example, in 1978, librarians working for the federal government, who were mostly female, had their salaries raised to the level of those of historical researchers, who were mostly male.[38] Quebec had passed similar legislation in 1976 covering both private and public sectors, as did Ontario in 1987. Manitoba's legislation, passed in 1985, affected only the public sector. Equal value legislation was still largely untested at the end of the 1980s. At its best, it was limited by being set in an equal rights framework, in some cases embedded in human rights legislation, so that it could not allow for specific problems that the workplace might pose for women, or for special measures to allow for domestic responsibilities.

Women's lower wages remained a central fact of their working lives, affecting their standard of living and that of their children, and dooming many to an impoverished old age. Women's increasing life expectancy, together with low wages, produced a new class of poor in Canada: widows and elderly single women. Existing pension plans, such as the Canada Pension Plan, were based on earnings calculated on the basis of a continuous lifelong involvement in the labour force. The assumption was that approximately 70 percent of lifetime average earnings should be enough to support a retired worker. But what if she had low income to start with, and no opportunity for savings? And what if she took years out of the labour force to raise children, as so many women had? Pensions for housewives became a major issue in the 1970s and 1980s, although some considered it a discriminatory measure, since by this time only the well–to–do could afford to have wives full-time in the home for all of their adult lives. This argument disregarded the needs of the still-surviving older women who had spent relatively little time in the workforce. Provincial governments gradually agreed to a "drop out provision," which meant that up to seven years could be dropped from Canada (or Quebec) Pension Plan calculations on account of absence from the workforce to care for children. There was at the same time a movement towards adapting pensions and other benefits to the pattern of women's working life. By the end of the 1980s, there were just beginning to be legal requirements of pro-rated benefits to part-time workers and other provisions useful to women.

For most women workers, maternity leave was granted under provincial legislation put in place in the 1960s and 1970s, which entitled pregnant employees to leave and then resume their jobs without loss of position or seniority; payment replacing wages was given separately, under the federal program of unemployment insurance. The initial legislation provided for a longer qualifying period than was required for unemployment on other grounds, apparently on the assumption that women already pregnant might take jobs just to get support. Maternity leave, sometimes even with full replacement of pay, was also on occasion negotiated as part of union contracts. Most women workers, however, had to rely on the provisions of the combined federal and provincial legislation, and in the 1970s it had paradoxical implications, as Stella Bliss discovered.

In 1976 Bliss was unemployed, having been fired. She had at that point worked long enough to be eligible for normal benefits; she did not apply for them because she was pregnant and did not intend to seek work until after the baby was born. Then, ready and eager to work, unable to find a job, she was refused benefits on the grounds that, having been pregnant when she became jobless, the only unemployment benefits she was entitled to were the pregnancy ones—for which she had not worked long enough to be eligible. This, she claimed, discriminated against women. The Supreme Court of Canada disagreed in 1978, arguing that Bliss was denied benefits, not because she was a woman, but because she was pregnant. The discrimination was not made by law, but by nature, which decreed that only women became pregnant.[39] This situation got a certain amount of public attention. With the assistance of pressure from women's organizations, it produced two legal changes in 1983: an amendment to the Unemployment Insurance Act so that it was not necessary to be in the workforce longer for pregnancy than for other unemployment benefits, and an amendment to the Canadian Human Rights Act so that discrimination because of pregnancy was no longer allowed. Ontario followed suit in the 1986 amendments of its Human Rights Code.

Work in the family

Government legislation to improve wages and provide for paid maternity leave was of little benefit to the many women who continued to toil long hours at home at piecework rates, unprotected by labour laws. Little had changed for industrial home workers over the course of the past century.[40] Many were recent immigrants whose lack of fluency in English, childcare responsibilities, or sometimes their status as illegal immigrants, prevented them from obtaining employment outside their homes. Over 52 000 other Canadian women laboured long hours as unpaid workers in family enterprises, accounting in 1981 for nearly three-quarters of such workers. Nearly 33 000 of these women worked on family farms, and countless others in small retail establishments such as corner variety stores. Although amendments to the federal Income Tax Act in 1981 permitted the payment of salaries to spouses working in unincorporated family businesses, thereby entitling them to contribute to the Canada Pension Plan, many women were unable to take advantage of the change, since financially hard-pressed family businesses could not afford to pay them wages.[41] A Quebec study in 1973 showed that these women worked an average of 23 hours per week in the family enterprise.[42]

For farm women, the 1980s were particularly difficult. The trend towards the ownership of land by large agricultural enterprises seemed to be gaining momentum as the proportion of family-owned farms declined. Squeezed by rising interest rates and production costs, and by declining commodity prices and agricultural land values, farmers' incomes plummeted and bankruptcies soared. While there were 623 000 farms in 1951, by 1981 there were only 318 361. In many instances, farm families survived precariously, thanks to the income wives obtained from paid employment off the farm. A 1982 survey of farm wives in Grey and Bruce counties in Ontario reported that 60 percent of them had had off-farm employment during the previous ten years.[43] Many farm women were thus compelled to work, not just a double day, but what could be termed a triple day. Not only did they hold down full-time jobs and perform the bulk of the household work, but they also did their share of the farm chores; 55 percent of the women in the Grey–Bruce survey performed farm work.[44]

Given the economic crisis confronting many farm families, rural women coped with high levels of stress, and with little access to support services such as daycare centres or health clinics. Contrary to the idyllic image of rural life, wife and child abuse, alcoholism, inter-generational conflict, and medical problems such as heart disease and ulcers were increasingly frequent in rural areas. "Jane's" story was not atypical. She was married to a full-time Ontario farmer, but in 1986, in order to pay the bills, the family of four depended upon the weekly salary of $200 she earned as an office worker. Her marriage was strained, and she was under medical care for stomach trouble.[45] Women in several provinces organized to save the family farm. These included Saskatchewan's Farm Women's Action, instrumental in lobbying politicians for assistance to farm families reeling from the ravages of drought, high interest rates, and low commodity prices, Ontario's Women for the Survival of Agriculture (1975) and Concerned Farm Women (1981). The continued migration of the rural population to urban centres also resulted in a reduction in the community services and facilities that past generations of farm women had fought so hard to obtain. As rural post offices, stores, schools, and churches disappeared from the countryside, women were active in groups such as Rural Dignity for Canada, created to protest the closing of rural post offices.

Like farm families, families working in the fishing industry experienced enormous economic and social dislocation. The number of family fishing enterprises on both the Atlantic and Pacific coasts declined dramatically because of environmental and economic factors such as depleted fish stocks, low fish prices, competition from large corporate-owned ships and factory freezer ships, and government policies, including the forced relocation of the inhabitants of many Newfoundland outports. The failure of governments to provide alternate employment created enormous hardship and frustration for the displaced families. In many communities, it was women's wage labour in fish processing plants during the summer that enabled them to claim the unemployment benefits needed to support their families during the rest of the year. When these plants closed — usually the only source of paid employment for women — the workers were unable to qualify for unemployment benefits. The resulting anger and desperation of some workers in Newfoundland led, in November 1985, to a hunger strike in which over 100 women and men protested the lack of job creation projects. Within two hours the federal government pledged its support and the strike was called off. Another widely publicized dispute between Newfoundland women and the federal bureaucracy occurred when "squidjigging" women were denied unemployment insurance benefits because government officials refused to believe that these women actually performed the heavy physical labour involved in the catching and preparation of squid. "Well, the men got their unemployment [benefits]," said Betty Burt, one of the leaders of the group, "and the women who had a man's name, such as Georgie, Frances, they got their money." When confronted by an angry deputation of "Squid Women," a Revenue Canada representative hastily declared that one of the women qualified for unemployment benefits — after he felt the muscles in her arm! In the end, about four-fifths of the women were deemed to qualify on the basis of their previous season's work, but the criteria for receiving unemployment benefits in subsequent years were made more restrictive.[46]

No government official would have doubted that it was women of all regions, classes, and ethnic origins who performed the bulk of domestic labour. Such work, however, continued to go largely unrecognized and unrewarded. Economists estimated that, were the unpaid services Canadian women provided in the home to be assigned a value, they would account for about one-third of the Gross National Product.[47] For housewives, there were none of the usual benefits of full-time employment — salary, vacation, sick leave, social security provisions—and, in spite of the introduction of labour-saving devices, the time women spent performing housework was not significantly reduced. While the work was not as physically taxing as it once was, the absence of full-time domestic help and constantly rising standards of performance intensified the homemaker's responsiblity for housework, and for consumption and family management. For many wives housework continued to be rendered more difficult by the fact that their husbands worked shifts, so that they had to juggle different schedules in order to accommodate the conflicting needs of husband, children, and household. As one Flin Flon, Manitoba wife explained:

Those changing shifts are awful. It's a constant reminder that his work comes first over any other needs this family might have. We can never get ourselves organized into any regular pattern because our lives are always being turned upside down.[48]

Even when women took on paid employment, they continued to perform most of the domestic labour. A Vancouver study conducted in the 1970s revealed that, in families with no children, husbands increased their contribution to household work an average of six minutes per week after their wives became employed; if there were children, the husbands averaged one hour more per week. Later studies also indicated that the wife still had the major responsibility for housework, despite a shift in public opinion in favour of sharing domestic duties between spouses. In 1981 seven out of ten Canadians indicated that husbands should share in housework, yet only slightly more than one in three women polled reported that men helped with housework on a regular basis.[49]

Through their childrearing and housekeeping, women continued to contribute directly to the functioning of the economy. They replenished the labour supply on a daily basis by attending to the physical needs of the workers, including preparing their meals and washing their clothes, and also on a long-term basis by giving birth to and raising the next generation of workers. It was their unpaid labour that permitted employers to pay lower wages than would have been required if workers had to purchase these services. The failure to include housewives' unpaid labour in calculations of the Gross National Product reflected the low value assigned to domestic work, and the low status women derived from it. Although home-makers' work involved many different skills acquired through years of experience, it was fragmented and easily interrupted, and considered low skilled. The under-valuation of women's work in the home, in turn, tended to depress their wages in the paid economy. Many of the positions women held in the workforce were viewed as similar to that of the housewife. A professional cook recounted that, as a woman, she was expected to do tasks men did not do: "If you're cooking in kitchens in big places and if you are working with men, men won't clean up. It's the women's job."[50] Furthermore, there was growing evidence that the home was not the relaxing, safe haven it has often been portrayed. Like other industrial workers, the woman working in the home had to contend with workplace hazards that in her case included stress, exposure to the pollutants and toxic substances in household cleaning products, and home accidents, which could be disabling.[51]

The economic consequences of the under-valuation of women's work, both at home and in the workplace, were only too evident. In 1986 six out of every ten families headed by female single parents under the age of sixty-five lived below the poverty line, compared to two out of ten headed by male single parents. The daily physical and emotional toll that these families experienced has been vividly described by a mother of three living on mother's allowance. She did not become a single parent by choice but was forced to leave an alcoholic and abusive husband, and resorted to mother's allowance only after she destroyed her own physical health working nights at the minimum wage.

I get behind on bills and we eat a lot of cheap meals. My kids wear second-hand clothing and ride second-hand bikes. They take a lot of abuse from other kids because of it. . . . We don't go out to movies or dinner or even to the Dairy Queen, it's just not in our budget.[52]

For half of the elderly, unattached women in Canada, poverty was also a way of life; seven out of every ten poor senior citizens were women. Statistics such as these led the National Council of Welfare to identify "the feminization of poverty" as a major social problem.[53] From 1969 to 1987, the jobless rate was usually higher among Canadian women than among men. Higher rates of female unemployment reflected the end of the rapid growth of clerical and service jobs, especially within the public sector, that occurred in the 1970s. Women's unemployment rate was undoubtedly higher than the official figures indicated because married women were often not counted as actively seeking work. Statistics Canada also distinguished between "unemployed" workers — those actively seeking work — and "discouraged" workers — those who had given up the search for jobs because they had abandoned hope of finding anything. In May 1987, there were some 94 000 discouraged workers in addition to the 1.3 million unemployed, and women made up proportionately more of the discouraged than they did of the unemployed.[54]

Women working for women

As awareness of their specific economic problems grew, so did the efforts of Canadian women to resolve them. In the workplace women increasingly used their collective strength to improve wages and working conditions, and to address other issues such as daycare and sexual harassment. After World War II, and especially after 1961, women increasingly became unionized — after 1971, more rapidly than men. Between 1965 and 1981, union membership more than tripled among female workers. Most of the increase occurred among public sector workers, a large proportion of whom were women. In 1980 nearly 68 percent of the female workers in public administration, which incorporated all levels of municipal, provincial, and federal government administration, were unionized. Women workers were also actively courted by large industrial unions such as the United Auto Workers (now the Canadian Auto Workers), and the United Steel Workers of America. These unions sought to maintain their numerical strength in the face of a shrinking manufacturing sector by organizing workers in the clerical and service sectors. However, overall, only one in four women workers was organized by 1980, compared to nearly half of all male workers.[55]

The division of the labour force along gender lines also resulted in different patterns of union membership for women and men. Whereas in 1980 the majority of male unionists belonged to international unions, only three out of ten female union members did. Nearly half of all unionized women were in national unions representing employees such as hospital workers and janitors. Predictably, within all unions women remained under-represented in top-level positions. However, they were relatively more successful in national and government unions, where they held 22 and 11.5 percent of the top positions respectively.[56] Of 106 executive board members representing American-based international unions, only four were women. On a more encouraging note, women's representation at the level of the local executives was growing.

In unions, special women's committees and women's caucuses were also influential in defining issues and developing policies of importance to women in relation to maternity leave, childcare, equal pay, occupational health and safety, sexual harassment, and the elimination of discrimination against women workers. The success of these groups was especially noteworthy within the militant, nationalist trade union movement in Quebec.[57] In 1979 Quebec unions were the first to succeed in obtaining paid maternity leave for their female members in place of the partially paid leave available under the federal Unemployment Insurance Plan. Federal post office workers received seventeen weeks of paid maternity leave as part of a strike settlement in 1981, over the opposition of the Treasury Board, which saw it as a precedent for federally employed workers; in fact, the clerical group, translators, home economists, and historical researchers for the federal government all negotiated the same agreement without strikes.[58] Trade union feminists were also successful in making connections across union boundaries by means of organizations such as Saskatchewan Working Women, Union Sisters in Vancouver, Organized Working Women in Ontario, and the Women's Bureau of the Canadian Labour Congress, and established ties to the broader-based contemporary women's movement.

Union women, both as leaders and rank–and–file activists, assumed a more visible role during the 1970s and 1980s. Textile organizers Madeleine Parent and Kent Rowley worked to establish the nationalist Canadian Confederation of Unions in 1969. Grace Hartman, a mother of two who began work as a typist in 1954 to help supplement the wages of her husband, rose through the ranks to become by 1985 the head of the largest national union, the Canadian Union of Public Employees. The links between the union movement and the women's movement were illustrated by Parent and Hartman, both of whom were actively involved with the National Action Committee on the Status of Women, the largest grouping of women's organizations in Canada. In fact, Hartman served as the first president of this new organization, founded in 1972. In 1986, another historic moment occurred when Shirley Carr became the first woman president of the influential Canadian Labour Congress. One year later Gwen Wolfe, a laboratory technologist, was the first woman to head a provincial labour organization in Atlantic Canada, when she became the president of the Nova Scotia Federation of Labour.

On the picket lines, by their determination and courage, militant rank–and–file women won a grudging new respect from their employers, and substantial public support. In a number of bitter strikes, characterized by employer intransigency and marred by picket-line violence, working women fought to improve their situation. Among the most well-known of these disputes were the 1981

On the picket line.

B.C. Telephone strike, the 1978 Fleck strike (Exeter, Ontario), the Radio Shack strike (Barrie, Ontario, 1979–80), and the Eaton's strike (six Ontario locations, 1984–85).[59] In these disputes, workers were seeking union recognition, first contracts, equal pay, and improved wages and working conditions. Each dispute lasted for several months, and each was a remarkable demonstration of women's solidarity, not only among the workers themselves but also within the women's movement. Women of many different social and ethnic backgrounds walked the picket lines with the strikers and gave them financial support. Frances Lankin underlined the importance of the "Women's Solidarity Picket" for the Fleck strike:

As we climbed aboard the yellow and black schoolbus we could feel the excitement. There was an electric charge in the air — the kind of thing that occurs when you sense something important is happening . . . the growing alliance between women's movement activists and trade union women activists was making an impression on the labour movement.

She noted with satisfaction that "Fleck was a woman's strike."[60] Women's solidarity pickets were also organized during the Radio Shack and Eaton's strikes, and additional support for the Eaton's workers was demonstrated on March 9, 1985 when the International Women's Day march made its way into Eaton's showplace store in downtown Toronto. During the Fleck and Radio Shack strikes, public support was also generated by managements' heavy-handed attempts to use strikebreakers and police to break the strikes. During the Fleck dispute, which lasted just over five months and involved 75 female strikers, 7000 police days were logged at a cost of over $2 million.[61]

Less dramatic but of equal significance were the first partially successful attempts to organize clerical and retail workers into small independent unions operating along feminist principles. In 1972 the Service, Office, and Retail Workers' Union of Canada (SORWUC) was created to organize workers in banks, offices, and restaurants, and subsequently made news by setting up unions in some bank branches. Unfortunately, SORWUC did not have the experience or financial resources necessary to wait out the lengthy periods involved in first-contract negotiation. In this instance, the interest of the women's movement and the trade union movement did not coalesce, since the Canadian Labour Congress opposed the independent union and was running its own organizational campaign among bank workers.[62] In the end, SORWUC was no match either for the nation's most powerful financial institutions or for its largest labour federation, and by 1978 many of its locals had been decertified.

In contrast, unionization made major inroads among professional women, especially nurses and teachers. In several provinces, they exchanged their goal of developing traditional professional associations in favour of trade union affiliation and a more militant approach. An important change occurred for teachers when membership in teachers' associations became compulsory. In Ontario, this requirement came into effect in 1944, and greatly enhanced the prestige and power of the Federation of Women Teachers' Associations of Ontario, which became the official bargaining unit for all female elementary teachers in the public school system. By the 1960s, the federation was playing a leading role in addressing issues of importance to all women, such as sex-role stereotyping and affirmative action. In the 1980s, the federation itself became the object of a precedent-setting case involving a Windsor elementary school principal, Margaret Tolmen, who challenged the provincial legislation requiring female and male teachers to belong to separate unions, invoking the Canadian Charter of Rights and Freedoms to support her request to join the male teachers' organization, the Ontario Public School Teachers' Federation. In 1987 a lower court ruling blocked amalgamation of the women's and men's associations, an objective actively pursued by the 14 000-member men teachers' organizations for more than two decades. The majority of the 33 000 women members of the Federation of Women Teachers' Associations were opposed to amalgamation, fearing that men would assume control of an integrated association and weaken the new feminist agenda.[63] On the other hand, female and male teachers in Quebec belonged to the same professional association, the *Centrale des Enseignants du Québec* (CEQ), one of the most militant of all teachers' organizations and one that has co-operated closely with other trade unionists in that province. The leftist orientation of CEQ undoubtedly enabled its women members to win support for a comprehensive and radical feminist agenda. Its call for equality extended well beyond the workplace, and included demands such as the recognition of a woman's right to decide if and when to have children, and the reorganization of housework along egalitarian lines.[64]

Business women also realized the benefits to be gained from mutual support; new organizations such as the Canadian Association of Women Executives and Entrepreneurs, and directories such as Montreal's *Bottin des femmes* emerged to facilitate networking among their members. Contacts between women in the corporate and business world were extremely important because women often lacked the role models and mentors that male executives have found so important. As one female vice-president commented, "There's still that old-boys' network when you're reaching above middle management."[65]

Finally, during the 1970s and 1980s — as earlier — working class women played an important role in supporting the men in their families during the trying circumstances of prolonged strikes. When the workers at INCO in Sudbury went on strike in 1979, a group of local feminists and workers' wives set up a special committee to support the strikers by mobilizing community resources and promoting solidarity among the workers' families. Like the traditional union ladies' auxiliaries, "Women Supporting the Strike" organized clothing drives, community dinners, and Christmas parties for the strikers' families. They also raised money and travelled widely to win public support for the strikers. However, unlike its predecessors, the wives' committee sought to assert its financial and political autonomy from the union, an objective that led to frequent tension within the committee itself and with the striking local of the United Steelworkers of America. The wives' committee not only demonstrated the importance of mobilizing women's support for the strike, but also underlined the connections between wage work and domestic work by demonstrating the extent to which women were directly affected by the strike. Cathy Mulroy, a woman who worked in the INCO plant, reported with admiration the way "the wives of workers got together":

I liked that these women were interested in what their husbands were doing. I went to a meeting about bargaining, and these women were at the door giving out pamphlets saying "come to the bean supper." . . . This man behind me says to one of the women, "What are you doing here? You have no business in the union hall." I turned around and said, "Of course they have. They're on strike just like their husbands are. They're going to have to go through a lot too."

Mulroy was invited to the wives' group and found "it was exciting! All these women. Really huffing and puffing. Now *this* was a union meeting."[66] After the strike was successfully concluded, several of the women involved in the wives' committee become active in the local women's movement. The experience of the Sudbury wives was very useful to the women who formed the "United Miners' Wives Association" during the 1981 miners' strike in Cape Breton. Once again it was striking workers' wives and local feminists who organized to represent women's interests. As in Sudbury, the activities of the wives' group had a transforming effect at both an individual and a collective level. As one participant pointed out, it "seemed like a new thing, women holding a bake sale to raise money to send themselves, not their husbands, to the Labour Day rally in Sydney."[67]

But it was not new, merely part of the tradition of Canadian women helping themselves as well as others. Women of all classes now increasingly combined forces to pressure governments into moving in the direction of affirmative action and pay equity schemes, and employers into first contracts and the elimination of discriminatory practices. The resolution and creativity of individual working women, both in the home and at the workplace, the growing collective strength of women workers, and their involvement in the contemporary women's movement gave them a firmer base for the continuing struggle.

16 "The personal is political"

In the 1970s, many women reacted to the women's movement slogan, "the personal is political," by beginning a painstaking and often painful reappraisal of their own attitudes and those of the people around them. The result was a more or less formal "consciousness-raising" that showed that women's difficulties were not the result of individual bad luck or incompetence, but shared by others. A personal awareness of women's subordination was often sparked by the most routine and unlikely incidents. One woman recalled a group of women "checking neurotic hostess reflexes when a male dinner guest complains there are no serviettes on the table: knuckles white with the effort not to jump up when he could more easily reach them, we mystify him with roars of laughter at our shared struggle."[1]

For many women, an enhanced consciousness led them to work for a public and political response to their personal situation. As a result, there was an amazing proliferation of pressure and service organizations set up by different groups of women, often not consciously feminist, but all concerned to provide voices, places, activities, and support for women. This process accelerated towards the end of the 1970s as many women who had been members of more ideological and change-oriented groups shifted to direct action with and for women. These actions, and the many changes they provoked, demonstrate the impact of the women's movement.

Bodies and language

In 1986 the highly acclaimed Quebec film, *Le Déclin de l'Empire Américain*, showed its women characters running, swimming, and weight-lifting with the trendy Nautilus machines, while the men cooked; both groups talked obsessively about the pleasures and dangers of sex. The image of the attractive female was increasingly athletic, and women of all sorts turned enthusiastically to fitness classes and health clubs. Some analysts took this positively, linking it to women's liberating themselves from the confining clothes, images, and attitudes of earlier times; others interpreted it more pessimistically as the co-option of feminism by commercialism, capitalism, patriarchy, or all three.[2] Even the most optimistic had to recognize the continuing emphasis on a standard of beauty that was unattainable for most women.

The insistence on femininity continued, even if its forms changed. The mini-skirts of the late 1960s and early 1970s were followed by an unsuccessful attempt to promote maxi-skirts. Women in business were at first steered into a sort of uniform that directed attention away from their gender. "Any time you look 'sweet' and 'pretty', you are in trouble," said one authoritative source that also told women executives: "Don't wear anything that jingles, wiggles, clanks, or glitters. Executive insignia are silent, understated, and unobtrusive — never sexy."[3] But by the 1980s, career women had largely abandoned their bowed ties and their mannish suits for dresses and high fashion. More generally, requirements of conformity in women's dress relaxed by the 1980s to a degree that the permanent-waved, girdled, and nylon-stockinged woman of the 1950s would not have expected.

The emphasis on visible physical fitness, however, was related to new sorts of clothes, which were often unstructured and unlined, and therefore clinging, or cut revealingly high at the thighs or low at the neck and armhole. All were expected to be worn without assistance from the substantial foundation garments that had helped earlier generations of women to conform to a womanly ideal. In these years, the quest for the perfect body became obsessive for many women. Anorexia or self-starvation became a serious health hazard, especially for younger women, and was paired with a new disease, bulimia, characterized by binge-eating between compulsive dieting, purges, and self-induced vomiting. Fat women were treated as if they were diseased, and were made to feel like outcasts; in the 1970s, a movement for Fat Liberation announced that "fat is a feminist issue."[4]

Among feminists, views about dress and bodily adornment changed. Women's liberation had insisted on a militant uniform of jeans or overalls and work boots, arguing that make-up or jewellery meant acceptance of sex stereotyping. In the 1970s and 1980s, women began to work out notions about the relationship between self-respect and the esthetics of adornment. The goal should be to please one's self and those one cared for, an expression of autonomy.

The quest for autonomy also led women to challenge what they identified as sexist language. Questions of naming and the related ones of language were not trivial, though feminists were often chided for their attention to them. They were an aspect of women's personal and economic independence, since a woman labelled "Mrs." had customarily been denied access to financial services and credit in her own right. Questions of titles reflected and legitimized the growing diversity of marital and "common law" arrangements. Many were uneasy at the indeterminacy of the term "Ms," now increasingly used to address a woman formally without identifying her relationship to a man, but by the 1970s even banks and department stores were permitting Ms on accounts and credit cards.

In general, there was growing sensitivity to the role of sexist language in reflecting and perpetuating notions of women's inferiority. Public organizations responded more quickly than private ones; the federal government adopted regulations about avoiding stereotypes in language in 1982; in 1986, after great pressure from feminists, the renovated Museum of Man was renamed the Museum of Civilization. In English, linguistic sexism could be reduced by using impersonal substitutes such as "letter carrier" for "postman." In French, the problems were admittedly more difficult, as all nouns were gendered and so were many other parts of speech. In suggesting terms such as *"auteure"* and *"professeure,"* Quebec feminists were inventive and influential, even more so than those in France from whom they adapted important ideas about the role of language in the construction of patriarchy.[5]

In Quebec, women's maiden names, which feminists preferred to call birth names, were established in 1980 as their continuing legal ones even after marriage; at the same time, women were granted long overdue rights in relation to their children. In addition, children's surnames could henceforth be a range of choices and combinations between the names of the legally declared father and mother. In the common-law provinces, the question of women's and children's names was more complex. There had not been any legal requirement previously that women adopt their husbands' names, though a powerful array of expectations and policies pretty much obliged them to do so. It was not until the 1980s that the provinces gradually began to move on this issue.

Sexuality and health

In the 1970s women became aware that "sexual liberation" had been less than satisfactory: the established patterns of male initiative and domination in sexual matters were difficult to counter. Younger women continued to be sexually active at a very young age, an age that decreased along with the age of puberty.[6] A related problem was the increasing population of very young prostitutes, mostly girls, who appeared in Canada's major cities.[7] In the 1980s specific physical hazards emerged as a result of the new sexual freedom. The number of sexually transmitted diseases expanded, and affected women particularly severely. The old curses of syphilis and gonorrhea were now more easily diagnosed and treated, but infectious diseases such as genital herpes, chlamydia, and pelvic infectious disease (PID) were increasingly recognized as threats, likely to interfere with women's fertility, and likely also to be transmitted to children. By the middle of the decade, acquired immune deficiency syndrome (AIDS) appeared, with no known cure. Condoms, now technically much improved, had a revived popularity as prophylactics, but the use of the Pill had encouraged aversion to them.

The new forms of birth control led men to expect that women would take responsibility for contraception. But the available choices for women were inadequate.[8] Although the Pill was now available with smaller doses of hormones, its side-effects ranged from depression and obesity to such potentially fatal conditions as blood clots and heart disease. The concentration of the more serious conditions among certain high risk groups such as heavy smokers was little comfort: by 1981 young women aged fifteen to nineteen were smoking as much as men of the same age.[9] In any case, many women distrusted such substantial chemical intervention in their bodies over a period of fertility that could be as long as thirty years. The use of the intra-uterine device (IUD) had also proved to be dangerous, sometimes producing ectopic pregnancy, and even sterility. Tubal ligation was still a surgical operation involving a hospital stay; in Quebec in 1976, it was used twice as frequently as the far simpler vasectomy for sterilizing men, which could be carried out in a doctor's office.[10] Many doctors and hospitals continued to require the husband's or father's consent to female sterilization as well as for abortion, even though the law made no such requirement. As part of doctors' resistance in 1986 to the nation-wide ban on charging patients more than the medical plan fees, Alberta physicians insisted on exacting additional fees for the requisite letters to make a case for an abortion to hospital abortion-assessment committees.[11] Progress on the development of a male contraceptive was unnoticeable. In reaction, some women returned to such earlier contraceptive contrivances as sponges, diaphragms, or douches.

Inadequate medical responses to sexually transmitted disease or contraception could be seen as countered by the vast leap in potential solutions to infertility. But this also meant an increase in medical control of women's bodies, as researchers learned how to flush out human eggs, fertilize them outside the body (*in vitro*), and implant them, sometimes in a different woman's womb. Canada's 100th test tube baby was born in 1987. This and other related processes were costly, and were subject to decisions by doctors on who were "fit" subjects for the procedures. The new reproductive technology alarmed feminists by its implications for treatment of the female body as a "baby-making" machine. In the context of problems related to women's status, artifical insemination assumed an importance far in excess of its frequency: it was the one reproductive technology amenable to self-help.[12] By the 1980s, some lesbians had conceived in this way with the assistance of male friends. Such cases separated sexuality and reproduction in the most extreme way yet, and also seemed to reassert women's claim to define the identity of both children and families. As lesbianism became more public and dissociated itself from male homosexuality, key questions related to sexuality and to family composition were raised again from a different perspective. One lesbian attempted to designate her partner and her partner's children as dependents; the Canadian Union of Public Employees supported the effort, and the lesbian couple obtained some of the contractual benefits available to common-law couples. In 1987 lesbians were still seeking other benefits, such as access to medical and insurance plans.[13]

Women's increased autonomy was more widely expressed in demands for less mechanized childbearing and childrearing. The use of forceps and total anesthesia were no longer seen as the ideals of "modern" childbirth. Experiments with less alienating forms of delivery were very influential, and were expounded by lay as well as medically trained practitioners. In the 1960s, women welcomed partial anesthesia such as spinal blocks, which left them conscious of the birthing process and able to apply the lessons of the widely attended pre-natal classes held for both mothers and fathers. By the next decade, fathers were encouraged to assist in labour and delivery; babies were allowed to be bigger and less fragile; babies staying in their mothers' hospital rooms had become a routine practice in hospitals. And by the 1980s, a small but significant number of women were opting for home births or childbirth without medication.

After birth, conditions had also improved. The energetic efforts of La Leche League helped promote breast-feeding as the preferred form of infant feeding, at least for the first few months. Disposable diapers and bottle-liners, as well as better formulas and baby food, made childcare easier, and so did a relaxation of the insistence on either total permissiveness or complete regimentation in childcare. Dr. Spock, remarried and a peace activist, issued a new, more flexible, and less sexist edition of his book. The ancient profession of midwifery, now accepted in all industrialized areas except North America, began to be revived; in 1987 an Ontario taskforce headed by feminist lawyer Mary Eberts recommended a system of licencing.[14]

The reassertions of traditional, woman-controlled patterns in medicine and family life should not be exaggerated. The percentage of births by Caesarean section actually increased in the period between 1970 to 1981, rising from 6 percent to just under 15 percent.[15] The cause was probably in part the increased use and efficiency of new fetal monitoring devices, which could show when infants were in distress; feminists were convinced that the causes also included doctors' convenience and their fear of malpractice suits. The large majority of births, like deaths, continued to take place in hospitals.

Furthermore, in a period when most women still completed their families before the age of thirty, "older" pregnant women provoked increased medical supervision, and doctors warned about the risk of abnormalities such as Down's Syndrome. Doctors tended to see the age of thirty as a cut-off for safe conception, though even women over forty had only approximately one chance in sixty of bearing a chromosomally abnormal child.[16] Amniocentesis became routine for pregnant women over thirty, as well as ultra-sound tests, internal and external fetal monitoring during birth, and an even higher incidence of Caesareans than for younger women. Women accordingly acquired a whole new range of anxieties and stresses, beginning with the feeling of a "biological clock" ticking away during childless years, and continuing through agonizing decisions about whether or not to abort an abnormal fetus. The biological impact of older fathers was overlooked in the discussions, which in effect put all the blame on women. Wendy Lill, who had a Down's Syndrome child when she was thirty-four, wrote angrily, "Instead of buying the theory about maternal age hook, line and sinker, I think we should be demanding more investigation on links between radiation, environmental pollutants, and all sorts of birth defects. . . . "[17]

The medical profession in general persisted in treating menopause as a medical problem requiring treatment by hormones. The recognition of premenstrual syndrome as a genuine medical problem was a mixed blessing, as it once again stigmatized women as physiologically defective. Even in the 1980s, women continued to be prescribed tranquillizers far more often than men.[18]

The women's movement responded to medical and political indifference to women's wishes by setting up women's clinics or health centres where women could diagnose and treat themselves, as well as carrying out preventive activities. All across the country, in small communities as well as large urban centres, they established "well women clinics." In Yarmouth, Nova Scotia, 500 women led by three nurses founded a Well-Women and Health Awareness Association in 1977. Sixty volunteers were able to operate no less than twelve separate services, including sex education and support for breast feeding.[19] These, along with rape crisis centres and support for battered or homeless women, were created and staffed by women who wished, by the mid-1970s, to move from consciousness raising to some more concrete activity. Many feminists felt that the services provided by such groups should be provided by the state, and as the 1970s and 1980s progressed, governments did indeed begin to provide more funds and facilities. The results were not entirely positive, since government support often entailed women losing control over projects they had initiated. Government involvement could also be seen, cynically, as a way of avoiding a more basic commitment to ongoing change in the situation of the women who were victims of violence and poverty. On the other hand, it could be viewed as linked to a greater awareness of women's problems, as well as to a wider public interest in health and well-being. Certainly, the initiatives of individual women as well as groups of women remained crucial.

Personal action

Native women were among the first to mount campaigns on their own behalf. The most active seem to have been Iroquois women, who reasserted their ancient right to participate in policy making, invoking "the matriarchal roots of the Six Nations Iroquois Confederacy."[20] Two contrasting cases were those of Mary Two-Axe Early and Kahn-Tineta Horn, both Mohawks from the Caughnawaga reserve in Quebec. Early, a widow, was barred from the home she inherited on the reserve because her late husband was not a status Indian. This was the effect of the notorious clause 12(1)(b) of the Indian Act, which gave Indian status to wives and children of Indian men, but denied it to Indian women marrying non-status men. The children of the latter were also classified as non-status. The Royal Commission on the Status of Women had criticized this as "a special kind of discrimination," and as early as 1968, Mohawk wives of non-status husbands organized under Early's leadership a group called Indian Rights for Indian Women.[21]

Most activist Indian women felt serious conflicts as they attempted to assert their claims. Was it not a denial of cultural autonomy to appeal to white women and the white men's government over the heads of their own native leaders? Nevertheless, groups of native women managed to develop an acceptable rationale for organizing separately. Feeling that "nothing would get done" until they organized, one group initiated "*Anishinabequek* [Indian women] locals in the communities. [They] had tea parties, bannock-making sessions, knitting sessions and beading sessions. Women started talking, not about their beading designs, but about what was happening in their families and in other families in the community."[22] This process produced the Ontario Native Women's Association, founded in 1972 with its headquarters in Thunder Bay, and including Métis or mixed-blood and non-status Indian women as well as status women. Sexist components of the Indian Act, they argued, came from white legislators attempting to assimilate the native population, rather than from native men: "Aboriginal women must provide the direction that encourages the Nation's warriors to respond as is appropriate to protect our children. . . . "[23]

The statement made by the Ontario Native Women's Association was a reminder that native women organized not just for their own entitlement, but also in an attempt to deal concretely with problems like disease and alcoholism, the assimilationist system of education that shipped children off reserves and ignored native traditions, and attitudes towards health care that condemned tubercular or pregnant native persons to long hospital sessions away from home. Groups with similar goals included the Indian Homemakers of British Columbia, Paktuutit (Inuit Women's Association), and the Nova Scotia Native Women's Association, founded by Micmac women.

Other Indian women chose to act within the existing male-dominated Indian organizations. Prominent among those was Kahn-Tineta Horn. Articulate and impassioned, she focussed on the need for her race to reproduce, and consequently she opposed not just inter-racial marriage, but also birth control and abortion. In 1971 Horn urged Indian groups to appeal to the Supreme Court of Canada against a Federal Appeal Court decision restoring Indian status to Jeannette Corbière Lavell from the Wikwemikong Band in Ontario. In 1973 the Supreme Court of Canada confirmed that Lavell had forfeited her status by marrying a white man; the same decision was given in the case of Yvonne Bédard, who had attempted to return to the Six Nations Reserve after a failed marriage to a non-Indian. The Supreme Court found that Indian women were entitled only to "equality in administration and enforcement of the law." The Bill of Rights enacted in 1960 did not forbid "inequality within a group or class by itself, by reason of sex."[24]

With the court route blocked, Indian women who had lost their status turned to other approaches, including lobbying, sit-ins, and appealing to international organizations. The most widely publicized case was that of Sandra Lovelace of the Tobique Reserve in New Brunswick. After camping out on the reserve with her small son, she joined a three-month occupation of the band office by Indian women trying to draw attention to the hardships faced by non-status Indian women, and finally took her case to the United Nations Human Rights Committee. In spite of the publicity and public pressure generated by a native Women's Walk to Ottawa in July 1979, the Canadian government was unresponsive. In 1981 the UN Committee found the Canadian government in breach of the International Covenant on Civil and Political Rights.[25]

The Canadian government, reluctant to provoke the hostility of Indian band leaders, professed itself helpless. Band membership had significant economic and political implications; along with the rights that came with Indian status—residence on the reserve, free medical treatment, and free education—band membership entailed the right to a share in what were sometimes substantial resources, as well as a voice in native self-government.[26] In 1981 the government gave permission to individual Indian bands to request that subsection 12(1)(b) not apply to them; by February 1984, only ninety-five of the 577 Indian bands in Canada had made that request. In 1987 the process of re-integrating women into the reserves was still lagging, although a 1985 law had repealed the offending clauses of the Indian Act.[27]

For most Canadian women, the problems of women like Early, Lavell, Bédard, and Lovelace were fairly remote even if they showed the inadequacy of the 1960 Bill of Rights. In contrast, the case of Irene Murdoch aroused considerable attention. Murdoch was an Alberta farm wife who could represent all wives who worked only "in the home." On the breakdown of her marriage in 1968, a violent event during which her jaw was broken, she claimed a share of the family ranch on the basis of her contributions to it. The Supreme Court, with future Chief Justice Bora Laskin dissenting, denied her claim. Urban feminists were stunned to learn that Murdoch's work included "haying, raking, swathing, mowing, driving trucks and tractors and teams, quietening horses, taking cattle back and forth to the reserve, dehorning, vaccinating, branding," and that she even ran the ranch for about five months out of each year. The courts, like the Murdochs, felt that Irene did the work of "any ranch wife." But they did not feel that such work "would give any farm or ranch wife a claim in partnership."[28]

In 1973 Murdoch was finally granted a lump-sum maintenance payment, but it implied no recognition of her role in the economic unit of the household. The assumptions of the law were manifest: women were entitled to support during marriage and to appropriate maintenance after its break-up, for a return obligation of domestic duties and sexual availability on an exclusive basis for the duration of the marriage. The Murdoch case helped to alter both law and

A demonstration in support of native women's rights.

attitudes about family property, for it mobilized women and women's groups to press for change. Beginning in 1977 with Manitoba, most provinces approved legislation giving concrete recognition to the fact that domestic activities, usually carried on by women, were what made it possible for wage earners to acquire money and property for the family. The new Ontario Family Law Reform Act (1978) stated that "child care, household management and financial provision" were "the joint responsibility of the spouses." In addition it declared that the marital relationship entailed a "joint contribution, whether financial or otherwise, by the spouses . . . entitling each spouse to an equal division of the family assets."[29] The revised version of this law, passed in 1986, explicitly classified business assets accumulated by members of a household during marriage as joint property resulting in part from the domestic activities still usually performed by women.

The new legislation on family property thus embodied the feminist insistence that domestic work was as valuable as public work. What was not yet fully accepted, in either attitudes or law, was the combination of family and public responsibilities by the same person. In the 1980s, men raising children alone were still considered ineligible for the sort of welfare payments made to women in the same circumstances, while only a fraction of childcare expenses were allowed as part of the legitimate expenses of mothers working outside the home. Nor was paid paternity leave yet generally available. In 1987 a Toronto man whose wife had just given birth complained to the Canadian Human Rights Commission because he was not granted time off with pay to help with his fourth child. "I was told by my employer that men cannot biologically get pregnant," said Tom Lenathen, a 41-year-old mechanic. "I told him I was quite relieved to hear that, but I needed leave."[30]

Politics

It was issues such as these that motivated activist women to seek direct involvement in the formulation of public policy. Governments continued to be unimaginative about people's lives; perhaps it was partly because of the relative absence of women in decision-making positions. Although there were no longer legal barriers to women's holding office, expectations continued to be against it. In 1966 a publication of the Department of Citizenship and Immigration stated flatly that "winter weather is a limiting factor [to Canadian women's political activity] as well as household duties and farm chores."[31] When the Royal Commission on the Status of Women was set up, there were only two women in the House of Commons, plus four more in the Senate. After the resignation of Liberal MP and cabinet minister Judy LaMarsh in 1968, New Democrat Grace MacInnis was for four years the only woman in the House. As late as 1975, a national survey showed Canadians tending to believe that "the average man" would make a better politician than the "average woman."[32] But 1972 was a turning point: Progressive Conservative Flora MacDonald and Liberals Jeanne Sauvé, Albanie Morin, and Monique Bégin were elected to join MacInnis. MacInnis retired in 1974; Morin died in 1976; Bégin, MacDonald, and Sauvé all became cabinet ministers, holding among them some very powerful ministries that were not conventionally female. Sauvé also became the first women to be Speaker of the House and then governor general, in 1980 and 1984 respectively. The Parliament of 1974 was modestly encouraging; all the women who ran for re-election were returned, and five more women, all Liberals, were added. A steady increase at by-elections and regular elections meant a total of fourteen women sitting in the 1980 Parliament.[33]

At the same time, feminism emerged as an issue in the *Parti québécois* referendum about a new constitutional arrangement for *souveraineté-association*. Lise Payette, Quebec Minister Responsible for the Status of Women, well-known broadcaster and committed independentist, caused a commotion early in 1980 by accusing *Québécoises* who opposed independence of being "Yvettes." Yvette and Guy were the Dick and Jane of Quebec schoolbooks, and Payette used the name to stand for the traditional submissive wife-and-mother who does what her husband and father tell her. Women's groups, headed by women in the Quebec Liberal party, responded vigorously, organizing first a lunch, and then a series of public meetings, ending with a vast one in the Montreal Forum. There, more than 14 000 women cheered federalist and feminist women such as Monique Bégin and Thérèse Casgrain, who talked about the role of women in building Quebec and Canada, and the way future generations in Quebec would benefit from federally provided opportunities and social services. Polls showed a significant shift in women's votes, and analysts agreed that women were largely responsible for the 10 percent victory of federalism in the referendum.[34]

Many interpreted the whole episode as a rejection of feminism in favour of traditional values, while others saw it as a manipulation of women by the Liberal party. A third interpretation was that women had made a rational policy choice related to their own interests. One Quebec feminist described "the movement of 'Yvettes' " as the symbol of a major shift in the feminist movement:

The image of the emancipation of women by paid labour and by incorporation into the capitalist system gives way to revaluing traditional feminine activities. The housewife reappears as a central figure in the women's movement, not as a symbol of oppression as had been the case in the 1970s but as a role to revalue/re-evaluate in all senses of the term.[35]

During the referendum, the federal government had promised redress of Quebec's persistent grievances about the structure of Confederation; after the defeat of sovereignty-association, the government accordingly pressed for a reformulated and "patriated" Constitution. The Constitution proposed by the federal government included a Charter of Rights and Freedoms as well as, for the first time, a formal judicial review of law in terms of basic principles. As many cases, including those of Bliss, Lavell, Bédard, and Murdoch, had shown, the 1960 Bill of Rights was virtually useless. It was clear by the end of the 1970s that, generally speaking, unequal laws would be upheld by the courts, the only remedy being the slow process of legislative change. Women's organizations reacted with enthusiasm to the suggestion that women's rights to equality might be enshrined in fundamental law. Individual legislative or administrative acts could then be challenged directly and possibly ruled unacceptable.

The 1980–81 campaign for the inclusion of women's rights in the Constitution became a landmark similar to the Persons' Case of 1929, an icon of feminist effectiveness. According to a feminist journalist, "A political earthquake occurred in Canada in 1981, dramatically changing the foundation for government policy making."[36] The reality, while important, was less clear cut. In 1980 women's organizations, including NAC and a large number of its member groups, made detailed presentations during the public hearings on the proposed Constitution, focussing particularly on the Charter of Rights and Freedoms. The legislative committee's co-chairman, Senator Harry Hays, provoked feminist ire when he asked plaintively who would take care of the children while "you girls" were out running the country.[37] When NAC delegates were able to meet with the Minister Responsible for the Status of Women, Lloyd Axworthy, in the fall of 1980, they were told to "trust" him. The federal Advisory Council on the Status of Women prepared full and useful documentation, and organized a mailing of tear-offs supporting entrenchment of strong equality clauses in the Constitution. In January 1981, Justice Minister Jean Chrétien announced in response that Article 15 of the Charter was now to read as follows: "Every individual is equal before and under the law and has the right to equal protection of the law and equal benefit of the law."[38] The experience of many women was behind that seemingly clumsy formulation, which attempted to ensure not just that laws were equally enforced, but also that they would have no discriminatory provisions, and no discriminatory impact.

Then, in a confused flurry, the National Conference on Women and the Constitution, scheduled for February, 1987 by the federal Advisory Council on the Status of Women, was cancelled. The council's chair, Doris Anderson, resigned dramatically with the charge that the cancellation had been ordered by Lloyd Axworthy. Her vice president, Lucie Pépin of the *Fédération des femmes du Québec*, assumed the presidency, and announced that the conference would take place in May. But a small group of feminists moved in as an ad hoc committee to hold the conference as scheduled. They surprised themselves and many others by holding, in February 1981, without government funding, a successful three-day meeting of some 1300 women from across Canada. Anderson's resignation, followed by bitter accusations and counter-accusations attracted enormous publicity, as did the counter-conference.[39] Feminist journalists such as Michele Landsberg and Penney Kome helped turn the affair into a national issue.

At its 1981 annual general meeting, NAC, which had previously been divided in its views about the charter, voted to support the ad hoc conference's resolutions, including its final call for Lloyd Axworthy's resignation and a public investigation of the federal Advisory Council on the Status of Women. Supporting Pépin, the *Fédération des femmes du Québec* left the meeting and NAC, as it had earlier threatened to do; provincial rights were also at issue, since Quebec had not given approval to the patriated constitution.[40] Then, in April, after continued lobbying by members of the ad hoc committee, the guarantees of equality in Article 15 were backed up by Article 28, which stated that "Notwithstanding anything in this Charter, the rights and freedoms referred to in it are guaranteed equally to male and female persons."

That fall, a federal–provincial conference bypassed Quebec to work out an "override" arrangement that would allow provinces to pass special, limited-term legislation in any area, "notwithstanding" any guarantees in the Charter. So little importance was attached to the special provision of Article 28 that it was not even discussed, and only several days later was it clear that the override applied to that section also. "This ill-conceived decision led to an explosion of all-party political activity, the likes of which I've never seen before," wrote Sheila Copps, an Ontario MPP at the time. Describing one of the many rallies that helped to mobilize public response, she reported:

The room was packed. . . . Were we going to sit back and allow a couple

*of male premiers to railroad through a constitution which denied basic
equality to the majority of people in our country? . . . That night, telegrams
went out, hotline shows buzzed, letters were sent, phones rang.*[41]

In their opposition to the override, NAC and the federal Advisory
Council on the Status of Women under Pépin were in agreement
with the newly appointed Minister Responsible for the Status of
Women, Judy Erola, the first woman to hold the position. So were
the many women's groups and individual women already sensitized
by the previous events surrounding the Constitution. The ad hoc
committee once more served as a rallying point and, with the help
of provincial groups, including advisory councils on the status of
women, and a massive public pressure campaign of telegrams and
phone calls, the provincial premiers were finally persuaded to exempt
Article 28 from the override. Feminists were jubilant.

But Marilou McPhedran, a well-known feminist lawyer who
played an important role in the ad hoc committee, summed up the
results as follows: "To make any lasting change you have to participate in the workings of the institution and that's *not* what the ad
hoc committee did; we assaulted the institution and forced it to
respond."[42] Many women felt pride for precisely that reason: the
assault, the assumption and use of power, and the visible, if limited
success — even if the process of long-term institutional change was
far from finished. Only an accumulation of court decisions would
settle what articles 15 and 28 of the Charter really meant. A certain
number of the more egregiously sexist items of law and public policy
were modified in anticipation of Charter obligations: in 1985, Bill
C-31 removed the Indian Act clauses that deprived Indian women
of their status upon marriage to non-status men. In 1987 the Canadian armed forces dropped their bar on the participation of women
in combat roles, and in 1988 the Supreme Court of Canada invoked
section 7 of the Charter—on the rights to life, liberty, and security
of person—to invalidate the federal law on abortion.

For the 1984 federal election, NAC pulled off the considerable
coup of sponsoring a nationally televised debate on women's issues
among the leaders of the three major parties. Ed Broadbent looked
like the winner as he presented the NDP's progressive positions on
issues such as day care. In contrast, the debate provoked from the
leaders of the Liberals and the Progressive Conservatives a frantic
effort to make sure that women would not be able to distinguish
between the parties. Chaviva Hošek, president of NAC, commented
diplomatically that "the leaders were better briefed then ever before.
We saw real discussion of women's issues."[43]

Parties did run more women candidates; after the election,
twenty-seven women were in the House—almost 10 percent of the
members. Of these women, six were awarded cabinet positions. By
this time virtually all women were being elected as candidates in their
own right; after 1964 only two women were elected as political
"widows." Younger women began to be elected, and Sheila Copps

provided two landmarks for women in Parliament: she was the first woman member of Parliament to get married and have a baby while in office. Feminist political scientists had already concluded that the main barrier to the increase of women in elective office was the difficulty of access to winnable ridings.[44] Most of the increase in women MPs in 1984 came from Conservative women who had been run in Quebec ridings where their party had not expected victory.

Moreover, there was clearly still a "glass ceiling" for women attempting to acquire a real share in power. Flora MacDonald, the popular MP from Kingston and the Islands, former secretary of the Conservative party, had been overwhelmingly defeated in an attempt at the party's leadership in 1976. Although public opinion polls had shown that 86 percent of the public would be willing to vote for a party with a woman leader, it was quite clear that MacDonald's sex had been a major element in her defeat.[45] As late as 1984, the Petroleum Club in Calgary showed the depth of male unwillingness to share power: Energy Minister Pat Carney was refused entry to the main dining room and bar because she was a woman. In 1986 the club reaffirmed its policy.[46]

At provincial and municipal levels, women had somewhat more success. Women headed provincial parties on occasion, and served as mayors of cities and towns, as well as increasing their representation on city councils and school boards. Ottawa had a succession of women mayors, and in 1987 May Cutler was elected to run Quebec's upper class suburb of Westmount. Cutler, who had become Canada's first woman publisher when she founded Tundra Books, was a newcomer to politics; she attributed her stunning victory to the support of Westmount's "tenants, small businessmen, feminists, and dog owners." She epitomized the sort of concerns that continued to make women active in municipal and local politics.[47]

Although the number of women lawyers continued to increase, women were not numerous or influential in the courts. Only in 1982 was Bertha Wilson appointed to the Supreme Court, to be followed four years later by Claire L'Heureux-Dubé; in 1987 Alice Desjardins was the first woman appointed to the Federal Appeals Court. But feminist activity concerning legal matters continued. Lawyers active in the National Association of Women and the Law, and in the constitutional struggle, organized an ambitious legal aid fund dedicated to fighting significant cases: the Legal Education and Action Fund (LEAF) was granted substantial funds by the province of Ontario. LEAF began by adopting a limited number of causes important for advancing the status of women, including girls' access to all sports organized for boys, the man–in–the–house rule as applied to welfare mothers, and cessation of sterilization of mentally handicapped girls.[48] In 1987 an analyst in the *Canadian Journal of Political Science* noted admiringly that "the best organized interest group use of the Charter has been mounted by Canadian feminists." Referring to the constitutional battles and to LEAF, he wrote that "More than any other interest group . . . Canadian feminists have done their homework and are now poised to use Charter litigation to advance their policy objectives."[49]

"We're not feminists but . . . "

In a variety of settings, women continued to organize to bring about fundamental change. Many of them rejected identification with feminism or with the women's movement, but their actions often belied their words. Women's caucuses or committees attached to mixed-sex institutions such as unions and churches represented one form of collective action. Such groups multiplied in the 1970s and 1980s, as did a new generation of separate women's organizations. For example, in 1973 members of the Canadian Women's Negro Association called together the first national Conference of Black Women. After seven years of annual meetings, they formed the Canadian Congress of Black Women "to provide a network of solidarity for Black Women in Canada, and to be a united voice in the defence and extension of human rights and liberties for Blacks in Canada." According to Dr. Dorothy Wills, the featured speaker at the fifth conference of the group, "Black Women must continue to remember . . . and to relive the slave and peasant experience of [their] ancestors."[50]

Some of the new groups represented the first attempts at self-expression by particular groups of women. Prostitutes organized to resist police harassment: since selling sex was not illegal but soliciting was, their demand was the right to work under conditions where violence, criminal exploitation, and the recruitment of under-age women could be controlled. Wives of the Canadian military organized to claim the right simply to meet and discuss their needs, a right denied under the blanket prohibition of political activity on armed forces property. Farm women organized to express their concern about the decline of the family farm and their own uncertain role in agricultural production. Immigrant women organized to obtain better facilities for language training and work. On both local and national levels, the 1970s and 1980s also saw new groups of native women, unemployed women, domestics, welfare mothers, lesbians and lesbian mothers, disabled women, and many others who felt the need to organize on their own.

While a major part of women's collective action focussed on entering and influencing existing institutions, there were also deliberate efforts to create environments where women could be free of male presence and influence; one commentator called them "liberated territory."[51] Women's centres in universities became visible in the middle of the 1970s, often in association with the new Women's Studies programs then emerging, but universities were reluctant to accept the notion that women needed a place of their own. As late as 1987, the student government at the University of Toronto cancelled its financial contribution to the Women's Centre because the centre's board did not include any men.[52]

The same time period also saw the beginning of a wide variety of community-based centres. In British Columbia, native and white women in Burns Lake worked together to design a centre. The Fraser Lake Women's Centre was represented on town and council planning committees, and active in providing mental health services, and speakers, courses, and counselling for women. Thunder Bay women established the Northern Women's Centre, the Thunder Bay Physical and Sexual Abuse Centre, the Faye Peterson Transition Home, and *The Northern Women's Journal* — all in 1972–73. In Montreal, the *Maison des femmes* grew out of a women's bookstore; its projects included writing, music, women's medicine, and self-defense. Women's centres in Montreal's industrial Côte-Nord and in Bas-du-Fleuve, Rimouski, and Sept-Iles were retreats where women could gather undisturbed. In Sherbrooke, the women's centre served as a location for pre-existing women's organizations, and included a women's cafe. In Quebec City, a women's centre was the first project of a group of women leaving mixed-sex community associations.[53] Many such women's centres were founded, largely unrecorded except in their own archives; in 1986 it was estimated that Quebec alone had over a hundred, each of which received about two hundred hours of volunteer support per month.[54]

Many of these organizations were able to carry on their activities because of the funding they received from the Women's Program created in 1973 in the Department of the Secretary of State. In 1986 this program disbursed over $12 400 000 — about 1 dollar per Canadian woman, not a vast sum.[55] Also calling on the Secretary of State's funds were the women's magazines and journals and presses, as well as women's music and arts centres and companies. Financially hardpressed, liable to burnout from a combination of overwork and the strains of attempts to develop feminist, non-hierarchical forms of organization, such groups were nevertheless vital and influential.[56]

The search for an environment sympathetic to women led some women towards feminist religions, including groups that drew on ancient traditions of witchcraft. By the 1980s, there was an eclectic range of various feminist, non-hierarchical Goddess cults made up of women only. Goddess-worshippers were the most extreme example of women who organized outside of mixed-sex groups. For such women, the problem of conflict between male standards and female autonomy was solved; their separate organization asserted their legitimate interests as women.[57]

Within the established churches, women also organized for reform, but progress varied from faith to faith. In Canada as elsewhere, the Roman Catholic church stood fast in its opposition to many of women's aspirations. The female religious orders felt the consequences as recruitment dwindled and, between 1968 and 1986, nearly 4000 nuns in Quebec broke their vows, leaving religious communities.[58] Official opposition to contraception and abortion continued, even though by the 1980s most Canadian Catholics were close to the views of the rest of the country on these issues.[59] There was still no possibility of ordaining women or even allowing lay-women a larger official role in the church: in Toronto in 1987, girls who had been serving at the altar were barred from doing so during the visit of senior church dignitaries. Judaism was almost as resistant to change, in spite of the pressures exerted by feminists who wished to remain within the community. Although some Reconstructionist and Reform Jewish congregations instituted bat mitzvah ceremonies for girls, and hired women rabbis or, more often, assistant rabbis, Orthodox women saw no changes. They continued to have to supplement legal divorce with the ex-husband's permission to remarry; some among them wondered if they had a case of discrimination under the Charter of Rights. "I have a lot of problems," said Norma Joseph, appointed scholar–in–residence to the Women's Federation of Montreal's Jewish Community Services, "but I am not willing to give up my religion because I see it as difficult."[60]

The Anglican Church of Canada made some reforms; its first women ministers were ordained in 1976, and Elizabeth Kilbourn was a serious candidate for a bishopric in 1986. Church officials now had to struggle with new issues: "I don't think when they first ordained women they thought about them getting pregnant," said one of the newest of Toronto's thirty-five Anglican women priests in 1986 when, aged thirty-one, she was within three months of needing maternity leave.[61] The largest Protestant denomination in the country, the United Church of Canada, was also increasingly responsive, and in 1982 peace activist Lois Wilson was elected moderator. Religion, the last of the great male establishments, was feeling the impact of women, as economics, law, and politics already had.

At her installation ceremony, Lois Wilson used a benediction typical of the feminist reinterpretations of Christianity, calling on "the God of Sarah and of Abraham," the "Son, born of the woman Mary," and, finally, the "Holy Spirit who broods over us like a mother with her children . . . ."[62] Sarah, Mary, or the Great Mother—they were probably not images of womanhood that all Canadians would have accepted. History and the efforts of feminists had made clear the way such roles limited women. By the 1980s, fewer Canadians were involved in organized religion than in earlier times, and their religious traditions, like their cultural ones, were infinitely varied. Yet Canada was Christian in heritage, and religion was still one of the major sources of public authority. When the moderator of the United church was a woman who used a blessing that was no longer exclusively patriarchal, it mattered. Surely Aataentsic would have been pleased, as would the Canadian women who came after her.

Appendix

Table A.1	Immigrants by sex, 1608–1759		
	Women	Men	Total
Before 1630	6	15	21
1630–1639	51	88	139
1640–1649	86	141	227
1650–1659	239	403	642
1660–1669	623	1075	1698
1670–1679	369	429	798
1680–1689	56	486	542
1690–1699	32	490	522
1700–1709	24	283	307
1710–1719	18	293	311
1720–1729	14	420	434
1730–1739	16	576	592
1740–1749	16	1699	1751
1750–1759	17	27	44
Total	1619	6908	8527

Source: R. Cole Harris, ed., *Historical Atlas of Canada* (Toronto: University of Toronto Press, 1987) vol. 1, plate 45.

Table A.2		Urban population by age and sex, 1921–1981 (thousands)			
		under 14	15–29	over 30	Total
1921	male	686	518	943	2147
	female	688	602	915	2205
1931	male	803	714	1256	2773
	female	796	791	1214	2801
1941	male	768	831	1480	3079
	female	756	915	1503	3174
1951	male	1194	977	2051	4222
	female	1156	1100	2150	4406
1961	male	2085	1324	1890	5299
	female	2268	1381	1767	5416
1971	male	2374	2167	3564	8105
	female	2274	2190	3842	8306
1981	male	2005	2630	4379	9014
	female	1909	2646	4867	9422

Source: F.H. Leacy, ed.,
Historical Statistics of Canada,
2nd ed. (Ottawa: Statistics
Canada, 1983) A94–109.

Figure A.3　　　　　**Life expectancy by sex, 1931–1981**

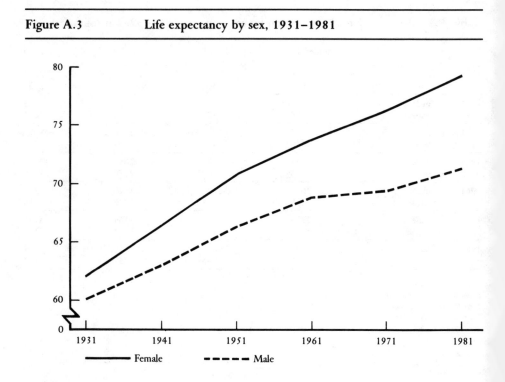

Sources: Based on data from
F.H. Leacy, ed., *Historical
Statistics of Canada* 2nd ed.
(Ottawa: Statistics Canada,
1983) B 65–74; Statistics
Canada, *Vital Statistics*
(1981).

Figure A.4	Percentage of population aged 65 or over, 1851–1981

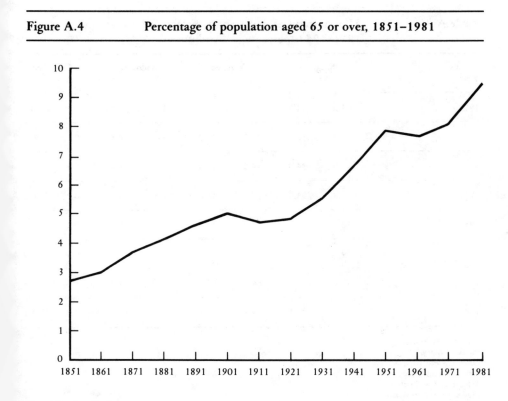

Source: Based on data from
John Kettle, *The Big
Generation* (Toronto:
McClelland and Stewart,
1980) 251–52.

Table A.5		Marital status of males and females, fifteen years and over, 1911–1981 (percentage distribution)						
Census Year	Single		Married		Widowed		Divorced	
	M	F	M	F	M	F	M	F
1911	45.0	34.9	51.5	56.9	3.4	8.2	0.1	0.1
1921	39.2	32.0	56.7	59.2	4.0	8.6	0.1	0.1
1931	41.0	34.0	54.9	57.4	4.0	8.5	0.1	0.1
1941	39.8	33.0	56.1	58.0	4.0	8.8	0.2	0.2
1951	32.1	25.7	63.9	64.5	3.8	9.4	0.3	0.4
1961	29.9	23.7	66.4	66.8	3.6	9.7	0.4	0.5
1971	31.6	25.0	64.9	63.9	2.5	9.8	1.0	1.3
1981	31.3	24.5	64.3	62.4	2.2	10.0	2.2	3.1

From: Roy H. Rodgers, and Gail Witney, "The Family Cycle in Twentieth Century Canada," *Journal of Marriage and the Family* (August 1981) 732; *Women of Canada: A Statistical Report* (Ottawa: Statistics Canada, 1985).

Marriage rates per 1000 population, 1901–1981

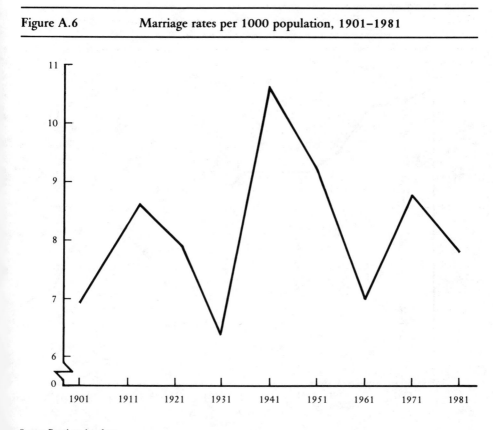

Source: Based on data from
Daniel Kubat and David
Thornton, *A Statistical
Profile of Canadian Society*
(Toronto: McGraw-Hill
Ryerson, 1974) 102.

Figure A.7   Fertility rates per 1000 women, 1851–1981

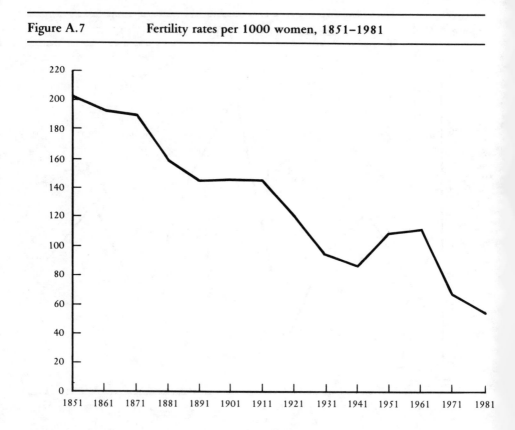

Total number of live births per 1000 women aged 15 to 49

Sources: Based on data from
1851–1961: Jacques
Henripin, *Tendances et
facteurs de la fécondité au
Canada* (Ottawa: Bureau
fédéral de la statistique,
1968) 21; 1971–1981:
*Women of Canada: A
Statistical Report* (Ottawa:
Statistics Canada, 1985)
tables 13, 14.

Table A.8		Fertility rates per 1000 married women, by age group, 1921–1969					
Year	15–19	20–24	25–29	30–34	35–39	40–44	45–49
1969*	350.4	249.5	172.5	91.1	47.7	13.3	1.2
1966	465.8	280.2	187.3	112.5	62.5	21.0	2.0
1961	541.2	374.4	255.6	161.4	89.9	32.1	2.8
1956	551.5	381.7	265.5	169.8	101.0	35.6	3.4
1951	498.5	350.4	218.1	168.7	100.8	36.6	3.7
1941	453.1	340.2	237.8	158.3	99.1	38.9	4.5
1931	485.0	357.6	257.7	180.9	123.1	52.5	6.5
1921	472.9	396.7	300.7	225.6	152.8	70.6	9.5

Note: Excludes Newfoundland for all years and the Yukon and Northwest Territories through 1941.
*Reporting of legitimate fertility discontinued as of 1970.

From: Daniel Kubat and
David Thornton, *A Statistical
Profile of Canadian Society*
(Toronto: McGraw Hill
Ryerson, 1974) 39.

Table A.9	Average number of children born to ever-married women, by mother tongue			
Period of birth of women (approx.)	English	French	Other	All languages
Before 1896	3.23	6.37	4.70	4.04
1896–1901	2.90	5.58	3.81	3.65
1901–1906	2.69	5.05	3.46	3.39
1906–1911	2.58	4.61	3.17	3.15
1911–1916	2.68	4.33	3.03	3.11
1916–1921	2.87	4.13	2.92	3.19
1921–1926	3.09	4.12	2.90	3.32
1926–1931	3.29	3.92	3.08	3.41
1931–1936	3.25	3.48	3.01	3.26
1936–1941[1]	2.88	2.83	2.76	2.84
1941–1946[1]	2.35	2.23	2.43	2.33

[1] *The fertility of these women was not complete in 1981; women born between 1941–1946, for example, would be 35–40 years old in 1981.*

From: A. Romaniuc, *Fertility in Canada: From Baby-Boom to Baby-Bust* (Ottawa: Statistics Canada, 1984) 16.

Table A.10			Percentage distribution of ever-married women who have reached the end of childbearing by number of children born						

Period of birth of women (approx.)	0	1	2	3	4	5	6+	Average number of children per married woman
Prior to 1876	12.83	9.23	11.08	10.86	9.99	8.65	36.89	4.818
1877–1886	13.20	11.16	13.46	12.31	10.38	8.16	31.01	4.398
1887–1896	12.31	12.36	15.44	13.32	10.55	7.96	27.77	4.167
1897–1901	12.62	14.11	17.31	13.85	10.30	7.52	24.04	3.795
1902–1906	15.48	14.99	19.04	14.40	9.90	6.81	19.38	3.385
1907–1911	15.25	15.76	21.32	14.92	9.76	6.56	16.43	3.154
1912–1916	13.12	15.12	22.48	16.82	10.85	6.75	14.87	3.110
1917–1921	11.77	13.14	22.41	17.96	12.24	7.66	14.83	3.189
1922–1926	9.59	11.26	22.00	19.62	13.96	8.45	15.12	3.315
1927–1931	8.35	9.43	21.23	20.80	15.43	9.47	15.29	3.407
1932–1936	7.20	8.98	22.88	22.89	16.53	9.30	12.22	3.260
1937–1941	7.34	9.64	28.52	24.83	14.92	7.26	7.49	2.934
1942–1946	9.31	12.83	38.00	23.62	9.87	3.57	2.79	2.405

From: A. Romaniuc, *Fertility in Canada: From Baby-Boom to Baby-Bust* (Ottawa: Statistics Canada, 1984) 31.

Figure A.11	Maternal mortality rates per 1000 live births, 1921–1981

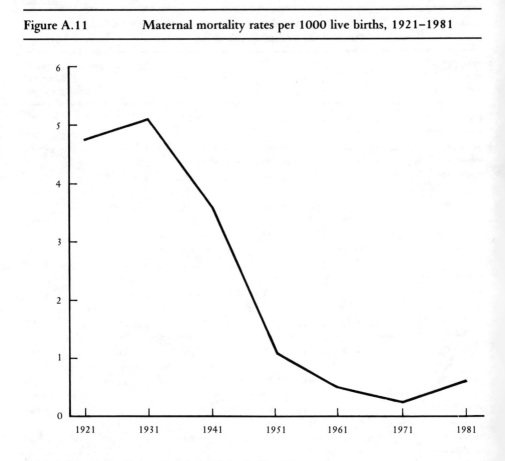

Excludes the Yukon Territory, Northwest Territories, and Newfoundland for 1921.

Source: Based on data from
F.H. Leacy, ed., *Historical Statistics*, 2nd ed., (Ottawa: Statistics Canada, 1983), Table B51–58; *1981 Census*, Cat. 84–204.

Table A.12	Percentage of births occurring in hospitals, 1931–1971

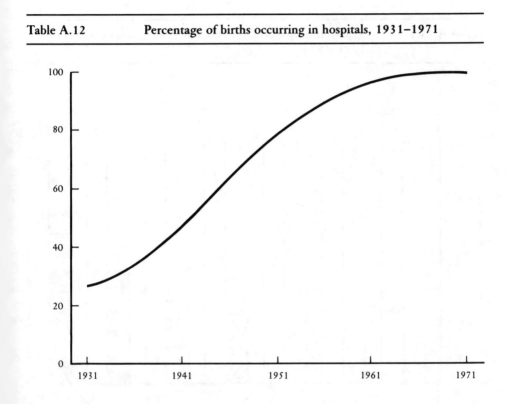

Comparable figures for 1981 are not available.

Source: Based on data from
F.H. Leacy, ed, *Historical
Statistics*, 2nd ed. (Ottawa:
Statistics Canada, 1983)
Table B1–14.

Figure A.13.1   Labour force participation rates of women and men, 1921–1981

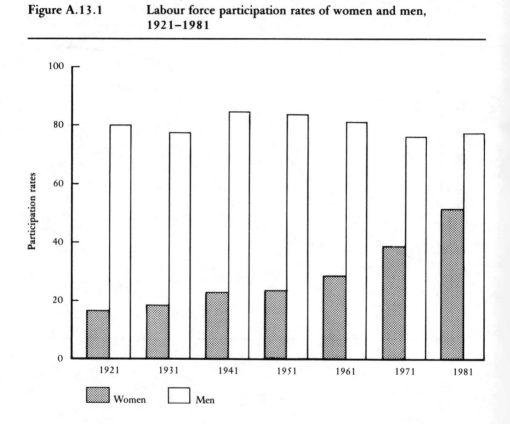

Excludes Newfoundland 1901–1961.

Source: Based on data from
F.H. Leacy, ed., *Historical
Statistics*, 2nd ed., (Ottawa:
Statistics Canada, 1983);
Statscan Cat. 71–201, 1971
and 1981.

Figure A.13.2   **Women as a percentage of the labour force, 1921–1981**

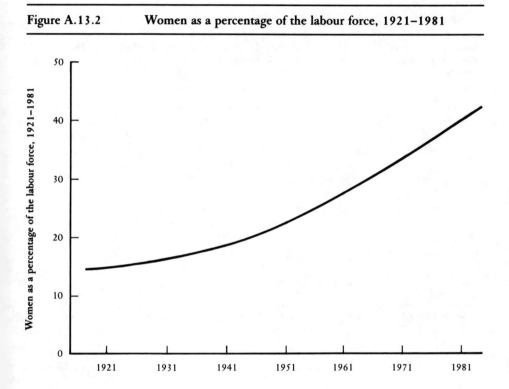

Excludes Newfoundland 1921–1961.

Source: Based on data from
F.H. Leacy, ed., *Historical
Statistics*, 2nd ed., (Ottawa:
Statistics Canada, 1983);
Statscan Cat. 71–201, 1971
and 1981.

Table A.14	Women's participation in the labour force, 1921–1985							
Year	1921	1931	1941	1951	1961	1971	1981	1985
Total %	18	20	21	24	30	39	52	55
Age category					percentages			
15–24	29	33	41	42	41	49	61	71
25–34	17	24	25	24	30	44	66	69
35–44	11	13	16	22	31	44	64	69
45–54	11	13	13	20	33	44	56	60
55–64	10	13	10	14	24	34	42	34

From: Canadian Congress for Learning Opportunities, *Decade of Promise: An Assessment of Canadian Women's Status in Education, Training and Employment, 1976–1985* (Toronto: Avebury Research, 1986) 61.

Table A.15   **Women as a percentage of the labour force, by occupation, 1901–1980**

Occupation	1901	1911	1921	1931	1941	1951	1961	1971	1980
Managerial	3.6	4.5	4.3	4.9	7.2	8.9	10.3	15.7	25.2
Professional	42.5	44.6	54.1	49.5	46.1	43.5	43.2	48.1	41.3
Clerical	22.1	32.6	41.8	45.1	50.1	56.7	61.5	68.4	78.2
Sales	10.4	20.2	25.6	26.0	32.1	38.3	40.3	30.4	39.6
Service	68.7	64.8	58.6	62.1	65.0	47.8	50.0	46.2	54.0
Primary	1.1	1.5	1.6	1.9	1.5	3.1	9.2	16.4	18.3
Blue collar	12.6	10.2	10.1	8.5	11.0	11.5	10.6	12.0	—
All occupations	13.4	13.2	15.4	17.0	19.9	22.0	27.3	34.3	39.7

From: Rosalie Silberman
Abella, *Equality in Employ-
ment: A Royal Commission
Report* (Ottawa: Ministry of
Supply and Services, 1984)
vol. 2.

Figure A.16 Women's and men's average annual earnings, in thousands of dollars, 1971, 1982

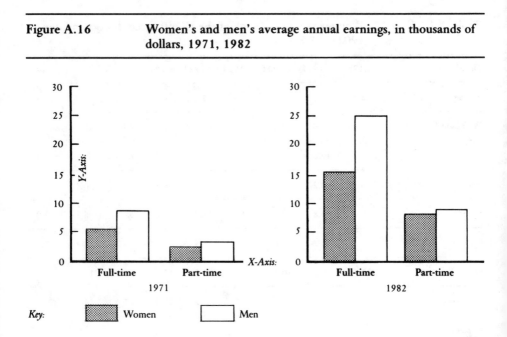

A full-time worker is a person who worked, mostly full-time, 50-52 weeks in 1971, and 49-52 weeks in 1982.
A part-time worker is a person who worked mostly part-time, 50-52 weeks in 1971, and 49-52 weeks in 1982.

From: *Women in Canada:*
A Statistical Report (Ottawa:
Information Canada,
1985)61.

| Table A.17 | Women's full-time[1] earnings as a percentage of men's, by age group, 1971, 1982 |

	1971	1982
Age group		
Under 20	--[2]	88.0
20–24[3]	74.5	78.2
25–34	65.8	71.3
35–44	57.9	61.6
45–54	55.5	58.7
55–64	64.5	62.2
Total	59.7	64.0

[1] *A full-time worker is a person who worked, mostly full-time, 50-52 weeks in 1971, and 49-52 weeks in 1982.*
[2] *Figures not available.*
[3] *In 1971, this age group includes those persons aged 24 years and under.*

From: *Women in Canada:*
A Statistical Report
(Ottawa: Statistics Canada,
1985) 61.

Table A.18	Percentage distribution of women by leading occupational groups,[1] 1901–1971							
Occupational group	1901[4]	1911	1921	1931	1941[5]	1951	1961	1971
Clerical	5.3	9.4	18.7	17.7	18.3	27.5	28.6	32.7
Personal service	42.0	37.1	25.8	33.8	34.2	21.0	22.1	22.3
Professional	14.7	12.7	19.1	17.8	15.7	14.4	15.5	17.5
Commercial and financial[6]	2.4	6.8	8.5	8.3	8.8	10.5	10.2	8.3
Manufacturing and mechanical[2]	29.6	26.3	17.8	12.7	15.4	14.6	9.9	11.2
Other[3]	6.0	7.8	10.1	9.6	7.7	11.9	13.6	7.7
Total[3]	100.0	100.1	100.0	99.9	100.1	99.9	99.9	99.7

[1] *Includes Newfoundland (1951 on), but not Yukon and Northwest Territories.*
[2] *Includes stationary enginemen and occupations associated with electric power production.*
[3] *Includes armed forces.*
[4] *10 years of age and over in 1901; 15 years of age and over 1911–1971.*
[5] *Not including active service, 1941.*
[6] *Includes saleswomen.*

From: Janice Acton, *et al*,
Women at Work, Ontario,
1850–1930 (Toronto: Canadian Women's Educational
Press, 1974) 280.

Table A.19		Female enrolment as a percentage of full-time university undergraduate enrolment, 1891–1975					
Field of specialization	1891	1920	1930	1945	1961	1971	1981
Arts, science, letters	21.8	31.6	32.6	26.6	29.3	40.6	49.1
Agriculture	—	1.3	1.1	4.0	4.2	13.1	36.6
Commerce and business administration	—	3.0	14.3	8.9	7.0	13.9	38.7
Education	—	61.8	64.4	48.0	48.1	55.8	69.2
Engineering and applied sc.	0.0	0.1	0.2	0.6	0.7	2.4	10.6
Fine and applied arts	—	—	91.7	80.6	66.4	53.9	62.2
Dentistry	0.0	1.8	1.3	1.2	4.5	7.5	22.7
Medicine	3.1	4.6	4.2	7.3	9.8	20.3	38.5
Nursing	—	100.0	100.0	100.0	99.8	97.9	97.4
Pharmacy	0.0	5.9	6.1	25.9	27.3	52.5	64.2
Misc. health professions	—	—	—	100.0	82.6	72.7	82.8
Household science	—	100.0	100.0	100.0	100.0	98.9	97.2
Law	0.4	3.7	3.4	4.4	5.3	14.9	39.9
Religion and theology	—	1.9	1.9	2.4	1.3	28.7	30.9
Veterinary medicine	0.0	0.0	0.0	2.3	5.9	16.1	48.8
Unclassified	0.0	—	—	—	55.2	34.0	48.1
Female % of total undergraduate enrolment	11.6	16.3	23.5	20.8	26.2	37.7	46.7

From: Rosalie Silberman Abella, *Equality in Employment: A Royal Commission Report* (Ottawa: Ministry of Supply and Services, 1984) 139.

Table A.20   Degrees granted by Canadian universities, 1920–1985

Academic Year	Bachelor and first professional degrees[1] Total	% Earned by women	Master and license[2] Total	% Earned by women	Doctorates Total	% Earned by women
1920–21	3 627	18.3	218	22.0	24	1
1930–31	5 290	25.3	468	21.4	46	7
1940–41	6 576	24.1	673	10.6	75	5
1945–46	8 192	26.9	877	11.3	104	11.5
1950–51	15 754	20.3	1 632	13.9	202	5.5
1955–56	13 770	22.9	1 459	20.8	366	4.6
1960–61	20 240	25.8	2 447	19.0	305	8.5
1965–66	38 470	32.9	5 233	19.0	697	10.9
1970–71	67 200	38.1	9 638	22.0	1625	9.3
1975	80 754	44.4	11 068	28.2	1840	16.1
1981	84 926	50.3	12 903	39.2	1816	24.2
1985	87 474	51.9	15 194	42.0	2000	26.4

[1] *Includes equivalent diplomas, as, for example, in theology, and honours degrees.*
[2] *The license in the French-language universities is the next degree after the Bachelor, as the Masters degree is in the English-language universities. This category excludes Masters and license degrees (i.e., in law, optometry) which are in reality the first professional degree and which are included in that column.*

From: Daniel Kubat and
David Thornton, *A Statistical
Profile of Canadian Society*
(Toronto: McGraw Hill-
Ryerson, 1974) 124;
Women in the Labour Force,
1986–1987 ed. (Ottawa:
Labour Canada, Women's
Bureau, 1987) tables iii–4,
70; iii–8, 74; iii–10, 76.

Notes

THE FOUNDING MOTHERS: BEGINNINGS TO THE MID-NINETEENTH CENTURY

1 Bruce Trigger, *The Children of Aataentsic* (Montreal: McGill-Queen's University Press, 1976) vol. 1, 77; Anne Cameron, *Daughters of Copper Woman* (Vancouver: Press Gang Publishers, 1981).

2 R. Cole Harris, ed., *Historical Atlas of Canada* (Toronto: University of Toronto Press, 1987) vol. 1, especially 5–6, and plate 18. See also J. Helm, ed., *Handbook of North American Indians* (Washington: Smithsonian Institution, 1981) vol. 6; B.G. Trigger, *Handbook of North American Indians* (Washington: Smithsonian Institution, 1978) vol. 15.

3 Harris, *Historical Atlas of Canada*, vol. 1, plates 9–13.

4 Jean Johnston, *Wilderness Women: Canada's Forgotten History* (Toronto: Peter Martin Associates, 1973) 1–22.

5 Harris, *Historical Atlas of Canada*, vol. 1, plates 33, 47, and 69; Ellice B. Gonzales, *Changing Economic Roles for Micmac Men and Women: an Ethnohistorical Analysis* (Ottawa: National Museums of Canada, 1981).

6 See W.J. Eccles, *Canada Under Louis XIV, 1663–1701* (Toronto: McClelland and Stewart, 1964); and *The Canadian Frontier, 1534–1760* (New York: Holt, Rinehart and Winston, 1969).

7 See Andrew H. Clark, *Acadia: The Geography of Early Nova Scotia to 1760* (Madison: University of Wisconsin Press, 1968); Eccles, *The Canadian Frontier*.

8 Naomi Griffiths, "The Acadians," *Dictionary of Canadian Biography* (Toronto: University of Toronto Press, 1979), vol. 4, xvii–xix.

9 See Harris, *Historical Atlas of Canada*, vol. 1, 113–17 and plate 45.

10 See Harris, *Historical Atlas of Canada*, vol. 1, 171–73, and plates 30–32, 46, 54, and 68.

11 Sylvia Van Kirk, *"Many Tender Ties": Women in Fur Trade Society, 1670–1870* (Winnipeg: Watson & Dwyer, 1980) chap. 4.

1 The first women

1 Sylvia Van Kirk, "Thanadelthur," *The Beaver* (Spring 1974) 40–45.

2 R. Cole Harris, ed., *Historical Atlas of Canada* (Toronto: University of Toronto Press, 1987) vol. 1, plate 12; Somer Brodribb, "The Traditional Roles of Native Women in Canada and the Impact of Colonization," *The Canadian Journal of Native Studies* 4, 1 (1984) 86; Karen Anderson, "A Gendered World: Women, Men, and the Political Economy of the Seventeenth Century Huron," *in* Heather Jon Maroney and Meg Luxton, eds., *Feminism and Political Economy: Women's Work, Women's Struggles* (Toronto: Methuen, 1987) 125. Estimates of numbers are difficult and accounts vary on this point.

3 Judith K. Brown, "A Note on the Division of Labour by Sex," *American Anthropologist* 72 (1970) 1073–78.

4 Brown, "A Note on the Division of Labour by Sex," 1076.

5 Judith K. Brown, "Economic Organization and the Position of Women Among the Iroquois," *Ethnohistory* 17 (1970) 151–67; Karen Anderson, "Commodity Exchange and Subordination: Montagnais-Nascapi and Huron Women, 1600–1650," *Signs* 11, 1 (Autumn 1985) 48–62.

6 Brown, "A Note on the Division of Labour by Sex," 1076. The document is reproduced in James Axtell, ed., *The Indian Peoples of Eastern America: A Documentary History of the Sexes* (New York: Oxford University Press, 1981) 138–39.

7 Eleanor Leacock and Jacqueline Goodman, "Montagnais Marriage and the Jesuits of the Seventeenth Century: Incidents from the *Relations* of Paul Le Jeune," *The Western Canadian Journal of Anthropology* 6, 3 (1976) 77–91; Leacock, "Women in Egalitarian Societies," *in* Renate Bridenthal and Claudia Koonz, eds., *Becoming Visible: Women in European Society* (Boston: Houghton-Mifflin, 1977) 11–35; Leacock, "Class, Commodity, and the Status of Women," *in* Ruby Rohrlich-Leavitt, ed., *Women Cross-Culturally: Change and Challenge* (The Hague: Mouton, 1975) 601–16; Leacock, "Montagnais Women and the Jesuit Program for Colonization," *in* Mona Etienne and Eleanor Leacock, eds., *Women and Colonization* (New York: Praeger, 1980) 25–42.

8 Glyndwr Williams, ed., *Andrew Graham's Observations on Hudson's Bay, 1767–91* (London: The Hudson's Bay Record Society, 1969) 177–78.

9 W. Kaye Lamb, ed., *The Journals and Letters of Sir Alexander Mackenzie* (Cambridge, England: Published for the Hakluyt Society at Cambridge Press, 1970) 135; Sylvia Van Kirk, *"Many Tender Ties": Women in Fur Trade Society, 1670–1870* (Winnipeg: Watson & Dwyer, 1980) 17–21.

10 Van Kirk, *"Many Tender Ties,"* 18.

11 Ellice B. Gonzales, *Changing Economic Roles for Micmac Men and Women: An Ethnohistorical Analysis* (Ottawa: National Museums of Canada, 1981) especially 15; Andrew Hill Clark, *Acadia: The Geography of Early Nova Scotia to 1760* (Madison: University of Wisconsin Press, 1968); Virginia P. Miller, "The Decline of Nova Scotia Micmac Population, A.D. 1600–1850," *Culture* 2, 3 (1982) 107–20.

12 Gonzales, *Changing Economic Roles,* 18.

13 Ruth Holmes Whitehead, *Micmac Quillwork* (Halifax: The Nova Scotia Museum, 1982).

14 Williams, ed., *Andrew Graham's Observations*, 177.

15 Van Kirk, *"Many Tender Ties,"* 21 and 86.

16 Leacock, "Montagnais Women and the Jesuit Program for Colonization," 26–27.

17 Leacock, "Montagnais Women and the Jesuit Program for Colonization"; Leacock and Goodman, "Montagnais Marriage and the Jesuits," 80–82.

18 Van Kirk, *"Many Tender Ties,"* 24–25; Sylvia Van Kirk, "Towards a Feminist Perspective in Native History," Centre for Women's Studies, Ontario Institute for Studies in Education, *Occasional Paper* No. 14 (1987) 7. Most of the following discussion draws on the work of Sylvia Van Kirk.

19 Marjorie Mitchell and Anna Franklin, "When You Don't Know the Language, Listen to the Silence: An Historical Overview of Native Indian Women in B.C.," *in* Barbara K. Latham and Roberta J. Pazdro, eds., *Not Just Pin Money: Selected Essays on the History of Women's Work in British Columbia* (Victoria: Camosun College, 1984) 17–35.

20 Jan Gould, *Women of British Columbia* (Saanichton: Hancock House, 1975) 13–14.

21 Mitchell and Franklin, "When You Don't Know the Language," 24.

22 Leacock and Goodman, "Montagnais Marriage and the Jesuits," 82–88.

23 Cornelius J. Jaenen, *Friend and Foe: Aspects of French-Amerindian Cultural Contact in the Sixteenth and Seventeenth Centuries* (Toronto: McClelland and Stewart, 1976) 76; *Dictionary of Canadian Biography* (Toronto: University of Toronto Press, 1966) vol. 1, 635–36.

24 Anderson, "Commodity Exchange and Subordination," 62.

25 Diane Rothenberg, "The Mothers of the Nation: Seneca Resistance to Quaker Intervention," *in* Etienne and Leacock, eds., *Women and Colonization*, 63–87.

26 Van Kirk, *"Many Tender Ties,"* 76.

27 Van Kirk, *"Many Tender Ties,"* especially chap. 4.
28 Van Kirk, *"Many Tender Ties,"* chap. 4; Jennifer Brown, "Ultimate Respectability: Fur Trade Children in the 'Civilized World'," *The Beaver* (Winter 1977) 4–10 and (Spring 1978) 48–55.
29 Van Kirk, *"Many Tender Ties,"* chaps. 5–10.
30 Van Kirk, *"Many Tender Ties,"* chap. 1; Mitchell and Franklin, "If You Don't Know the Language," 25–26.
31 Whitehead, *Micmac Quillwork*, 24.
32 Whitehead, *Micmac Quillwork*, chap. 3.
33 Douglas Saunders, "Indian Women: A Brief History of their Roles and Rights," *McGill Law Journal* 21 (1975) 656.
34 Mrs. Jameson, *Winter Studies and Summer Rambles in Canada* (London: Saunders and Otley, 1838; reprint edition, Toronto: Coles Canadiana Collection, 1972) vol. 3, 305, 308.
35 See Marilyn Ravicz, Diane Battung, and Laura Baker, "Rainbow Women of the Fraser Valley: Lifesongs through the Generations," *in* Latham and Pazdro, eds., *Not Just Pin Money*, 37–52.

2 French women in the New World

1 Silvio Dumas, *Les Filles du roi en Nouvelle-France* (Québec: Société d'histoire du Québec, 1972) 114–15.
2 Raymond Douville and Jacques Casanova, *Daily Life in Early Canada*, trans. by Carola Congreve (London: George Allen and Unwin, 1968) 27.
3 *Dictionary of Canadian Biography* (Toronto: University of Toronto Press, 1966), vol. 1, 578, 110.
4 Micheline Dumont-Johnson, "Les communautés religieuses et la condition féminine," *Recherches Sociographiques* 19 (janvier/avril 1978) 80.
5 François Rousseau, "Hôpital et société en Nouvelle-France: L'Hôtel Dieu de Québec à la fin du XVIIe siècle," *Revue d'histoire de l'Amérique française* 31 (juin 1977) 29–30.
6 Le Collectif Clio, *L'histoire des femmes au Québec depuis quatre siècles* (Montréal: Quinze, 1982) 38; Joyce Marshall, ed., *Word from New France: The Selected Letters of Marie de l'Incarnation* (Toronto: Oxford University Press, 1967); Dom Guy Oury, *Marie de l'Incarnation, 1599–1672*, 2 vols. (Québec: Presses de l'Université Laval, 1973).
7 Le Collectif Clio, *L'histoire des femmes*, 40–41; Soeur Marguerite Jean, "L'Etat et les communautés religieuses féminines au Québec, 1639–1840," *Studia Canonica* 6, 1 (1972) 166.
8 Le Collectif Clio, *L'histoire des femmes*, 43; Hélène Bernier, ed., *Marguerite Bourgeoys* (Montréal: Fides, 1958).
9 Dumas, *Les filles du roi en Nouvelle-France*, 70. Authors' translation.
10 Le Collectif Clio, *L'histoire des femmes*, 48–52.
11 Dumas, *Les filles du roi*, chap. 2; "Les soeurs Raclot," *Nos Ancêtres* 4 (1983).
12 Douville and Casanova, *Daily Life in Early Canada*, 32; Dumas, *Les filles du roi*, 320–21.
13 Louise Dechêne, *Habitants et marchands de Montréal au XVIIe siècle* (Montréal: Plon, 1974) 45.
14 Jacques Henripin, *La population canadienne au début du XVIIIe siècle*, Institut national d'études démographiques: Travaux et documents, Cahier No. 20 (Presses Universitaires de France, 1954); A.J.B. Johnston, *Religion and Life at Louisbourg, 1713–1758* (Kingston and Montreal: McGill-Queen's University Press, 1984) 5.
15 Yves Landry and Jacques Légaré, "Le cycle de vie familiale en Nouvelle-France: méthodologie et application à un echantillon," *Histoire sociale/Social History* 17 (May 1984) 7–20; Isabel Foulché-Delbosc, "Women of Three Rivers: 1651–63," *in* Susan Mann Trofimenkoff and Alison Prentice, eds., *The Neglected Majority: Essays in Canadian Women's History* (Toronto: McClelland and Stewart, 1977) vol. 1, 16–18.
16 Foulché-Delbosc, "Women of Three Rivers," 18.

17 Landry and Légaré, "Le cycle de vie familiale," 11; Alan Greer, *Peasant, Lord, and Merchant: Rural Society in Three Quebec Parishes, 1740-1840* (Toronto: University of Toronto Press, 1985) 51; John Bosher, "The Family in New France," *in* B.M. Gough, ed., *In Search of the Visible Past* (Waterloo, Ontario: Wilfrid Laurier University Press, 1975) 1–13.

18 See Henripin, *La population canadienne*, 90; P. A. Leclerc, "Le mariage sous le régime français," *Revue d'histoire de l'Amérique française* 13/14 (1959–60) 230–46, 374–406, 525–43.

19 Naomi Griffiths, "The Acadians," *Dictionary of Canadian Biography*, vol. 4 (1978) xvii–xxxi; Henripin, *La population canadienne*, 49–53; Robert V. Wells, "Quaker Marriage Patterns in Colonial Perspective," *William & Mary Quarterly* 3rd Series, 24 (July 1972); Roderic Beaujot and Kevin McQuillan, *Growth and Dualism: The Demographic Development of Canada* (Toronto: Gage, 1982) 6–9.

20 Hélène Rioux, "Les amours québecoises au XVIIIe siècle," *Histoire*, 11 (avril 1979) 71; Beaujot and McQuillan, *Growth and Dualism*, 9.

21 Hélène Laforce, *Histoire de la sage-femme dans la région de Québec* (Québec: Institut Québecois de recherche sur la culture, 1985) 30–64.

22 Greer, *Peasant, Lord, and Merchant*, chap. 2; Andrew Hill Clark, *Acadia* (Madison, Wisconsin: University of Wisconsin Press, 1968) 165.

23 *Dictionary of Canadian Biography*, vol. 3 (1974) 308–13; vol. 1 (1966) 383.

24 Robert–Lionel Séguin, "La canadienne au XVIIe et XVIIIe siècles," *Revue d'histoire de l'Amérique française* 13 (1959–60) 492–508; Clark, *Acadia*, 165, 168, 177 and 377; Foulché-Delbosc, "Women of Three Rivers," 25.

25 Clark, *Acadia*, especially 176, 377–78, 243–44; Naomi Griffiths, "The Acadians," xix–xxi; Greer, *Peasant, Lord, and Merchant*, 14.

26 Le Collectif Clio, *L'histoire des femmes*, 23.

27 Greer, *Peasant, Lord, and Merchant*, 49–51; Leclerc, "Le mariage sous le régime français," 375–76.

28 Yves F. Zoltvany, "Esquisse de la Coutume de Paris," *Revue d'histoire de l'Amérique française* 25, 3 (décembre 1971) 366–83.

29 Dechêne, *Habitants et marchands de Montréal*, 419; Louis Lavallée, "Les archives notariales et l'histoire sociale de la Nouvelle-France," *Revue d'histoire de l'Amérique française* 28, 3 (décembre 1974) 388–89; Johnston, *Religion in Life at Louisbourg*, chap. 5; Cameron Nish, *Les bourgeois-gentilhommes de la Nouvelle-France, 1729-1748* (Montréal: Fides, 1968), chap. 10.

30 Greer, *Peasant, Lord, and Merchant*, 34.

31 *Dictionary of Canadian Biography*, vol. 3, 580–81.

32 Liliane Plamondon, "Une femme d'affaires en Nouvelle-France: Marie-Anne Barbel, veuve Fornel," *Revue d'histoire de l'Amérique française* 31, 2 (septembre 1977) 165–86.

33 *Dictionary of Canadian Biography*, vol. 3, 421; Douville and Casanova, *Daily Life in Early Canada*, 201; Noel, "Les femmes favorisées," *in* Prentice, *The Neglected Majority*, 25–6.

34 Noel, "Les femmes favorisées," 32; Terence Crowley, "Thunder Gusts: Popular Disturbances in Early French Canada," Canadian Historical Association, *Historical Papers* (1979) 19–20.

35 Laforce, *Histoire de la sage-femme*, 138–200.

36 Rousseau, "Hôpital et société," 36–47.

37 Micheline d'Allaire, "Les prétensions des religieuses de l'hôpital-général de Québec sur le palais épiscopal de Québec," *Revue d'histoire de l'Amérique française* 13, 1 (juin 1969) 53–67.

38 Johnston, *Religion in Life at Louisbourg*, chap. 4.

39 Micheline Dumont-Johnson, "History of the Status of Women in the Province of Quebec," *in* Margaret W. Labarge *et al.*, *The Cultural Tradition and Political History of Women in Canada*, Study No. 8 of the Royal Commission on the Status of Women (Ottawa: Information Canada, 1971) 6.

40 Johnston, *Religion in Life at Louisbourg*, 96.
41 Antonio Drolet, "Quelques remèdes indigènes à travers la correspondance de Mère Sainte-Hélène," *Trois siècles de médicin Québecoise*, Société historique de Québec, No. 22 (Québec, 1972); Soeur Morin, "Annales de l'Hôtel-Dieu de Montréal," *Mémoires de la société historique de Montréal*, vol. 12 (1921).
42 Douville and Casanova, *Daily Life in Early Canada*, 210.
43 Johnston, *Religion in Life at Louisbourg*, 8 and 93; Esmerelda Thornhill, "Black Women's Studies in Teaching related to Women: Help or Hindrance to Universal Sisterhood?" *Fireweed* (Spring 1983) 81; Adrienne Shadd, "Three Hundred Years of Black Women in Canadian History: Circa 1700 to 1980," *Tiger Lily* 1, 2 (1987).
44 Nadia Fahmy-Eid, "L'éducation des filles chez les Ursulines de Québec sous le régime français," *in* Nadia Fahmy-Eid and Micheline Dumont, eds., *Maîtresses de maison, maîtresses d'école: femmes, famille et éducation dans l'histoire de Québec* (Montréal: Boréal Express, 1983), especially 66–67.
45 Johnston, *Religion in Life at Louisbourg*, 91. See also Johnston's "Education and Female Literacy at Eighteenth-Century Louisbourg: The Work of the *Soeurs de la Congrégation de Notre Dame*," *in* J. Donald Wilson, ed., *An Imperfect Past: Education and Society in Canadian History* (Vancouver: Centre for the Study of Curriculum and Instruction, University of British Columbia, 1984).
46 Fahmy-Eid, "L'éducation des filles," 53.
47 Fahmy-Eid, "L'éducation des filles."
48 Johnston, *Religion in Life at Louisbourg*, 107; Alan Greer, "The Pattern of Literacy in Quebec, 1745–1899," *Histoire sociale/Social History* 11, 22 (November 1978) 299.
49 Soeur Morin, *Annales*; Ghislaine Légendre, ed., "Relation de Soeur Cuillerier," *Ecrits du Canada français* 42 (Montréal 1979); Elisabeth Bégon, *Lettres au cher fils. Correspondance d'Elisabeth Bégon avec son gendre, 1748–1753* (Montréal: Editions Hurtubise, 1972); Douville and Casanova, *Daily Life in Early Canada*, 202–16.
50 Francine Barry, "Familles et domesticité féminine au milieu du 18e siècle," *in* Fahmy-Eid et Dumont, *Maîtresses de maison, maîtresses d'école*," 223–36.
51 See Naomi Griffiths, "The Acadians."
52 Andrée Morel, "Réflexions sur la justice criminelle canadienne au 18e siècle," *Revue d'histoire de l'Amérique française* 29, 2 (septembre 1975) 241–53.
53 Peter Gossage, "Foundlings and the Institution: The Case of the Grey Nuns of Montreal," paper presented to the Canadian Historical Association, Winnipeg, June 1986.
54 On dowries, see Dechêne, *Habitants et Marchands de Montréal*, 478; Jean, "L'état et les communautés religieuses féminines au Québec," 166–68.
55 Greer, *Peasant, Lord, and Merchant*, 25–28 and 55–56.

3 Carders of wool, drawers of water: women's work in British North America
1 Marilyn Porter, "She Was Skipper of the Shore Crew: Notes on the Sexual Division of Labour in Newfoundland," *Labour/le travail* 15 (Spring 1985) 109.
2 Diane Bélanger and Lucie Rozon, *Les Religieuses au Québec* (Montréal: Libre Expression, 1982) 294; Sister Maura, *The Sisters of Charity, Halifax* (Toronto: Ryerson Press, 1956).
3 W. A. Spray, "The Settlement of the Black Refugees in New Brunswick, 1815–1836," *The Acadiensis Reader* 1; see also Spray, *The Blacks in New Brunswick* (Brunswick Press, n.p., n.d.).
4 Beth Light and Alison Prentice, eds., *Pioneer and Gentlewomen of British North America* (Toronto: New Hogtown Press, 1980) 1–12; Elisabeth de Moissac, "L'éducation à la Rivière Rouge (1844–1870): Les Soeurs Grises," Canadian Catholic Historical Association, *Report* (1948–49) 39–45; Jan Gould, *Women of British Columbia* (Saanichton: Hancock House, 1975) chap. 2.

5   L. Lee, "The Myth of Female Equality in Pioneer Society: The Red River Colony as a Test Case," (University of Manitoba: M.A. Thesis, 1978) 14.

6   H.C.Burleigh, "A Tale of Loyalist Heroism," *Ontario History* 42, 2 (1950) 91–99.

7   *Canadian Encyclopedia* (Edmonton: Hurtig Publishers, 1985) vol. 1, 431.

8   Wallace Brown, *The Good Americans: The Loyalists in the American Revolution* (New York: Morrow, 1969) 140–41 and 206.

9   Mary Beacock Fryer, "Sarah Sherwood: Wife and Mother and Invisible Loyalist," *in* Phyllis R. Blakely and John N. Grant, eds., *Eleven Exiles: Accounts of Loyalists and the American Revolution* (Toronto: Dundurn Press, 1982) 245–64.

10 Susanna Moodie, *Roughing it in the Bush or Forest Life in Canada* (Toronto: McClelland and Stewart, 1970) especially 167; Elizabeth Hopkins, "A Prison-House for Prosperity: the Immigrant Experience of the Nineteenth Century Upper Class British Woman," *in* Jean Burnet, ed., *Looking into My Sister's Eyes: An Exploration in Women's History* (Toronto: The Multicultural History Society of Ontario, 1986); Marian Fowler, *The Embroidered Tent: Five Gentlewomen in Early Canada* (Toronto: Anansi, 1982); Carl Ballstadt, Elizabeth Hopkins, and Michael Peterman, eds., *Susanna Moodie: Letters of a Lifetime* (Toronto: University of Toronto Press, 1985).

11 Diary of Anne Powell, Diaries Collection, Public Archives of Ontario.

12 See, for example, Suzanne D. Cross, "The Neglected Majority: The Changing Role of Women in 19th Century Montreal," *in* Susan Mann Trofimenkoff and Alison Prentice, eds., *The Neglected Majority: Essays in Canadian Women's History* (Toronto: McClelland and Stewart, 1977) vol. 1, 66–86; Michael B. Katz, *The People of Hamilton, Canada West: Family and Class in a Mid-Nineteenth-Century Canadian City* (Cambridge, Mass.: Harvard University Press, 1976) 265.

13 Sylvia Van Kirk, " 'Women in Between': Indian Women in Fur Trade Society in Western Canada," *Historical Papers* (1977) 30–47; Sylvia Van Kirk, " 'What if Mama is an Indian?': The Cultural Ambivalence of the Alexander Ross Family," *in* John Foster, ed., *The Developing West* (Edmonton: University of Alberta Press, 1983) 125–36; Sylvia Van Kirk, *"Many Tender Ties": Women in Fur Trade Society in Western Canada, 1700–1850* (Winnipeg: Watson and Dwyer, 1980).

14 Sylvia Van Kirk, "The Impact of White Women on Fur Trade Society," *in* Trofimenkoff and Prentice, eds., *The Neglected Majority*, vol. 1, 27–48; and Van Kirk, *"Many Tender Ties,"* chap. 8.

15 See Jennifer S.H. Brown, "Ultimate Respectability: Fur Trade Children in the 'Civilized World'," *The Beaver* (Winter 1977) 4–10 and (Spring 1978) 48–55.

16 Van Kirk, *"Many Tender Ties,"* 111–13, 156, 208–9, 237; Van Kirk, " 'Women in Between';" Gould, *Women of British Columbia*, chap. 2.

17 Ingeborg Marshall, "Disease as a Factor in the Demise of the Beothuck Indians," *Culture* 1, 1 (1981) 71–77; Virginia P. Miller, "The Decline of Nova Scotia Micmac Population, A.D. 1600–1850," *Culture* 2, 3 (1982) 107–20; Ruth Holmes Whitehead, "Christina Morris: Micmac Artist and Artist's Model," *Material History Bulletin* 3 (Spring 1977) 1–14; Keith Winter, *Shawanditti: The Last of the Beothucks* (North Vancouver: J.J. Douglas, 1975). On peoples of the Northwest who managed to remain relatively isolated and escape the worst aspects of cultural conflict, see Julie Cruikshank, "Becoming a Woman in Athapaskan Society: Changing Traditions on the Upper Yukon River," *Western Canadian Journal of Anthropology* 5, 2 (1975) 1–14; Robin Ridington, "Stories of the Vision Quest Among Dunne-Za Women," *Atlantis* 9, 1 (1983) 68–78.

18 Ellen M. Thomas Gee, "Marriage in Nineteenth-Century Canada," *Canadian Review of Sociology and Anthropology* 19, 3 (August 1982) 315–20; Michael B. Katz, *The People of Hamilton, Canada West*, 271–72.

19 Jacques Henripin, *La Population Canadienne au XVIII siècle*, Institut
    nationale d'études démographiques, Cahier No. 22 (Presses Universitaires
    de France, 1954); David Gagan, *Hopeful Travellers: Families, Land, and
    Social Change in Mid-Victorian Peel County, Canada West* (Toronto:
    University of Toronto Press, 1981) 70–73; Chad Gaffield, "Canadian
    Families in Cultural Context: Hypotheses from the Mid-Nineteenth
    Century," *Historical Papers* (1979), especially graph 4; Katz, *The People of
    Hamilton*, 34, 233; Roderick P. Beaujot and Kevin McQuillan, "Social
    Effects of Demographic Change: Canada 1851–1981," *Journal of
    Canadian Studies* 2 (Spring 1986) 57–59.
20 Margaret Angus, "A Gentlewoman in Early Kingston," *Historic Kingston*
    24 (1976) 73–95.
21 Katz, *The People of Hamilton*, 255.
22 Katz, *The People of Hamilton*, 223; Gagan, *Hopeful Travellers*, 64–65;
    Sheva Medjuck, "Family and Household Composition in the Nineteenth
    Century: The Case of Moncton, New Brunswick, 1851–1871,"
    Canadian Journal of Sociology 4, 3 (1979) 275–86.
23 Katz, *The People of Hamilton*, 249, 255.
24 F.K. Donnelly, "Occupational and Household Structures of a New
    Brunswick Fishing Settlement: Campobello Island, 1851," *in* R.
    Chanteloup, ed., *Labour in Atlantic Canada* (Saint John: Social Service
    Monographs, 1981), vol. 4, 55–63; Katz, *The People of Hamilton*, 250.
    See also Gagan, *Hopeful Travellers*, 65–67.
25 J.M. Bumsted, "The Household and Family of Edward Jarvis, 1828–
    1852," *The Island* 14 (Fall-Winter 1983) 22–28.
26 Claudette Lacelle, "Les domestiques dans les villes Canadiennes au XIXe
    siècle: effectifs et conditions de vie," *Histoire sociale/Social History* 15
    (1982) 181–207; Katz, *The People of Hamilton*, 27.
27 Frances Stewart, *Our Forest Home, Being Extracts from the Correspondence of
    the Late Frances Stewart*, compiled and edited by her daughter, E.S.
    Dunlop (Toronto, 1889) 78–79; A.S. Miller, ed., *The Journals of Mary
    O'Brien* (Toronto: Macmillan, 1968).
28 Moodie, *Roughing It in the Bush* (Toronto: McClelland and Stewart,
    1923) 458–73.
29 Elsie Gregory MacGill, *My Mother the Judge: A Biography of Judge Helen
    Gregory MacGill* (Toronto: PMA Books, 1981) 6, 9, 32.
30 Stewart, *Our Forest Home*, 80–81.
31 Lacelle, "Les domestiques;" Katz, *The People of Hamilton*, 260, 270.
32 Leone Banks Cousins, "Woman of the Year — 1842: The Life of
    Eliza Ruggles," *Nova Scotia Historical Quarterly* 6, 4 (December 1976)
    349–76.
33 Elizabeth Muir, "Delayed but Not Forgotten: Methodist Women Called
    to Preach," unpublished paper (Faculty of Religious Studies, McGill
    University, 1980) 35.
34 John E. McDowell, "Madame La Framboise," *Michigan History* 56, 3
    (1972) 271–86; McDowell, "Thérèse Schindler of Mackinac: Upward
    Mobility in the Great Lakes Fur Trade," *Wisconsin Magazine of History*
    61 (Winter 1977–78) 125–43.
35 W. Kaye Lamb, "The Mystery of Mrs. Barkley's Diary," *British Columbia
    Historical Quarterly* 6, 1 (1942) 31–59; Margaret Conrad, "Recording
    Angels: Private Chronicles of Maritime Women, 1800–1950," *in*
    Prentice and Trofimenkoff, eds., *The Neglected Majority*, vol. 2, 41–60.
36 Porter, "She Was Skipper of the Shore Crew," 105–23.
37 Ephraim W. Tucker, *Five Months in Labrador and Newfoundland During
    the Summer of 1838* (Concord: 1838) 119–20.
38 Marjorie Griffin Cohen, *The Razor's Edge Invisible: Women, Markets and
    Economic Development in Ontario, 1800–1911* (York University: Ph.D.
    Thesis, 1985). See also Cohen, "The Decline of Women in Canadian
    Dairying," *in* Prentice and Trofimenkoff, eds., *The Neglected Majority*,
    vol. 2, 61–83.
39 Conrad, "Recording Angels," 44–45.

40 Conrad, "Recording Angels," 44.

41 *Census Reports of the Canadas*, 1851. Upper Canada, vol. 1, 520; Lower Canada, vol. 1, 546.

42 Christina Bates, "Blue Monday: A Day in the Life of a Washerwoman, 1840 . . . " *Canadian Collector* (July/August 1985) 44–48.

43 Susan E. Houston and Alison Prentice, *Schooling and Scholars in Nineteenth Century Ontario* (Toronto: University of Toronto Press, 1988) chap. 3.

44 Donald Chaput, "The 'Misses Nolin' of Red River," *The Beaver* (Winter 1975) 14–17.

45 Grace McLeod Rogers, "Kate Andrews, Schoolmistress," *The Maritime Advocate and Busy East*, 32 (1942) 5–10.

46 H.H. Langton, ed., *A Gentlewoman in Upper Canada: The Journals of Anne Langton* (Toronto: Clarke, Irwin, 1950).

47 Light and Prentice, eds., *Pioneer and Gentlewomen*, 73–74.

48 Phyllis R. Blakely, "And Having a Love for People," *Nova Scotia Historical Quarterly* 5 (June 1975) 165–75.

49 Elizabeth McCallum, "Catharine Parr Traill, A Nineteenth Century Ontario Naturalist," *The Beaver* (Autumn 1975) 39–45.

50 Katz, *The People of Hamilton*, 222.

51 Katz, *The People of Hamilton*, 348.

52 In the list of occupations for Hamilton, twenty-one appear to be clearly women's; men's occupations numbered several hundred. Katz, *The People of Hamilton*, appendix two.

53 Catharine McKenna, "Options for Elite Women in Early Upper Canadian Society: The Case of the Powell Family," paper presented to the Canadian Historical Association, Winnipeg, 1986.

54 Moodie, *Roughing It in the Bush* (Toronto: McClelland and Stewart, 1962) 142 and 167.

4 Women and the public order

1 Beth Light and Alison Prentice, eds., *Pioneer and Gentlewomen of British North America, 1713–1867* (Toronto: New Hogtown Press, 1980) 213–14.

2 Sylvia Van Kirk, *"Many Tender Ties": Women in Fur-Trade Society, 1670–1870* (Winnipeg: Watson & Dwyer, 1980) 175–77. See also Malvina Bolus, "The Son of I. Gunn," *The Beaver* (Winter 1971) 23–26.

3 Light and Prentice, eds., *Pioneer and Gentlewomen*, 215–16.

4 Frances Brookes, *The History of Emily Montague* (London, 1769; Toronto: McClelland and Stewart, 1961).

5 Van Kirk, *"Many Tender Ties,"* 154–57.

6 Light and Prentice, eds., *Pioneer and Gentlewomen*, 120.

7 Peter Ward, "Courtship and Social Space in Nineteenth Century English Canada," *Canadian Historical Review* 68, 1 (March 1987) 35–62; Madeleine Ferron et Robert Cliché, *Les Beaucerons ces insoumis* suivi de *Quand le peuple fait la loi* (Québec: Hurtubise, 1982) 279–80.

8 Light and Prentice, eds., *Pioneer and Gentlewomen*, 99–101.

9 Audrey S. Miller, ed., *The Journals of Mary O'Brien* (Toronto: Macmillan, 1968) 84, 88–89.

10 Byran D. Palmer, "Discordant Music: Charivaris and Whitecapping in Nineteenth-Century North America," *Labour/le travail* 3 (1978) 5–62.

11 Louis Knafla, "Marriage Customs, Law, and Litigation in the Northwest, 1800–1870," Paper presented to the Canadian Historical Association, London, 1978. The paper deals, in part, with the Lower Canadian laws that affected marriages of traders who returned to the province.

12 Constance B. Backhouse, "Married Women's Property Law in Nineteenth-Century Canada," unpublished paper (July 1987) 3.

13 See Rosemary Ball, " 'A Perfect Farmer's Wife': Women in 19th Century Rural Ontario," *Canada: An Historical Magazine* 3 (1975) 2–21.

14 Constance B. Backhouse, " 'Pure Patriarchy': Nineteenth Century

Canadian Marriage," *McGill Law Journal* 31 (March 1986) 264–312.

15 B. Hovius, *Family Law* (Toronto: Carswell, 1987) 110.

16 Light and Prentice, eds., *Pioneer and Gentlewomen*, 119.

17 Light and Prentice, eds., *Pioneer and Gentlewomen*, 125.

18 Margaret Conrad, "Recording Angels: The Private Chronicles of Women from the Maritime Provinces of Canada, 1750–1950," *in* Alison Prentice and Susan Mann Trofimenkoff, eds., *The Neglected Majority: Essays in Canadian Women's History* (Toronto: McClelland and Stewart, 1985) vol. 2; Light and Prentice, eds., *Pioneer and Gentlewomen*, 125–26 and 163–64.

19 Light and Prentice, eds., *Pioneer and Gentlewomen*, 163.

20 Constance B. Backhouse, "Desperate women and compassionate courts: Infanticide in nineteenth-century Canada," *University of Toronto Law Journal* 34, 4 (Fall 1984) 447–78; Backhouse, "Involuntary Motherhood: Abortion, Birth Control and the Law in Nineteenth Century Canada," *The Windsor Yearbook of Access to Justice* 3 (1983) 61–130; Backhouse, "The Tort of Seduction: Fathers and Daughters in Nineteenth Century Canada," *Dalhousie Law Journal* 10, 1 (June 1986) 45–80.

21 Backhouse, "Desperate Women," 450–52.

22 Backhouse, "Involuntary Motherhood," 61–130.

23 Richard A. Leonardo, *History of Gynecology* (New York: Froben Press, 1944) 255.

24 Ruth A. Olson, "Rape—An 'Un-Victorian' Aspect of Life in Upper Canada," *Ontario History* 68, 2 (June 1976) 75–79.

25 Backhouse, "The Tort of Seduction," 50.

26 Light and Prentice, eds., *Pioneer and Gentlewomen*, 208–10.

27 Abraham Gesner, *New Brunswick: With Notes for Emigrants* (London 1847) 241.

28 Susan E. Houston and Alison Prentice, *Schooling and Scholars in Nineteenth Century Ontario*, (Toronto: University of Toronto Press, 1988), chap. 3.

29 Light and Prentice, eds., *Pioneer and Gentlewomen*, 75–78.

30 Alison Prentice, "The Feminization of Teaching," *in* Prentice and Trofimenkoff, eds., *The Neglected Majority*, vol. 1, 49–65.

31 Marta Danylewycz, Beth Light, and Alison Prentice, "The Evolution of the Sexual Division of Labour in Teaching: A Nineteenth Century Ontario and Quebec Case Study," *Histoire sociale/Social History* 16, 31 (May 1983) 81–109. For urban teachers, see Alison Prentice, "The Feminization of Teaching," *in* Trofimenkoff and Prentice, eds., *The Neglected Majority*, vol. 1, especially 56–59; and Marta Danylewycz and Alison Prentice, "Teachers, Gender, and Bureaucratizing School Systems in Nineteenth Century Montreal and Toronto," *History of Education Quarterly* 24 (Spring 1984) 75–100.

32 Houston and Prentice, *Schooling and Scholars in Nineteenth Century Ontario*, chap. 3.

33 Elsie Pomeroy, "Mary Electa Adams," *Ontario History* 41, 3 (1949) 106–17.

34 Diane Bélanger and Lucie Rozon, *Les religieuses au Québec* (Montréal: Libre Expression, 1982) Annexe 2, 294–315; Sister Marthe Baudoin, "The religious of the Sacred Heart in Canada, 1842–1980," Canadian Catholic History Association *Study Sessions* 48 (1981) 43–60; Sister Maura, *The Sisters of Charity, Halifax* (Toronto: Ryerson Press, 1956).

35 Jeanette Letourneau, *Les écoles normales de filles au Québec* (Montréal: Fides, 1981), especially chaps. 1 and 2.

36 Alison Prentice, " 'Friendly Atoms in Chemistry': Women and Men at the Toronto Normal School," *in* David Keane and Colin Read, eds., *A Festschrift for J.M.S. Careless* (Toronto: Dundurn Press, forthcoming); Light and Prentice, eds., *Pioneer and Gentlewomen*, 216–18.

37 G.A. Rawlyk, *Ravished by the Spirit: Religious Revivals, Baptists and Henry Alline* (Kingston: McGill-Queen's University Press, 1984) especially 76–79 and 120–28.

38 Jean Bannerman, *Leading Ladies: Canada 1639–1867* (Belleville: Mika Publishing, 1978) 25; Elizabeth Muir, "Delayed But Not Forgotten: Methodist Women Called to Preach," unpublished paper (Faculty of Religious Studies, McGill University, 1980); *Dictionary of Canadian Biography* (Toronto: University of Toronto Press, 1985), vol. 8, 200–1. See also Muir, "The Bark Schoolhouse: Methodist Episcopal Female Missionaries in Early Nineteenth Century Upper Canada," *in* John Moir, ed., *A Festschrift for John Webster Grant* (forthcoming).

39 John Garner, *The Franchise and Politics in British North America 1755–1867* (Toronto: University of Toronto Press, 1969) 156.

40 William Renwick Riddell, "Woman Franchise in Quebec a Century Ago," Royal Society of Canada, *Proceedings and Transactions* Series 3, 22 (1928) 87–88.

41 Garner, *The Franchise and Politics*, 157.

42 Garner, *The Franchise and Politics*, 88–89; Light and Prentice, eds., *Pioneer and Gentlewomen*, 211–13.

43 Garner, *The Franchise and Politics*, 155.

44 Garner, *The Franchise and Politics*, 156.

45 Garner, *The Franchise and Politics*, 156–58.

46 Le Collectif Clio, *L'histoire des Femmes au Québec depuis quatre siècles* (Montréal: Quinze, 1982) 126.

47 H. Pearson Gundy, "Molly Brant—Loyalist," *Ontario History* 45, 3 (1953); Helen Caister Robinson, "Molly Brant: Mohawk Heroine," *in* Phyllis R. Blakely and John R. Grant, eds., *Eleven Exiles: Accounts of Loyalists and the American Revolution* (Toronto: Dundurn Press, 1982); Jean Johnston, *Wilderness Women: Canada's Forgotten History* (Toronto: Peter Martin Associates, 1973).

48 *Dictionary of Canadian Biography* (Toronto: University of Toronto Press, 1976), vol. 9, 405–7; John S. Moir, "An Early Record of Laura Secord's Walk," *Ontario History* 51, 2 (1959) 105–8.

49 Le Collectif Clio, *L'histoire des femmes*, 144–49; Marcelle Reeves-Morache, "La canadienne pendant les troubles de 1837–1838," *Revue d'histoire de l'Amérique française* 5 (1951–52).

50 Light and Prentice, eds., *Pioneer and Gentlewomen*, 165–66.

51 Light and Prentice, eds., *Pioneer and Gentlewomen*, 191–92.

52 Light and Prentice, eds., *Pioneer and Gentlewomen*, 193–96.

53 Alan Greer, "The Sunday Schools of Upper Canada," *Ontario History* 67 (September 1975) 169–84.

54 G.A. Rawlyk, *Ravished by the Spirit*, 124–27.

55 Marta Danylewycz, *Taking the Veil: An Alternative to Marriage, Motherhood and Spinsterhood in Quebec, 1840–1920* (Toronto: McClelland and Stewart, 1986), introduction.

56 Roger Lane, *Policing the City: Boston 1822–1885* (Cambridge, Mass.: Harvard University Press, 1967).

57 John Weaver, "Crime, Public Order and Repression," *Ontario History* 78, 3 (September 1984) 191–92.

58 J.T. McNeil, *The Presbyterian Church in Canada 1875–1925* (Toronto: General Board of the Presbyterian Church in Canada, 1925) 140.

59 *Halifax Woman's Christian Temperance Union* (1890), 40; McNeil, *The Presbyterian Church*, 142; Haley P. Bamman, "The Ladies' Benevolent Society of Hamilton, Ontario: Form and Function in Mid-Nineteenth Century Urban Philanthropy," *in* Michael B. Katz and Paul H. Mattingly, eds., *Education and Social Change: Themes from Ontario's Past* (New York: New York University Press, 1975); Robin Winks, *The Blacks in Canada: A History* (New Haven: Yale University Press, 1971) 328–29.

60 Le Collectif Clio, *L'histoire des femmes*, 124; Danylewycz, *Taking the Veil*, 47.

61 D. Suzanne Cross, "The Neglected Majority: The Changing Role of Women in 19th Century Montreal," *in* Trofimenkoff and Prentice, eds., *The Neglected Majority*, vol. 1, 79.

62 Danylewycz, *Taking the Veil*, 20.

63 Maritime Woman's Christian Temperance Union, *Annual Report* (1890)
    40.

THE NEW PIONEERS: THE MID-NINETEENTH CENTURY TO THE END OF THE GREAT WAR
 1 Bryan D. Palmer, *Working-Class Experience: the Rise and Reconstitution of
    Canadian Labour, 1800–1980* (Toronto: Butterworth, 1983) 67.
 2 F.H. Leacy, ed., *Historical Statistics of Canada*, 2nd ed. (Ottawa: Statistics
    Canada, 1983) A1–14.
 3 Leacy, *Historical Statistics of Canada*, A125–63.
 4 *Canadian Annual Review* (1905) 589.
 5 L.O. Stone, *Urban Development in Canada*, 1961 Census Monograph,
    Dominion Bureau of Statistics (Ottawa: Queen's Printer, 1967) 29.
 6 Ellen M. Thomas Gee, "Marriage in Nineteenth-Century Canada,"
    Canadian Review of Sociology and Anthropology 19, 3 (1982) 318, 320.
 7 Catherine Cleverdon, *The Woman Suffrage Movement in Canada*
    (Toronto: University of Toronto Press, 1974) 108.
 8 Nancy M. Sheehan, "Women's Organizations and Educational Issues,
    1900–1930," *Canadian Woman Studies* 7, 3 (Fall 1986) 91.

 5 Continuity and change in women's work
 1 Margaret Conrad, " 'Sunday Always Makes Me Think of Home': Time
    and Place in Canadian Women's History," *in* Veronica Strong-Boag and
    Anita Clair Fellman, eds., *Rethinking Canada: The Promise of Women's
    History* (Toronto: Copp Clark Pitman, 1986) 72.
 2 Beth Light and Joy Parr, eds., *Canadian Women on the Move, 1867–1920*
    (Toronto: New Hogtown Press and OISE Press, 1983) 169–70.
 3 Linda Rasmussen, *et al.*, eds., *A Harvest Yet to Reap: A History of Prairie
    Women* (Toronto: The Women's Press, 1976) 26.
 4 Dominion Bureau of Statistics, *Origin, Birthplace, Nationality and
    Language of the Canadian People* (Ottawa: Printer to the King, 1929) 42.
 5 Dominion Bureau of Statistics, *Origin, Birthplace, Nationality*, 42.
 6 F.H. Leacy, ed., *Historical Statistics of Canada* 2nd ed. (Ottawa: Statistics
    Canada, 1983) A110–53; Howard Palmer, *Patterns of Prejudice: A History
    of Nativism in Alberta* (Toronto: McClelland and Stewart, 1982) 39.
 7 Tamara Adilman, "A Preliminary Sketch of Chinese Women and Work
    in British Columbia 1858–1950," *in* Barbara K. Latham and Roberta J.
    Pazdro, eds., *Not Just Pin Money: Selected Essays on the History of Women's
    Work in British Columbia* (Victoria: Camosun College, 1984) 54–57.
 8 Information provided by Ottilia Doering's great-granddaughter, Bonnie
    Shettler.
 9 Joy Parr, *Labouring Children: British Immigrant Apprentices to Canada,
    1869–1924* (Montreal: McGill-Queen's University Press,1980) 88.
10 Rasmussen *et al.*, eds., *A Harvest Yet to Reap*, 22.
11 Paul Phillips and Erin Phillips, *Women and Work: Inequality in the Labour
    Market* (Toronto: James Lorimer, 1983) 6.
12 Leacy, ed., *Historical Statistics of Canada*, A94–109.
13 Warren E. Kalbach and Wayne W. McVey, *The Demographic Bases of
    Canadian Society*, 2nd ed. (Toronto: McGraw-Hill Ryerson, 1971) 136.
14 Emily Nett, "Canadian Families in Social-historical Perspective,"
    Canadian Journal of Sociology 6, 3 (1981) 245.
15 *Sixth Census of Canada* (1921) vol. 4, xiv.
16 G.G. Campbell, "Susan Dunlap: Her Diary," *Dalhousie Review* 46, 2
    (1966) 218–19.
17 E.B. Gonzalez, *Changing Economic Roles for Micmac Men and Women*
    (Ottawa: National Museums, 1981) 86, 91.
18 Anne B. Woywitka, "Homesteader's Woman," *Alberta History* 24, 2
    (Spring 1976) 21.
19 Harriet Neville, "Pioneering in the North-West Territories, 1882–1905,"
    Canada, An Historical Magazine 2, 4 (June 1975) 29.

20 Sarah Kolasiewicz, "Outstanding Women of Oxford County," *Canadian Women's Studies* 3, 1 (1981) 50–1; Marjorie Cohen, "The Decline of Women in Canadian Dairying," *in* Susan Mann Trofimenkoff and Alison Prentice, eds., *The Neglected Majority: Essays in Canadian Women's History* (Toronto: McClelland and Stewart, 1985), vol. 2, 71–83.

21 Beth Light and Alison Prentice, eds., *Pioneer and Gentlewomen of British North America, 1713–1867* (Toronto: New Hogtown Press, 1980) 160.

22 Susan Jackel, "Introduction," Georgina Binnie-Clark, *Wheat and Woman* (Toronto: University of Toronto Press, 1979) xvii.

23 Light and Parr, eds., *Canadian Women on the Move*, 189–90.

24 Anita Penner, "Emily Murphy and the Attempt to Alter the Status of Canadian Women, 1910–31," (Carleton University: M.A. Thesis, 1979) 46.

25 Nanciellen Davis, " 'Patriarchy from the Grave': Family Relations in 19th Century New Brunswick Wills," *Acadiensis* 13, 2 (1984) 95.

26 Mary Rubio and Elizabeth Waterson, eds., *Selected Journals of L. M. Montgomery vol. 1 (1889–1910)* (Toronto: Oxford University Press, 1986) 310.

27 "How the Chamberlains Found Canada," *Women's Work in Western Canada* (Canadian Pacific Railway, 1906) 63–66; Georgina Binnie-Clark, *Wheat and Woman* (Toronto: William Heinemann, 1914).

28 Rasmussen *et al.*, eds., *A Harvest Yet to Reap*, 60.

29 Jorgen Dahlie, "Learning on the Frontier: Scandinavian Immigrants and Education in Western Canada," *Canadian and International Education* 1, 2 (December 1972) 64.

30 Light and Parr, eds., *Canadian Women on the Move*, 168.

31 Letitia Youmans, *Campaign Echoes: The Autobiography of Letitia Youmans* (Toronto: William Briggs, 1893) 81.

32 Sylvia Van Kirk, "The Impact of White Women on Fur Trade Society," *in* Susan Mann Trofimenkoff and Alison Prentice, eds., *The Neglected Majority* (Toronto: McClelland and Stewart, 1977) vol. 1, 27–48.

33 Gonzalez, "Changing Economic Roles," 94.

34 Bettina Bradbury, "The Fragmented Family: Family Strategies in the Face of Death, Illness and Poverty, Montreal, 1860–1885," *in* Joy Parr, ed., *Childhood and Family in Canadian History* (Toronto: McClelland and Stewart, 1982) 109–28; Bettina Bradbury, "Pigs, Cows and Boarders: Non-Wage Forms of Survival Among Montreal Families 1861–1891," *Labour/Le Travail* 14 (Fall 1984) 9–48.

35 Light and Parr, eds., *Canadian Women on the Move*, 27; Rasmussen *et al.*, eds., *A Harvest Yet to Reap*, 70.

36 See Ruth Schwartz Cowan, *More Work for Mother: The Ironies of Household Technology from the Open Hearth to the Microwave* (New York: Basic Books, 1983).

37 Nellie McClung, *The Stream Runs Fast* (Toronto: Thomas Allen, 1945) 47.

38 Light and Parr, eds., *Canadian Women on the Move*, 61.

39 Ian Davey, "Educational Reform and the Working Class: School Attendance in Hamilton, Ontario, 1851–1891," (University of Toronto: Ph.D. Thesis, 1975) 175.

40 Phillips and Phillips, *Women and Work*, 12.

41 Phillips and Phillips, *Women and Work*, 12.

42 Cassie Palamar, "The Treatment of Issues Affecting Women by the Knights of Labor in the *Palladium of Labor*, 1883–86," unpublished paper, Ontario Institute for Studies in Education, 12.

43 McClung, *The Stream Runs Fast*, 259.

44 Peter Gossage, "Absorbing Junior: The Use of Patent Medicines as Abortifacients in Nineteenth Century Montreal," *The Register* 3, 1 (March 1982) 2–3.

45 Genevieve Leslie, "Domestic Service in Canada, 1880–1920," *in* Janice Acton *et al.*, *Women at Work: Ontario 1850–1930* (Toronto: Canadian Women's Educational Press, 1974) 94.

46 Lori Rotenberg, "The Wayward Worker: Toronto's Prostitute at the Turn of the Century," *in* Acton *et al.*, eds., *Women at Work*, 33–69; Constance B. Backhouse, "Nineteenth-Century Canadian Prostitution Law: Reflection of a Discriminatory Society," *Histoire Sociale/Social History* 18, 36 (November 1983) 387–423.

47 Phillips and Phillips, *Women and Work*, 8.

48 Albert Faucher, "Explication socio-économique des migrations dans l'histoire du Québec," *in* Normand Séguin, *Agriculture et Colonisation au Québec* (Montréal: Boréal Express, 1980) 114.

49 Light and Parr, eds., *Canadian Women on the Move*, 100–1.

50 Ceta Ramkhalawansingh, "Women During the Great War," *in* Acton *et al.*, eds., *Women at Work*, 281.

51 Wayne Roberts, "Honest Womanhood: Feminism, Femininity and Class Consciousness Among Toronto Working Women 1893–1914," *in* R. Douglas Francis and Donald B. Smith, eds., *Readings in Canadian History: Post Confederation*, 2nd ed. (Toronto: Holt, Rinehart and Winston Canada, 1986) 240; Terry Copp, *The Anatomy of Poverty: The Condition of the Working Class in Montreal 1897–1929* (Toronto: McClelland and Stewart, 1974) 45.

52 Susan Trofimenkoff, "One Hundred and Two Muffled Voices: Canada's Industrial Women in the 1880's," *Atlantis* 3, 1 (Fall 1977) 67–68.

53 *Census of Canada* (1891), 186.

54 Phillips and Phillips, *Women and Work*, 22.

55 Wayne Roberts, *Honest Womanhood: Feminism, Femininity and Class Consciousness Among Toronto Working Women 1893 to 1914* (Toronto: New Hogtown Press, 1976) 37; J. T. Copp, "The Conditions of the Working Class in Montreal, 1897–1920," *in* Francis and Smith, eds., *Readings in Canadian History*, 2nd ed., 227.

56 Rotenberg, "The Wayward Workers," 48–49.

57 Roberts, "Honest Womanhood," 242.

58 Barbara Hansen, "A Historical Study of Women in Canadian Banking, 1900–1975," *Canadian Women's Studies* 1, 2 (Winter 1978/79) 17.

59 Ramkhalawansingh, "Women During the Great War," 280–81.

60 Judith Fingard, "The New Woman Goes to College: Dalhousie Coeds, 1881–1921," unpublished paper (1986) 9.

61 Kennethe Haig, "E. Cora Hind," *in* Mary Quayle Innis, ed., *The Clear Spirit: Twenty Canadian Women and Their Times* (Toronto: University of Toronto Press, 1966) 120–41.

62 Graham Lowe, "Class, Job, and Gender in the Canadian Office," *Labour/Le Travail* 10 (Autumn 1982) 20, 28.

63 Phillips and Phillips, *Women and Work*, 25.

64 Linda Bohnen, "Women Workers in Ontario: A Socio-Legal History," *University of Toronto Faculty of Law Review* 31 (1973) 47.

65 *Census of Canada* (1921), vol. 4, 6–7.

66 Donald J. Wilson *et al.*, *Canadian Education: A History* (Scarborough: Prentice Hall, 1970) 317.

67 Alison Prentice and Marta Danylewycz, "Teachers' Work: Changing Patterns and Perceptions in the Emerging School Systems of Nineteenth- and Early Twentieth-Century Central Canada," *Labour/Le Travail* 17 (Spring 1986) 65.

68 W.L. Morton, "Furrow's End," *Journal of Canadian Studies* 21, 3 (Fall 1986) 29.

69 Elizabeth Graham, "Schoolmarms and Early Teaching in Ontario," *in* Acton *et al.*, eds., *Women at Work*, 194.

70 Saskatoon Women's Calendar Collective, "Medical Women of Prince Edward Island," *in Herstory*, (Sidney, B.C.: Gray's Publishing, 1981) 12.

71 Margaret Gillett, *We Walked Very Warily: A History of Women at McGill* (Montreal: Eden Press Women's Publications, 1981) 227, 306.

72 Sr. Marie Bonin, "The Grey Nuns and the Red River Settlement," *Manitoba History* 11 (Spring 1986) 13.

73 Judi Coburn, " 'I See and am Silent': A Short History of Nursing," *in* Acton *et al.*, eds., *Women at Work*, 150.

74 Colin Howell, "Reform and the Monopolistic Impulse: The Professionalization of Medicine in the Maritimes," *Acadiensis* 11, 1 (Autumn 1981) 20.

75 Heather MacDougall, " 'Guides, Philosophers and Friends': The Development of Public Health Nursing in Toronto, 1907–1932," paper presented to the Canadian Historical Association, Winnipeg, 1986, 1–2.

76 A.A. Travill, "Early Medical Co-Education and Women's Medical College, Kingston, Ontario, 1880–1894," *Historic Kingston* 30 (January 1982) 86; Micheline D.-Johnson, "History of the Status of Women in the Province of Quebec," *in Cultural Tradition and Political History of Women in Canada*, Study 8, Royal Commission of the Status of Women in Canada (Ottawa: Information Canada, 1971) 29; see also Veronica Strong-Boag, "Canada's Women Doctors: Feminism Constrained," *in* Linda Kealey, ed., *A Not Unreasonable Claim: Women and Reform in Canada, 1880s-1920s* (Toronto: The Women's Press, 1979) 109–29.

77 A Bystander, "The Woman's Rights Movement," *The Canada Monthly!* (March 1872) 255.

78 Constance B. Backhouse, " 'To Open the Way for Others of My Sex': Clara Brett Martin's Career as Canada's First Woman Lawyer," *Canadian Journal of Women and the Law* 1, 1 (1985) 1–41.

79 Micheline D.-Johnson, *Cultural Traditions*, 28–29.

80 Fingard, "The New Woman Goes to College," 46.

81 Our thanks to Margaret Conrad for this information.

82 Isabel Bassett, *The Parlour Rebellion: Profiles in the Struggle for Women's Rights* (Toronto: McClelland and Stewart, 1975) 154.

83 Barbara Freeman, " 'Every Stroke Upward': Women Journalists in Canada, 1880–1906," *Canadian Woman Studies* 7, 3 (Fall 1986), 44–45.

84 Paula Giddings, *When and Where I Enter: the Impact of Black Women on Race and Sex in America* (New York: Bantam Books, 1984) 69.

85 Mary Jean Green, "The Literary Feminists in the Fight for Women's Writing in Quebec," *Journal of Canadian Studies* 21, 1 (Spring 1986) 129.

86 Laura Jones, "Rediscovery," *Canadian Women's Studies* 2, 3 (1980) 5–6; Diana Pedersen and Martha Phemister, "Women and Photography in Ontario, 1839–1929: A Case Study of the Interaction of Gender and Technology," *Scientia Canadensis* 9, 1 (June 1985) 34.

87 *The Canadian Encyclopedia* (Edmonton: Hurtig, 1985) vol. 1, 35.

88 Carol Budnick, "The Performing Arts as a Field of Endeavour for Winnipeg Women, 1870–1930," *Manitoba History* 11 (Spring 1986) 51.

89 Maria Tippett, *Emily Carr: A Biography* (Toronto: Oxford University Press, 1979) 118–19; Angela E. Davis, "Mary Riter Hamilton: Manitoba Artist 1873–1954," *Manitoba History* 11 (Spring 1986) 23–25.

90 Laurie Albert, "Petticoats and Pickaxes," *Alaska Journal* 7, 3(1972) 146–59.

91 Gregory S. Kealey and Bryan D. Palmer, *Dreaming of What Might Be: The Knights of Labor in Ontario, 1880–1900* (New York: Cambridge University Press, 1982) 106.

92 Jacques Ferland, "When the Cotton Mills 'Girls' Struck for the First Time: A Study of Female Militancy in the Cotton and Shoe Factories of Quebec (1880–1910)," paper presented to the Canadian Historical Association, Winnipeg, 1986, 18–19.

93 Joan Sangster, "The 1907 Bell Telephone Strike: Organizing Women Workers," *Labour/Le Travail* 3 (1978) 109–30.

94 Ruth Frager, "Sewing Solidarity: The Eaton's Strike of 1912," *Canadian Woman Studies* 7, 3 (Fall 1986) 96–97.

95 Star Rosenthal, "Union Maids: Organized Women Workers in Vancouver, 1900–1915," *BC Studies* 41 (Spring 1979) 50.

96 Roberts, "Honest Womanhood," 243.

97 Margaret McCallum, "Keeping Women in Their Place: The Minimum Wage in Canada 1910–25," *Labour/Le Travail* 17 (Spring 1986) 37.

98 Palamar, "The Treatment of Issues Affecting Women by the Knights of Labor," 9.

99 Ruth Frager, "No Proper Deal: Women Workers and the Canadian Labour Movement, 1870–1940," *in* Linda Briskin and Lynda Yanz, eds., *Union Sisters: Women in the Labour Movement* (Toronto: The Women's Press, 1983) 52.

100 Prentice and Danylewycz, "Teacher's Work," 76.

101 Alison Prentice, "Themes in the Early History of the Women Teachers' Association of Toronto," *in* Paula Bourne, ed., *Women's Paid and Unpaid Work: Historical and Contemporary Perspectives* (Toronto: New Hogtown Press, 1985) 97–121; Pat Staton and Beth Light, *Speak with Their Own Voices: A Documentary History of the Federation of Women Teachers' Associations of Ontario and the Elementary Public School Teachers of Ontario* (Toronto: Federation of Women Teachers' Associations of Ontario, 1987) chap. 3.

102 Apolonja Maria Kojder, "In Union There is Strength: the Saskatoon Women Teachers' Association," *Canadian Woman Studies* 7 (Fall 1986) 82–84.

103 P.B. Waite, *The Man from Halifax: Sir John Thompson Prime Minister* (Toronto: University of Toronto Press, 1985) 61–65.

104 Marta Danylewycz, *Taking the Veil: An Alternative to Marriage, Motherhood and Spinsterhood in Quebec, 1840–1920* (Toronto: McClelland and Stewart, 1987) 95.

105 Margaret Street, *Watch-Fires on the Mountains: The Life and Writings of Ethel Johns* (Toronto: University of Toronto Press, 1973) 43.

106 Mary Quayle Innis, *Unfold the Years: A History of the Young Women's Christian Association in Canada* (Toronto: McClelland and Stewart, 1949) 80.

107 Ramkhalawansingh, "Women during the Great War," 279.

108 Ramkhalawansingh, "Women during the Great War," 275.

109 Graham S. Lowe, "Women, Work and the Office: The Feminization of Clerical Occupations in Canada, 1901–1931," *in* Strong-Boag and Fellman, eds., *Rethinking Canada* 109–14.

110 Ramkhalawansingh, "Women during the Great War," 276.

111 John Herd Thompson, *The Harvests of War: The Prairie West, 1914–1918* (Toronto: McClelland and Stewart, 1978) 110.

112 G.W.L. Nicholson, *Canada's Nursing Sisters* (Toronto: Samuel Stevens Hakkert, 1975) 4, 98.

113 See Patricia Connelly, *Last Hired, First Fired: Women and the Canadian Work Force* (Toronto: The Women's Press, 1978) 10–22.

114 Margaret McCallum, "Keeping Women in Their Place," 34.

6 Women's sphere

1 Anton Wagner, ed., *Women Pioneers: Canada's Lost Plays* (Toronto: Canadian Theatre Review Publications, 1979) vol. 2, 94–5, (author's emphasis); 136–37.

2 Paul Phillips and Erin Phillips, *Women and Work: Inequality in the Labour Market* (Toronto: James Lorimer, 1983) 8.

3 Ramsay Cook and Wendy Mitchinson, eds., *The Proper Sphere: Woman's Place in Canadian Society* (Toronto: Oxford University Press, 1976) 9.

4 "Woman's Sphere," *The Harp* (December 1874) 25.

5 Diane Bélanger and Lucie Rozon, *Les Religieuses au Québec* (Montréal: Libre Expression, 1982) 294–319 and annexe 2.

6 Cook and Mitchinson, eds., *The Proper Sphere*, 86–87 (authors' translation).

7 Michael Owen, "Keeping Canada God's Country: Presbyterian Perspectives on Selected Social Issues 1900–1915," (University of Toronto: Ph.D. Thesis, 1984) 114.

8 M.L. Holbrook, "Parturition without Pain," *in* George Napheys, *The Physical Life of Woman* (Toronto, 1890) 312.

9 *Canadian Practitioner* (January 1886) 43.

10 J. Thoburn, *A Practical Treatise of the Diseases of Women* (London, 1885) 192–93. See also Wendy Mitchinson, "Causes of Disease in Women: The Case of Late 19th Century English Canada," *in* Charles G. Roland, ed., *Health, Disease, and Medicine: Essays in Canadian History* (Toronto: Clarke, Irwin, 1984) 381–95.

11 Wendy Mitchinson, "Gynecological Operations on Insane Women, London, Ontario, 1895–1901," *Journal of Social History* 15, 3 (Spring 1982) 467–84; Public Archives of Ontario, Case Files of London Ontario Asylum for the Insane, Case #4269, E.F.

12 Constance B. Backhouse, "Nineteenth-Century Canadian Prostitution Law: Reflection of a Discriminatory Society," *Histoire sociale/Social History* 18, 36 (November 1985) 416–17.

13 Linda Silver Dranoff, *Women in Canadian Life: Law* (Toronto: Fitzhenry and Whiteside, 1977) 62, 64.

14 Sally Weaver, "The Status of Indian Women," *in* Jean Leonard Elliott, ed., *Two Nations, Many Cultures: Ethnic Groups in Canada* (Scarborough: Prentice-Hall, 1983) 58–59.

15 Douglas Saunders, "Indian Women: A Brief History of their Roles and Rights," *McGill Law Journal* 21, 4 (1975) 663.

16 Erin Breault, "Educating Women About the Law: Violence Against Wives in Ontario, 1850–1920," (University of Toronto: M.A. Thesis, 1986) especially 39.

17 Dranoff, *Women in Canadian Life: Law*, 20–23.

18 Dranoff, *Women in Canadian Life: Law*, 58.

19 Constance B. Backhouse, "Nineteenth Century Canadian Rape Law 1800–92," *in* David Flaherty, ed., *Essays in the History of Canadian Law* (Toronto: The Osgoode Society, 1983) vol. 2, 200–47.

20 Karen Sanders, "Margaret Marshall Saunders: Children's Literature as an Expression of Early Twentieth-Century Social Reform," (Dalhousie University: M.A. Thesis, 1978) 20.

21 Maud Rankin to Elizabeth Smith, September, 1877. Elizabeth Smith Shortt Papers, Doris Lewis Rare Book Room, University of Waterloo.

22 Alice Chown, *The Stairway* (Boston: The Cornhill Company, 1921) 11.

23 Janet McPhee, "The Campbellville Chronicles," unpublished paper, 1987.

24 Barbara Hansen, "A Historical Study of Women in Canadian Banking, 1900–1975," *Canadian Women's Studies* 1, 2 (Winter 1978/79) 18.

25 Michael Piva, *Conditions of the Working Class in Toronto—1900–1921* (Ottawa: University of Ottawa Press, 1979) 125.

26 Veronica Strong-Boag, *Introduction, in* Nellie McClung, *In Times Like These* (Toronto: University of Toronto Press, 1972) 22.

27 Alison L. Prentice and Susan E. Houston, eds., *Family, School and Society in Nineteenth-Century Canada* (Toronto: Oxford University Press, 1975) 267.

28 Owen, "Keeping Canada God's Country," 85.

29 John Abbott and Alison Prentice, "Policy, Gender and Conflict: Teachers and Inspectors in Ontario and Quebec in the 1870s and 1880s," Paper presented to the Canadian History of Education Association, Halifax, October 1986.

30 Elizabeth Smith, *"A Woman with a Purpose:" The Diaries of Elizabeth Smith 1872–1884*, edited and with an introduction by Veronica Strong-Boag, (Toronto: University of Toronto Press, 1980) 22.

31 Robin Winks, *The Blacks in Canada: A History* (Montreal: McGill-Queen's University Press, and New Haven: Yale University Press, 1971) 243.

32 Beatrice Brigden, "One Woman's Campaign for Social Purity and Social Reform," *in* Richard Allen, ed., *The Social Gospel in Canada* (Ottawa: National Museums of Canada, 1975) 36–62.

33 Marta Danylewycz, *Taking the Veil: An Alternative to Marriage, Motherhood and Spinsterhood in Quebec, 1840–1920* (Toronto: McClelland and Stewart, 1987) 134–37.

34 Henriette Dessaulles, *Hopes and Dreams: The Diary of Henriette Dessaulles, 1874–1881*, translated by Liedewy Hawke, (Willowdale, Ont.: Hounslow Press, 1986) especially 64; Mary Rubio and Elizabeth Waterson, eds., *Selected Journals of L.M. Montgomery vol. 1 (1889–1910)* (Toronto: Oxford University Press, 1986) 263.

35 Jean Cochrane, Abby Hoffman and Pat Kincaid, *Women in Canadian Life: Sports* (Toronto: Fitzhenry and Whiteside, 1977) 25–27; Honora M. Cochrane, ed., *Centennial Story: Board of Education for the City of Toronto, 1850–1950* (Toronto: Thomas Nelson, 1950) 173.

36 Cochrane, Hoffman and Kincaid, *Women in Canadian Life: Sports*, 25–27.

37 National Council of Women of Canada, *Annual Report* (1911) 68–69.

38 *Dominion Medical Monthly and Ontario Medical Journal* (February 1897) 146-47.

39 Jay Cassel, *Venereal Disease in Canada, 1838–1939* (Toronto: University of Toronto Press, 1987) 156. See also Suzann Buckley and Janice Dickin McGinnis, "Venereal Disease and Public Health Reform in Canada," *Canadian Historical Review* 63, 3 (September 1982) 337–54.

40 Rubio and Waterson, eds., *Selected Journals*, 209-10.

41 Eliane Leslau Silverman, "Women's Perceptions of Marriage on the Alberta Frontier," *in* David C. Jones and Ian MacPherson, eds., *Building Beyond the Homestead* (Calgary: University of Calgary Press, 1985) 55.

42 Mary Horodyski, "Women and the Winnipeg General Strike of 1919," *Manitoba History* 11 (Spring 1986) 29.

43 Backhouse, "Nineteenth Century Canadian Prostitution Law," 404–5.

44 Frederick Elkin, *The Family in Canada* (Ottawa: Vanier Institute of the Family, 1964) 113; Jean Barman, "Youth, Class and Opportunity in Vancouver," paper presented to the Canadian Historical Association, Vancouver, 1983, 5.

45 Ian Davey, "Educational Reform and the Working Class: School Attendance in Hamilton, Ontario, 1851–1891," (University of Toronto: Ph.D. Thesis, 1975) 134–35.

46 Joy Parr, *Labouring Children: British Immigrant Apprentices to Canada, 1869–1924* (Montreal: McGill-Queen's University Press, 1980) 109.

47 Marion V. Royce, "Arguments over the Education of Girls — their Admission to Grammar Schools in This Province," *Ontario History* 67 (March 1975) 1–13.

48 Donna Varga Heise, "Gender Differentiated Teacher Training: the Toronto Normal School, 1877–1902," (University of Toronto: M.A. Thesis, 1987).

49 Dunham Ladies' College *Calendar* (1883–84) 7.

50 Jean Barman, "Separate and Unequal: Indian and White Girls at All Hallows School, 1884–1920," *in* Jean Barman *et al.*, eds., *Indian Education in Canada. Volume I: The Legacy* (Vancouver: University of British Columbia Press, 1986) 114.

51 Joyce Taylor Dawson, "A Note on Research in Progress: The Needlework of the Ursulines of Early Quebec," *Material History Bulletin* 5 (Spring 1978) 73–80.

52 Barbara Riley, "Six Saucepans to One: Domestic Science vs the Home in British Columbia 1900-1930," *in* Barbara Latham and Roberta Pazdro, eds., *Not Just Pin Money* (Victoria: Camosun College, 1984) 168 and 100; Marta Danylewycz, Nadia Fahmy-Eid and Nicole Thivierge, "L'enseignement menager et les "home economics" au Québec et en Ontario au début du 20e siècle: une analyse comparées," *in* J. Donald Wilson, ed., *An Imperfect Past: Education and Society in Canadian History* (Vancouver: Centre for the Study of Curriculum and Instruction, University of British Columbia, 1984) 109.

53 Linda Rasmussen *et al.*, eds., *A Harvest Yet to Reap: A History of Prairie Women* (Toronto: The Women's Press, 1976) 132.

54 Beth Light and Alison Prentice, eds., *Pioneer and Gentlewomen of British North America, 1713–1867* (Toronto: New Hogtown Press, 1980) 82.

55 Hugh Ernest MacDermot, *Maude Abbott: A Memoir* (Toronto: Macmillan, 1941) 10.

56 *Christian Guardian* (October 30, 1872) 346.

57 Alan A. Brookes, "The Golden Age and the Exodus," *Acadiensis* 11, 1 (Fall 1981) 67.

58 Judith Fingard, "The New Woman Goes to College: Dalhousie Coeds 1881–1921," unpublished paper, 1986, 15.

59 Sister Maura, *The Sisters of Charity, Halifax* (Toronto: Ryerson Press, 1956) 24, 34, 77–78.

60 Danylewycz, *Taking the Veil*, 146.

61 Donna Ronish, "The Development of Higher Education for Women at McGill University from 1857 to 1907," (McGill University: M.Ed Thesis, 1972); Paula J.S. LaPierre, "Separate or Mixed: The Debate over Co-Education at McGill University," (McGill University: M.A. Thesis, 1983); Margaret Gillett, *We Walked Very Warily: The History of Women at McGill* (Montreal: Eden Press, 1984).

62 Catherine Cleverdon, *The Woman Suffrage Movement in Canada* (Toronto: University of Toronto Press, 1974) chap. 2; Deborah Gorham, "Singing Up the Hill," *Canadian Dimension* 10, 8 (June 1975) 29; Carlotta Hacker, *The Indomitable Lady Doctors* (Toronto: Clarke Irwin, 1974) chap. 2; Veronica Strong-Boag, "Canada's Women Doctors: Feminism Constrained," *in* Linda Kealey, ed., *A Not Unreasonable Claim: Women and Reform in Canada* (Toronto: Canadian Women's Educational Press, 1979) 109–30; J.E. Thompson, "The Influence of Dr. Emily Howard Stowe on the Woman Suffrage Movement in Canada," *Ontario History* 54, 4 (December 1962) 253–66.

63 A.A. Travill, "Early Medical Co-Education and Women's Medical College, Kingston, Ontario, 1880–1894," *Historic Kingston* 30 (January 1982) 72.

64 *Canada Year Book* (1918–19); Canada, Royal Commission on the Status of Women in Canada, *Report* (Ottawa: Information Canada, 1970) 68; see also John A. Reid, "The Education of Women at Mount Allison, 1854–1914," *Acadiensis* 12, 2 (Spring 1983) 38.

65 Danylewycz, *Taking the Veil*, 146–47.

66 Peter Laslett, "Age at Menarche in Europe Since the Eighteenth Century," *in* Theodore K. Rabb and Robert I. Rotberg, eds., *The Family in History: Interdisciplinary Essays* (New York: Harper and Row, 1971) 29.

67 Ellen M. Gee, "Marriage in Nineteenth Century Canada," *Canadian Review of Sociology and Anthropology* 19, 3 (1982) 315; Ellen M. Gee, "Female Marriage Patterns in Canada: Changes and Differentials," *Journal of Comparative Family Studies* 11, 4 (Autumn 1980) 460.

68 Lorne Tepperman, "Ethnic Variations in Marriage and Fertility: Canada, 1871," *Canadian Review of Sociology and Anthropology* 11, 4 (November 1974) 331.

69 A. Romaniuc, *Fertility in Canada: From Baby-Boom to Baby-Bust* (Ottawa: Statistics Canada, 1984) 19.

70 Jacques Henripin, *Trends and Factors of Fertility in Canada* (Ottawa: Federal Census Bureau, 1972) 39.

71 Roderick P. Beaujot and Kevin McQuillan, "Social Effects of Demographic Change: Canada 1851–1981," *Journal of Canadian Studies* 21 (Spring 1986) 57–59.

72 Gee, "Marriage in Nineteenth Century Canada," 315.

73 Gee, "Female Marriage Patterns," 460.

74 Terry Chapman, "Women, Sex, and Marriage in Western Canada, 1890–1920," *Alberta History* 33, 4 (Fall 1985) 8; Rasmussen, *et al.*, eds., *A Harvest Yet to Reap*, 72.

75 Daniel Scott Smith, "Family Limitation, Sexual Control, and Domestic Feminism in Victorian America," *Feminist Studies* 1 (Winter-Spring 1973) 40–57.

76 Gilbert Malcolm Sproat, *The Nootka: Scenes and Studies of Savage Life*, (1868) West Coast Heritage Series, (Victoria: Sono Nis Press, 1987) 169.

77 Peter Gossage, "Absorbing Junior: The Use of Patent Medicines as Abortifacients in Nineteenth Century Montreal," *The Register* 3, 1 (March 1982) 6.

78 Angus McLaren and Arlene Tigar McLaren, *The Bedroom and the State: The Changing Practices and Politics of Contraception and Abortion in Canada 1880–1980* (Toronto: McClelland and Stewart, 1986) 19.

79 Henripin, *Trends and Factors*, 81.

80 Joy Parr, "Hired Men: Ontario Agricultural Wage Labour in Historical Perspective," *Labour/le travail* 15 (Spring 1985) 91–103.

81 Beaujot and McQuillan, "Social Effects of Demographic Change," 59.

82 Margaret Conrad, " 'Sunday Always Makes Me Think of Home': Time and Place in Canadian Women's History," *in* Veronica Strong-Boag and Anita Clair Fellman, eds., *Rethinking Canada: the Promise of Women's History* (Toronto: Copp Clark Pitman, 1986) 74.

83 Beth Light and Joy Parr, eds., *Canadian Women on the Move, 1867–1920* (Toronto: New Hogtown Press and OISE Press, 1983) 112.

84 *The Canadian Lancet* 7 (October 1874) 57.

85 Light and Parr, eds., *Canadian Women on the Move*, 153.

86 See, for example, Edward Sapir, "A Girl's Puberty Ceremony Among the Nootka Indians," Royal Society of Canada, *Proceedings and Transactions* Series 3, 7, Part 2 (1930) 67.

87 F.H. Leacy, ed., *Historical Statistics of Canada* 2nd ed. (Ottawa: Statistics Canada, 1983) A78–93; Tom Belton, "Homes for the Aged in Ontario, 1870–1920," unpublished paper, (University of Waterloo, 1986); Teresa A. Bishop, "Peel Industrial Farm and House of Refuge: A Case Study in Institutional Development," (University of Toronto: M.A. Thesis, 1982) 35–75.

7 The "woman movement"

1 Letitia Youmans, *Campaign Echoes* (Toronto: William Briggs, 1893) 42.

2 Naomi Black, *Social Feminism: Theory and Practice in Four Countries* (Ithaca, New York: Cornell University Press, forthcoming).

3 Deborah Gorham, "English Militancy and the Canadian Suffrage Movement," *Atlantis* 1, 1 (Fall 1975) 83–112; "WSPU Deputation to Prime Minister Borden, 1912," *Atlantis* 5, 2 (Spring 1980) 188–95.

4 E.C. Merrick, *These Impossible Women: The Story of the United Baptist Woman's Missionary Union of the Maritime Provinces* (Fredericton: Brunswick Press, 1970) 13–16.

5 Wendy Mitchinson, "Aspects of Reform: Four Women's Organizations in Nineteenth Century Canada," (York University: Ph.D. Thesis, 1977) 69, 76.

6 Wendy Mitchinson, "Canadian Women and Church Missionary Societies," *Atlantis* 2, 2 (Spring 1977) 60–62.

7 Carlotta Hacker, *The Indomitable Lady Doctors* (Toronto: Clarke Irwin, 1974) 68–69; Loraine Gordon, "Doctor Margaret Norris Patterson: First Woman Police Magistrate in Eastern Canada—Toronto—January 1922 to November 1934," *Atlantis* 10, 2 (Autumn 1984) 97.

8 Ruth Compton Brouwer, "Canadian Women and the Foreign Missionary Movement: A Case Study of Presbyterian Women's Involvement at the Home Base and in Central India, 1876–1914," (York University: Ph.D. Thesis, 1984).

9 Wendy Mitchinson, "The Woman's Christian Temperance Union: A Study in Organization," *International Journal of Women's Studies* 4, 2 (1981) 143–56.

10 Youmans, *Campaign Echoes*, "Introduction," 18.

11 Mitchinson, "The Woman's Christian Temperance Union," 148–49.

12 Youmans, *Campaign Echoes*, 106–7.

13 Wendy Mitchinson, "The WCTU: For God, Home and Native Land:
A Study in Nineteenth-Century Feminism," *in* Linda Kealey, ed., *A Not
Unreasonable Claim: Women and Reform in Canada, 1880s-1920s*
(Toronto: The Women's Press, 1979) 155.

14 Communication from Mary Jane Mossman; Constance B. Backhouse,
"Married Women's Property Law in Nineteenth-Century Canada,"
unpublished paper (July 1987) 79, fn. 76.

15 *The Globe* (9 January, 1857) 1.

16 Backhouse, "Married Women's Property Law."

17 Jim Bearden and Linda Jean Butler, *Shadd: the Life and Times of Mary
Shadd Cary* (Toronto: NC Press, 1977) 160–61.

18 Elizabeth Forbes, *Wild Roses at Their Feet: Pioneer Women of Vancouver
Island* (Vancouver: Evergreen Press, 1971) 27–28.

19 Forbes, *Wild Roses*, 7; Michael H. Cramer, "Public and Political:
Documents of the Woman's Suffrage Campaign in British Columbia,
1871–1917: The View from Victoria," *in* Barbara Latham and Cathy
Kess, eds., *In Her Own Right: Selected Essays on Women's History in B.C.*
(Victoria: Camosun College, 1980) 79–100.

20 Edith M. Luke, "Woman Suffrage in Canada," *Canadian Magazine* 5
(1895) 330.

21 Luke, "Woman Suffrage in Canada," 330.

22 See Linda S. Dranoff, *Women in Canadian Life: Law* (Toronto: Fitzhenry
and Whiteside, 1977) 45–59.

23 Marta Danylewycz, *Taking the Veil: An Alternative to Marriage,
Motherhood, and Spinsterhood in Quebec, 1840–1920* (Toronto: McClelland
and Stewart, 1987) especially chap. 5.

24 See D. Suzanne Cross, "The Neglected Majority: The Changing Role of
Women in 19th Century Montreal," *in* Susan Mann Trofimenkoff and
Alison Prentice, eds., *The Neglected Majority: Essays in Canadian Women's
History* (Toronto: McClelland and Stewart, 1977) vol. 1, 75–77;
Micheline Dumont-Johnson, "Des garderies au XXIXe siècle: Les salles
d'asile des Soeurs Grises à Montréal," *Revue d'histoire de l'Amérique
française* 34, 1 (juin 1980) 27–55.

25 Diana Pedersen, " 'Keeping Our Good Girls Good': The YWCA and the
'Girl Problem' 1870–1930," *Canadian Woman Studies* 7, 4 (Winter
1986) 20–24; Josephine P. Harshaw, *When Women Work Together: A
History of the Young Women's Christian Association in Canada, 1870–1966*
(Toronto: Ryerson Press, 1966); Mary Q. Innis, *Unfold the Years: A
History of the Young Women's Christian Association in Canada* (Toronto:
McClelland and Stewart, 1949).

26 Joanne Emily Thompson, "The Influence of Emily Howard Stowe on
the Woman Suffrage Movement in Canada," *Ontario History* 54, 4
(1962) 259.

27 Thompson, "The Influence of Emily Howard Stowe on the Woman
Suffrage Movement in Canada," 260–61.

28 Catherine L. Cleverdon, *The Woman Suffrage Movement in Canada*
(Toronto: University of Toronto Press, 1974) 22–26.

29 Carlotta Hacker, *The Indomitable Lady Doctors*, 26–35.

30 Veronica Strong-Boag, *The Parliament of Women: The National Council of
Women of Canada 1893–1929* (Ottawa: National Museums of Canada,
1976) 81.

31 Strong-Boag, *The Parliament of Women*, 131–46.

32 Mitchinson, "The Woman's Christian Temperance Union," 152–53; and
Strong-Boag, *The Parliament of Women*, 78–79.

33 Lady Aberdeen, *The Canadian Journal of Lady Aberdeen*, edited by J.T.
Saywell (Toronto: University of Toronto Press, 1960) 258, 2 August
1895.

34 Ruth Howes, "Adelaide Hoodless," *in* Mary Q. Innis, ed., *The Clear
Spirit* (Toronto: University of Toronto Press, 1966) 114.

35 Terry Crowley, "Madonnas before Magdalenes: Adelaide Hoodless and the Making of the Canadian Gibson Girl," *Canadian Historical Review* 67, 4 (1986) 520–47; "The Origins of Continuing Education for Women: The Ontario Women's Institutes," *Canadian Woman Studies* 7, 3 (Fall 1986) 78–81.

36 Robert Stamp, "Teaching Girls Their 'God Given Place In Life': The Introduction of Home Economics in the Schools," *Atlantis* 2, 2, part 1 (Spring 1977) 18–34.

37 Cleverdon, *The Woman Suffrage Movement*, chap. 3.

38 Mary Kinnear, "The Icelandic Connection: *Freyja* and the Manitoba Woman Suffrage Movement," *Canadian Woman Studies* 7, 4 (Winter 1986) 25–28.

39 Yolande Pinard, "Les débuts du mouvement des femmes à Montréal," *in* Marie Lavigne and Yolande Pinard, eds., *Travailleuses et féministes: Les femmes dans la société québécoise* (Montréal: Boréal Express, 1983) 194–96; le Collectif Clio, *L'histoire des femmes au Québec depuis quatre siècles* (Montréal: Quinze, 1982) 329; Marie Lavigne, Yolande Pinard and Jennifer Stoddart, "The Fédération Nationale Saint-Jean-Baptiste and the Women's Movement in Quebec," *in* Kealey, ed., *A Not Unreasonable Claim*, 71–88.

40 Margaret Conrad, "Recording Angels: The Private Chronicles of Women from the Maritime Provinces of Canada, 1750–1950," Paper No. 4 (Ottawa: Canadian Research Institute for the Advancement of Women, 1983) 12.

41 Luke, "Woman Suffrage in Canada," 335–36.

42 Ernest Forbes, "The Ideas of Carol Bacchi and the Suffragists of Halifax," *Atlantis* 10, 2 (Spring 1985) 119–26.

43 Pierre M. Gérin and Pierre Gérin, "Une femme à la recherche et la défense de l'identité acadienne à la fin du XIXᵉ siècle, Marichette," *La Revue de l'Université de Moncton* 11 (mai 1978) 22, (authors' translation).

44 Elspeth Tulloch, *We, the Undersigned: A Historical Overview of New Brunswick Women's Political and Legal Status, 1784–1984* (Moncton: New Brunswick Advisory Council on the Status of Women, 1985) 43; Pierre M. Gérin and Pierre Gérin, "Qui êtes-vous Marichette?" *Cahiers de la société historique acadienne* 8, 4 (décembre 1977) 165–72; Gérin and Gérin, "Une femme à la recherche," 17–26.

45 Tulloch, *We, the Undersigned*; Cleverdon, *The Woman Suffrage Movement*, chap. 6.

46 Susan Altschul and Christine Carron, "Chronology of Some Legal Landmarks in the History of Canadian Women," *McGill Law Journal* 21, 4 (Winter 1975) 476–94.

8 **Marching into the twentieth century**

1 National Council of Women of Canada, *Women of Canada: Their Life and Work* (Ottawa: National Council of Women of Canada, 1900, reprinted 1975).

2 National Council of Women of Canada, *Women of Canada*, 3.

3 Beth Light and Joy Parr, eds., *Canadian Women on the Move 1867–1920* (Toronto: New Hogtown Press and OISE Press, 1983) 187–88.

4 Mary Kinnear and Vera Fast, *Planting the Garden: An Annotated Archival Bibliography of the History of Women in Manitoba* (Winnipeg: University of Manitoba Press, 1987) 209.

5 Robin Winks, *The Blacks in Canada: A History* (Montreal: McGill-Queen's University Press, 1971) 348.

6 Jean Bannerman, *Leading Ladies Canada* (Belleville, Ont.: Mika Publishing, 1977) 67; P. R. Blakeley, "Anna of Siam in Canada," *Atlantic Advocate* (January 1967) 41–45; and especially, Ernest Forbes, "Edith Archibald and the Feminist Movement in Halifax, Nova Scotia," draft chapter for proposed book, *Canada and the Great War* (1987).

7   Catherine L. Cleverdon, *The Woman Suffrage Movement in Canada* (Toronto: University of Toronto Press, 1974) 29–33.

8   Deborah Gorham, "Flora MacDonald Denison: Canadian Feminist," *in* Linda Kealey, ed., *A Not Unreasonable Claim: Women and Reform in Canada, 1880s–1920s* (Toronto: The Women's Press, 1979) 47–70.

9   Gorham, "Flora MacDonald Denison," 56–57.

10 Gorham, "Flora MacDonald Denison," 58–60; Cleverdon, *The Woman Suffrage Movement*, 36; Deborah Gorham, "English Militancy and the Canadian Suffrage Movement," *Atlantis* 1 (Fall 1975) 83–112; Carol Bacchi, *Liberation Deferred? The Ideas of the English-Canadian Suffragists 1877–1918* (Toronto: University of Toronto Press, 1983) 37–38.

11 Veronica Strong-Boag, "Canada's Women Doctors: Feminism Constrained," *in* Kealey, ed., *A Not Unreasonable Claim*, 124–26; Kathleen McConnachie, "Methodology in the Study of Women in History: A Case Study of Helen MacMurchy, M.D.," *Ontario History* 75 (March 1983) 61–70; Angus McLaren, "The Creation of a Haven for 'Human Thoroughbreds': The Sterilization of the Feeble-Minded and the Mentally Ill in British Columbia," *Canadian Historical Review* 67, 2 (June 1986) 127–50; Terry L. Chapman, "The Early Eugenics Movement in Western Canada," *Alberta History* 25 (1977) 9–17.

12 Carol Bacchi, "Race Regeneration and Social Purity: A Study of the Social Attitudes of Canada's English-Speaking Suffragists," *Social History/histoire sociale* 11 (November 1978) 460–74.

13 Canada, *Census*, 1901, Table XI, "Origins of the People." It is possible that census takers underestimated the size of the community.

14 Carrie Best, *That Lonesome Road* (New Glasgow, N.S.: Clarion Publishing, 1977) 189.

15 Richard Allen, ed., *The Social Gospel in Canada* (Ottawa: National Museums of Man, 1975) particularly Beatrice Brigden, "One Woman's Campaign for Social Purity and Social Reform," 36–62.

16 Paul Voisey, "The 'Votes for Women' Movement," *Alberta History* 23, 2 (Summer 1975) 17.

17 Candace Savage, *Our Nell: A Scrapbook Biography of Nellie L. McClung* (Saskatoon: Western Producer Prairie Books, 1979) 89.

18 Donald McCaig, *A Reply to John Stuart Mill on the Subjection of Women* (Philadelphia: J.B. Lippincott, 1870).

19 Goldwin Smith, "Woman Suffrage," *in* his *Essays on the Questions of the Day, Political and Social* (New York, 1893).

20 Stephen Leacock, "The Woman Question" *in* his *Essays and Literary Studies* (New York: John Lane, 1916).

21 Susan Mann Trofimenkoff, "Henri Bourassa and 'the Woman Question'," *Journal of Canadian Studies* 10, 4 (November 1975) 3–11.

22 Terry Crowley, "Madonnas before Magdalenes: Adelaide Hoodless and the Making of the Canadian Gibson Girl," *Canadian Historical Review* 67, 4 (December 1986) 532.

23 Carol Bacchi, "Divided Allegiances: The Response of Farm and Labour Women to Suffrage," *in* Kealey, ed., *A Not Unreasonable Claim*, 89–108; Christine MacDonald, "How Saskatchewan Women Got the Vote," *Saskatchewan History* 1, 3 (October 1948) 1–9; Voisey, "The 'Votes for Women Movement'," 10–23; Cleverdon, *The Woman Suffrage Movement*, chap. 3; Nellie McClung, *In Times Like These*, introduction by Veronica Strong-Boag, (Toronto: University of Toronto Press, 1972) 54–55.

24 Janice Newton, "Women and *Cotton's Weekly*: A Study of Women and Socialism in Canada, 1909," paper presented at the fifth conference on Workers and their Communities, Toronto, 1984; Linda Kealey, "Prairie Socialist Women and WWI: The Urban West," paper presented to the Canadian Historical Association, Winnipeg, 1986.

25 Veronica Strong-Boag, " 'Ever a Crusader': Nellie McClung, First-Wave Feminist," *in* Veronica Strong-Boag and Anita Clair Fellman, eds., *Rethinking Canada: The Promise of Women's History* (Toronto: Copp Clark Pitman, 1986) 178–90.

26 McClung, *In Time Like These*, 48.
27 McClung, *In Times Like These*, 87.
28 Linda Silver Dranoff, *Women in Canadian Life: Law* (Toronto: Fitzhenry and Whiteside, 1977) 49.
29 Georgina Binnie-Clark, *Wheat and Woman*, introduction by Susan Jackel (Toronto: University of Toronto Press, 1979), and *A Summer on the Canadian Prairie* (London: Edward Arnold, 1910).
30 Elsie Gregory MacGill, *My Mother the Judge*, introduction by Naomi Black (Toronto: Peter Martin Associates, 1981) 115.
31 Susan Wade, "Helena Gutteridge: Votes for Women and Trade Unions," in Barbara Latham and Cathy Kess, eds., *In Her Own Right: Selected Essays on Women's History in B.C.* (Victoria: Camosun College, 1980) 187–204; Dranoff, *Women in Canadian Life: Law*, 70–73.
32 Wade, "Helena Gutteridge"; Cleverdon, *The Woman Suffrage Movement*, chap. 4.
33 Elspeth Tulloch, *We, the Undersigned: A History of New Brunswick Women, 1784–1984* (Moncton: New Brunswick Advisory Council on the Status of Women, 1985) 44–45.
34 Tulloch, *We, the Undersigned*, 47–48.
35 Ernest Forbes, "The Ideas of Carol Bacchi and the Suffragists of Halifax," *Atlantis* 10, 2 (Spring 1985) 121.
36 Forbes, "Edith Archibald and the Feminist Movement in Halifax, Nova Scotia."
37 Cleverdon, *The Woman Suffrage Movement*, 201–2.
38 For a recent overview, see Susan Mann Trofimenkoff, *The Dream of Nation: A Social and Intellectual History of Quebec* (Toronto: Macmillan, 1982) chap. 6. On lay and religious women, see Marta Danylewycz, *Taking the Veil: An Alternative to Marriage, Motherhood, and Spinsterhood in Quebec, 1840–1920* (Toronto: McClelland and Stewart, 1987) especially chap. 5.
39 Marie Lavigne, Yolande Pinard, and Jennifer Stoddart, "The Fédération Nationale Saint-Jean-Baptiste and the Women's Movement in Quebec," in Kealey, ed., *A Not Unreasonable Claim*, 71–88; Yolande Pinard, "Les débuts du mouvement des femmes à Montréal, 1893–1902," in Marie Lavigne and Yolande Pinard, eds., *Travailleuses et féministes: les femmes dans la société québécoise* (Montréal: Boréal Express, 1983) 177–98.
40 Christine Mander, *Emily Murphy: Rebel* (Toronto: Simon and Pierre, 1985); Byrne Hope Sanders, *Emily Murphy Crusader* (Toronto: Macmillan, 1945).
41 Barbara M. Wilson, *Ontario and the First World War* (Toronto: Champlain Society, 1977) lxxxv–xcv and 101–47.
42 Wilson, *Ontario and the First World War*, lxxxvi.
43 Forbes, "The Ideas of Carol Bacchi and the Suffragists of Halifax," 121–22.
44 Strong-Boag, *The Parliament of Women*, 323–24.
45 Strong-Boag, *The Parliament of Women*, chap. 7.
46 *Canadian Annual Review* (1917) 432.
47 Crowley, "Madonnas before Magdalenes," 520–47.
48 *Canadian Annual Review* (1915, 1916, 1917).
49 Strong-Boag, *The Parliament of Women*, 329.
50 *Canadian Annual Review* (1916) 419.
51 Judith Fingard, "The New Woman Goes to College: Dalhousie Coeds 1881–1921," unpublished paper (1986) 37–38; and Ernest Forbes, "Edith Archibald and the Feminist Movement in Halifax, Nova Scotia."
52 Strong-Boag, *The Parliament of Women*, 324–25.
53 Strong-Boag, *The Parliament of Women*, 305, 329–32.
54 Tulloch, *We, the Undersigned*, 61.
55 Ernest Forbes, "The Ideas of Carol Bacchi and the Suffragists of Halifax," 122.

56 Flora Denison, "War and Women," *in* Ramsay Cook and Wendy
   Mitchinson, eds., *The Proper Sphere: Women's Place in Canadian Society*
   (Toronto: Oxford University Press, 1976) 249–52; Deborah Gorham,
   "Vera Brittain, Flora MacDonald Denison and the Great War: The
   Failure of Non-Violence," *in* Ruth Roach Pierson, ed., *Women and Peace:
   Theoretical, Historical and Practical Perspectives* (London: Croom Helm,
   1987) 137.
57 McClung, *In Times Like These*, 15.
58 Savage, *Our Nell*, 109–10.
59 Gloria Geller, "The Wartimes Elections Act of 1917 and the Canadian
   Women's Movement," *Atlantis* 2, 1 (Autumn 1976) 88–106.
60 *Canadian Annual Review* (1917) 428.
61 Cleverdon, *The Woman Suffrage Movement*, chap. 5.
62 Neil Sutherland, *Children in English-Canadian Society: Framing the
   Twentieth-Century Concensus* (Toronto: University of Toronto Press, 1976).
63 John Herd Thompson, *The Harvests of War. The Prairie West, 1914–1918*
   (Toronto: McClelland and Stewart, 1978) 98–106.
64 Marjorie MacMurchy, *The Woman Bless Her* (Toronto: S. B. Gundy,
   1916).

THE PROMISED LAND? THE END OF THE GREAT WAR TO THE BEGINNING OF WORLD WAR II

   1 G.W.L. Nicholson, *Canada's Nursing Sisters* (Toronto: Samuel Stevens,
      Hakkert, 1975) 92–93.
   2 A.E. Safarian, *The Canadian Economy In The Great Depression* (Toronto:
      McClelland and Stewart, 1970) 196, 202.

**9 New opportunities, old obstacles: women in the corporate economy,
1918–1939**

   1 Marjory MacMurchy, *Women and Reconstruction* (Toronto: Canadian
      Reconstruction Association, n.d.) 9.
   2 Ceta Ramkalawansingh, "Women during the Great War," *in* Janice
      Acton *et al.*, eds., *Women at Work: Ontario, 1850–1930* (Toronto:
      Canadian Women's Press, 1974) 288.
   3 Ontario, Department of Labour, *Vocational Opportunities in the Industries of
      Ontario*, 1 (1920) iii.
   4 *What Shall I Do Now? How to Work for Canada in Peace* (Toronto:
      Canadian Reconstruction Association, Women's Department, 1919) 7.
   5 *What Shall I Do Now?*, 3.
   6 Juliet Stuart Poyntz, "Problems of the Working Woman," *The New
      Democracy* (May 29, 1919).
   7 Mary Horodyski, "Women and the Winnipeg General Strike of 1919,"
      Manitoba History, 11 (Spring 1986) 28–37.
   8 Elaine Bernard, "Last Back: Folklore and the Telephone Operators in the
      1919 Vancouver General Strike," *in* Barbara K. Latham and Roberta
      J.Pazdro, eds., *Not Just Pin Money: Selected Essays On The History Of
      Women's Work In British Columbia* (Victoria: Camosun College, 1984)
      279–86.
   9 James Naylor, "Toronto 1919," *Historical Papers/Communications
      historiques* (1986) 44, 50.
  10 "Vancouver Working Women, 1920," *Herstory* (1982) 96.
  11 Gail Cuthbert Brandt, " 'Weaving it Together': Life Cycle and the
      Industrial Experience of Female Cotton Workers in Quebec, 1910–
      1950," *Labour/Le Travail*, 7 (Spring 1981) 164–66; Ruth Frager,
      "Uncloaking Vested Interests: Class, Ethnicity and Gender in the Jewish
      Labour Movement of Toronto, 1900–1939," (York University: Ph.D.
      Thesis, 1986) 320, 365–66; for Edmonton see Rebecca Coulter, "Teen-
      Agers in Edmonton, 1921–1931: Experiences of Gender and Class,"
      (University of Alberta: Ph.D. Thesis, 1987) 56.
  12 Elizabeth Goudie, *Woman of Labrador* (Toronto: Peter Martin Associates,
      1975) 7–8.

13 Marilyn Barber, "The Gentlewomen of Queen Mary's Coronation Hostel," *in* Latham and Pazdro, eds., *Not Just Pin Money*, 141–58.

14 Varpu Lindström-Best, "I Won't Be a Slave! Finnish Domestics in Canada, 1911–30," *in* Jean Burnet, ed., *Looking into My Sister's Eyes: an Exploration in Women's History* (Toronto: The Multicultural History Society of Ontario, 1986) 33–53.

15 Helen Potrebenko, *No Streets of Gold: A Social History of Ukrainians in Alberta* (Vancouver: New Star Books, 1977) 180.

16 Tamara Adilman, "A Preliminary Sketch of Chinese Women and Work in British Columbia 1858–1950," *in* Latham and Pazdro, eds., *Not Just Pin Money*, 53–78; Mahinder Kaur Doman, "A Note on Asian Indian Women in British Columbia 1900–1935," *in* Latham and Pazdro eds., *Not Just Pin Money*, 99–104.

17 Potrebenko, *No Streets of Gold*, 186.

18 Joy Parr, "Hired Men: Ontario Agricultural Wage Labour in Historical Perspective," *Labour/Le Travail*, 15 (Spring 1985) 102.

19 Margaret E. McCallum, "Separate Spheres: The Organization of Work in a Confectionery Factory. Ganong Bros., 1900–1945," paper presented to the Canadian Historical Association, Hamilton, 1987; Frager, "Uncloaking Vested Interests," 220; Gail Cuthbert Brandt, "The Transformation of Women's Work in the Quebec Cotton Industry 1920–1950," *in* Bryan Palmer, ed., *The Character of Class Struggle, Essays in Canadian Working-Class History, 1850–1950* (Toronto: McClelland and Stewart, 1986), 115–37; Joy Parr, "Disaggregating the Sexual Division of Labour: a Transatlantic Case Study," unpublished paper (November 1986).

20 Andrée Lévesque, "Putting It Out: Social Reformers' Efforts to Extinguish the Red Light in Montreal," paper presented to the Canadian Historical Association, Hamilton, 1987, 29; "Le Bordel: Milieu de Travail Contrôlé," forthcoming, *Labour/Le Travail*.

21 Jack Gregg, "Girls live only to create profits for a Boss," *The Young Worker* (May 1926) 2.

22 Franc Sturino, "The Role of Women in Italian Immigration to the New World," *in* Burnet, *Looking into My Sister's Eyes*, 27–28.

23 Graham S. Lowe, "Women, Work and the Office: The Feminization of Clerical Occupations in Canada, 1901–1931," *in* Veronica Strong-Boag and Anita Clair Fellman, eds., *Rethinking Canada: The Promise of Women's History* (Toronto: Copp Clark Pitman, 1986) 116.

24 Veronica Strong-Boag, "The Girl of the New Day: Canadian Working Women in the 1920s," *Labour/Le Travail* (1979) 146.

25 M.E. Clark, "Woman in Business is Still At Heart a Woman," *Canadian Magazine*, 69 (January 1928) 27.

26 Dora Nipp, " 'But Women Did Come': Working Chinese Women in The Interwar Years," *in* Burnet, *Looking into My Sister's Eyes*, 189.

27 Marilyn Porter, " 'She was Skipper of the Shore-Crew:' Notes on the History of the Sexual Division of Labour in Newfoundland," *Labour/Le Travail* 15 (Spring 1985) 112–16.

28 Margaret M. Street, *Watch-fires on the Mountains: the Life and Writings of Ethel Johns* (Toronto: University of Toronto Press, 1973) 128–29.

29 Yolande Cohen and Michèle Dagenais, "Infirmière: un métier ou une carrière? Savoirs féminins et reconnaissance professionnelle," paper presented to the Canadian Historical Association, Hamilton, 1987, 41–45.

30 Judy Coburn," 'I See and am Silent': A Short History of Nursing in Ontario," *in* Acton *et al.*, eds., *Women at Work*, 142–47; Barbara A. Keddy, "Private Duty Nursing Days of the 1920s and 1930s in Canada," *Canadian Woman Studies* 7, 3 (Fall 1986) 99–102.

31 Coburn, " 'I See and am Silent'," *in* Acton *et al.*, eds., *Women at Work*, 148.

32 Meryn Stuart, " 'Let Not the People Perish For Lack of Knowledge':
    Public Health Nursing in Ontario, 1920–1925," paper presented to the
    Canadian Society for the History of Medicine, Hamilton, 1987, 8–9, 12.

33 Ontario, *Sessional Papers*, Annual Report of the Minimum Wage
    Commission (1920) 5.

34 Alice Klein and Wayne Roberts, "Beseiged Innocence: The 'Problem' and
    Problems of Working Women—Toronto, 1896–1914," *in* Acton *et al.*,
    eds., *Women at Work*, 211–12.

35 E. M. Murray and Maude Pettit Hill, "Do Women Want Protection? Yes
    and No," *Chatelaine* 1, 6 (August 1928) 7.

36 Susan Wade, "Helena Gutteridge: Votes for Women and Trade Unions,"
    in Latham and Kess, eds., *In Her Own Right*, 196–97.

37 Ontario, *Sessional Papers*, Annual Report of the Minimum Wage
    Commission (1921) 14.

38 Louise Watson, *She Never Was Afraid: The Biography of Annie Buller*
    (Toronto: Progress Books, 1976) 1–11, 82.

39 Joan Sangster, "The Communist Party and the Woman question, 1922–
    1929," *Labour/Le Travail* 15 (Spring 1985) 34.

40 H.A. Spencer, "Minimum Wage Laws for Women," *Canadian Congress
    Journal* 4 (March 1925) 37.

41 Frager, "Uncloaking Vested Interests," 37.

42 Soeur Marie Gérin-Lajoie, "Le syndicalisme féminin," *in* Michèle Jean,
    ed., *Québécoises au XXᵉ Siècle* (Montréal: Editions du Jour, 1974) 104–6.

43 Strong-Boag, "The Girl of the New Day," 155–56; Michelle Lapointe,
    "Le syndicat catholique des allumetières de Hull, 1919–1924," *Revue
    d'histoire de l'Amérique française* 32, 4 (mars 1979) 603–28.

44 Gérin-Lajoie, "Le syndicalisme féminin," 107.

45 Pat Staton and Beth Light, *Speak with Their Own Voices: A Documentary
    History of Women Teachers' Associations of Ontario and the Women
    Elementary Public School Teachers of Ontario* (Toronto: FWTAO, 1987)
    chap. 3; Apolonja Kojder, "In Union There is Strength: The Saskatoon
    Women Teachers' Association," *Canadian Woman Studies/les cahiers de la
    femme* 7, 3 (Fall 1986) 82–84; Doris French, *High Button Bootstraps*
    (Toronto: Ryerson Press, 1968) 43.

46 The Registered Nurses' Association of Ontario Foundation, *1987
    Appointment Book* (Toronto: RNAO Foundation, 1986).

47 Potrebenko, *No Streets of Gold*, 169; Anne B. Woywitka, "A Pioneer
    Woman in the Labour Movement," *in* Strong-Boag and Fellman, eds.,
    Rethinking Canada, 196–97.

48 Canada, House of Commons, Special Committee on Price Spreads and
    Mass Buying, *Proceedings and Evidence*, vol. 1, 113.

49 Sybil Shack, *Saturday's Children: Canadian Women in Business* (Toronto:
    Faculty of Education, University of Toronto, 1977) 29.

50 Brandt, "The Transformation of Women's Work," 128; Joy Parr,
    "Factory Work, Out Work, Household and Me: The Life Cycle Work
    Experience of Female Small Town Hosiery and Knit Goods Employees,
    1919–1949," paper presented to the Canadian Historical Association,
    Montreal, 1985.

51 Canada, Royal Commission on Price Spreads, *Minutes of Proceedings and
    Evidence* (1935) 4410, 4433, 4569, 4554.

52 Canada, *Report of the Royal Commission on Price Spreads* (Ottawa: King's
    Printer, 1935) 110.

53 L. Richter, ed., *Canada's Unemployment Problem* (Toronto: Macmillan,
    1939) 118.

54 "Single Women on Relief," *Canadian Forum* 16, 15 (March 1937).

55 Rebecca Coulter, "Teen-Agers in Edmonton, 1921–1931," 36.

56 Barry Broadfoot, *Ten Lost Years, 1929–1939: Memories of Canadians Who
    Survived The Depression* (Toronto: Doubleday Canada, 1973) 280, 74–75.

57 L.M. Grayson and Michael Bliss, eds., *The Wretched of Canada: Letters to
    R.B. Bennett 1930-1935* (Toronto: University of Toronto Press, 1971)
    75–77.

58 Potrebenko, *No Streets of Gold*, 250–52.
59 James Gray, *The Winter Years: The Depression on the Prairies* (Toronto: Macmillan, 1966) 63–66.
60 Dorothy Kidd, "Women's Organization: Learning from Yesterday," *in* Acton *et al.*, eds., *Women at Work*, 340.
61 Le Collectif Clio, *Histoire des femmes au Québec*, 299–300.
62 Evelyn Dumas, *The Bitter Thirties in Quebec* (Montreal: Black Rose Books, 1975) 49.
63 Frager, "Uncloaking Vested Interests," 289–91, 357.

10 At home
1 A.J. Pelletier, F.D. Thompson, and A. Rochon, *The Canadian Family*, Census Monograph no. 7 (Ottawa: J.O. Patenaude for the Dominion Bureau of Statistics, 1938) 19.
2 Roy H. Rogers and Gail Whitney, "The Family Cycle in Twentieth Century Canada," *Journal of Marriage and the Family* 43, 3 (August 1981) 734.
3 Canada, Dominion Bureau of Statistics, *Vital Statistics 1964* (Ottawa: Queen's Printer, 1966) L2, 212.
4 Rogers and Whitney, "The Family Cycle," 729.
5 Rebecca Coulter, "Rhetoric and Reality: The Experience of Teenagers in Edmonton," paper presented to the Canadian Historical Association, Vancouver, 1983, 14; and "The Working Young of Edmonton, 1921–1931," *in* Joy Parr, ed., *Childhood and Family in Canadian History* (Toronto: McClelland and Stewart, 1982) 146; Joy Parr, "Introduction," *in* Parr, ed., *Childhood and Family*, 14; Neil Sutherland, *Children in English-Canadian Society* (Toronto: University of Toronto Press, 1976) 165.
6 Frederick Elkin, *The Family in Canada* (Ottawa: The Vanier Institute of the Family, 1964) 113.
7 Beth Light and Ruth Roach Pierson, eds., *No Easy Road* (Toronto: New Hogtown Press, forthcoming) chap. 1; J.D. Wilson *et al.*, *Canadian Education: A History* (Scarborough: Prentice-Hall, 1970) 364–65.
8 Light and Pierson, eds., *No Easy Road*, chap. 1.
9 F.H. Leacy, ed., *Historical Statistics of Canada*, 2nd ed. (Ottawa: Statistics Canada, 1983) W340-438.
10 Marta Danylewycz, Nadia Fahmy-Eid, and Nicole Thirièrge, "L'enseignement ménager et les 'home economics' au Québec et en Ontario au début du 20e siècle: une analyse comparée," *in* J. Donald Wilson, ed., *An Imperfect Past: Education and Society in Canadian History* (Vancouver: Centre for the Study of Curriculum and Instruction, University of British Columbia, 1984) 72.
11 Barbara Riley, "Six Saucepans to One: Domestic Science vs. the Home in British Columbia 1900-1930," *in* Barbara K. Latham and Roberta J. Pazdro, eds., *Not Just Pin Money: Selected Essays on the History of Women's Work in British Columbia* (Victoria: Camosun College, 1984) 168.
12 Riley, "Six Saucepans to One," 172.
13 Riley, "Six Saucepans to One," 159–94; and Marta Danylewycz *et al.*, "L'enseignement ménager," 65–119.
14 *4-H Clubs in Manitoba* (Winnipeg: Historic Resources Branch, 1983) 8.
15 Gertrude E.S. Pringle, "Is the Flapper a Menace?" *Maclean's Magazine* (June 15, 1922).
16 Emily F. Murphy, *The Black Candle* (Toronto: Thomas Allen, 1922, reprinted Toronto: Coles Canadiana Collection, 1973).
17 Mary Vipond, "The Image of Women in Mass Circulation Magazines in the 1920s," *in* Susan Mann Trofimenkoff and Alison Prentice, eds., *The Neglected Majority: Essays in Canadian Women's History* (Toronto: McClelland and Stewart, 1977) vol. 1, 118–24.
18 Marjorie Harris, "Fifty Golden Years of *Chatelaine*," *Chatelaine* (March 1978) 43.

19 Christine Foley, "Consumerism, Consumption and Canadian Feminism," (University of Toronto: M.A. Thesis, 1979) 23, 58–59.

20 Margaret Hobbs and Ruth Roach Pierson, "When is a Kitchen Not a Kitchen?" *Canadian Woman Studies/Les Cahiers de la femme* 7, 4 (Winter 1986) 71–76.

21 Suzann Buckley, "Efforts to Reduce Infant Matern[al] Mortality in Canada Between the Two World Wars," *Atlantis* 2, 2, part 2 (Spring 1977) 76.

22 Norah L. Lewis, "Reducing Maternal Mortality in British Columbia: An Educational Process," *in* Latham and Pazdro, eds., *Not Just Pin Money*, 344; Jo Oppenheimer, "Childbirth in Ontario: The Transition from Home to Hospital in the Early Twentieth Century," *Ontario History* 75, 1 (March 1983) 36; France Laurendeau, "La médicalisation de l'accouchement," *Recherches sociographiques* 24, 2 (mai–août 1983) 204; Veronica Strong-Boag and Kathryn McPherson, "The Confinement of Women: Childbirth and Hospitalization in Vancouver, 1919–1939," *BC Studies* 69–70 (Spring-Summer 1986) 142–74.

23 Diary of Leila Middleton, 29 March 1930, courtesy of her granddaughter Sharon Trewartha.

24 Veronica Strong-Boag, "Intruders in the Nursery: Childcare Professionals Reshape the Years One to Five, 1920–1940," *in* Parr, *Childhood and Family in Canadian History*, 160–78; Norah L. Lewis, "Creating the Little Machine: Child Rearing in British Columbia, 1919–1939," *BC Studies* 56 (Winter 1982–1983) 44–60.

25 Phyllis Knight and Rolf Knight, *A Very Ordinary Life* (Vancouver: New Star Books, 1974) 165.

26 C.V. Madder, *History 1895–1963: The Canadian Home and School Parent-Teacher Federation* (The Federation, c. 1964) n.p.

27 L.J. Wilson, "Educational Role of the United Farm Women of Alberta," *in* David C. Jones *et al.*, eds., *Shaping the Schools of the Canadian West* (Calgary: Detselig Enterprises, 1979) 124–35.

28 R. Coulter, "Rhetoric and Reality."

29 Murphy, *The Black Candle*; Pringle, "Is the Flapper a Menace?"

30 Lola Martin Burgoyne, *History of the Home and School Movement in Ontario* (n.p., n.d.) 27.

31 Rebecca Coulter, "Rhetoric and Reality," 12; Helen Lenskyj, *Out of Bounds: Women, Sport and Sexuality* (Toronto: Women's Press, 1986).

32 Lenskyj, *Out of Bounds*, 33–53.

33 *Women at Acadia University: The First Fifty Years, 1884–1934* (Wolfville, N.S.: Acadia University, 1984) 12.

34 Katherine Arnup, "Education for Motherhood: Government Health Publications, Mothers and the State," paper presented to the Canadian Sociology and Anthropology Association, Winnipeg, 1986, 21.

35 *La Presse* (2 janvier 1930) 1 (authors' translation).

36 Mabel Crews Ringland, "What About Father?" *Maclean's Magazine* (August 1, 1928) 59–61. See also Stella E. Pines, R.N., "We Want Perfect Parents!" *The Chatelaine* (September 1928) 12–13.

37 A.H. Tyrer, *Sex, Marriage and Birth Control* (Toronto: Marriage Welfare Bureau, 1936) xiii.

38 Margaret Currie, *Margaret Currie—Her Book* (Toronto: Hunter-Rose, 1924).

39 See, for example, "How to Be a Good Wife," *Chatelaine* (February 1940).

40 Light and Pierson, eds., *No Easy Road*, chap. 1.

41 Inez Houlihan, "The Image of Women in *Chatelaine* Editorials March 1928 to September 1977," (University of Toronto: M.A. Thesis, 1984) 31–32.

42 89.2 percent of farm families used outhouses, compared to only 11.9 percent of urban dwellers; 57.1 percent of farm households depended on outside water pumps, versus 7 percent of households in urban areas. *Census of Canada 1941* (Ottawa: Dominion Bureau of Statistics, 1949), vol. 9, Table 16, 73, and Table 14, 66.

43 "Gwen Lefort, War Bride in WWI," *Cape Breton's Magazine* 35 (1984) 49.

44 Bryan D. Palmer, *Working-Class Experience: The Rise and Reconstitution of Canadian Labour, 1800–1980* (Toronto and Vancouver: Butterworth (Canada), 1983) 192–93.

45 Margaret Stewart and Doris French, *Ask No Quarter: A Biography of Agnes Macphail* (Toronto: Longmans, Green, 1959) 92.

46 *Winnipeg Free Press* (December 18, 1934) as quoted in the *House of Commons Debates* (January 22nd, 1935) 84–85.

47 Light and Pierson, eds., *No Easy Road*, chap. 2.

48 Angus McLaren and Arlene Tigar McLaren, *The Bedroom and the State: The Changing Practices and Politics of Contraception and Abortion in Canada, 1880–1980* (Toronto: McClelland and Stewart, 1986) 67.

49 Angus McLaren, " 'What Has This To Do With Working Class Women?': Birth Control and the Canadian Left, 1900–1939," *Histoire sociale/Social History* 14 (November 1981) 435–54. See also McLaren and McLaren, *The Bedroom and the State*, chap. 4.

50 Angus McLaren, "The First Campaigns for Birth Control Clinics in British Columbia," *Journal of Canadian Studies* 19, 3 (Fall 1984) 50–64; McLaren and McLaren, *The Bedroom and the State*, chap. 3.

51 Angus McLaren, " 'What Has This To Do With Working Class Women?' " 445.

52 McLaren and McLaren, *The Bedroom and the State*, 64.

53 Marjorie Wild, *Elizabeth Bagshaw* (Toronto: Fitzhenry and Whiteside, 1984) 97.

54 Le Collectif Clio, *L'histoire des femmes au Québec* (Montréal: Quinze, 1982) 250–51.

55 Diane Dodd, "The Canadian Birth Control Movement on Trial, 1936–1937," *Histoire sociale/Social History* 16, 32 (November 1983) 411–28.

56 National Archives of Canada, Canadian Council on Social Development, MG 28, I 10, vol. 13, file 497, *Aid to Dependent Mothers and Children in Canada: Social Policy Behind our Legislation.*

57 Pierre Berton, *The Dionne Years* (Toronto: McClelland and Stewart, 1977) 81.

58 Allan Roy Dafoe, *Dr. Dafoe's Guidebook for Mothers* (New York: Julian Messner, 1936) xii.

59 Andrée Lévesque, "Deviant Anonymous: Single Mothers at the *Hôpital de la Miséricorde Montreal, 1929–39*," *Historical Papers* (1984) 175.

60 Angus McLaren, " 'The Creation of a Haven for Human Thorough-breds': The Sterilization of the Feeble-Minded and the Mentally Ill in British Columbia," *Canadian Historical Review* 67, 2 (June 1986) 146.

61 Light and Pierson, eds., *No Easy Road*, chap. 3.

62 Varpu Lindström-Best, " 'I Won't Be A Slave!' Finnish Domestics in Canada 1911–30," *in* Jean Burnet, ed., *Looking into My Sister's Eyes: an Exploration in Women's History* (Toronto: Multicultural History Society of Ontario, 1986) 35.

63 Micheline Dumont-Johnson, "Les communautés religieuses et la condition féminine," *Recherches sociographiques* 19, 1 (janvier–avril 1978) 90; Marta Danylewycz, *Taking the Veil: an Alternative to Marriage, Motherhood, and Spinsterhood in Quebec, 1840–1920* (Toronto: McClelland and Stewart, 1987) 17.

64 Patricia T. Rooke, "Public Figure, Private Woman: same-sex support structures in the life of Charlotte Whitton," *International Journal of Women's Studies* 6, 5 (November/December 1983) 412–28.

65 E.R. Forbes and A.A. Mackenzie, eds., *Four Years with the Demon Rum 1925-1929: The Autobiography and Diary of Temperance Inspector Clifford Rose* (Fredericton: Acadiensis Press, 1980) 32-34, 42-43.
66 Thérèse Casgrain, *A Woman in a Man's World*, translated by Joyce Marshall (Toronto: McClelland and Stewart, 1972) 112-14.
67 Brigitte Kitchen, "The Introduction of Family Allowances in Canada," *in* Allan Moscovitch and Jim Albert, eds., *The Benevolent State: The Growth of Welfare in Canada* (Toronto: Garamond Press, 1987) 222-41.

11 Proving themselves in public life
1 Elizabeth Forbes, *comp.*, *With Enthusiasm and Faith, Book 1* (Ottawa: The Canadian Federation of Business and Professional Women's Clubs, 1974) 7.
2 Diane Crossley, "The BC Liberal Party and Women's Reforms, 1916-1928," *in* Barbara Latham and Cathy Kess, eds., *In Her Own Right: Selected Essays on Women's History in B.C.* (Victoria: Camosun College, 1980) 229.
3 Gail Brandt, "Organizations in Canada: The English Protestant Tradition," *in* Paula Bourne, ed., *Women's Paid and Unpaid Work: Historical and Contemporary Perspectives* (Toronto: New Hogtown Press, 1985) 89.
4 Marjorie Wild, *Elizabeth Bagshaw* (Toronto: Fitzhenry and Whiteside, 1984) 57-58; Clara Thomas, "Women Writers of the Twenties: The Dynamics of Community," paper presented to the York-University of Toronto Women's Studies Colloquium, November 1978; Doris French, *High Button Bootstraps* (Toronto: Ryerson Press, 1968) 48; Pat Staton and Beth Light, *Speak With Their Own Voices: A Documentary History of the Federation of Women Teachers' Associations of Ontario and the Women Elementary Public School Teachers* (Toronto: The Federation of Women Teachers' Associations of Ontario, 1987); Marion V. Royce, *Eunice Dyke* (Toronto and Charlottetown: Dundurn Press, 1983) chap. 7.
5 Judi Cumming, "The Canadian Federation of Business and Professional Women's Clubs," *The Archivist* 14, 1 (January-February 1987) 4-5; Forbes, *comp.*, *With Enthusiasm and Faith*, 15-32.
6 Forbes, *With Enthusiasm and Faith*, 28-29, 15-17.
7 Thomas,"Women Writers of the Twenties"; Joan Murray, "Isabel McLaughlin," *Resources for Feminist Research* 13, 4 (December/January 1984/5) 17-20.
8 Natalie Luckyj, *Visions and Victories: 10 Canadian Women Artists 1914-1945* (London, Ont.: London Regional Art Gallery, 1983), 13-14.
9 Frances Rooney, "Frances Loring and Florence Wyle, Sculptors," *Resources for Feminist Research* 13, 4 (December/January 1984/85) 21-23; Rebecca Sisler, *The Girls: A Biography of Frances Loring and Florence Wyle* (Toronto: Clarke, Irwin, 1972).
10 Luckyj, *Visions and Victories*, 16.
11 Dorothy Livesay, *Right Hand, Left Hand* (Erin, Ont.: Press Porcepic, 1977) 48.
12 Luckyj, *Visions and Victories*, 109.
13 Jean Bannerman, *Leading Ladies Canada* (Belleville, Ont.: Mika Publishing Company, 1977) 309.
14 Veronica Strong-Boag, *The Parliament of Women: The National Council of Women of Canada 1893-1929* (Ottawa: National Museums of Canada, 1976) 444.
15 National Council of Women of Canada, *Yearbook* (1935, 1936).
16 Strong-Boag, *The Parliament of Women*, 357-58.
17 Christine Foley, *Consumerism, Consumption and Canadian Feminism 1900-1930* (University of Toronto: M.A. Thesis, 1979); Strong-Boag, *The Parliament of Women*, 364-67.
18 Rosa L. Shaw, *Proud Heritage: A History of the National Council of Women of Canada* (Toronto: The Ryerson Press, 1957).

19 Nancy M. Sheehan, "Temperance, Education and the WCTU in Alberta, 1905-1930," *Journal of Educational Thought* 14, 2 (August 1980) 108-24; Nancy M. Sheehan, " 'Women Helping Women': The WCTU and the Foreign Population in the West, 1905-1930," *International Journal of Women's Studies* 6, 5, 395-411; Sheehan, "The WCTU and Educational Strategies on the Canadian Prairie," *History of Education Quarterly* (Spring 1984) 101-19; Sheehan, "The WCTU on the Prairies, 1886-1930: An Alberta-Saskatchewan Comparison," *Prairie Forum* 6, 1 (1981) 17-33.

20 L.J. Wilson, "Educational Role of the United Farm Women of Alberta," *Alberta History* 25, 2 (Spring 1977) 35.

21 Wilson, "Educational Role of the United Farm Women of Alberta," 30.

22 Alexandra Zacharias, "British Columbian Women's Institutes in the Early Years: Time to Remember," *in* Latham and Kess, eds., *In Her Own Right*, 69.

23 Le Collectif Clio, *L'Histoire des femmes au Québec depuis quatre siècles* (Montréal: Editions Quinze, 1982) 307-9.

24 Beth Light and Ruth Roach Pierson, eds., *No Easy Road* (Toronto: New Hogtown Press, forthcoming) chap. 5.

25 Mary Prokop, "Looking Back on Fifty Years," *Ukrainian Canadian* (March 1972) 7-14.

26 Robin Winks, *The Blacks in Canada* (Montreal: McGill-Queen's University Press, 1971) 417; Adrienne Shadd, "300 Years of Black Women in Canadian History: circa 1700-1980," *Tiger Lily* 1, 2, (1987) 11.

27 "History of Hour-A-Day Study Club," *Impetus — The Black Woman: Proceedings of the 4th National Congress of Black Women in Canada* (1977) 8.

28 Lillian Petroff, "Macedonian Women in Toronto in 1940," *Polyphony* vol. 8, 1-2 (1986) 24-28.

29 Isabel Kaprielian, "Armenian Refugee Women and the Maintenance of Identity and Heritage," *Polyphony* 8, 1-2 (1986) 33; for a discussion of these and other ethnic organizations, see Jean Burnet, ed., *Looking Into My Sister's Eyes: An Exploration in Women's History* (Toronto: Multicultural History Society of Ontario, 1986); Robert F. Harney, ed., *Gathering Place: Peoples and Neighbourhoods of Toronto, 1834-1934* (Toronto: Multicultural History Society of Ontario, 1985).

30 Paula J. Draper and Janice B. Karlinsky, "Abraham's Daughters: Women, Charity and Power in the Canadian Jewish Community," *in* Burnet, *Looking Into My Sister's Eyes*, 75-90.

31 Florence Bird, *Anne Francis: An Autobiography* (Toronto: Clarke, Irwin, 1974) 114.

32 Bird, *Anne Francis*, 119.

33 Bird, *Anne Francis*, 141, 149.

34 Margaret Prang, " 'The Girl God Would Have Me Be': The Canadian Girls in Training, 1915-39," *Canadian Historical Review* 66, 2 (1985) 154-84.

35 Jean Cochrane et al., *Women in Canadian Life: Sports* (Toronto: Fitzhenry and Whiteside, 1977); Helen Lenskyj, *Out of Bounds: Women, Sport and Sexuality* (Toronto: Women's Press, 1986); Lenskyj, "We Want to Play...We'll Play: Women and Sport in the Twenties and Thirties," *Canadian Woman Studies* 4, 3 (Spring/May 1983) 11-18.

36 Anne Rochon Ford, *A Path Not Strewn With Roses: One Hundred Years of Women at the University of Toronto 1884-1984* (Toronto: Governing Council, University of Toronto, 1985) 65-72; Margaret Gillett, *We Walked Very Warily: A History of Women at McGill* (Montreal: Eden Press Women's Publications, 1981) 245-46.

37 Paul Axelrod, "Moulding the Middle Class: Student Life at Dalhousie University in the 1930s," *Acadiensis* 15, 1 (Fall 1985) 117; Gillett, *We Walked Very Warily*, 231-32.

38 Elizabeth Anderson, "Women in the Student Christian Movement of Canada 1921-1949," unpublished student paper, University of Toronto, n.d.

39 Joan Sangster, " 'Women and the New Era': The Role of Women in the Early CCF, 1933–1940," *in* J. William Brennan, ed., *"Building the Co-operative Commonwealth": Essays on the Democratic Socialist Tradition in Canada* (Regina: Canadian Plains Research Centre, University of Regina, 1985) 72.

40 Diane Haglund, "Side Road on the Journey to Autonomy: The Diaconate Prior to Church Union," *in* S. Davy, ed., *Women, Work and Worship in the United Church of Canada* (Toronto: United Church of Canada, 1983) 206–27; John D. Thomas, "Servants of the Church: Canadian Methodist Deaconess Work, 1890–1926," *Canadian Historical Review* 65, 2 (1984) 371–95.

41 Marlene Epp, "The Changing Role of Mennonite Women in Canada," paper presented at the Symposium on Mennonites in Canada, University of Winnipeg, May 1987, 10.

42 F. H. Eva Hasell, *Canyons, Cans and Caravans* (London: Society for the Propagation of Christian Knowledge, 1930); W. L. Morton, ed., *God's Galloping Girl: The Peace River Diaries of Monica Storrs, 1929–1931* (Vancouver: University of British Columbia Press, 1979).

43 Mary E. Hallett, "Nellie McClung and the Fight for the Ordination of Women in the United Church of Canada," *Atlantis* 4, 2 (Spring 1979) 2–16.

44 Shelagh Parsons, "Women and Power in the United Church of Canada," *in* S. Davy, *Women, Work, and Worship in the United Church of Canada*, 172–88.

45 William E. Mann, *Sect, Cult and Church in Alberta* (Toronto: University of Toronto Press, 1955) 40.

46 Alvyn Austin, *Aimee Semple McPherson* (Toronto: Fitzhenry and Whiteside, 1980).

47 Evelyn M. Brown, *Educating Eve* (Montreal: Palm Publishers, 1957) xiv–xv.

48 Diane Bélanger and Lucie Rozon, *Les Religieuses au Québec* (Montréal: Libre Expression, 1982), annexe 2, 294–319.

49 Carol Lee Bacchi, *Liberation Deferred? The Ideas of the English-Canadian Suffragists, 1877–1918* (Toronto: University of Toronto Press, 1983) 129–30.

50 Strong-Boag, *The Parliament of Women*, 438–39; Ramsay Cook and Wendy Mitchinson, eds., *The Proper Sphere. Woman's Place in Canadian Society* (Toronto: Oxford University Press, 1976) 324–27.

51 Douglas Baldwin, *Abegweit. Land of the Red Soil* (Charlottetown: Ragweed Press, 1985) 328.

52 M. Janine Brodie and Jill McCalla Vickers, *Canadian Women in Politics: An Overview*, The CRIAW Papers No. 2 (Ottawa: Canadian Research Institute for the Advancement of Women, 1982) 6.

53 Joan Sangster, "The Communist Party and the Woman Question, 1922–1929," *Labour/le travail* 15 (Spring 1985) 25–56; John Manley, "Women and the Left in the 1930s: The Case of the Toronto CCF Women's Joint Committee," *Atlantis* 5 (Spring 1980) 100–19.

54 Georgina M. Taylor, "Gladys Strum: Farm Woman, Teacher and Politician," *Canadian Woman Studies* 7, 4 (Winter 1986) 89–93; J. F. C. Wright, *The Louise Lucas Story* (Montreal: Harvest House, 1963).

55 Joan Sangster, "The Communist Party and the Woman Question," 27.

56 Her life story was told by her son, Craig Fraser, 1987.

57 Irene Howard, "The Mothers' Council of Vancouver: Holding the Fort for the Unemployed, 1935–1938," *BC Studies* 69–70 (Spring–Summer 1986) 249–87.

58 Margaret Stewart and Doris French, *Ask No Quarter: A Biography of Agnes Macphail* (Toronto: Longmans, Green, 1959) 74.

59 Sylvia B. Bashevkin, "Independence versus Partisanship: Dilemmas in the Political History of Women in English Canada," *in* Veronica Strong-Boag and Anita Clair Fellman, eds., *Rethinking Canada: The Promise of Women's History* (Toronto: Copp Clark, Pitman, 1986) 258.

60 Martha Louise Black, *My Ninety Years* (Anchorage: Alaska Northwest Publishing Company, 1976) 137.

61 Susan Walsh, "The Peacock and the Guinea Hen: Political Profiles of Dorothy Gretchen Steeves and Grace MacInnis," *in* Alison Prentice and Susan Mann Trofimenkoff, eds., *The Neglected Majority: Essays in Canadian Women's History* (Toronto: McClelland and Stewart, 1985) vol. 2, 144–59.

62 Linda Louise Hale, "Appendix: Votes for Women: Profiles of Prominent British Columbia Suffragists and Social Reformers," *in* Latham and Kess, *In Her Own Right*, 294.

63 Olive M. Stone, "Canadian Women as Legal Persons," *Alberta Law Review* 17, 3 (1979) 370–71; Catherine Cleverdon, *The Woman Suffrage Movement in Canada* (Toronto: University of Toronto Press, 1974) 143–55.

64 Franca Iocavetta, "The Political Career of Senator Cairine Wilson, 1921–1961," *Atlantis* 11, 1 (Fall 1985) 108–23; Marion C. Wilson, ed., *Women in Federal Politics: A Bio-Bibliography* (Ottawa: National Library of Canada, 1975) 1.

65 Luigi Trifiro, "Une intervention à Rome dans la lutte pour le suffrage féminin au Québec (1922)," *Revue d'histoire de l'Amérique française* 32, 1 (juin 1978) 3–18.

66 Thérèse F. Casgrain, *A Woman in a Man's World*, translated by Joyce Marshall (Toronto: McClelland and Stewart, 1972) 54.

67 Marie Lavigne, Yolande Pinard, and Jennifer Stoddart, "The Fédération Nationale Saint-Jean-Baptiste and the Women's Movement in Quebec," *in* Linda Kealey, ed., *A Not Unreasonable Claim: Women and Reform in Canada, 1880s to 1920s* (Toronto: Women's Press, 1979) 79.

68 Susan Mann Trofimenkoff, "Thérèse Casgrain and the CCF in Quebec," *Canadian Historical Review* 66, 2 (1985) 125–53; Casgrain, *A Woman in a Man's World*.

69 Cleverdon, *The Woman Suffrage Movement*, 232.

70 Jennifer Stoddart, "Quebec's Legal Elite Looks at Women's Rights: The Dorion Commission 1929–1931," *in* D.H. Flaherty, ed., *Essays in the History of Canadian Law* (Toronto: The Osgoode Society, 1981) vol. 1, 342.

71 Casgrain, *A Woman in a Man's World*, 62–63.

72 Donald M. Page, "The Development of a Western Canadian Peace Movement," *in* S.M. Trofimenkoff, ed., *The Twenties in Western Canada*, Mercury Series, paper no. 1, (Ottawa: National Museum of Man, 1972) 81–89. Thomas Paul Socknat, *"Witness Against War": Pacifism in Canada, 1900–1945* (Toronto: University of Toronto Press, 1987); Veronica Strong-Boag, "Peace-making Women: Canada 1919–1939," *in* Ruth Roach Pierson, ed., *Women and Peace: Theoretical, Historical and Practical Perspectives* (London: Croom Helm, 1987) 169–90.

73 Candace Savage, *Our Nell: A Scrapbook Biography of Nellie McClung* (Saskatoon: Western Producer Prairie Books, 1979) 171.

74 Elsie Gregory MacGill, *My Mother The Judge. A Biography of Helen Gregory MacGill*, with an introduction by Naomi Black (Toronto: Peter Martin Associates, 1981) 218–19.

12 The "Bren gun girl" and the housewife heroine

1 Ruth Roach Pierson, *"They're Still Women After All": The Second World War and Canadian Womanhood* (Toronto: McClelland and Stewart, 1986) 36–37.

2 Geneviève Auger and Raymonde Lamothe, *De la poêle à frire à la ligne de feu* (Montréal: Boréal Express, 1981) frontispiece (authors' translation).

3 Auger et Lamothe, *De la poêle à frire*, 53.

4 Pierson, *"They're Still Women,"* 33.

5 Barry Broadfoot, *Six War Years, 1939–1945: Memories of Canadians at Home and Abroad* (Toronto: Paperjacks, 1974) 355–56.

6 Pierson, *"They're Still Women,"* 48.

7   Pierson, *"They're Still Women,"* 50.
8   Auger and Lamothe, *De la poêle à frire,* 128 (authors' translation).
9   Auger and Lamothe, *De la poêle à frire,* 128 (authors' translation).
10 Pierson, *"They're Still Women,"* 47.
11 Pierson, *"They're Still Women,"* 71.
12 National Archives of Canada, RG 3614, vol. 135, McTague Commission Inquiry, *Proceedings,* 2263–79.
13 Pierson, *"They're Still Women,"* 71.
14 *Financial Post* (February 24, 1951).
15 Sheila Kieran, *The Family Matters: Two Centuries of Family Law and Life in Ontario* (Toronto: Key Porter Books, 1986) 125.
16 This discussion of women in the armed forces relies extensively on Pierson, *"They're Still Women,"* chap. 3.
17 Carolyn M. Gossage, "Never The Same Again: Canada's Women in the Armed Forces, 1939–45," unpublished manuscript (1985) 116–17, 192.
18 Gossage, "Never the Same Again," 123.
19 Pierson, *"They're Still Women,"* chaps. 5 and 6.
20 Paul Ward, "Women in World War II: Focus on the Women's Royal Canadian Naval Service," unpublished paper, April 1987, 27.
21 Canada, House of Commons, *Debates* (1944) 2629.
22 Claire Booth Luce, "Women Can Win the Peace," *Chatelaine* (February 1944) 3.
23 "Will Women Go Back to the Kitchen?" *Canadian Home Journal* 40 (January 1944) 3.
24 The other members included Margaret Mackenzie (Fredericton), Thaïs Lacoste Frémont (Quebec City), Margaret Wherry (Montreal), Dr. A. Vibert Douglas (Kingston), Helen Smith Agnew and Marion Findlay (Toronto), Susan Gunn (Lloydminster), Grace MacInnis and Evelyn Lett (Vancouver); see Gail Cuthbert Brandt, " 'Pigeon-Holed and Forgotten': The Work of the Subcommittee on the Post-War Problems of Women, 1943," *Histoire sociale/Social History* 15, 29 (March–May 1982) 239–59.
25 *Saturday Night* (June 24, 1944) 6; *Halifax Herald* (February 2, 1944) 8.
26 Pierson, *"They're Still Women,"* 49.
27 National Archives of Canada, MG 28, I-10, vol. 104, file 777, 1947.
28 Pierson, *"They're Still Women,"* 82.
29 Agnes Macphail, "Men Want to Hog Everything," *Maclean's* (September 15, 1949) 71–72.
30 Pierson, *"They're Still Women,"* 91.
31 Auger et Lamothe, *De la poêle à frire,* 215.
32 Canada, House of Commons, *Debates* (July 4, 1946) 3182.
33 Ruth Pierson, " 'Home Aide': A Solution to Women's Unemployment After World War II," *Atlantis* 2, 2 (Spring 1977) 85–96.
34 M.A.C. Francis, "Will Married Women Go To War Again?" *Saturday Night* 66 (January 30, 1951) 21–22.
35 Yvonne Mathews-Klein, "How they saw us: Images of Women in National Film Board films of the 1940s and 1950s," *Atlantis* 4, 2 (1979) 26.
36 M. Susan Bland, "Henrietta the Homemaker, and Rosie the Riveter: Images of Women in Advertising in Maclean's Magazine, 1939–50," *Atlantis* 8, 2 (Spring 1983) 70.
37 Susan M. Hartmann, *The Homefront and Beyond: American Women in the 1940s* (Boston: Twain Publishers, 1982) 203.
38 *Chatelaine* (August 1951); *Chatelaine* (October 1948) 59; *Chatelaine* (March 1958) 78.
39 *Maclean's* (June 15, 1951).
40 Hilda Neatby, "Are Women Fulfilling Their Obligations to Society?" *Food For Thought* 13 (November 1952) 20–21.
41 Deborah Findlay, "Professional Interests in Medicine's Construction of Women's Reproductive Health," a paper presented to the Canadian Sociology and Anthropology Association, Winnipeg, 1986, 29, 10, 21.

42 Ruth Adam, *A Woman's Place, 1910–1975* (London: Chatto and Windus, 1975) 165–67.

43 Pierson, *"They're Still Women,"* 215.

44 Victor Koby, "The ladies, bless 'em, can ease the squeeze," *Financial Post* (February 24, 1951).

45 Alice Kessler-Harris, *Out to Work* (New York: Oxford University Press, 1985) 277.

46 Pierson, *"They're Still Women,"* 216.

47 Monica Boyd, Margrit Eichler, John R. Hofley, "Family: Functions, Formations, and Fertility," *in* Gail Cook, ed., *Opportunity for Choice* (Ottawa: Statistics Canada, 1976) 18.

48 "You'll Hire Older Women, Miss Giggles will Marry," *Financial Post* (May 4, 1957) 1.

49 Warren E. Kalbach and Wayne W. McVey, *The Demographic Bases of Canadian Society* (Toronto: McGraw-Hill, 1971) 61.

50 *Canada Yearbook, 1976–77, Special Edition* (Ottawa: Ministry of Supplies and Services, 1977) Table 4.35.

51 Omer Leroux, "All This and Suffrage Too," *Financial Post* (September 4, 1954) 22.

52 Pat Armstrong and Hugh Armstrong, *The Double Ghetto*, rev. ed. (Toronto: McClelland and Stewart, 1984) 20–21.

53 "Save Your Tears—Watch the Girls," *Financial Post* (November 16, 1957) 1.

54 Patricia Marchak, "Rational Capitalism and Women as Labour," *in* Heather Jon Maroney and Meg Luxton, eds., *Feminism and Political Economy: Women's Work, Women's Struggles* (Toronto: Methuen, 1987) 197–212.

55 Interview with Florence Mowatt, former school teacher in Hants County, Nova Scotia, March 10, 1987.

56 Canada, Department of Labour, *Married Women Working for Pay in Eight Canadian Cities* (Ottawa, 1958) 52.

57 Franca Iacovetta, "From *Contadina* to Worker: Southern Italian Immigrant Women Working in Toronto, 1947–62," *in* Jean Burnet, ed., *Looking Into My Sisters' Eyes: An Exploration in Women's History* (Toronto: The Multicultural History Society of Ontario, 1986) 209–11.

58 Canada, Department of Labour, *Married Women Working for Pay*, 52.

59 Canada, Department of Labour, *Labour Gazette* (1954) 1513.

60 Dorothy Manning, "I Quit My Job to Save My Marriage," *Chatelaine* (June 1955).

61 John Kenneth Galbraith, *Economics and the Public Purpose* (New York: New American Library, 1973) 29–37.

62 Wayne Roberts, ed., *Where Angels Fear To Tread: Eileen Tallman and the Labor Movement* (Hamilton: McMaster University, n.d.) 23; Eileen Sufrin, *The Eaton Drive: The Campaign to Organize Canada's Largest Department Store 1948 to 1952* (Toronto: Fitzhenry and Whiteside, 1982).

63 Sara Diamond, "A Union Man's Wife: The Ladies' Auxiliary Movement in the IWA, the Lake Cowichan Experience," *in* Barbara K. Latham and Roberta J. Pazdro, eds., *Not Just Pin Money: Selected Essays on the History of Women's Work in British Columbia* (Victoria: Camosun College, 1984) 287.

64 Broadfoot, *Six War Years*, 358.

13 Prelude to revolution

1 John R. Miron, *Demographic Change, Household Formation and Housing Demand: Canada's Postwar Experience* (Toronto: University of Toronto, Centre for Urban and Community Studies, 1985) 7.18, table 7.3.2.

2 *Canada Yearbook, 1976–77, Special Edition* (Ottawa: Minister of Supply and Services Canada, 1977) 169.

3 F.H. Leacy, ed., *Historical Statistics of Canada*, 2nd ed. (Ottawa: Statistics Canada, 1983) B75–81.

4 Monica Boyd, Margrit Eichler, John R. Hofley, "Family: Functions, Formation, and Fertility," *in* Gail Cook, ed., *Opportunity for Choice* (Ottawa: Statistics Canada, 1976) 18.

5 Miron, *Demographic Change*, 3, 16–17.

6 Miron, *Demographic Change*, 4.20, 7.21.

7 *Canada Yearbook, 1976–77*, 171.

8 Leacy, *Historical Statistics*, 2nd ed., B1–14.

9 Warren E. Kalbach and Wayne W. McVey, *The Demographic Bases of Canadian Society* (Toronto: McGraw–Hill, 1971) 298, 293–95.

10 *Canada Yearbook, 1976–77*, 197–98.

11 James S. Frideres, *Canada's Indians: Contemporary Conflicts* (Scarborough: Prentice–Hall, 1974) 17.

12 Angus McLaren and Arlene Tigar McLaren, *The Bedroom and the State: The Changing Practices and Politics of Contraception and Abortion in Canada, 1880–1980* (Toronto: McClelland and Stewart, 1986) 125.

13 Le Collectif Clio, *L'histoire des femmes au Québec depuis quatre siècles* (Montréal: Quinze, 1984) 249.

14 McLaren and McLaren, *The Bedroom and the State*, 132–33.

15 Jacques Henripin et Evelyne Lapierre-Adamcyk, *La Fin de la Revanche des Berceaux: qu'en Pensent les Québécoises?* (Montréal: Les Presses de l'Université de Montréal, 1974).

16 McLaren and McLaren, *The Bedroom and the State*, 136, 52–53.

17 Boyd, Eichler, Hofley, "Family," *in* Cook, *Opportunity for Choice*, 22–23.

18 McLaren and McLaren, *The Bedroom and the State*, 44.

19 Ellen M. Gee and Meredith M. Kimball, *Women and Aging* (Toronto and Vancouver: Butterworths, 1987).

20 Frideres, *Canada's Indians*, 19.

21 Marlene Mackie, *Exploring Gender Relations: A Canadian Perspective* (Toronto: Butterworths, 1983) 185.

22 Le Collectif Clio, *L'Histoire des Femmes au Québec*, 439.

23 Shirley Stokes, *The Shortest Shadow: A Descriptive Study of the Members of the Federation of Women Teachers' Associations of Ontario* (Toronto: FWTAO, 1969) 3.

24 Ontario, Department of Education, *Courses of Study Grades IX, X, XI and XII, Home Economics, General and Commercial and Vocational Courses*, 1945; *Courses of Study in Grades XI and XII, The Home Economics Option of the General Course, The Commercial Course and The Art Course*, 1955; *Home Economics, Intermediate Division*, 1964.

25 Micheline Dumont-Johnson, "La parole des femmes. Les revues féminines, 1938–68," *in* Fernand Dumont, Jean Hamelin, Jean-Paul Montminy, eds., *Idéologies au Canada Français, 1940–1976*, (Québec: Les Presses de l'Université Laval, 1981) tome 2, 5–45.

26 Gertrude Joch Robinson, "The Media and Social Change: Thirty Years of Magazine Coverage of Women and Work (1950–1977)," *Atlantis* 8, 2 (Spring 1983) 87–111.

27 Nancy Kiefer, "The Impact of World War II on Female Students at the University of Toronto, 1939–49" (University of Toronto: M.A. Thesis, 1984).

28 Interview with Dr. Marjorie Moore, Toronto, April 16, 1987.

29 Judy LaMarsh, *Memoirs of a Bird in a Gilded Cage* (Toronto: McClelland and Stewart, 1969).

30 Leacy, ed., *Historical Statistics*, 2nd ed., W340–57.

31 Jill Vickers and June Adam, *But can you type? Canadian universities and the status of women* (Ottawa: Canadian Association of University Teachers, 1977) 59.

32 "Women Still Choose Traditional Studies," *University Affairs* (October 1987) 10.

33 Canadian Congress for Learning Opportunities for Women, *Decade of Promise: An Assessment of Canadian Women's Status in Education, Training and Employment, 1976–1985* (Toronto: Avebury Research and Consulting, 1986) 31–35; *Women in Canada: A Statistical Report* (Ottawa: Statistics Canada, 1985), 24–26.

34 *Insight, 1975*, published by the Public Relations and Development Office of Mount Saint Vincent University.

35 Evelyn M. Brown, *Educating Eve* (Montreal: Palm Publishers, 1957) xiv–xv, 92–115.

36 Leacy, *Historical Statistics*, 2nd ed., W389–94, W405–8, W436–42.

37 *Women in Canada*, 32, 33, 25; CCLOW, *Decade of Promise*, 36–37.

38 Thomas H.B. Symons and James E. Page, *Some Questions of Balance: Human Resources, Higher Education and Canadian Studies* (Ottawa: Association of Universities and Colleges of Canada, 1984) 193, table 43.

39 Margaret Gillett, *We Walked Very Warily: A History of Women at McGill* (Montreal: Eden Press, 1981) 404.

40 Helen Lenskyj, *Out of Bounds: Women, Sport and Sexuality* (Toronto: The Women's Press, 1986) 70.

41 Jean Cochrane *et al.*, eds., *Women in Canadian Life: Sports* (Toronto: Fitzhenry and Whiteside, 1977) 54, 56.

42 M. Ann Hall and Dorothy A. Richardson, *Fair Ball: Towards Sex Equality in Canadian Sport* (Ottawa: Canadian Advisory Council on the Status of Women, 1982) 38–48.

43 Lenskyj, *Out of Bounds*, 84–85.

44 Cochrane *et al.*, eds., *Women in Canadian Life: Sports*; and Hall and Richardson, *Fair Ball*.

45 David MacDonald, "Powerful Woman's Lobby in Canada," *Chatelaine* (June 1957) 58.

46 Dean Beeby, "Women in the Ontario C.C.F., 1940–1950," *Ontario History*, 74, 4 (December 1982) 275–76.

47 Elizabeth Forbes, *With Enthusiasm and Faith: The History of the Canadian Federation of Business and Professional Women's Clubs* (Ottawa: 1974) 56–111; MacDonald, "Powerful Woman's Lobby in Canada," 58.

48 Le Collectif Clio, *L'histoire des Femmes au Québec*, 426–29.

49 Ethel Vineberg, *The History of the National Council of Jewish Women of Canada* (Montreal: National Council of Jewish Women of Canada, 1967) 58.

50 Cathy Kennedy and Chris Stirling, *The Junior League of Toronto, Diamond Jubilee 1926–1986* (Toronto: 1986) 12.

51 Robert Collins, "The Biggest Country Club in Canada," *Maclean's Magazine* (July 5, 1958) 48.

52 Helen F. Morton, "Women on the Land," *Food For Thought* (April 1950) 7.

53 Shirley Davey, ed., *Women, Work and Worship in the United Church of Canada* (Toronto: United Church of Canada, 1983) 54.

54 Collins, "The Biggest Country Club in Canada," 48.

55 Muriel Duckworth, *in* "Voice of Women Dialogue," *Atlantis* 6, 2 (Spring 1981) 172; Kay Macpherson and Meg Sears, "The Voice of Women: A History," *in* Gwen Matheson, ed., *Women in the Canadian Mosaic* (Toronto: Peter Martin Associates, 1976) 71–89.

56 Eileen Morris, "Canada . . . a Woman's World!" *Saturday Night* (May 31, 1952) 34.

57 Sandra Gwyn, *Women in the Arts in Canada* (Ottawa: Information Canada, 1971) 21.

58 Barbara Moore, "Canadian Theatre's Fiery Godmother," *Maclean's* (February 15, 1958) 19.

59 Gwyn, *Women in the Arts*, 31.

60 Frances Rooney, "The Montreal Women's Symphony," *Atlantis* 5, 1 (Fall 1979) 70–82.

61 Gwyn, *Women in the Arts*, 36.
62 Gwyn, *Women in the Arts*, 13.
63 Paul-Emile Borduas, "Refus Global," *in* Ramsay Cook, ed., *French Canadian Nationalism* (Toronto: Macmillan, 1969) 280.
64 Gwyn, *Women in the Arts*, 18.
65 Marie Fleming, "A Tribute Whose Time Has Come," *Art Gallery of Ontario News* 9, 4 (April 1987) 1.
66 Maryon Kantaroff, "Breaking Out of the Female Mould," *in* Matheson, *Women in the Canadian Mosaic*, 287.
67 Robin Winks, *The Blacks in Canada: A History* (Montreal and New Haven: McGill–Queen's, Yale University Press, 1971) 407–8.
68 Rella Braithwaite, ed., *The Black Woman in Canada* (n.p.,n.d.)

14 A bomb already primed and ticking
1 Patricia Carey, "The Personal is Political," *Canadian Women's Studies/ Les cahiers de la femme* 2, 2 (1980) 6.
2 Le Collectif Clio, *L'Histoire des femmes au Québec depuis quatre siècles* (Montréal: Quinze, 1984) 450–57; Michèle Lamont, "Les rapports politiques au sein du mouvement des femmes au Québec," *Politiques* 5 (hiver 1984) 75–106; Azilda Marchand, "Les femmes au foyer: hier et demain," *Canadian Women's Studies/Les cahiers de la femme* 2, 4 (1980) 46–48; Martine Lanctôt, "La genèse et l'évolution du mouvement de libération des femmes à Montréal, 1969–79" (Université du Québec à Montréal: thèse de maîtrise, 1982) 35.
3 Le Collectif Clio, *L'histoire des femmes*, 489.
4 *Chatelaine* (July 1966); Cerise Morris, " 'No More Than Simple Justice': The Royal Commission on the Status of Women and Social Change in Canada" (McGill University: Ph.D. dissertation, 1982) 114.
5 Sylvia Fraser, "Laura Sabia: Not Exactly Mom & Apple Pie," *Chatelaine* (November 1975) 100; "How Laura built a lobby," *Saturday Night* (September 1978) 4; June Callwood, "Scream Bloody Murder," *The Globe and Mail* (25 October, 1984).
6 Cerise Morris, " 'Determination and Thoroughness': The Movement for the Royal Commission on the Status of Women in Canada," *Atlantis* 5, 2 (Spring 1980) 1–21; Penney Kome, *Women of Influence: Canadian Women and Politics* (Toronto: Doubleday, 1985) 76–87.
7 The brief was presented by Sabia, Laberge–Colas, Margaret Hyndman for the Canadian Federation of Business and Professional Women's Clubs, Julia Schwartz for the National Council of Jewish Women, and Margaret MacLellan for the National Council of Women of Canada. Morris, " 'Determination and Thoroughness'," 121.
8 Barry Craig, "Women's March May Back Call for Rights Probe," *The Globe and Mail* (January 5, 1967); Michael Sabia, "Growing Up Feminist," *Chatelaine* (May 1986) 44.
9 Judy LaMarsh, *Memoirs of a Bird in a Gilded Cage* (Toronto: McClelland and Stewart, 1969) 316.
10 News Release, "Text of an Address prepared for Delivery by Miss Sylva M. Gelber, Director, Women's Bureau, Canada Department of Labour" (December 8, 1969).
11 John Terry, "Male–Female Differences in Voting Turnout and Campaign Activities, Canada and Ontario" (Ottawa: Library of Parliament, Research Branch, Political and Social Affairs Division, 1982) 4.
12 Florence Bird, *Anne Francis, An Autobiography* (Toronto: Clarke Irwin, 1974) 8.
13 *Report of the Royal Commission on the Status of Women in Canada* (Ottawa: Information Canada, 1970) vii.
14 Humphrey replaced Donald Gordon, a professor of political science, who resigned without becoming active.

15 Elsie Gregory MacGill, "Legalist Feminism," presentation to a conference on the Canadian Women's Movement, York University (September 1977) 6–7.

16 Christine Newman, "What's So Funny About the Royal Commission on the Status of Women?" *Saturday Night* (January 1969) 22, 24.

17 *Report of the Royal Commission on the Status of Women*, xii.

18 Anthony Westell, "Report is more explosive than any terrorists' time bomb," *Toronto Star* (December 8, 1970).

19 Submission of the National Ad Hoc Committee on the Status of Women to the government of Canada, February, 1972.

20 Canadian Research Institute for the Advancement of Women, "Women's Involvement in Political Life: A Pilot Study," research report submitted to the United Nations Educational, Scientific, and Cultural Organization (April 1986) 24–29.

21 "Lise Payette par Lise Payette," *Féminin Pluriel* 1, 1 (septembre 1981); Nicole Boily, "Les femmes en politique, encore une exception," entrevue réalisée par Carolle Simard et Denis Monière, *Politiques* 5 (hiver 1984); Lanctôt, "La genèse et l'évolution du mouvement de libération des femmes," 175.

22 *The Toronto Sun* (July 7, 1976).

23 Naomi Wall, "The Last Ten Years. A Personal/Political View," *in* Maureen Fitzgerald *et al.*, eds., *Still Ain't Satisfied! Canadian Feminism Today* (Toronto: The Women's Press, 1982) 16.

24 Satu Repo, "Are Women Necessary?" *Saturday Night* (August 1969) 30.

25 *Women Unite! An Anthology of the Canadian Women's Movement* (Toronto: Canadian Women's Educational Press, 1972); Fitzgerald *et al.*, *Still Ain't Satisfied!*; Sara Evans, *Personal Politics: The Roots of Women's Liberation in the Civil Rights Movement and the New Left* (New York: Vintage Books, 1980) 208; Marylee Stephenson, "Being in Women's Liberation: A Case Study in Social Change," (University of British Columbia: Ph.D. Dissertation, 1975); Daryl Webber, "The Women's Movement in Northern Ontario: Its History, Growth and Current Affairs" (Glendon College, York University: Women's Studies Honours Thesis, 1986); Francie Ricks, George Matheson, and Sandra W. Pyke, "Women's Liberation: A Case Study of Organizations for Social Change," *The Canadian Psychologist* 13, 1 (January 1972) 31–40; Cheryl Lynne Malmo–Levine, "Behavior of Women in Consciousness-Raising Groups" (University of Alberta: M.Ed. Thesis, 1972); correspondence in the New Feminists' files.

25 Donna Cherniak and Allan Feingold, "Birth Control Handbook," *in Women Unite!* 109–12; Véronique O'Leary and Louise Toupin, *Québécoises debboutte!* (Montréal: Editions du remue-ménage, 1982); Diane Lamoureux, *Fragments et collages: Essai sur le féminisme québécois des années 70* (Montréal: Editions du remue-ménage, 1986); Lanctôt, "La genèse et l'évolution du mouvement de libération des femmes."

27 Cerise Morris, "Diary of a Feminist," *in* Margret Anderson, ed., *Mother Was Not A Person* (Montreal: Content Publishing/Black Rose, 1972) 182, 184.

28 Krista Maeots, "Abortion Caravan," *Canadian Forum* (July–August 1970) 15; Phyllis Waugh, "Movement Comment: Choice Description," *Broadside* 9, 2 (November 1987) 6.

29 Judy Bernstein, Peggy Morton, Linda Seese, Myrna Wood, "Sisters, Brothers, Lovers . . . Listen . . .," *in Women Unite!* 39; Myrna Kostash, *Long Way from Home* (Toronto: James Lorimer, 1980) 168.

30 Un groupe de femmes de Montréal, *Manifeste des femmes québécoises* (Montréal: Editions L'Etincelle, 1971) 52; O'Leary and Toupin, *Québécoises debboutte!* 1, 53.

31 Diane Lamoureux, "Nationalism and Feminism in Quebec: An Impossible Attraction," in Heather Jon Maroney and Meg Luxton, eds., *Feminism and Political Economy: Women's Work, Women's Struggles* (Toronto: Methuen, 1987) 51–68.

32 Gwen Matheson and V.E. Lang, "Nellie McClung: 'Not a Nice Woman'," in Matheson, ed., *Women in the Canadian Mosaic* (Toronto: Peter Martin Associates, 1976) 1–22; Gloria Geller, "The Wartime Elections Act of 1917 and the Canadian Women's Movement," *Atlantis* 2, 1 (Autumn 1976) 88–106; Linda Kealey, ed., *'A Not Unreasonable Claim': Women and Reform in Canada, 1880s–1920s* (Toronto: The Women's Press, 1979).

33 Michèle Jean, Jacqueline Lamothe, Marie Lavigne, and Jennifer Stoddart, "Nationalism and Feminism in Quebec: The 'Yvettes' Phenomenon," in Roberta Hamilton and Michèle Barrett, eds., *The Politics of Diversity: Feminism, Marxism and Nationalism* (Montreal: Book Center, 1986) 331.

34 O'Leary and Toupin, *Québécoises deboutte!* 1, 70–71; Lamoureux, *Fragments et collages*, 85.

35 Pierrette Bouchard, "Féminisme et marxisme; un dilemme pour la Ligue communiste," *Canadian Journal of Political Science* 20, 1 (March 1987) 57–78.

36 The Toronto Women's Liberation Group, "Is Feminism Necessary for Women's Liberation?" (Canadian Union of Students, 1969) 3.

37 Bonnie Kreps, "Radical Feminism," in *Women Unite!* 74.

38 Peggy Morton, "Women's Work is Never Done," in *Women Unite!* 46.

39 Naomi Black, *Social Feminism: Theory and Organization in England, France, and the United States* (Ithaca, New York: Cornell University Press, forthcoming, 1989).

40 Letter from Bonnie Kreps, November 1986.

41 Sherill Cheda, Johanna Stuckey, Maryon Kantaroff, "New Feminists Now," *Canadian Women's Studies/Les cahiers de la femme*, 2, 2 (1980) 27–31.

42 *The New Feminist* 1 (November 17, 1969).

43 Bonnie Kreps, *Guide to the Women's Movement in Canada: A Chatelaine Cope Kit* (Toronto: n.d.) 8, 2.

44 Lanctôt, "La genèse et l'évolution du mouvement de libération des femmes," 119.

45 "WAVAW Demands," *Broadside* 3, 2 (November 1981) 19.

46 Feminist Party of Canada *News/Nouvelles* 2, 1 (March 1980); Trish Wells, "Towards A Canadian Feminist Party," flyer (April 1979).

47 Eileen Morris, "The Case Against Women's Studies," *Homemaker's Magazine* 10, 5, (September 1975) 26–27.

48 Margaret Benston, "The Political Economy of Women's Liberation," *Monthly Review* 21, 4 (September 1969) 13–29; Linda Briskin, "The Women's Movement: Where is it Going?" *Our Generation* 10, 3 (Fall 1974) 23–34; Hamilton and Barrett, *The Politics of Diversity: Feminism, Marxism and Nationalism.*

49 Micheline de Sève, *Pour un féminisme libertaire* (Montréal: Boréal Express, 1985); Ginette Legault, "L'institutionalisation du mouvement féministe" (Université du Québec à Montréal: thèse de maîtrise, 1982).

50 Pol Pelletier, "Petite Histoire du théâtre des femmes au Québec," *Canadian Women's Studies/Les cahiers de la femme*, 2, 2 (1980) 85–87; Jeanne Demers et Line McMurray, eds., *Femmes scandales 1965–1985* (Outremont, Québec: La nouvelle barre du jour, 1987).

51 corrective collective, *she named it Canada because that's what it was called* (Vancouver: Press Gang, 1972); Women's Calendar Collective, *Herstory: A Canadian women's calendar* (Toronto: Canadian Women's Educational Press, 1974).

52 Margie Wolfe, "Feminist Publishing in Canada," *Canadian Women's Studies/Les cahiers de la femme* 2, 2 (1980) 11–14; and "Working with Words: Feminist Publishing in Canada," in Fitzgerald et al., *Still Ain't Satisfied!* 265–75.

53 *Women Unite!* 12.

54 Julie McLean, "Militantly Impotent: Has the Women's Movement Come to This?" *Branching Out* (April–June 1976) 9.

55 Varda Burstyn, ed., *Women Against Censorship* (Toronto: Douglas and McIntyre, 1985); Susan Cole, review of Burstyn, *Canadian Journal of Women and the Law* 1, 1 (1985) 226–39.

56 Michèle Lamont, "Les rapports politiques au sein du mouvement," 95; Claire Duguay and Micheline de Sève, "Tant d'amarres à larguer: une analyse des pratiques du mouvement des femmes," 67–69, both *in* "Femmes et pouvoir," *Politiques* 5 (hiver 1984) (authors' translation).

57 Jan Lancaster, "British Columbia Federation of Women," *Canadian Women's Studies/Les cahiers de la femme* 2, 2 (1980) 35–36; Bev Le Francois and Helga Martens Ens, *Story of a Women's Centre* (Vancouver: Press Gang, n.d.) 108.

58 Maureen Fitzgerald, "Toronto International Women's Day Committee," *Canadian Women's Studies/Les cahiers de la femme* 11, 2 (1980) 34; Nancy Adamson, "What Are Our Options?" *in* Fitzgerald *et al.*, *Still Ain't Satisfied!* 300–12; Carolyn Egan, "Toronto's International Women's Day Committee: Socialist Feminist Politics," *in* Maroney and Luxton, *Feminism and Political Economy*, 109–18.

59 Lamoureux, *Fragments et collages*, 134 (authors' translation).

60 Eleanor Wright Pelrine, *Abortion in Canada* (Toronto: New Press, 1972); and *Morgentaler: The Case That Rocked Canada* (Toronto: Gage Educational Publishing/Signet–New American Library, 1976); Anne Collins, *The Big Evasion: Abortion, The Issue That Won't Go Away* (Toronto: Lester Orpen and Denis, 1985).

61 Ellen Long, "Traditionalist Women's Groups in the 1980s: A Case Study of the Alberta Federation of Women United for the Family," (University of Alberta: Honours Thesis, 1986).

62 REAL Women of Canada, "Presentation to the Standing Committee on the Secretary of State" (December 11, 1986); Jackie Smith, "The women alienated by feminism," *Toronto Star* (February 21, 1985); Stevie Cameron, "Homey muffins, pink brochures belie REAL Women's focus," *The Globe and Mail* (December 18, 1986); Cathie Dunphy, "Don't lower your standards, MP Urges REAL Women," *Toronto Star* (February 15, 1987); C. Gwendolyn Landolt, "REAL Women fights to obtain genuine options," *The Globe and Mail* (April 23, 1987); Judy Erola speaking at York University, *in The Second Decade/La deuxième décennie* 1, 2 (December 1986).

63 "Radical feminists blocking bids for financing, group says," *The Globe and Mail* (December 12, 1986); Maureen McTeer, "Federal funds for women's groups," *Chatelaine* (April 1986) 40.

64 Val Sears, "Will the real women please stand up?" *Toronto Star* (January 3, 1987).

65 Gallup poll taken for CARAL, June 1972; "Canadians receptive to NAC's views, poll shows," *Feminist Action* (April 1987).

66 "Womanpoll: Women's roles and rights," *Chatelaine* (May 1986) 42.

67 Christy McLaren, "Environment tops free trade in poll of Canadians," *The Globe and Mail* (January 15, 1987).

15 **Work in the electronic era**

1 Canadian Congress for Learning Opportunities for Women, *Decade of Promise: An Assessment of Canadian Women's Status in Education, Training and Employment, 1976–1985* (Toronto: Avebury Research and Consulting, 1986) 61, table 15.

2 Monica Boyd, "English-Canadian and French-Canadian Attitudes Toward Women: Results of the Canadian Gallup Polls," *Journal of Comparative Family Studies* 6, 2 (Autumn 1975) 157, table 1; Gertrude Joch Robinson, "The Media and Social Change: Thirty Years of Magazine Coverage of Women and Work (1950–1977)," *Atlantis* 8, 2 (Spring 1983) 108.

3 "Irene Desjarlais," *in Speaking Together: Canada's Native Women* (Toronto: Hunter Rose, 1975) 46.

4 Canadian Congress for Learning Opportunities for Women, *Decade of Promise*, 65.

5 The Royal Bank, *Report* (Spring 1986) 19.

6 S.J. Wilson, *Women, The Family And The Economy* (Toronto: McGraw–Hill Ryerson, 1982) 96.

7 Pat Armstrong and Hugh Armstrong, *A Working Majority: What Women Must Do For Pay* (Ottawa: Advisory Council on the Status of Women, 1983) 36.

8 Statistics Canada, *Women in Canada: A Statistical Report* (Ottawa: Statistics Canada, 1985) 10, 11, 12, tables 9, 10, 11; "Divorce statistics not all that bad, U.S. pollster says," *The Globe and Mail* (June 29, 1987).

9 Pat Armstrong, *Labour Pains: Women's Work in Crisis* (Toronto: The Women's Press, 1984) 198.

10 Sybil Shack, *Saturday's Stepchildren: Canadian Women in Business* (Toronto: Faculty of Education, University of Toronto, 1977) 42.

11 Armstrong, *Labour Pains*, 234.

12 Sheila Amato and Pat Staton, *Making Choices! Women in Non-Traditional Jobs* (Toronto: Green Dragon Press, 1987).

13 Marina Strauss, "Hygienists seek slice of tooth turf," *The Globe and Mail* (June 4, 1987) B1–B2.

14 Strauss, "Hygienists" *The Globe and Mail*.

15 Jeannette Easson, Debbie Field, and Joanne Santucci, "Working Steel," *in* Jennifer Penney, *Hard Earned Wages: Women Fighting for Better Work* (Toronto: The Women's Press, 1983) 200, 211.

16 "Today's Woman," supplement to *The Halifax Chronicle–Herald* and *The Mail–Star* (March 10, 1987) 8, 14.

17 Ann Rauhala, "Job Quota for Women is Upheld," *The Globe and Mail* (June 26, 1987).

18 Doris Anderson, "How a tiny women's group defeated a corporate giant," *The Toronto Star* (July 18, 1987) K1.

19 Canadian Congress for Learning Opportunities for Women, *Decade of Promise*, 83–91.

20 "Women make inroads into 'male' professions," *The Globe and Mail* (May 29, 1987) A1–A2; Bonnie J. Fox and John Fox, *Occupational Gender Segregation of the Canadian Labour Force, 1931–1981* (Toronto: Institute for Social Research, York University, 1987) 28–29.

21 Ellen Roseman, "More women entering the business world, determined to overcome cautious attitudes," *The Globe and Mail* (May 29, 1987) C7.

22 Catharine W. Warren, *Vignettes of Life: Experiences and Self Perceptions of New Canadian Women* (Calgary: Detselig Enteprises, 1986) 48; Charlene Gannagé, *Double Day, Double Bind: Women Garment Workers* (Toronto: The Women's Press, 1986).

23 Anne Noonan, "Autonomy for Native Women," *Tiger Lily* 1, 1 (November–December 1986) 19.

24 Marion Pollack, "Under Attack: Women, Unions and Micro-technology," *in* Linda Briskin and Lynda Yanz, eds., *Union Sisters* (Toronto: The Women's Press, 1983) 104.

25 Judith Gregory, "The Electronic Sweatshop," *in* Joan Turner and Lois Emery, eds., *Perspectives on Women in the 1980s* (Winnipeg: The University of Manitoba Press, 1983) 99–112; Heather Menzies, *Women and the Chip: Case Studies of the Effects of Informatics on Employment in Canada* (Montreal: The Institute for Research on Public Policy, 1981).

26 Armstrong, *Labour Pains*, 167.

27 Pat Armstrong and Hugh Armstrong, *The Double Ghetto: Canadian Women and Their Segregated Work*, rev. ed. (Toronto: McClelland and Stewart, 1984) 48.

28 Gina Vance and Anne Bishop, "No More Lobsters for Lizmore," *in* Penney, *Hard Earned Wages*, 42–43.

29 Fox and Fox, *Occupational Gender Segregation*, 1.

30 "Canadian women trail Europeans in earning power, conference told," *The Globe and Mail*, (June 11, 1987); Eric Beauchesne, "Women Losing Battle of the Wage Gap," *The Globe and Mail* (March 13, 1987).

31 Wilson, *Women, the Family, and the Economy*, 106.

32 Armstrong, *Labour Pains*, 22.

33 Morley Gunderson, "Work Patterns," *in* Gail Cook, ed., *Opportunity for Choice* (Ottawa: Statistics Canada, 1976) 119–26.

34 Statistics Canada, *Women in the World of Work* (September 1984), chart 12.

35 Ontario, "Green Paper on Pay Equity — Fact Sheet," 1986.

36 Armstrong and Armstrong, *The Double Ghetto*, 45.

37 Lorna R. Marsden, "The Role of the National Action Committee on the Status of Women in Facilitating Equal Pay Policy in Canada," *in* Ronnie Ratner Steinberg, ed., *Equal Employment Policy for Women: Strategies for Implementation in the United States, Canada, and Western Europe* (Philadelphia: Temple University Press, 1980) 242–60.

38 Armstrong, *Labour Pains*, 59.

39 Leslie A. Pal and F.L. Morton, "*Bliss v. Attorney General of Canada*: From Legal Defeat to Political Victory," *Osgoode Hall Law Journal* 24, 1 (Spring 1986) 141–60.

40 Laura C. Johnson and Robert Johnson, *The Seam Allowance: Industrial Home Sewing in Canada* (Toronto: The Women's Press, 1982).

41 Armstrong and Armstrong, *The Double Ghetto*, 45.

42 Azilda Marchand, "Les femmes au foyer hier et demain," *Canadian Women's Studies/Les cahiers de la femme* 2, 2 (1980) 48.

43 Gisele Ireland, *The Farmer Takes a Wife* (Chesley: Concerned Farm Women, 1983) 14.

44 Ireland, *The Farmer Takes a Wife*, 15.

45 Muriel Lush, "The Family Farm is Dying," *Women's Concerns*, Division of Mission in Canada of the United Church in Canada, 31 (Winter 1986) 8.

46 Betty Burt and Loretta Burt, "Squidjigging Women," *in* Penney, *Hard Earned Wages*, 228.

47 Gail C.A. Cook and Mary Eberts, "Policies Affecting Work," *in* Cook, *Opportunity for Choice*, 148.

48 Meg Luxton, *More Than a Labour of Love: Three Generations of Women's Work in the Home* (Toronto: The Women's Press, 1980) 48.

49 Armstrong and Armstrong, *The Double Ghetto*, 66; Meg Luxton, "Two Hands for the Clock: Changing Patterns in the Gendered Division of Labour in the Home," *in* M. Luxton and Harriet Rosenberg, *Through the Kitchen Window: The Politics of Home and Family* (Toronto: Garamond Press, 1986) 17–36.

50 Armstrong and Armstrong, *A Working Majority*, 196.

51 Harriet Rosenberg, "The Home is the Workplace: Hazards, Stress, and Pollutants in the Household," *in* Luxton and Rosenberg, *Through the Kitchen Window*, 37–61.

52 "Living on mother's allowance no bed of roses: single mother," *Peterborough Examiner* (July 18, 1987) 8.

53 National Council of Welfare, *Progress Against Poverty*, rev. ed. (Ottawa: 1987).

54 " 'Discouraged worker' is redefined," *The Globe and Mail* (May 23, 1987) A3.

55 Linda Briskin, "Women and Unions in Canada: A Statistical Overview," *in* Briskin and Yanz, *Union Maids*, 28–43; Heather Jon Maroney, "Feminism at Work," *in* Bryan D. Palmer, ed., *The Character of Class Stuggle: Essays in Canadian Working Class History, 1850–1985* (Toronto: McClelland and Stewart, 1986) 160–75.

56 Briskin, "Women and Unions," *in* Briskin and Yanz, *Union Maids*, 37.

57 Martine Lanctôt, "Le genèse et l'évolution du mouvement des femmes à Montréal, 1969–79" (Université du Québec à Montréal: thèse de maîtrise, 1982).

58 M. Elizabeth Atcheson, Mary Eberts, and Beth Symes with Jennifer Stoddart, *Women and Legal Action: Precedents, Resources and Strategies for the Future* (Ottawa: Canadian Advisory Council on the Status of Women, 1984) 31.

59 Lynda Yanz and David Smith, "Annotated List of Women's Strikes," *Resources for Feminist Research* 10, 2 (July 1981) 77–83.

60 Frances Lankin, "Foreword," *in* Carole Conde and Karl Beveridge, *First Contract: Women And The Fight To Unionize* (Toronto: Between The Lines, 1986) 6–7.

61 Conde and Beveridge, *First Contract*, 72.

62 Laurell Ritchie, "Why are so many women unorganized?" *in* Briskin and Yanz, *Union Sisters*, 208–9.

63 Dorothy Lipovenko, "Women Teachers' Bastion under Assault," *The Globe and Mail* (May 9, 1987).

64 Maroney, "Feminism at work," *in* Palmer, *The Character of Class Struggle*, 162.

65 Rona Maynard, "Why Women Still Fail To Reach The Top," *Report on Business Magazine* (May 1985) 80–85.

66 Cathy Mulroy, "Miner's Daughter," *in* Penney, *Hard Earned Wages*, 182.

67 Luxton, "From Ladies' Auxiliaries to Wives' Committees: Housewives and the Unions," *in* Luxton and Rosenberg, *Through the Kitchen Window*, 63–81.

16 "The personal is political"

1 Patricia Carey, "Personal is Political," *Canadian Women's Studies/Les cahiers de la femme* 2, 2 (1980), 6.

2 M. Ann Hall, ed., "Special Issue: The Gendering of Sport, Leisure, and Physical Education," *Women's Studies International Forum* 10, 4 (1987), particularly Helen Lenskyj, "Female Sexuality and Women's Sport," 381–86.

3 Betty Lehan Harragan, *Games Mother Never Taught You: Corporate Gamesmanship for Women* (New York: Warner Books, 1977) 346, 345.

4 L. Schoenfielder and B. Wieser, eds., *Shadow on a Tightrope* (Iowa City, Iowa: Aunt Lute Book Company, 1983); C.M. Donald, *The Fat Woman Measures Up* (Charlottetown, P.E.I.: Ragweed Press, 1986).

5 Gouvernement du Québec, L'Office de la langue française, "Titres et fonctions: essai d'orientation et d'usage," 1986; Margrit Eichler and Jeanne Lapointe, "The Treatment of the Sexes in Research/Le traitement objectif des sexes dans la recherche" (Ottawa: Social Sciences and Humanities Research Council of Canada, 1985) 15–17 in English, 17–19 in French.

6 Esther Greenglass, *A World of Difference: Gender Roles in Perspective* (Toronto: John Wiley, 1982) 115–16.

7 Robin F. Badgley, "Report of the Committee on Sexual Offenses Against Children and Youths" (Toronto: August 1984).

8 Ann Rauhala, "Women will pay price for society's confusion, apathy on birth control," *The Globe and Mail* (October 12, 1987).

9 *Women in Canada: A Statistical Report* (Ottawa: Statistics Canada, 1985) 87, table 5.

10 A. Romaniuk, *Fertility in Canada: From Baby-Boom to Baby-Bust* (Ottawa: Statistics Canada, 1984).

11 Derek Ferguson, "Women victims as Alberta MDs fight billing ban," *Toronto Star* (December 11, 1986).

12 "Women and Reproduction," *Canadian Journal of Women and the Law* 1, 2 (1986).

13 "Same Sex Spousal Benefits," *Broadside* 8, 10 (August/September 1987) 6.

14 Ann Rauhala, "Task force calls for training and licencing of midwives," *The Globe and Mail* (October 16, 1987).

15 *Women in Canada*, 93, table 14.

16 Rona Maynard, "Can We Avoid The Heartbreak Of Birth Defects?"
   Chatelaine (September 1983) 215.
17 Wendy Lill, "Celebrating Sam's Birth," *Herizons* 4, 8 (December 1986)
   20.
18 *Women in Canada*, 96, table 17.
19 Jane L. Haliburton, "Establishing a Well-Women Clinic in Yarmouth,
   Nova Scotia," *Atlantis* 4, 2, 2 (Spring 1979) 141.
20 Judy Steed, " 'Mohawk beauty' paid high price in fight for Indian
   rights," *The Globe and Mail* (May 8, 1987).
21 *Report of the Royal Commission on the Status of Women* (Ottawa:
   Information Canada, 1970) 237–38; The Mohawk Women of
   Caughnawaga, " 'The Least Members of Our Society'," *Canadian
   Women's Studies/Les cahiers de la femme* 2, 2 (1980).
22 Marlene Pierre-Aggawamay, "Native Women and the State," *in* Joan
   Turner and Lois Emery, eds., *Perspectives on Women in the 1980s*
   (Winnipeg: University of Manitoba Press, 1984) 67.
23 Daryl Webber, "The Women's Movement in Northern Ontario: Its
   History, Growth and Current Affairs" (Glendon College, York
   University: Women's Studies Honours Thesis, 1986) 16–22.
24 Kathleen Jamieson, *Citizens Minus: Indian Women and the Law* (Ottawa:
   Advisory Council on the Status of Women, 1978) 82; Paula Bourne,
   Women in Canadian Society (Toronto: OISE Press, 1975) 111–31; Elizabeth
   Atcheson, Mary Eberts, and Beth Symes, *Women and Legal Action:
   Precedents, Resources, and Strategies for the Future* (Ottawa: Canadian
   Advisory Council on the Status of Women, 1984) 14–15.
25 Atcheson *et al.*, *Women and Legal Action*, 17–18; Caroline Lachapelle,
   "Beyond Barriers: Native Women and the Women's Movement," *in*
   Maureen Fitzgerald, Connie Guberman, and Margie Wolfe, eds., *Still
   Ain't Satisfied! Canadian Feminism Today* (Toronto: The Women's Press,
   1982) 257–64.
26 Sherill Cheda, "Indian Women: An Historical Example and a
   Contemporary View," *in* Marylee Stephenson, ed., *Women in Canada*,
   2nd ed. (Don Mills: General Publishing, 1978) 195–208; Le Collectif
   Clio, "La Femme autotochtone face à la loi sur les indiens," *Canadian
   Women's Studies/Les cahiers de la femme* 2, 4 (1980) 37–41.
27 Atcheson *et al.*, *Women and Legal Action*, 18; Matthew Fisher, "Indian
   wives remain in limbo over status despite altered law," *The Globe and
   Mail* (October 16, 1987); "Loophole in reserve," editorial in *The Globe
   and Mail* (November 4, 1987).
28 Linda Silver Dranoff, *Women in Canadian Life: Law* (Toronto: Fitzhenry
   and Whiteside, 1977) 52–53.
29 Goverment of Ontario, Ministry of the Attorney General, "Family Law
   Reform: Your New Rights" (Toronto, n.d.) 43.
30 Heather Mallick, "Father of four pressses for paid child-care leave," *The
   Globe and Mail* (August 5, 1987).
31 Rosamonde Ramsay Boyd, "Women and Politics in the United States and
   Canada," *Annals of the American Association of Political and Social Science*
   (January 1968) 56.
32 Decision Marketing Research Limited, *Women in Canada* (Ottawa: Office
   of the Co-ordinator, Status of Women, 1976) 120.
33 Penney Kome, *Women of Influence: Canadian Women and Politics*
   (Toronto: Doubleday Canada, 1985) appendix 1.
34 Evelyne Tardy, "Les femmes et la campagne référendaire," *in Québec: Un
   pays incertain* (Montréal: Editions Québec-Amérique, 1980) 183–203;
   Michèle Jean, Jacqueline Lamothe, Marie Lavigne and Jennifer Stoddart,
   "Nationalism and Feminism in Quebec: The 'Yvettes' Phenomenon," *in*
   Roberta Hamilton and Michèle Barrett, eds., *The Politics of Diversity:
   Feminism, Marxism and Nationalism* (Montreal: Book Center, 1986) 322–
   38.

35 Diane Lamoureux, *Fragments et collages: Essai sur le féminisme québécois des années 70* (Montréal: Éditions du remue-ménage, 1986) 148 (authors' translation).

36 Penney Kome, *The Taking of Twenty-Eight: Women Challenge the Constitution* (Toronto: The Women's Press, 1983) 23.

37 Kome, *The Taking of Twenty-Eight*, 36.

38 Walter Tarnopolsky, "The Constitution and Human Rights," *in* Keith Banting and Richard Simeon, eds., *"And No-one Cheered": Federalism, Democracy and the Constitution Act* (Toronto: Methuen, 1983) 272.

39 Beverly Baines, "Women, Human Rights and the Constitution," (Ottawa: Advisory Council on the Status of Women, 1980); Lynn McDonald, "The Charter of Rights and the Subjection of Women," *Canadian Forum* (June–July 1981) 17–18; Chaviva Hošek, "How Women Fought for Equality," *in* Banting and Simeon, *"And No One Cheered,"* 280–300; Sandra Burt, "Women's Issues and the Women's Movement in Canada," *in* Alan Cairns and Cynthia Williams, eds., *The Politics of Gender, Ethnicity and Language* (Toronto: University of Toronto Press, 1986) 156–58.

40 Colette Beauchamp, "Anderson vs. Axworthy," *Féminin Pluriel* 1, 1 (septembre 1981), especially 17; "La navigation du féminisme," *Revue d'information pour les femmes* (avril 1987) 15.

41 Sheila Copps, *Nobody's Baby* (Toronto: Deneau, 1986) 87.

42 Anne Collins,"Which Way to Ottawa?" *City Woman* (Holiday, 1981) 30.

43 Ross Howard, "Credibility on line as politicians face women's debate," *The Globe and Mail* (August 13, 1984); John Cruikshank *et al.*, "Issue of trust left hanging after debate," *The Globe and Mail* (August 16, 1984).

44 M. Janine Brodie and Jill McCalla Vickers, "Canadian Women in Politics: An Overview," CRIAW paper no. 2 (Ottawa: Canadian Research Institute for the Advancement of Women, 1982).

45 73 percent said it would make no difference and 13 percent said they would be more likely to support such a party. Canadian Institute of Public Opinion poll, 382; Val Ross, "The Honorable Flora," *Chatelaine* (January 1980) 36.

46 Donn Downey, "Men-only restrictions in club prompts affiliate to sever ties," *The Globe and Mail* (November 7, 1986); "Sexism in the Club," editorial in *The Globe and Mail* (December 10, 1986).

47 Paul Delean, "Cutler brings a new style to Westmount city hall," *The Gazette* (November 9, 1987).

48 Doris Anderson, "Women need money to test Charter," *Toronto Star* (May 23, 1987).

49 F.L. Morton, "The political Impact of the Canadian Charter of Rights and Freedoms," *Canadian Journal of Political Science* 20, 1 (March 1987) 41–42.

50 Report of the sixth conference of the Congress of Black Women of Canada, 1984; Report of the fifth conference of the Congress of Black Women of Canada, 1982, Dr. Dorothy Wills, "The Challenge for Black Women in the Eighties," 3.

51 Lamoureux, *Fragments et collages*, 110 (authors' translation).

52 Hugh Filman, "SAC rejects bid for Women's Centre funds," *The Varsity*, University of Toronto (August 5, 1987).

53 Bev Le Francois and Helga Martens Enns, *Story of a Women's Centre* (Vancouver: Press Gang, n.d.) 5; Webber, "The Women's Movement in Northern Ontario," 11; Lamoureux, *Fragments et Collages*, 110–12.

54 Final Report, "Emergency Consultation Between Groups Receiving Women's Program Funds and the Secretary of State" (Ottawa: June 25–27, 1986).

55 Sue Findlay, "Facing the State: The Politics of the Women's Movement Reconsidered," *in* Heather Jon Maroney and Meg Luxton, eds., *Feminism and Political Economy: Women's Work, Women's Struggles* (Toronto: Methuen, 1987) 31–50.

56 Margie Wolfe, "Feminist Publishing in Canada," *Canadian Women's Studies/Les cahiers de la femme* 2, 2 (1980) 11–14; and "Working with Words: Feminist Publishing in Canada," *in* Fitzgerald *et al.*, *Still Ain't Satisfied!*, 265–75.

57 Naomi R. Goldenberg, *Changing of the Gods: Feminism and the End of Traditional Religions* (Toronto: Fitzhenry and Whiteside, 1979) 85–114.

58 Bernard Marotte, "Once pervasive Quebec nuns seek renewal," *The Globe and Mail* (October 1, 1987).

59 Reginald Bibby, "Religion à la carte," *The Globe and Mail* (September 12, 1987).

60 Susan Schwartz, "She's reclaiming women's roots," *The Gazette* (November 9, 1987).

61 "Anglican women celebrate first decade in priesthood," *The Globe and Mail* (December 6, 1986).

62 *Canadian Woman Studies/Les cahiers de la femme* 5, 2 (Winter 1983) 89.

Selected Bibliography

Bibliographies and historiographical studies

Bradbury, Bettina. "Women's History and Working Class History," *Labour/le travail* 19 (Spring 1987) 23-43.

Cohen, Yolande. "L'histoire des femmes au Québec 1900-1950," *Recherches sociographiques* 21, 3 (septembre-décembre 1980) 339-45.

Cohen, Yolande. "La recherche universitaire sur les femmes au Québec (1929-1980). Répertoire de thèses de maîtrise et de doctorat déposées dans les universités du Québec: présentation thématique," *Resources for Feminist Research/documentation sur la recherche féministe* 10, 4 (December 1981-January 1982) 5-24.

Conrad, Margaret. "The Re-Birth of Canada's Past: a Decade of Women's History," *Acadiensis* 12 (Spring 1983) 140-62.

Jackel, Susan. "Canadian Prairie Women's History: a Bibliographic Survey," CRIAW Paper No. 14 (April 1987) 1-22.

Lemieux, Denise, and Lucie Mercier. *La Recherche sur les femmes au Québec. Bilan et bibliographie* (Québec: Institut Québécois de recherche sur la culture, 1982).

Light, Beth, and Veronica Strong-Boag. *True Daughters of the North. Canadian Women's History: an Annotated Bibliography* (Toronto: OISE Press, 1980).

Mazur, Carol, and Sheila Pepper. *Women in Canada: a Bibliography, 1965-1982* (Toronto: OISE Press, 1984).

Pierson, Ruth. "Women's History: the State of the Art in Atlantic Canada," *Acadiensis* 7 (Autumn 1977) 121-31.

Pierson, Ruth, and Beth Light. "Women in the Teaching and Writing of Canadian History," *The History and Social Science Teacher* 17, 2 (Winter 1982) 83-95.

Prentice, Alison. "Writing Women into History: the History of Women's Work in Canada," *Atlantis* 32, 2 (Spring 1978) 72-83.

Prentice, Alison. "Towards a Feminist History of Education," *in* D.G. Jones *et al*, eds., *Approaches to Educational History* (Winnipeg: University of Manitoba Monographs in Education, 1980) 39-64.

Silverman, Eliane Leslau. "Writing Canadian Women's History, 1970-82: an Historiographical Analysis," *Canadian Historical Review* 63, 4 (December 1982) 513-33.

Strong-Boag, Veronica. "Raising Clio's Consciousness: Women's History and Archives in Canada," *Archivaria* 6 (Summer 1978) 70-82.

Van Kirk, Sylvia. "What Has the Feminist Perspective Done for Canadian History?" *in* Ursula M. Franklin *et al.*, eds. *Knowledge Reconsidered: a Feminist Overview* (Ottawa: Canadian Research Institute for the Advancement of Women, 1984) 43-58.

Van Kirk, Sylvia, ed. "Canadian Women's History: Teaching and Research," special issue of *Resources for Feminist Research/dcocumentation sur la recherche féministe* (July 1979) 5-71.

Walsh, Susan. "Studying Women at Home and Abroad: a Bibliographical Guide to English-Language Sources, 1970-1982," *The Journal of Educational Thought* 17, 2 (August 1983) 187-200.

Collections of Essays

Acton, Janice *et al.*, eds. *Women at Work: Ontario 1850-1930* (Toronto: Canadian Women's Press, 1974).

Bourne, Paula, ed. *Women's Paid and Unpaid Work: Historical and Contemporary Perspectives* (Toronto: New Hogtown Press, 1985).

Burnet, Jean, ed. *Looking into My Sister's Eyes: an Exploration in Women's History* (Toronto: Multicultural History Society of Ontario, 1986).

Demers, Jeanne, et Lijne McMurray, eds. *Femmes scandales 1965-1985* (Montréal: La nouvelle barre du jour, 1987).

Dumont, Micheline, et Nadia Fahmy-Eid, eds. *Les couventines: l'éducation des filles au Québec dans les congrégations religieuses enseignantes 1840-1960* (Montréal: Boréal Express, 1986).

Fahmy-Eid, Nadia, et Micheline Dumont, eds. *Maîtresses de maison, maîtresses d'école: femmes, famille et éducation dans l'histoire du Québec* (Montréal: Boréal Express, 1983).

Identités féminines: mémoire et création. Questions de culture, no. 9 (Québec: Institut québécoise de recherche sur la culture, 1986).

Innis, Mary Quayle. *The Clear Spirit: Twenty Canadian Women and their Times* (Toronto: University of Toronto Press, 1973).

Kealey, Linda, ed. *A Not Unreasonable Claim: Women and Reform in Canada 1880s-1920s* (Toronto: Canadian Women's Press, 1979).

Kinnear, Mary, ed. *First Days, Fighting Days: Women in Manitoba History* (Regina: Canadian Plains Research Centre, University of Regina, 1987).

Lacelle, Elizabeth J., ed. *La femme et la religion au Canada français* (Montréal: Bellarmin, 1979).

Latham, Barbara, and Cathy Kess, eds. *In Her Own Right: Selected Essays on Women's History in B.C.* (Victoria: Camosun College, 1980).

Latham, Barbara, and Roberta Pazdro, eds. *Not Just Pin Money: Selected Essays on the History of Women's Work in British Columbia* (Victoria: Camosun College, 1984).

Lavigne, Marie, et Yolande Pinard, eds. *Les femmes dans la société québécoise: aspects historiques* (Montréal: Boréal Express, 1977).

Lavigne, Marie *et al.*, eds. *Travailleuses et féministes: les femmes dans la société québécoise* (Montréal: Boréal Express, 1983).

Prentice, Alison, and Susan Mann Trofimenkoff, eds. *The Neglected Majority: Essays in Canadian Women's History* (Toronto: McClelland and Stewart, 1985) vol. 2.

Strong-Boag, Veronica, and Anita Clair Fellman, eds. *Rethinking Canada: the Promise of Women's History* (Toronto: Copp Clark Pitman, 1986).

Trofimenkoff, Susan Mann, and Alison Prentice, eds. *The Neglected Majority: Essays in Canadian Women's History* (Toronto: McClelland and Stewart, 1977) vol. 1.

Documentary Collections

Cook, Ramsay, and Wendy Mitchinson, eds. The Proper Sphere: Woman's Place in Canadian Society (Toronto: Oxford University Press, 1976).

Jackel, Susan, ed. *A Flannel Shirt and Liberty: Emigrant British Gentlewomen in the Canadian West 1880-1914* (Vancouver: University of British Columbia Press, 1982).

Jean, Michèle, ed. *Québécoises du XXe siècle* (Montréal: Editions du Jour, 1974).

Light, Beth, and Joy Parr, eds. *Canadian Women on the Move, 1867-1920* (Toronto: New Hogtown Press and OISE Press, 1983).

Light, Beth, and Ruth Pierson, eds. *No Easy Road: Women in Canada, 1920s to 1960s* (Toronto: New Hogtown Press, 1988).

Light, Beth, and Alison Prentice, eds. *Pioneer and Gentlewomen of British North America, 1713-1867* (Toronto: New Hogtown Press, 1980).

McGahan, Elizabeth, ed. *Whispers from the Past: Selections from the Writings of New Brunswick Women* (Fredericton: Goose Lane Editions, 1986).

O'Leary, Véronique, et Louise Toupin, eds. *Québécoises deboutte! tome 1: une anthologie de textes du Front de libération des femmes (1969-1971) et du Centre des femmes (1972-1975)* (Montréal: Les editions du remue-ménage, 1982).

Rasmussen, Linda *et al*, eds. *A Harvest Yet to Reap* (Toronto: Canadian Women's Press, 1976).

Silverman, Eliane Leslau. *The Last Best West: Women on the Alberta Frontier 1880-1930* (Montreal: Eden Press, 1984).

Photo Credits

Page 16: Courtesy of the Royal Ontario Museum; p. 19: Public Archives Canada PA 129588; p. 27; Metropolitan Toronto Library; p. 29: National Gallery of Canada 6663; p. 30: Courtesy of the Royal Ontario Museum; p. 35. Public Archives Canada C-2821; p. 43: Public Archives Canada C1549; p. 49: Courtesy of Jean-Claude Dupont; p. 57: Archives Nationales du Québec à Québec GH 670-177; p. 58: Archives of the Congregation de Notre-Dame; p. 63: Collection Gagnon, Bibliothèque de la ville de Montréal 4510; p. 66: from William Still, *The Underground Railroad* (Philadelphia: Porter & Coates, 1872); p. 69: Public Archives Canada C 2001; p. 78: Public Archives Canada C-11224; p. 86: Courtesy of the Royal Ontario Museum; p. 87: Public Archives Canada C 43906; p. 100: Courtesy of the Royal Ontario Museum; p. 106: Glenbow Archives; p. 117: National Museums of Canada 18818; p. 119: Manitoba Archives; p. 126: Provincial Archives of New Brunswick, Taylor Photograph Collection, P. 198–2; p. 134: Courtesy of the Royal Ontario Museum; p. 140: Courtesy of Alexander Graham Bell National Historic Park; p. 144; Metropolitan Toronto Library Board; p. 149; Public Archives Canada PA-13284; p. 152: Public Archives Canada C 30935; p. 160: Public Archives Canada PA 32891; p. 161: Public Archives Canada PA 122876; p. 163: Public Archives of Nova Scotia, Notman 25815; p. 173: Women's and Labour Studies Resource Room, Monarch Park Collegiate, Toronto; p. 180: Public Archives Canada PA 27434, p. 181: Postcard Courtesy of Betty Tomlinson Anderson, photograph courtesy of Manitoba Archives N7573; p. 195: Canadian Women's Movement Archives; p. 196: Thunder Bay Finnish Canadian Historical Society; p. 198: Provincial Archives of British Columbia HP 39854; p. 212: Woodland Indian Cultural Education Centre; p. 220: Provincial Archives of Newfoundland and Labrador, Hayword 1546; p. 232: Manitoba Archives; p. 233: Public Archives Canada C53850; p. 253: Women's and Labour Studies Resource Room, Monarch Park Collegiate, Toronto; p. 254: Notman Photographic Archives, McCord Museum, McGill University 234, 097-II; p. 264: Art Gallery of Ontario; p. 273: Courtesy of Katharine N. Hooke; p. 278: Manitoba Archives N9343; p. 280: Vancouver Public Library; p. 288: Eleanor Sim; p. 296: Public Archives Canada C33442; p. 309: Courtesy of Miles Laboratories Canada Inc.; p. 313: Provincial Archives of Alberta H. Pollard Collection, P 8682; p. 317: Public Archives Canada PAC 24452; p. 325: Records, Archives and Museum, Toronto Board of Education; p. 341: Archives of Ontario; p. 351: Courtesy of Moira Armour; p. 361: Claudine Kurtzman; p. 370: The Royal Bank of Canada; p. 375: Toronto Star; p. 377: George Brown College; p. 387: Canadian Women's Movement Archives; p. 399: Canadian Women's Movement Archives.

Every effort has been made to obtain permission for copyright material used in this book and to acknowledge all such indebtedness accurately. Any errors and omissions called to our attention will be corrected in future printings.

Index

Faye Peterson Transition House, 406
federalism, 355, 400
Federated Women's Institutes of Canada. *See* Women's Institutes.
Fédération catholique des institutrices rurales, 238
Fédération des femmes du Québec, 343–4, 346, 348, 351–2, 402
Fédération Nationale Saint-Jean-Baptiste, 185, 203, 231, 283
Federation of Liberal Women of Canada, 277, 283
Federation of Medical Women of Canada, 263
Federation of Women Teachers' Associations of Ontario, 138, 231, 263, 324, 388
Female Employees Fair Remuneration Act, 333
femininity, 309–10, 325–6, 330, 361, 391–2
feminism, 12–5, 39, 123, 164, 169–71, 175–7, 179, 185–7, 191–4, 197–8, 201–3, 206–7, 210–1, 217, 251, 262, 270, 279–82, 284–5, 287–9, 294, 337, 340, 342–3, 346–7, 357–61, 366, 388–9, 392–3, 395, 398, 400–1, 405
  anti-, 202–3, 364–5
  chronology of, 344–5
  equal rights or political, 169, 177, 191–2, 199, 202
  and film, 362
  maternal- or social-, 169, 177, 198–9, 201, 361
  Marxist, 355–6
  and publishing, 360–1
  radical, 349, 357–62
  socialist, 355, 357, 359, 360–1, 364
Feminist Action League, 353
Feminist Communication Collective, 358
Feminist Party of Canada, 359
Fergusson, Muriel McQueen, 332
Ferron, Marcelle, 339
fertility, 72, 86, 134, 146, 162–4, 166, 289, 295, 322, 369, 394
fertility rates, 321, 369. *See also* birth rate
field work, 27, 48, 79, 119, 223
filles à marier, 44
filles du roi, 45–6
film, 235, 362, 391
finances
  educational, 97, 156, 159, 242
  family, 255, 269, 297, 299, 314, 370
  farm, 117
  political, 277

wartime, 205–6, 297
women's organizations', 181, 183, 190, 270, 335, 365
Financial Post, 313–4
financing, 42–4, 55, 134, 219
  of birth control clinics, 258
  culture 266, 337–9
  of home purchases, 246
  missions, 42–3, 171, 275
Finnish women, 196, 222, 261, 278
fishing, 17, 19–21, 26–7, 29, 34–5, 53, 74, 77–8, 104, 125, 225, 377–8, 382–3
flappers, 13, 244
Flatheads, 34
Flin Flon, Man., 232, 283
food, 14, 17, 21, 26, 28–9, 40, 43, 47–9, 52–4, 60, 73, 77–8, 84, 122, 157, 190, 205, 219, 221, 224, 236–8, 242–3, 270
  distribution of, 26, 28
  preserving, 49, 76–8, 116, 122, 204, 233
Forbes, Mary Frances, 128
Forbes Shorthand School, 128
Fornel, Jean-Louis, 53
Forrester, Maureen, 339
Forrestier, Marie, 42
Foster, Veronica, 300
4-H Club, 243
Franca, Celia, 339
France, 19, 22, 41–2, 43–44, 47, 51, 54–5
  franchise, 98–9, 109, 170, 178, 186, 191, 193, 203
  municipal, 159, 178, 185, 187
Francis, Anne. *See* Bird, Florence
Francophone women, 19, 41, 176, 186, 213, 229, 238
Fraser, Nellie, 279
Fraser Lake Women's Centre, 406
Frechette, Pierre, 85
Fredericken, Johanne, 120
Fredericton, N.B., 70, 97
Free Press (Manitoba), 196
Free Press (Winnipeg), 133
French, Mabel, 201
Freydis, 19
Freyja, 185, 197
friendship, 42, 75, 103, 150–1, 167, 193, 254, 264, 266, 270, 319, 342
Front commun contre la Pornographie, 362
Front pour la libération des femmes du Québec, 354–5
Front pour la libération du Quebec, 355–6
Frost, Leslie, 332
Fun With Dick and Jane, 324
fur trade, 19–22, 24–5, 33–4, 36–8, 44, 47, 50, 67, 70–1, 80

Gaelic, 21
Gamelin, Emelie, 104
gardening, 48, 76–9, 116, 122, 241
garment industry, 121, 191, 201, 220, 224, 230, 238–9, 298, 378
gathering, 14, 17, 21, 25–9, 33, 40, 78, 116, 225, 241
Gaudreault, Laure, 238
Gauld, Bella Hall, 229
Gauthier, Monique Comeau, 306
Gauthier, Monseigneur Georges, 251
Gazette (Montreal), 136
Gelber, Sylva, 347
gender relations, 33, 45–7, 56
gender structures, 357
genocide, 72
gentlewomen, 13, 69, 81, 222
Gérin-Lajoie, Marie, 185, 283
German, 21, 66–7, 163, 222
Gervais, Lise, 339
Girl Guides of Canada, 243, 271, 274
girls, 31, 48, 76, 94, 123, 128–9, 145–6, 151, 155–6, 158–9, 236, 241, 243–4.
Girls' and Boys' Clubs of Canada, 243
Girls' Friendly Society, 177, 182
Glace Bay, N.S., 256
Globe (St. John), 201
Goldman, Emma, 257
Gordon, Hortense, 340
Gordon, Lady Ishbel Marjoribanks. *See* Aberdeen, Countess of
Gore, Upper Canada, 102
Gorman, Mary, 154–5, 157
Goudie, Elizabeth, 221
gouttes de laits, 203
government, 54, 85
  exclusion of women from, 36, 98–9, 270
Graham, Andrew, 28, 30
Graham, Gwethalyn, 336
Graham, Isabel, 196, 199
Grain Growers' Association, 197, 200
Grain Growers' Guide, 133, 154, 158, 196–7, 199
Les Grand Ballets Canadiens, 339
Grant, Isabel, 133
Great Deportation or Expulsion, 21, 61
Gregg, Milton, 333
Grey Co, Ont., 198, 382
Grey Nuns, 61–2, 67, 138, 159, 177, 299
Grier, Margaret, 261
Group of Seven, 265–6
Gruchy, Lydia, 274–5
Grunet, Marie, 42
Gudrid, 19

Guelph, Ont., 157, 232, 353
Guèvremont, Germaine, 340
Gunn, Isabel, 85
Gunn, Susan, 268
Gutteridge, Helena Rose, 200–1, 207, 227
Guy et Yvette, 324, 400
gynecology, 309–10

Haida, 26, 34–5
hairdressers, 252
Halfbreed, 341
Halifax, 68, 70, 85, 96, 128, 138, 148, 185, 202, 204–6, 263, 336, 353, 374
Hamel, Marie-Angélique, 60
Hamilton, 72, 74–6, 82, 96, 104, 182, 200, 219, 230, 258, 263, 339, 353, 373
Hamilton, Mary Riter, 135
handicrafts. *See also* sewing
    carving, 34
    embroidery, 55, 59, 100, 157
    knitting, 59, 76, 94, 158, 204, 235, 266, 297, 397
    needlework, 94, 157
    quillwork, 29, 39
    quilting, 103, 266
    weaving, 34–5, 50, 52, 63, 69–70, 79–80, 82, 90, 116, 118, 136
harassment, 175, 201–2, 230, 237, 280, 361, 373, 385–6
Harris, Bella, 154
Hartman, Grace, 386
Hasell, Eva, 274
Hatheway, Ella, 202
Haviland, Laura, 151
Hawkins, Mary, 258
Hawley, Elizabeth L., 174
Hawthorn Women's Club, 266
health, 44, 47, 71, 75, 78, 81–2, 109, 120, 122–3, 126, 130–1, 145, 179, 182, 227, 247–8, 256, 268, 281, 315, 334, 372, 392–6
    insurance, 265, 305
    public, 123, 131, 191, 202, 225–6, 240, 249, 263, 323
    rural, 268, 328
    workers', 224, 235, 376
Hearne, Samuel, 28
Hearst, William, 208
Hébert, Anne, 340
Hebert, Elizabeth, 151
Hébert, Louis, 41
Heck, Barbara, 98
Heliconian Club, 266
Henderson Secretarial School, 313
Heneker, Dorothy, 264
Henripin, Jacques, 348
Henry, Alexander, 33
Hepburn, Mitchell, 216
heroines, 142, 225, 355
Herstory, 360
L'Heureux-Dubé, Claire, 404

Heyman, Jane, 338
hierarchy, 33, 56, 85, 129–30, 145, 170–1, 177, 273–6, 334–5, 371–2
high school, 156–7, 159
Hill, Maud Petitt, 227
Hind, Cora, 128, 133, 184, 207
historical interpretation, 13–4, 24–5, 28, 31, 52, 82–3, 97, 112, 217, 293–4
historical sources, 13, 22–3, 40, 51–2, 59, 80–1, 101, 111–2, 217, 293–4
Hoffman, Abby, 330
Home Aide, 307
Home and Domestic Employees Union, 136
home economics. *See* domestic science
Home Improvement Plan, 246
home, woman's place in, 142, 218, 303–4, 318
Homemakers' Clubs, 268
Homemaker's Magazine, 359
homesteading, 108, 113, 115, 119–20, 176, 196, 199–200
homosexuality, 150–1, 261, 360, 365, 394, 405
Hoodless, Adelaide, 182–3, 195
Hôpital-Général, 45, 55
Hôpital de la Miséricorde, 260
Horn, Kahn-Tineta, 396–7
Hošek, Chaviva, 403
Hospitalières, 42
Hospitalières de Saint Joseph de la Flèche, 44
hospitals, 42, 54, 61–2, 130–2, 153, 167, 204, 248, 260, 268, 321, 323, 327, 375, 385, 397
hostels, 179, 222
Hôtel-Dieu, 42, 44, 54–5, 60
Hour-A-Day Study Club, 269
household, 31, 36, 40–1, 45, 52, 54, 73–4, 89, 96, 136, 247, 319–20
    head of, 51, 73, 99
    management, 75, 122, 183, 217, 242–3, 245, 247, 315
    production, 37, 107, 116–8, 123, 235
    size of, 216–7
    structure, 32
Household Finance Corporation, 247
Household Leagues, 205
housing, 219, 317, 319–20
housewives, 15, 42, 52, 78–9, 121–8, 157–8, 241, 295, 307, 315, 321, 380
Housewives' League, 205
housework, 12, 48, 75–7, 83, 116–8, 122–3, 158, 300, 359–60, 382
Hudson's Bay Company, 24, 33, 39, 67, 71, 85
Hughes, Laura, 207

Hull, Que., 230
Human Rights Code, 358, 361, 381
Human Rights Commission, 373–4
Humphrey, John, 348
hunting, 14, 17, 21, 25–9, 31, 33–6, 40
Hurons, 17, 25–6, 31–2, 34, 36, 39, 44
husbands, 32, 34, 36, 41, 45, 88, 99, 102, 121, 147–8, 153, 164, 236–7, 247, 252–3, 284–5, 367, 374
    absences of, 50
    cruelty of, 41, 56, 89–90, 147, 188
    fur trader, 25, 71
    supportive, 177, 184
hygiene, 151, 183, 308
hygienist, dental, 373
Hyndman, Margaret, 331–3

Icelandic, 184–5, 191, 197
Icelandic Suffrage Association, 191
idealization, 112–3, 122, 143–8, 261, 307
Île de France, 20
illness, 12, 69, 82, 104, 122, 161. *See also* disease; health; tuberculosis
image
    professional, 225–6
    women, 132, 143–8, 153, 225–6, 307, 311, 366–7, 382
    women in armed forces, 302–3
immigrants, illegal, 381
immigration, 19–20, 41, 47, 65, 69, 93, 107–8, 110, 114–21, 123–4, 141, 151, 179, 189, 192–3, 197, 215, 219, 222, 228, 236, 259, 283, 289–90, 314, 321, 374–5, 381, 405
    agencies, 114–5, 123, 155–6
    of children, 155–6
    policy, 181–2, 222
    of single women, 42, 44–6, 66, 70, 222
Imperial Order Daughters of the Empire, 110, 205, 209, 346
imperialism, 36, 110, 204, 271
In Times Like These, 206
Incarnation, Marie de l', 43, 55–6, 59–60, 355
incest, 147
INCO, 389
independence, 117, 152, 160, 171–2, 243–4
    economic, 245, 392
Indian Act, 396–8, 403
Indian Homemakers of B.C., 397

newspapers, 111, 133–5, 154, 186, 196–7, 200–2, 240
Niagara, Upper Canada, 102
Nightingale, Florence, 131
Nolin, Angélique and Marguerite, 80, 82
Nootka, 17, 35, 164
Noranda, Que., 229
normal school, 96–7, 156, 159, 190. *See also* teachers, training of
Norris, Hannah, 170–1
Norse, 19
Northern Women's Centre, 406
The Northern Women's Journal, 406
Northwest Company, 33, 37
Norwich, Ont., 160
Not a Love Story, 362
notaries, 85, 328. *See also* lawyers.
notarial records, 22, 51–2
Nova Scotia, 21–2, 25, 38, 46, 53, 61, 65–6, 68, 70, 72, 76, 81, 85, 89–92, 94, 96, 99, 103, 107, 114, 116, 121, 125, 128, 138, 140, 148, 158, 163, 166, 177, 185–6, 190, 201–2, 204–7, 227, 241, 249, 255, 258, 263, 278, 314, 336, 353, 374, 386, 390, 396–7
Nova Scotia Federation of Labour, 386
Nova Scotia Gazette and Weekly Chronicle, 90
Nova Scotia Native Women's Association, 397
Novascotian, 99
nuns, 20, 22, 41, 43–4, 46, 51, 54–8, 60, 62, 66–7, 95, 130, 151–2, 160, 176–7, 203, 260–1, 276, 324–5, 327–8, 346, 406
nurses, 76, 113, 122, 128, 130–1, 138, 141, 180, 183, 212–3, 225–6, 228, 232, 242–3, 262, 263–4, 266, 305–6, 325, 369, 388, 396, 372–3
professionalization of, 131
public health, 122, 225–6, 310. *See also* health, public
nutrition, 157, 182–3, 218, 242–3, 246, 297
Nuu-Chah-Nulth. *See* Nootka

Obomsawin, Alanis, 340
O'Brien, Mary, 75, 88
occupation, 12, 80, 83, 109, 123, 125. *See also* work; labour force; employment
Ogilvie, Judge Doris, 348
Ojibway, 33–4
Okanagan Valley, 39
old age pensions. See pensions, old age
older women, 99, 113, 122,

151, 163, 167, 237, 281, 319, 337, 380
Oliphant, Betty, 339
Olympics, 250, 330
On the Subjection of Women, 194
One Big Union, 214
Ontario, 21–2, 39, 69–70, 72–6, 82, 92–3, 95–6, 98–9, 101, 104, 107–8, 110, 126–7, 130–1, 134–8, 148, 150, 153–5, 171, 182, 187, 191, 199, 200–1, 205, 207–9, 216, 219–21, 223, 227–8, 230–2, 234, 238, 241–2, 247–8, 258, 263, 266, 269–70, 279, 287, 289–90, 297–300, 314–6, 321, 325, 332–5, 338–9, 353, 357–8, 364, 373, 380, 382, 386–7, 397
Ontario Ladies College, 96
Ontario Native Women's Association, 397
O'Reilly, Jane, 76
organizations, 101, 103–5, 107, 109, 112, 114, 123, 128, 138–9, 150–1, 159, 175, 185, 189–211, 215, 217, 238, 242, 248–50, 263–87, 294, 297, 319–21, 331–7, 381, 393–407. *See also* feminism; women's movement
for adolescents, 243–4, 250, 271, 274
co-operation between, 279, 356, 361–4. *See also* feminism; sisterhood; women's movement
divisions within, 184–5, 201, 205–7, 266–7, 277, 287
maids', 222
membership in, 172–3, 178, 182–5, 187, 189, 191, 193, 205, 210, 263, 265–7, 269–71, 275, 286, 335, 364
mixed sex, 265, 356, 405
Organized Working Women, 386
organizers, 178, 219, 230, 238–9, 278–9, 315–6, 346
orphans, 36, 45, 76, 103–5, 259, 310
Oshawa, Ont., 358
Ottawa Home for Friendless Women, 180
Ottawa, Ont., 130, 224, 258, 263, 353–4, 365
Owen Sound, Ont., 172, 231
Oxford County, Ont., 118

Packwood, Anne, 341
Paine, Hilda, 244
painting, 73, 83, 134–5, 253
Paktuutit (Inuit Women's Association), 397
Palladium of Labour, 137
Palmer, Dorothea, 258
Palmer, Mary, 85

Pankhurst, Christabel, 192
Pankhurst, Emmeline, 192
Pankhurst, Sylvia, 192, 201
Papineau family, 98, 100, 102
Parent, Madeleine, 315–6, 386
parents, 34, 43, 45, 47–8, 51, 74, 81, 87–8, 92, 95, 109, 156, 221, 250–2, 259, 310, 324–5
single, 370, 384. *See also* mothers, unmarried
Parents' Information Bureau, 258
Paris, Ontario, 235
Parlby, Irene, 268, 281–2
Parti québécois, 350–1, 400–1
patriarchy, 15, 32, 36, 38, 90, 103, 295, 346, 356, 358, 360, 391, 407
patriotes, 101–2
patriotism, 203–10, 300
Patullo, Duff, 216
Paubst, Alma, 241
Payette, Lise, 351, 400
peace and pacifism, 21, 24, 37, 65, 110, 206–7, 240, 267, 270–1, 279–81, 285–8, 293, 303, 330–1, 334–6, 355. *See also* Voice of Women; League of Nations Society; Women's International League for Peace and Freedom
Peace Study Group, 270–1
Pean, Madame, 53
Pearson, Lester B., 293, 336, 346–8
Pearson, Maryon, 336
Peel County, Ont., 73–4
Peltrie, Mme de la, 43
Pendant que les hommes travaillaient, les femmes elles. . ., 345
pensions, 52, 101, 203, 280, 380–1
old age, 217, 237, 259, 380
Pépin, Lucie, 402
periodization, historical, 13
Perrault, Louis, 102
Persons Case, 281–2, 401
Peterborough, Ont., 69
petitions, 70, 81, 99, 102, 105, 170, 173–4, 177–8, 184, 186–7, 194, 201, 304
philanthropy. *See* charity; social welfare
Phinney, Gertrude, 250
photographers, 134
Phyllis Wheatley Art Club, 269
physical education, 157, 250, 271–2, 330. *See also* sports
picketing, 220, 231–2, 238–9, 386–7
Pickford, Marie, 134
Picton Lady's Academy, 96
Picton, Ont., 172, 174
piecework, 121, 127, 223, 228, 235, 376–7, 381
Pilotte, Angélique, 91

feminist, 406
revivals, 97, 103
sects, 97, 145, 275–6
religious orders, 44, 54, 95–6,
105, 138, 144–5, 151, 176–
7, 260–1, 276, 324, 327–8,
406
uncloistered, 44
Repentigny, Madame de. *See*
Saint-Père, Agathe de
reproduction, 12, 34, 92, 126,
145–6, 309, 359. *See also*
childbearing
reproduction rights, 357
reproductive system, 145–6
resistance, 37–8, 42–3, 53–4,
56, 90, 92, 101–2, 114,
124, 151–2, 222
retail, 127–8, 218, 231, 339
Retail, Wholesale and Department Store Union, 316
revolution, 289, 352, 355
Le revue populaire, 326
Richelieu Valley, 49, 52
Richibucto, N.B., 118
Le Rideau Vert, 338
Riel, Louis, 130
Riel Rebellions, 110, 141
Rigeault, Judithe, 46
riots, 52–3, 88, 102
Ritchie, Eliza, 202, 206
Roback, Lea, 238–9
Roberts, Lillie, 152
Roblin, Rodmond, 194
roles, 27, 142–3, 189, 214, 217,
240–62
domestic, 154, 158, 180, 241–
3, 328
maternal, 151, 168, 179, 194–
5, 211, 308–9
gender, 289, 357
native women's, 26, 30–1
sex, 358
wives', 172, 341
women's, 144–5, 150, 169,
179, 184, 240–62, 276,
326
Rollet, Marie, 41
"rolling pin brigade," 317
Roman Catholic, 20, 33, 36,
42–4, 48, 51, 54, 56, 62–3,
66, 80, 85, 95–6, 103–4,
111, 129–30, 138, 144–5,
150, 156, 181, 185–6, 202–
3, 230, 251, 254, 257, 260,
276, 283, 307, 316, 322,
328, 350, 406
Rose, Clifford, 261
Roshko, Dominko, 116
Ross, Mrs. J.D., 334
Roughing It in the Bush, 69
Rowley, Kent, 315–6, 386
Roy, Gabrielle, 340
Roy, Marguerite, 55
Royal Commission on National
Development in the Arts,
Letters and Sciences, 337
Royal Commission on Price

Spreads, 233–5
Royal Commission on the Relations of Capital and Labor,
127
Royal Commission on the Status
of Women in Canada, 270,
345–9, 352, 354, 358, 397,
400
Royal Commission on Technical
Education, 202
Royal Winnipeg Ballet, 338
Royce, Marion, 272–3, 314
Rubes, Susan, 338
Ruggles, Eliza, 76–7
rum running, 261–2
rural, 22, 51, 59, 73, 75, 81, 94,
108–9, 113, 123, 129–30,
155, 166, 171–2, 182–3,
189, 193, 196–7, 221, 238,
241, 245–6, 250, 268–9,
297, 321–2, 334, 345, 382,
398–9, 305
Rural Dignity for Canada, 382
Ruthenian, 150
Rutherford, Lillian, 269

Sabia, Laura, 345–7, 349, 352
St. Catharines, Ont., 131, 346
Saint-Germain, Eugénie, 102
St. Hyacinthe, Que., 151
Saint-Hélène, Mère, 55
Saint-Jean, Idola, 284
Saint John, 79, 192, 201, 206,
263
Saint John Ladies' Total Absti-
nence Society, 104–5
St. John's, Nfld., 127
St. Lawrence River, 17, 20–1,
25, 27, 60–1, 65
Saint-Père, Agathe de, 52
Ste. Anne de Bellevue, Que.,
157
Sainte-Thérèse, Soeur, 130
Salish, 26, 35–6
Salvation Army, 283
Sanger, Margaret, 256–8
sanitation, 109, 122, 129, 179,
182–3, 242, 245
Sarnia, Ont., 358
Saskatchewan, 118, 120, 138,
187, 197, 200, 207–10,
215, 221, 227–8, 231, 237,
241, 257–9, 272, 274, 279–
80, 303, 308, 353, 358,
360, 370, 382, 386
Saskatchewan Working Women,
386
Saskatoon, Sask., 138, 231, 360
Saskatoon Women's Calendar
Collective, 360
Saskatoon Women Teachers'
Association, 138
satire, 184, 186, 194, 198
Saturday Night, 191
Saunders, Bryne Hope, 297
Saunders, Margaret
Marshall, 133, 148
Sauvé, Jeanne, 400

Savariat, Olive, 124
Scandinavian, 222. *See also*
Finnish women.
Schlinder, Thérèse, 77
school, 44, 57–9, 68, 76, 80–1,
83, 94, 97, 101, 110, 120,
122, 129, 135, 168, 174,
183, 268, 276, 305, 314,
324–5, 328, 346
attendance at, 94, 155–6, 241,
249, 259
boarding, 38, 44, 57, 59, 71,
77, 148
convent, 44, 55, 81, 95, 152,
157, 160, 346
household, 94
nursery, 305
secretarial, 128, 191, 313
Sunday, 103, 172, 174, 271,
274, 297
science, 14, 55–6, 82, 111, 130,
132, 167, 183, 245, 325,
327, 336, 348
Scott, Barbara Ann, 330
sculptors, 264–5, 340
Sculptors Society of Canada, 265
seamstresses, 59, 80
Second Awakening, 97
Secord, Laura, 101, 142
secretaries, 242–3, 376
Sedgwick, Rev. Robert, 143–4
seduction, 92–3
Selkirk, 67
Senate, 282–3
senators, 216, 277, 332, 335
Senecas, 26–7, 37
separation, 36, 38, 75, 89–90,
284, 370
separatism, 323, 355, 398, 400–1
servants, 24, 28, 40–1, 46, 50,
60, 62, 66, 70, 74–7, 79,
81, 83, 91–3, 95, 104, 113–
5, 121–4, 126, 128–31,
136, 139, 155, 157, 183,
185, 219–23, 228, 235–6,
241, 243, 245, 266, 290,
305–6, 318, 361, 375
Service, Office and Retail Workers' Union of Canada, 388
settlement, 20, 25, 32, 36, 44–5,
65, 67–8, 101, 108–9, 114–
5, 181, 190
sewing, 12, 19, 45, 50, 58–9,
76, 80, 94–5, 103, 121,
125, 130, 135, 153, 157,
183, 190, 204, 221, 224,
247, 266, 274, 297, 328
sex, 151, 164, 237, 252, 361,
391
abuse, 260
education. *See* education, sex
extramarital, 261, 320
role stereotyping, 324–6, 331,
358, 361–2, 388
ratios, 45, 70, 108, 116, 165,
215
Sex, Marriage and Birth Control,
252

Sexton, May, 206
sexual exploitation, 124
sexual freedom, 31
sexuality, 31–2, 35, 38, 86–7, 91, 93, 132, 146–7, 153–4, 167, 261, 302–3, 309, 319–20, 352–3, 356–7, 362, 393–4
Shadd, Mary Ann, 134, 175
Shakespearean Society, 191
shamans, 32, 35
Shanks, Ola., 341
Shaw, Dr. Anna Howard, 178
Shawandithit, 72
She Named It Canada, 360
Sherwood, Sarah, 68–9, 73, 79
Sillery, Que., 36–7, 42
Similkameen, 39
Simon Fraser University, 353
Simpson, Frances, 71
Simpson, Sir George, 71
Simpson's 191, 229
Sinclair, Adelaide, 335
single women, 36, 41, 44–6, 59, 62, 72, 76, 80–3, 91–4, 99, 104, 108, 113–5, 119, 124–5, 130, 135, 141, 149–51, 154, 159, 163, 175, 177, 181, 199, 201, 218–9, 221, 227, 234, 244, 260–1, 264, 280, 290, 298, 308, 385
Sir George Williams University, 353
sisterhood, 109–10, 148, 150–1, 167, 179, 188, 192, 358, 361–2
sisters, 42, 52, 69, 75, 77, 80, 103, 130, 148, 236
Sisters of Charity. *See* Grey Nuns
Sisters of Providence, 104
Six Nations. *See* Iroquois
"Slave Woman." *See* Thanadelthur
slavery, 20, 33, 36, 39, 56, 66, 68, 102, 115, 151, 331
Smith, Donald, 159
Smith, Elizabeth, 148–9, 151, 161
Smith, Goldwin, 132, 194
Smith, Silvestria Theodora, 175
smoking, 34, 49, 244, 394
Snyder, Edna, 241
social activities, 120–1, 127, 135, 189–90, 243, 265, 331
Social Credit, 238, 352
Social Gospel, 145, 151, 193, 272
social structure, 20, 36
social welfare, 42, 56, 103, 169, 174, 320, 356, 380–1, 399
social work, 191, 218, 261, 271, 305, 325, 334
Socialist Party of Canada, 197, 278
socialists, 110, 196–7, 215, 229, 257, 278–9, 281, 353
Soeurs de la Miséricorde, 105
Le Sont, Anne, 46

Sorel, Q., 46
spheres
  private, 14, 31, 82
  public, 14, 31, 93, 96
  woman's proper, 95, 111, 137–8, 143, 168, 175
  separate, 14, 83, 97, 142–3, 156, 269, 273
  separate, ideology of, 168, 210
spinning, 19, 50, 79, 93, 116, 118, 126, 137, 150, 234
Split Lake, Man., 190
Spock, Dr. Benjamin, 310, 395
sports, 145–6, 153, 157, 250, 253, 271–3, 319, 329–31, 391, 404
  facilities, 272, 329
  team, 152–3, 272, 330
  Olympics, 250, 330
spouses, 77, 79, 130, 197
  choice of, 31, 33–8, 49, 51, 87, 153–4
"Squid Women," 383
standard of living, 214, 227, 235, 299–300, 315, 380
Stark, Ethel, 338
starvation, 24, 37, 41, 66, 68, 72, 75, 103
status, 14, 21, 36, 189, 217, 244
  domestic servants', 157, 267
  housewives', 305
  Indian, 396–7
  married women's, 34, 51, 147–8, 244
  native women's, 22, 26, 28, 34, 37
  professional, 95, 138–9, 141, 145, 225, 232
  widows', 118–9
  women workers', 224, 378–9
  women's, 184, 200, 331
  Woodland Cree women's, 28
Status of Women groups, 350–2
Steeves, Dorothy, 281
stenographers, 127, 218, 224, 306
sterilization, 193, 257, 260, 394, 404
Stevens, H.H., 216
Stewart, Ann, 94, 96
Stewart, Anna Marie, 76
Stewart, Bessie, 76
Stewart, Ellen, 76
Stewart, Frances, 75–6
Stewiacke, N.B., 116
Stone, Lucy, 175
Storrs, Monica, 274
Stowe, Emily Howard, 131–2, 160, 175, 178, 191
Stowe-Gullen, Dr. Augusta, 178
Stratford, Ont., 231, 338
Stratford Shakespearean Festival, 338
Strategy for Change, 350
strikes, 135–6, 206, 219–20, 231–2, 238, 255, 316, 357, 383, 386–8

women supporting, 219–20, 232, 279–80, 357, 389–90
Strum, Gladys, 278, 280
student movement, 352, 355–6
Student Christian Movement, 272–3
Studio D, 362
Subcommittee on the Post-war Problems of Women, 304–5
suburb's, 291, 315, 321, 367
Sudbury, Ont., 353, 389–90
suffrage, 13, 109, 177–9, 181, 184–5, 189, 191–2, 200–1, 204, 206–7, 210, 217, 263, 265, 280, 283, 343, 346
  opposition to, 185–6, 189, 192, 194–5, 201–3
suffragettes, 192, 196, 200, 202, 354
suffragists, 175, 178
Suffragists' War Auxiliary, 204
suicide, 38–9, 68, 256, 345
A Summer on the Canadian Prairie, 199
Summerside, P.E.I., 202
Sunday School, 103, 172, 271, 274, 297
Sunnyside, N.B., 114
support, emotional, 12, 33, 120, 236, 254–5, 261, 308
surgery, 146–7
sweated labour, 107, 191, 224

Tadoussac, 53
"Take Back the Night" marches, 359
Tallman, Eileen, 316
Talon, Jean, 45
taxation, 298, 305, 331, 365, 370, 381
teachers, 44, 58–9, 66, 68, 70, 76, 80–3, 93–7, 101, 103, 113, 115, 128–9, 131, 138, 140, 152, 156–7, 160, 170–2, 179, 185, 191, 194, 203, 225–6, 228, 231–2, 238, 241–3, 249, 263–4, 266, 268, 297, 305, 314, 324, 331, 334, 372, 385, 388
  training of, 96–7, 156, 159. *See also* normal school.
technology, 15, 122–3, 127, 158, 214, 216–7, 223, 245, 291, 376–7
  reproductive, 394
T.E. Eaton Co., 136, 229, 235, 238, 316, 387
Tekakwitha, Kateri, 36–7
telephone, 293
telephone operators, 136, 206, 219–20, 225, 302, 306
television, 291, 315, 334, 337
temperance, 104, 169, 172–4, 175, 178–9, 184, 193, 202, 209–10, 263, 267, 331
La Terre et le Foyer, 307